Feminism

Feminism

June Hannam

Longman
is an imprint of

Harlow, England • London • New York • Boston • San Francisco • Toronto • Sydney • Singapore • Hong Kong
Tokyo • Seoul • Taipei • New Delhi • Cape Town • Madrid • Mexico City • Amsterdam • Munich • Paris • Milan

PEARSON EDUCATION LIMITED

Edinburgh Gate
Harlow CM20 2JE
United Kingdom
Tel: +44 (0)1279 623623
Fax: +44 (0)1279 431059
Website: www.pearson.com/uk

First edition published in Great Britain in 2012

© Pearson Education Limited 2012

The right of June Hannam to be identified as author of this work has been asserted by her in accordance with the Copyright, Designs and Patents Act 1988.

Pearson Education is not responsible for the content of third-party internet sites.

ISBN: 978-1-4082-5557-5

British Library Cataloguing in Publication Data
A CIP catalogue record for this book can be obtained from the British Library

Library of Congress Cataloging in Publication Data
A CIP catalog record for this book can be obtained from the Library of Congress

10 9 8 7 6 5 4 3 2 1
16 15 14 13 12

Set in 10/13.5pt Berkeley Book by 35
Printed in Malaysia, KHL-CTP.

Introduction to the series

History is narrative constructed by historians from traces left by the past. Historical enquiry is often driven by contemporary issues and, in consequence, historical narratives are constantly reconsidered, reconstructed and reshaped. The fact that different historians have different perspectives on issues means that there is also often controversy and no universally agreed version of past events. *Seminar Studies* was designed to bridge the gap between current research and debate, and the broad, popular general surveys that often date rapidly.

The volumes in the series are written by historians who are not only familiar with the latest research and current debates concerning their topic, but who have themselves contributed to our understanding of the subject. The books are intended to provide the reader with a clear introduction to a major topic in history. They provide both a narrative of events and a critical analysis of contemporary interpretations. They include the kinds of tools generally omitted from specialist monographs: a chronology of events, a glossary of terms and brief biographies of 'who's who'. They also include bibliographical essays in order to guide students to the literature on various aspects of the subject. Students and teachers alike will find that the selection of documents will stimulate discussion and offer insight into the raw materials used by historians in their attempt to understand the past.

Clive Emsley and Gordon Martel
Series Editors

Contents

Acknowledgements

Thanks to Arthur for all the practical and emotional support that made this book possible.

PUBLISHER'S ACKNOWLEDGEMENTS

We are grateful to the following for permission to reproduce copyright material:

Documents

Document 3 from *Women, the Family, and Freedom: The Debate in Documents Volume One, 1750–1880*, Stanford University Press (Bell, Susan Groag and Karen M. Offen (eds), 1983), Copyright © 1983 by the Board of Trustees of the Leland Stanford Junior University. All rights reserved. Used with the permission of Stanford University Press, www.sup.org; Document 6 from National Archive of New Zealand, *The Women's Suffrage Petition 1893* [Archives Reference: LE 1 1893/7a] Archives New Zealand The Department of Internal Affairs Te Tari Taiwhenua; Document 17 excerpts from *The Harem years: The Memoirs of an Egyptian Feminist 1879–1924*, Feminist Press (Sha'rawi, H. and (trans) Badran, M. 1987) 112–13, edited and translated by Margot Badran, Translation copyright © 1986 by Margot Badran. Reprinted with the permission of The Feminist Press, www.feminist.org; Document 19 from *Conversations with Alice Paul: Woman suffrage and the Equal Rights Amendment: oral history transcript*, BANC MSS 76/177. The Bancroft Library, University of California, Berkeley; Document 22 from *The Second Sex*, Knopf (de Beauvoir, S. 1953), "Introduction" from THE SECOND SEX by Simone De Beauvoir, translated by H.M. Parshley, copyright 1952 and renewed 1980 by Alfred A. Knopf, a division of Random House, Inc. Used by permission of Alfred A. Knopft, a division of Random House, Inc.; Document 24 from Editorial, *The Times*, 21 November 1970, 13, with the permission of News International Syndication

Ltd.; Document 26 from *Feminism in France*, Routledge (Duchen, C. 1988) 23–4; Document 27 from Western feminism and women in the third world, *The Guardian*, 2 October 1984 (Yoon, S.-Y.), Copyright Guardian News & Media Ltd 1984; Document 29 from *Implementation of the Nairobi Forward-looking Strategies for the Advancement of Women to the Year 2000*, United Nations Publications (United National General Assembly)

Plates

The publisher would like to thank the following for their kind permission to reproduce their photographs:

Plate 1: Kansas State Historical Society; Plate 2: Alexander Turnbull Library, Wellington, New Zealand; Plate 3: Bibliothèque Nationale de France; Plate 4: Greater Manchester Police Museum and Archive; Plate 5: Bath in Time; Plate 6: Schwimmer-Lloyd collection, Manuscripts and Archives Division, The New York Public Library, Astor, Lennox and Tilden Foundations; Plate 7: © Bettmann/Corbis; Plate 8: Carrie Chapman Catt Albums, Bryn Mawr College Library, Special Collections; Plate 9: © The British Library Board (*Votes for Women*, 24 May 2912); Plate 10: Bibliotheque Marguerite Durand, Paris, France/Archives Charmet/The Bridgeman Art Library Ltd; Plate 11: INTERFOTO/Sammlung Rauch/Mary Evans

In some instances we have been unable to trace the owners of copyright material, and we would appreciate any information that would enable us to do so.

Abbreviations

Chronology

1908	Women's Anti-Suffrage League formed, London
1909	First hunger strikes of suffrage prisoners in Britain
1911	First Proletarian Women's Day, Germany
1912	Men's International Alliance for Woman's Suffrage formed
1913	'Cat and Mouse' Act (Prisoner's temporary Discharge for Ill health) passed in Britain Suffrage Pilgrimage, Britain
1914	(March) Germany's Red Week
1915	Women's International League formed
1918	Women over 30 gain vote in Britain Women gain vote in Canada, Austria and Germany
1919	Women gain the vote in Czechoslovakia and the Netherlands Egyptian women take part in uprising against the British WIL renamed Women's International League for Peace and Freedom
1920	Nineteenth Amendment gives women the vote in the United States
1922	Pan-American Association for the Advancement of Women, formed
1923	Egyptian Feminist Union founded
1925	Sarojini Naidu president of Indian National Congress
1926	Civil Code revised in Argentina IWSA renamed International Alliance of Women
1928	Women in Britain gain vote on same terms as men Pan-Pacific and South East Asia Women's Association formed
1929	Women in Ecuador gain the vote
1931	Indian Women's delegation attends Round Table Conference, London
1932	Women gain vote in Brazil and Uruguay
1934	Women gain vote in Turkey
1944	Women gain vote in France and Bulgaria
1945	Women gain vote in Italy and Hungary Women's International Democratic Federation formed, Paris
1946	Women gain vote in Romania
1948	Women gain vote in Belgium
1949	Simone de Beauvoir, *The Second Sex*, published
1956	Women gain vote in Egypt
1963	Betty Frieden, *The Feminine Mystique*, published
1966	National Organization of Women founded, US
1968	Demonstration against Miss America Beauty Contest, Atlantic City, US

1969   Kate Millett, *Sexual Politics*, published

1970   First Women's Liberation Conference, Oxford
Disruption of Miss World Competition, London

1971   'Whore's Manifesto' signed, France
Germaine Greer, *The Female Eunuch*, published

1974   Juliet Mitchell, *Woman's Estate*, published

1975   United Nations International Women's Year
UN World Conference on Women, Mexico City

1976   United Nations Decade of Women begins

1977–8   Reclaim the Night marches

1981   Susie Orbach, *Fat is a Feminist Issue*, published
First Latin American encuentro (convention) held in Bogotá
Women only peace camp established at Greenham Common, England

1988   Denise Riley, *Am I That Name?*, published

1991   Naomi Wolf, *The Beauty Myth*, published

1995   United Nations sponsors World Conference on Women, Beijing

Who's who

Anthony, Susan B. (1820–1906): Leading American suffrage campaigner, Quaker and abolitionist; worked closely with Elizabeth Cady Stanton, founding the American National Woman Suffrage Association in 1869, co-editing the influential journal, *The Revolution* and founding the International Council of Women, 1888; president of National American Woman Suffrage Association, 1892–1906.

Auclert, Hubertine (1848–1914): French militant suffrage campaigner; edited and founded the newspaper, *La Citoyenne* (the Citizeness); formed group Suffrage des Femmes (Women's Suffrage).

Augspurg, Anita (1857–1943): With Lida Heymann formed the German Union for Women's Suffrage, 1902; active in Women's International League for Peace and Freedom.

Bebel, August (1840–1913): Marxist politician and writer; leader of German Social Democratic Party; author of *Woman and Socialism*, 1879, a key text for socialists on the woman question.

Billington-Greig, Teresa (1877–1964): British socialist; one of the founders and leader of the militant suffrage group, Women's Freedom League; left the WFL in 1911 and attacked militancy in her book *The Militant Suffrage Movement*, 1911.

Bingen, Hildegard of (1098–1179): German mystic, visionary, writer and composer of music; abbess of an independent convent and outspoken critic of male secular and religious leaders.

Boyle, Nina (1865–1943): British journalist and campaigner for women's equal rights; secretary of Women's Freedom League, 1912; active in Save the Children Fund.

Butler, Josephine (1828–1906): Formed and led the Ladies National Association for the Repeal of the Contagious Diseases Acts in Britain.

Carpenter, Mary (1807–77): Daughter of a Unitarian minister based in Bristol, England, who gained a national reputation for the establishment of ragged schools and reformatories for juvenile delinquents. Committed to the cause of anti-slavery and worked to expand women's education in India.

Catt, Carrie Chapman (1859–1947): Influential suffragist in the United States and internationally; president of the National American Woman Suffrage Association, 1900–4 and 1915–20; founded League of Women Voters, 1920; first president of International Woman Suffrage Alliance, 1904–23.

Campoamor, Clara (1888–1972): Leading Spanish feminist and member of the Radical Party; elected to the first Parliament of the Second Republic, 1931; fell out with her own party over her support for women's suffrage.

Cobbe, Frances Power (1822–1904): Irish writer and women's rights' activist; executive member of the London National Society for Women's Suffrage; used journalism to campaign against domestic violence and vivisection.

Craigen, Jessie (1835/5–99): British working-class suffrage campaigner and speaker.

De Beauvoir, Simone (1908–86): French novelist, political theorist, essayist and biographer; had a lifetime relationship with Jean Paul Sartre and contributed to the development of existentialist philosophy; wrote *The Second Sex*, 1949, a key text for 'second wave' feminism.

Deraismes, Maria (1828–94): French author and pioneer of women's rights who worked closely with Leon Richer; they founded *L'Association pour le droit des femmes* (Association for women's rights), 1869 and organized the first International Women's Rights Congress, Paris 1878.

Deroin, Jeanne (1805–94): French Utopian Socialist, prominent in the revolutions of 1848; campaigner for the rights of working women.

Despard, Charlotte (1844–1939): British socialist and one of founders of the militant suffrage group, Women's Freedom League; a pacifist, she formed the Women's Suffrage National Aid Corps in the First World War.

Fawcett, Millicent Garrett (1847–1929): Leader of the British constitutional suffrage movement; president of the National Union of Women's Suffrage Societies, 1897–1919.

Ford, Isabella (1855–1924): British socialist, suffragist and peace campaigner; member of National Administrative Council of Independent Labour Party, 1903–07; a member of the executive committee of the National Union of Women's Suffrage Societies, 1907–15; member of executive of British branch of the Women's International League, 1915–24.

Fourier, Charles (1772–1837): French Utopian Socialist, philosopher and supporter of women's rights.

Friedan, Betty (1921–2006): American author of *The Feminine Mystique*, 1963, a key text for 'second wave' feminism; one of the founders of the National Organization of Women, 1966.

Gay, Désirée (1810–91): French seamstress, follower of Saint-Simon and a founder of *Tribune des femmes*, 1834; president of women's section of International Working Men's Association, 1866.

Goldstein, Vida (1869–1949): Australian socialist feminist; founded Women's Federal Political Association 1903 and launched journal, *The Woman Voter*, 1909; pacifist in the First World War.

Gouges, Olympe de (1748–93): French playwright and advocate of the abolition of slavery and of women's rights. Wrote Declaration of the rights of woman and the citizen, 1791; executed 1793.

Greer, Germaine (b. 1939): Australian academic, writer and journalist. Achieved notoriety with her book *The Female Eunuch*, 1970; her arguments, language and combative style ensure she continues to be a controversial figure.

Gripenberg, Alexandra (1859–1913): Leader Finnish Women's Association and a nationalist; treasurer of International Council of Women, 1893–99.

Heymann, Lida Gustava (1868–1943): With Anita Augspurg formed the German Union for Women's Suffrage, 1902 and active in Women's International League for Peace and Freedom.

hooks, bell (b. 1952): Black American writer and social critic; born Gloria Watkins she took the name of her maternal great grandmother; most influential writings include *Ain't I a Woman? Black Women and Feminism*, 1981 and *Feminism is for Everybody: Passionate About Politics*, 2000.

Jacobs, Aletta (1854–1929): Leading Dutch suffragist and peace activist; founding member of the Woman Suffrage Association, 1894 and national president 1903–19; active in IWSA; organized the International Congress of Women at the Hague, 1915; helped establish the Women's International League.

Kauffmann, Caroline (c.1840s–1926): French militant suffrage campaigner; leader of La solidarité des femmes (Women's Solidarity), 1898 and after 1906 staged a protest at the Chamber of Deputies.

Kenney, Annie (1879–1953): British working-class suffragette; organizer and charismatic speaker for the Women's Social and Political Union.

Knight, Anne (1786–1862): British Quaker, anti-slavery campaigner and supporter of Chartism; wrote a pamphlet on women's suffrage, 1847 and established the Sheffield Female Political Association, 1851.

Kollontai, Alexandra (1872–1952): Russian Communist; founded Zhenotdel (Women's Department), 1919, to improve women's position; 1923 appointed Soviet ambassador to Norway.

Kramers, Martina (1863–1934): Dutch suffragist and socialist; 1899–1909 member of the board of International Council of Women; secretary of International Woman Suffrage Alliance, 1906–11; edited *Jus Suffragii*, newspaper of IWSA, 1904–13.

Krog, Gina (1847–1916): Leader of the Norwegian suffrage movement and editor of the feminist periodical *Nylaende* (New Frontiers); founded a Norwegian branch of the International Council of Women, 1904.

Leavitt, Mary (1830–1912): Founder member of Woman's Christian Temperance Union and honorary life president; travelled the world speaking for temperance and women's suffrage.

Luisi, Paulina (1875–1940): Leading women's rights advocate in Uruguay; first woman to gain a medical degree, 1909; attended international conferences and an honorary vice-president of the Pan American Conference of Women.

Lutz, Bertha (1894–1976): Founder and president of the Brazilian Federation for the Advancement of Women, 1922; elected to Chamber of Deputies, 1936 – served for a year until the new regime restricted women's political activities.

Macmillan, Chrystal (1892–1937): British suffragist, peace activist and lawyer; 1913–23 vice-president of International Woman Suffrage Alliance; delegate to the Paris Peace Conference 1919; co-founder 1929 and president of Open Door International.

Mill, John Stuart (1806–73): British MP and eminent liberal philosopher; presented 1866 suffrage petition to Parliament; wrote influential book, *On the Subjection of Women*, 1869; with his stepdaughter Harriet Taylor he played a controversial role in the London women's suffrage movement.

Millett, Kate (b. 1934): American feminist theorist and activist; wrote *Sexual Politics*, 1969; committee member of National Organization of Women.

Montefiore, Dora (1851–1933): British socialist, suffragette and internationalist; leading member of Women's Social and Political Union until 1907; joined Adult Suffrage Society and honorary secretary, 1909; active in International Bureau for Socialist Women; founder member of British Communist Party, 1921.

Mott, Lucretia Coffin (1793–1880): Quaker minister, abolitionist and pioneer of the American women's rights movement; with Elizabeth Cady Stanton organized the first Women's Rights Convention at Seneca Falls, 1848.

Mozzoni, Anna Maria (1837–1920): Italian feminist and suffragist; translated Mill's *On the Subjection of Women* and wrote regularly for the feminist journal, *La Donna* (Woman).

Myrdal, Alva (1902–86): Swedish sociologist and politician; writings, with husband Gunnar, influenced welfare state; 1950–55 first woman to chair UNESCO's Social Science section; elected to Parliament 1962; advocate of disarmament and awarded Nobel Peace Prize 1982.

Nabarawi, Saiza (1897–1985): Egyptian feminist and national liberation leader; journalist and editor of *L'Egyptienne* (Egyptian Woman); co-founder of Egyptian Feminist Union.

Naidu, Sarojini (1879–1949): Indian nationalist and suffragist; educated in England; second woman president of the Indian National Congress, 1925; representative of Indian women's organizations to the 1931 Round Table Conference in London, where she demanded adult suffrage.

Nassef, Malak (1886–1918): Egyptian journalist and poet who contributed to debates on the woman question.

Otto-Peters, Louise (1819–95): Founded the General German Women's Association, 1865 and the Federation of German Women's Associations, 1894.

Owen, Robert (1771–1835): Mill owner who established a model village at New Lanark, Scotland; influenced the founding of village communities based on communitarian principles in Britain and the United States.

Paine, Tom (1737–1809): English radical political theorist who welcomed the American Revolution; wrote *The Rights of Man*, 1791–2, in support of French Revolution; accused of sedition he fled to France and was elected to the Convention; wrote *The Age of Reason*, 1793, when in prison after refusing to support the execution of the King.

Pankhurst, Christabel (1880–1958): British militant suffragette who, with her mother, led the Women's Social and Political Union; founded the Women's Party in 1917.

Pankhurst, Emmeline (1858–1928): British militant suffragette and most well-known, charismatic leader of the Women's Social and Political Union; repeatedly arrested and forcibly fed; with her daughter Christabel, formed the Women's Party in 1917.

Paul, Alice (1885–1977): Leader of militant wing of American suffrage movement; with Lucy Burns formed the Congressional Union, 1913, to work for a federal amendment and in 1915 established the National Woman's Party; campaigned for an equal rights amendment; formed the World Woman's Party, 1938 that worked with the United Nations to promote women's equality.

Pelletier, Madeleine (1874–1939): French socialist, journalist and militant suffrage campaigner; secretary of the small group La solidarité des femmes (Women's Solidarity) and founder of journal, *La suffragiste* (The Suffragist) in 1908.

Pizan, Christine de (1365–c. 1434): Born in Venice, as an adult she lived in Paris where she wrote poetry and other texts that challenged contemporary views about a woman's role and nature.

Plamínková, Františka (1875–1942): Czech women's rights campaigner and suffragist; founded the Women's Club in Prague, 1901, and the Committee for Women's Suffrage, 1905; a radical and a nationalist she became a senator in the new republic, formed in 1918, and was executed by the Nazis in 1942.

Ransome-Kuti, Funmilayo (1900–78); women's rights activist in Nigeria; founder and president of Nigerian Women's Union, 1949, and Federation of Nigerian Women's Societies, 1954.

Rathbone, Eleanor (1872–1946): British suffragist; executive member of National Union of Women's Suffrage Societies; president of National Union of Societies for Equal Citizenship, 1919–29; independent MP for Combined British Universities, 1929–46; campaigner for family allowances and educational reform for Indian women; author of *The Disinherited Family*, 1924.

Richer, Leon (1824–1911): French journalist and supporter of women's rights; edited the journal, *Le droit des femmes* (Right of Women); worked closely with Maria Deraismes; they founded The Association for the Right of Women, 1869 and organized the first International Women's Rights Congress, Paris 1878.

Roosevelt, Eleanor (1884–1962): Influential wife of the American President, Franklin D. Roosevelt, 1933–45 and supporter of his New Deal policies; delegate to United Nations General Assembly, 1945–52; chaired the important 1961 Presidential Commission on the Status of Women.

Rousseau, Jean-Jacques (1712–78): Political philosopher and author, born in Geneva but influenced by Enlightenment thinkers in Paris; wrote novels including *Emile*, 1762 and political texts, such as *The Social Contract*, 1762, a key text in social and political thought.

Saint-Simon, Henri de (1760–1825); French social theorist and Utopian socialist who argued that science was the key to progress and the reorganization of society.

Sanger, Margaret (1879–1966): American birth control campaigner; launched journals such as *Birth Control Review*; founder of birth control organizations and chair of the Birth Control Council of America, 1937.

Schwimmer, Rosika (1877–1948); Hungarian suffragist and international peace activist; formed the Hungarian Council of Women and the Hungarian Feminist Association, 1904; international press secretary of International Woman Suffrage Alliance, 1914; appointed ambassador to Switzerland 1918–20; emigrated to United States and worked for peace as a member of the Women's International League for Peace and Freedom and the Campaign for World Government, that she helped to found, 1937.

Scott, Rose (1847–1925): Australian suffrage leader; founded Womanhood Suffrage League in New South Wales, 1891.

Shafik, Doria (1908–1975): Egyptian militant feminist; educated in France; founded a magazine, *Daughter of the Nile*, 1948 and the Bint al-Nil Union, 1948, a party committed to women's suffrage and women's rights.

Sha'rawi, Hudá (1879–1947): Egyptian feminist and nationalist; prominent in the Egyptian Nationalist Party; co-founder of Egyptian Feminist Union, 1923; active in International Woman Suffrage Alliance.

Sheppard, Kate (1848–1934): Suffragist and leader of New Zealand Woman's Christian Temperance Union from the 1880s until the vote was achieved in 1893; popular speaker in Britain and the United States.

Stanton, Elizabeth Cady (1815–1902); American suffrage leader; with Lucretia Mott called Seneca Falls Convention 1848; worked closely with Susan Anthony, forming the National Woman Suffrage Association, 1869, co-editing the journal *The Revolution* and founding the International Council of Women, 1888; first president of the National American Woman Suffrage Association, 1890–2, and one of the authors of *History of Woman Suffrage*, 1886.

Stone, Lucy (1818–92): American suffragist; established National Woman Suffrage Association, 1869; with husband, published the influential *Woman's Journal*, 1872.

Stritt, Marie (1855–1928): German suffragist; president of the Federation of German Women's Associations in 1899.

Truth, Sojourner (c. 1797–1883): Self given name of Isabella Baumfree, born into slavery in New York; an abolitionist and women's rights activist; dictated memoir, *The Narrative of Sojourner Truth: A Northern Slave* (1850); delivered 'Ain't I a Woman' speech at Ohio Woman's Rights Convention, 1851.

Tristan, Flora (1803–44): French socialist, writer and propagandist who tried to link the emancipation of women and the working class.

Voilquin, Suzanne (1801–78): French working-class feminist, follower of Saint-Simon and founder of newspaper *Tribune des femmes*, 1834.

Ward, Mary Augusta (Mrs Humphrey) (1851–1920): British novelist, author of best selling *Robert Elsmere*; a founder of the Women's National Anti-Suffrage League, 1908.

Wolstenholme-Elmy, Elizabeth (1833–1918): British suffrage supporter from 1866; paid secretary of Women's Franchise League and founder of Women's Emancipation Union 1891; controversial figure through radical politics and unconventional private life.

Wollstonecraft, Mary (1759–97): Member of influential radical group of thinkers in London, including Tom Paine and William Godwin; her book, *A Vindication of the Rights of Woman*, 1792, is considered to be the founding text of feminism in Britain and America; married Godwin in 1897 and died in childbirth the same year.

Zetkin, Clara (1857–1933): German theoretician and activist in the Social Democratic Party; leader of its women's organization and editor of its journal, *Die Gleichheit* (Equality); secretary of the International Bureau of Socialist Women from 1907.

Glossary

Adult suffrage: The demand that all men and women over a certain age should be able to vote.

Anti-Corn Law League: Formed 1838 to gain repeal of the Corn Laws and to establish free trade to ensure low priced food. Many women gave support.

Cat and Mouse Act, 1913: Popular name given to the British Prisoner's Temporary Discharge for Ill Health Act; empowered the Home Secretary to release a hunger-striking prisoner until her health improved after which she could be re-arrested and imprisoned.

Chartism: Extensive British working-class movement, lasting over ten years, organized around The Charter of 1838. This had six aims, one of which was universal male suffrage.

Civil rights: The legal rights women gained in areas such as education, employment and the family, including divorce, custody of children and ownership of property.

Consciousness raising: A group discussion with each member sharing personal experiences in order to enlighten the group as a whole, as well as the individual, about social and political realities.

Contagious Diseases Acts: A series of Acts passed in Britain in the 1860s that applied to garrison towns. Police could arrest any woman suspected of prostitution. She was medically examined to see if she had venereal disease and could be sent to a Lock hospital for up to nine months for treatment. The Acts did not apply to male clients.

Declaration of the Rights of Man and the Citizen (1791–2): A fundamental document of the French Revolution defining individual and collective rights. Influenced by the doctrine of natural and universal rights of man, but did not address women's status.

Dissenter: Name given to religious groups such as Quakers, Baptists and Presbyterians who did not conform to all the practices of the Church of England.

Enlightenment: A series of philosophical and political debates in the eighteenth century that criticized the monarchy and the established church and was optimistic about the potential of human reason to reshape the political order on the basis of an understanding of the natural world.

Family wage: The assumption that men should earn a higher wage than women because they either had, or would have in the future, a dependent family to support.

Feminism: A recognition of an imbalance of power between the sexes with women in a subordinate role to men and a belief that women's condition is socially constructed and can therefore be changed. Emphasis is placed on female autonomy.

French Revolution (1789–99): A period of radical social and political upheaval in which the monarchy was overthrown and a republic established on the basis of citizenship and inalienable rights.

Independent Labour Party: British socialist group formed in 1893. Played a key role in the establishment of the Labour Party to which it was affiliated until 1932.

Limited suffrage: The demand for votes for women on the same terms as men was described as a limited suffrage when not all men were eligible to vote. Thus only some categories of women would have been enfranchised.

Manhood suffrage: The demand that all men over a certain age should be entitled to vote.

Marriage bar: In the context of mass unemployment in the inter-war years many governments in Europe, at both a national and a local level, sought to prevent married women from working in occupations such as the civil service, teaching and nursing.

Napoleonic Code (1804): The Code gave a husband full legal powers over his wife, her property and her children and there were harsh penalties if she committed adultery. It was widely adopted in countries other than France, including Italy, Belgium, Holland and the German States.

National Organization of Women: Formed in 1966 by leading American feminists; spearheaded campaign for equal opportunities; has mobilized many demonstrations, including a March for Women's Lives, for reproductive rights, in 2004 that involved 1.15 million people; a membership of 500,000.

Patriarchy: Term used by 'second wave feminists' to describe and analyse a social system in which men had power over women in key social organizations and in personal life.

Post-modernism: A set of concepts that critique broad explanatory theories such as Marxism or Feminism; emphasizes the role of language in constructing our understanding of social reality.

Second International (1889–1916): An umbrella group to which European socialist and labour parties affiliated. Its congresses provided the opportunity for delegates to formulate policy that would guide, rather than bind, members. It had a permanent executive, the International Socialist Bureau. In 1910 declared 8 March International Women's day.

Seneca Falls Convention, 1848: Attended mainly by Quaker women, produced a Declaration of Sentiments on women's rights that included the controversial demand for the vote.

Separate spheres: A term used in the nineteenth century to describe the identification of women with the private space of the family and men with the public world of work. It was assumed this was based on natural biological and social differences between the sexes.

Socialist Women's International: First met in 1907 in Stuttgart before the full Second International Congress; established an International Bureau for Socialist Women to maintain contact between national groups.

Suffragette: First used in Britain as a pejorative term by the *Daily Mail* in 1906. The Women's Social and Political Union then adopted the word for themselves, although it was soon used more widely to include all those engaged in militant activities.

Suffragist: Used in the nineteenth century to describe men and women who supported women's suffrage. After 1905 it was applied more specifically to those who used constitutional or legal methods.

Unitarian: Christian theology based on the view that God is one person (rather than the Trinity); its members were prominent in campaigns against slavery and for women's rights.

Utopian Socialism: Vision of a new way of organizing society based on a transformation of all oppressive institutions, including marriage.

White Slave Trade: This term was used to refer to women, in particular girls, who were sold into prostitution across national borders. An International Conference to suppress the 'white slave traffic' was held in London, 1899.

Woman's Christian Temperance Union: Founded 1874 in the United States to combat the effects of alcohol and led by Frances Willard; an important pressure group for women's suffrage, especially in Canada, Australia, New Zealand and the American mid west.

Women's Liberation Movement: Name given to a series of campaigns on diverse issues such as abortion rights, domestic violence and equal pay in the 1970s that challenged discrimination against women. It was characterized by grass-roots consciousness raising groups and the slogan 'the personal is political'.

World Anti-Slavery Convention, 1840: A meeting of abolitionists held in London. The British Foreign Anti-Slavery Society refused to allow American women delegates to take their seats; this was a pivotal moment in highlighting women's rights.

Part 1

ANALYSIS AND ASSESSMENT

1

The Problem

TURNING THE WORLD UPSIDE DOWN

Millicent Fawcett, a leader of the British campaign for women's suffrage, claimed in 1913 that the women's movement was one of the 'biggest things that has ever taken place in the history of the world'.

> Other movements towards freedom have aimed at raising the status of a comparatively small group or class. But the women's movement aims at nothing less than raising the status of an entire sex – half the human race – to lift it up to the freedom and value of womanhood. It affects more people than any former reform movement, for it spreads over the whole world. It is more deep-seated, for it enters into the home and modifies the personal character.
>
> (Fawcett, 1913: xii)

Fawcett's words remind us of why feminism, both as an ideology and as a political practice, has been such an important and controversial issue in most countries of the world since at least the eighteenth century. At many different times and places individuals and organized groups have demanded reforms that would improve women's lives. Feminism, however, has always had the potential of doing more than that – of quite simply 'turning the world upside down'. Feminism is a cultural as well as a political movement. It changes the way women think and feel and affects how women and men live their lives and interpret the world. For this reason it has provoked lively debates and fierce antagonisms that have continued to the present day. Contemporary feminism and its concerns, therefore, are rooted in a history stretching over at least two centuries.

The mid-eighteenth century is used here as the starting point for a history of feminism. In earlier centuries individual women did debate women's social position. The most well known of these are Hildegard of Bingen, founder of a vibrant convent in the twelfth century, and the fourteenth-century poet and writer, Christine de Pizan. Through their writings and actions they challenged contemporary views about a woman's place and sought greater equality for women, in particular in education. In the period in which they were writing, however, their ideas had little impact beyond a small, educated elite. It was not until the eighteenth century that there was a marked shift in the extent and nature of the development of feminism. The number of texts dealing with women's emancipation increased and the audience for them began to grow. Women were excited by the new ideas of the **Enlightenment** and the upheavals of the **French Revolution**. They began to imagine alternative social and gender relations and came together in various forms of association to challenge male domination and to reject contemporary definitions of what it meant to be female. By the mid-nineteenth century women in Europe, North America and the white-settler colonies of Canada, New Zealand and Australia began to organize together for the first time in societies and groups whose sole purpose was to achieve changes and improvements in the social, political and economic lives of women.

Enlightenment: A series of philosophical and political debates in the eighteenth century that criticized the monarchy and the established church and was optimistic about the potential of human reason to reshape the political order on the basis of an understanding of the natural world.

French Revolution (1789–99): A period of radical social and political upheaval in which the monarchy was overthrown and a republic established on the basis of citizenship and inalienable rights.

HISTORIES OF FEMINISM

This organized movement takes centre stage in most histories of feminism. The educated, articulate women who led the movement were aware that they were making history. They wanted their achievements to be recognized by future generations and to tell their own story. So they wrote autobiographies, memoirs and histories that have helped to shape the way in which we view the characteristics and aims of early feminism. This close relationship between feminist politics and the development of a history of feminism continued with the Women's Liberation Movement of the 1960s and 70s. Activists were keen to trace the origins of their movement and constructed and reconstructed their own history and traditions in line with their contemporary preoccupations. This has had important implications for the ways in which the history of organized feminism has been understood and for the framework within which the story has been told. Thus some ideas, individuals and campaigns have been privileged over others. The suffrage movement, in particular, has held a central place in histories of feminism, especially in Britain and the United States where it was a strong and highly visible campaign. A focus on suffrage, however, can be a distorting lens through which to view feminism as a whole. Many women had other priorities, in particular if they were involved in nationalist, anti-colonial and revolutionary struggles, and we need to make sure that their attempts to pursue women's social, economic and political rights are not lost from view.

A focus on well-organized women's movements has led to the development of a common narrative in histories of feminism that identifies two key periods of activism – 'first wave' feminism, c. 1860s to 1920 and 'second wave' feminism in the 1960s and 70s. This has been adapted slightly to fit the context of some other European countries. In Denmark, for example, three waves have been identified. The first in the late nineteenth century, before demands were made for the suffrage, the second, suffrage phase, just before and during the First World War and the third wave in the 1970s. In Norway there was a long first wave, going up to the end of the Second World War and then a second wave from the 1960s to the 1980s, but with two 'crests' in the 1880s and 1970s. The use of waves as a metaphor can, however, be problematic. A focus on 'ebbs and flows' draws attention away from continuities and lines of tradition and reinforces the assumption that in periods of 'ebb' little feminist activity took place. This means that we can miss the variety of ways in which feminists continued to press for change in a hostile political climate, for example in the inter-war years (Legates, 2001: 282). The 'two wave' model, drawn from the experiences of Britain and the United States, provides a chronological framework that is misleading when applied to other countries. It assumes that the main gains for women's suffrage had been won by 1920, after which the movement fragmented, and yet in South America the inter-war years proved far more significant, while in the 1940s over half the female population of the world still did not have the vote.

These are important reminders that we need to take care that the metaphors that we use, such as 'waves', illuminate rather than constrain our understanding of feminist activities. Thus women's attempts to challenge aspects of their social role in 'quieter' periods need to be rescued from obscurity and seen as a key part of the history of feminism. At the same time we should not underestimate the impact of high-profile, public campaigns which raised 'feminist consciousness' in an explicit way. The suffrage campaign and the **Women's Liberation Movement**, for instance, generated widespread publicity, influenced contemporary politics and affected the ways in which women and men thought about themselves and their place in the world. Historians have therefore searched for other ways to describe 'phases' in feminist history that can differentiate between periods of intense activity, while at the same time not ignoring that there were continuities in feminist campaigns or privileging one chronological framework over another.

An important and influential American historian of feminism, Karen Offen, prefers a metaphor derived from the study of volcanoes. Her comparative study of European feminisms has led her to suggest that feminism is a 'rather fluid form of discontent that repeatedly presses against . . . weak spots in the sedimented layers of a patriarchal crust', with the task of the historian, like

Women's Liberation Movement: Name given to a series of campaigns on diverse issues such as abortion rights, domestic violence and equal pay in the 1970s that challenged discrimination against women. It was characterized by grass-roots consciousness raising groups and the slogan 'the personal is political'.

that of the geologist, to 'map and measure the terrain, to locate the fissures, to analyse the context in which they open . . . and to evaluate the shifting patterns of activity over time' (2000: 25–6). A senior scholar with the Institute for research on Women and Gender at Stanford University, Offen is also a founder and past secretary-treasurer of the International Federation for Research in Women's History. Her comparative work raises many issues that are examined in the course of this book which will explore the history of feminism in a range of countries spanning several continents.

Comparative studies are only possible because of the growing number of histories of feminism that have been produced in recent years for countries outside Western Europe and North America. A broad, comparative approach highlights the varieties of feminism and the different political and social contexts in which they developed across the world. Too often the priorities of white, middle-class Western women, in particular, the achievement of the vote and equal rights, are used as a lens through which to view feminism as a whole. The concerns of women in other parts of the world – for clean water, decent food and access to health care – are then either marginalized or seen as somehow 'less feminist'. Comparative work draws attention to the ethnocentrism and racism of Western feminism and questions the notion of a 'universal sisterhood'. Comparisons between countries put national peculiarities to the test and highlight cross-cultural similarities and differences. They also shift the focus away from a definition of feminism that is based on an Anglo-American model (Blom, 1998). Comparative studies have contributed to an understanding of the complexity of feminism as a theory and as a political practice. Rather than identifying distinctive strands within feminism, such as an emphasis on equality or sexual difference, or between socialist feminism and radical feminism, historians are now more likely to suggest that there was a shifting and complicated interrelationship between various ideas and that these could change over time.

Although feminist campaigns were usually targeted at specific governments, there was a strong international dimension to the movement. The development of industrial capitalism, imperialism and colonialism from the late nineteenth century onwards ensured that women's lives would be woven together on a global scale, while feminists actively sought to make links with each other across national boundaries. It was commonly thought that feminists in Western Europe and North America took the lead in this process, and that there was 'a simple one way move from imperial center to periphery and colony' (DuBois and Oliviero, 2009: 2). Recent studies, however, have shown that the flow of ideas and organizational practice was far more fluid than this might imply. The imperialist nations of Britain, the United States and The Netherlands did not present a monolithic view, but differed amongst themselves, while feminist ideas could also originate outside of these areas. In the inter-war years this was expressed in the growth of international organizations that had their focus outside of Europe and North America.

DEFINITIONS OF FEMINISM

What do we mean by feminism? Does 'feminism' exist today or are the differences among feminists so great that we should speak of 'feminisms'? In fact, such differences are nothing new; the movement has always encompassed a wide range of attitudes, concerns and strategies. This raises the question, therefore, of whether it is possible to come up with a working definition that can be applied to a variety of contexts and periods of time. Feminists themselves, and commentators on their campaigns, are bound to emphasize different issues as lying at the heart of 'modern feminism'. For some it is the demand for women's rights or the quest for female autonomy, whereas for others it is the emphasis on the common bonds uniting women in a critique of male supremacy. It is rare to find any political label that is not controversial, but to jettison labels 'would leave one without any signposts in a sea of chaos' (Caine, 1997: 7).

In this book the term **feminism** will be used to describe a set of ideas that recognize in an explicit way that women are subordinate to men and seek to address imbalances of power between the sexes. Central to feminism is the view that women's condition is socially constructed, and therefore open to change. At its heart is the belief that women's voices should be heard – that they should represent themselves, put forward their own view of the world and achieve autonomy in their lives.

Feminism: A recognition of an imbalance of power between the sexes with women in a subordinate role to men and a belief that women's condition is socially constructed and can therefore be changed. Emphasis is placed on female autonomy.

The word *féminisme*, meaning women's emancipation, was initially used in political debates in late nineteenth-century France and the first woman to proclaim herself a *féministe* was the French women's suffrage advocate, Hubertine Auclert. Earlier in the nineteenth century it was common to refer to the 'woman movement', the 'women's movement' or to 'women's rights'. Even after 1900 when the word feminism was in more general use in Europe women might still prefer to describe themselves as suffragists rather than as feminists. In some cases, as in the United States after 1910, feminism was used by those who wanted to distinguish themselves from the 'woman movement' with its emphasis on suffrage and equal rights. The term feminism was preferred because it implied a more far-reaching revolution in relationships between the sexes, in particular, within the family. How appropriate is it, therefore, to use the word feminist when contemporaries did not describe themselves in that way? It is obviously important to take account of the language used by women themselves in specific historical periods since it helps us to understand their aims and objectives. On the other hand, the term feminist does provide a useful shorthand to convey a set of meanings that are instantly recognizable, in particular, if feminism is defined as broadly as possible. It will, therefore, be used throughout this book to refer to individual women and to social movements that challenged gender inequalities.

Women's rights, women's emancipation and the women's or woman movement were all used by feminists at different times and places to describe their movements and goals. These labels had complex meanings which could change over time. Women's rights campaigners demanded that women should have formal equality with men in the law, politics and in civil society. In the course of making these demands, however, some began to question whether women should simply be seeking to enter a world that was defined by men and shaped by male values. Instead they argued that women were different from men and that 'feminine' qualities should be valued in the public as well as in the private sphere. This tension between equality and difference has been present in feminist debates since the late eighteenth century and will be a persistent theme in this book.

Women's emancipation implies that broader change was needed once formal equality had been achieved. Women were unlikely to be able to take advantage of equal rights while other aspects of their social position remained the same, for example their responsibility for child care. For socialist women full emancipation could only be achieved once women were liberated from economic and class oppression. It was imperative therefore to work for the overthrow of capitalism. During the twentieth century terms such as the women's movement or women's groups took on a different meaning from the one that was common in nineteenth-century Europe. In the earlier period the women's movement was used as a term to refer to those women who acted together to challenge women's subordination. In Latin America in the 1980s and 1990s, however, the term women's movement was used to distinguish groups that made demands on behalf of the community, or who sought to uphold the status quo, from feminist movements that sought to challenge gender roles and inequalities. We need to be careful, therefore, to be clear about what particular groups and movements aimed to achieve.

THEMES

In a book of this size it is not possible to provide a detailed account of the development of feminism in individual countries. Emphasis is placed, therefore, on identifying broad trends and changes over time and on introducing recent interpretations and approaches. There are a number of key themes. Firstly, the challenge made by feminists to prevailing ideas about a 'woman's place'. From the late eighteenth century onwards it was assumed that there was a separation between public and private space. Women's identification with the family and domesticity, or the private sphere, was then used to justify their exclusion from the public world of work and politics. For feminists it was important to contest these ideas and to dispute their exclusion from public life, in particular from the exercise of citizenship. In doing so they challenged contemporary definitions of masculinity and femininity, re-defined what it meant to be female, and used imagination to look forward to a society in which gender relations would be transformed (Yeo, 1997: Introduction).

Feminists did not develop their ideas in a vacuum but had to engage with an existing framework of social and political thought – this in turn helped to shape the characteristics of feminism at different times and places. The complex relationship between equality and difference, a second theme in the book, provides a good example. Feminists did not necessarily challenge the view that women had different qualities and characteristics from men, but used this to their own advantage. They argued that because women were different then they needed to exert an influence for good in the world beyond the family and so they needed equal rights in politics, employment and the law. There could be tensions, however, in bringing these perspectives together and also between the demand for personal autonomy and collective responsibility towards others. These tensions were then worked out in different ways by individual feminists and by the movements of which they were a part.

A further theme will focus on sisterhood. Feminists attempted to develop a politics based on women's solidarity with each other at both a national and at an international level. 'Sisterhood is powerful' was one of the key slogans of the Women's Liberation Movement of the 1960s and 70s. And yet differences of class, race, nation and sexual orientation constantly threatened to undermine this solidarity. Separate women's organizations played a key role in developing a sense of collective identity and a 'feminist consciousness', but did not provide the only space in which women could make their demands. Many feminists sought to achieve their goals through mixed-sex political parties and viewed their feminist causes as inextricably linked to a broader political agenda. Thus, they had to juggle competing loyalties and political identities, often making difficult choices over the course of a lifetime. Some feminists prioritized gender issues throughout their lives, while others shifted the focus of their political interests over time, in some periods prioritizing the fight against racism or class exploitation rather than women's subordination to men. Therefore, the relationship between feminism and other social and political reform movements, including nationalist struggles, socialist politics and anti-colonial movements will form a major theme for this study.

Contagious Diseases Acts: A series of Acts passed in Britain in the 1860s that applied to garrison towns. Police could arrest any woman suspected of prostitution. She was medically examined to see if she had venereal disease and could be sent to a Lock hospital for up to nine months for treatment. The Acts did not apply to male clients.

Feminist ideas, in theory and in practice, were complex. It is important, therefore, not to be too quick to label individuals as feminist or non-feminist on the basis of an ideal model of what a feminist should look like. Women expressed a variety of ideas, and took many different routes, as they tried to challenge inequalities in their lives. Whether they worked in single-sex groups or in mixed-sex political parties feminists had to develop effective tactics. This meant making compromises and negotiating with others who had a different agenda. What they had in common, however, was a vision of a different world for women in which they could imagine possibilities that were not confined by rigid sex roles. To achieve this world they were ready to risk imprisonment, ill health and public ridicule. As Josephine Butler, leader of the British campaign to repeal the **Contagious Diseases Acts**, wrote in 1871: 'English women will be found ready again and again to agitate, to give men no repose, to turn the world upside down if need be, until impurity and injustice are expelled from our laws' (Summers, 2000: 126).

2

The beginnings of modern feminism

THE ENLIGHTENMENT AND THE FRENCH REVOLUTION

When and where did modern feminism begin? What did feminists hope to achieve? Did they see themselves as feminists? It was not until the middle of the nineteenth century that women began to organize themselves into groups with the purpose of challenging their subordinate position and achieving improvements in their lives. They faced a formidable task since legal barriers, religious beliefs, economic interests and political systems all stood in their way. Nevertheless, some women in Western Europe and North America began from the late eighteenth century to demand that their voices be heard.

The ferment of new ideas, political upheavals and economic change in late eighteenth-century Europe provided the perfect conditions for feminist ideas to develop. Gender issues were at the heart of contemporary debates known as the Enlightenment. Political thinkers and philosophers expressed optimism in the potential of human reason to understand the natural world and human behaviour. To achieve this potential, individuals needed freedom of speech and religious belief. They also needed a voice in politics so that they could reshape the political order on the basis of the natural world, thus challenging hierarchical political structures such as monarchies that were inherited from the past.

Emphasis was placed on the importance of a universal human nature and the ability to reason. Universality, however, did not seem to encompass women since most writers claimed that there were physical and intellectual differences between the sexes. Medical and scientific opinion was used to support the view that social and cultural differences were natural, or biologically based, rather than socially constructed. Men were thought to be rational, objective and scientific in their thinking, whereas women were seen as emotional, sensual, lacking in innate reason and a barrier to social progress. These different characteristics were used as the basis for definitions of masculinity and femininity well into the nineteenth century and beyond.

They did not, however, go unchallenged. Women expressed alternative views on marriage, education and politics in an outpouring of novels, articles and pamphlets from the mid-eighteenth century. In salons in France or in literary circles in England small groups of well-educated women began to meet together in an attempt to influence intellectual and cultural life. They drew a response from the French writer Jean Jacques Rousseau whose influential text on education, *Emile* (1762), explored the socio-political implications of sexual difference. For him, boys needed education to develop their natural instincts for independence, autonomy and freedom which in turn suited them for public life and citizenship. In contrast, education for women should be designed to fit them for a domestic role where they could concentrate on motherhood and act as 'the carriers . . . of a new morality through which the unnaturalness of civilisation . . . could be transcended' (Outram, 1995: 84). Within this domestic space women were to be subordinate legally and politically to their husbands.

The French Revolution of 1789 added a new dimension to these debates. It raised the question of what it meant to be an active citizen in the new republic and opened a space for women to take political action. In the **Declaration of the Rights of Man and the Citizen** it was declared that 'men are born free and equal in rights', and yet when the revolutionaries drew up their first constitution a distinction was drawn between active citizens, who were property-owning males over the age of 21, and passive citizens, such as women and domestic servants. Political activists and commentators were quick to challenge this definition. The monarchist Olympe de Gouges, for example, in her book, *Declaration of the Right of Woman and the Citizeness* (1791), called for women to enjoy equality with men in the public sphere. She accepted that men and women had different social roles but thought that this was a sign of strength rather than a weakness. She argued that women would play a more conciliatory role in the Assembly and that this would be good for the nation.

Mary Wollstonecraft's book, *A Vindication of the Rights of Woman* (1792), was the most influential text written by a woman to come out of the French Revolution. Wollstonecraft worked as a writer, critic and translator for the London publisher Joseph Johnson who introduced her to an influential group of radical thinkers, including her future husband William Godwin, and Tom Paine, author of *The Rights of Man*, a text that defended the Revolution against its critics. In her book Wollstonecraft argued that women were just as capable as men of exercising reason and virtue but had been encouraged to see themselves as governed by their feelings and as existing only to please a man. [**Doc. 1, pp. 98–9**] In her view, women needed education to develop their

Declaration of the Rights of Man and the Citizen (1791–2): A fundamental document of the French Revolution defining individual and collective rights. Influenced by the doctrine of natural and universal rights of man, but did not address women's status.

character and to enable them to contribute to shaping the new social order. In common with many other writers of the time Wollstonecraft also believed that equal intellectual capabilities could sit side by side with different social roles. She suggested, therefore, that women's sphere of expertise was motherhood and that the raising of children could contribute to the development of the republic.

Mary Wollstonecraft's powerful message, that a change in women's 'character' and outlook would transform the social order for everyone, inspired many nineteenth-century feminists in Britain. But her unconventional private life – she lived for a time with Gilbert Imlay outside marriage and bore him an illegitimate daughter – and her republican politics meant that her influence was rarely acknowledged at the time. Her reputation was partly rehabilitated when Millicent Fawcett, leader of the British suffrage movement, wrote a sympathetic preface to a new edition of A Vindication in 1891, but it was not until the twentieth century that her importance for the development of feminist ideas, and her influence on the women's movement, was given greater recognition.

The explicit exclusion of women from active citizenship during the French Revolution encouraged them to make demands on behalf of their sex. They established their own organizations to call for government support for educational and social work and also for women's complete equality with men. These activities aroused so many suspicions that in 1793 women were banished from public life. They no longer had the right to attend meetings or to parade in the streets and this was later reinforced when Napoleon came to power. And yet the revolutionaries did see women as having a key part to play in developing the new republic. Through their role as 'patriotic mothers' they would educate their children into the values of republican citizenship. This emphasis on mother educators might seem to give a boost to the notion that women should be identified largely with home and family, but it also gave women an innovative and semi-public role. The notion of 'patriotic motherhood', which was also a feature of nationalist movements in the nineteenth century, could then be used by feminists to promote women's education and to demand equal access to the public sphere.

In the short term, however, legal, economic and social changes reinforced women's identification with domesticity. Their subordination to men within marriage and the family was at the heart of the **Napoleonic Code**, introduced in France in 1804 and then widely adopted by other countries across Europe, including Italy, Belgium and the German states, either as a result of their being conquered by Napoleonic armies or through choice. Britain had its own framework of laws that gave men ownership of their wives' persons, property and earnings and denied women most rights over their children.

Napoleonic Code (1804): The Code gave a husband full legal powers over his wife, her property and her children and there were harsh penalties if she committed adultery. It was widely adopted in countries other than France, including Italy, Belgium, Holland and the German States.

Rapid urbanization and industrialization also led to an emphasis on women's domestic role, although the pace and timing of this varied in different countries. Waged work increasingly took place away from the family and became identified with men and masculinity. This had the dual effect of ensuring that women's paid employment was seen as marginal, thereby justifying low pay, and reinforcing the view that women's natural role was in the home. Working-class women still needed to contribute to family income, but their right to employment was challenged as men sought to achieve a '**family wage**'. For the middle class, who were growing in wealth and influence during these years, the withdrawal of women from making an active contribution to family income was seen as a mark of status and was integral to the way in which they developed a class identity. Even if middle-class women needed, or wanted, paid employment they found that they were hampered by their lack of education and were excluded from most professions. An ideology of domesticity, therefore, based on the concept of a separation of spheres between the sexes, came to dominate political and social thought during the first half of the nineteenth century. It was assumed that biological and social differences affected the personalities of men and women and their suitability for particular tasks. Men were seen as aggressive, competitive and rational, and therefore fitted for the world of paid work and public activity, whereas women were thought to be emotional, nurturing and passive, traits which made them most suited to care for a family in a domestic setting. **Separate spheres** for the sexes were thought to be natural and ordained by God. These ideas then underpinned republican and liberal political theories and were used to justify women's economic and legal dependence on men.

On the other hand, the concept of separate spheres did not necessarily reflect the reality of women's lives since it was employed in complex and contradictory ways and could be affected by class, religion and nationality. In practice, of course, women were not entirely constrained by the private world of the family. There was no hard and fast dividing line between the public and the private. The home itself can be seen as a 'political space' since it was the 'the site of salons, informal discussion groups, political correspondences, ideologically motivated consumer choices . . . all of which were crucial to the emergence of specific radical political cultures' (Gleadle, 2001: 151). Family and friendship networks, and the sociability that was an integral part of these, could facilitate women's involvement in public life. For example, women who were active in the anti-slavery movement in Britain and America, met in each others' homes, made articles for sale at bazaars and then went on to boycott goods produced using slave labour. Such activities remind us that women could be inspired by contemporary definitions of femininity, in particular, their caring and moral qualities, to

Family wage: The assumption that men should earn a higher wage than women because they either had, or would have in the future, a dependent family to support.

Separate spheres: A term used in the nineteenth century to describe the identification of women with the private space of the family and men with the public world of work. It was assumed this was based on natural biological and social differences between the sexes.

attempt to make a difference in the world and could use their distinctiveness from men to justify a role in social and moral reform movements, such as temperance and philanthropy.

EARLY NINETEENTH-CENTURY SOCIAL AND POLITICAL REFORM MOVEMENTS

Did involvement in social, political and moral reform movements lead to an interest in women's rights? Some women were far more concerned with moral and religious questions than with gender inequalities, while others might be just too busy to get involved with women's rights. The British **Unitarian** Mary Carpenter, for example, a leading social reformer, was willing to speak in favour of women's suffrage, but gave most of her energies to the cause of destitute children. Nonetheless, many of the women who were inspired to work with her, including the journalist Frances Power Cobbe, also became convinced that the vote was necessary so that they could influence social legislation and went on to play an active part in the women's movement. In her autobiography Cobbe claimed that

Unitarian: Christian theology based on the view that God is one person (rather than the Trinity); its members were prominent in campaigns against slavery and for women's rights.

> It was not until I was actively engaged in the work of Mary Carpenter at Bristol, and had begun to desire earnestly various changes of law relating to young criminals and paupers that I became an advocate of "Women's Rights". It was good old Samuel J. May of Syracuse, New York, who, when paying us a visit pressed on my attention the question "Why should you not have a vote?" Why should not women be enabled to influence the making of laws in which they have as great an interest as men?
>
> (Cobbe, 1904: 583)

This complex relationship is also mirrored in the anti-slavery campaign. In Britain, a commitment to anti-slavery work delayed women's involvement in feminist politics until the cause had been won. But women did gain experience of working together, corresponded with each other across the Atlantic and developed friendship networks they could draw on in developing an organized women's movement (Midgley, 1992: 174).

Involvement in the anti-slavery campaign also encouraged women to question aspects of their own social position. They drew an analogy between the position of slaves on plantations and their own sexual, legal, emotional and physical slavery to men within marriage. This could then inspire them to make demands on behalf of their sex, whether at home or in European colonies. Feminists continued to draw on the metaphor of slavery to describe their own position in the late nineteenth and early twentieth centuries. They felt able to identify, as women, with the sufferings of others, including those in countries subject to colonial rule, and used this in making a claim for political rights (Burton, 2002: 19).

Utopian socialists added a further dimension to the debates around women's emancipation in the 1820s and 30s. Charles Fourier and Henri de Saint-Simon, political theorists from France, both envisaged a new communal society that would be free from all inequalities, including sex inequality. They were committed to a general movement for 'human liberation' that would include changes in women's social position. Indeed, Fourier argued that the degree to which women were emancipated provided a measure of how far general emancipation had been achieved. Socialists wanted to put their ideas into practice and formed communities in France, Britain and the United States. Rather than focusing exclusively on new forms of production, they sought a transformation in all areas of life, including marriage and the organization of the household. Women took an active part as speakers and as members of the communities. The most well-known female propagandist was the French socialist, Flora Tristan, who argued in her writings and speeches to working men that the emancipation of women and of workers was inextricably linked. In Britain, where the movement was associated with the cotton manufacturer Robert Owen, many female propagandists came from working-class backgrounds, while in France the Saint-Simonians Suzanne Voilquin, Désirée Gay and Jeanne Deroin were all young, working women. Although **Utopian socialism** declined in the 1840s, the links made between the emancipation of women and of workers were to re-surface during the socialist revival of the late nineteenth century. In Britain a number of women influenced by Owenite socialism took their radical views and unconventional behaviour with them into the feminist campaigns of the 1850s and 60s.

Utopian Socialism: Vision of a new way of organizing society based on a transformation of all oppressive institutions, including marriage.

Socialist women also took part in the revolutions of 1848 in Europe that challenged conservative regimes and sought to achieve representative governments and a range of civil liberties. In the process women again raised their own demands. In France Jeanne Deroin called for women's participation in public affairs and argued that only with the end of male privileges in politics could a new society be achieved. She disseminated her views through her own journal, *La Voix des Femmes* (Women's Voice). After declaring that she would stand as a candidate for office she was arrested, with Pauline Roland, and imprisoned for trying to organize male and female workers. Using arguments that were common in the French Revolution, Deroin claimed that women, as 'humanitarian mothers', needed a political voice to safeguard the future of their children and to show men how to achieve harmony. In Germany, Louise Otto-Peters, a well-educated woman from an upper-middle-class background, was also radicalized by the events of 1848.

She drew attention to the need to organize women workers and, a year later, took advantage of the liberal climate to found a weekly women's newspaper that called for social reforms to improve women's position. [**Doc. 3, pp. 100–1**] Otto-Peters insisted that women could make a distinctive contribution to the building of a German nation. For her, womanly qualities included courage, patriotism and the desire for peace and morality. However, if they were to develop their 'true womanliness' to the full women needed education and economic independence.

In Britain women formed female associations to support **Chartism**, a working-class movement that called in 1838 for all men to have the vote. When Chartism declined in the early 1850s, supporters in Sheffield set up a suffrage society to demand votes for women. They were influenced by the radical Quaker, Anne Knight, an anti-slavery campaigner, who wrote one of the first pamphlets calling for women's suffrage. She had connections with outspoken abolitionists in the United States, including Lucretia Mott and Elizabeth Cady Stanton. The two women had met at the **World Anti-Slavery Convention**, held in London in 1840, where they had been incensed by the decision of male delegates that women should not be allowed to play a full part in the conference even if, as in the case of Lucretia Mott, they had been nominated to serve as official delegates by their respective abolitionist organizations. This was the first time that the question of accepting or rejecting women had been raised explicitly and it provided an opportunity for women reformers from Britain and America to meet together to consider issues that they faced as women. As a result of this experience Mott and Stanton were determined to hold a convention on women's rights when they returned home. This was finally held at **Seneca Falls**, New York, in 1848 – a key event in the history of organized feminism. Three hundred delegates passed resolutions on married women's rights, divorce and the need for employment and educational opportunities. Stanton's resolution that it was women's duty to secure the franchise was the most controversial, but it was accepted with a narrow majority. [**Doc. 2, pp. 99–100**]

The interconnections between anti-slavery, women's rights and race are exemplified in the life and activism of Sojourner Truth. A former slave, she took part in the abolitionist movement from the late 1840s. In her speeches she drew on her own personal experiences of slavery that were then published in the form of a memoir entitled *The Narrative of Sojourner Truth: A Northern Slave* (1850). She has become most well known, however, for the speech that she made to the Ohio Woman's Rights Convention in 1851. She criticized men who denied women's claim for rights on the grounds that they needed male protection by detailing all of the physical labour that she had performed and ending with the phrase and 'Ain't I a Woman?' Newspaper accounts do not mention this phrase, and no formal record of the speech was

Chartism: Extensive British working-class movement, lasting over ten years, organized around The Charter of 1838. This had six aims, one of which was universal male suffrage.

World Anti-Slavery Convention, 1840: A meeting of abolitionists held in London. The British Foreign Anti-Slavery Society refused to allow American women delegates to take their seats; this was a pivotal moment in highlighting women's rights.

Seneca Falls Convention, 1848: Attended mainly by Quaker women, produced a Declaration of Sentiments on women's rights that included the controversial demand for the vote.

made until over ten years later when Frances Gage, who helped to organize the Ohio meeting, wrote down her own recollections of what was said. This version varied considerably from contemporary reports, and included the phrase four times. It is Gage's account, however, that has become the standard version and 'Ain't I a Woman' has been used as an inspiration for subsequent generations of feminists. [**Doc. 4, pp. 101–3**]

The demand for women's emancipation, therefore, developed as part of a much broader radical campaign – to free slaves, to introduce representative government, to advance the rights of workers and to achieve property reforms. Links were already being made between like-minded women in different countries. In 1851, for example, Jeanne Deroin and Pauline Roland wrote from their prison in France to the Second National Women's Convention held in the United States, sending greetings to their sisters of America and Great Britain who were united with them 'in the vindication of the right of woman to civil and political equality' (Rendall, 1985: 320). In the political upheavals of the period women from all social classes found a space to articulate their own demands. They challenged the legal, political and economic constraints on their lives, but also used notions of difference to support their demands for a public role.

Did the mid-nineteenth-century women's movement arise from a reaction against the restrictions placed on women, in particular unmarried middle-class women who needed to gain employment? Or did it arise from an attempt by women to extend a public role that was already enjoyed by many? The answer is a complex one lying somewhere between these two positions. As already noted, women were involved in a range of social and political reform movements and organizations which gave them political skills and established a network of contacts. But the restrictions that they experienced, along with the belief that they should use their female values for the good of the community, also provided an impetus towards involvement in feminist politics.

THE ORGANIZED WOMEN'S MOVEMENT IN THE MID-NINETEENTH CENTURY

The precedent set by the United States was soon followed in Europe. The first women to establish organizations to demand their rights and to gain improvements in their social position were to be found in Britain, France and Germany, but these were followed swiftly after 1870 by Italy, Belgium, the Netherlands and Scandinavia. Well-educated, middle-class women predominated in these organizations, although the term 'middle-class' covered a wide range of backgrounds. The unmarried daughters of low-income clergymen worked together with the wives of wealthy industrialists and with women in professional employment such as school teaching or medicine. Men, in particular the relatives of women activists, often gave practical and emotional support. In France, for example, the republican journalist Leon Richer established a newspaper, *Le Droit des Femmes* (*The Right of Women*) (1869) to campaign for women's legal rights and approximately 50 per cent of the members of French feminist groups were male. Individual working-class women did take part in the movement and gained a reputation for their propaganda skills but their numbers remained small. After the political upheavals of 1848 there was a conservative backlash against radical, feminist and socialist politics. This made it difficult to sustain the 'challenging and subversive' side of feminism (Taylor, 1983: xvii). The leaders of the women's movement were anxious to emphasize the moderation and respectability of their movement and to distance themselves from political and sexual radicalism.

In the mid-nineteenth century single, middle-class women were in a diffi-cult position if they had no male relatives to support them. Their education did not prepare them for employment and they were hampered by legal and other restrictions. Thus, key demands of the women's movement at this stage were the provision of secondary and higher education for women and access to professional employment. [**Doc. 5, p. 103**] Women's suffrage was also high-lighted in Britain and the United States but was seen as a more controversial demand in France and Germany. Here it was feared that support for suffrage might harm other causes. Feminists were not, however, just narrowly focused on equal rights. They also took an interest in the family and in moral issues, including the legal position of married women, marital violence and the double standard of morality between the sexes.

The regulation of prostitution by the state came in for particular criticism. In Britain a number of groups were formed in the late 1860s to campaign for the repeal of the Contagious Diseases Acts. The Acts gave extensive powers to the police in garrison towns to detain prostitutes who were suspected of having venereal disease. They could be forced to have a medical examina-tion and then to undergo treatment in a Lock hospital. Repeal campaigners argued that the Acts infringed civil liberties and sanctioned vice. An all-female group, the Ladies National Association, led by Josephine Butler, added a feminist dimension to the campaign by criticizing the power that the Acts gave to men to control women's bodies and highlighting the double standard of morality between the sexes. Campaigners argued that sexual relations should take place within marriage and refuted the belief that men were less able than women to curb their sexual desires. The Acts were finally repealed in 1886 although they still applied to India and other British colonies. Butler formed the International Abolitionist Federation in 1875 to take her campaign to other countries and there was an active abolitionist movement in France, Germany, Finland, the Netherlands and Italy. This had different degrees of success depending on national political, religious and social structures. After 1895, for example, most Dutch municipalities, faced with abolitionist pressure and new medical views about the effectiveness of the system, no longer regulated prostitution, whereas in Italy regulation continued until 1958. For many women the double standard of morality, domestic violence and marital relationships were the areas that concerned them the most, and it was involvement in campaigns around these issues that drew them into feminist activism, not just in Europe and North America but also in countries such as India.

Although feminists were united in their opposition to the double standard of morality and generally disagreed with state regulation of prostitution, they differed on how prostitution should be managed after repeal. Towards the end of the nineteenth century some feminists began to look to the state to play a positive role in protecting young girls from sexual abuse, in reducing prostitution and in preventing the **white slave trade**. In Britain, for example, they joined social purity groups to ensure that the provisions of the 1885 Criminal Law Amendment Act, that raised the age of consent and gave the police powers to shut down brothels, were enforced. Although feminists still attempted to challenge the sexual basis of male power, their actions were often repressive towards working-class women. Moreover, the abolitionist emphasis on the human rights of the prostitute, and critique of male power, often became lost in a general attack on vice in which women were seen as victims.

The women's movement in different countries shared many goals and characteristics in common, but there were also national differences. In the United States native born women of rural New England predominated and they used the language of the Declaration of Independence to claim individual, natural rights, including the suffrage. Inspired by the view that it was women's special mission to undertake moral reforms they were very active in temperance, social reform and anti-slavery movements. Similarly in Britain women were extensively involved in philanthropic work, but feminists were largely drawn from urban industrial and professional families who were rooted in a dissenting reform tradition. Aware of class differences, they took an interest in industrial reform and the position of working-class women as well as a range of equal rights campaigns, including women's suffrage. In Catholic France there was far less opportunity for women to organize together for philanthropic purposes and there was 'no easy route to humanitarian and political activity, such as the anti-slavery or **anti-Corn Law movements** in Britain' (Rendall, 1985: 299). The women's movement was far weaker in terms of support and was to become a moderate, bourgeois

White Slave Trade: This term was used to refer to women, in particular girls, who were sold into prostitution across national borders. An International Conference to suppress the 'white slave traffic' was held in London, 1899.

Anti-Corn Law League: Formed 1838 to gain repeal of the Corn Laws and to establish free trade to ensure low priced food. Many women gave support.

movement linked with republicanism. Emphasis was placed on educational and legal reforms rather than the franchise since republicans feared that women would use their votes to support the monarchy and the church.

Women met regularly in small groups to discuss ideas and to give each other support. Sometimes, as in Britain, there were separate committees to campaign for specific issues such as women's suffrage, the expansion of secondary education, the promotion of employment opportunities or the repeal of the Contagious Diseases Acts. At others, for instance in France and Germany, there were general associations that took up a range of causes. Tactics included lobbying politicians, gathering signatures for petitions, and publicizing ideas through public meetings, pamphlets and newspapers. Petitioning was a key campaign method used throughout the world by women committed to gaining the suffrage. Petitions could demonstrate the strength of support of individual men and women and helped to raise the profile of the movement. In New Zealand a women's suffrage petition was used in a dramatic way when the liberal politician Sir John Hall unrolled a petition 300 yards long, signed by 25,000 women, on the floor of the House of Commons in 1893. [**Doc. 6, p. 104**]

It was a radical and courageous act for women to address an audience outside the home, since their appearance in a public space was equated with immorality. Public meetings with women speakers were most likely to be found, therefore, in the 'liberal' societies of Britain and the United States. It was far more common for feminists to publish their own journals. Amongst the most well known were the *Englishwoman's Journal* (1858) and *The Revolution*, founded in the United States in 1868 by Elizabeth Cady Stanton and Susan B. Anthony. But nearly every country had its own publication including the Spanish Journal *La Voz de la Mujer* (Woman's Voice), *Nylaende* (New Frontiers) published in Norway in 1887 and *La Donna* (Woman), which appeared in Italy between 1868 and 1892. There could be tensions over finance and editorial control that influenced the content of the paper. Also, when the women's movement split in some countries, especially over women's suffrage, different groups used their publications to demonstrate the strength of their own particular strategies and to justify their own position. Nonetheless, with the growth of education and literacy the importance of these journals cannot be overstated. They provided a space for feminists to challenge prevailing ideas about appropriate social roles for women and brought like-minded women in touch with each other. For a minority of women there were also opportunities to gain skills as editors, journalists and financial managers.

Liberal democracies provided the most fertile ground in which feminism could flourish and it was difficult for a women's movement to develop in the context of authoritarian political systems. In Germany, for instance, it was illegal for women to become involved in political meetings or to join political groups. Thus, the General German Women's Association, founded by Louise Otto-Peters in 1865, concentrated on philanthropy and the expansion of educational and employment opportunities for women. In Russia women's public activity was equated with sexual promiscuity and with oppositional politics and was looked on with suspicion by the state. Nonetheless, women did benefit from the government's modernizing agenda. Educational reforms to ensure that girls would be better mothers had the unintended effect of fostering independence and raising expectations. Feminists were then able to build on this to demand access to higher education. By 1900 women had gained entry to most professions except for the law and, through their work as teachers and doctors, were increasingly seen by the state as a force for stability.

Many countries were still subject to the rule of a foreign power. How far did this affect the growth of a women's movement? To what extent did demands for national autonomy and liberal, representative governments stimulate feminism? Women were often encouraged to take part in nationalist struggles. As mothers, it was assumed that they would educate children in the language and culture of their nation, thereby helping to develop a sense of national identity. It was then only a small step before women began to raise their own demands. Alexandra Gripenberg, a leading feminist in Finland, recognized this connection when she observed that the nationalist movement, by encouraging mothers to teach their children the Finnish language, 'became also an indirect means of awakening the women to a sense of their rights and responsibilities' (Evans, 1977: 86). In Norway, for example, women played a part in the struggle with the Swedish Crown to establish independent political institutions. When this succeeded in 1884 they formed the Norwegian Feminist Society, a moderate group open to both sexes, that aimed to achieve economic and educational reforms. Women involved in nationalist and feminist movements could find their loyalties divided, in particular if they had to make the decision to prioritize one over the other. Nonetheless, in Iceland, Norway and Czechoslovakia women's rights were presented as a nationalist issue and this helped to drive forward the struggle for women's suffrage. The links with nationalism were especially strong in Czechoslovakia that was part of the Hapsburg Empire. Here women joined in the campaign in the 1890s to gain parity for the Czech language in the civil service and in 1909 demanded that the International Woman Suffrage Alliance should use Czech as a fourth language in its proceedings.

How far did women gain a sense of sisterhood from working together for their rights? Campaigns that challenged their unequal and dependent position highlighted the difficulties that women shared in common. Close friendships, forged in committee work, added an emotional dimension to feminist politics that helped to sustain individuals as they faced hostility and criticism for flouting conventions. A distinct feminist culture developed based on an alternative set of values that included a critique of male conduct and morality. Women did not, however, just move in a female world. They worked closely with male sympathizers, many of whom were family members. In a movement that roused such strong passions and commitment a sense of sisterhood could be fragile. Some women were difficult to work with and others, including the British feminist Elizabeth Wolstenholme-Elmy, came under criticism because of their unconventional private lives. Disagreements were frequent and could undermine personal friendships, while class, religion and party political differences could cut across and conflict with a sense of common sisterhood. In the United States, for example, Elizabeth Cady Stanton and Lucy Stone set up rival suffrage organizations because of their disagreements over whether to support the Fifteenth Amendment which prohibited disenfranchisement on the grounds of race, but excluded women. Despite her earlier support for the abolition of slavery Stanton was incensed by women's failure to gain the vote and opposed the amendment. She then accepted financial backing from the racist Democratic senator George Francis Train for her journal, the *Revolution*, in which suffrage was connected with a wide range of other reforms. Stone, on the other hand, accepted the amendment and worked with republicans in the mistaken belief that women would gain their support in the future.

Class differences in particular could undermine gender solidarities. In Britain and France feminists argued that they had a common sisterhood with working-class women over the question of employment. They defended women's right to work against attempts by the state, through 'protective legislation', to limit hours of employment or to prohibit women from particular types of work. Drawing parallels with women's exclusion from professional work, they argued that protective legislation was an infringement of women's liberties. Socialist and trade union women took a different view. They looked to legislation and trade unionism as a solution for the long hours and low pay suffered by working women. In the late nineteenth century, when opposition to protective legislation became less pronounced, there was space for greater cooperation between the women's movement and the labour movement.

International sisterhood was also difficult to achieve. News of events and activities in different countries, carried in journals and by propagandists on world-wide speaking tours, did help to stimulate the development of a women's movement, in particular, in places where the political climate was difficult. [**Doc. 9, p. 107**] For example, the United States envoy of the Woman's Christian Temperance Union, Mary Leavitt, travelled throughout the world and left behind 86 women's organizations that aimed to achieve votes for women. The establishment of the International Council of Women (ICW) in Washington in 1888, an initiative of the American suffrage leaders Elizabeth Cady Stanton and Susan B. Anthony, then provided the possibility of a more formal link being made. The Council was an umbrella group for a wide range of women's associations and by 1914 23 national councils had affiliated, mostly from Europe. By aiming to foster unity among its members, however, the ICW avoided controversial issues such as women's suffrage and gained a reputation for moderation and respectability. When the demand for the suffrage became more urgent any pretence at unity collapsed as many individuals and groups left the ICW to pursue their interests in other organizations.

The mainstream women's movement can be characterized as moderate in its aims, ideas and tactics. But this does not tell the whole story. Throughout the period there were dissenting voices, in particular from those who maintained links with an earlier, radical tradition and were prepared to use less conventional methods to achieve their aims. What meanings does the term radical have in the context of the women's movement of the nineteenth century? One of the most influential historians of British suffrage, Sandra Holton, has been instrumental in drawing our attention to a radical tradition within the suffrage movement and has, therefore, changed the way in which it has been viewed. For her, a woman could be defined as a radical if she was impatient with the social conventions of the day, was committed to a radical current of politics outside the women's movement and took up controversial questions such as opposition to the state regulation of prostitution (Holton, 1996). In Britain radicals included Elizabeth Wolstenholme-Elmy, the working-class propagandist Jessie Craigen and members of leading Quaker families such as the Brights and the Priestmans. At a time when there was fierce debate in the suffrage movement about which women should be enfranchised and whether links should be made between suffrage and other political parties, they supported the enfranchisement of married women, attempted to make alliances with working class women and with the labour movement and campaigned for a range of other radical causes. Some of them refused to pay their rates because they were disenfranchised, while Elizabeth Wolstenholme lived in a 'free union' before being pressurized by members of the women's movement to marry Ben Elmy.

In France and Germany, however, where women's suffrage was viewed as a particularly controversial demand, women could be described as radical largely because they were willing to prioritize the vote. Hubertine Auclert, for instance, criticized the moderate outlook of feminist organizations in France because they did not demand the vote for women. In 1870, therefore, she established her own suffrage group and aimed to attract support from women of all social classes. In common with her British counterparts she carried out direct actions to achieve her aims. With other members of her group she tried to add her name to the electoral roll and, when refused, announced that she would withhold payment of taxes. In the 1880s her broad radicalism went beyond suffrage when she carried out other forms of protest, including attending civil marriage ceremonies where she addressed brides on the iniquities of the marriage law. Auclert founded a magazine, *La Citoyenne* (Citizeness), that lasted from 1881 to 1891, but at this stage she was only able to attract a few hundred women to her organization. The German suffragists Anita Augspurg and Lida Gustava Heymann also established their own suffrage group at the turn of the century. They lived together as a couple and combined suffrage activities with demands for sex reform and work for international peace. Heymann also refused to pay her taxes while she was denied the right to vote.

Feminists not only had different priorities, but also had different understandings about what was meant by women's emancipation and how to achieve it. Early histories of feminism tried to make sense of these differences by identifying strands – in a pioneering study Olive Banks, for example, pointed to an equal rights, an evangelical and a socialist tradition in British feminism (Banks, 1980). Feminists certainly had different ideas and strategies, but attempting to fit them too neatly into strands can be constraining. Individuals could draw on a complex set of ideas that often cut across each other and changed as alliances, priorities and tactics shifted over time.

JOHN STUART MILL AND AUGUST BEBEL

Two key texts that helped to stimulate debates on the 'woman question' and provided a framework of ideas for feminists, were both written by men. One was John Stuart Mill's *On the Subjection of Women* (1869). An eminent liberal philosopher and politician, Mill was influenced in his intellectual development by Harriet Taylor, a married woman with whom he began a long friendship in 1830. They married in 1851 after the death of her husband and in the same year she published an article on 'The enfranchisement of women' in the *Westminster Review*. They moved in radical intellectual circles that were sympathetic to rethinking the social position of women, but it was not until after his wife's death that Mill began to write his book. It was to be a groundbreaking text proposing the legal and political emancipation of women.

Mill rejected the view that women were biologically inferior to men and argued that their social upbringing was responsible for any special characteristics that they displayed. Only if women were able to develop fully as human beings, free of legal and cultural restrictions, would it be possible to know what women's nature was really like. Mill emphasized the importance of individual 'self development and the cultivation of individual faculties' and insisted that women should be able to play a full part in political life (Rendall, 2001: 172). Mill's ideas were not always in tune with those of the women's movement. He criticized marriage as a form of slavery for women, but did not challenge the sex division of labour and assumed that women with young children would remain within the home. He also said little about single women, who were central to the concerns of the nineteenth-century women's movement. Mill assumed that domesticity made women unsuited for public roles and, therefore, they needed to be exposed to public life before they could participate in it. This was in complete contrast to feminists who argued that the skills and qualities developed by women within the home qualified them for public and political life.

Contemporaries therefore had mixed reactions to his book but it had a considerable impact that went beyond Britain. In the first year of publication it appeared in the United States, Australia and New Zealand and in translation in France, Germany, Austria, Sweden and Denmark. The leading Italian women's rights advocate, Maria Mozzoni, translated Mill's book, while in 1884 the Finnish Women's Association was founded by a group of women in Helsinki who had met to discuss Mill's ideas. The Association demanded equal rights in education and employment, sought legislation to end the double standard of morality and supported the demand for votes for women. On a practical level Mill, who was elected as an MP in 1865, attempted to further the cause of women's suffrage by presenting a petition comprising 1,499 signatures to the House of Commons in 1866 and in the following year proposing an amendment to include women in the Second Reform Bill.

A second key text, based on a very different set of political assumptions and ideas, was *Woman and Socialism* (1879) written by August Bebel, a leader of the influential German Social Democratic Party (SPD). Bebel argued that a woman in capitalist society was doubly disadvantaged since she suffered economic and social dependence on a man within the family as well as from economic exploitation at the workplace. He explored the social construction of gender and claimed that the 'domination of women by men was rooted not in biology but in history and was thus capable of resolution in history' (Sowerwine, 1987: 403). On the other hand, by using economic definitions of class to describe women's role within the family, or a sex/class analogy, he argued that women would only gain emancipation if they worked alongside men to achieve a socialist society. Bebel's writings provided 'no clear space to develop an understanding of **patriarchy**, as either a separate or a related system to capitalism' (Hunt, 1996: 25) and, therefore, had an ambivalent and contradictory impact on the socialist construction of the woman question. By asserting the primacy of class he enabled socialists to

Patriarchy: Term used by 'second wave feminists' to describe and analyse a social system in which men had power over women in key social organizations and in personal life.

marginalize women's concerns, but by recognizing that women had specific experiences he also ensured that the woman question would be debated extensively in socialist circles.

Bebel's book was translated into several languages and went into numerous editions. His ideas about the relationship between sex and class were then developed further by Clara Zetkin, a leader of the women's section of the German SPD. [**Doc. 11, pp. 109–10**] She popularized her views in a pamphlet on the woman question in 1889 and through her editorship of the newspaper *Die Gleichheit* (Equality), first published in 1891. In 1896 she made an influential speech at the Congress of the Socialist **Second International** where, while sympathetic to the aims of the 'bourgeois women's movement', she opposed any attempts to cooperate with them and set out to show that the interests of women workers lay with their class. In practice, however, socialist women adopted a variety of strategies to achieve their goals; they challenged the preoccupation of their own organizations with the interests of the male worker and sought to foreground the specific needs of women. They also, on occasion, joined with 'bourgeois' women over specific campaigns, although there was often mutual hostility between women who had very different political agendas. [**Doc. 8, pp. 106–7**]

Irrespective of any differences in political perspective, feminists did share a number of common assumptions. They recognized that it was crucial to contest contemporary definitions of masculinity and femininity and to engage in what Offen describes as 'knowledge wars' (Offen, 2000). They denied that women were suited only for domestic life and challenged the liberal assumption that the private world of the home was separate from the public world of work. In doing so they drew upon the language of liberalism and socialism to condemn the restrictions that women faced, but added a new dimension by addressing the 'central question of sexual oppression, as distinct from political or social oppression' (Caine, 1992: 41). They also demonstrated how work and family roles structured female subordination. In demanding a role for women outside the home feminists used Victorian domestic ideology and notions of sexual difference to their own advantage. If women possessed distinct virtues and values then these needed to be used for the good of society as a whole and justified a role for women in public life. Negotiating this complex relationship between 'equality' and 'difference' was something feminists continued to do well beyond the nineteenth century.

At the start of the new century the women's movement in Europe and North America was many faceted. Despite disagreements over theory, tactics and strategies feminists did share many similarities as they confronted a common set of ideas about women's nature and their social roles. As well as seeking equal rights for women in employment, education and the law, they also claimed a role for women in public life on the basis of sexual

Second International (1889–1916): An umbrella group to which European socialist and labour parties affiliated. Its congresses provided the opportunity for delegates to formulate policy that would guide, rather than bind, members. It had a permanent executive, the International Socialist Bureau. In 1910 declared 8 March International Women's day.

difference and the positive qualities possessed by their sex. They challenged male dominance, or patriarchy, in all spheres of life, exposed male violence within the family and contested the double standard of morality. By 1900 women in most countries had greater access to education and professional employment, while married women had an improved legal status. These changes were achieved through a combination of feminist campaigns and broader economic and social developments, including the willingness of some governments to improve women's education in the interests of the state. The one demand that still remained elusive, however, was the right to vote, and at the end of the nineteenth century this increasingly came to the foreground of feminist campaigning.

3

Women's suffrage, 1860s–1920s

ORIGINS OF WOMEN'S SUFFRAGE

Why was women's suffrage such a controversial issue and why did it take so long to achieve? Why did women want the vote so badly and why has it had such a central place in histories of feminism? To what extent did suffrage campaigns make a difference to the achievement of the vote? Both supporters and opponents believed that women would use the vote to bring about social and political change. But more than that contemporaries feared that if women had a political voice then the 'traditional' relationship between men and women in the family and the workplace would come under threat. Feminists certainly recognized the symbolic importance of the vote. It signified the possibility of women acting together across national boundaries to transform the world in which they lived. This helps to explain why it evoked such strong feelings on both sides.

Sex was a key factor in deciding who should, or should not, be included in the franchise. The demand for women's suffrage, therefore, highlighted women's common interests and raised the possibility of a 'universal sisterhood'. It was the one issue that brought women from a variety of backgrounds together in organized groups and in highly public campaigns. This in turn could foster a sense of solidarity among women as they faced intransigent opposition to their cause. Organized suffrage movements developed first in the 'liberal democracies' of Europe, North America and the white-settler colonies of Australia and New Zealand and in most cases reached a peak in the decade before the First World War. Given their size and 'militancy', the British and American movements took centre stage among contemporaries and also in later suffrage histories. But this should not lead us to neglect suffrage movements in other countries. They had their own priorities, aims and tactics which need to be recognized and should not simply be viewed through the eyes of Anglo-American campaigners.

The first women's suffrage organizations were formed in the 1860s in the context of broader political developments. Although women's suffrage was raised in the United States at the Seneca Falls Convention in 1848, it was not until the Civil War that organizations were formed at state level with the specific aim of campaigning for the vote. Once hostilities were over, two national groups were established: the National Woman Suffrage Association, led by Elizabeth Cady Stanton and Susan B. Anthony, and the American Woman Suffrage Association led by Lucy Stone. In Britain women raised their own demands when working-class men, who were excluded from a property-based franchise, campaigned for political reforms in the late 1860s. Women's suffrage societies were formed in large provincial cities as well as in London and in 1868 these joined together in a loose federation called the National Society for Women's Suffrage (NSWS). Despite a hard-fought campaign women were not included in the 1884 Franchise Act. In the bleak years that followed the movement was weakened by disagreements, in particular over whether party political groups that included suffrage within their aims should be able to affiliate to the National Society for Women's Suffrage. As tensions came to a head the NSWS split into two groups until the late 1890s.

In Australia, New Zealand, France, Canada and Scandinavia an organized movement for women's suffrage developed slightly later, in the 1880s and 90s, and the numbers involved tended to be small. In New Zealand the **Woman's Christian Temperance Union** (WCTU) took up the suffrage question. One of its leaders, Kate Sheppard, promoted press campaigns and produced suffrage literature, while the WCTU put strong pressure on parliament by sending in resolutions and petitions. [**Doc. 6, p. 104**] Similarly in Australia the WCTU began to canvass support for women's suffrage in 1888 and was then joined by the Womanhood Suffrage League, formed by Rose Scott in 1891.

Woman's Christian Temperance Union: Founded 1874 in the United States to combat the effects of alcohol and led by Frances Willard; an important pressure group for women's suffrage, especially in Canada, Australia, New Zealand and the American mid west.

In Scandinavia and parts of the Austro-Hungarian Empire there were close connections between liberal nationalist movements and women's suffrage. In Norway, for example, Gina Krog, who was inspired by events in the United States, formed the Female Suffrage Union in 1885. But it was not until radical liberal nationalists, who thought that women would support them in their goal of independence from Sweden, took up the demand for women's suffrage in the 1890s that it became a key political issue. Women who took part in nationalist struggles and were inspired to demand political rights for themselves often found that their own needs were neglected once national independence had been achieved. But this was not invariably the case. In Finland and Norway women gained the vote in 1906 and 1913 respectively and this was closely related to their support for the nationalist movement. Similarly in Czechoslovakia women who took part in the nationalist movement in the 1890s began to raise demands on behalf of their sex. They organized a petition for women's suffrage and in 1905 Františka Plamínková formed the Committee for Women's Suffrage. Women used the argument that their demands were integral to Czech democratic traditions, which were contrasted with those of more repressive governments. They benefited from the support of the liberal nationalist leader Masaryk, president of the post-war republic that introduced women's suffrage.

It was difficult for women to demand the vote in countries with authoritarian political systems. Nonetheless, the departure of the German Chancellor, Bismarck, in 1890 did create a space for groups demanding liberal reforms. The Federation of German Women's Associations (BDF), formed in 1894, did not at first include women's suffrage in its official programme. The affiliated groups had such a wide range of aims that the BDF only represented views acceptable to the majority. Once Marie Stritt became president in 1899, however, women's suffrage was pushed higher up the agenda. In Russia women were inspired to demand the suffrage as part of the political upheavals of the period 1904–5, when the Tsar was forced to call a Duma (parliament) and also by the success of the women's suffrage movement in Finland. Women were so infuriated by their exclusion from the Duma that they formed the All-Russian Union of Equal Rights for Women, led by professional and literary women in Moscow, to achieve equality before the law, including voting rights.

Many moderate women's associations, especially in countries outside Britain and North America, concentrated on civil rather than political rights. They were reluctant to include women's suffrage in their aims because it was seen as a particularly radical demand. Those women who became frustrated with this cautious outlook and wanted to prioritize the vote had to form their own organizations. In France, for example, Hubertine Auclert broke her association with the moderate feminists and formed a group called Women's Suffrage in 1876. Similarly in Denmark a minority of members of the Danish Women's Association left to form suffrage groups in the mid-1880s, while Gina Krog left the Norwegian Feminist Society, whose members showed little interest in participating in politics, to form the Female Suffrage Union in 1885.

As noted in Chapter 2, however, the term radical could have multiple meanings. Just to take up the cause of women's suffrage could be seen as radical in some countries. In others, where the campaign for the vote was stronger, there were differences between suffrage supporters themselves. Gina Krog, for example, can be seen as a moderate because she advocated a property-based franchise, even after **adult suffrage** for men had been achieved, since she believed that the middle-class parties of the Norwegian parliament would be more likely to enfranchise women of their own class. In

Adult suffrage: The demand that all men and women over a certain age should be able to vote.

Britain the term radical has been used to describe different groups of suffrage supporters. Sandra Holton (1996), for example, has traced a radical strand of suffragism throughout the nineteenth century (see Chapter 2) whereas Jill Liddington and Jill Norris (1978), in a pioneering and influential study, use the term radical suffragist in a very specific way to describe Lancashire working-class women at the turn of the century. Rejecting the demand for votes for women on the same terms as men, which would have enfranchised propertied women, in favour of a demand for womanhood suffrage to include all women, they saw women's suffrage as inextricably linked to the broader aims of the labour movement and sought to build a mass movement of working women. What this shows is the importance of exercising caution in the use of terms such as radical or moderate and being clear about their meaning in specific contexts.

In most countries women were enfranchised long after at least some men were enabled to vote. In France all adult males were enfranchised in 1848, while in Britain the franchise for men was broadened by successive franchise reform acts in 1832, 1867 and 1884, and yet women had to wait until the twentieth century to take part in elections for their respective national representative bodies. Why did women face so much opposition to their claim for the vote? Some of the answer lies in the specific political and social contexts of individual countries and whether it was considered that women's votes would favour one party over another. Women were usually associated with conservative attitudes and therefore liberal and left-wing groups, who would normally be expected to support the development of more representative governments, were often half hearted in their attitudes towards women's suffrage. Race could also be an issue. In Texas, for example, it was feared that the enfranchisement of women would increase the Black vote. Other arguments were far more universal. Drawing on the notion of separate spheres it was suggested that women were suited to the domestic world and that their femininity would be threatened by the rough and tumble of politics. Their experience of homemaking and child care meant that they were unsuited to make decisions about imperial affairs or foreign policy. This was reinforced by the belief that women were by nature weak, temperamental and likely to be overcome by emotions, all characteristics that were at odds with the rational decision making expected of voters. It was also feared that the vote would encourage women to argue with their husbands and to neglect their domestic duties which would threaten the stability of the family. Opponents put forward their case in pamphlets, letters to the press and in newspaper articles. Ridicule was a powerful weapon in the attempts made to undermine suffrage supporters. Cartoonists used their drawings to show that the vote would bring domestic chaos and to depict suffragists as unsexed, mannish creatures who found it difficult to attract a husband.

Women as well as men came out in opposition and in some countries formed organizations to campaign against the suffrage movement. In Britain, the novelist Mrs Humphrey (Mary) Ward, who, along with many other well known women, had signed an 'Appeal against Women's Suffrage' in 1889, formed the Women's National Anti-Suffrage League in 1908 which had 10,000 members organized in over 100 branches by 1910. Anti-suffragists feared that full voting rights might disrupt family life and lead men to withdraw their protection which would make women's lives more insecure. It was also suggested that women could play a much more influential role in public life if they did not have the vote.

Faced with such hostility and derision suffrage campaigners gained much needed emotional support from the close friendships that were formed with other like-minded women. It has been suggested that the dynamic of women's political activity cannot be understood simply through a study of organizations but should be seen as rooted in 'personal value systems and in the bonds of family, friendship and community' (Holton, 1994: 213). In the nineteenth century the suffrage movement drew most of its support from well-educated, urban middle-class women whose existing family and friendship networks often formed the basis of their involvement in the suffrage movement and then sustained their commitment through long years of campaigning. In other instances a close, lifelong friendship, such as that between Elizabeth Cady Stanton and Susan B. Anthony, could grow out of a shared commitment to gaining the suffrage and helped to contribute to the success of the movement. Intense friendships, often sustained by letter writing, developed in international organizations – for example between Carrie Chapman Catt, Aletta Jacobs and Rosika Schwimmer of the International Woman Suffrage Alliance. Such friendships reinforced a commitment to internationalism and encouraged women to carry on when the cause seemed hopeless in their own countries (Rupp, 1997: 203–4).

Suffragists used a variety of methods to further their cause. They petitioned governments, lobbied elected representatives, held public meetings and placed their newspapers in public libraries. They also put forward powerful arguments as to why women should have the vote in order to counter those of their critics. [**Doc. 10, p. 108**] It was claimed that women should have the vote as a natural right based on their common humanity with men since, it was argued, they could not be fully human unless they had citizenship rights. For some the claim to political rights was rooted in property ownership, whereas for others it rested on humanity alone, that is the individual's ability to reason. [**Doc. 10**]

By demanding that women should have a role as active citizens in formal political life, suffragists challenged the ideology of separate spheres at the heart of liberal political thought. At the same time they drew on gender differences to support their case by arguing that women would bring particular qualities to politics, and demanded that 'their differences from men should be acknowledged in their citizenship' (Pateman, 1992: 19). In doing so they denied that enfranchisement would undermine 'womanliness'. Instead they argued that their 'womanliness' could be used in the service of the community.

On the surface it might seem that there was a dichotomy between arguments based on equal rights and those based on women's difference from men, but the ideas put forward were complex and interlinking rather than mutually exclusive. Liberalism itself emphasized civic responsibilities, combining the notion of individual rights with the language of duty, responsibility and public service. Women simply re-worked this to suit their own purposes. Millicent Fawcett, a leader of the British suffrage movement, was typical of many in arguing that the right to vote would not only contribute to women's self-development and personal fulfilment, but would also lead to an unselfish public spirit in which women could help those less fortunate than themselves.

Equal rights were always central to the arguments used by suffragists to demand the vote, but after the turn of the century there was a change in emphasis. Politicians and social commentators increasingly saw motherhood as vital for the strength of the nation and the future of the 'race'. Suffragists then took up these issues when making their own demands. They argued that women, with their maternal and domestic qualities, would support reforms to help women and children and would seek to achieve a moral regeneration of society. Up to a point anti-suffrage women shared similar attitudes about women's active citizenship. They feared that women voters would have little say in a male dominated political world but they were anxious to ensure that women could exert influence in other ways. The Women's Anti-Suffrage League argued strongly that women, as mothers, should play a key role in Britain's 'imperial destiny' since the 'whole "future of the race" turned upon women's caring work in their home and communities' (Bush, 2002: 433). Their involvement in social welfare work and 'enthusiasm for advancing women's interests' meant that anti-suffragists could work alongside moderate suffragists, despite their differences on the franchise question.

Both groups of women were ethnocentric in their outlook and in the meaning that they gave to women's citizenship. In Britain, for example, suffragists and anti-suffragists argued that women had a role to play in the Empire through their civilizing mission that would mitigate the harsher aspects of colonial rule and therefore strengthen the Empire. [**Doc. 15, pp. 113–14**] Suffragists saw themselves, in liberal terms, as part of a 'progressive movement of civilization' that could be measured by the improvements that had occurred in women's social position. They believed that they could take the lead in encouraging women's emancipation in the colonies and also that their own enfranchisement would enable them to press for reforms to improve the lives of indigenous populations of the Empire. Suffragists talked of reaching out to their suffering sisters, but there were limits to the extent to which they could connect with women in the colonies on equal terms. Indeed, they were most likely to view themselves as part of a mother–daughter relationship, with the unequal positions of power that this entailed, and to construct a picture of Indian women as helpless victims of oppression rather than as active participants in political struggles to improve their social position.

Women in Western societies were, therefore, often complicit with the racism of colonial regimes at home and abroad. Australian feminists, for instance, were so keen to join the nation that they colluded with racism when they accepted the exclusion of aboriginal women from the franchise. Only a few suffragists, including Rose Scott, protested at this exclusion and sought to protect and encourage the culture of Aboriginal women. Similarly in South Africa suffragists rarely alluded to issues of race except when the 'native question' dominated national politics. When they did so they argued that women as mothers were uniquely qualified to legislate on issues affecting the black population who were akin to children. Thus, they appealed for the vote in ways that could 'reinforce both gendered stereotypes of women's capacities as well as entrenched ideas in the white communities about the supposed political immaturity of black South Africans' (Scully, 2000: 68). For the most part, suffragists avoided race by demanding votes for women on the same terms as men, but they had little difficulty in accepting the exclusion of Cape Africans, defined as people of mixed descent, from voting rolls in the 1920s.

WIDENING THE BASIS OF SUPPORT AFTER 1900

Women had made little headway by the end of the nineteenth century in their campaign to have a voice in national politics. In 1893 New Zealand became the first country to give all women the vote in national elections, while by the 1890s women were able to vote at state level in Wyoming, Utah, Colorado and Idaho in the United States and in South Australia, West Australia and New South Wales. In 1902 Australia introduced adult suffrage for all federal elections in the newly formed nation. There was intense excitement when women first went to the polls in these areas, partly because of the novelty, but partly because it was a way to show that the former colonies were in advance of the European 'mother country' and less bound by old conventions and ideas. [**Doc. 7, pp. 105–6**] Patricia Grimshaw has suggested that although there were specific political issues that explain enfranchisement in different states, places where women were enfranchised at an early date all had common features. They were colonial farming societies, often with a more egalitarian social structure than in Europe. The preponderance of men in the population meant that they felt less threatened by women's enfranchisement and, alongside women's own pressure for the vote, the support of key male legislators could be vital (Grimshaw, 1987). Elsewhere voting rights were confined to local politics where it was thought that women would bring the skills of good housekeeping to the running of local or municipal services. In Sweden and Britain, for example, single women who fulfilled the property qualifications were able to vote for municipal councils in 1862 and 1869 respectively.

A new sense of excitement was generated by the suffrage campaign, however, after the turn of the century. Recently formed organizations attracted a broadly based membership and began to develop different methods and political strategies. This meant that the demand for women's suffrage had a far greater impact on national politics than ever before. In the United States, although the politics of race and class did cause divisions, there were greater efforts to involve more black and working-class women in the suffrage movement. Leaders of a nationally organized black women's club movement that developed in the 1890s encouraged black women to participate in the suffrage campaign. They also attempted to counter the tendency among white northern suffragists to support restrictions such as literacy qualifications on the grounds of political expediency since this would limit the voting rights of black women. The National American Woman Suffrage Association (NAWSA), formed from a merger of existing groups in 1890, expanded its membership and began to work more closely with the women's trade union movement, in particular, in New York, where working-class trade union leaders such as Rose Schneiderman and Leonora O'Reilly spoke on suffrage platforms. After 1912 there was also a change in tactics when there was a far more concerted effort to campaign for a federal amendment to the constitution rather than seeking voting rights at a state level. Similarly in Britain provincial organizations came together in 1897 to form the National Union of Women's Suffrage Societies (NUWSS) under the leadership of Millicent Fawcett. The basis of support began to widen. Women who had taken advantage of greater educational opportunities and were employed in the expanding areas of teaching, nursing and clerical work took up the suffrage cause alongside some groups of industrial workers. In Lancashire, where textile workers took the lead, new methods of campaigning were used, including open-air meetings, leafleting at factory gates and public demonstrations, while in 1900 29,300 signatures were obtained for a suffrage petition.

Elsewhere in Europe, including Germany, France, Denmark and Sweden, new organizations were formed. Membership was smaller than in Britain and the United States but should not be underestimated. In Germany, the Union for Women's Suffrage, established by Anita Augspurg and Lida Heymann in 1902, had only 2,500 members by 1908, but when the ban on women's participation in politics was lifted in that year its membership expanded rapidly and reached 9,000 by 1913. In Denmark the two largest suffrage groups had 23,000 members between them by 1910, a significant proportion of the small female population of 1.5 million. Here a broad coalition of women's organizations supported the campaign for the vote, including nurses, teachers, girl scouts and deaconesses' associations as well as the suffrage groups themselves. They also managed to cooperate with women from trade unions and the Social Democratic Party.

Men also gave their support. Women's exclusion from national representative institutions meant that they needed sympathetic men to introduce suffrage bills. Keir Hardie, the British socialist MP, Sir John Hall in New Zealand and Hadji Vakil el Rooy from Iran, all presented the case for women's suffrage. They had a strong personal conviction that women should have the right to vote as a matter of natural justice, but there were other politicians and political parties that took up the cause as a matter of expediency. Thus in Sweden before the First World War both the Liberal Party and the Social Democrats supported a measure of women's suffrage because they thought the women's vote would strengthen their parties against the conservatives.

Male journalists used their access to the media to spread suffrage propaganda. Tom Johnston, editor of the Scottish socialist newspaper *Forward*, and the Czech nationalist leader Tomas Masaryk, editor of *Our Era*, both gave sympathetic coverage to women's suffrage in their newspapers, while others, such as Henry Blackwell and Frederick Pethick-Lawrence, edited suffrage papers jointly with their wives. Married couples had often worked together for political or social reform, but the suffrage movement did provide a different context for this shared activity and challenged the roles that men and women were expected to play in politics and in the family, with many couples using both surnames as a mark of equality.

Nonetheless, the struggle for the vote in this period was a female-dominated movement with leadership firmly in the hands of women. Male supporters were expected to be in an auxiliary position. In France, for example, the suffrage movement was largely comprised of women by 1900, with men forming approximately 15–20 per cent of the membership of feminist societies compared to almost half earlier in the century (Hause with Kenney, 1984: 44). Some suffrage groups excluded men from holding office while others were closed to men altogether, including the British Women's Social and Political Union, the Norwegian Female Suffrage Union, the National Woman Suffrage Association in America and the Female Progressive Association in Denmark. In a number of countries, therefore, men established their own organizations to support the campaign for women's suffrage and in 1912 groups from the Netherlands, France, Sweden, Britain, Hungary, the United States and Denmark came together to form the Men's International Alliance for Woman Suffrage.

SOCIALISM AND SUFFRAGE

There was more ambivalent support from within the socialist movement. If some feminists increasingly emphasized male power over women, others continued to focus on class as well as sex oppression and drew attention to the difficulties faced by working-class women. They were often suspicious of suffrage groups that were set up ostensibly to cater for the needs of all women but were in fact run by middle-class women who controlled the agenda and direction of the organizations. [**Doc. 8, pp. 106–7**] Socialist women thought that women's emancipation should be seen as part of the struggle for socialism but could not agree on how much importance to give the vote. The suffragists amongst them argued that political equality would raise women's industrial and social status and would give them greater power to influence social reforms. Socialist women found it difficult to juggle between competing loyalties – to class, party and gender – but managed to make a significant contribution to the suffrage campaign. Encouraged by socialist rhetoric of equality women demanded political rights for themselves. They argued that if women did not have political equality they would be unable to take part in the struggle to achieve socialism or to influence the shape of the new socialist society. [**Doc. 11, pp. 109–10**]

Socialist groups were committed in principle to women's suffrage, but in practice they rarely gave priority to the question. At the Second International meeting in Stuttgart in 1907, however, a resolution was passed calling on members to 'struggle energetically' for women's suffrage as part of a broad demand for all men and women to have the vote. This caused tensions between socialists and women's suffrage groups in countries where the male franchise was a restricted one. In the latter suffragists called for votes for women on the same terms as men, or a **limited suffrage [franchise]**, even if this meant that only propertied or educated women would be enfranchised, since it was argued that the principle of removing a restriction based simply on sex was all important. Socialists on the other hand claimed that this would not benefit working-class women and called instead for adult suffrage, a demand that many suffragists feared could easily turn into support for **manhood suffrage**. Nonetheless, in countries such as Norway and Austria, it was socialist women who were instrumental in ensuring that franchise reforms that had given women the vote on a restricted basis were extended to include all women.

Limited suffrage: The demand for votes for women on the same terms as men was described as a limited suffrage when not all men were eligible to vote. Thus only some categories of women would have been enfranchised.

Manhood suffrage: The demand that all men over a certain age should be entitled to vote.

In Britain, the **Independent Labour Party** was unusual amongst European socialist parties in giving formal support at annual conferences to the demand for a limited suffrage. Many of its members were active in suffrage organizations and this pattern was repeated elsewhere in Europe. In Austria and Germany, however, it was the socialist women's organizations, the largest and most well organized on the Continent, which took a leading role in the suffrage movement. [**Doc. 11, pp. 109–10**] In Germany they campaigned vigorously in the pre-war years, organizing the first Proletarian Women's Day in 1911 when demonstrations in favour of women's suffrage were held throughout the country. Street marches, with women carrying placards and banners, provided a contrast to the moderate methods of the liberal feminist suffrage groups. Socialist women, in particular in Britain, Austria, Germany and Italy were able to put pressure on labour and socialist parties to give support to the cause of women's suffrage. This became increasingly important as the electoral support for such parties began to increase. There could be considerable hostility between socialist women and the 'bourgeois' women's movement, although the intensity of this varied in different countries, while close links were made and sustained between individual activists, in particular at a local level.

Independent Labour Party: British socialist group formed in 1893. Played a key role in the establishment of the Labour Party to which it was affiliated until 1932.

INTERNATIONAL WOMEN'S ORGANIZATIONS

The fresh lease of life gained by the women's suffrage movement could also be seen at an international level. For the first time an international organization devoted specifically to the campaign for the vote was established. The International Woman Suffrage Alliance (IWSA) was formed in Berlin in 1904 after the International Council of Women (ICW) failed to give wholehearted support to the suffrage cause. The aim of the IWSA was to act as a central bureau to collect, exchange and disseminate information about suffrage work and to stimulate national suffrage activities. It could be a lifeline for women in countries such as Russia, who were struggling against repressive regimes, to know that they had the support of others in more fortunate circumstances. Under the leadership of the American Carrie Chapman Catt, president from 1904 to 1923, the IWSA provided an important space for women to meet with each other across national boundaries. Congresses were held in different countries every two years until the outbreak of war and members could keep in touch with international developments in the years in between through reading, and contributing to, the IWSA journal, *Jus Suffragii* (The right of suffrage), launched in 1906. At the same time their own suffrage newspapers reported at length on the campaign in other countries. National women's suffrage organizations that had suffrage as a sole objective could affiliate to the IWSA. The definition of a national group was ambiguous, however, and led to controversy in later years when there were splits in national suffrage movements. It was agreed that suffrage would be pursued as a matter of human rights and justice. This contrasted with the emphasis of some national groups on women's special qualities, derived from the domestic sphere, as a justification for the vote.

There were tensions though, even in a group based on white, middle-class women who shared similar liberal and imperialist assumptions. Many women from continental Europe distrusted the extent to which Britain dominated the international women's suffrage movement, while individual women could find the private lives or radical causes taken up by others difficult to deal with. In her biography of Carrie Chapman Catt, written in 1944, Mary Peck noted that 'As one of the earliest and most outspoken advocates of birth control and pacifism, and also as a bitter critic of England in the Boer War, [Aletta Jacobs] was a good deal of a trial to Mrs. Fawcett in the International Women Suffrage Alliance' (quoted in Bosch, 2009: 9). In 1913, Martina Kramers, a Dutch socialist, was asked by Carrie Chapman Catt to give up her position as editor of the IWSA journal *Jus Sufragii* both because of her private life (she lived with a married man) and also because of her socialist politics.

Socialist Women's International: First met in 1907 in Stuttgart before the full Second International Congress; established an International Bureau for Socialist Women to maintain contact between national groups.

In many respects there was a huge gulf between the IWSA, with its largely moderate, educated, middle-class membership and the **Socialist Women's International** with its emphasis on class oppression and exploitation. Nonetheless, individual socialist women such as Isabella Ford from Britain and Martina Kramers from the Netherlands took an active part in the IWSA, although it is significant that neither of them were simultaneously heavily involved in the Socialist Women's International. The hostility between some international leaders of both movements, and the ideological differences between them, should not be underestimated. On the other hand there was often a complex interchange of ideas between socialists and feminists across national boundaries. For example, it was the arrival of the Dutch feminist Wilhelmina Drucker at the Brussels Congress of the Second Socialist International in 1891 that led to the development of an organized feminist movement in Belgium. At the same time, Drucker's successful challenge to male socialists at the Congress to give formal support to full equality for women meant that she made numerous international contacts with women's rights campaigners and began to move away from socialist politics (Aerts, 2005).

MILITANCY

Although the campaign for women's suffrage grew in strength in many different countries in the decade before the First World War, it was the

British suffrage movement which took centre stage as 'militant' methods caught women's imagination throughout the world. Militancy has given us the most enduring images of the campaign – women being arrested and forcibly fed – that are instantly recognizable to a wide public. Britain, rather than the United States, was now looked to for leadership and inspiration from women in other countries who faced greater political and social restrictions on their activities and their lives. The new tactics were initiated by the Women's Social and Political Union (WSPU), an organization established in 1903 by Emmeline Pankhurst, along with other members of the Manchester branch of the socialist group, the Independent Labour Party.

Inspired by the suffrage activities of women workers in Lancashire the WSPU sought initially to carry out propaganda for socialism and for suffrage and for two years remained as a small, locally based group. All this was to change in 1905 when the WSPU came into the limelight in a dramatic way. During the General Election campaign of that year two WSPU members, Annie Kenney and Christabel Pankhurst, disrupted a meeting by shouting Votes for Women and were promptly arrested. This led to further disruptive activities, including heckling speakers and mass lobbying of parliament, as well as to the organization of large demonstrations and processions in London. [**Doc. 12, pp. 110–11**] Other organizations followed suit, including the Women's Freedom League (WFL), a breakaway group formed in 1907 by Teresa Billington-Greig and Charlotte Despard. As frustration mounted the WSPU, whose members were called **suffragettes** to distinguish them from **suffragists** who used constitutional methods, escalated their tactics. Their new campaign involved the smashing of windows, setting fire to empty buildings and destroying mail in post boxes. Approximately 1,000 women were imprisoned for their suffrage activities and after 1909 many went on hunger strike to protest at being denied the status of political prisoners. [**Doc. 13, pp. 111–12**] They were forcibly fed and in 1913 the '**Cat and Mouse' Act** enabled the government to release prisoners until their health had recovered and then to re-arrest them.

Militancy has always provoked passionate debate. Suffrage campaigners, for example, disagreed about whether militancy was either effective or legitimate. In their autobiographies, often written in the inter-war years, suffragettes created a view of 'authentic militancy' which they associated with destruction of property, imprisonment and hunger striking. This has had a long-lasting influence on the way the public and historians have looked at the movement (Kean, 1994; Mayhall, 2003). But, how should we define militancy? What did it mean to those who took part? If we look closely at the different organizations and individual activists then it becomes clear that militant actions were very diverse and also changed over time. When WSPU members first heckled cabinet ministers at meetings their action was considered as militant, but

Suffragette: First used in Britain as a pejorative term by the *Daily Mail* in 1906. The Women's Social and Political Union then adopted the word for themselves, although it was soon used more widely to include all those engaged in militant activities.

Suffragist: Used in the nineteenth century to describe men and women who supported women's suffrage. After 1905 it was applied more specifically to those who used constitutional or legal methods.

Cat and Mouse Act, 1913: Popular name given to the British Prisoner's Temporary Discharge for Ill Health Act; empowered the Home Secretary to release a hunger-striking prisoner until her health improved after which she could be re-arrested and imprisoned.

this was a far cry from the window breaking and arson that was a feature of the campaign just before the war. WFL members looked for other ways to express their militancy that did not involve the destruction of property, including tax resistance and a boycott of the 1911 census. Within the WSPU itself women could choose which type of activity they wanted to engage in and not all volunteered for 'active service'. The Blathwayt family who lived near Bath, for example, put their large house at the disposal of suffragettes who needed to recuperate after speaking campaigns in all weathers or after a spell in prison. Women were encouraged to plant a tree in an area of the grounds that came to be known as the suffragette field, or Annie's arboretum, after Annie Kenney who was the district organizer, while Colonel Linley Blathwayt sought to provide a record for posterity by taking photographs of all who stayed in his home. It was less a question of whether a specific activity was undertaken and more a matter of the spirit in which women approached their political activism. The intensity of feeling and the daring of suffragettes inspired women from a variety of social and political backgrounds to give up everything for the cause and transformed the lives of those who took part. For suffragettes, militancy was a way of expressing active citizenship, perhaps best encapsulated in the phrase, 'Deeds not Words', the motto of the WSPU.

The terms constitutionalist and militant provide us with useful labels to distinguish between different tactics and strategies, but they do not describe completely distinct positions. In the early years, in particular, many women were members of both the WSPU and the NUWSS, while other organizations such as the Actresses' Franchise League and the Artists' Franchise League cooperated with both groups. The tactics and methods adopted by organizations changed over time as they were influenced by each other. Inspired by the flamboyance of the WSPU, the NUWSS began to hold large demonstrations, pageants and processions, including the 1913 Pilgrimage in which thousands of women marched from all over Britain to a rally in London. The NUWSS found new ways to spread ideas, such as the suffrage caravan in which speakers toured through towns and villages. Suffrage activists may have disagreed about the effectiveness of militancy, but the publicity generated by the campaign boosted the membership of all suffrage groups. By 1914 the NUWSS had 380 affiliated societies with over 53,000 members. The WSPU was smaller, with 88 branches and an active membership of less than 5,000, but its newspaper had a circulation of 30,000–40,000.

The new militant tactics also affected suffrage campaigners in other countries. In France Madeleine Pelletier and Caroline Kauffman disrupted a meeting of the Chamber of Deputies on 3 June 1906 when they showered delegates with leaflets which led to their arrest. In China members of the Women's Suffrage Alliance armed themselves with pistols and stormed the parliament for three days. The Irish Women's Franchise League harassed visiting English politicians, resisted the 1911 census and in 1912 began to smash windows, leading to the arrest and imprisonment of those who took part. The American, Alice Paul, was introduced to militant methods when she was studying in London, 1907–10. She joined the WSPU and was imprisoned twice, on one occasion going on hunger strike for three days. When she returned to the United States she sought to bring new methods to the American movement. Along with a friend, Lucy Burns, whom she had met in a London police station, she organized a suffrage parade of 5,000 women in Washington in 1913 on the day before the inauguration of the new president, Woodrow Wilson. Through a new group, the National Woman's Party, formed in 1916, she organized parades, demonstrations, automobile petition drives throughout the west and picketed the White House. Many women were arrested for obstruction and were imprisoned, which led to hunger strikes and forcible feeding. The WSPU clearly inspired all these actions, but in most countries outside Britain they were confined to a minority. [**Doc. 14, p. 112**]

Propaganda became increasingly important for suffrage campaigners. Posters, plays, novels and newspapers were used to counter the view that engagement in politics would make women less womanly. In place of the embittered, masculine spinster or the domineering wife that appeared in the imagery of their opponents, they put the womanly woman who protected the interests of working-class women and children or the educated professional woman such as the teacher, nurse or midwife. Heroines from the present and the past were also used to inspire rank and file activists. Emmeline Pankhurst, for example, was a tireless campaigner and gave rousing speeches at meetings throughout the country. She was arrested, imprisoned and forcibly fed on numerous occasions. Her physical courage inspired devotion from her followers and gave her the status of a 'heroine'. Her photograph, and those of other leaders, were then sold to the membership which enabled them to show their devotion and loyalty as well as raising money for the cause. Images of well-known historical figures such as Joan of Arc were used on banners, posters and in the newspapers to represent powerful women operating in a political context. Joan of Arc was a potent symbol, a maiden warrior who had overcome the limitations of her sex to fight for a higher cause which brought her martyrdom and then sainthood. Such propaganda, in particular imagery, was a powerful tool to challenge contemporary notions of how women should behave and of what it meant to be a 'political' woman. As Lisa Tickner argues, suffrage imagery was not just a 'footnote' to the real political history going on elsewhere, but an integral part of the fabric of social conflict with its own power to 'shape thought, focus debates and stimulate action' (Tickner, 1987: ix).

It became an important part of the suffrage campaign in other countries of the world, although the imagery was not always the same. In Austria and Germany the images used reflected a more 'traditional' view of femininity since suffragists were anxious to counter arguments that women would become too masculine if they entered politics. In contrast, socialist women highlighted women's strength and bravery. They were prepared to take to the streets to gain the suffrage. A poster advertising Women's Day in Germany's red week, March 1914, depicted a woman of strength, who was bare-footed and plainly dressed, holding a flag and standing above the slogan 'Come Out For Women's Right to Vote'. Thus suffrage campaigners both used, and subverted, contemporary definitions of femininity and adopted those images which best suited their particular national contexts.

The campaign for the vote also generated intense debate about the causes of women's subordination, the meaning of emancipation and what feminists hoped to do once they were enfranchised. A minority of radical feminists criticized the constraints of marriage and, inspired by sexual psychologists such as Havelock Ellis, took an interest in sexual freedom and pleasure for women. The mainstream suffrage movement was also interested in sexual issues and saw them as linked to the vote. But they remained suspicious of demands for greater sexual freedom and called instead for men to exercise self control and for an end to the double standard of morality. Fearing the spread of venereal disease and male promiscuity, Christabel Pankhurst, after fleeing to Paris in 1912, wrote a famous series of articles for the *Suffragette*, later turned into a pamphlet entitled *The Great Scourge and How to End It* (1913), which claimed that the majority of men suffered from a sexually transmitted disease. She advised women to cease from sexual relations with men until they had the vote and the WSPU came up with the well known slogan 'Votes for women, chastity for men'. By this stage Christabel Pankhurst and other members of the Union saw male power over women as encompassing personal as well as political and economic life and argued that women's exclusion from politics left them powerless in their sexual lives. Controversially, they drew a parallel between married women's exchange of sexual services for economic support with the prostitute's sale of her body and sex to male clients.

ACHIEVEMENT OF THE VOTE

By 1920 women had gained the vote in most countries in Europe and North America. Suffragists in France and Italy had to wait until after the Second World War and it was not until 1971 that Switzerland finally conceded voting rights. What explains the timing of women's achievement of the vote and why did some governments resist women's demands for so long? The favourable conditions in colonial farming countries have already been noted. Religion could also play a part. In general, Catholic countries were more resistant to women's suffrage than Protestant ones. In France, for example, Republicans feared that women were controlled by parish priests and might wish to restore the monarchy and so they were wary of any demand for the vote. Similarly in Spain there was an emphasis on women's 'traditional' role in the family. When it was suggested that widows should be able to vote in municipal elections in 1908 this was opposed on the grounds that it would be like handing the vote over to the priest. And yet in Czechoslovakia, a predominantly Catholic country, the Czechs associated the Habsburgs with loyalty to Rome and supported women's suffrage as a way to strengthen the nationalist movement. In Ireland also the church did little to prevent the development of a strong, militant movement.

A long-held assumption is that women achieved the vote as a reward for their war services, but this does not stand up to close scrutiny. In France and Italy women were not enfranchised, despite their efforts during the war, while in Britain politicians were reluctant at first to include women in proposals made in 1916 to extend the male franchise. When British women did achieve a measure of suffrage in 1918, it was restricted to those over 30 who had been far less involved in the war effort than younger women. Where the war did have an impact was in creating political and social upheavals that led to the development of new political systems. Thus women gained the vote in the liberal democratic governments created after the war, including Czechoslovakia, Austria, Hungary and Germany where it was assumed that women would support moderate governments against attack from both the left and the right.

What is clear is that no one single explanation will suffice, and that the achievement of the franchise must be understood within the complex political, religious and social context of individual countries. It is important though not to lose sight of women's agency and the extent to which they played an active role in their own emancipation. By itself, the existence of a strong suffrage movement was clearly not enough to guarantee success. In Switzerland, for example, women did not gain the vote until long after other Western European countries, but there had been an active suffrage movement since the early twentieth century. Women also gained the vote relatively early in countries where the suffrage movement was weak or non-existent. Elsewhere, however, suffrage campaigning and the publicity generated did ensure that politicians were not able to ignore the demand for the vote. There was no guarantee, for example, that women in Britain would have been included in the 1918 Franchise Bill if they had not continued to lobby the government and to make their presence felt. They also maintained their pressure until an equal franchise was granted in 1928. Similarly in the United States it was women's hard work at a national and at a state level that ensured that the Senate would ratify the Nineteenth Amendment, giving women the vote, in 1920, albeit with the narrowest of margins.

The suffrage campaign was a key moment in the development of a feminist consciousness. Suffrage activists, organized in groups that were predominantly female, gained a heightened sense of solidarity with other women as they battled against hostile governments to achieve their aims. This could lead, as in the case of the WSPU, to an emphasis on the oppression of all women as a sex by men and an appeal to put gender loyalty above class and party. Although they were inspired by individual acts of courage, the emphasis was on women acting together and many suffrage campaigners gave a full-time commitment to the cause in the years immediately before the First World War. On the other hand, the suffrage movement revealed, and at times exacerbated, the differences between women. Suffrage groups were often hostile to each other and failed to agree on political strategies and on methods of action. At the IWSA meeting of 1906, for example, Millicent Fawcett challenged the credentials of Dora Montefiore, a member of the WSPU. Dora was only allowed to speak after the Dutch and Hungarian delegates wrote to the president asking that she should be heard on behalf of the 'insurgent women of England'. Suffrage groups had their own colours and slogans that reinforced a sense of identification with a particular group rather than to suffragists more generally. As the social and political backgrounds from which suffrage campaigners were drawn began to widen, tensions increased between them and the leaders of the movement who were still largely well educated, middle class and moderate in outlook. For those women who remained politically active once the vote was won differences could be exacerbated as they sought to pursue their feminism through mainstream political parties as well as through women's organizations. At the same time there was a grow-ing tension between women's involvement in nationalism and anti-colonial struggles and the internationalism of the women's movement. These issues will be considered in the next chapter.

4

Feminism, internationalism and nationalism in the twentieth century

WOMEN'S SUFFRAGE BEYOND EUROPE AND NORTH AMERICA

L atin America, the Caribbean, Asia and parts of the Middle East took centre stage in the inter-war years in the struggle for women's suffrage and women's rights. Feminists here were often involved in nationalist and anti-colonial struggles and had a complicated relationship with Western feminism. To what extent was it possible to link a nationalist with an internationalist consciousness and how does this affect our understanding of the term 'universal sisterhood' (Sinha, Guy and Woollacott, 1998: 345, 350)?

After the upheavals of the First World War issues of race and the need for self-determination came to the fore. Within the British Empire India demanded a larger degree of self-government, while countries in Latin America expressed nationalist and anti-imperialist sentiments when the United States increased its military and economic presence. The Russian and Mexican revolutions also inspired many to seek a far-reaching transformation of economic and social structures. In this uncertain time women increasingly tried to make their voices heard and demanded change in all areas of their lives, including the right to vote.

Feminist campaigns gathered momentum in the inter-war years in Latin America and parts of the Caribbean. Women had already begun to organize together to demand reforms in the early 1900s. It was in the 1920s and 30s, however, that organized women's groups in Argentina, Uruguay, Brazil, Chile and Mexico expanded in number and gained greater publicity. The characteristics of these groups varied a great deal from country to country – so much so that Latin America can be described as a site of 'competing feminisms' (Ehrick, 1998: 415). Brazil and Uruguay, for instance, had very different suffrage campaigns although women were enfranchised in both countries in 1932. The suffrage movement in Brazil was unusual since it was led by a small group of upper- and middle-class urban women, with close ties to the country's political elite, who used their influence with members of the government as a way to achieve their aims. In an attempt to mobilize more women, however, they did expand their activities to include letter campaigns, press releases, petitions and the holding of public forums. The most well-known women's rights organization, the Brazilian Federation for the Advancement of Women, was formed in 1922 by Bertha Lutz who had been educated in Europe and had personal friendship links with women in the International Woman Suffrage Alliance to which the Federation was affiliated. The leaders of the Federation were moderate in their arguments. They attempted to allay the fears of their opponents by suggesting that the vote would enhance women's role as mothers and enable them to use their special qualities of morality and care for others for the good of the community. A breakthrough came after a revolution in 1930 which brought in a new regime, under the leadership of President Getúlio Vargas, that set about redrafting the electoral code. After protracted negotiations and a delegation from the Federation to the president, it was finally conceded that women should have votes on the same terms as men.

In Uruguay, where the church was weak, the women's movement followed a liberal feminist pattern that was familiar in Europe. Women's organizations, including the Uruguayan National Council of Women (1916) and the Uruguay Alliance of Women for Suffrage (1919) were established. Led by a doctor, Paulina Luisi, they drew their members initially from the educated and professional middle class but then sought to expand their membership base by appealing to literate working-class women. As elsewhere the movement was hampered by opposition from conservative political parties who feared the links that had been made between socialist groups and feminist causes. Luisi's domination of the movement also caused internal splits and conflicts. After 1928, however, the Alliance, inspired by gains women had made in other countries of the region and by pan-American women's conferences, launched a new women's rights campaign that emphasized reforms in education and the family as well as the suffrage. There was considerable press support and a bill to enfranchise women was finally approved in December 1932.

Feminists argued about aims, priorities and tactics and often shifted their position over time. Equality for women in education, the family and the law was a key objective for all of them, but the vote, and the basis on which to demand the franchise, was far more contentious. Class differences were especially important. In Puerto Rico, for example, it was working women from the trade union movement who, in 1908, first lobbied for a bill to give women all the rights enjoyed by men under the law. From this point on both working- and upper-class women gave priority to the suffrage. But they campaigned from separate platforms and could not agree about whether to ask for a limited or an adult franchise. In Mexico too class proved to be divisive. In the 1920s working-class and peasant women formed groups associated with trade unions or the Communist Party and were concerned with economic questions, while urban middle-class women concentrated on the vote. In the mid-1930s, however, they joined together in an umbrella group, the Sole Front for Women's Rights. This gave priority to women's suffrage and at its peak had 50,000 members organized in 800 societies, although women did not gain the vote until 1958.

The suffrage might have proved elusive in several countries in the 1920s, but feminists did manage to achieve many **civil rights** for women – in Argentina, for example, the Civil Code was revised in 1926. In the period 1929 to the mid-1930s, however, the vote was gained in a number of countries, including Ecuador, Uruguay, Brazil and Cuba. Women's enfranchisement was closely linked to the interests of the mainstream political parties. In Uruguay members of the government became more sympathetic to women's suffrage once they were convinced that women would be a force for stability rather than being associated with socialism or anarchism, while in Brazil and Cuba suffragists benefited from the introduction of liberal and reforming governments who sought their support. Viewed either as reactionary conservatives or as dangerous radicals, women found themselves in a contradictory position. Sometimes this helped, and at other times it hindered, their campaign for the vote. For example, the deeply conservative pro-Catholic country of Ecuador was the first to enfranchise women in Latin America in 1929, albeit on a limited basis. The ruling coalition faced a threat from socialists and saw women as compliant and loyal to the status quo. In Mexico, however, women's association with conservatism worked against them. Congress refused to ratify a suffrage amendment to the constitution in 1939 because it was feared that women would support the conservative opposition party.

Women did not gain the vote in the other major countries in the region, including Argentina, Bolivia, Peru, Nicaragua and Mexico until after the Second World War. A liberal political climate again proved to be important. In Costa Rica, for example, women were finally able to vote and stand for election in 1949 after the Partido Liberación Nacional had come to power and the Assembly of Representatives had drafted a new constitution. In Argentina it was the election of General Perón as president that was to lead to women's suffrage in 1947 after his wife, Eva, mobilized the support of working-class women. Nonetheless, feminists opposed many of the arguments that she used, in particular the assertion that political participation would make women more attractive.

Civil rights: The legal rights women gained in areas such as education, employment and the family, including divorce, custody of children and ownership of property.

NATIONALISM AND ANTI-COLONIALISM

Nationalist and anti-colonial struggles provided the context for women to raise their own demands in countries subject to formal colonial rule, including India, Egypt, Tunisia and Syria. Women had engaged in debates about their social position during the nineteenth century. In India, for example, women from the educated elite 'articulated the rudiments of feminist thought publicly through negotiation with the Raj and Indian male reformers', and sought to put their ideas into practice by working with women's organizations to improve women's lives within the home (Anagol, 2010: 541). In Egypt the first women's periodicals were established in the 1890s and again debate centred on women's position within the family. It was not until the early twentieth century that women began to pursue a broader range of civil and political rights and to develop an organized movement. Educated upper- and middle-class women influenced both by the European women's movement and by nationalism, took the lead. In India, for example, Sarojini Naidu was a key figure. Born in Hyderabad into a Brahmin family she was educated in London and Cambridge before marrying a doctor, G.R. Naidu in 1898. She was involved in nationalist politics before the First World War and also took up the cause of women, addressing a meeting of the British Dominions Woman Suffrage Movement in London in 1914 on the topic of 'ideals of Indian womanhood'.

In 1917 Naidu led an all-India women's delegation to ask the Montagu-Chelmsford Committee on constitutional reform to enfranchise Indian women on the same terms as men. This was not accepted, but women's protests did lead to the concession that women who possessed the requisite educational and property qualifications could vote for representatives to provincial legislatures. Throughout the inter-war years she continued to pursue the two causes of Indian independence and women's rights and demanded that all women, regardless of religious affiliation, should be able to vote. From the early 1920s women gradually entered public life as members of provincial councils and as magistrates. A number of women's organizations, including the All-India Women's Conference, continued to press for social reforms and for women's suffrage, but they were expected to give priority to the cause of national independence. This caused tensions when Indian political parties boycotted British Commissions appointed to look at constitutional questions. Nonetheless, Indian women's organizations sent representatives, including Naidu, to the series of Round Table conferences held in London between 1930 and 1932 to discuss dominion status. They were consistent in their demand for full adult suffrage but had to accept a compromise in 1935 whereby women with educational and property qualifications became eligible to vote. Women finally gained full adult suffrage in 1949 as a result of the new constitution adopted after independence, but those living in the newly created Pakistan had to wait until 1956 before they were fully enfranchised, although no elections were held until 1970.

In a volatile political situation feminists often had to change the nature of their demands and to shift their priorities. In Egypt, for example, women were initially involved in nationalist politics (Phillip, 1978). Hudá Sha'rawi, the daughter of a wealthy landowner and provincial administrator, was married to a leading member of the Wafd, the Egyptian Nationalist Party. She was expected to help her husband in organizing resistance to British rule and in 1919 took part with many other women in the uprising against the British, becoming the first president of the Ladies central committee of the Wafd party [**Doc. 17, pp. 116–17**]. Women became disillusioned, however, when, after independence in 1922, the suffrage was restricted to men. In the following year, therefore, after the death of her husband, Hudá Sha'rawi founded the Egyptian Feminist Union (EFU) to campaign for a range of reforms, including political rights.

It was not easy to maintain a commitment to political rights. Nationalists increasingly emphasized women's social role rather than their individual rights and so the EFU gave greater attention to women's education and the reform of the personal status law. There was some success for this tactic in the 1920s; equal secondary school education for girls, the entry of women into the state university and the raising of the minimum marriage age for both sexes were all introduced.

The political climate changed in 1934 with a return to liberalism. In the same year the IWSA held its congress in neighbouring Istanbul and women gained the suffrage in Turkey. This gave a new impetus to the suffrage campaign in Egypt and the EFU demanded votes for educated women. In the late 1930s, however, the Palestine question dominated politics for men and women and it was not until towards the end of the Second World War that a more sustained attempt was made to raise the issue of women's political rights. Sha'rawi spoke eloquently at the Arab Women's Congress in Cairo in 1944 in favour of political rights for all Arab women. Two other suffrage groups that aimed to attract a broader middle-class membership now joined the EFU in its campaign. One of the leaders, Doria Shafik, employed militant methods. She led an invasion by 1,500 women of the Egyptian parliament in 1951 and was one of eight women who went on hunger strike three years later. Shafik's arguments, emphasizing the freedom of the individual and a secular approach, were in the tradition of liberal feminism and she was placed under house arrest by President Nasser in 1957. A younger generation of university students linked women's liberation with socialism and communism, but in a context of increasing nationalist pressure to expel British troops from Egypt feminists joined forces with fundamentalist women in a common nationalist cause. The pressure of suffrage campaigners, combined with the needs of a modernizing state, did lead President Nasser to introduce votes for women in 1956, but women still had to make a special request to register their votes.

When feminists took part in mixed-sex politics they were often torn in their loyalties. What should come first – loyalty to their sex, or their party or their class? Or was it likely to be more complicated than that? There was usually a balancing act at any one time as priorities and tactics shifted. This could mean that feminists had differing views about what was meant by women's emancipation and how best to achieve it in specific political contexts. In China, for example, Xiang Jingyu, leader of the women's section of the Communist Party in the 1920s, argued that the vote was irrelevant to women under the current social system and urged them to join with working men to overthrow imperial rule which would then be a prerequisite for the suffrage. Similarly in Chile, liberal feminists refrained from campaigning for the vote in the 1920s because they feared the influence of the Catholic Church among women. Teachers attending feminist congresses in Mexico viewed the vote with suspicion since they believed that women should not become involved with corrupt masculine regimes.

In some instances, as in Sierra Leone and Ghana in the 1950s, women found it difficult to make their voices heard in nationalist, anti-colonial and revolutionary struggles and suppressed their own demand for political equality in order to give priority to other struggles. In contrast, in Vietnam, the Communist Party emphasized the importance of women's participation in politics in order to strengthen the revolutionary movement in 1937 and 1938. Party branches formed women's committees and at a May Day rally in Hanoi in 1938 thousands of women marched through the streets. In her speech to the rally Bao Tam demanded the 'progressive eradication of barriers differentiating men and women' (Jayawardena, 1986: 210).

It was common for individual women to shift their political positions over time. Ofelia Domínguez Navarro, a Cuban lawyer from a lower-middle-class background, provides a good example of this. She was involved in the feminist movement and then became increasingly drawn to revolutionary politics. In the late 1920s she joined other politically active women in opposing Machado's dictatorship and in 1928 left the Cuban Feminist National Alliance to form the Women's Labour Union that had links with the Communist Party. During a second term in prison she wrote that the feminist movement 'with its political and civic aspirations now seems to me too narrow a mould within which to struggle . . .' Ehrick makes the interesting point that whereas liberal feminists thought that a concern with class or nationalist politics was a less progressive position, 'now we see a Cuban feminist coming to the conclusion that it is being solely concerned with women's issues which is confining and backward, and that the incorporation of class issues was what the historical moment required' (Ehrick, 1998: 416).

Indeed, contemporaries often equated nationalism with progress since it highlighted questions of citizenship and political representation that could be seen as part of a modernizing agenda. It is not surprising that feminists also looked at women's suffrage in this light. In countries such as New Zealand and Australia the early enfranchisement of women was viewed with some pride as an indicator of civilization and of the progress that these young nations had achieved. In India too feminists expressed pride that the provincial legislatures had unanimously agreed to remove the sex disqualification for the vote. One suffragist claimed that 'while in the European countries women had to struggle hard for the attainment of their political rights women of India experience no difficulty in securing the same' (Sinha, 2000: 231).

Feminists used a variety of arguments to justify their demands for greater public influence. Where cultural and religious values reinforced women's identification with the home, and male authority within the household, as in Latin America, feminists linked together nationalism, women's role as mothers and women's suffrage. They argued that if women realized the connection between home and the public world they would try to influence collective action, in particular the achievement of social reforms to solve social problems, and that this would ensure the development of the nation as well as civic rights for women (Lavrin, 1995). In Syria and Lebanon, on the other hand, feminists avoided controversial questions such as the vote in the 1930s in the hope that they would gain support for other social reforms affecting women's social position. They praised domestic work and philanthropy as a national service and called for social rather than political rights to be able to carry out this task. It was a tactic designed to broaden the appeal of women's organizations, to mobilize mothers and to give them an influence in the growing movement for independence from France (Thompson, 2000). This form of 'patriotic motherhood', in which it was assumed that women, as the educators of their children, could play a vital role in forging a sense of national identity and patriotism, has echoes of the 'republican' and 'patriotic' motherhood that was a feature of the French Revolution and of nineteenth-century liberal nationalist movements in Europe. Although it was an argument associated with anti-suffragists, feminists could also use their patriotic role to demand political rights.

In countries subject to colonial rule, in particular where Islam was the predominant religion, feminist arguments and demands had to be developed in a context in which many nationalist and religious leaders sought to distance themselves from the West. Thus, respect for women's traditional roles in Muslim families and support for practices such as veiling were seen as a rejection of the influence of the colonial power. In Algeria 'women found themselves trapped by a conservative vision of their role in society justified by anti-colonialism' (Gadant, 1995: 122). Two competing feminist arguments can be identified. One took a secularist approach to politics and looked to the West as representing progress. Its upper-class adherents had usually been educated in Europe and had friendship links with European feminists. Hudá Sha'rawi and Saiza Nabarawi, for example, were closely associated with the IWSA and, after attending its congress in Rome in 1923, removed their veils when they returned to Egypt. Although Shar'awi was a nationalist who opposed British domination, she accepted many Western ideas and argued that there should be gradual reforms towards adopting Western institutions and a secularist understanding of the state. The other feminist argument sought to affirm women's sense of self within Islam and to see it as part of a renovation of the whole society. This was expressed by the writer Malak Nassef who opposed unveiling, arguing that those who unveiled were upper-class women who were not motivated by a desire for liberty or the pursuit of knowledge, but were obsessed by fashion. Her views on veiling were, however, complex, since she was critical of men who sought to impose their own views on the subject onto women. She argued 'we must be wary of man being as despotic about liberating us as he has been about our enslavement' (Ahmed, 1992: 182). Although Sha'rawi's brand of feminism, which looked to the West, was the most prominent perspective during the period, those who campaigned for women and the nation in Islamist terms became more potent in the latter decades of the twentieth century.

INTERNATIONALISM AND 'UNIVERSAL SISTERHOOD'

Did these national tensions, in particular between those subject to colonial rule and women in Western societies, undermine the notion that there could be a 'universal sisterhood' that crossed national boundaries? The suffrage campaign, in particular, did encourage women to see themselves as part of an international movement. As already noted in Chapter 3, formal links were made through the establishment of transnational organizations before the First World War, including the International Council of Women and the International Woman Suffrage Alliance. During the inter-war years the number of national affiliates to the IWSA almost doubled, from 26 to 51, and now included Egypt, India, Japan and countries in Latin America as well as the pre-war groups from Europe, North America and Australia. Those who already had the suffrage took up other campaigns, in particular peace, and in 1926 the IWSA took the new name of the International Alliance of Women for Suffrage and Equal Citizenship with a programme of peace, democracy and women's rights.

Women met regularly at international meetings and forged strong friendships. They kept in touch by writing copious letters which encouraged feelings of solidarity and enabled them to deepen personal relationships. For example, the American Carrie Chapman Catt, the Dutch suffragists Aletta Jacobs and Rosa Manus and the Hungarian Rosika Schwimmer were particularly close friends. At first friendships tended to be between women in the United States and Europe, but by the inter-war years Bertha Lutz from Brazil and the Egyptian feminist leaders Hudá Sha'rawi and Doria Shafik, among others, were included in these networks.

Familial language was used by women to express their connections with each other. Bertha Lutz, for example, addressed Carrie Chapman Catt as 'my dear mother Mrs Catt' and signed herself as Catt's Brazilian daughter. This could imply that feminists were challenging the view that 'the only families were national families' (Rupp, 1997: 199) but familial terms could also reinforce power relationships between women based on age and nationality. European feminist leaders, for instance, figure prominently in the autobiographies and memoirs of Egyptian suffragists, although this is not the case the other way round (Badran, 1995).

Travel was also a means by which women could make contact with, and influence each other, across national boundaries. In some instances women travelled on behalf of their national group. The publicity generated by the militant suffrage campaign, for example, meant that British suffragettes such as Mrs Pankhurst were in great demand as speakers in the United States and were able to use their speaking tours to raise money for the cause. Women's international organizations saw travel as particularly important in order to gather information on women's lives and to make contact with, or to establish, new groups that might result in affiliations from a wider range of countries. The ability to travel was largely restricted to women who had resources and leisure time and therefore women active in international organizations were predominantly from middle-class or upper-class backgrounds. They shared the assumptions of their class and generation that the West signified pro-gress and civilization, in particular, in relation to the position of women, and therefore it was part of their role to stimulate suffrage activity elsewhere. Nonetheless, feminists from the United States and Western Europe could also find their own preconceptions challenged when they travelled widely. British suffragists, for example, were surprised to find Iranian women making demands for the vote in their country's constitutional crisis of 1906–11, while the suffrage movement was still at its height in Britain.

One of the most well known world tours was undertaken in 1911 by Aletta Jacobs and the IWSA president Carrie Chapman Catt who visited South Africa,

Sri Lanka, Indonesia, China and Japan. They did not have much success in gaining new affiliations for the IWSA, but their accounts of their travels provide important insights into the complex relationship between feminism, colonialism and race. Carrie Chapman Catt, for instance, claimed that she had not expected to find that women in Burma had the right to own property, engage in business and vote in municipal elections and, therefore, in many respects were better off than women in the West. And yet at the same time that she made this observation she also noted 'the languor of people in such sunshine' and the fact that in the Orient women were often held in 'most pitiful tutelage, and denied every vestige of personal liberty' (Rupp, 1997: 76–7).

TENSIONS WITHIN THE IWSA

Was it possible for feminists from across the world to share common interests despite their national differences? Transnational groups took pride in the international flavour of their proceedings and argued that women, as the guardians and nurturers of life, were committed to peace and international understanding. Leila Rupp suggests that the well-educated upper- and middle-class Christian women of European origins who dominated the ICW and IWSA saw their internationalism as a 'stitched together quilt of existing differences rather than a wholly new piece of cloth' (Rupp, 1997: 108–9). They displayed national pride through cultural symbols such as national costume and dance but believed that they could talk across their differences and achieve a broad unity of purpose. [**Doc. 18, p. 117**] Taking a slightly different perspective, Bosch suggests that the IWSA used exaggerated images of difference to point up the essential unity of women (Bosch, 1990). Unity, however, was difficult to sustain. There were immediate conflicts with socialists, many of whom chose to pursue the fight for women's right to vote from within their own organization, the Socialist Women's International. In the inter-war years further conflicts arose as women from outside Europe and North America demanded that their voices and perspectives be heard.

The First World War gave an impetus to international feminist activities as women from many nations joined together in a new organization, the Women's International League (WIL), to campaign for a peace by negotiation. In 1919 the WIL changed its name to the Women's International League for Peace and Freedom (WILPF), established a headquarters in Geneva and reaffirmed its aims of achieving peace and women's emancipation. [**Doc. 16, pp. 114–15**] In the 1920s the League sought to increase women's influence in the League of Nations, and to be a force for peace and disarmament. It was the only women's organization that set policy at an international level and expected the national sections to follow its lead.

Given that in the aftermath of the war women had gained the right to vote in many countries, there was some discussion about whether the IWSA should be disbanded. At the 1920 Congress, however, it was decided that the Alliance would make more effort to extend its influence and to support those countries that were still fighting for the suffrage. At the same time it would broaden its remit to campaign for a range of other reforms that would establish equality for women, including educational opportunities, marital law reform and a change in the laws governing nationality for women who married someone from a different country.

The IWSA, the International Council of Women and WILPF all made great efforts to extend their influence in South America where the struggle for the vote and for enhancing women's rights was beginning to grow. Extensive tours were made in the region in the 1920s by leaders of these groups. Carrie Chapman Catt, accompanied by Rosa Manus, spoke at meetings across the continent and helped to support groups that had already affiliated as well as recruiting new ones, while the ICW sent one of its senior members, Louise van Eeghen, on a similar trip. The ICW enjoyed greater popularity than the Alliance in South America and Marie Sandell suggests that this was 'linked to its reputation for being the most conservative international women's association at that time' (Sandell, 2007: 186). Its Christian ethos, for example, enabled the Council to interrelate with Catholic women and with other Christian groups, such as the Woman's Christian Temperance Union, that were well established in the region.

As their geographical scope broadened, so tensions increased within international women's organizations. Those still excluded from the franchise wanted the IWSA to concentrate on women's suffrage and it was feared that, by widening the range of their activities to encompass peace and social reform, the Alliance would lose its distinctiveness and its focus on equal rights. Within the IWSA there was now a situation in which, instead of women campaigning together against their common exclusion from political rights, some women, mainly from Europe and North America, were working for the rights of others. This reinforced the assumption that women from the West were there to teach their non-Western sisters how to move forward to emancipation. It also implied that Western women were modern, educated and in control of their own lives and bodies in contrast to those in Arab countries or in colonial contexts who were not (Woollacott, 1998).

Nonetheless, as DuBois and Oliviero have recently suggested, it would be a mistake to assume that ideas, strategies and leadership simply flowed outwards from Europe and North America. Instead, there was a far more complex interaction between feminists from different parts of the world. Thus, women from Australia and New Zealand, who already had the vote, were welcomed as speakers in the imperial heartland. In 1911, for example, the

Women's Social and Political Union invited the Australian Vida Goldstein to address numerous meetings in Britain in order to encourage suffrage campaigners who were facing strong resistance. She met all the main suffrage leaders and offered them advice and support, but also found that her experience of the British militant campaign then affected many of her own ideas, in particular over the extent to which male and female socialists could cooperate together in a common struggle. Women from outside Europe and North America also travelled extensively and exerted an influence on each other. For instance Sarojini Naidu of the Indian National Congress inspired Sri Lankan middle-class women to demand the vote when she visited their country in 1922. In Uruguay, Mexico, Brazil and Argentina, suffragists built on friendship links that they had already made in congresses held in South America before the First World War. They carried out an extensive correspondence in which they began to develop their own methods and political strategies.

The views of the IWSA leadership were also increasingly criticized in the inter-war years. Hudá Sha'rawi, who was elected vice-president of the IWSA in 1923, voiced the concerns of the Muslim women of Palestine against Jewish immigration and challenged the Christian assumptions that lay behind the Alliance. Meanwhile, feminists in colonial contexts began to assert their own distinctive voices as their countries sought greater independence and self-determination. [**Doc. 21, pp. 120–1**] Indian women, for example, challenged the right of newly enfranchised British women to speak for them on the Commission, established in 1927, to recommend future political reforms in India. They demanded their own place on the Commission and clashed with the dominant British women's organizations over the nature of the proposals that were made to extend Indian women's franchise (Sinha, 2000). At the same time Indian women used the international arena to 'reformulate Indian nationalism so as to highlight female citizenship' (DuBois and Oliviero, 2009: 2).

New organizations were formed that challenged the dominance of the IWSA and WILPF. This has been seen as marking a break from the assumptions and leadership of Western feminists and of marking a change towards an international feminism based on many different voices. On the other hand recent studies have shown that Western feminism was not monolithic and also that there were many continuities in aims and ideas across international women's organizations throughout the twentieth century. The Pan-American Association for the Advancement of Women, established in 1922 sought a wide range of reforms, including women's suffrage, and aimed to improve communications among all American countries and to exert an influence on policy within the region. Feminists in the Americas were able to work together for a number of common goals, but the dominance of the United

States caused discontent. The American Carrie Chapman Catt who had founded the Association was looked on with suspicion because of her self-proclaimed missionary role to countries where feminist movements were less well developed. Feminists in South America, therefore, asserted their independence by joining with their Iberian counterparts to form the International League of Iberian and Hispanic American Women in 1923. Tensions were, though, also present within Latin America itself. Feminists from Uruguay sought to link with their counterparts in Chile, Cuba and Mexico, but they were suspicious of Argentina and feared that their own nation could be threatened as much by their close neighbours as by the United States.

As the ties binding the constituent parts of the British Empire began to loosen in the inter-war years, the self-governing Dominions, including Canada, Australia and New Zealand began to build distinct national identities for themselves within the new Commonwealth. Feminists wanted to ensure that they would have an influence over this process and raised their own issues, such as the nationality of married women and maintenance payments to deserted wives, in London and in Dominion capitals. Now that Australia and New Zealand were represented in their own right at the League of Nations women were aware that their citizenship status within the Empire had changed and they set out with a new sense of confidence to influence the shape of 'imperial feminism'. [**Doc. 15, pp. 113–14**] The first step was to form new organizations – the British Commonwealth League (BCL) and the Pan-Pacific and South East Asia Women's Association (PPSEAWA) – to bring women together from across the Empire, the Commonwealth and the Pacific Rim to discuss issues that affected them all. This helped to shift the focus and perspectives of feminist campaigning away from the heartland of Europe.

The PPSEAWA, for instance, helped women in Asia to strengthen their national organizations. It also sought to inform European based groups about the conditions of women's lives in Pacific Rim countries and in many respects encouraged women from India, Japan and the Philippines to speak for themselves. On the other hand, Angela Woollacott, a leading historian in the field, argues persuasively that PPSEAWA members from Australia and New Zealand saw themselves as 'protecting less forward races' while in the BCL white women who could vote thought that it was their responsibility to look after the interests of native peoples. She suggests, therefore, that they substituted a new brand of 'Commonwealth feminism' for the older-style Imperial feminism (Woollacott, 1998).

In the inter-war years, therefore, feminism was fractured in multiple ways – national, class, religious and racial differences could all undermine solidarity. On the other hand, feminists also sought to work together internationally and spoke a language of universal sisterhood. This could be seen as an example of the difficulties involved in creating a politics around the category 'woman', but in practice the situation was far more complex. Many feminists had a modest goal of working together over specific issues while accepting limitations to the notion of universal sisterhood. Nationalism and internationalism, for example, were not necessarily mutually exclusive concepts and it was possible to find space within them to build notions of 'sisterhood' and female solidarity. For the Dutch feminist Aletta Jacobs, for instance, internationalism was an intrinsic part of her national and imperial identity and was not something separate from it. Too small to rule their empire by force the Dutch claimed that they sought to foster international cooperation and peace while at the same time respecting local customs (Bosch, 1999). On her travels in Africa and Asia, 1911–12, Jacobs expressed national pride in this outlook, which was compared favourably with the British attempt to 'civilize' the indigenous population. She then drew upon this concept of nationalism to support her international work as a member of the IWSA and as an organizer of the Women's Peace Congress at The Hague in 1915.

Feminists active in North American and European based international organizations such as the IWSA tended to view their demands for suffrage or for peace as universal issues, transcending differences between women. They were critical of feminists in Asia and the Middle East for being too 'nationalist' in their politics, but, as Leila Rupp points out in her path-breaking study of transnational women's organizations, that was only because they took their own nationalist interests for granted (Rupp, 1997). If looked at from the perspective of women elsewhere then internationalism has a different meaning but could still encompass the concept of a universal sisterhood. Indian women, for instance, developed complex arguments about nationalism, colonialism and feminism. Although they were deeply engaged in the nationalist movement for independence from British rule, Indian feminists were also internationalist in outlook. Nonetheless, they had their own ideas about the meaning of feminist internationalism and objected when newly enfranchised British feminists assumed that they could speak for Indian women. They drew attention within organizations such as the IWSA and WILPF to the problems posed by European imperialism for notions of inter-national solidarity while simultaneously developing their ideas in meetings outside European influence, such as the first All Asian Women's Conference held in Lahore in 1931 (Sinha, 2000). Indian feminists thought that it would be possible to create a universal sisterhood but only if British feminists recognized their own failure to live up to this ideal. Thus they noted that British feminists, rather than supporting Indian women's demand for an equal franchise, took the same line as the British government in calling for a qualified franchise for women in India.

After the First World War organized feminist movements began to grow in strength outside Europe and North America. They developed in a context of nationalist and anti-colonial movements that sought greater independence and autonomy from Imperial rule, but feminists still asserted the right to speak for themselves. They challenged the colonial and racial assumptions of their counterparts in Europe and North America while also contesting attitudes about women's social role held by many male political and religious leaders in their own countries. Although they often appeared to put nationalism before other causes, feminists did pursue the interests of women and sought a role for themselves in building a national identity. At the same time they also made links with women from other countries and aimed to develop their own version of a 'universal sisterhood'. A focus on these struggles provides a new lens through which to view the history of feminism. It reveals the rich variety of different feminisms and reinforces the argument that we should be wary of assuming that only certain aims, objectives and strategies deserve the label feminist. Despite differences in national cultures, as well as divisions based on class, race and political beliefs, in certain contexts women still expressed solidarity with each other on the grounds of a shared oppression as women.

5

Citizenship in North America and Europe in the inter-war years

POLITICAL REPRESENTATION AND IMPACT

After campaigning for so long to achieve the vote, feminists now had to decide how to move forward from their new position as 'active citizens'. What goals and strategies should they adopt? Could they agree on a common outlook and act together? What kind of women's emancipation did they want to see? In comparison to the flamboyant and highly visible pre-war suffrage campaign, the women's movement in the inter-war years seemed more fragmented and to have less influence. The First World War had raised expectations that women's 'traditional' social roles could change, but once the conflict was over there was a desire to get back to 'normal' as quickly as possible. Domesticity and motherhood were emphasized as essential for the good of the family and of the state. Economic depression, high unemployment and fears about the quality and quantity of the population reinforced the assumption that women should devote their energies to family life, as did the development of conservative and fascist regimes that were explicitly anti-feminist in outlook.

War had encouraged the view that men and women, with their complementary roles, could work together for a common goal. It is hardly surprising, therefore, that individuals and organizations were reluctant to describe themselves as feminists, a label associated with a radical upheaval in family life and conflict between the sexes. Generation played a key role here. Young women had enjoyed greater personal freedoms during the War and tended to view feminist organizations as dull and old-fashioned. Former suffrage campaigners, therefore, complained that the young were only interested in personal fulfilment and pleasing men.

In this context it was difficult for feminists to make an impact on politics, either as individuals or collectively. Only a few women were elected to representative assemblies. In Norway women never held more than 2.5 per cent of seats on local councils in the inter-war years and gained only 3 out of the 150 seats in the Storting, the national parliament. In Austria eight women were elected to a Constituent Assembly of 170 deputies in 1919 and ten to the National Assembly in 1920. South Australia did not elect its first woman to parliament until 1959 and in Britain women comprised only a handful of MPs until the 1990s. Throughout the world women had to wait until the last two decades of the twentieth century before their representation on elected bodies showed any substantial increase. Embarking on a political career was not an easy option for women. Working practices in male-dominated representative assemblies made it difficult to combine a career with family life and women were reluctant to put themselves forward as candidates in a context in which national politics was still identified with masculinity. When they did seek to become candidates they found that the established political parties were unwilling to support the adoption of women as candidates in seats that could be won. Many of those who *were* successful in being elected did not adopt a feminist perspective or else found it difficult to work together because of conflicting party loyalties. In Germany, for example, where they comprised 10 per cent of the Reichstag deputies in the 1920s, socialist and Catholic women disagreed about married women's employment and protection for unmarried mothers, although they cooperated on maternity benefits and protective legislation for women at the workplace.

How far, therefore, did women's social, economic and legal status improve after their enfranchisement? Legislation that enhanced their civil status was introduced in many countries while social welfare benefits such as family allowances and maternity pay provided economic support for married women. In Sweden, for example, married women obtained full legal equality in 1920 while in Britain the 1919 Sex Disqualification (Removal) Act provided for women to be admitted to the legal profession, to be eligible for jury service and to enter the civil service. In the new constitutions drawn up for the Weimar Republic in 1919 and the Irish Free State in 1922 it was declared that all citizens were equal under the law regardless of sex.

There was no guarantee, however, that legal equality would be put into practice, in particular when governments were anxious to reinforce male authority in the family. A strong, united feminist movement might have made a difference but this was largely absent. In Ireland for example, when the suffrage movement disintegrated, women no longer had an independent voice and found it difficult to resist new legislation designed to emphasize women's domesticity. In 1935, after pressure from the Catholic Church, legislation was introduced to restrict women's employment outside the home and in 1937 the constitution was re-written. Feminists managed to resist attempts to remove the clause 'without distinction of sex', but new articles were added that emphasized women's importance to the state as mothers and homemakers. This example provides a useful reminder that the gains women made could also be lost. In Hungary, for instance, women received the vote on equal terms with men in 1919, but were disenfranchised when the conservative wing of the nationalist movement came to power. After 1921 the vote was restricted to women over 30 who fulfilled educational and economic qualifications and full suffrage was not regained until 1945. In Spain women were successful in their campaign to ensure that the new constitution of the Second Republic, ratified in 1931, would include women's enfranchisement. There was fear among liberals that women would be a force for conservatism, but socialists and Catholics supported the measure. Clara Campoamor of the Radical Party was a particularly influential voice in the debate, arguing that Spain should provide an example of the best, most modern form of democracy. The Republic also introduced other reforms that benefited women, including a secularized marriage law, civil divorce and the end of regulated prostitution. When Franco came to power in 1936, however, women were disenfranchised and emphasis was placed on their role within the home, reinforced by legislative changes that made divorce illegal and restored male authority within marriage.

How far should we see the results of women's enfranchisement as meagre and how did these compare with the hopes of suffrage campaigners? Suffragists themselves did not necessarily expect that there would be rapid changes in women's position as a result of gaining the vote. In Britain, for example, Millicent Fawcett wrote that while the vote was the 'very foundation stone of political freedom' and would bring 'enlarged opportunities' and an 'improved status of women', she did not believe that this would happen overnight (Fawcett 1920 in Thane, 2001: 258).

There was a great deal to be done even to achieve formal equality between men and women. In many countries in Europe feminists still had to campaign for the franchise. In France the movement extended beyond Paris and in 1929 the most important moderate suffrage group, the Union française pour le suffrage des femmes (French Union for Women's Suffrage) had 100,000 members. Up to 1936 the question was practically never off the political agenda as time and again the Chamber of Deputies expressed their support, only to find any proposals blocked by the Senate. In Britain suffragists had to work hard to ensure that all women were finally included in the franchise, regardless of age, in 1928. A mass meeting in London in 1926 was supported by 40 women's groups and over 3,000 women attended the first suffrage procession held since the war. At the same time there was a great deal of lobbying behind the scenes to persuade a reluctant Conservative Party Cabinet that they might benefit from an increase in women voters.

In the inter-war years feminists were active in seeking improvements in women's lives both at the workplace and in the home. They lobbied politicians, took part in government inquiries and, on occasion, organized demonstrations in support of causes as diverse as the right of married women to work, access to birth control information and equality for married women under the law. The feminist movement, as a movement, however, seemed to lack coherence and strength. In this context many of those who had been involved in the suffrage campaign, and who still took an active part in feminist causes, attempted both to ensure that the excitement generated by the pre-war movement was not forgotten, and also to inspire a new generation of younger women to challenge gender inequalities. As Hilda Kean argues, they chose the genre of autobiography or biography to do this because the suffrage campaign had transformed their personal lives which were in turn intertwined with political goals. Some histories of the suffrage struggle were themselves largely autobiographical. Sylvia Pankhurst's *The Suffragette Movement*, for example, published in 1931, told the story of the militant campaign from the perspective of a socialist feminist and provided a space in which she could work out her troubled personal relationship with her mother and sister (Pankhurst, 1931). Such accounts must be read with care as 'a representation of experience within the suffrage movement rather than as a quasi objective historical account' (Kean, 1994: 61). It is not surprising that women who had often been engaged in acrimonious debate and splits with others in the movement should be selective in the events and people that they chose to include, while in some cases personal issues were downplayed. Dutch suffragist Aletta Jacobs, for example, developed a wide friendship network with women from many countries, but this is rarely discussed in her autobiography which is organized around key events and journeys. Nonetheless, autobiographies provide unique insights into the meaning of the suffrage campaign for those who took part and also remind us that, for feminists, the writing of history, in particular the celebration of what could be achieved through collective struggle, had relevance to contemporary politics.

In Britain in particular feminists made a conscious effort to collect source material for historians of the future. The Suffragette Fellowship was established in 1926 to perpetuate the memory of the pioneers, especially those from the militant movement. The Fellowship held a series of commemorative events and acquired written and oral personal testimony from those who had been imprisoned, as well as encouraging activists to write autobiographies. A Women's Service Library was also established to gather material from the constitutionalist side of the movement and this laid the foundations of the Fawcett library, subsequently the Women's Library, London, which now has one of the most extensive collections of sources for feminist and women's history in the world.

Despite such efforts membership of general feminist organizations declined in the inter-war years and the existence of numerous small, single-issue pressure groups confirmed the impression of fragmentation. Many feminists chose to pursue their goals through mixed-sex political parties, in particular social democratic and communist parties, but found it difficult to maintain a distinctive presence. Single-sex organizations, such as suffrage groups, encouraged a sense of solidarity among women and the development of a 'feminist consciousness'. Once they left this environment it was difficult for women to retain their confidence and a sense of autonomy. Moreover, European social democratic parties and other groups on the Left were ambiguous in their attitudes towards women's emancipation. There were extensive debates on the 'woman question' and it was common to find socialists using a rhetoric of sex equality, but in practice these male-dominated, class-based organizations were reluctant to give priority to gender issues.

Feminist activists were prepared, however, to fight their corner within the mainstream political parties and saw them as a vehicle for advancing their aims. In Britain over half of the individual members of the Labour Party were women – in 1929 there were 250,000 women in 1,867 sections, while in the Netherlands women's share of the membership of the Social Democratic Workers' Party increased from 20 per cent in 1920 to 33 per cent in 1938. In Austria and Holland just over a third of Social Democratic Party members were women, while in Norway and Sweden the figure was 16 per cent and 14 per cent respectively. In contrast, the proportion of women members was much smaller in France and Belgium, where socialist groups were hostile to gender issues, and in Italy and Spain where fascism was the deciding factor.

Engagement in mixed-sex politics raised a complex set of issues for feminists. What should they do when loyalty to class and party conflicted with their commitment to fight against gender inequalities? What kind of relationship should they have with women involved in feminist organizations? Some issues, such as protective legislation, led to fierce disagreements, whereas campaigns to extend the franchise or to gain access to birth control advice brought women together across party and organizational boundaries. Within their own parties socialist women, in particular, raised feminist concerns, but the extent to which they were willing to press their demands varied between individuals and also between countries.

In Sweden, where the social democrats played an important part in the achievement of political and civil rights for women in the early 1920s, socialist women were successful in ensuring that issues such as birth control, improved housing and the social welfare needs of working-class mothers were placed on the social democratic agenda, and Sweden was one of the first countries to legalize abortion in 1938. This can be contrasted with Norway where women had gained civil rights as early as the nineteenth century in the context of liberal politics. Socialism developed after these gains had been made and there was little cooperation between party members and liberal feminists. This continued into the twentieth century when social democrats remained far less supportive of women's rights than their counterparts in Sweden. Debates over the **marriage bar** in employment illustrate the differences between them. In Sweden left-wing socialists, social democrats and liberal feminists joined together to wage a strong campaign to ensure that a marriage bar would not be implemented. In Norway, however, the social democrats actually introduced a marriage bar and opposition came from liberal women rather than from socialists (Hagemann, 2002).

Marriage bar: In the context of mass unemployment in the inter-war years many governments in Europe, at both a national and a local level, sought to prevent married women from working in occupations such as the civil service, teaching and nursing.

It was common for feminists within socialist organizations to find themselves adopting complex and varied positions. In Denmark, for example, women had little success in persuading the male leadership to adopt their women-centred agenda. In this case socialist women from middle-class backgrounds joined with feminists in the Danish Women's Society to press for reforms for all women, regardless of class, but this led to conflict with many working-class women in the trade union movement and the Working Women's Association. In Britain the conflicts did not follow class lines in such a clear cut way. Within the Labour Party it was women in official leadership positions who were reluctant to cause disunity by supporting controversial questions such as birth control and they placed emphasis on the importance of women's role within the home as the basis of their citizenship. Other women, in particular, those associated with the socialist group, the Independent Labour Party, fought a sustained campaign in the 1920s to persuade the Labour Party leadership to support birth control and family allowances, to oppose the marriage bar in employment, and to give increased power to the Women's Conference, although they found it difficult to make much headway. Alberti (1989) suggests that the involvement of women in the labour movement strained feminist solidarity in the 1920s while Smith (1984) argues that the leaders of the Labour Party were actively hostile to feminists outside the movement and ensured that class interests would be paramount within the party. Pat Thane on the other hand suggests that Labour women wanted women to have real choices in their lives, put social welfare on the Labour Party agenda, helped to improve local welfare services and brought more women into public life (Thane, 1993).

WOMEN'S ORGANIZATIONS

What other spaces could women voters use to make their voices heard? How far can they be viewed as part of the history of feminism? Many women's organizations were formed after the First World War to appeal largely to wives and mothers. There had long been a debate, especially in social democratic and other parties of the left, about the potential of housewives and mothers for political activism. During the First World War the high cost of living and food shortages led women in many cities including Barcelona, Berlin,

Petrograd, Melbourne and New York to carry out street protests, some of which turned into riots, to demand that governments take action to lower prices and to provide adequate supplies of food and fuel. In some cities they acted alone, whereas in others they were joined by seasoned campaigners from established political parties. In her study of Barcelona in 1918 Temma Kaplan suggests that through their collective action women demonstrated a 'female consciousness', that is the belief that they had fulfilled their obligations as wives and mothers and now had the right to a guaranteed subsistence. Thus they drew on a traditional sex division of labour rather than challenging it. Nonetheless, Kaplan also suggests such collective action had a revolutionary potential since it politicized everyday life.

Although women's organizations based on housewives and mothers in the inter-war years did not encourage the same methods of direct action, they did have complex aims and believed it was important to ensure that women within the home saw politics as relevant to their daily lives. They were reluctant to identify themselves with the feminist movement but their activities challenged gender inequalities and, in some instances, conventional gender roles. They all aimed to educate women in the rights and duties of citizenship and provided an avenue through which women could take part in public life. In Denmark, for example, women's organizations, including housewives' associations and women's sections in political parties, ensured that a growing number of women would be drawn into political activity. Reaching a peak in the 1940s and 50s these groups gained representation for their organizations in the official committee system. They might have refused the label feminist, but some of their members had the courage to express support for contraception and abortion. Similarly in England groups such as the Townswomen's Guild and the Women's Institute supported a range of social and economic reforms that would improve women's position, in particular, within the home. By distancing themselves from feminist organizations they were able to attract a large number of housewives and mothers who would otherwise have been put off by negative publicity and they campaigned to remove gender inequalities as well as challenging the imbalance of power between men and women.

It would be a mistake to assume that there was a hard and fast line between feminist and non-feminist organizations. Nonetheless, a failure to identify with feminism meant that there was little sense that women's organizations were part of a collective movement that questioned 'traditional gender' roles and developed a consciousness of solidarity among women. A similar point can be made about the plethora of women's organizations established as part of reconstruction in Germany after the Second World War. Karen Offen argues that their 'failure to re-define a woman's place in society and the family meant that women's "organisations" had replaced the (feminist) women's "movement"' (Offen, 2000: 389).

Plate 1 Lucy Stone wearing bloomers – a fashion that some feminists wore to give themselves more freedom, *Illustrated News* (New York), 28 May 1853

Source: Kansas State Historical Society

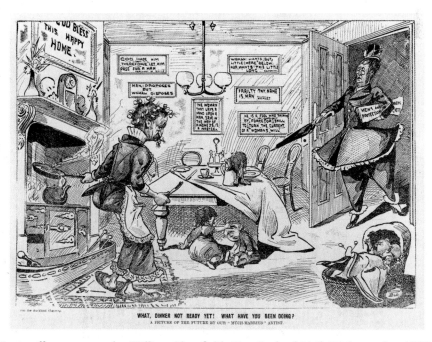

Plate 2 Anti-suffrage cartoon by William Blomfield, *New Zealand Mail*, 29 September 1893, p. 17

Source: Alexander Turnbull Library, Wellington, New Zealand

Plate 3 Portrait of the French suffragette, Hubertine Auclert, 1910

Plate 4 A suffragette is arrested in Manchester for causing obstruction at Manchester University

Source: Greater Manchester Police Museum and Archives

Plate 5 Annie Kenney, Mary Blathwayt and Emmeline Pankhurst at Eagle House, Batheaston, near Bath. Emmeline Pankhurst has just planted a tree in the suffragette field

Source: Bath in Time

Plate 6 International Woman Suffrage Alliance Congress, 1913. Peasant women delegates from Balmazujvaros with Jane Dirnfield and Miss Nellie Schnur

Source: Schwimmer-Lloyd collection, Manuscripts and Archives Division, The New York Public Library, Astor, Lenox and Tilden Foundations

Plate 7 Members of the New Women's (Femme-Nouvelle) Organization demand the right for French women to have the vote, 1934

Source: © Bettmann/CORBIS

Plate 8 Nabawiyya Musa, Hudá Sha'rawi and Saiza Nabarawi at the International Woman Suffrage Alliance Conference, Rome, 1923

Source: Carrie Chapman Catt Albums, Bryn Mawr College Library, Special Collections

"Votes for Women," May 24, 1912. Registered at the G.P.O. as a Newspaper.

VOTES FOR WOMEN

VOL. V. (New Series), No. 220. FRIDAY, MAY 24, 1912. Price 1d. Weekly (Post Free 1½d.)

AT THE OLD BAILEY, MAY 22, 1912.

The Jury: "We desire unanimously to express the hope that, taking into consideration the undoubtedly pure motives that underlie the agitation which has led to this trial, you would be pleased to exercise the utmost leniency in dealing with the case."

The Judge: "Nine months in the Second Division with the costs of the prosecution."

PRISONERS OF WAR

WSPU

Poyntz Wright

"We wage war, O disciples; therefore are we called warriors.
Wherefore, Lord, do we wage war?
For lofty virtue, for high endeavour, for sublime wisdom;
Therefore are we called warriors."

— Sayings of Buddha —

Plate 9 From the cover of *Votes for Women*, 24 May 1912

Source: © The British Library Board (*Votes for Women*, 24 May 1912)

Plate 10 Poster of the French Union of Woman's Suffrage suggesting that women's votes would be used against war, the use of alcohol and the slums

Source: 'Against Alcohol, the Slums and the War. The Women Must Vote', poster for the feminist movement, *c.* 1910 (litho) by Chavannas (20th century)
Bibliotheque Marguerite Durand, Paris, France / Archives Charmet / The Bridgeman Art Library
Nationality / copyright status: French / in copyright

Heraus mit dem Frauenwahlrecht

FRAUEN-TAG!
8. MÄRZ 1914

Den Frauen, die als Arbeiterinnen, Mütter und Gemeindebürgerinnen ihre volle Pflicht erfüllen, die im Staat wie in der Gemeinde ihre Steuern entrichten müssen, hat Voreingenommenheit und reaktionäre Gesinnung das volle Staatsbürgerrecht bis jetzt verweigert.

Dieses natürliche Menschenrecht zu erkämpfen, muß der unerschütterliche, feste Wille jeder Frau, jeder Arbeiterin sein. Hier darf es kein Ruhen kein Rasten geben. Kommt daher alle, ihr Frauen und Mädchen in die am

Sonntag den 8. März 1914 nachmittags 3 Uhr stattfindenden

9 öffentl. Frauen-Versammlungen

Plate 11 Poster advertising Women's Day, 8 March 1914 was produced by the German Social Democratic Party. It depicts a proletarian woman of strength and calls for votes for women

Source: INTERFOTO / Sammlung Rauch / Mary Evans

These ambivalent attitudes draw attention to the difficulties of using the label feminist in any rigid or prescriptive sense and to the diverse ways in which women could view their active citizenship. The impulse to be of service to the broader community could be seen to override the selfish individualism of women's rights and enabled women from different political perspectives to work together for social change, including improvements in women's position. The importance or otherwise of women's self-identification as feminists is then further complicated by the differences between members of those organizations that *were* explicitly feminist. They all had to grapple with the same issues – population questions, motherhood and female employment – that also pre-occupied politicians and social reformers in Europe and North America. They could not agree, however, about whether to pursue women's equal rights and personal autonomy or whether to emphasize their needs as mothers and the vital role that they could play in society through their position in the family.

These differing perspectives can be explored through the British context in the 1920s. Many pre-war suffrage organizations continued into the inter-war years – for example, the National Union of Women's Suffrage Societies changed its name to the National Union of Societies for Equal Citizenship (NUSEC) in 1919 to reflect its broader agenda. Its declared aim was to achieve equal suffrage and 'all other reforms, economic, legislative and social as are necessary to secure a real equality of liberties, status and opportunities between men and women' (Kent, 1993: 115). The meaning of equality, however, was hotly contested. The president of NUSEC, Eleanor Rathbone, argued that women could never achieve equality unless their special needs as mothers were addressed, in particular their economic dependence on men, and she advocated a range of social reforms, including family allowances, to improve women's status within the home. This position has been labelled as 'new feminism'.

Others, who have been described as 'old' feminists, continued to focus on equal rights. Differences between the two groups should not be exaggerated, since in practice most feminists sought to extend equal rights and also supported welfare measures that would improve the lives of working-class mothers. Nonetheless, there were differences in the assumptions underlying those reforms. 'New' feminists referred to maternity as 'the most important of women's occupations', while 'equality' feminists were concerned that a focus on motherhood would make it difficult for women to escape from traditional roles and preferred to emphasize the 'common humanity of men and women' (Smith, 1990: 47–65).

SOCIAL WELFARE

Similar debates took place elsewhere. Protective legislation for women workers was particularly contentious, causing disagreements between feminists from all shades of the political spectrum. In the United States, for example, Alice Paul proposed an Equal Rights Amendment to the constitution in 1923 which read that 'men and women shall have equal rights throughout the United States'. She argued that this would remove legal barriers to women's advancement in the public sphere and that this would then be followed by changes in the family and the relationship between the sexes. Her views were bitterly opposed by other groups, such as the League of Women Voters, who thought priority should be given to the welfare needs of working-class mothers and to women's role within the family [**Doc. 19, pp. 118–19**]. They pushed for more rather than less protective legislation to shorten hours of work and to regulate the conditions of women's employment. In Britain protective legislation was one of the issues that made it difficult for feminists within the labour movement to work with those who were outside. It also created a split within the feminist organization, NUSEC, when those opposed to protective legislation established the Open Door Council in 1927. These conflicts spilled over into feminist international organizations as laws regulating women's labour became an international issue. Disagreements came to a head at the 1926 IWSA Congress when Alice Paul's National Woman Party applied to affiliate. Subsequently new organizations, such as the Open Door International, were formed to lead the fight against protective legislation.

Protective legislation was so contentious because it raised the difficult question of whether women, because of their marginal position in employment, should be treated differently from men. Disagreements over other social welfare proposals tended to focus on the form that they took rather than on whether they should be introduced in the first place. The state provision of economic assistance to families was a common demand from feminists in countries as diverse as Britain, Germany and Scandinavia. They added their voices to a more general demand that family allowances should be introduced but disagreed on how such allowances should be financed and what they hoped to achieve by their introduction. In Norway, for instance, liberal and conservative women argued that regular wages should support only one individual with allowances given for the number of children in a household, whereas socialist women wanted a 'mother's wage' financed through the tax system. They saw this as a means to free women from work outside the home, enabling them to devote more time to their children. Liberal feminists, however, saw child allowances as a way that mothers could pay for child care and therefore continue with paid employment. In Britain, Eleanor Rathbone thought that family allowances would bring economic independence for mothers within the home and would strengthen the case for equal pay at the workplace. She accepted that some married women might wish to seek paid employment, but her emphasis was on the importance of women from all social classes placing greater value on motherhood.

The feminist dimension of proposals for family allowances could easily get lost within arguments that emphasized the relationship between welfare policies, child poverty and population growth. In contrast, campaigns for reproductive rights appeared to have a greater potential for challenging traditional structures since they raised issues about women's autonomy and personal freedom. The 1920s provided a new context for advocates of birth control. The First World War had brought a change in attitudes to sex and morality, while for a brief period debates on the 'woman question' in Bolshevik Russia included an emphasis on sexual freedoms. Alexandra Kollontai's writings expressed the view that men and women could be 'lovers and comrades outside structures that formalised relationships characterised by domination and subordination' (Offen, 2000: 268) and legislation was introduced on birth control and abortion. However, the association of birth control with 'free love', coupled with the opposition of governments anxious to promote more births, meant that feminist groups were cautious in their approach to the question. It was often individuals, such the American Margaret Sanger, who were the most outspoken advocates for birth control, while in many countries it was socialist women who took the lead in demanding the provision of free contraceptive advice. [**Doc. 20, pp. 119–20**] Nonetheless, both feminist groups and socialist women downplayed the importance of women achieving sexual autonomy and emphasized the health and welfare aspects of birth control, with socialist women raising the class dimensions of the issue. Indeed, many feminists were still more concerned with controlling male sexuality than with seeking sexual freedom for women.

Welfare feminism did have a radical potential, since it raised fundamental questions about the role of women in the family and could draw working-class women into a feminist constituency. However, this potential was rarely realized. Few analytical connections were made between the family and other social structures, while the critical edge of 'new feminists' was blunted by using women's needs as mothers, rather than their rights as women, as a basis on which to demand reform. As Susan Kingsley Kent, a leading historian of the war and post-war period notes, when 'new feminists made demands based upon women's traditional, special needs and special functions, when they ceased to challenge the dominant discourses on sexuality, their ideology often became confused with anti-feminists' (Kent, 1993: 118). Eleanor Rathbone's arguments for family allowances are a case in point. Although she believed that allowances would provide economic independence for married women, she also suggested that they would alleviate child poverty and improve the quality of the population – views that were indistinguishable from reformers who did not have a feminist perspective.

In Scandinavian countries, however, women played an important part in shaping the social welfare measures that were introduced by social democratic parties in the 1930s. In Sweden these included job protection for pregnant women, the legalization of contraception and maternity benefits that were paid to mothers, while in Sweden and Denmark abortion based on a restricted set of criteria was also made legal. It was the Swedish feminist Alva Myrdal who made some of the most radical suggestions for enabling women to combine motherhood and paid employment. She called for child care facilities, a range of social services, social support for domestic labour and a change in the division of labour within the home so that women would no longer have a 'double burden'. She framed her proposals in terms of Sweden's national interest, since mothers would not only have economic independence but would live in stable heterosexual partnerships and bear healthy children. Her views were too radical for the inter-war years, but many of her ideas were implemented in Sweden in the 1960s.

How far were women's campaigns responsible for the welfare reforms that were introduced? It was far easier for feminists to make gains when their aims coincided with those of the parties in power. In the United States, where women had a high public visibility in the 1930s, Eleanor Roosevelt was able to take advantage of a favourable political climate to gain humanitarian reforms. In Denmark, Sweden and Norway social democratic parties introduced social welfare reforms that benefited women, but they were financed through direct taxation and were intended to redistribute resources as well as to improve the lives of the poor. Feminists within these parties had to battle much harder to gain support for the legalization of birth control information and abortion. In Britain too it was not until 1930 that the Labour government finally conceded that local authority clinics could give birth control information to married women in a context in which many doctors now argued that it was necessary to improve women's health. Family allowances were resisted in the inter-war years and faced considerable opposition from the trade union movement. When they were finally introduced after the Second World War the intention was to reduce wage inflation rather than to ensure the economic independence of married women. The key issue was not whether social welfare measures were introduced, but whether they shifted the power relationship between men and women and challenged gender divisions. Many feminists were clear that an emphasis on social welfare did neither of these things and that feminist goals could easily be subsumed within a broader movement.

FEMINISM, PEACE AND INTERNATIONAL ACTIVISM

Similar issues were raised by the involvement of women in the movement for disarmament and peace. The Women's International League for Peace and

Freedom was the main rallying point for those feminists who sought to focus their efforts on peace, democracy and freedom, although the International Women Suffrage Alliance, later the International Alliance of Women (IAW), also worked for peace as one of its aims. There had been a long-standing connection between feminism and peace, stretching back to the nineteenth century. During the First World War it was difficult for all but a minority of women to make a stand for peace, but in the aftermath of that conflict women joined in vigorously to add their voices to those who insisted that such a war should never happen again. Peace raised in an acute form the different positions of men and women. War was seen to be an outcome of male values of aggression and ambition compared with female values of care for others, sacrifice and love.

Feminists who took a more radical perspective also drew attention to the violence that men perpetrated against women in time of war. It was assumed that men actually enjoyed fighting and conquest. Carrie Chapman Catt expressed the views of many in the days before women were enfranchised that 'all wars are men's wars. Peace has been made by women, but wars never' (quoted in Rupp, 1997: 84). Suffragists, in particular, argued that once women were able to influence foreign policy then they would be a force for peace, progress and civilization against war and barbarism. It became more common for peace campaigners during and after the First World War to argue that mothers in particular had a horror of war since they created the life that wars destroyed. Even those who were not mothers could empathize with this argument since all women were viewed as having a caring and nurturing role, both in the family and in the wider community. It was assumed therefore that a hatred of war had the potential to unite women across national boundaries in a common action.

Nonetheless, peace was another issue that strained the common bonds between women. The 'equal rights' activist Nina Boyle, for example, argued that feminists were diverted away from a focus on women's legal and material subordination to men if they took up causes such as pacifism and social reform. It was suggested that if women's emancipation became tied up with the defence of democracy and freedom for both sexes then gender inequalities and issues around male power over women could easily slip from view. Others disagreed and positively welcomed the idea that feminism should encompass a broad agenda. Indeed, Carrie Chapman Catt claimed that 'I have personally moved on and become a humanist since the vote came to me', but 'I have not ceased to be a feminist nor to be less sympathetic with protests against women's wrongs' (Offen, 2000: 375, 371).

Such arguments were increasingly played out at an international level, in particular through the League of Nations based at Geneva. At the 1919 Paris Peace conference when the League was formed members of women's international organizations pushed for the League to accept women as delegates and to open up employment to them in the secretariat. Faced with a hostile climate in their respective countries feminists sought to use the League to gain improvements in the status of women as well as to further their campaign for peace. Those who aimed for full legal, political and economic equality for women lobbied hard for the League to adopt a Treaty on Equal Rights but this proved a controversial proposal for those who wanted to ensure that women's different needs were also recognized. Despite a failure to agree on priorities and demands, the pressure from feminist organizations and individual women did have an impact. As a result of a campaign by Alice Paul and Chrystal Macmillan, a British lawyer and leading member of the IAW, it was agreed in 1931 that the League Assembly would discuss equal nationality rights for married women, the first time that an issue of equal rights had been considered in any detail. By the end of the decade the League established an inquiry into the rights and status of women, although its work was halted by the outbreak of war. Nonetheless, Carole Miller concludes that in a context in which national governments jealously guarded their own control over the status of women, 'it was a real achievement for women's groups to have convinced League member states that the position of women in society could be construed as a problem for international attention' and that this 'paved the way for post-war developments' (Miller, 1994: 238).

In a hostile political and economic climate feminists did continue to campaign for reforms and to challenge gender inequalities. They worked through a wide range of groups, including single-sex feminist organizations, women's groups, political parties and peace organizations. This meant that they were less visible as part of a vibrant movement, but it did give them a platform from which to raise issues of concern to women. Feminists debated what it meant to be a citizen and tried to extend the gains already made in equal rights. Many also focused on the needs of the working-class woman and campaigned for social welfare reforms, ranging from improved health care facilities to reproductive rights. For some feminists women's role as wives and mothers provided the basis from which they could play a part as active citizens, although this was a controversial point of view. In several countries women's groups, representing housewives, were drawn into the official committee system and were called on to give advice to governments. It was far more difficult for women to assert their rights to active citizenship as waged workers, in particular in the context of economic depression and the rise of conservative and fascist governments. It was not until the 1960s and 70s that feminists were able to make a sustained challenge to women's identification with the home and to put to the test contemporary assumptions about appropriate male and female roles.

6

'The personal is political': women's liberation and 'second wave' feminism

ORIGINS OF 'SECOND WAVE FEMINISM'

In 1968 women in Atlantic City decided to stage a protest against the Miss America beauty contest. They invited women to throw their bras and girdles, symbols of the pressures on women to conform to unrealistic standards of beauty, into a 'freedom trash bucket'. This was the start of a new and explosive period in feminist history. A series of provocative direct actions followed and soon attracted the attention of the world's media. The women's liberation movement, as it was popularly called, swept through North America and Western Europe. For almost a decade this vibrant political force was rarely out of the headlines. It was the first time in two generations that women 'unapologetically declared their feminism' (Legates, 2001: 327) and the movement soon became known as 'second wave' feminism.

What led women to take such flamboyant and public actions? Why was 1968 a crucial turning point? Some of the answers must be looked for as far back as the Second World War. Women's expectations were raised as a result of their extensive participation in the war effort – as workers, members of the armed forces and as activists in the resistance. At the end of the First World War women were enfranchised in several European countries and a similar pattern can be seen after the Second World War. Women gained the vote in France and Bulgaria (1944), Italy and Hungary (1945), Romania (1946) and Belgium (1948), often after pressure from communist politicians. In the atmosphere of liberation after the war feminists demanded full civil rights for women and encouraged them to take part in the political process. In France, for instance, pre-war suffragists, resistance workers and Catholic women joined together to ensure that the new Constitution would include a clause on sexual equality in all areas of life, including family law, as well as a guarantee that mothers and their children would receive protection. In Germany there was considerable opposition from politicians to women's rights, but after vigorous lobbying from a socialist politician and lawyer, Elisabeth Selbert, women were granted unconditional rights in the new Constitution.

Formal equality, however, did not automatically mean that women experienced a fundamental change in their political, social and economic position. In the immediate aftermath of war women turned out to vote in similar numbers to men and also stood for election in increasing numbers. Nonetheless, women faced structural barriers to full participation in the political arena, as well as a continuation of older, gender-based assumptions. The numbers present in representative assemblies remained low and female politicians were expected to deal largely with 'women's issues' such as welfare, health and children. Within political parties women tended to be marginalized into single-sex organizations that had little influence on policy making and priorities. A fear of social instability after the upheavals of war led governments to emphasize the importance of 'traditional' gender roles. Social welfare policies, including family allowances and social security payments, which were driven by population issues and the need for reconstruction after the war, were based on the assumption that there was a male breadwinner. Women rarely had full legal rights within marriage even if they had equal rights under their country's constitution. In West Germany, for example, equality in marriage was not accepted until 1957 and fathers could still have the final say on matters relating to children. In Spain, under the authoritarian regime of General Franco, women were expected to devote themselves to the family and had few personal or social rights. In Catholic countries such as Italy and Ireland women were subordinate to male relatives within the family and in the 1950s and 60s suffered from discriminatory legislation relating to divorce, adultery and abortion.

As the political landscape became more conservative it proved increasingly difficult for feminists to find a space to put forward alternative views. This was exacerbated by the onset of the Cold War during the 1950s when governments in the West became suspicious of any movements that appeared radical. One of the first casualties in this climate of fear and mounting tension was the attempt by women after the war to make new links with each other across national boundaries. Older international groups, notably WILPF and the International Alliance of Women, were still active and were joined by a new group, the Women's International Democratic Federation (WIDF). The Federation was formed at an international congress in Paris in 1945, which attracted delegates from countries throughout Europe, including Russia, Bulgaria, Hungary, France, Spain and Britain. Many of those present had been actively engaged in the fight against Nazism and they were passionate about the four aims of WIDF – to fight fascism, and to promote the rights of women, a lasting peace and better conditions for children. A close relationship was formed in the following year with a newly established organization in the United States, the Congress of American Women, a cross-class, racially integrated group that aimed to fight for the rights of women workers, racial and social justice, peace and women's rights.

All of these groups were involved in campaigns within the United Nations, established in 1945, to ensure that women's rights were recognized as part of a broader commitment to human rights. They served on the Status of Women Commission, set up in 1946 as a separate group to focus on women's rights, and also achieved consultative status B within the UN which gave them access to documents and the possibility of addressing sessions. The WIDF in particular recruited women from Africa and Asia and sought to bring them into the ambit of the UN. One of these was Funmilayo Ransome-Kuti, a teacher from Nigeria who saw women's rights as inextricably linked with opposition to racism and imperialism. She was active in organizing women at a grass-roots level to demand political and social rights. Attending a meeting in London in 1947 she met members of the WIDF and worked closely with them when they set up a commission to investigate the conditions of women in Africa and Asia. This period of international cooperation was, however, difficult to sustain during the period of the Cold War when any individuals or groups suspected of communist sympathies were thought to be subversives. The WIDF lost its consultative status at the UN in 1954 and was not reinstated until 1967.

In countries dominated by the Soviet Union only Communist Party sponsored organizations that promoted Party policies among women were allowed to thrive. Women found themselves in a complex position. Communist rhetoric was based on equality between the sexes. Women were expected to participate in the labour force, were able to enjoy mixed, free and accessible education and often found a role within politics. On the other hand little was done to alter gender relationships in the family, while in the workplace there was a hierarchy of jobs that gave men greater power and resources than women. In non Communist countries the image of the contented wife and mother, giving all her attention to housework, children and the care of her husband predominated and was widespread in popular magazines and advertisements. It is hardly surprising, therefore, that in the West the 1950s has been described as the 'decade of the housewife'.

And yet women did not remain silent. They continued to organize together to demand improvements in their employment and family lives, working through trade unions and political parties as well as their own single-sex organizations. Debates about gender roles were fuelled by key pieces of writing. Simone de Beauvoir's *The Second Sex* (1949) was a particularly influential text. She argued that the assumption that men represented the norm, and that women, throughout history, had been seen to deviate from this, limited women's sense of themselves and the possibilities open to them since they were always viewed as 'the other'. [**Doc. 22, pp. 121–2**] She emphasized that the roles and characteristics assigned to women were socially constructed. In a famous passage she concluded that 'one is not born, but rather becomes, a woman', since a woman's 'destiny is imposed upon her by her teachers and her society' (De Beauvoir, 1953: 315). De Beauvoir did not see herself as writing in a feminist tradition but tried to understand women's subordination in the context of her broader interest in existentialist philosophy. Nonetheless, she provided feminists with a new way of understanding the social position of women and her book was to become a key foundation text for 'second wave' feminism.

The image of the perfect wife and mother was increasingly at odds with the realities of women's lives in the late 1950s and 1960s. As young women took advantage of the opportunities offered by an expansion in higher education they were less content than their mothers to accept a future bounded by domesticity. At the same time married women began to enter the labour force in larger numbers. They were clustered in part-time and low-paid work that prompted extensive public debates and government inquiries into gender inequalities at the workplace, many of which resulted in legislation. In Norway, for example, the principle of equal pay was adopted in 1958 and a new taxation system for married couples was introduced, weakening the male breadwinner system. In Canada a number of women's organizations came together in 1966 to put pressure on the government to appoint a Royal Commission on women, while in France public discussion on women's work outside the home contributed to a reform of the law on marriage in 1965.

The 1960s also saw the publication of another key text, Betty Friedan's *The Feminine Mystique* (1963). This seemed to encapsulate the frustrations of white, middle-class housewives in suburban America who, when interviewed, suggested that their lives had not been fulfilled. Friedan labelled this as 'the problem with no name'. She explored how women had come to believe that they should be good wives and mothers and therefore blamed themselves if they failed to be contented with their roles. Friedan's solution for this problem was to encourage women to take up paid employment, although she perhaps underestimated the difficulties of combining paid work and child care. She also gave too much emphasis to the bored housewife and said little about those women who were active outside the home in voluntary social or political work. Nonetheless, she was important in drawing attention to 'sex role conditioning' and to the fact that nurture, rather than nature, had assigned women to domestic roles. She stimulated debates about the position of women, in particular, on women's experiences within the family – a question that was to be central for 'second wave feminism'.

PROTEST IN THE 1960S AND WOMEN'S LIBERATION

It was the black civil rights movement, however, that provided the main impetus for women to organize together and to challenge contemporary gender roles. By taking part in the movement they established networks, learned new tactics and also began to raise questions about their own lack of rights. In 1966 Betty Friedan, along with labour and civil rights activists, established the **National Organization of Women** (NOW). Its aims were to 'bring women into full participation in the mainstream of American society now' (Legates, 2001: 348), so that they could reach their full potential as human beings. [**Doc. 23, pp. 122–3**] It sought to use the law to gain equality of opportunity in employment and education and to achieve equal civil and political rights and responsibilities for women.

NOW can be located in many respects in a long-standing liberal tradition that emphasized the importance of men and women working together to achieve change through legislation. Nonetheless, its statement of purpose also drew attention to the importance of the mass media in creating images of women that were derogatory and that reduced women's self confidence, and therefore it was argued that women's own view of themselves needed to be changed from within. By 1967 its members had begun to take more radical direct action, picketing government offices to ensure that laws were complied with. Just as pressure began to mount for more attention to be paid to gender inequalities, student unrest and demonstrations against the Vietnam War in 1968 were to transform the political landscape.

Across Europe and North America students took to the streets to protest against the Vietnam War, to call for reforms in education and to demand civil freedoms. Inspired by revolutionary struggles elsewhere in the world they criticized the capitalist system and, in Paris, were joined by workers from a range of industries who went on strike. Grass-roots action and street demonstrations, in which there were violent confrontations with the police, characterized the movement. Women joined into these activities with enthusiasm but too often ended up as caterers and minute takers rather than as speakers and decision takers. Their frustration at being marginalized was increased by the fact that this was 'flagrantly contradicting the anti hierarchical and participatory ideals of the 1968 movements' (Eley, 2002: 366). When they demanded a greater role women found that men, who claimed to be their comrades, did not take them seriously and were 'sexist' in their attitudes. This prompted women to draw attention to the specific problems that they faced as women and to question the priorities and concerns of a male-defined left politics.

It is hardly surprising, therefore, that women began to meet together in autonomous single-sex groups to discuss issues that concerned them

National Organization of Women: Formed in 1966 by leading American feminists; spearheaded campaign for equal opportunities; has mobilized many demonstrations, including a March for Women's Lives, for reproductive rights, in 2004 that involved 1.15 million people; a membership of 500,000.

and to raise their own demands. Inspired by the demonstration against the Miss America contest in Atlantic City, women in America and elsewhere took direct action to draw attention to their grievances. In Germany women members of the Socialist German Student Federation met to discuss their specific problems, in particular child care, and argued that the family, as well as the workplace or the university, should become a site of political activity. When they met with derision from men at a subsequent conference one woman pelted her critics with tomatoes. French women also rejected the 'sexism' of the Left. They formed numerous women-only groups, including the MLF (Mouvement de libération des femmes). Some of these groups wanted to work anonymously underground whereas others, following the provocative style of May '68, carried out spectacular public actions, using 'transgression, insolence and caustic humour to win the media's attention' (Picq, 2002: 316). The most famous example was when one woman laid a wreath of flowers under the Arc de Triomphe for the wife of the Unknown Soldier. In 1971 over 300 French women signed a newspaper article, known as the 'Whore's Manifesto', declaring that they had had an illegal abortion and this was followed by a similar public declaration in West Germany.

In Britain the women's liberation movement gained an impetus from the campaign of women factory workers for equal pay as well as from disillusion with the attitudes of men in the anti-Vietnam War protests. The first Women's Liberation Conference, attended by over 600 women, was held at Ruskin College, Oxford, early in 1970. A National Women's Coordinating Committee was formed to demand equal pay, equal education and employment opportunities, free contraception and abortion on demand and 24-hour nurseries. Disruptive actions were also common. In 1969 the Tufnell Park women's liberation group leafleted the Ideal Home Exhibition and a year later there was a protest against the televised Miss World Competition at the Albert Hall in which protesters threw smoke bombs and bags of flour. [**Doc. 24, pp. 124–5**]

The women's liberation movement was not just confined to Europe and North America. Japanese feminists, for example, highlighted inequalities in family law and the problems of working women. They organized demonstrations and sit-ins and campaigned to have a 'sexist' television commercial for instant noodles removed. In Scandinavia, however, where legal equalities in marriage and the right to abortion had already been achieved, and where social welfare legislation enabled women to combine work and family, a women's liberation movement was far less evident.

Feminists did not always agree on the best way to organize and on the demands that they wanted to make. In France, Germany, Italy and the United States there was an emphasis on women working autonomously in single-sex groups. In the United States, in particular, feminists tried to develop a separate women's culture and placed emphasis on sex oppression. In Britain, however, class politics exerted more influence and many feminists sought to maintain links with the trade union and labour movement. And yet with their slogan 'sisterhood is powerful' women sought to transcend their differences and had a sense that they were part of an international movement with shared characteristics.

Autonomous women's groups were at the heart of the women's liberation movement. Formed at a grass-roots level and outside of existing political parties, they deliberately rejected hierarchies and national leaders. At meetings individual women were encouraged to speak about their own experiences. **Consciousness raising**, as it was termed, was intended to help women to develop an awareness of their position and to take control over their own lives and aspirations. As they talked about the frustrations that they experienced in their private lives women came to realize that their difficulties were not just individual ones but arose from social conditions that were shared by others. This self-knowledge was then a springboard for taking collective actions to achieve change. These could be spontaneous, unplanned actions including 'sudden outbreaks of anger, gatherings with singing, dancing through the streets, impromptu speeches and exuberant expressions of solidarity' (Kaplan, 1992: 19). They could also be well-organized events such as sit-ins, marches and demonstrations. For example, in 1977–8 women marched through the streets in Britain, West Germany and Italy in 'Reclaim the Night' actions to assert their right to be in public spaces in safety after dark.

> **Consciousness raising:** A group discussion with each member sharing personal experiences in order to enlighten the group as a whole, as well as the individual, about social and political realities.

The 'personal is political' was one of the most famous slogans of the movement. Women were expected to conform to particular ideals of femininity and this affected the ways in which they thought about themselves as well as simply being imposed from outside. Feminists consistently drew attention to the way in which consumerism and advertising used women's sexuality to sell goods and conditioned them into believing that only a particular kind of beauty had value. This encouraged women to spend a great deal of money on the latest fashions and beauty products. It also fed into anxieties about ageing and the 'ideal body shape' that could lead to cosmetic surgery and eating disorders so graphically portrayed in Susie Orbach's *Fat is a Feminist Issue* (1981). Areas once thought as private, including anxieties about the body, sexuality and relationships between men and women were all viewed as political issues within 'second wave feminism'. The pleasures of sex and women's erotic desires were emphasized as well as women's right to define their own sexuality and the demand that there should be an end to discrimination against lesbians. Consciousness raising played a central role in ensuring that the personal would become political and women were encouraged to 'reassess their personal and emotional lives, their relation to their families, their lovers and their work' and to 'negotiate an autonomous identity beyond those associated with family duties' (Whelehan, 1995: 13).

The family was viewed as a key site of women's oppression. Alongside more conventional demands for equal pay and an end to sex discrimination at work feminists called for paid housework, child-care facilities, and contraceptive advice. Reproductive rights, including free contraception and abortion on demand, were central issues for the women's liberation movement. Campaigns to legalize abortion, and to ensure that women had the right to choose whether to have an abortion, took place in most countries in Europe and North America in the early 1970s. It was the one issue that managed to bring women from different generations, social groups and political backgrounds together at a national level to work for a reform of common concern. For the most part, these campaigns were successful in legalizing abortion, but the legislation often fell short of the demand for a woman's right to choose.

Feminists communicated their ideas through an array of newspapers, newsletters and journals and also through women's presses, such as Virago in Britain and Arlen House in Ireland. Education also provided an important space for feminists to challenge conventional wisdoms about gender roles and contemporary definitions of femininity. As more women entered higher education, they highlighted the fact that women were invisible in academic disciplines that had been defined by men. They demanded women's studies courses to provide information about women's lives and to raise new questions about how knowledge had been constructed. This in turn affected the nature of the academic disciplines themselves. Women's studies courses also had a role to play in the political struggle for women's liberation. An important part of the academic project, for example, was to re-discover women's political activism in the past – pioneering texts included Sheila Rowbotham's *Hidden From History* and Gerda Lerner's *The Majority Finds Its Past*. As feminists found out more about the varied activities in which women had been involved in the past so they were able to question the view that women's roles were natural and could not be changed.

DEBATING FEMINISM

A number of key texts helped to shape the ideas and characteristics of the early years of the women's liberation movement. 'Liberal feminists' still focused on individual rights and equal opportunities and argued that legal and social policy changes would help women to achieve these. More characteristic of 'second wave feminism', however, was the 'radical feminist' attempt to find new ways of theorizing women's relationship to men. They looked in particular at 'men's social control of women through various mechanisms of patriarchy . . . especially violence, heterosexuality and reproduction, where men as a group are seen as responsible for maintaining women's oppression'

(Maynard, 1998: 253). Kate Millett's influential book *Sexual Politics* (1969) argued that patriarchy, or male power over women, underpinned all social forms including the family, religion and the workplace. The fact that patriarchy was all pervasive and also operated at the level of ideas meant that it had the power to shape how women thought as well as how they lived their lives. By suggesting that personal lives were affected by the state and by patriarchy, Millett opened the way for feminists to challenge the division between the public and the private that was central to liberal political thought. Millett's scathing attack on male authors for glorifying sexual brutality against women in literature brought her considerable notoriety and criticism for being anti-male.

Germaine Greer, an Australian academic living in England, also became the centre of controversy for her book *The Female Eunuch* (1971). This was a provocative text that led to criticism from both within and outside the women's liberation movement. Greer produced a polemic about the ways in which women had been conditioned to accept a sense of inferiority to men and argued for sexual liberation outside the monogamous family. She made a spirited attack on the constraints women faced in their lives but was criticized by many feminists for blaming women themselves for failing to grasp the opportunities that were offered. She complained that women were 'frigid' and argued that 'the cage door has been opened but the canary has refused to fly out' (p. 14). With her tall, striking figure and her views on the enjoyment of heterosexual sex, Greer was described by *Life* magazine as the 'saucy feminist that even men like' and it is not surprising that she stood outside the mainstream.

Within Britain, in particular, women who had taken part in left politics attempted to bring together a Marxist and a feminist approach in which the economic roots of women's exploitation within capitalism could be linked with more personal forms of oppression. In her influential text *Woman's Estate* (1971), for example, Juliet Mitchell revised standard Marxist accounts by analysing the position of women not just in terms of relations of production or of private property but also by looking at sexual differences through the insights offered by psychoanalytic theory.

The lively debate among feminists about the root causes of women's oppression and about the nature and importance of patriarchy provides just one example of the vibrancy of the women's movement in the early 1970s. This was a time of exceptional activity as women mobilized across several countries. Contemporaries self-consciously described themselves as feminists and felt that they were taking part in a new phenomenon. In France, for example, feminists proclaimed 'women's liberation, year zero' in 1970 to demonstrate that they had different goals and a different way of thinking than the liberal feminists who had preceded them. Clearly there were many similarities with feminist campaigners of previous generations. 'Second wave' feminists pursued a variety of equal rights campaigns alongside other demands and some of the direct actions and use of spectacle evoked the militancy of the British suffragettes. Nonetheless, there were differences. In Britain, young middle-class women did support campaigns for equal rights at work, but their passionate, personal concerns were about 'images in advertising, child care, the response of left-wing men to women's liberation' (Rowbotham, 1989: 166). The language used was significant; emancipation implied freedom from constraints and the achievement of social policies to enable women to fulfil their potential. Liberation, on the other hand, implied a greater sense of personal empowerment and choice, adventure and sexual power free from prevailing ideas of what it meant to be a woman. More women were now prepared to take part in exuberant actions. They organized from the grass roots, were suspicious of charismatic leaders and put 'personal' issues such as the control of their own bodies and sexual freedoms at the forefront of their politics. The style of the movement was subversive. 'It meant taking the culture's trappings and symbols, its most cherished beliefs and disordering them, playing with them, turning their meanings around in acts of public transgression. It was a calculated acting out, a purposeful disobedience, a misbehaving in public' (Eley, 2002: 372).

What had the movement achieved? It has been estimated that in Western Europe at least a million women were activists and a further 12 million were sympathizers and supporters (Kaplan, 1992: 17). In most countries the movement contributed towards legislation that aimed to enhance women's position, including equal pay, sex discrimination laws and, most important of all, the legalization of abortion. A key feature of 'second wave' feminism, however, was women's attempt to set up their own support networks outside mainstream political and social institutions. Women's health centres encouraged self-awareness about the female body and sexuality, while rape crisis centres provided practical help for women. In 1972 the first refuge in the world for battered women was established in Britain.

Feminists showed that domestic violence and rape were not just the actions of violent individuals but were caused by social structures and expectations about male and female roles. In doing so they ensured that support would be forthcoming from state agencies in the future. Perhaps the most important aspect of the 1970s, however, was changing the terms in which the woman question was debated and encouraging women to think differently about themselves and their place in the world. A new language had to be developed in order to make sense of the all-pervasive discrimination that women faced. It was argued that 'sexism' was embedded not just in the structures of institutions such as the workplace or the family, but also in the ways in which the roles of men and women, and the meaning of masculinity and femininity, were constructed in the media, in advertising and in everyday language. This ensured that the next generation of women would enter a very different world from the one that their mothers had struggled to change.

FEMINISM ON A GLOBAL SCALE

The mobilization of so many women, and the publicity given to the inequalities and discrimination faced by women throughout the world, brought more attention to their cause within the United Nations. There, it was the WIDF president, Hertta Kuusinen from Finland, who proposed to the UN Commission on the Status of Women that there should be an International Women's Year. This was held in 1975 and was followed by the Decade for Women, 1976–85. The UN called on governments to improve health, employment and educational levels of women under the banner of equality, development and peace. [**Doc. 29, pp. 128–9**] There were still debates about whether the focus should be on rights or whether, as many Third World women argued, it was important to first address structural forces of oppression. Nonetheless, UN initiatives provided a stimulus for women across the world to set up women's groups and to make their own demands. In Japan, for example, the International Women's Year Action Group was able to exert pressure for change on the government at home as well as raising issues in the International Women's Decade conferences held at Copenhagen, Mexico and Nairobi. In Brazil the military government allowed International Women's Day to be celebrated in 1975 since women were not seen as 'political'. This gave a stimulus to feminist demands. At first these focused on women's work and production, but at the 1978 International Women's Day the politics of the private sphere, the family and reproductive rights were highlighted.

Women in Third World countries had their own independent goals and strategies. In India, for example, a countrywide movement of women emerged on a mass scale in 1979–80 when the Supreme Court acquitted a policeman accused of raping a young woman who was in custody. Women took part in mass demonstrations and established organizations such as the Joint Women's Programme (1981) and the India Democratic Women's Association (1981) to fight all forms of violence against women, including the practice of sati and dowry deaths. Some groups were locally based and autonomous, drawing their active supporters from young, educated urban feminists who had worked with women in rural areas, slums and trade unions. Others were affiliated with various political parties and sought to make gains for women through existing political channels as well as through direct actions.

Women also mobilized on a large scale in Latin America in the 1970s and 80s. Their political strategies, however, were complex and their movements arose within a very different context to that found in Europe and North America. The repression of political parties and trade unions opened up a space for women to play a key role in campaigns to achieve democracy and they were then inspired to raise their own demands as a sex. Women were involved in three different types of action. In response to the economic difficulties facing their families working-class women joined together at a grass-roots level to ensure access to basic services that were being neglected by their governments. Women also organized as mothers to demand information about missing relatives, in particular their children and grandchildren, and raised human-rights questions. The most famous of the groups were the *Madres de la Plaza de Mayo* in Argentina. In both of these cases women used their traditional role as wives and mothers as a justification for their political activism and did not initially draw attention to gender-specific issues.

Alongside these groups, however, educated middle-class women, many of whom were active in left opposition parties, began to raise questions about sex discrimination in the context of the larger class struggle and also established separate women's groups. For example, when the Echeverría regime in Mexico allowed new opposition parties to form from 1970–6 young professional women and students formed feminist organizations. They emphasized the need for consciousness raising and held workshops and demonstrations, often criticizing consumerism and its exploitation of women. In raising the question of what democratization would mean for women, feminists in Latin American countries linked the authoritarianism of the state with authoritarianism in society, in particular the family, and argued that sex oppression lay at the root of most social structures. Their demands mirrored those of their counterparts in the West, ranging from economic and equal rights issues to questions of reproduction and male violence.

The dynamism and variety of the feminist movement in Latin America can be seen in the debates at the biennial *encuentros* (conventions) held in the area during the 1980s. These provided a stimulus to movements in particular countries and also revealed the changing concerns of feminists over time as attendance expanded to include women from Central and South America and from the Caribbean. In Bogotá in 1981 the key debates were over autonomy from mainstream politics and whether feminist objectives could be separated from the class struggle. In Lima in 1983 the theme was patriarchy. The inclusion of members of the popular, grass-roots women's movements expanded the parameters of the debate about autonomy since for some it 'opened up the possibility that women could define and act on their own interests' (Jaquette, 1994: 5). In São Paulo, Brazil, in 1985 race and sexual preference were part of the agenda in an explicit way for the first time, although class remained a central issue.

For Third World feminists it was impossible to disentangle sex from race and class oppression. In South Africa, for example, black women took part in the struggle against apartheid and also had to cope with the absence of male members of the family. Their priorities were to ensure the economic and physical survival of their families. This entailed working long hours for low pay as well as providing many of the primary health-care services. Thus, the dichotomy between public and private spheres, and between masculine and feminine domains, was less marked in African societies than in many other countries. African feminism therefore stressed 'human totality, parallel autonomy, co-operation, self reliance, adaptation, survival and liberation' (Steady, 1996: 18). Women's role in ensuring family survival led to grass-roots organizing at community level and then to involvement in national and international politics.

In practice there were many overlaps between women's groups that had practical goals, such as the protection of families, and those that highlighted gender inequalities. Women in opposition movements in Latin America used their 'traditional' social role as mothers as a source of strength and were able to create a new feminist practice as they politicized everyday life. In Brazil, for example, housewives who engaged in community politics also began to discuss family, love and childbearing and increasingly focused on women's subordination. This in turn had an influence on the agenda of the middle-class feminist movement. By the late 1970s the feminist movement had reached women from all social classes, had expanded the definition of feminist struggle and had formed new groups, including those based on the needs and specific agendas of Afro-Brazilians and lesbians (Alvarez, 1994: 25).

DIVISIONS IN 'SECOND WAVE' FEMINISM

A sense of 'sisterhood', so integral to the women's liberation movement in Europe and North America, was difficult to sustain as differences based on class, race and sexual orientation increasingly came to the surface. 'Second wave feminism' was dominated by white, educated, middle-class, heterosexual women and their concerns. The methods used, in particular, consciousness raising, and the emphasis on sexual freedom and personal autonomy alienated working-class women who were never drawn to the movement in large numbers. Other groups, such as lesbian feminists and black feminists, challenged the claims of the women's liberation movement to speak for all women and sought to bring their own experiences and priorities to the fore. [**Doc. 26, p. 126**] Thus, in contrast to white middle-class women's criticism of the patriarchal nature of the family, black women were more likely to see the family as a source of strength and support against systematic racism. They were concerned that Reclaim the Night Marches and debates about rape reproduced stereotyped views of the sexualized black man who posed a threat to white women. Similarly, demands for legalized abortion failed to address issues such as forced sterilization that had a specific impact on black women. Black women found it difficult to accept that sexism was a more fundamental form of oppression than racism and sought to develop their own theories that would link gender and race. [**Doc. 25, pp. 125–6**] The American writer bell hooks has been particularly influential in challenging the racist assumptions of white feminism and in tracing black women's political and historical invisibility to the beginnings of slavery (hooks, 1981). Using lower case for her name in order to put the emphasis on her writing she has criticized the feminist movement for claiming to speak for all women. She argues that race, sex, class and sexual orientation are all inextricably linked and that social change requires them to be dealt with as a whole.

Lesbian feminists argued that it was heterosexuality and not just male economic power that underpinned male supremacy. Authors such as Adrienne Rich and Mary Daly celebrated women's difference and argued that women could identify with each other in a variety of ways including the emotional as well as the political. For some activists, particularly in the United States, this implied the need for a separatist form of politics that would concentrate on women-identified concerns such as domestic violence. [**Doc. 26, p. 126**] Some lesbians then suggested that heterosexual women could not be feminists since they collaborated with patriarchy and with men. This in turn led to acrimonious debates and splits in the movement in the late 1970s, in particular, over attitudes towards male violence, rape and pornography.

Divisions based on class, race, religion and ethnicity were just as common in the Third World as in Western societies. Community based working-class women's movements in Latin America, for example, tended to view feminist groups as middle class or as representing the interests of white women. In Asia feminists were conscious of the extent to which industrialized, wealthy countries in the region exploited women in less developed, neighbouring states and this contributed to the development of a complex feminist politics. Japanese women, for instance, linked their own oppression, in particular domestic violence, with the oppression of other women in South East Asia that resulted from Japanese attempts to find cheap labour. As members of the Asian Women's Association Japanese feminists drew attention to the plight of women in the Philippines, Korea and Indonesia who were faced with either low pay in sweated industries or else work providing sexual services for tourists. They attempted to act in solidarity with Asian women rather than to see them as passive victims. In Islamic societies religious differences could lead to complex feminist alliances and strategies. In Iran, for example, the establishment of an Islamic republic in 1976 led to a loss of many rights that had been won over the course of the century. Nonetheless, Islamic feminists used their knowledge of the Koran to justify their arguments that women should have access to greater educational and employment opportunities. At the same time secular feminists reluctantly agreed to take up the veil as part of a bargaining strategy to enable them to make gains in employment, education and welfare.

The three International conferences held during the UN decade of women brought feminists together from different parts of the world, but they also revealed growing tensions between them. White, middle-class Western feminists were criticized for seeing their own goals and assumptions as universal ones. [**Doc. 27, pp. 126–7**] Muslim women, in particular, challenged the view that Islamic societies, with their emphasis on the patriarchal family, were repressive to women and that practices such as veiling were examples of women's lack of personal freedoms. Instead, they pointed to the ways in which Western feminists had been implicated in colonialism and suggested that their personal freedoms were illusory since women were used as sex objects in the media and in advertising. In contrast, Islamic feminists claimed that wearing the veil should be seen in a positive light, since it 'liberates them from the dictates of the fashion industry and the demands of the beauty myth' (Afshar, 1996: 124).

SETBACKS AND NEW INITIATIVES

As early as the 1980s, therefore, 'second wave' feminists in Europe and North America could see that their movement was losing momentum and had become more fragmented. The slogan 'sisterhood is universal' was difficult to sustain when differences between women – including race, religion, ethnicity and sexual orientation – seemed more significant than their common interests as a sex. New ways of thinking appeared to confirm this. **Post-modernism**, in particular, led feminists to question whether it was possible to speak of 'woman' as a distinct category. In her influential book, *Am I That Name?*, Denise Riley suggested that '"woman" is historically, discursively constructed and always relatively to other categories which themselves change' (Riley, 1988 in Hall, 1991: 205). If the individual self is fragmented and likely to have multiple identities that change over time, it would be difficult to find a straightforward link between experience and political activity or to conceive of a politics based on collective interests as a sex – both of which had been crucial for 'second wave' feminism.

Post-modernism: A set of concepts that critique broad explanatory theories such as Marxism or Feminism; emphasizes the role of language in constructing our understanding of social reality.

A hostile political climate also made it difficult for a women's movement to flourish. A move to the right in politics led to a new emphasis on the importance of the traditional family and to attacks on some of the gains made by women, in particular, abortion rights. This 'backlash' against 'second wave' feminism was then reinforced by the popular media which used the term post-feminism – not to describe something that occurred after feminism, but to imply that there was an active rejection of 'second wave' feminism and its outmoded ideas. Younger women were encouraged to exercise personal choice, in particular, as consumers of clothes and beauty products, and to react against the stereotype of the serious feminist who wore dungarees, used little make up and was anti-male. This attack on feminism can be seen as a defensive reaction of a male establishment against the threat of change that 'second wave' feminism had posed. On the other hand, there were also feminist authors who criticized 'second wave' feminism, in particular, for its preoccupation with rape and sexual harassment that implied women were victims. The most well known of these authors – who was taken up extensively by the media – was Naomi Wolf, the author of *The Beauty Myth* (1991) and *Fire Within Fire* (1993). Although she argued that the media were largely responsible for creating a negative image of feminism, she also blamed the movement itself for being too rigid in its definitions and for holding back women from doing whatever they wanted.

Despite these uncertainties and the critique of tenets that had been fundamental to 'second wave' feminism, such as the importance of experience and women's solidarity, women did continue to take action outside formal political and professional structures. They organized self-help groups at a local level, took part in campaigns over specific issues, such as child-care facilities and tried to get their message across by forming publishing collectives, theatre groups or organizing other cultural activities. There were moments when women could be mobilized in larger numbers. In Britain, for example, a women-only peace camp was set up at the Greenham Common nuclear base in 1981. In the following year over 30,000 women encircled the base and left personal items such as photographs or children's clothes tied to the fence. This provides a good example of how informal networks could be effective in leading to the organization of a large-scale protest. Similarly in the United States, three quarters of a million women were still prepared to march on Washington in 1992 when abortion rights were under threat. Nonetheless, while women might join together in specific identity groups, or in single-issue protests, this seemed like a far cry from the mass mobilization to challenge a common oppression that had characterized the earlier women's liberation movement.

The term post-feminism, used so frequently in the media, seemed to imply that there was no longer a need for feminism now that women had made so many gains in legal, economic, political and reproductive rights. Indeed, throughout the world girls and women took full advantage of an increase in educational and employment opportunities and began to make inroads into positions of power in many organizations. Feminism as an approach and a category of analysis became more embedded in academic subjects and women were able to gain positions of influence in higher education and in the media. Publishing houses and journals established by women then provided an important outlet for feminist scholarship.

Women were also able to make their voices heard within formal political structures. Working through political parties, trade unions and the professions feminists attempted to influence policies affecting the lives of women, in particular in the area of social welfare. In Ireland, for instance, women took an active part in the referenda in the 1980s on abortion and the removal of the constitutional ban on divorce. Women did not necessarily use their positions of power and influence within such organizations, however, to challenge gender inequalities. They were more likely to press for social welfare reforms to improve women's health or their housing conditions rather than to focus on empowering women to take control over their lives. The subversive, questioning side of feminism, therefore, appeared to be lost. A feminist perspective was perhaps more in evidence at an international level. Women continued to exert pressure within international bodies, notably the European Union and the United Nations, to ensure that gender inequalities would remain high on the agenda. After many decades of effort women appeared to make a political breakthrough at the UN sponsored World Conference on Women held in Beijing, 1995. A statement was made that 'women's rights are human rights'. Further, it was agreed that, as well as making broad inquiries into the extent to which women's rights were violated, individual complaints would be received and investigated (Gaer, 2009: 68).

Not all women benefited from the social and economic changes of the last two decades of the twentieth century. In the year 2000 women, who were just over half of the world's population, still performed two thirds of the world's work hours, earned less than one tenth of its income and owned less than 1 per cent of its property. Of the estimated 1.3 billion people living in poverty, over 70 per cent were female and there were still vast differences in the maternal mortality rates and general health statistics between sub-Saharan Africa, East Asia and industrialized countries. The World Health Organization, for instance, estimated in 2000 that one in five women globally had been physically or sexually abused at some time in her life, while in countries such as Thailand and the Philippines child sex tourism was widespread (Billson and Fluehr-Lobban, 2005: 5–6). Even in the West there were paradoxes. Young women were told that they had 'never had it so good' and were doing well in education and in employment. But violence against women, exploitative advertising, pornography and prostitution were still endemic. The freedom to express sexual desire and to have relationships outside marriage without a social stigma were positive developments for young women, but were accompanied by a greater risk of sexually transmitted diseases and a greater respectability for pornography in the public sphere.

Changes that might on the surface have brought benefits for women could prove to be contradictory in their effects. Without the context of a strong women's movement, for instance, it was difficult to frame reforms in feminist terms. Thus, professional women who sought improvements in social welfare services such as reproductive rights emphasized health and the well-being of families rather than women's right to choose and sexual autonomy. Similarly, the introduction of democratic governments could, paradoxically, marginalize women's needs and feminist demands. In Latin America, for example, political parties took up feminist demands around employment and social welfare, but were reluctant to pursue reproductive rights, sexuality and domestic violence. Women became less significant as political actors, their activities were more diffuse and there was little sense that the reforms introduced were designed to challenge male power. In Eastern Europe, democratization in the 1980s opened up a space for women to organize together in feminist groups that were independent of the state. They debated women's rights, produced books on the subject and introduced courses on women's studies in schools and colleges. On the other hand, the new, male-dominated parliaments increasingly questioned the reproductive rights women had enjoyed under socialism and an emphasis was placed on women's role within the family rather than the workplace. [**Doc. 28, pp. 127–8**] Lack of economic opportunities meant that young women and girls, lured to wealthier countries by the promise of financial gain and employment, often found themselves forced to become prostitutes. It has been estimated that two-thirds of women trafficked for sex purposes worldwide come from Central and Eastern Europe.

In the face of so many examples of ongoing economic and social inequalities in women's lives on a global scale, in particular the widespread domestic violence and sexual exploitation, as the new millennium approached there were signs of a new vitality in feminist politics. Collective actions by women and debates about the future of feminism raised the possibility that we were entering a period of 'third wave' feminism in the twenty-first century. This suggests that for a new generation of women, as well as for many older campaigners, feminism still has a place in their lives and certainly is neither dead nor irrelevant.

7

Assessment

W
hat has happened to feminism since the heady days of the women's liberation movement? Is there still a space for feminist politics in a world in which older political certainties appear to have collapsed with the fall of the Berlin Wall and the end of the Cold War? How should feminists deal with new political allegiances and conflicts – fundamentalist Islam against the corruption of the West, civil wars between ethnic groups or the increasing gap between rich and poor nations? Throughout the history of feminism there has always been debate about what it means to be a feminist, which goals should be pursued and which tactics should be used. Feminism in the twenty-first century is no exception. It simply has to deal with different patterns, priorities and contradictions which are going to affect the ways in which women act politically.

There have been numerous disagreements about the meaning of 'third wave' feminism, and indeed whether there is something distinctive that can be assigned that label. But all participants in the debate contest the view that we are living in a post-feminist age. It is surely significant that Germaine Greer, author of *The Female Eunuch*, a key text of the women's liberation movement once again came to the fore in 1999 with another book *The Whole Woman*. In this she argued that post-feminism had encouraged women to think they could have it all – a career, motherhood, beauty and a good sex life. Their role as consumers and the importance of personal lifestyle choices had been emphasized at the expense of politics. And yet, as she pointed out, this applied largely to the affluent West where 'the exercising of one person's freedom may be directly linked to another's oppression'. Thus, a collapse in economic power of the majority of women in the world has been a direct consequence of Western power and control. In this situation, she asked, how could a woman believe that she has passed beyond feminism (Gamble, 2001: 51)?

If feminism is still alive and well in the twenty-first century, what does it aim to do and does it have a different character from the feminisms that have gone before? Generation is a key issue. Young women who have benefited from social changes since 'second wave' feminism focus on the body and sexuality as areas where struggle still has to take place. They have also joined into campaigns around global issues including environmentalism, anti-capitalist and anti-corporate activities, cultural production and human-rights questions. They perceive these as women's issues but do not see them in isolation from human issues – a perspective that would have been familiar to peace and human rights campaigners in the inter-war years.

Feminists active in the women's liberation movement of the 1970s have also attempted to develop different strategies for the new millennium. Elaine Showalter, for example, an American author and feminist campaigner suggests community activists, seeking to improve women's lives through better child-care or health facilities, should use the political and economic power that women now hold to help their cause. Debates around the best strategies to follow are not new and echo concerns that feminists have expressed from the mid-nineteenth century onwards. Should women organize together in women only groups, both as the most effective way to make an impact and also because this provides a safe environment in which consciousness of what it means to be a woman can be raised? Or is it better, in a mixed-sex world, to work with men in organizations addressing common concerns? Should women work through formal structures to achieve change or does this dilute the whole meaning of feminism with its emphasis on non-hierarchical ways of acting together and informal networks of support?

What has emerged from these debates is the importance of developing a variety of strategies for achieving change; women in parliaments through-out the world are likely to be more effective in raising feminist issues if they have the support of an autonomous women's group outside. Involvement in community struggles over child care, school closures or health facilities, which do not at first appear to have a feminist agenda, can lead to links being made between local activists and feminist groups. Moreover, whether structures are formal or informal collective campaigns lead to networks of support being developed at all levels. In a new political context, and with the distance that enables feminists to re-appraise 'second wave' feminism, many issues can be approached in far more complex ways than in the past. Instead of using the slogan a 'woman's right to choose', campaigners around reproductive rights are likely to look at the language of rights that has framed the debates and to consider compromises that might need to be made to ensure legislative success.

'Third wave' feminism might be difficult to define – and indeed the label may have very little meaning. But debates around this issue show that feminism still has vitality and that it is possible for women to take common action for political purposes and not just for individual, personal fulfilment. Women have found, and continue to find, a variety of spaces in which to operate and have expressed greater optimism that both identity politics and single-issue campaigns can be a springboard for broader actions. In France, for example, debate over the small number of women elected to representative institutions has reinvigorated the women's movement and brought a new visibility to feminist politics. Third World feminists, in particular, have argued that it is possible to conceive of a different type of universal feminism that is no longer rooted within the norms and perspectives of white, Western feminists. They suggest that if emphasis is placed on the great variety of feminisms and on an understanding of the specific contexts in which women develop their strategies and their priorities, feminists would be able more easily to speak to each other across national and cultural barriers. In many instances, such as the women of Burundi who have organized committees to bring together villagers engaged in ethnic disputes, there is an attempt to find common ground as women despite differences.

Feminism has never been a monolithic movement. There have always been many feminisms united by the fact that at their heart they recognize men's power over women and seek to challenge women's subordination. Feminism is not necessarily synonymous with a highly organized and visible women's movement that explicitly challenges gender inequalities and seeks to 'turn the world upside down'. This is not likely to happen very often. As Showalter notes, 'movements by their nature are infrequent and localised events' with a 'specific and attainable goal' (Gillis and Munford, 2004: 60). The absence of a well organized and seemingly united women's movement, however, does not mean a corresponding absence of feminist activity. In the twenty-first century there are still 'persistent, patterned inequalities' (Jackson and Jones, 1998: 10) between men and women throughout the world. This makes it imperative not to lose sight of the category 'woman' and to continue to expose the unequal power relationship between the sexes. It is likely that women will find many different sites, as they have done in the past, in which to make their voices heard and to put forward their demands. Debates will continue about how best to develop a 'feminist consciousness', about the aims and objectives to be pursued and about whether to organize in single or in mixed-sex groups. The many differences between women are bound to lead to a variety of feminisms, but this does not have to prevent women from working collectively. Political and economic globalization are increasingly linking women together across national boundaries and raise the possibility of joint actions in the future against common forms of oppression. As one author notes, in a recent collection of essays on 'third wave' feminism: 'never mind which number we're on, we need to be making waves' (Spencer, 2004: 12).

Part 2

DOCUMENTS

Document 1   MARY WOLLSTONECRAFT ON THE RIGHTS OF WOMAN

This pioneering text, with its powerful message that women's 'characters' were socially constructed and, if changed, would benefit society as a whole, influenced the development of feminist thought. Note the complex ways in which their role as wives and mothers is discussed.

Women are, in common with men, rendered weak and luxurious by the relaxing pleasures which wealth procures; but added to this they are made slaves to their persons, and must render them alluring that man may lend them his reason to guide their tottering steps aright. Or should they be ambitious, they must govern their tyrants by sinister tricks, for laws respecting women, which I mean to discuss in a future part, make an absurd unit of a man and his wife; and then, by the easy transition of only considering him as responsible, she is reduced to a mere cipher.

The being who discharges the duties of its station is independent; and, speaking of women at large, their first duty is to themselves as rational creatures, and the next, in point of importance, as citizens, is that, which includes so many, of a mother. The rank in life which dispenses with their fulfilling this duty, necessarily degrades them by making them mere dolls. Or, should they turn to something more important than merely fitting drapery upon a smooth block, their minds are only occupied by some soft platonic attachment; or the actual management of an intrigue may keep their thoughts in motion; for when they neglect domestic duties, they have it not in their power to take the field and march and counter-march like soldiers, or wrangle in the senate to keep their faculties from rusting. . . .

But, to render her really virtuous and useful, she must not, if she discharge her civil duties, want, individually, the protection of civil laws; she must not be dependent on her husband's bounty for her subsistence during his life, or support after his death – for how can a being be generous who has nothing of its own? or virtuous, who is not free? The wife, in the present state of things, who is faithful to her husband, and neither suckles nor educates her children, scarcely deserves the name of wife, and has no right to that of a citizen. But take away natural rights, and duties become null. . . .

Still to avoid misconstruction, though I consider that women in the common walks of life are called to fulfil the duties of wives and mothers, by religion and reason, I cannot help lamenting that women of a superior cast have not a road open by which they can pursue more extensive plans of usefulness and independence. I may excite laughter, by dropping a hint, which I mean to pursue, some future time, for I really think that women ought to have representatives, instead of being arbitrarily governed without having any direct share allowed them in the deliberations of government. . . .

Would men but generously snap our chains, and be content with rational fellowship instead of slavish obedience, they would find us more observant daughters, more affectionate sisters, more faithful wives, more reasonable mothers – in a word, better citizens. We should then love them with true affection, because we should learn to respect ourselves. . . .

Source: Mary Wollstonecraft, *A Vindication of the Rights of Woman*, Miriam Brody Kramnick (ed.), Harmondsworth, 1975 (1st edn, 1792), pp. 257–63.

THE DECLARATION OF SENTIMENTS, SENECA FALLS CONFERENCE, 1848 **Document 2**

This early demand that women's rights as individuals should be acknowledged and respected was based on the model of the US Declaration of Independence. It was signed by sixty-eight women and thirty-two men.

We hold these truths to be self-evident: that all men and women are created equal; that they are endowed by their Creator with certain inalienable rights; that among these are life, liberty, and the pursuit of happiness; that to secure these rights governments are instituted, deriving their just powers from the consent of the governed. Whenever any form of government becomes destructive of these ends, it is the right of those who suffer from it to refuse allegiance to it, and to insist upon the institution of a new government, laying its foundation on such principles, and organizing its powers in such form, as to them shall seem most likely to effect their safety and happiness. Prudence, indeed, will dictate that governments long established should not be changed for light and transient causes; and accordingly all experience hath shown that mankind are more disposed to suffer, while evils are sufferable, than to right themselves by abolishing the forms to which they are accustomed. But when a long train of abuses and usurpations, pursuing invariably the same object, evinces a design to reduce them under absolute despotism, it is their duty to throw off such government, and to provide new guards for their future security. Such has been the patient sufferance of the women under this government, and such is now the necessity which constrains them to demand the equal station to which they are entitled. The history of mankind is a history of repeated injuries and usurpations on the part of man toward woman, having in direct object the establishment of an absolute tyranny over her. To prove this, let facts be submitted to a candid world.

He has never permitted her to exercise her inalienable right to the elective franchise.

He has compelled her to submit to laws, in the formation of which she had no voice.

He has withheld from her rights which are given to the most ignorant and degraded men – both natives and foreigners.

Having deprived her of this first right of a citizen, the elective franchise, thereby leaving her without representation in the halls of legislation, he has oppressed her on all sides.

He has made her, if married, in the eye of the law, civilly dead.

He has taken from her all right in property, even to the wages she earns.

He has made her, morally, an irresponsible being, as she can commit many crimes with impunity, provided they be done in the presence of her husband. In the covenant of marriage, she is compelled to promise obedience to her husband, he becoming, to all intents and purposes, her master – the law giving him power to deprive her of her liberty, and to administer chastisement.

He has so framed the laws of divorce, as to what shall be the proper causes, and in case of separation, to whom the guardianship of the children shall be given, as to be wholly regardless of the happiness of women – the law, in all cases, going upon a false supposition of the supremacy of man, and giving all power into his hands. . . .

He has monopolized nearly all the profitable employments, and from those she is permitted to follow, she receives but a scanty remuneration. He closes against her all the avenues to wealth and distinction which he considers most honourable to himself. As a teacher of theology, medicine, or law, she is not known.

He has denied her the facilities for obtaining a thorough education, all colleges being closed against her. . . .

He has endeavoured, in every way that he could, to destroy her confidence in her own powers, to lessen her self-respect, and to make her willing to lead a dependent and abject life.

Now, in view of this entire disfranchisement of one-half the people of this country, their social and religious degradation – in view of the unjust laws above mentioned, and because women do feel themselves aggrieved, oppressed, and fraudulently deprived of their most sacred rights, we insist that they have immediate admission to all the rights and privileges which belong to them as citizens of the United States.

Source: Elizabeth Cady Stanton, *A History of Woman Suffrage*, Vol. 1, Rochester, NY, 1889, pp. 70–1. Part of the Internet Modern History Sourcebook, copyright © Paul Halsall Aug 1997, updated November 1998, halsall@murray.fordham.edu

Document 3   LOUISE OTTO PETERS FOUNDS *FRAUEN ZEITUNG* (WOMEN'S NEWSPAPER) 1849

Louise Otto Peters was radicalized by the revolutions of 1848. She linked the demand for women's rights in Germany with other political causes and emphasized the importance of organizing working-class women. She hoped that her newspaper would enable progressive women to spread their ideas in a hostile political climate.

The history of all ages, especially that of the present, teaches us that those who forget to think of themselves be forgotten! Thus I wrote in May 1848, when I was addressing myself primarily to the men who were concerned with the labor question in Saxony. I drew their attention to the poor women workers, by speaking out on behalf of my sisters so that they should not be forgotten!

The same experiences have inspired me to publish a woman's journal. In the midst of the great revolutions in which we find ourselves, women will find themselves forgotten, if they forget to think of themselves!

Come along then, my sisters, unite with me, so that we do not remain behind while everything around and about us is pressing forward and struggling. We must also demand and earn our part of the great World-Deliverance that must at last come to the whole of humanity, of which we constitute one-half.

We shall demand to have as our share the right to accomplish with all our strength and in unrestricted development that in us which is purely human, and the right to come of age and enjoy independence within the State.

We shall earn our share as follows: we shall offer our forces to advance the work of world salvation, first by promoting the great ideals of the future – Liberty and Humanity (in fact these are synonymous terms) – in all those circles that are accessible to us, in the circles of the world-at-large through the press, and in those of the immediate family through example, instruction, and education.

However, we shall also earn our part by not struggling in isolation – not everyone for herself, but rather everyone for all the others – and by concerning ourselves primarily with those women who are languishing forgotten and neglected in poverty, misery, and ignorance.

Come, my sisters, help me with this work! Help me first of all to further the ideas here suggested through this journal!

I invite all of you who think alike to subscribe so that this undertaking may thrive!

Source: Louise Otto, *'Program' Frauen-Zeitung, Ein Organ für die hoheren weiblichen Interessen*, No.1, 21 April 1849. From Susan Groag Bell and Karen M. Offen (eds), *Women Family and Freedom: The Debate in Documents Volume 1*, Stanford, CA, 1983.

SOJOURNER TRUTH'S SPEECH, 'AIN'T I A WOMAN?'   **Document 4**

This speech by the African American ex slave Sojourner Truth was delivered at a Women's Convention in Akron Ohio, 1851. The famous phrase 'Ain't I a Woman' only appeared in this later account written by one of the organizers, Frances Gage, who also added the dialect. The phrase 'Ain't I a Woman', however, has been used as a powerful slogan by feminists up to the present day.

There were very few women in those days who dared to "speak in meeting"; and the august teachers of the people were seemingly getting the better of us, while the boys in the galleries, and the sneerers among the pews, were hugely enjoying the discomfiture, as they supposed, of the "strong-minded." Some of the tender-skinned friends were on the point of losing dignity, and the atmosphere betokened a storm. When, slowly from her seat in the corner rose Sojourner Truth, who, till now, had scarcely lifted her head. "Don't let her speak!" gasped half a dozen in my ear. She moved slowly and solemnly to the front, laid her old bonnet at her feet, and turned her great speaking eyes to me. There was a hissing sound of disapprobation above and below. I rose and announced "Sojourner Truth," and begged the audience to keep silence for a few moments.

The tumult subsided at once, and every eye was fixed on this almost Amazon form, which stood nearly six feet high, head erect, and eyes piercing the upper air like one in a dream. At her first word there was a profound hush. She spoke in deep tones, which, though not loud, reached every ear in the house, and away through the throng at the doors and windows.

"Wall, chilern, whar dar is so much racket dar must be somethin' out o' kilter. I tink dat 'twixt de niggers of de Souf and de womin at de Nork, all talkin' 'bout rights, de white men will be in a fix pretty soon. But what's all dis here talkin 'bout?

"Dat man ober dar say dat womin needs to be helped into carriages, and lifted ober ditches, and to hab de best place everywhar. Nobody eber helps me into carriages, or ober mud-puddles, or gibs me any best place!" And raising herself to her full height, and her voice to a pitch like rolling thunders, she asked "And a'n't I a woman? Look at me! Look at me! Look at my arm! (and she bared her right arm to the shoulder, showing her tremendous muscular power). I have ploughed, and planted, and gathered into barns, and no man could head me! And a'n't I a woman? I could work as much and eat as much as a man – when I could get it – and bear de lash a well! And a'n't I a woman? I have borne thirteen chilern, and seen 'em mos' all sold off to slavery, and when I cried out with my mother's grief, none but Jesus heard me! And a'n't I a woman? . . .

"Den dat little man in black dar, he say women can't have as much rights as men, 'cause Christ wan't a woman! Whar did your Christ come from?" Rolling thunder couldn't have stilled that crowd, as did those deep, wonderful tones, as she stood there with outstretched arms and eyes of fire. Raising her voice still louder, she repeated, "Whar did your Christ come from? From God and a woman! Man had nothin' to do wid Him." Oh, what a rebuke that was to that little man. . . .

Amid roars of applause, she returned to her corner, leaving more than one of us with streaming eyes, and hearts beating with gratitude. She had taken us up in her strong arms and carried us safely over the slough of difficulty turning the whole tide in our favor. I have never in my life seen anything like the magical influence that subdued the mobbish spirit of the day, and turned the sneers and jeers of an excited crowd into notes of respect and admiration. Hundreds rushed up to shake hands with her, and congratulate the glorious old mother, and bid her God-speed on her mission of "testifyin' agin concerning the wickedness of this 'ere people."

Source: Elizabeth Cady Stanton, Susan B. Anthony and Matilda Joslyn Gage (eds) *The History of Woman Suffrage*, Vol. 1, New York, 1981, pp. 114–17.

SURPLUS WOMEN AND EMPLOYMENT   **Document 5**

In this article Jessie Boucherett puts forward arguments for increasing access for single middle-class women to paid employment, a key demand of the nineteenth-century women's movement. The English Woman's Journal *provided an important space for women to air their views.*

The fact revealed in the census of 1851, and brought into notice by the article on female employment in the *Edinburgh Review* for April, 1859, that two million of our countrywomen are unmarried and have to maintain themselves, startled every thinking mind in the kingdom, and has done much to effect a change in public opinion, with regard to the expediency of opening fresh fields of labour to the industry of the weaker sex . . . it was at once perceived that to make all social arrangements on the supposition that women were almost invariably married, and supported by their husbands, was to build on a fallacy. . . .

But change our present plan, grant to women the means of a special education, and so raise them to an intellectual equality with men, and give them, as much as the difference in their strength allows, an equal chance of earning their bread, and at once their position will be infinitely improved. If, in addition to this, the powerful protection of the law were extended to those women who are either deprived of their tools or forcibly prevented from working by their male competitors, immense benefit would be conferred on the two millions of our countrywomen who, as the census tells us, are unmarried and have to maintain themselves by their labour, while men would be subjected to no more inconvenience than is necessary to enable us to maintain our national defences without recourse to the aid of foreign mercenaries.

Source: Jessie Boucherett, 'On the obstacles to the employment of women', *The English Woman's Journal*, February 1860, cited in Candida Ann Lacey (ed.) *Barbara Leigh Smith Bodicchon and the Langham Place Group,* London, 1986.

Document 6   NEW ZEALAND SUFFRAGE PETITION

This is the first sheet of the Canterbury section of the huge 1893 suffrage petition, which was signed by nearly 32,000 women, almost a quarter of the adult European female population of New Zealand. Suffrage leader Kate Sheppard's signature appears about halfway down the left column.

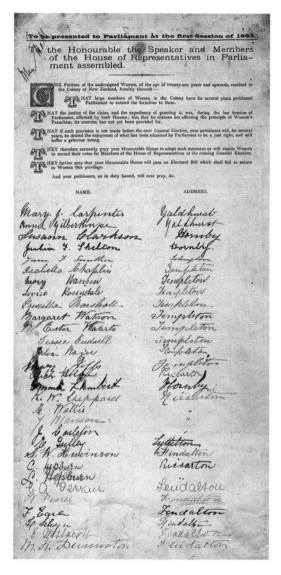

Source: National Archive of New Zealand, *The Women's Suffrage Petition 1893* [Archives Reference: LE1 1893/7a] Archives New Zealand, The Department of Internal Affairs Te Tari Taiwhenua

WOMEN VOTE IN SOUTH AUSTRALIA   **Document 7**

This extract from a contemporary newspaper conveys the excitement when women voted for the first time and the sense of South Australia being a pioneer.

Voters in the 1896 South Australian election

Women			Men		
Enrolments	Voters	% voted	Enrolments	Voters	% voted
59 166	39 312	66.4%	77 752	51 572	66.3%

THE GENERAL ELECTIONS
POLLING-DAY.
INTENSE EXCITEMENT – SOME SURPRISES – HOW THE WOMEN VOTED – TEN OLD MEMBERS REJECTED – STATE OF PARTIES – INTENSE EXCITEMENT

. . . But the magnitude of what is left to be accomplished before the millennium arrives, which will witness the extinction of politics, with its pettiness and tricks, should not obscure the greatness of what has been done, and well done. So many steps have been taken to perfect the system of government that the terms Conservative and Liberal as understood in the mother country are altogether inappropriate here. In the democratic constitution of the Legislature the adoption and form of the ballot, the extension of local government, the simplification of land transfers, and in many other reforms South Australia has stood prominently in the front rank.

And now the colony is the first in Australia to rest the government of the people upon an adult suffrage. Memorable in the history of the southern continent must be the general election in South Australia of 1896 as the first in which women took part. . . .

Women were everywhere, and their presence in the streets, and leavening the lumps of humanity in the crowded polling-places, no doubt had a refining influence. Never have we had a more decorous gathering together of the multitude than that which distinguished the first exercise of the female franchise on Saturday, April 25, 1896; and rarely since the days of open voting has there been so much excitement, albeit well under control. The charming spectacle of –

Lovely woman, hesitating
Round the booths in sweet dismay
Her gentle bosom palpitating
Lest she cast her vote away

was presented throughout the livelong day, but it would be a base libel upon a sex whose instinct is less liable to err than man's reason to assert that the women failed to realize their responsibilities – quite the contrary; they did themselves infinite credit, displaying a level-headedness and self-possession that called for admiration. . . .

Even the nuns exercised the franchise, and at North Adelaide the sisters of the Dominican Convent created a picturesque feature in the proceedings by filing solemnly into the Temperance Hall, led by the Mother Superior, dressed in their distinctive garb, grave, kindly, and silent. The scene was peculiarly impressive. The ladies, regaled in their Sunday best, rolled up in large numbers, many arriving in cabs, while others were content to come on foot. Cabby must have reaped quite a harvest. Sometimes there were as many as a score of cabs drawn up in front of the hall. It was quite a study to watch the women as they went in to exercise their right of franchise for the first time. On the faces of some the air of responsibility was writ so large that something like an intellectual pallor had been imparted thereto.

Source: *The Adelaide Observer*, 2 May 1896, p. 141. Copyright © 2001 State Library of South Australia.

Document 8   SOCIALIST AND BOURGEOIS WOMEN CLASH

In this extract from her autobiography, published in 1912, Therese Schlesinger-Eckstein (1863–914), a middle-class Austrian woman who became a socialist leader, recalls her difficulties with 'bourgeois' feminists at the International Women's Congress in Berlin, 1896. She joined the Austrian Social Democratic Party in 1897.

The first International Women's Congress took place in Berlin the late summer of 1896. It was organised by bourgeois women and I was sent as a delegate of the general Austrian Women's Association. I was to give two talks, first a report about the women's movement in Austria and then one on the Inquiry about working women which I have already mentioned. As I was making my first report – I had already talked about various facets of the bourgeois women's movement – I turned to the subject of the social democratic women's movement and the *Women Workers Newspaper* when the chairwoman, Lina Morgenstern, suddenly informed me that my time had run out despite the fact that those who had spoken before me had been given unlimited time. I saw in this action – whether I was right or not doesn't matter – an anti-working-class bias and I let it be known I wanted to leave the Congress and sought to take my second talk off the agenda. There was a storm. The co-chairwoman, Minna Cauer, and several other women, urged me to give up my protest saying it was all a misunderstanding and trying to convince me that I could use my material on the women workers in my second talk. So I gave my talk on the Inquiry two days later. My description of the misery and privations to which the women workers were exposed shocked the audience, which was for the most part composed of teachers, officials and writers of both sexes . . . I also spoke out during a discussion on the morality question and, amid vigorous protests, expressed my conviction, which was only in partial agreement with the speaker's moral preaching, that prostitution is directly connected to the capitalist system itself. . . .

Source: Adelheid Popp (ed.), *A Commemorative Book; Twenty Years of the Austrian Women Workers' Movement* (1912), reproduced in Eleanor Reimer and John C. Fout (eds), *European Women: A Documentary History, 1789–1945*, Brighton, 1980, pp. 97–8.

FINNISH WOMEN INSPIRED BY ELIZABETH CADY STANTON   **Document 9**

This greeting published in the New York Times demonstrates the influence of American feminism in other parts of the world.

Finland's Greeting to Mrs. Stanton
Baroness Gripenberg Sends Good Wishes from Finland.

Mrs. Elizabeth Cady Stanton, whose birthday anniversary is to be celebrated on Tuesday next at the Metropolitan Opera House, has just received the following letter from Baroness Gripenberg:

Helsingfors, Finland, Oct. 19, 1895:

Dear Madam: The earliest founded Woman's Rights Association in Finland, Einsk Kvinnoforsning, sends you a respectful greeting on your eightieth birthday. The work you have done to raise and enlighten womanhood has influenced the work done for women all over the world. Our little country shows a reflex of it in our association, whose platform is almost the same as that published by the first woman's rights meeting in Seneca Falls in 1848.

Accept our most respectful thanks for the inspiration your noble work has been for all laborers in our common cause.

Alexandra Gripenberg, President.

Source: *New York Times*, 7 November 1895. http://www.slsa.sa.gov.au/women_and_politics/suffr3.htm

Document 10   WHY WOMEN NEED THE VOTE

The French suffrage activist, Hubertine Auclert, suggests that the vote would raise women's status as citizens which would then enable them to improve their economic and social position.

Men buck at the idea of women having equal rights! Instead of seeing women as their helpers, enabling them to attain a better quality of life, men seem to think something is going to be taken away from them.

Frenchmen are imploring Frenchwomen not to try to become citizens. They tell them nothing would be gained by universal suffrage and that their superiority lies in remaining enslaved.

Similar language was used by eligible voters on those who didn't get the vote before 1848. The "Remain women!" of today is the equivalent of the "Remain workers!" of yesterday, and it has the same meaning: stay incapable of bettering your condition.

Those women who see the social and economic advantages obtained by the voters, those women who notice that in every country men deprived of suffrage are desperately trying to claim it, are beginning to understand that this paper power, this voting ballot, is just as necessary to them as paper money. For possessing one makes it easier to get the other. The voter's registration card will make housework pay and include housewives among retired workers.

Work is, in effect, assessed according to the condition of the person accomplishing it. Women's work is so belittled and given such a derisory salary because these women are outside the law; they are slaves whose efforts are not judged worthy of reward. Let women enter into common political rights and soon their economic situation will be changed; their work, ennobled by citizenship, will receive a lucrative salary.

Women will not escape oppression from their husbands or exploitation from their employers until they become their equals at the ballot box.

Source: Hubertine Auclert, *Le Vote des femmes*, Paris: n.p., 1908. Reproduced in Jennifer Waelti-Walters and Steven C. Hause (eds) *Feminisms of the Belle Epoque: A Historical and Literary Anthology*, translated by Jette Kjaer, Lydia Willis and Jennifer Waelti-Walters, Lincoln and London, University of Nebraska Press, 1994, pp. 266–76.

CLARA ZETKIN DISCUSSES THE RELATIONSHIP BETWEEN SOCIALISM AND   **Document 11**
WOMEN'S RIGHTS

In this article, published in Justice, *the newspaper of the British Social Democratic Federation, Clara Zetkin, a leading figure in the European socialist movement, highlights the successes of socialist women in Germany and explores how the 'woman question' and socialism are linked.*

In 1907 the Social-Democratic Party of Germany embraced 29,458 women members, in 1908 they numbered 62,257. These figures show the practical result of political propaganda in favour of Socialism during the last twelve months. 1908 was the first year in which the new law of association for the whole Empire allowed women to join political organisations. . . .

Socialist propaganda amongst the workers' wives and women wage-earners has been carried on by many hundred public meetings, in which women comrades addressed more particularly working-class women. Over a million copies of a leaflet were distributed amongst them which, in a simple and popular manner, analysed the political events of the day, showing for what reasons women as well as men are interested in politics and must join the S.D.P. Since 1892 "Gleichheit," the organ of the Socialist women, and which is the property of the Party, has spread Socialist ideas amongst working-class women, and has provided for the theoretical education of the women comrades. Several trade unions with a great women membership give the paper free of cost to their women members; "Gleichheit" had a circulation last year of 73,000 copies.

Besides their activity in that line, the Socialist women have continued their propaganda in favour of the full political emancipation of their sex. The struggle for universal suffrage, vigorously maintained, particularly in Prussia, was a struggle for adult suffrage for both sexes, vindicated in meetings and leaflets. Public and factory meetings in great number; and an indefatigable activity in other different forms, have served the trade union organisations of the women workers. The number of women trade unionists has increased from 136,429 in 1907 to 138,443 in 1908. The work of our trade unions to enlighten, train and organise wage-earning women is not smaller nor less important than what the S.D.P. has done to induce women to join in political struggles of the working class. . . .

The most prominent feature of the Socialist women's movement in Germany is its clearness and revolutionary spirit as to Socialist theories and principles. The women who head it are fully conscious that the social fate of their sex is indissolubly connected with the general evolution of society, the most powerful moving force of which is the evolution of labour, of economic life. The integral human emancipation of all women depends in consequence on the social emancipation of labour; that can only be realised by the class-war of the exploited majority. Therefore, our Socialist women oppose strongly the bourgeois women righters' credo that the women of all classes must gather into an unpolitical, neutral movement striving exclusively for women's rights. In theory and practice they maintain the conviction that the class antagonisms are much more powerful, effective and decisive than the social antagonisms between the sexes, and that thus the working-class women will never win their full emancipation in a struggle of all women without difference of class against the social monopolies of the male sex, but only in the class-war of all the exploited, without difference of sex, against all who exploit, without difference of sex. That does not mean at all that they undervalue the importance of the political emancipation of the female sex. On the contrary, they employ much more energy than the German women-righters to conquer the suffrage. But the vote is, according to their views, not the last word and term of their aspirations, but only a weapon – a means in struggle for a revolutionary aim – the Socialistic order.

Source: Clara Zetkin, 'German socialist women's movement', *Justice,* 9 October 1909; Marxist International Archive.

Document 12   MILITANT ACTIONS

Militant activities were reported regularly in Votes for Women, *the newspaper of the British Women's Social and Political Union.*

Breaking a Barricade.

On May 14, at Bristol, Miss Ada Flatman, made a spirited protest before Mr. Birrell at the Chamber of Commerce banquet at the Royal Hotel. She had taken a room at the hotel the day previously, and watched with grow-ing despair the strong wooden barricades, 10 ft. high, ready to be placed at every approach to the balcony overlooking the banqueting hall, and the strong force of men arriving, ranging from the chief of police to detectives, and plain clothes constables, who literally thronged the lounge, stairs, and corridors.

After dinner, when the speeches were being made, she spent the time wandering from corridor to corridor, followed all the time by detectives. When she arrived back at her first pitch by the barricade, the detective on guard turned his head to speak to someone, and she dashed the barrier down, and reaching the other side shouted "Give Votes to Taxpaying Women," and flung into the hall below hundreds of purple, green, and white handbills, asking Liberal men to support women in their fight for freedom. A hand was put over her mouth, and she was dragged away amidst the clapping and cheering of the men, having overcome the 10 ft. barricades and outwitted hundreds of police.

Source: Votes for Women, 18 February 1909.

LETTERS FROM A SUFFRAGETTE PRISONER   **Document 13**

Suffragettes who were imprisoned wrote letters to family and friends. These reveal their passionate support for the movement and also their concern to continue to give practical support to the campaign. The following extracts are from letters sent by Alice Ker, a Liverpool suffragette, to her daughters from Holloway prison where she was awaiting trial for smashing windows at Harrod's store, Knightsbridge. She had become a militant early in 1912 when the Government dropped the Conciliation Bill.

March 7 1912

Go often to Renshaw Street. I am sure that there will be much to hear. From March 9 to 16 is a self denial week. Try to do without some things and keep account of how much. You need not actually pay the money in just now, as you may be short, but keep the reckoning, and we will pay it into the War Chest later on. For instance, I think you might sell your theatre tickets for Saturday. I feel now as if I would never spend an unnecessary penny on anything else.

16 March 1912

A great many have gone out on bail, which is apparently being allowed at Bow Street (Magistrates Court). We poor Westminsters were not allowed it. Lady Conny tried for me and Mrs Abraham for Dolly. Did you see the *Courier* of Wednesday, I think, with a description of us all? That ought to have been quoted to your man who called us Howling Dervishes. If he could only see the sedate old ladies who are in! Make the most of all these evidences of respectability at any further debates or discussions. I believe the descriptions were put into the *Courier* to dispose of the hooligan cry. Some at the Artists' Club expressed great surprise that Miss Palethorpe should have been drawn into a Society which they understood, consisted chiefly of charwomen and persons of loose character! When I come out, I think I am going to let the Nationals know what I think of them, as well as the men. One sees clearly in this atmosphere, and, what makes even more difference, one has nothing left to be afraid of in speaking one's mind. Why should they not only not support us, the advance guard, as the rear guard should, but even fire into us from behind. No, I am associating with heroines here, and I don't feel inclined to suffer cowards so gladly as I have hitherto done.

Notes: Renshaw Street – WSPU shop; Dolly – daughter of Mrs Abraham, arrested at the same time as Alice; Lady Conny – Lady Constance Lytton; The Nationals – National Union of Women's Suffrage Societies.

Source: Letters from Alice Ker, reprinted in Krista Cowman, *Votes for Women: The Events on Merseyside, 1870–1928*, National Museums and Galleries on Merseyside, 1992, pp. 61, 62.

Document 14   INTERNATIONAL SUFFRAGE ACTIVITY

This report from the International Woman Suffrage Alliance congress of 1907 shows both how suffrage groups in different countries varied in their characteristics and methods and also how militant action was viewed at that time. Rosika Schwimmer was prominent in the suffrage movement in Hungary. She moved to London in 1914 to work as international press secretary for the IWSA.

June 18th. Afternoon Session.

The President called upon Hungary for suggestions as to methods of work and Miss Rosika Schwimmer responded as follows:

She advised to work actively during the elections, question candidates and get them to declare themselves publicly. Use woman suffrage stamps as they attract attention and bring about discussion. Wear a woman suffrage badge. Many people in Hungary are "mad for decorations" and very few women get them, so when people see the badge they think it is a decoration and immediately ask about it. This gives a chance to talk to them of women suffrage. Talk about it in season and out of season and thus you will make an impression on those who hear you.

Do woman suffrage work in a way to make as much noise and attract as much attention as possible. An article in a Vienna paper says the English suffragettes and those in France who follow their example have hurt the cause and that other women ought to follow the example of the Hungarian suffragists and work in a ladylike manner. But at home we are thought anything but quiet in our methods and some people criticise them. . . .

Source: *Report of the 4th Annual Congress of the International Woman's Suffrage Alliance, 1907*, LSE Library, pp. 37–8.

SUFFRAGE AND EMPIRE DURING AND AFTER THE FIRST WORLD WAR   **Document 15**

*To counter the arguments of their opponents that women were unsuited to deal
with imperial questions, suffragists argued that, on the contrary, women had
a central role to play in Empire. In a period of consolidation rather than conquest they would support social reforms to strengthen the British race. This was
needed after the losses of war time. The Vote was the newspaper of the Women's
Freedom League and the article, written by one of its leaders, Charlotte
Despard, notes how women from the Dominions attempted to act together.*

When the anti-suffrage agitation was at its height, women were accused by
the enlightened leaders of that movement of being incapable of "thinking
imperially," and the phrase was eagerly caught up and passed from mouth to
mouth. At every anti-suffrage meeting it was quoted, and the downfall of the
Empire was dolefully predicted as the inevitable result of entrusting women
with political power, for they were intellectually incapable of realising either
the importance or the responsibilities of an Empire. . . .

To the British women of our Dominions scattered all over the world one
instinct is common. These, though under alien skies and in strange, new lands,
have preserved in the depths of their hearts the old love of "home," and cherish
a keen desire to maintain and to improve the race to which they are proud to
belong. Their eyes are not fixed admiringly on the symbols of potential military
and naval triumphs, but are dilated with horror at the enormous increase in
the rate of infant mortality, which shows that last year more children died in
infancy than there were men slain on the battlefield. The rising generation is
paying a heavy price for the prospective victory of the British race. These women
of the Dominions Overseas, as their suffragist sisters in these islands, have the
keen foresight of the goddess Frigga, worshipped by their ancestors. They
see the dread doom of this Empire not in a German victory, but in the steady
degeneration in numbers and stamina of the race to which they belong.

The meeting of the second biennial Conference of the British Dominions
Woman Suffrage Union, now taking place (July 5 to 7 inclusive), is a great
episode in this age, which is fraught with so many dramatic and startling
events. In the midst of the most terrible war that the world has ever seen the
women are sending representatives from the remotest parts of our Empire to
discuss the really great and permanently important questions of the day and
to prepare for the rebuilding of the social structure on a sounder and more
reliable foundation. When this war-fever has passed away, how much will have
been destroyed in the great cataclysm, and who will rebuild the shattered
ruins? The women must be the Empire-builders – as they have been, in truth,
through all the ages. They have followed in the wake of the conqueror – healing
the wounds, creating order out of chaos, bringing love to banish hatred,
striving to preserve the race. Their work has been purely altruistic, for they

have been most unselfishly oblivious of their own personal loss in their eagerness to serve their generation and posterity. The subjects discussed at the Conference are sufficiently significant. They show how the women, with marvellous foresight, are determined to warn the unthinking opportunists, and thus to endeavour to avert the great evils which menace the human race.

Women's suffrage takes the first and last place in the discussions, for it is the crux of the whole matter. If then women have the vote in all parts of the Empire, they will be able to deal effectively with the threatening evils, possible even to avert them. The crying injustice of the British law, which forces a woman to sacrifice her nationality on her marriage with an alien, is being discussed from the legal and the human point of view, and the terribly distressing cases of women who have suffered under this law since the out-break of the war presented to the audience. The question of sex morality and sex education will be ably dealt with by specially competent speakers; it is a subject that this war, as all wars have done in the past, has brought specially into prominence. The dark menace of venereal disease, increased a hundred-fold under a military *régime*, will be treated of as a grave danger to the continuance of the race. Women and children in the industrial world is another theme which the true guardians of the race can fitly deal with; over-work and under-payment for women and children are the main causes of the degeneracy of the rising generation.

Source: Charlotte Despard, 'Thinking Imperially', *The Vote*, 7 July 1916, p. 1086.

Document 16   FEMINISM AND PEACE

Many feminists during and after the First World War thought that women had a special role to play in maintaining world peace. During the congress of the Women's International League for Peace and Freedom in 1921 Aletta Jacobs, a leading suffragist and peace campaigner from Holland, assesses the post war situation and indicates the role that she thought women could play in ensuring peace.

Dr. Aletta Jacobs, Holland, seconding the resolution, said:

Last September for the first time the League of Nations assembled in Geneva. In one of the first sessions, Mr. Motta, President of the Swiss Republic, pro-posed to amend some of the articles of the League. The French delegate at once objected that the Assembly was not allowed to bring in amendments. Mr. Motta said he did not wish to amend the articles of the Peace Treaty, that could only be done by the Council, but some of the articles of the Covenant of the League, which Switzerland, as one of the signatories, had a right to do.

When I read the official notes of that session, I immediately began to ask myself "Who can bring sufficient pressure upon the Council of the League of Nations to revise all the Peace Treaties that need revision?" I could not think of any organization that had the power, and I realized that it was only the women of the world who could accomplish it. We have heard from Miss Marshall that the Council is sometimes open to the wishes of women. If the women understand what the terms of the Peace Treaty mean to the world, and if they will use their combined power, I believe a revision of the Peace Treaties could be accomplished.

We have come here to consider how to prevent future wars and to propagate the means of prevention, but let us not forget that we are still living in the midst of war in all parts of the world, and that the present terms of peace will soon be producing a new war, more immense and more inhuman than the last one. While we are discussing problems of Education and how to use literature about internationalism, we do not realize that we are sitting on the edge of a volcano which can at any moment completely destroy us. Peace has not come. Under the existing Peace Treaties, not only the peoples who have been conquered, but also those that are supposed to be the victors, and also the Neutral Countries, live under a terrible pressure of anxiety about the future, that prevents them from developing and progressing.

The general belief is that it is for the Entente to revise the Peace Treaties, but as long as the whole world suffers from them, the world should have the right to compel the Entente to make this revision and to appoint representatives from the different nations to assist in the revision.

The peace terms should be such as will help the nations to live together in friendship, and to develop in happiness and prosperity along their own lines. But if we really wish this, we must for one or two years devote all the time, strength, and money of our League to this great task. We must create public opinion. We must teach the women of the world to demand revision. We must hold meetings in all parts of our own countries. We must make clear to the working people how the peace terms affect them. The International Bureau must send out letters to all women's organizations with instructions what to do. We must prepare literature and get hold of the Press and influence the next Assembly of the League of Nations. After a year or two of this simultaneous propaganda a large Women's Congress should be held on this subject alone, at which resolutions would be passed to be sent to the respective governments. If we do this we shall really be doing Peace work, we shall be serving the world, and posterity will bless us.

Source: Report of the International Congress of Women, Vienna, 1921. From the BLPES Library.

Document 17   EGYPTIAN WOMEN'S ACTIVISM IN NATIONALIST STRUGGLES

In her memoirs Hudá Sha'rawi, a leading Egyptian nationalist and feminist, recalls a demonstration that took place after the Wafd (The Delegation Party, a nationalist, liberal party) had demanded independence from British rule for Egypt in 1919. The leader of the Wafd, Saad Zaghlul, was arrested and deported. This led to approximately 150 upper-class women going into the streets in their veils to demonstrate.

We women held our first demonstration on 16 March to protest the repressive acts and intimidation practised by the British authority. In compliance with the orders of the authority we announced our plans to demonstrate in advance but were refused permission. We began to telephone the news to each other, only to read in *al-Muqattam* that the demonstration had received official sanction. We got on the telephone again, telling as many women as possible that we would proceed according to schedule the following morning. Had we been able to contact more than a limited number of women, virtually all the women of Cairo would have taken part in the demonstration.

On the morning of 16 March, I sent placards to the house of the wife of Ahmad Bey Abu Usbaa, bearing slogans in Arabic and French painted in white on a background of black – the colour of mourning. Some of the slogans read, 'Long Live the Supporters of Justice and Freedom', others said 'Down with Oppressors and Tyrants' and 'down with Occupation' . . . No sooner were we approaching Zaghlul's house than British troops surrounded us. They blocked the streets with machine guns, forcing us to stop along with the students who had formed columns on both sides of us.

I was determined the demonstration should resume. When I advanced, a British soldier stepped toward me pointing his gun, but I made my way past him. I shouted in a loud voice, 'Let me die so Egypt shall have an Edith Cavell'.

This second extract shows women's disillusion when it was thought that the Wafd had ignored their views.

12 December 1920. Hudá signs a letter sent from the Wafdist Women's Central Committee to Saad Zaghlul:

We are surprised and shocked by the way we have been treated lately, in contrast to previous treatment and certainly contrary to what we expect from you. You supported us when we created our Committee. . . . What makes us all the more indignant is that by disregarding us the Wafd has caused foreigners to disparage the renaissance of women. They claim that our participation in the nationalist movement was merely a ploy to dupe civilized nations into believing in the advancement of Egypt and its ability to govern itself. Our women's renaissance is above that as you well know. At this moment when the future of Egypt is about to be decided, it is unjust that the Wafd, which stands for the rights of Egypt and struggles for its liberation, should deny half the nation a role in that liberation.

Source: Hudá Sha'rawi, *The Harem Years: Memoirs of an Egyptian Feminist*, London, 1986, pp. 112–13, 122.

NATIONALISM AND INTERNATIONALISM   **Document 18**

In her memoirs Shizue Ishimoto, an upper-class feminist and birth control advocate from Japan, considers the significance of wearing national costume when women came together from different countries at meetings of the International Council of Women in the inter-war years. She notes the extent to which this encouraged, rather than hindered, international friendship.

Always for public lectures and for formal dinners I wore my native costume. It seemed to create the best atmosphere for friendship. Since I wore western costume at other times I often felt as exotic in my native dress as I doubtless looked to others. However, I felt utterly at home in it during a convention at Chicago, which I attended. This had been called by the National Council of Women, and women from many foreign lands were present to give it an international flavour. Some of these guests were, like myself, in native apparel. Thus I had the pleasure of feeling rather more dignified than exotic as I sat beside Selma Ekrem of Turkey, for example, who wore her fascinating native dress. She is the author of that important book on Turkish women, *Unveiled*. I was deeply impressed by her skill at handling the English language, by her directness of expression, and by her knowledge. But I did the best I could to represent my race too. Since the general theme set by this conference was "Our Common Cause – Civilization", the speeches all revolved around the idea of women in a changing world. And since they were delivered by such forceful women as Mrs Carrie Chapman Catt, Jane Addams and Margaret Bondfield of England, I derived from them a stronger determination than ever to face the modern world courageously and as intelligently as possible.

Source: Shizue Ishimoto, *Facing Two Ways: The Story of My Life*, 1935, pp. 381–2, quoted in Marie Sandell, 'International sisterhood?: International women's organisations and cooperation in the interwar period', PhD thesis, Royal Holloway, University of London, 2007, p. 108.

Document 19   EQUAL RIGHTS IN AMERICA AFTER THE VOTE

In an interview with Amelia Fry, 1972–3, Alice Paul, the militant suffrage leader, recalls the bitter debates in the US women's movement about which causes feminists should support in the inter-war years. This came to a head at the National Woman's Party's convention, held in Washington, 15 February 1921.

Paul: At this convention, it was a large convention held in the big hall of the Washington Hotel. Representatives came and were given every chance to talk. [Small interruption.] Oh, is it dinner? Let me just tell you quickly then. Miss Jane Addams came and sat in the front row. I remember I presided at this convention and she was right down in front of me. She said that she hoped – and she was a very beloved person by the National Woman's Party because she stood by us always so strongly and faithfully when we were being – usually when we were being attacked by somebody, she certainly didn't vary in her support. So, she said, "Now, I hope you'll all join us in coming into the Women's International League for Peace and Freedom." That was a very *strong* feeling among most of the delegates, that peace was, after all, the next thing to work for.

We had succeeded when they didn't think we *could* succeed in such a short time in getting the Equal Rights Amendment in the Constitution.

Fry: You mean the suffrage amendment.

Paul: I mean the suffrage amendment. So, for the moment, we were regarded with some respect and as powerful people that they'd like to have take up their reform. That was I would think the strongest effort that was made: to get us to become affiliated with or in some relationship with the Women's International League for Peace and Freedom, of which Miss Jane Addams was the international president.

Crystal Eastman, who was much more to the left I would say than most of us, drew up a whole program of all kinds of social reforms that she wanted us – a very good program, she thought it was. Maybe it was, but it was sort of more like – well, we'll say the program that had been adopted by Russia in general. And these people were not only wanting it, but they wanted it with such intensity, the different ones, that they were *full* of almost *rage* [laughter] when we didn't at once leap into taking up another one of these measures. . . .

Fry: What about birth control?

Paul: [Simultaneously.] Some were all for throwing all our effort into the Republican party. Some were for throwing all our effort into the Democratic party. Many were for throwing all our effort into the Socialist party and into the Labor party, whatever labor group there was. Oh, that was an enormous, *enormous* campaign to get us to go into the field that the Consumers League, with Florence Kelley, was into. That was *tremendous* because so many of our women had helped put through these special labor laws for women.

Fry: Yes, right. And Florence Kelley – I've seen her name in the suffrage books. She used to help with the suffrage campaign.

Paul: Oh yes. She was one of our strong members in the suffrage campaign. She was a leader in the campaign and had a meeting in Washington to which she invited *all* women's organizations to try to get them all to form a sort of coalition to work together for what the Consumers League was working for. She was one of the *strongest* people in trying to get this put in our program. Well, we kept saying, "But we stand for *equality* and your special labor laws are not in harmony with the principle that we're standing for."

So we had these debates day after day, people coming to our headquarters and asking us to meetings over in the country where they were discussing what to do next, just because it was a group of women who were being credited with having won something that was important to win and maybe we'd win something for them. [Dinner is called again.] I remember these just bitter fights with the special-labor-laws-for-women people.

Source: Conversations with Alice Paul. An interview with Amelia R. Fry, 1972–3, as part of the Suffrage Oral History Project, The Bancroft Library of the University of California. http://content.cdlib.org/view?docId=kt6f59n89c;NAAN=13030&doc.view=frames&chunk.id=d0e18400&toc.depth=1&toc.id=d0e18400&brand=calisphere

BIRTH CONTROL CAMPAIGN   **Document 20**

Margaret Sanger became one of the best known birth control campaigners. She challenged the Comstock laws, 1873, that made dissemination of birth control information in the US illegal and was an inspiration to others around the world. In her publication, Birth Control Review, *she comments on the letters received from working-class women pleading for birth control information.*

"For the children's sake" is the plea that rings again and again through the letters of suffering and sorrowing mothers; letters that come daily to the offices of THE REVIEW; letters asking for information concerning contraceptives.

"For the children's sake" plead the mothers, "tell us how we may prevent more children than we can care for".

Upon the necks of these mothers, upon the necks of their children rests the barbarous yoke of the laws and customs which would deny to them the knowledge by which they may be free. It is not only for themselves that they ask freedom; it is for their helpless infants, doomed to neglect, hunger, ignorance and disease.

Nothing that a writer may pen, nothing that an editor may conceive, can be so bitter and so unanswerable an arraignment of the laws and customs of yesterday – persisting viciously today – as are these simple letters from mothers.

Can you masculine minded moralists, you conventional minded puritans carrying over dark age laws and customs from a past which even you are only too happy to forget, read these letters unmoved?

Can you persist in your mistaken, abstract convictions, in the face of this concrete evidence of your error? Can you look undisturbed upon the fruits of your determination to force your own ideas upon a suffering womanhood and a starved and diseased and broken childhood?

Source: Birth Control Review, 3, January 1919, reproduced in Ruth Barnes Moynihan, Cynthia Russett and Laurie Crumpacker (eds), Second To None: A Documentary History of American Women, Vol. 11, Lincoln, 1993, pp. 173–4.

Document 21　　CRITICISMS OF WESTERN FEMINISM

During the inter-war years there were criticisms from women outside of Europe and North America that Western feminists had stereotyped views about the difficult lives of women in other societies, and yet, it was suggested, they had problems of their own. This is expressed by Mrs S. W. Hangakoon of Ceylon at the All-Asia Women's Committee in 1931.

In the West individuality has been carried on to such a point that observers admit that the family system has broken down. We see it in the worst form in the increase of divorce, in estrangements between husbands and wives; in the declining birth rate, and the reluctance of men and women to take the responsibilities of parenthood. In the face of these stern facts it used to be the fashion in the West to disparage Eastern civilization. Miss Mayo's "Mother India" is a notorious example of the libels perpetrated on Indian civilizations. The suggestion behind the book is the time-honoured libel that women of India are helpless chattels bought and sold, according to the whims of their masters. Nobody who knows anything of the East could make such a stupid mistake. The women of the East have, usually, not ventured to cross the seas, and have preferred to exert their influence in shaping, influencing and directing the destinies of their husbands, sons, and daughters over the sea of life. But they have seldom been backward, when the need arose, in the more perilous adventures of life to play their part bravely and selflessly . . . the attitude of women in the West which is to a greater or lesser degree the result of feminine antagonism to man's claim of overlordship. In the East, women are in no sense antagonistic to men, but they are now only exerting in the political field the benevolent influences they have always exerted in the home for the betterment, upliftment and preservation of their country and nation. Unless the women of each Asian country work side by side with their men to preserve the national and moral qualities of their individual civilisations, it is not only possible but probable that every nation or race in the East will be effectively wiped out in the near or distant future.

Source: All Asia Women's Committee, *Report*, 1931. Quoted in Marie Sandell, 'International sisterhood? International women's organisations and cooperation in the interwar period', PhD thesis, Royal Holloway, University of London, 2007, p. 227.

SIMONE DE BEAUVOIR AND WOMAN AS THE OTHER   **Document 22**

Simone de Beauvoir's book, The Second Sex, *was a key text that provided a new way of understanding women's subordinate social position and inspired 'second wave feminism'.*

If her functioning as a female is not enough to define woman, if we decline also to define her through 'the eternal feminine', and if nevertheless we admit, provisionally, that women do exist, then we must face the question, what is a woman?

To state the question is, to me, to suggest, at once, a preliminary answer. The fact that I ask it is itself significant. A man would never get the notion of writing a book on the peculiar situation of the human male. But if I want to define myself I must first of all say: 'I am a woman'; on this truth must be based all further discussion. A man never begins by presenting himself as an individual of a certain sex; it goes without saying that he is a man. . . .

Thus humanity is male and man defines woman not in herself but as relative to him; She is not regarded as an autonomous being. Michelet writes: 'Woman the relative being . . .' And Benda is most positive in his *Rapport d'Uriel* 'The body of man makes sense in itself quite apart from that of woman, whereas the latter seems wanting in significance by itself . . . Man can think of himself without woman. She cannot think of herself without man'. And she is simply what man decrees; thus she is called 'the sex', by which is meant that she appears essentially to the male as a sexual being. For him she is sex-absolute sex, no less. She is defined and differentiated with reference to man and not he with reference to her; she is the incidental, the inessential as opposed to the essential. He is the Subject, he is the Absolute – she is the Other.

Source: Simone de Beauvoir, 'Introduction', *The Second Sex*, 1949, reprinted in Kelly Oliver (ed.), *French Feminism: A Reader*, Oxford, 2000, pp. 7–8.

Document 23   NATIONAL ORGANIZATION OF WOMEN STATEMENT OF PURPOSE

The National Organization of Women adopted its statement of purpose at its organizing conference in Washington DC, 29 October 1966. It suggests that, despite many changes, women still suffered from discrimination in employment and in the home.

We, men and women, who hereby constitute ourselves as the National Organization for Women, believe that the time has come for a new movement toward true equality for all women in America, and toward a fully equal partnership of the sexes, as part of the world-wide revolution of human rights now taking place within and beyond our national borders. . . .

Despite all the talk about the status of American women in recent years, the actual position of women in the United States has declined, and is declining, to an alarming degree throughout the 1950's and '60s. Although 46.4% of all American women between the ages of 18 and 65 now work outside the home, the overwhelming majority – 75% – are in routine clerical, sales, or factory jobs, or they are household workers, cleaning women, hospital attendants. About two-thirds of Negro women workers are in the lowest paid service occupations. Working women are becoming increasingly – not less – concentrated on the bottom of the job ladder. As a consequence full-time women workers today earn on the average only 60% of what men earn, and that wage gap has been increasing over the past twenty-five years in every major industry group. In 1964, of all women with a yearly income, 89% earned under $5,000 a year; half of all full-time year round women workers earned less than $3,690; only 1.4% of full-time year round women workers had an annual income of $10,000 or more.

Discrimination in employment on the basis of sex is now prohibited by federal law, in Title VII of the Civil Rights Act of 1964. But although nearly one-third of the cases brought before the Equal Employment Opportunity Commission during the first year dealt with sex discrimination and the proportion is increasing dramatically, the Commission has not made clear its intention to enforce the law with the same seriousness on behalf of women as of other victims of discrimination. Many of these cases were Negro women, who are the victims of the double discrimination of race and sex. Until now, too few women's organizations and official spokesmen have been willing to speak out against these dangers facing women. Too many women have been restrained by the fear of being called "feminist.". . . . There is no civil rights movement to speak for women, as there has been for Negroes and other victims of discrimination. . . .

WE REJECT the current assumptions that a man must carry the sole burden of supporting himself, his wife, and family, and that a woman is automatically entitled to lifelong support by a man upon her marriage, or that marriage, home and family are primarily woman's world and responsibility – hers to dominate – his to support. We believe that a true partnership between the sexes demands a different concept of marriage an equitable sharing of the responsibilities of home and children and of the economic burdens of their support. We believe that proper recognition should be given to the economic and social value of homemaking and child-care. To these ends we will seek to open a re-examination of laws and mores governing marriage and divorce, for we believe that the current state of "half-equality" between the sexes discriminates against both men and women, and is the cause of much unnecessary hostility between the sexes. . . .

IN THE INTERESTS OF THE HUMAN DIGNITY OF WOMEN, we will protest, and endeavor to change, the false image of women now prevalent in the mass media, and in the texts, ceremonies, laws, and practices of our major social institutions. Such images perpetuate contempt for women by society and by women for themselves. We are similarly opposed to all policies and practices – in church, state, college, factory, or office – which, in the guise of protectiveness, not only deny opportunities but also foster in women self-denigration, dependence, and evasion of responsibility, undermine their confidence in their own abilities and foster contempt for women. . . .

WE BELIEVE THAT women will do most to create a new image of women by acting now, and by speaking out in behalf of their own equality, freedom, and human dignity – not in pleas for special privilege, nor in enmity toward men, who are also victims of the current, half-equality between the sexes – but in an active, self-respecting partnership with men. By so doing, women will develop confidence in their own ability to determine actively, in partnership with men, the conditions of their life, their choices, their future and their society.

Source: National Organization for Women. Statement of Purpose 1966, Excerpts from the Original Electronic Text at the website of the Feminist Chronicles.

Document 24   PRESS REACTIONS TO WOMEN'S LIBERATION

When feminists began to take direct action to draw attention to their concerns, in particular the disruptions to the Miss World competition, the press reacted with arguments that were similar to those of anti-suffragists earlier in the century. The extract below shows dislike of the 'revolutionary' aspects of the women's movement.

Six months have passed since the successful agitation against the South African cricket tour, and now the call has gone out for an end to the Miss World competition. There have been some of the old faces back again and some of the same scenes. Against the complacent democracy, idly viewing "a degrading and debasing spectacle" (not Mrs Whitehouse speaking but the Young Liberal leader of the anti Miss World demonstration) only the tactics of direct action seem proper. Once again an activity considered quite harmless by most people has been denounced as an offensive exploitation of a wronged community. Then it was race; now it is sex. Community politics set out to the rescue of women, the oppressed majority.

The neo feminist case against the Miss World competition starts from the view that it is a "symptom of society's attitude towards women . . . which portrays them as sex-symbols". A women's liberationist ideology has been developed to explain and expose these social attitudes, drawing heavily on academic analysis of cultural deprivation in other distinctive communities – the young, the black, the urban poor. Miss Kate Millett, the leading American liberationist theoretician, identifies the underlying cause of feminist subjection as the principle of patriarchy – "the most pervasive ideology of our culture".

Among the manifestations of patriarchal power exercised by men over women are inequality in job opportunities, the prevalence of female sexual inhibition, and the commercial exploitation of feminine sex appeal. . . . According to this analysis a profound cultural revolution, shattering the traditional family and altering every aspect of economic, social and political relationships is the only way to secure relief for women, as for all other oppressed communities.

It is true that women experience a number of disabilities, notably in connection with social security benefits, taxation and equal pay. We wholeheartedly support the abolition of these restrictions, to the removal of which the government is pledged. . . . But it is hard to support the view of women as an oppressed majority moving towards a revolutionary deliverance. Many are content simply to be different from men, with few feelings of subordination or inferiority. And a powerful antidote to Women's Liberation lies in the plain fact of differentiation of biological function with all the deep differences in behaviour and life experience which this entails. Perhaps the real criticism of the Miss World competition should also be applied to the Women's Liberation movement: that they both exalt an essentially function-less feminism.

Source: *The Times*, Editorial, 21 November 1970, p. 13.

THE VOICE OF BLACK AMERICAN FEMINISTS   **Document 25**

This statement from the Combahee River Collective, a Black feminist group that met in Boston from 1974 reveals some of the general characteristics of the Women's Liberation Movement as well as the specific position of Black feminists in the United States.

What we believe

Above all else, our politics initially sprang from the shared belief that Black women are inherently valuable, that our liberation is a necessity not as an adjunct to somebody else's but because of our need as human persons for autonomy. This may seem so obvious as to sound simplistic, but it is apparent that no other ostensibly progressive movement has ever considered our specific oppression as a priority or worked seriously for the ending of that oppression. Merely naming the pejorative stereotypes attributed to Black women (e.g. mamy, matriarch, Sapphire, whore, bulldagger), let alone cataloguing the cruel, often murderous treatment we receive, indicates how little value has been placed upon our lives during four centuries of bondage in the Western hemisphere. We realise that the only people who care enough about us to work consistently for our liberation are us. . . .

A political contribution which we feel we have already made is the expansion of the feminist principle that the personal is political. In our con-sciousness raising sessions, for example, we have in many ways gone beyond white women's revelations because we are dealing with the implications of race and class as well as sex. Even our Black women's style of talking/testifying in Black language about what we have experienced has a resonance that is both cultural and political . . .

As we have already stated, we reject the stance of Lesbian separatism because it is not a viable political analysis or strategy for us. It leaves out far too much and far too many people, particularly Black men, women and children. We have a great deal of criticism and loathing for what men have been socialized to be in the society. . . . But we do not have the misguided notion that it is their maleness, per se – i.e. their biological maleness – that makes them what they are. As Black women we find any type of biological determinism a particularly dangerous and reactionary basis upon which to build a politic. . . .

Source: The Combahee River Collective Statement, 1977, reproduced in Barbara Smith (ed.) *Home Girls: A Black Feminist Anthology*, New York, 1983, pp. 274–7.

Document 26   LESBIAN FEMINISTS

Lesbian feminists often criticized other feminists for marginalizing their concerns. For some their sexuality represented a political choice and this is discussed in the following letter to the feminist women's movement distributed by radical lesbians in France on an International Women's Day meeting at the Salle Wagram, 8 March 1981.

. . . radical lesbianism is not a 'sexual preference' or 'only liking to live with women'. It is a decisive political choice which is implicit in the analysis of sex class relations based on exploitation and oppression, and which have antagonistic interests. Lesbian political commitment is different from the feminism of 'homosexuals' or 'heterosexuals' because we choose to use the margins of freedom, of manoeuvre that the patriarchal system leaves us, to fight it at its roots. . . .

The lesbian choice is *mobilisation*, in a visible collective movement, and the transfer of all our creative powers, both intellectual and emotional, to women, because we all have the same class interests. Far from carving out spaces for ourselves in a hetero-patriarchal society which objectivises, oppresses and kills women, we want to fight the mechanisms of its power.

The lesbian choice is *awareness* that male violence against women is at work everywhere, especially in 'private' life, with its traps of emotional attachment or heterosexual 'desire'. . . .

Source: 'Letter to the feminist movement', 8 March 1981, quoted in Claire Duchen, *Feminism in France*, London, 1988, pp. 23–4.

Document 27   THIRD WORLD FEMINISM IN THE 1980S

This article, written in The Guardian *in 1984, discusses criticisms of the way in which western feminists still took leadership of the women's movement and asserted their own concerns in the late twentieth century.*

But in Mexico City and Copenhagen, many third world women rejected this leadership of the west. At the forthcoming UN conference on the decade of

Women in Nairobi they will probably do the same. They accuse American and European feminists of being obsessed with sexual issues and of paying too little attention to poverty and national liberation. They see the western initiatives as another example of high handed missionary zeal among the supposedly unknowing, and they resent what they see as feminist imperialism. . . .

Whether the issue is birth control, rape or circumcision, western feminists do not seem to understand the reluctance of third world women to 'go into the streets' or even to confront the problems openly in public debates. . . . the truth is that third world feminists are often isolated, but this has little to do with the states of consciousness, it has to do with survival. In Egypt Nawal El-Saadawi was imprisoned for her writings advocating feminism. In India girls may be impoverished and disinherited for open protests against dowry and arranged marriages . . .

As for an ideological unity, western feminists must acknowledge that 'political issues' such as the racism in South Africa and human rights in South Korea are feminist issues and that they have priority over other such as lesbian rights. An international list of feminist issues would show many common interests among women in all countries, such as the struggle against domestic violence. . . .

The problem is the unequal distribution of power and resources, for this has allowed the few to set the feminist agenda for the many. Third world women have recognised this, and demand a more equal share of both so that they can fight for their own causes, as they experience them, and as they wish to have them known. . . .

Source: Soon-Young Yoon 'Western feminism and women in the third world', *The Guardian*, 2 October 1984, Copyright Guardian News & Media Ltd 1984; reprinted in Kira Cochrane (ed.) *Women of the Revolution: Forty Years of Feminism*, London, 2010, pp. 101–5.

CHANGE FOR RUSSIAN WOMEN   **Document 28**

Personal account of Olga Bessolova, born 1949 in Russia, of her experiences of changes brought to women's lives during the period of political transition in the 1980s and 1990s. She was prominent in developing a political network of women in the Moscow region and then across Russia. She notes the complexity of these changes which did not always lead to improvement in women's lives.

As the majority of women became educated and active, they held major roles in the middle level of society. I think men are really afraid of women in these positions; they try to humiliate women and their roles to keep men in power, because power in my country is very connected to the acquisition of wealth. The second reason is economic. The cutting of military orders, the declining number of jobs resembles in reverse the situation of the 1950s and 60s. In those decades, women were invited to fill new jobs in the defense sector. Now when the jobs are cut, women are the first invited to leave. In a recessionary situation, women are the first who are forced to leave. The third complex of reasons is personal and derives from women themselves, their own capability and character. Women are thinking much more about the moral aspect of politics, about participating in this corrupted world of business and politicians. . . .

As a schoolgirl, there was no problem of choice, and if a girl expressed an ambition for entering the most prestigious professions . . . it was quite all right; it didn't surprise anybody; but now my eleven year old daughter wants to become a dress designer. Why? Because the mass media present this to us: A girl has to find a nice man, marry him and serve him. This change in psychology has been so quick, and it is difficult to define what has produced it. Before 1985, there were many educated women, and they were presented in the media with pride; more women had had a higher education than . . . men. But at some point, this seems to have frightened men, as if women needed to be stopped.

Source: Linda Racioppi and Katherine O'Sullivan, *Women's Activism in Contemporary Russia*, Philadelphia, Temple University Press, 1997, pp. 119–20, 124.

Document 29   UNITED NATIONS CALLS FOR ACTION

The United Nations has organized a series of conferences and initiatives to raise the status of women world-wide. Its various reports indicate that gender inequalities are prevalent in all areas of life. The following extract from a 1994 report seeks to promote increased women's access to science and technology training.

29. The United Nations Development Fund for Women (UNIFEM) stresses that major efforts should be made and effective incentives created to increase women's access to education and training in the fields of science and technology. The Expert Group Meeting on "Women's Science and Technology", convened by UNIFEM in December 1993 at the request of the secretariat for the Fourth World Conference on Women, recommended that Governments should be encouraged to set quotas for women at all levels in science and education to ensure that a critical mass of 30 per cent of professional women scientists and technologists is achieved. In order to encourage girls and young women to enter science education, efforts should

be made to de-mystify science and technology, to develop gender-neutral science curricula, and to promote images of women in scientific and technical professions and fields. Increased women's participation in science and technology could shift the mainstream towards being more people-centred and more focused on basic needs and sustainable development.

30. It was further recommended that UNESCO and other organizations of the United Nations system should give priority to eliminating female illiteracy and to monitoring efforts to ensure that women have equal access to all levels of education and training. UNESCO has organized, in cooperation with the United Nations Children's Fund (UNICEF), a Pan-African Conference on the education of girls held in Ouagadougou, Burkina Faso on 28 March–1 April 1993. This Conference marked another milestone in regional efforts to make education for all a reality in terms of quality, access and management. The main objectives of the Conference were to obtain a regional consensus on girls' education as priority for education development in Africa. The Conference adopted the Ouagadougou Declaration which calls upon Governments, international and bilateral agencies, NGOs and politicians to establish the education of girls as a priority, to set targets and to report regularly to the international Forum on Education for All (EFA). In the Delhi Declaration (16 December 1993), the leaders of nine high-population developing nations reaffirmed their commitment to EFA goals by, inter alia, recognizing that "the education and empowerment of girls and women are important goals in themselves and are key factors in contributing to social development, well-being and the education of present and future generations, and the expansion of the choices available to women for the development of their full potential" (paras 2–6).

Source: United Nations General Assembly, 30 August 1994, report of the Secretary General on Implementation of the Nairobi Forward-looking Strategies for the Advancement of Women to the Year 2000, 49th Session.

Guide to further reading

There is a vast literature on the history of feminism in Britain, North America and Australia. The suffrage movement in particular is one of the most well-known episodes in women's history and has been the focus of attention of historians for over half a century. The reading that follows, therefore, is, of necessity, selective for these areas. What follows is an attempt to identify those key texts that have brought a new perspective to the study of feminist history and the suffrage movement, or overviews that provide a guide to further reading. For other parts of the world, where an interest in feminist history developed later and only some texts are in English, as many studies as possible have been included. The place of publication is London unless otherwise indicated.

Sources

There are a large number of document collections for Britain and the United States. These focus on the nineteenth and early twentieth centuries and include extracts from speeches of women's rights campaigners and their opponents, journal articles, books, pamphlets and evidence to government inquiries. In Britain, specific issues are covered in an important series of books published by Routledge in the 1980s. They include: Jane Lewis (ed.), *Before the Vote was Won: Arguments for and against Women's Suffrage, 1864–1896* (1987); Candida Ann Lacey (ed.), *Barbara Leigh Smith Bodichon and the Langham Place Group* (1987); Dale Spender (ed.), *The Education Papers: Women's Quest for Equality in Britain 1850–1912* (1987); Carol McPhee and Ann Fitzgerald (eds), *The Non-Violent Militant: Selected Writings of Teresa Billington-Greig* (1987); Sheila Jeffrey (ed.), *The Sexuality Debates* (1987); Jane Marcus (ed.), *Suffrage and the Pankhursts* (1987). Two six-volume sets of documents *Sources of British Feminism* (1993) and *Perspectives on the History of British Feminism* (1994), both edited by Tamae Mizuta and Marie Mulvey-Roberts cover a wide range of topics pertaining to women's rights from the seventeenth century to the 1930s. Patricia Hollis (ed.), *Women in Public: The Women's Movement 1850–1900* (1979), provides documents on women's public activities. For the United States the two volume *Second to None: A Documentary History of American Women* (1993), edited by Ruth Barnes Moynihan, Cynthia Russett and Laurie Crumpacker covers varied aspects of women's political life from the sixteenth century to the present. A very varied and comprehensive selection of documents is provided in the three volume *Public Women, Public Words: A Documentary History of American Feminism* edited by Dawn Keetley and John Pettegrew (New York, 1997, 2002, 2003) which goes from the beginnings of feminism to the present day. See also Winston E. Langley and Vivian C. Fox (eds), *Women's Rights in the United States: A Documentary History* (Westport, CT, 1994); Bert James Loewenberg and Ruth Bogin (eds), *Black Women in Nineteenth-Century American Life: Their Words, Their Thoughts, Their Feelings* (Pennsylvania, 1976). Collections of the often ephemeral material produced by the Women's Liberation Movement can be found in Rosalyn Baxandall and Linda Gordon (eds), *Dear Sisters: Dispatches from the Women's Liberation Movement* (New York, 2000); Barbara Crow (ed.), *Radical Feminism: An Historical Reader* (New York, 2000); Robin Morgan (ed.), *Sisterhood is Powerful: An Anthology of Writings from the Women's Liberation Movement* (New York, 1970); Nancy Maclean, *The American Women's Movement, 1945–2000. A Brief History with Documents* (2009). Margaret Jolly, *In Love and Struggle: Letters in Contemporary Feminism* (New York, 2008) reprints letters between women in the 1960s and 70s.

For Australia, see Kay Daniels and Mary Murname, *Uphill All the Way: A Documentary History of Women in Australia* (St Lucia, 1980). For France, extracts from the personal and political writings of feminists including Tristan, Deroin and Pelletier can be found in Felicia Gordon and Maire Cross (eds), *Early French Feminisms: An Historical Reader* (Cheltenham, 1996). See also Jennifer Waelti-Walters and Stephen C. Hause (eds), *Feminisms of the Belle Epoque: A Historical and Literary Anthology* (Lincoln, 1994).

Other collections of documents cover more than one country, but the focus is usually Britain, France, Germany and the United States. See, for example, Susan Groag Bell and Karen M. Offen (eds), *Women, the Family and Freedom. The Debate in Documents* (Chicago, 1983); Erna Olafson Hellerstein, Lesley Parker Hume and Karen M. Offen (eds), *Victorian Women: A Documentary Account of Women's Lives in Nineteenth-Century England, France and the United States* (Brighton, 1981); Eleanor Riemer and John Fout (eds), *European Women: A Documentary History, 1789–1945* (New York, 1980).

There are numerous texts that provide extracts from the writings of key feminist theorists. They include Miriam Schneir (ed.), **Feminism: The Essential Historical Writings** (New York, 1972); Heidi Safia Mirza (ed.), **Black British Feminism: A Reader** (1997) contains extracts from classic texts and more contemporary debates; Alice Rossi (ed.), **The Feminist Papers: From Addams to de Beauvoir** (New York, 1971); Mari Jo Buhle and Paul Buhle (eds), **The Concise History of Woman Suffrage: Selections from the Classic Work of Stanton, Gage, and Harper** (Urbana, IL, 1978); Alma Garcia (ed.), **Chicana Feminist Thought: The Basic Historical Writings** (1997); Linda Nicholson (ed.), **The Second Wave: A Reader in Feminist Theory** (1997); Margot Badran and Miriam Cooke (eds.), **Opening the Gates: A Century of Arab Feminist Writing** (1990); Kelly Oliver (ed.), **French Feminism: A Reader** (Oxford, 2000); Norma Grieve and Ailsa Burns (eds), **Australian Women: Contemporary Political Thought** (Oxford, 1994).

There are many autobiographies and memoirs of those who took part in feminist campaigns. They need to be read with care since they construct a specific version of events, often in support of their own organizations. Nonetheless they also provide important insights into the relationship between public and private lives and into the different experiences of women from across the world. Examples include Elizabeth Cady Stanton, **Eighty Years and More: Reminiscences, 1815–1897** (New York, 1898); Millicent Garrett Fawcett, **The Women's Victory and After: Personal Reminiscences, 1911–1918** (1920); Aletta Jacobs, **Memories. My Life as an International Leader in Health, Suffrage and Peace** (1924, 1996); Alexandra Kollontai, **The Autobiography of a Sexually Emancipated Communist Woman** (New York, 1971. Memoir compiled 1926); Margaret Sanger, **An Autobiography** (New York, 1938). Many autobiographies were written by British suffragettes, including Emmeline Pankhurst, **My Own Story** (1915); Annie Kenney, **Memories of a Militant** (1924); Mary Richardson, **Laugh a Defiance** (1953); Mary Gawthorpe, **Up Hill to Holloway** (1962). Interesting insights are provided by militants who remained close to labour politics such as Emmeline Pethick Lawrence, **My Part in a Changing World** (1938) and Hannah Mitchell, **The Hard Way Up** (1968). Huda Sha'arawi, **Harem Years: The Memoirs of an Egyptian Feminist** (1986) and Shidzue Ishimoto, **Facing Two Ways: The Story of My Life** (1935) provide a rare, non western perspective. For a discussion of how women who were politically active constructed their autobiographies, see Pauline Polkey, 'Reading history through autobiography: politically active women of late nineteenth-century Britain and their personal narratives', **Women's History Review**, 9, 3 (2000).

Another key source is the suffrage histories written by participants; these blend personal reminiscences, partisan views and documentary evidence. They provide a rich mine of information for the historian but must again be approached with care. Helen Blackburn, **Women's Suffrage: A Record of the Women's Suffrage Movement in the British Isles** (1902); Sylvia Pankhurst, **The Suffragette Movement: An Intimate Account of Persons and Ideals** (1931); Ray Strachey, **The Cause: A Short History of the Women's Movement in Great Britain** (1928); E. Cady Stanton, Susan B. Anthony, Matilda Joslyn Gage and Ida Husted Harper, **History of Woman Suffrage** (New York, 1881–1922); Carrie Chapman Catt and Nettie Rogers Shuler, **Woman Suffrage and Politics: The Inner Story of the Suffrage Movement** (New York, 1938).

Laura E. Nym Mayhall, 'Creating the "suffragette spirit": British feminism and the historical imagination', **Women's History Review**, 4, 3 (1995) and Hilda Kean, 'Searching for the present in past defeat: the construction of historical and political identity in British feminism in the 1920s and 30s', **Women's History Review**, 3, 1 (1994) consider the ways in which suffragettes writing in the inter-war years shaped later histories of militancy. See also Kathryn Dodd, 'Cultural politics and women's historical writings: the case of Ray Strachey's *The Cause*', **Women's Studies International Forum**, 13, 1/2 (1990) and Kathryn Dodd (ed.), **A Sylvia Pankhurst Reader** (Manchester, 1991).

Comparative studies

For a stimulating discussion of new perspectives that arise when looking at feminism across national boundaries, see the special issue edited by Ann Taylor Allen, Anna Cova and June Purvis, International Feminisms, **Women's History Review**, 19, 4 (2010) and Anna Cova (ed.), **Comparative Women's History: New Approaches** (New York, 2006). A key text that provides a detailed and thought provoking comparison of feminist ideas and movements in a wide range of European countries is Karen Offen, **European Feminisms, 1700–1950: A Political History** (Stanford, CA, 2000). See also Karen Offen (ed.), **Globalising Feminisms, 1789–1845** (2000). Other comparative studies of Europe include: Gisela Bock, **Women in European History** (Oxford, 2002) and Barbara Caine and Glenda Sluga, **Gendering European History** (2000). Europe and North America are compared in Marlene Legates **In Their Time. A History of Feminism in Western Society** (2001). For a comparative study that not only looks at Europe, North America and Australia, but also goes further afield to include Japan, Argentina, Chile, Colombia and Uruguay, see Caroline Daley and Melanie Nolan (eds) **Suffrage and Beyond: International Feminist Perspectives** (Auckland, 1994). This was a pioneering study that drew attention to the extent to which the history of feminism had been viewed through the perspective of a model drawn from Britain and North America.

Definitions

The comparative texts referred to above all discuss different definitions of feminism. In addition, Barbara Caine suggests that women's rights were at the core of modern feminism in **English Feminism, 1780–1980** (Oxford, 1997). Jane Rendall also employs the term modern feminism to describe the late eighteenth century onwards and uses the word feminist 'to describe women who claimed for themselves the right to define their own place in society, and a few men who sympathised with them': Jane Rendall, **The Origins of Modern Feminism: Women in Britain, France and the United States, 1780–1860** (Houndmills, 1985: 1–2). For an argument that feminism can be used to describe periods when it was not employed by contemporaries, see Barbara Taylor, **Eve and the New Jerusalem. Socialism and Feminism in the Nineteenth Century** (1983). The opposite position is explored in Nancy Cott, **The Grounding of Modern Feminism** (New Haven, CT, 1986). The use of the term 'waves' in histories of feminism is discussed in: Karen Offen (2000); Drude Dahlerup, 'Three Waves of Feminism in Denmark'; and Beatrice Halsaa, 'The History of the Women's Movement in Norway' – both in Gabriele Griffin and Rosi Braidotti (eds) **Thinking Differently: A Reader in European Women's Studies** (2002) and in Nancy Hewitt, **No Permanent Waves: Recasting Histories of US Feminism** (Chapel Hill, NC, 2010).

Origins of modern feminism

For a discussion of the complex origins of modern feminism, see Jane Rendall, **The Origins of Modern Feminism: Women in Britain, France and the United States, 1780–1860** (Basingstoke, 1985) and Karen Offen, **European Feminisms, 1780–1950: A Political History** (Stanford, CA, 2000). Women's critique of their subordinate position before the late eighteenth century is explored in Gerda Lerner, **The Creation of Feminist Consciousness: From the Middle Ages to 1870** (Oxford, 1993). The ideas of the Enlightenment are explained in Dorinda Outram, **The Enlightenment** (Cambridge, 1995). The impact of the French Revolution is explored in Rendall and Offen, above. See also James F. McMillan, **France and Women, 1789–1914. Gender, Society and Politics** (2000) and Gisela Bock, **Women in European History**, (Oxford, 2002). Mary Wollstonecraft's ideas have been the subject of extensive debate and differing interpretations. For a recent discussion of her work, see Eileen Janes Yeo (ed.) **Mary Wollstonecraft and 200 Years of Feminisms** (1997) and Barbara Taylor, **Mary Wollstonecraft and the Feminist Imagination** (Cambridge, 2003). Lee Holcombe, **Wives and Property: Reform of the Married Women's Property Law in Nineteenth Century England** (Toronto, 1983) provides a detailed account of women's legal position. For an overview of the social and economic changes affecting women during industrialization and a guide to further reading, see Katrina Honeyman, **Women, Gender and Industrialisation in England, 1700–1870** (Basingstoke, 2000). An influential text exploring family, separate spheres and class is Leonore Davidoff and Catherine Hall, **Family Fortunes. Men and Women of the English Middle Class, 1750–1850** (1987). For a recent critique of their ideas, see Amanda Vickery, 'Golden age to separate spheres? A review of the categories and chronology of English women's history', **Historical Journal**, 36 (1993). The argument that women in the late eighteenth and nineteenth centuries remained active in the public sphere and that the women's movement was an attempt to extend this role is explored in: Kathryn Gleadle and Sarah Richardson (eds), **Women in British Politics, 1760–1860. The Power of the Petticoat** (Basingstoke, 2000); and in Kathryn Gleadle, 'British women and radical politics in the late nonconformist Enlightenment, c. 1780–1830', in Amanda Vickery (ed.), **Women, Privilege and Power. British Politics, 1750 to the Present** (Stanford, CA, 2001). They also raise questions about what should be defined as political. Ann Summers gives greater emphasis to the restrictions that women faced. See **Female Lives, Moral States** (Newbury, 2000).

For an overview of women's involvement in philanthropy, temperance and anti-slavery campaigns in the United States and a guide to further reading, see Jay Kleinberg, **Women in American Society, 1820–1920** (Brighton, 1990); and Christine Bolt, **The Women's Movements in the United States and Britain from the 1790s to the 1920s** (Hemel Hempstead, 1993). The relationship between anti-slavery campaigns, colonialism and the development of the women's movement in Britain is explored in: Clare Midgley, **Women Against Slavery: The British Campaigns, 1780–1870** (London, 1992); and Clare Midgley, 'British women, women's rights and Empire, 1790–1850', in Patricia Grimshaw, Katie Holmes and Marilyn Lake (eds), **Women's Rights and Human Rights** (Basingstoke, 2001). For a local example, see June Hannam, '"An enlarged sphere of usefulness": The Bristol women's movement, c. 1860–1914', in Madge Dresser and Philip Ollerenshaw (eds), **The Making of Modern Bristol** (Tiverton, 1996). The most stimulating discussion of the relationship between utopian socialism and women's emancipation is still Barbara Taylor, **Eve and the New Jerusalem. Socialism and Feminism in the Nineteenth Century** (1983). For France, see Susan Grogan, **Flora Tristan: Life Stories** (1998).

Nineteenth-century women's movement

For the women's movement in individual countries, see Linda Edmondson, 'Women's rights, gender and citizenship in Tsarist Russia, 1860–1920: The question of difference', in Patricia Grimshaw, Katie Holmes and Marilyn Lake (eds), *Women's Rights and Human Rights* (Basingstoke, 2001); Ute Gerhard, 'The women's movement in Germany', in Gabriele Griffin and Rosi Braidotti (eds), *Thinking Differently: A Reader in European Women's Studies* (2002); Eleanor Flexner, *Century of Struggle: The Woman's Rights Movement in the United States* (Cambridge, MA, 1959).

Olive Banks, *Faces of Feminism* (Oxford, 1980) was one of the first historians to identify separate strands in the women's movement. This view was later challenged by those who argued that feminist ideas were complex and that there were interconnections between individuals and movements, and between notions of equality and difference. For example, see Barbara Caine, *Victorian Feminism* (Oxford, 1992) and Joan Scott, 'Deconstructing equality-versus-difference: or the uses of post-structuralist theory for feminism', *Feminist Studies*, 14 (1988). The ideas of individuals and groups are explored in: Jane Rendall, 'Citizenship, culture and civilisation: the languages of British suffragists, 1866–1874', in Caroline Daley and Melanie Nolan (eds), *Suffrage and Beyond* (Auckland, 1994). For a discussion of John Stuart Mill's ideas, see Jane Rendall, *Origins*; and 'John Stuart Mill, Liberal politics, and the movements for women's suffrage, 1865–1873', in Amanda Vickery (ed.), *Women, Privilege and Power* (Stanford, CA, 2001).

The campaigns against state regulation and social purity movements are discussed in: Judith Walkowitz, *Prostitution and Victorian Society: Women, Class and the State* (Cambridge, 1980); Ute Frevert, *Women in German History: From Bourgeois Emancipation to Sexual Liberation* (Oxford, 1989); Lucy Bland, *Banishing the Beast: English Feminism and Sexual Morality, 1885–1914* (Harmondsworth, 1995). For an interesting set of articles on the European dimensions of Josephine Butler's work, see the special issue edited by Anne Summers, Gender, religion and politics; Josephine Butler's campaigns in international perspective (1875–1959), *Women's History Review*, 17, 2 (2008).

Women's friendships are discussed in Philippa Levine, 'Love, friendship and feminism in later nineteenth-century England', *Women's Studies International Forum*, 13, 1/2 (1990). The informal friendship links between women at an international level are discussed in Mineke Bosch with Annemarie Kloosterman (eds), *Politics and Friendship: Letters from the International Woman Suffrage Alliance, 1902–1942* (Columbus, OH, 1990).

Suffrage movement

For an overview of suffrage campaigns in different countries in the nineteenth and early twentieth centuries, see June Hannam, Mitzi Auchterlonie and Katherine Holden, *International Encyclopaedia of Women's Suffrage* (Santa Barbara, CA, 2000).

There is a vast literature on the history of the suffrage movements in Britain and the United States. The subject is best approached, therefore, through overview texts that provide a guide to further reading, for example: Christine Bolt, *The Women's Movements in the United States and Britain from the 1790s to the 1920s* (Hemel Hempstead, 1993); Harold L. Smith, *The British Women's Suffrage Campaigns, 1866–1928* (1998); Paula Bartley, *Votes for Women* (1998). Elizabeth Crawford, *The Women's Suffrage Movement. A Reference Guide* (1999) and *The Women's Suffrage Movement in Britain and Ireland: A Regional Survey* (2006) are invaluable reference guides to all aspects of the British suffrage movement. Sandra Stanley Holton's many publications have added new perspectives to British suffrage history. See, in particular, *Suffrage Days: Stories from the Women's Suffrage Movement* (1996) in which Holton explores the continuity between nineteenth-century radicalism and the militancy of the Edwardian suffrage movement and *Feminism and Democracy: Women's Suffrage and Reform Politics in Britain, 1900–1818* (Cambridge, 1986) in which attention is drawn to the relationship between suffrage campaigning and the political parties. A pioneering text on the involvement of working women in the campaign is Jill Liddington and Jill Norris, *One Hand Tied Behind Us. The Rise of the Women's Suffrage Movement* (1978). The debate on the impact of war is considered in Penny Summerfield, 'Women and war in the twentieth century', in June Purvis (ed.), *Women's History: Britain 1850–1945* (1995). A classic American text is Eleanor Flexner, *Century of Struggle: the Women's Rights Movement in the United States* (Cambridge, MA, 1975). For more recent scholarship see the collection of essays edited by Jean H. Baker, *Votes for Women: The Struggle for the Suffrage Re-visited* (Oxford, 2002); Ellen DuBois, *Woman Suffrage and Women's Rights* (New York, 1998) and Rosalyn Terborg Penn, *African American Women in the Struggle for the Vote, 1850–1920* (Bloomington, 1998).

Other countries are covered by the following: Steven C. Hause with Anne R. Kenney, *Women's Suffrage and Social Politics in the French Third Republic* (Princeton, NJ, 1984); Steven C. Hause, *Hubertine Auclert: The French Suffragette* (1987); Audrey Oldfield, *Woman Suffrage in Australia. A Gift or a Struggle* (Cambridge, 1992); Patricia Grimshaw, *Women's Suffrage in New Zealand* (Auckland, 1987); Janette Bomford, *That Dangerous and Persuasive Woman: Vida Goldstein* (Carlton, 1993); Ida Blom, 'The struggle for women's suffrage in Norway, 1885–1913', *Scandinavian Journal of History*, 5, 3 (1980); Katherine David, 'Czech feminists and nationalism in the late Habsburg Monarchy: "The First in Austria"', *Journal of Women's History*, 3, 2 (1991); Linda H. Edmondson, *Feminism in Russia, 1900–1917* (Stanford, CA, 1984); D. Dahlerup, 'Three Waves of Feminism in Denmark', in Gabriele Griffin and Rosie Braidotti (eds) *Thinking Differently: A Reader in European Women's Studies* (2002); Harriet Anderson, *Utopian Feminism: Women's Movements in Fin-de-Siècle Vienna* (New Haven, CT, 1992) and Werner Thönnesen, *The Emancipation of Women: The Rise and Decline of the Women's Movement in German Social Democracy, 1863–1933* (1976). The difficulties feminists encountered in societies where the Catholic Church and conservative governments emphasized traditional family structures and roles are explored in: Margaret Ward, '"Suffrage First – Above All Else!" An account of the Irish suffrage movement', in Alibhe Smyth (ed.), **Irish Women's Studies Reader** (Dublin, 1993) and Judith Keene, '"Into the clean air of the plaza": Spanish women achieve the vote in 1931', in Victoria Loree Enders and Pamela Beth Radcliff (eds), *Constructing Spanish Womanhood: Female Identity in Modern Spain* (Albany, NY, 1999).

For the different arguments of suffragists, see Les Garner, *Stepping Stones to Women's Liberty: Feminist Ideas in the Women's Suffrage Movement, 1900–1918,* (1984); Susan K. Kent, *Sex and Suffrage in Britain, 1860–1914* (1990); and Gayle Gullett, *Becoming Citizens: The Emergence and Development of the California Women's Movement, 1880–1911* (Champagne, IL, 2000). The arguments of anti-suffrage women are discussed in Julia Bush, *Edwardian Ladies and Imperial Power* (2000).

The iconic status of Emmeline Pankhurst is explored in two recent biographies: Paula Bartley, *Emmeline Pankhurst* (2002) and June Purvis, *Emmeline Pankhurst: A Biography* (2002). Martin Pugh, *The Pankhursts* (Harmondsworth, 2002) looks at the contribution of the family as a whole and the relationship between its members. Debates about the nature of militancy are considered in: Sandra S. Holton, 'Women and the vote', in June Purvis (ed.), *Women's History: Britain, 1850–1945* (1995) and Laura E. Nym Mayhall, *The Militant Suffrage Movement: Citizenship and Resistance in Britain, 1860–1930* (Oxford, 2003). The importance of paid organizers is explored in Krista Cowman, *Women of the Right Spirit. Paid Organisers of the Women's Social and Political Union, 1904–18* (Manchester, 2007),

A key text for understanding the imagery of the movement and the role that it played in suffrage politics is: Lisa Tickner, *The Spectacle of Women: Imagery of the Suffrage Campaign, 1907–1914* (1987). For propaganda, including plays, novels and poetry, see Alice Sheppard, *Cartooning for Suffrage* (Albuquerque, NM, 1994) and relevant essays in Maroula Joannou and June Purvis (eds), *The Women's Suffrage Movement: New Feminist Perspectives* (Manchester, 1998). For the importance of advertising and raising income, see Margaret Finnegan, *Selling Suffrage: Consumer Culture and Votes for Women* (New York, 1999) and John Mercer, 'Shopping for suffrage: the campaign shops of the Women's Social and Political Union', *Women's History Review*, 18, 2 (2009).

Socialism and the women's movement, 1880s–1920

For the impact of socialist ideas on nineteenth-century debates around the 'woman question', see Karen Honeycut, 'Clara Zetkin: A socialist approach to the problem of women's oppression', in Jane Slaughter and Robert Kern (eds), *European Women on the Left* (Westport, CT, 1981). The complex relationship between class and gender in socialist theory and practice is explored in June Hannam and Karen Hunt, *Socialist Women. Britain 1880s to 1920s* (2001); Marilyn J. Boxer and Jean H. Quataert (eds), *Socialist Women: European Socialist Feminism in the Nineteenth and Twentieth Centuries* (New York, 1978); Charles Sowerwine, 'The socialist women's movement from 1850–1940', in Renate Bridenthal, Claudia Koontz and Susan Stuard (eds), *Becoming Visible: Women in European History* (Boston, 1987); and Karen Hunt, *Equivocal Feminists: The Social Democratic Federation and the Woman Question, 1884–1911* (Cambridge, 1996). The international dimension is covered in Richard J. Evans, *Comrades and Sisters: Feminism, Socialism and Pacifism in Europe, 1870–1945* (Brighton, 1987); Ellen C. DuBois, 'Woman suffrage and the left: an international socialist-feminist perspective', *New Left Review*, 186 (1991) and 'Woman suffrage round the world: three phases of internationalism', in Caroline Daley and Melanie Nolan (eds), *Suffrage and Beyond* (Auckland, 1994). For a critique of the use of the term 'bourgeois feminism' and of conventional wisdoms about socialist attitudes to the women's movement, see Marilyn Boxer 'Rethinking the socialist construction and international career of the concept "bourgeois feminism"', *American Historical Review*, 112, 1 (2007): 131–58.

Feminism, nationalism and internationalism

The complex relationship between feminism and nationalism is explored in: Richard J. Evans, *The Feminists: Women's Emancipation Movements in Europe, America and Australasia, 1840–1920* (1977); Susan Zimmermann, 'The challenge of multinational Empire for the international women's movement: the Hapsburg monarchy and the development of feminist inter/national politics', *Journal of Women's History*, 17, 2 (2005): 87–117; Mrinalini Sinha, Donna J. Guy and Angela Woollacott (eds), Special Issue on Feminisms and Internationalism, *Gender and History*, 10, 3 (1998) and Margaret Ward, *Unmanageable Revolutionaries. Women and Irish Nationalism* (1983). Kumari Jayawardena examines feminism and nationalism in 12 countries in Asia and the Middle East in *Feminism and Nationalism in the Third World* (1986).

The relationship between nationalism, internationalism and feminism in the inter-war period is the subject of an important special issue of *Gender and History*, 10, 3 (1998). The debates are explored in the introduction written by the editors: Mrinalini Sinha, Donna J. Guy and Angela Woollacott, 'Introduction: why feminisms and internationalism?'. Kumari Jayawardena, *Feminism and Nationalism in the Third World* (1986) provides a comparison of several countries in Asia. The complicated relationship between Islam and women's rights, in particular the relationship between Westernization and feminism, is explored in: Margot Badran, *Feminists, Islam and Nation: Gender and the Making of Modern Egypt*, (Princeton, NJ, 1995) and Leila Ahmed, *Women and Gender in Islam* (New Haven, CT, 1992).

International women's organizations formed in Europe and North America have been the subject of a comprehensive study by Leila Rupp, *Worlds of Women: The Making of an International Women's Movement* (Princeton, NJ, 1997). See also Leila Rupp, 'Feminisms and internationalism: a view from the centre', *Gender and History*, 10, 3 (1998). For women's link with the League of Nations, see Carole Miller, 'Geneva – the key to equality: inter-war feminists and the League of Nations', *Women's History Review*, 3, 2 (1994): 218–245; For international organizations outside Europe, see Christine Ehrick, '"Madrinas and missionaries": Uruguay and the Pan-American Women's Movement', *Gender and History*, 10, 3 (1998); Angela Woollacott, 'Inventing Commonwealth and Pan-Pacific feminisms: Australian women's internationalist activism in the 1920s–30s', *Gender and History*, 10, 3 (1998). The special issue edited by Ellen Carol Dubois and Katie Oliviero, 'Circling the Globe: International feminism reconsidered', *Women's Studies International Forum*, 32, 1 (2009), has essays on women's activism in a variety of international organizations.

The special issue of *Women's History Review*, 19, 4 (2010) on International Feminisms, spans the nineteenth and twentieth centuries and includes articles on transnational feminist connections, national comparisons and international women's organizations.

Feminism, imperialism and colonialism

Studies of Western feminist involvement in the project of imperialism and colonialism reveal the multiple ways in which the local, the national and the global intersect. They also draw attention to the ethnocentrism and racism of Western feminism. See, for example, Catherine Hall, Keith Mclelland and Jane Rendall (eds), *Defining the Victorian Nation: Class, Race, Gender and the Reform Act of 1867* (Cambridge, 2000); Clare Midgley, 'White women, "race" and Empire', in June Purvis (ed.) *Women's History. Britain, 1850–1945* (1995). Key texts for understanding the relationship between feminist campaigners, colonialism and imperialism are: Antoinette Burton, *Burdens of History: British Feminists, Indian Women and Imperial Power, 1865–1914* (Chapel Hill, NC, 1994); Barbara Ramusack, 'Cultural missionaries, maternal imperialists, feminist allies: British women activists in India, 1865–1945', *Women's Studies International Forum*, 13, 2 (1990); Mineke Bosch, 'Colonial dimensions of Dutch women's suffrage; Aletta Jacobs's travel letters from Africa and Asia, 1911–12', *Journal of Women's History*, 11, 2 (1999).

The complicated relationship between feminists in the colonies and their counterparts in the imperial heartland is examined in Elizabeth Thompson, *Colonial Citizens: Republican Rights, Paternal Privilege and Gender in French Syria and Lebanon* (New York, 2000) and Ian C. Fletcher, Laura E. Nym Mayhall and Philippa Levine (eds), *Women's Suffrage in the British Empire: Citizenship, Nation and Race* (2002). The complexities of race are also considered in the latter and in: Vron Ware, *Beyond the Pale. White Women, Racism and History* (1992); Cheryl Walker, *The Women's Suffrage Movement in South Africa* (Cape Town, 1979); Marilyn Lake, 'The ambiguities for feminists of national belonging: race and gender in the imagined Australian community', in Ida Blom, Karen Hagemann and Catherine Hall (eds), *Gendered Nations: Nationalisms and Gender Order in the Long Nineteenth Century* (Oxford, 2000). Lake suggests that feminist concern with Aboriginal women led them to recognize their country's racism, whereas Woollacott (cited above) is more critical.

Women's movement in Europe and North America between the wars

For different views of the impact of war on British feminists see Johanna Alberti, *Beyond Suffrage: Feminists in War and Peace, 1914–28* (Houndmills, 1989) and Susan Kingsley Kent, *Making Peace: The Reconstruction of Gender in Inter-War Britain* (Princeton, NJ, 1993). A stimulating re-assessment of what suffrage campaigners in Britain hoped to achieve once the vote was won is put forward by Pat Thane, 'What Difference Did the Vote Make', in Amanda Vickery (ed.), *Women, Privilege and Power. British Politics 1750 to the Present* (Stanford, CA, 2001). Cheryl Law, *Suffrage and Power: The Women's Movement 1918–1928* (1998) examines the neglected campaign to extend the franchise to all adult women in Britain in the 1920s. The various contributors to Harold L. Smith (ed.), *British Feminism in the Twentieth Century* (Aldershot, 1990) urge caution in drawing a rigid distinction between 'old' and 'new' feminists and also between concepts of equality and difference in the inter-war years. Caitriona Beaumont extends the discussion about definitions of feminism by arguing that a wider range of women's organizations should be included: 'Citizens not feminists: the boundary negotiated between citizenship and feminism by mainstream women's organisations in England, 1928–39', *Women's History Review*, 9, 2 (2000).

The debates in European inter-war feminism about social welfare, protective legislation and reproductive rights are explored in Karen Offen, *European Feminisms* (Stanford, CA, 2000) and Susan Pedersen, *Family Dependence and the Origins of the Welfare State: Britain and France 1914–1945* (Cambridge, 1993). The relationship between feminism, social democratic parties and welfare is explored in a series of essays in Helmut Gruber and Pamela Graves (eds), *Women and Socialism, Socialism and Women. Europe Between the Two World Wars* (Oxford, 1998). See also, Pat Thane, 'Women in the British Labour Party and the construction of state welfare', in Seth Koven and Sonya Michel (eds) *Mothers of a New World: Maternalist Politics and the Origins of the Welfare States* (1993). For a comparison of social democratic parties in Norway and Sweden, see Gro Hagemann, 'Citizenship and social order: Gender politics in twentieth century Norway and Sweden', *Women's History Review*, 11, 3 (2002). The conflict in the United States over protective legislation is discussed in Barbara Ryan, *Feminism and the Women's Movement. Dynamics of Change in Social Movement, Ideology and Activism* (1992). Christine Bolt, *Sisterhood Questioned: Race, Class and Internationalism in the American and British Women's Movements c. 1800s–1970* (2004) discusses feminism and peace.

Women's movement in South America

For important comparative studies of the women's movement in South America, see Asunción Lavrin, *Women, Feminism and Social Change in Argentina, Chile and Uruguay, 1890–1940* (Lincoln, 1995) and Francesca Miller, *Latin American Women and the Search for Social Justice* (Hanover, NH, 1991). Individual countries are covered in June Hahner, *Emancipating the Female Sex: The Struggle for Women's Rights in Brazil, 1850–1940* (Durham, NC, 1990); Yamila Azize-Vargas, 'The emergence of feminism in Puerto Rico, 1870–1930', in Vikki L. Ruiz and Ellen C. DuBois (eds), *Unequal Sisters: A Multicultural Reader in US Women's History*, 3rd edn (2000); Anna Macías, *Against All Odds: The Feminist Movement in Mexico to 1940* (Westport, CT, 1982) and Manifran Carlson, *Feminismó! The Women's Movement in Argentina from its Beginnings to Eva Perón*, (Chicago, 1988).

Second wave feminism

An analysis of the women's movement in individual countries in the 1950s and 60s can be found in: Claire Duchen and Irene Bandhauer Schöffmann (eds), *When the War Was Over: Women, War and Peace in Europe, 1940–1956* (2000); Monica Threlfall (ed.), *Mapping the Women's Movement* (1996); Gabriele Griffin and Rosi Braidotti (eds), *Thinking Differently. A Reader in European Women's Studies* (2002) and Martin Pugh, *Women and the Women's Movement in Britain, 1914–1959* (Houndmills, 1992).

The characteristics of 'second wave' feminism are discussed in: Drude Dahlerup (ed.), *The New Women's Movement* (1986); Sheila Rowbotham, *The Past is Before Us. Feminism in Action since the 1960s* (1989); Jeska Rees, 'A look back at anger: the women's liberation movement in 1978', *Women's History Review*, 19, 3 (2010): 337–56; Françoise Picq, 'The history of the feminist movement in France', in Griffin and Braidotti (eds), *Thinking Differently* (above); and Ute Frevert, *Women in German History. From Bourgeois Emancipation to Sexual Liberation* (Oxford, 1989); Sara Evans, *Personal Politics: The Roots of Women's Liberation in the Civil Rights Movement and the New Left* (New York, 1980); Marilyn Lake, *Getting Equal: the History of Australian Feminism* (St Leonard's, 1999); Gisela Kaplan, *The Meagre Harvest: The Australian Women's Movement, 1950s–1990s* (St Leonard's, 1996). For a discussion of 'second wave' feminism in the context of left-wing politics in Europe, see Geoffrey Eley, *Forging Democracy. The History of the Left in Europe, 1850–2000* (Oxford, 2002).

Key texts of 'second wave' feminism include: Simone de Beauvoir, *The Second Sex*, (1953) (Translation: H.M. Parshley); Betty Friedan, *The Feminine Mystique* (New York, 1963); Germaine Greer, *The Female Eunuch* (1971); Juliet Mitchell, *Woman's Estate*, (Harmondsworth, 1971); bel hooks, *Feminist Theory from Margin to Centre* (Boston, 1984) and Kate Millett, *Sexual Politics* (New York, 1970).

For an overview of feminist theories in this period, see Imelda Whelehan, *Modern Feminist Thought. From the Second Wave to 'Post Feminism'* (Edinburgh, 1995): Gisela Kaplan, *Contemporary Western European Feminism* 1992) and Jane Freedman, *Feminism* (Buckingham, 2001). The attempts by feminists to integrate Marxism and feminism are explored in Heidi Hartmann, 'The unhappy marriage of Marxism and Feminism: towards a more progressive union', in Lydia Sargent (ed.), *Women and Revolution* (1981). Marxist feminists differed over whether patriarchy was a useful tool of analysis, for example, see Judith Newton, Mary Ryan and Judith Walkowitz (eds), *Sex and Class in Women's History* (1983) and Sheila Rowbotham, 'The trouble with patriarchy', in Mary Evans (ed.) *The Women Question* (1982). For a discussion of the concept of patriarchy, see Sylvia Walby, *Theorizing Patriarchy* (Oxford, 1990). Mary Maynard provides a useful explanation of the 'three strands' of feminist thought and also gives a critique of these categories: 'Women's Studies' in Stevi Jackson and Jackie Jones (eds) *Contemporary Feminist Theories* (Edinburgh, 1998) and 'Beyond the "Big Three": the development of feminist theory into the 1990s', *Women's History Review*, 4, 3 (1995). Jane Aaron and Sylvia Walby (eds) *Out of the Margins: Women's Studies in the Nineties* (1992) consider the extent to which, after two decades of scholarship, academic studies had been influenced by feminism.

Feminist theory and practice in Third World countries is discussed in: Chandra Talpade Mohanty, Ann Russo and Lourdes Torres (eds), *Third World Women and the Politics of Feminism* (Bloomington, IN, 1991); Haleh Afshar (ed.), *Women and Politics in the Third World* (1996); Leila Ahmed, *Women and Gender in Islam* (New Haven, CT, 1992); Barbara J. Nelson and Najma Chowdhury (eds), *Women and Politics Worldwide* (New Haven, CT, 1994); Jane S. Jaquette (ed.), *The Women's Movement in Latin America. Participation and Democracy* (Boulder, CO, 2nd edn 1994); Victoria E. Rodriguez, *Women's Participation in Mexican Political Life* (Boulder, CO, 1998); Rosalyn Terborg-Penn and Andrea Benton Rushing (eds), *Women in Africa and the African Diaspora* (Washington, DC, 1996); Z.A. Mangaliso, 'Gender and nation building in South Africa', in Lois A. West (ed.), *Feminist Nationalisms* (1997) and Maxine Molyneux, 'Mobilisation without emancipation? Women's interest, the state and revolution in Nicaragua', *Feminist Studies*, 11, 2 (1985).

Post-modernism and backlash

Key texts exploring the implications of post-modernism for feminist theory and practice are: Denise Riley, *Am I That Name? Feminism and the Category of 'Women' in History* (1988) and Joan Scott, *Gender and the Politics of History* (New York, 1988). The implications of their work for feminist history is discussed in June Purvis, 'From "women worthies" to post-structuralism? Debate and controversy in women's history in Britain', in June Purvis (ed.), *Women's History. Britain, 1850–1945* (1995). The 'backlash' against feminism in the late 1980s and 1990s is discussed in: Florence Rush, 'The many faces of backlash', in Dorchen E.H. Lendholt and Janice G. Raymond (eds), *The Sexual Liberal and the Attack on Feminism* (Oxford, 1990) and Susan Faludi, *Backlash: The Undeclared War Against Women* (1991). Two stimulating but controversial feminist texts in the 1990s were: Naomi Wolf, *The Beauty Myth: How Images of Beauty Are Used Against Women* (New York, 1991) and Germaine Greer, *The Whole Woman* (1999).

For the politics of women's rights in post communist states, see Susan Gal and Gail Kligman (eds), *Reproducing Gender: Politics, Publics and Everyday Life after Socialism* (Princeton, 2000); Chris Corrin (ed.), *'Superwoman' and the Double Burden: Women's Experience of Change in Central and Eastern Europe and the Former Soviet Union* (Toronto, 1992); Linda

Racioppi and Katherine O'Sullivan, *Women's Activism in Contemporary Russia* (Philadelphia, 1997); Mihaela Miroiu, '"Not the right moment!" Women and the politics of endless delay in Romania', *Women's History Review*, 19, 4 (2010), 575–93.

For a discussion of the continuing vitality of feminism in the 1990s and beyond, see Gabriele Griffin (ed.), *Feminist Activism in the 1990s* (1995); Breda Gray and Louise Ryan, 'The politics of Irish identity and the interconnections between feminism, nationhood and colonialism', in Ruth Roach Pierson and Nupur Chaudhuri (eds), *Nation, Empire, Colony: Historicizing Gender and Race* (Bloomington, IN, 1998); Vera Mackie, 'Feminist critiques of modern Japanese politics', in Monica Threlfall (ed.), *Mapping the Women's Movement* (1996); Sara Mills 'Post-colonial feminist theory' and Stevi Jackson and Jackie Jones, 'Thinking for ourselves: an introduction to feminist theorising', in Stevi Jackson and Jackie Jones (eds), *Contemporary Feminist Theories* (Edinburgh, 1998).

Global dimensions of feminism are considered in: Amrita Basu (ed.), *The Challenge of Local Feminisms* (Oxford, 1995). Information on women's lives worldwide can be found in Janet Mancini Billson and Carolyn Fluehr-Lobban (eds), *Female Well-Being. Toward a Global Theory of Social Change* (2005).

For an overview of contemporary feminist debates, see Valerie Bryson, *Feminist Debates; Issues of Theory and Political Practice* (Houndmills, 1999); Sarah Gamble (ed.), *Feminism and Postfeminism* (2001); Stacy Gillis, Gillian Howie and Rebecca Munford (eds), *Third Wave Feminism: A Critical Exploration* (Houndmills, 2004).

References

Aerts, Mieke (2005) 'Feminism from Amsterdam to Brussels in 1891: political transfer as transformation', *European Review of History*, 12, 2: 367–82.

Afshar, Haleh (ed.) (1996) *Women and Politics in the Third World*, London: Routledge.

Ahmed, Leila (1992) *Women and Gender in Islam*, New Haven, CT: Yale University Press.

Alberti, Johanna (1989) *Beyond Suffrage: Feminists in War and Peace, 1914–28*, Houndmills: Macmillan.

Alvarez, Sonia E. (1994) 'The (trans)formation of feminism(s) and gender politics in democratizing Brazil', in Jaquette, J.S. (ed.) *The Women's Movement in Latin America: Participation and Democracy*, Boulder, CO: Westview Press, pp. 13–63.

Anagol, Padma (2010) 'Feminist inheritances and foremothers: the beginnings of feminism in modern India', *Women's History Review*, 19, 4: 523–46.

Badran, Margot (1995) *Feminists, Islam and Nation: Gender and the Making of Modern Egypt*, Princeton, NJ: Princeton University Press.

Banks, Olive (1980) *Faces of Feminism*, Oxford: Martin Robertson.

Billson, Janet Mancini and Fluehr-Lobban, Carolyn (eds) (2005) *Female Well-Being: Toward a Global Theory of Social Change*, London: Zed Books.

Blom, Ida (1998) Conference report, Gendered Nations: Nationalisms and Gender Order in the Long Nineteenth Century – International Comparisons, www.h-netmsu.edu/~women/threads/report-nation.html

Bosch, Mineke, with Kloosterman, Anne Marie (eds) (1990) *Politics and Friendship: Letters from the International Woman Suffrage Alliance, 1902–1942*, Columbus, OH: Columbus University Press.

Bosch, Mineke (1999) 'Colonial dimensions of Dutch women's suffrage: Aletta Jacobs's travel letters from Africa and Asia, 1911–12', *Journal of Women's History*, 11, 2: 199–220.

Bosch, Mineke (2009) 'Between entertainment and nationalist politics: the uses of folklore in the spectacle of the International Woman Suffrage Alliance', *Women's Studies International Forum*, 32: 4–12. [The quotation is from Mary Peck (1944) *Carrie Chapman Catt: A Biography*, New York: H.W. Wilson, p. 435.]

Burton, Antoinette (2002) '"States of injury": Josephine Butler on slavery, citizenship, and the Boer War', in Fletcher, Ian C., Mayhall, Laura E.N. and Levine, Philippa (eds) *Women's Suffrage in the British Empire: Citizenship, Nation and Race*, London: Routledge, pp. 338–61.

Bush, Julia (2002) 'British women's anti-suffragism and the forward policy, 1908–14', *Women's History Review*, 11, 3: 431–54.

Caine, Barbara (1992) *Victorian Feminists*, Oxford: Oxford University Press.

Caine, Barbara (1997) *English Feminism, 1780–1980*, Oxford: Oxford University Press.

Cobbe, Frances Power (1904) *The Life of Frances Power Cobbe: As Told By Herself*, London: S. Sonnenschein.

De Beauvoir, Simone (1953) *The Second Sex*, London: Jonathan Cape.

Dubois, Ellen Carol and Oliviero, Katie (2009) 'Circling the globe: international feminism reconsidered', *Women's Studies International Forum*, 32, 1.

Edmondson, Linda H. (1992) *Women and Society in Russia and the Soviet Union*, Cambridge: Cambridge University Press.

Ehrick, Christina (1998) '"Madrinas and missionaries": Uruguay and the pan-American women's movement', *Gender and History*, 10, 3: 406–24.

Eley, Geoffrey (2002) *Forging Democracy: The History of the Left in Europe, 1850–2000*, Oxford: Oxford University Press.

Evans, Richard J. (1977) *The Feminists: Women's Emancipation Movements in Europe, America and Australasia, 1840–1920*, London: Croom Helm.

Fawcett, Millicent (1913) 'Introduction' to Helena M. Swanwick, *The Future of the Women's Movement*, London: G. Bell, p. xii; quoted in Offen (2000), p. 2.

Friedan, Betty (1963) *The Feminine Mystique*, New York: Dell.

Gadant, Monique (1995) *Le Nationalism Algérien et les Femmes*, Paris: Editions l'Harmattan.

Gaer, Felice (2009) 'Women, international law and international institutions: the case of the United Nations', *Women's Studies International Forum*, 32: 60–66.

Gamble, Susan (ed.) (2001) *Feminism and Postfeminism*, London: Routledge.

Gillis, Stacy and Munford, Rebecca (2004) 'An interview with Elaine Showalter', in Gillis, Stacy, Howie, Gillian and Munford, Rebecca (eds), *Third Wave Feminism: A Critical Exploration*, Houndmills: Palgrave Macmillan, p. 60.

Gleadle, Kathryn (2001) 'British women and radical politics in the Late Nonconformist Enlightenment, c. 1780–1830', in Vickery, Amanda (ed.), *Women, Privilege and Power: British Politics, 1750 to the Present*, Stanford, CA: Stanford University Press, pp. 123–51.

Greer, Germaine (1971) *The Female Eunuch*, London: Paladin.

Greer, Germaine (1999) *The Whole Woman*, London: Doubleday.

Grimshaw, Patricia (1987) *Women's Suffrage in New Zealand*, Auckland: University of Auckland Press.

Hagemann, Gro (2002) 'Citizenship and social order: gender politics in twentieth century Norway and Sweden', *Women's History Review*, 11, 3: 417–29.

Hall, Catherine (1991) 'Politics, post-structuralism and feminist history', *Gender and History*, 3, 2: 204–10.

Hannam, June and Hunt, Karen (2001) *Socialist Women: Britain, 1880s–1920s*, London: Routledge.

Hause, Stephen C. with Kenney, Anne R. (1984) *Women's Suffrage and Social Politics in the French Third Republic*, Princeton, NJ: Princeton University Press.

Holton, Sandra Stanley (1994) 'From anti-slavery to suffrage militancy: the Bright circle, Elizabeth Cady Stanton and the British women's movement', in Daley, Caroline and Nolan, Melanie (eds), *Suffrage and Beyond: International Feminist Perspectives*, Auckland: Auckland University Press.

Holton, Sandra Stanley (1996) *Suffrage Days: Stories from the Women's Suffrage Movement*, London: Routledge.

hooks, bell (1982) *Ain't I a Woman*, London: Pluto.

Hunt, Karen (1996) *Equivocal Feminists. The Social Democratic Federation and the Woman Question, 1884–1911*, Cambridge: Cambridge University Press.

Jackson, Stevi and Jones, Jackie (1998) 'Thinking for ourselves: an introduction to feminist theorising', in Jackson, Stevi and Jones, Jackie (eds) *Contemporary Feminist Theories*, Edinburgh: Edinburgh University Press, pp. 1–10.

Jacquette, Jane S. (ed.) (1994) *The Women's Movement in Latin America: Participation and Democracy*, Boulder, CO: Westview Press.

Jayawardena, Kumari (1986) *Feminism and Nationalism in the Third World*, London: Zed Books.

Kaplan, Gisela (1992) *Contemporary Western European Feminism*, London: UCL Press.

Kaplan, Temma (1992) 'Female consciousness and collective action: the case of Barcelona, 1910–18', *Signs*, 7: 545–66.

Kean, Hilda (1994) 'Searching for the present in past defeat: the construction of historical and political identity in British feminism in the 1920s and 30s', *Women's History Review*, 3, 1: 57–80.

Kent, Susan Kingsley (1993) *Making Peace: The Reconstruction of Gender in Inter-War Britain*, Princeton, NJ: Princeton University Press.

Lavrin, Asunción (1995) *Women, Feminism and Social Change in Argentina, Chile and Uruguay, 1890–1940*, Lincoln: University of Nebraska Press.

Legates, Marlene (2001) *In Their Time: A History of Feminism in Western Society*, London: Routledge.

Lerner, Gerda (1979) *The Majority Finds Its Past: Placing Women in History*, Oxford: Oxford University Press.

Levine, Philippa (1990) 'Love, feminism and friendship in later nineteenth-century England', *Women's Studies International Forum*, 13, 1/2: 63–78.

Liddington, Jill and Norris, Jill (1978) *One Hand Tied Behind Us: The Rise of the Women's Suffrage Movement*, London: Virago.

Mayhall, Laura E.N. (2003) *The Militant Suffrage Movement: Citizenship and Resistance in Britain, 1860–1930*, Oxford: Oxford University Press.

Maynard, Mary (1998) 'Women's studies', in Jackson, S. and Jones, J. (eds) *Contemporary Feminist Theories*, Edinburgh: Edinburgh University Press, pp. 247–59.

Midgley, Clare (1992) *Women Against Slavery: The British Campaigns, 1780–1870*, London: Routledge.

Midgley, Clare (2001) 'British women, women's rights and empire, 1790–1850', in Grimshaw, Patricia, Holmes, Katie and Lake, Marilyn (eds), *Women's Rights and Human Rights*, Houndmills: Palgrave Macmillan, pp. 3–15.

Mill, John Stuart (1869; 1985) *On the Subjection of Women*, London: Dent.

Miller, Carole (1994) 'Geneva – the key to equality: inter-war feminists and the League of Nations', *Women's History Review*, 3, 2: 218–45.

Millett, Kate (1969) *Sexual Politics*, London: Rupert Hart-Davis.

Mitchell, Juliet (1971) *Woman's Estate*, Harmondsworth: Penguin.

Offen, Karen (2000) *European Feminisms, 1700–1950: A Political History*, Stanford, CA: Stanford University Press.

Outram, Dorinda (1995) *The Enlightenment*, Cambridge: Cambridge University Press.

Pankhurst, Sylvia, E. (1931) *The Suffragette Movement: An Intimate Account of Persons and Ideals*, London: Longmans.

Pateman, Carole (1992) 'Equality, difference and subordination: the politics of motherhood and women's citizenship', in Bock, Gisela and James, Susan (eds), *Beyond Equality and Difference: Citizenship, Feminist Politics and Female Subjectivity*, London: Routledge, pp. 17–31.

Phillip, Thomas (1978) 'Feminism and nationalist politics in Egypt', in Beck, Lois and Keddie, Nikki (eds), *Women in the Muslim World*, Cambridge, MA: Harvard University Press, pp. 277–94.

Picq, Françoise (2002) 'The history of the feminist movement in France', in Griffin, Gabriele and Braidotti, Rosi (eds), *Thinking Differently: A Reader in European Women's Studies*, London: Zed Books, pp. 313–20.

Rendall, Jane (1985) *The Origins of Modern Feminism: Women in Britain, France and the United States, 1780–1860*, Houndmills: Macmillan.

Rendall, Jane (2001) 'John Stuart Mill, liberal politics and the movements for women's suffrage, 1865–1973', in Vickery, Amanda (ed.), *Women, Privilege and Power: British Politics, 1750 to the Present*, Stanford, CA: Stanford University Press.

Riley, Denise (1988) *Am I That Name? Feminism and the 'Category' of Women in History*, Houndmills: Macmillan.

Rowbotham, Sheila (1973) *Hidden from History: 300 Years of Women's Oppression and the Fight Against It*, London: Pluto.

Rowbotham, Sheila (1989) *The Past Is Before Us: Feminism in Action since the 1960s*, London: Pandora.

Rupp, Leila (1997) *Worlds of Women: The Making of an International Women's Movement*, Princeton, NJ: Princeton University Press.

Sandell, Marie (2007) 'International sisterhood? International women's organisations and cooperation in the interwar period', PhD thesis, Royal Holloway, University of London.

Scully, Pamela (2000) 'White maternity and black infancy: the rhetoric of race in the South African women's suffrage movement, 1890–1930', in Fletcher, Ian C., Mayhall, Laura E.N. and Levine, Philippa (eds), *Women's Suffrage in the British Empire: Citizenship, Nation and Race*, London: Routledge.

Sinha, Mrinalini (2000) 'Suffragism and internationalism: the enfranchisement of British and Indian women under an imperial state', in Fletcher, Ian C., Mayhall, Laura E.N. and Levine, Philippa (eds), *Women's Suffrage in the British Empire: Citizenship, Nation and Race*, London: Routledge.

Sinha, Mrinalini, Guy, Donna J. and Woollacott, Angela (1998) 'Introduction: why feminisms and internationalism?', *Gender and History*, 10, 3.

Smith, Harold L. (1984) 'Sex vs class: British feminists and the labour movement, 1919–29', *Historian*, 47.

Smith, Harold L. (ed.) (1990) *British Feminism in the Twentieth Century*, Aldershot: Edward Elgar.

Sowerwine, Charles (1987) 'The socialist women's movement from 1850–1940', in Bridenthal, Renate, Koontz, Claudia and Stuard, Susan (eds), *Becoming Visible: Women in European History*, Boston, MA: Houghton Mifflin.

Spencer, Jane (2004) 'Introduction: genealogies', in Cullis, Stacy, Howie, Gillian and Munford, Rebecca (eds), *Third Wave Feminism: A Critical Exploration*, Houndmills: Palgrave Macmillan.

Steady, Filomina C. (1996) 'African feminism: a worldwide perspective', in Terborg-Penn, Rosalyn and Rushing, Andrea B. (eds), *Women in Africa and the African Diaspora*, Washington, DC: Harvard University Press, 1996.

Summers, Anne (2000) *Female Lives, Moral States*, Newbury: Threshold Press.

Taylor, Barbara (1983) *Eve and the New Jerusalem. Socialism and Feminism in the Nineteenth Century*, London: Virago.

Thane, Pat (1993) 'Women in the British Labour Party and the construction of state welfare', in Koven, Seth and Michel, Sonya (eds), *Mothers of a New World: Maternalist Politics and the Origins of the Welfare States*, London: Routledge.

Thane, Pat (2001) 'What difference did the vote make?', in Vickery, Amanda (ed.) *Women, Privilege and Power: British Politics 1750 to the Present*, Stanford, CA: Stanford University Press.

Thompson, Elizabeth (2000) *Colonial Citizens: Republican Rights, Paternal Privilege and Gender in French Syria and Lebanon*, New York: Columbia University Press.

Tickner, Lisa (1987) *The Spectacle of Women: Imagery of the Suffrage Campaign, 1907–1914*, London: Chatto and Windus.

Whelehan, Imelda (1995) *Modern Feminist Thought: from the Second Wave to 'Post Feminism'*, Edinburgh: Edinburgh University Press.

Wolf, Naomi (1991) *The Beauty Myth: How Images of Beauty Are Used Against Women*, New York: Vintage.

Wolf, Naomi (1993) *Fire within Fire: New Female Power and How It Will Change the Twenty-First Century*, Toronto, Ontario: Random House.

Wollstonecraft, Mary (1792; 1993) *A Vindication of the Rights of Woman*, Harmondsworth: Penguin.

Woollacott, Angela (1998) 'Inventing Commonwealth and pan-Pacific feminisms: Australian women's internationalist activism in the 1920s–30s', *Gender and History*, 10, 3.

Yeo, Eileen Janes (ed.) (1997) *Mary Wollstonecraft and 200 Years of Feminisms*, London: Rivers Oram.

Index

The Robber Bride

BOOKS BY MARGARET ATWOOD

Fiction
The Edible Woman
Surfacing
Lady Oracle
Life Before Man
Bodily Harm
The Handmaid's Tale
Cat's Eye
The Robber Bride
Alias Grace

Short Fiction
Dancing Girls
Bluebeard's Egg
Wilderness Tips
Good Bones

Poetry
The Circle Game
The Animals in That Country
The Journals of Susanna Moodie
Procedures for Underground Power Politics
You Are Happy
Two-Headed Poems
Selected Poems
True Stories
Interlunar
Selected Poems II
Morning in the Burned House

Nonfiction
Survival: A Thematic Guide to Canadian Literature
Second Words
Strange Things: The Malevolent North in Canadian Literature

For Children
Princess Prunella and the Purple Peanut

The Robber Bride

Margaret Atwood

SEAL BOOKS
Toronto

THE ROBBER BRIDE
A Seal Book/published by arrangement with McClelland & Stewart, Inc.

PUBLISHING HISTORY
McClelland & Stewart edition published 1993
Seal edition/November 1994: reissued 1999

For information address:
Seal Books
105 Bond Street
Toronto, Ontario M5B 1Y3

ISBN 0-7704-2821-5

Printed and bound in Canada

UNI   10 9 8 7 6 5 4 3 2 1

For Graeme and Jess,
and for Ruth, Phoebe, Rosie, and Anna.

For Absent Friends.

Acknowledgements

I would like to thank the following for their help: my agents Phoebe Larmore and Vivienne Schuster; my editors Ellen Seligman, Nan A. Talese, and Liz Calder; David Kimmel, for helping with some of the historical details; Barbara Czarnecki, Judi Levita, Marly Rusoff, Sarah Beale, and Claudia Hill-Norton; Joan Sheppard, Donya Peroff, and Sarah Cooper; Michael Bradley, Garry Foster, Kathy Minialoff, Gene Goldberg, and Alison Parker; Rose Tornato. Thanks also to Charles and Julie Woodsworth, to Dorris Heffron, and to John and Christiane O'Keeffe, for premises rendered.

John Keegan's *The Face of Battle* and *The Mask of Command* were most useful for background, as were *None Is Too Many* by Irving Abella and Harold Troper and *The War Against the Jews,* by Lucy S. Dawidowicz; and also for specific battles and events, Richard Erdoes's *A.D. 1000* and *The Unknown South of France* by Henry and Margaret Reuss. The assassination of ballistics expert Gerald Bull is dealt with in *Bull's Eye,* by James Adams, and in *Wilderness of Mirrors,* by Dale Grant.

The image of the body as a lampshade is courtesy Lenore Mendelson Atwood; the expression "brain snot" is courtesy E.J.A. Gibson. The red-and-white footprints recall a story told to me by Earle Birney; the toboggan incident and the black-painted apartment, from Graeme Gibson; the ghost as dry rice was suggested by an episode recounted by P.K. Page; the notion of a flesh dress came from James Reaney's poem "Doomsday, or the Red-Headed Woodpecker"; the tale of the heroic German aunt was suggested partly by Thomas Karl Maria Schwarz; and the professor who disallowed military essay topics for women from an anecdote related by Susan Crean.

Zenia is pronounced with a long "e," as in "seen"; *Charis* with a hard "c" as in "karma." The Teutones (second century B.C.) are distinct from the Teutons (tenth century A.D.)

Contents

A rattlesnake that doesn't bite teaches you nothing.

—*Jessamyn West*

Only what is entirely lost demands to be endlessly named:
there is a mania to call the lost thing until it returns.

— *Günter Grass*

Illusion is the first of all pleasures.

—*Oscar Wilde*

Onset

1

The story of Zenia ought to begin when Zenia began. It must have been someplace long ago and distant in space, thinks Tony; someplace bruised, and very tangled. A European print, hand-tinted, ochre-coloured, with dusty sunlight and a lot of bushes in it—bushes with thick leaves and ancient twisted roots, behind which, out of sight in the undergrowth and hinted at only by a boot protruding, or a slack hand, something ordinary but horrifying is taking place.

Or this is the impression Tony has been left with. But so much has been erased, so much has been bandaged over, so much deliberately snarled, that Tony isn't sure any longer which of Zenia's accounts of herself was true. She can hardly ask now, and even if she could, Zenia wouldn't answer. Or she would lie. She would lie earnestly, with a catch in her voice, a quaver of suppressed grief, or she would lie haltingly, as if confessing; or she would lie with a cool, defiant anger, and Tony would believe her. She has before.

Pick any strand and snip, and history comes unravelled. This is how Tony begins one of her more convoluted lectures, the one on the dynamics of spontaneous massacres. The metaphor is of weaving or else of knitting, and of sewing scissors. She likes using it: she likes the faint shock on the faces of her listeners. It's the mix of domestic image and mass bloodshed that does it to them; a mix that would have been appreciated by Zenia, who enjoyed such turbulence, such violent contradictions. More than enjoyed: created. *Why* is still unclear.

Tony doesn't know why she feels compelled to know. Who cares why, at this distance? A disaster is a disaster; those hurt by it remain hurt, those killed remain killed, the rubble remains rubble. Talk of causes is beside the point. Zenia was a bad business, and should be left alone. Why try to decode her motives?

But Zenia is also a puzzle, a knot: if Tony could just find a loose end and pull, a great deal would come free, for everyone involved, and for herself as well. Or this is her hope. She has a historian's belief in the salutary power of explanations.

Where to start is the problem, because nothing begins when it begins and nothing's over when it's over, and everything needs a preface: a preface, a postscript, a chart of simultaneous events. History is a construct, she tells her students. Any point of entry is possible and all choices are arbitrary. Still, there are definitive moments, moments we use as references, because they break our sense of continuity, they change the direction of time. We can look at these events and we can say that after them things were never the same again. They provide beginnings for us, and endings too. Births and deaths, for instance, and marriages. And wars.

It's the wars that interest Tony, despite her lace-edged collars. She likes clear outcomes.

So did Zenia, or so Tony thought once. Now, she can hardly tell.

An arbitrary choice then, a definitive moment: October 23, 1990. It's a bright clear day, unseasonably warm. It's a Tuesday. The Soviet bloc is crumbling, the old maps are dissolving, the Eastern tribes are on the move again across the shifting borders. There's trouble in the Gulf, the real estate market is crashing, and a large hole has developed in the ozone layer. The sun moves into Scorpio, Tony has lunch at the Toxique with her two friends Roz and Charis, a slight breeze blows in over Lake Ontario, and Zenia returns from the dead.

The Toxique

2

Tony

Tony gets up at six-thirty, as she always does. West sleeps on, groaning a little. Probably in his dreams he's shouting; sounds in dreams are always louder. Tony inspects his sleeping face, his angular jaw-line relaxed to softness, his unearthly blue hermit's eyes so gently closed. She's happy he's still alive: women live longer than men and men have weak hearts, sometimes they just keel over, and although she and West aren't old—they're hardly old at all—still, women her age have awakened in the morning to find dead men beside them. Tony does not consider this a morbid thought.

She's happy in a more general way, too. She's happy that West is on this earth at all, and in this house, and that he goes to sleep every night beside her and not somewhere else. Despite everything, despite Zenia, he's still here. It seems a miracle really. Some days she can't get over it.

Quietly, so as not to wake him, she gropes for her

glasses on the night-table, then slides down out of the bed. She pulls on her Viyella dressing gown and her cotton socks and her grey wool work socks over them, and stuffs her bundled feet into her slippers. She suffers from cold feet, a sign of low blood pressure. The slippers are in the form of raccoons, and were given to her by Roz, many years ago, for reasons best known to Roz. They're the duplicates of the slippers Roz gave her eight-year-old twins at the time; they're even the same foot size. The raccoons are somewhat ratty by now and one of them is missing an eye, but Tony has never been good at throwing things out.

On her insulated feet she makes her way stealthily down the hall to her study. She prefers to spend an hour in there first thing every morning; she finds it concentrates her mind. There's an eastern exposure, so she catches the sunrise when there is one. Today there is.

Her study has new green curtains in a palm-tree-and-exotic-fruit print, and an easy chair with matching cushions. Roz helped her choose the print, and talked her into paying the price, which was higher than what Tony would have paid if she'd been alone. *Listen to me, sweetie,* said Roz. *Now this—this! is a bargain. Anyway, it's for the place where you think! It's your mental environment! Get rid of those dull old navy blue sailboats! You owe it to yourself.* There are days when Tony is overwhelmed by the trumpet vines and the orange mangoes, or whatever they are; but she's intimidated by interior decoration, and finds Roz's expertise hard to resist.

She feels more at home with the rest of the study. Books and papers are stacked in piles on the carpet; on the wall there's a print of the Battle of Trafalgar, and another one of Laura Secord, in unlikely white, driving her mythical cow through the American lines to warn the British during the War of 1812. Armfuls of dog-eared war memoirs and collections of letters and foxed volumes of front-line reportage by long-forgotten journalists are stuffed into the olive green bookcase, along with several copies of Tony's two published books, *Five Ambushes* and *Four Lost Causes*. *Meticulously researched; a refreshing new interpretation,* say the reviews quoted on the quality paperbacks. *Sensationalistic; overly digressive; marred by obsessive detail,* say those not quoted. Tony's face, owl-eyed and elf-nosed and younger than her face is now, goggles out from the back covers, frowning slightly in an attempt to look substantial.

In addition to a study desk she has an architect's drawing board with a high swivelling stool that renders her instantly taller. She uses it for marking student term papers: she likes to perch up there on the stool, swinging her short legs, with the papers on a slant in front of her, and correct from a judicious distance, as if painting. The truth is that she's getting far-sighted as well as the near-sighted she's always been. Bifocals will soon be her fate.

She marks with her left hand, using different-coloured pencils, which she holds between the fingers of her right hand like brushes: red for bad comments, blue for good ones, orange for spelling mistakes, and mauve for queries. Sometimes she reverses hands. When each paper is finished she drops it onto the floor, making a satisfying flurry. To combat boredom she occasionally reads a few sentences out loud to herself, backwards. *Seigolonhcet gnitepmoc fo ecneics eht si raw fo ecneics eht.* How true. She has said it herself, many times.

Today she marks quickly, today she's synchronized.

Her left hand knows what her right hand is doing. Her two halves are superimposed: there's only a slight penumbra, a slight degree of slippage.

Tony marks papers until quarter to eight. Sunlight floods the room, made golden by the yellow leaves outside; a jet flies over; the garbage truck approaches along the street, clanking like a tank. Tony hears it, slippers hastily down the stairs and into the kitchen, lifts the plastic sack from its bin, twist-ties it, runs to the front door with it, and scampers down the porch steps, hiking up her dressing gown. She has to sprint only a short distance before catching up with the truck. The men grin at her: they've seen her in her dressing gown before. West is supposed to do the garbage, but he forgets.

She goes back to the kitchen and makes the tea, warming the pot, measuring the leaves carefully, timing the steeping with her big-numbers wristwatch. It was Tony's mother who taught her about making tea; one of the few useful things she did teach her. Tony has known how to make tea since she was nine. She can remember standing on the kitchen stool, measuring, pouring, carrying the cup upstairs, tenderly balanced, to where her mother was lying in bed under the sheet, a rounded mound, white as a snowdrift. *How lovely. Put it there.* And finding the cup later, cold, still full.

Begone, Mother, she thinks. *Rehtom, enogeb.* She banishes her, not for the first time.

West always drinks the tea that Tony makes. He always accepts her offerings. When she goes upstairs with his cup he's standing by the back window, looking out over the neglected and derelict autumn yard. (Both of them say they will plant things in it, soon, later. Neither of them does.) He's already dressed: jeans, and a blue sweatshirt that says *Scales & Tails* and has a turtle on it. Some organization devoted to the saving of amphibians and reptiles, which—Tony imagines—doesn't have a very large membership, yet. There are so many other things, these days, that require saving.

"Here's your tea," she says.

West bends in several places, like a camel sitting down, in order to kiss her. She raises herself on tiptoe.

"Sorry about the garbage," he says.

"It's all right," she says, "it wasn't heavy. One egg or two?" Once, during the morning garbage race, she tripped on her dressing gown and took a header down the front steps. Luckily she landed on the bag itself, which burst. She didn't mention this to West, though. She's always careful with him. She knows how frangible he is, how subject to breakage.

3

While boiling the eggs Tony thinks of Zenia. Is it a premonition? Not at all. She frequently thinks of Zenia, more frequently than when Zenia was alive. Zenia dead is less of a threat, and doesn't have to be shoved away, shoved back into the spidery corner where Tony keeps her shadows.

Though even Zenia's name is enough to evoke the old sense of outrage, of humiliation and confused pain. Or at least an echo of it. The truth is that at certain times—early mornings, the middle of the night—she finds it hard to believe that Zenia is really dead. Despite herself, despite the rational part of herself, Tony keeps expecting her to turn up, stroll in through some unlocked door, climb through a window carelessly left open. It seems improbable that she would simply have evaporated, with nothing left over. There was too much of her: all that malign vitality must have gone somewhere.

Tony slides two slices of bread into the toaster, then rummages in the cupboard for the jam. Zenia *is* dead, of course. Lost and gone forever. Dead as a cinder. Every time Tony thinks this, the air goes into her lungs, then out in a long sigh of relief.

• • •

Zenia's memorial service was five years ago, or four and a half. It was in March. Tony can recall the day perfectly, a wet grey day that turned to sleet later. What surprised her at the time was that there were so few people there. Men, mostly, with their coat collars turned up. They avoided the front row and kept trying to get behind one another, as if they didn't want to be seen.

None of these men was Roz's runaway husband Mitch, Tony noted with interest and some disappointment, though she was glad for Roz. She could sense Roz craning her neck, riffling through the faces: she must have expected him to be there, and then what? Then there would have been a scene.

Charis was looking too, in a less obtrusive way; but if any of these men was Billy, Tony wouldn't have been able to tell, because she'd never met Billy. He'd arrived, then vanished, during the interval when she hadn't been in touch with Charis. True, Charis had shown her a photo, but the focus was bad and the top of Billy's head was cut off, and he'd had a beard then. Men's faces changed more than women's did, over time. Or they could change them more, at will. Add facial hair and subtract it.

There was no one at all that Tony knew; except Roz and Charis, of course. They wouldn't have missed it for anything, said Roz. They wanted to see the end of Zenia, make sure she was now fully (Tony's word) inoperational. Charis's word was *peaceful*. Roz's was *kaput*.

The service was unsettling. It seemed a patched-up affair, held at a funeral parlour chapel of a lumpy, magenta clumsiness that would have filled Zenia with scorn. There were several bunches of flowers, white chrysanthemums. Tony wondered who could have sent them. She hadn't sent any flowers herself.

A blue-suited man who identified himself as Zenia's lawyer—the same man, therefore, who had called Tony to tell her about the service—read out a short tribute to Zenia's good qualities, among which courage was listed foremost, though Tony didn't think the manner of Zenia's death had been particularly courageous. Zenia had been blown up during some terrorist rampage or other, in Lebanon; she hadn't been a target, she'd just been in the way. An innocent bystander, said the lawyer. Tony was sceptical about both words: *innocent* was never Zenia's favourite adjective for herself, and bystanding was not her typical activity. But the lawyer did not say what she'd really been doing there, on that unnamed street in Beirut. Instead he said she would be long remembered.

"Damn right she will be," Roz whispered to Tony. "And by *courage* he meant *big tits.*" Tony felt this was tasteless, as the size of Zenia's tits was surely no longer an issue. In her opinion Roz sometimes went too far.

Zenia herself was present only in spirit, said the lawyer, and also in the form of her ashes, which they would now proceed to the Mount Pleasant Cemetery to inter. He actually said *inter.* It had been Zenia's wish, as stated in her will, that the ashes should be interred under a tree.

Interred was very unlike Zenia. So was the tree. In fact, it seemed unlike Zenia to have made a will, or to have had a lawyer at all. But you never knew, people changed. Why, for instance, had Zenia put the three of them on the list of people to be informed in the event of her death? Was it remorse? Or was it some kind of last laugh? If so, Tony failed to get the point.

The lawyer had been no help: all he had was the list of names, or so he'd claimed. Tony could hardly expect him to explain Zenia to her. If anything it should be the other way around. "Weren't you her friend?" he'd said, accusingly.

"Yes," said Tony. "But that was so long ago."

"Zenia had an excellent memory," said the lawyer, and sighed. Tony had heard sighs like that before.

It was Roz who insisted they go on to the cemetery after the service. She drove them in her car, her large one. "I want to see where they're putting her, so I can walk the dogs there," she said. "I'll train them to widdle on the tree."

"It's not the *tree's* fault," said Charis indignantly. "You're being uncharitable."

Roz laughed. "Right, sweetie! I'm doing it *for* you!"

"Roz, you don't have any dogs," said Tony. "I wonder what kind of a tree it is."

"I'll get some, just for this," said Roz.

"Mulberry," said Charis. "It was in the vestibule, with a label on."

"I don't see how it can possibly grow," said Tony. "It's too cold."

"It'll grow," said Charis, "as long as the buds aren't out yet."

"I hope it gets blight," said Roz. "No, really! She doesn't deserve a tree."

Zenia's ashes were in a sealed metal canister, like a small land-mine. Tony was familiar with such canisters, and they depressed her. They did not have the grandeur of coffins. She thought of the people inside them as having been condensed, like condensed milk.

She thought there would be some sprinkling involved, of what the lawyer had referred to as the cremains, but the canister was not opened up and the ashes weren't sprinkled. (Afterwards—after the service, and after her October-morning egg-cooking as well—Tony had occasion to wonder what had really been in there. Sand, probably, or something disgusting, like dog turds or used condoms. That would have been the sort of gesture Zenia would have made, once, when Tony first knew her.)

They stood around in the fine cold drizzle while the canister was planted, and the mulberry tree on top of it. Earth was tamped down. There were no final words said, no words of dismissal. The drizzle began to freeze, and the men in their overcoats hesitated, then wandered off towards their parked cars.

"I have the uneasy feeling that we've left something out," said Tony, as they walked away.

"Well, there wasn't any singing," said Charis.

"So, like what?" said Roz. "A stake through her heart?"

"Maybe what Tony meant was that she was a fellow human *being,*" said Charis.

"Fellow human being, my fat fanny," said Roz. "If she was a fellow human being, I'm the Queen of England."

What Tony meant was less benevolent. She was thinking that for thousands of years, when people died—especially powerful people, especially people who were feared—the survivors had gone to a lot of trouble. They'd slit the throats of their best horses, they'd buried slaves and favourite wives alive, they'd poured blood into the earth. It hadn't been mourning, it had been appeasement. They'd wanted to show their good will, however spurious, because they'd known the spirit of the dead one would be envious of them for still being alive.

Maybe I should have sent flowers, thought Tony. But flowers wouldn't have been enough, for Zenia. She would have sneered at flowers. What was needed was a bowl of blood. A bowl of blood, a bowl of pain, some death. Then maybe she would stay buried.

Tony didn't tell West about the memorial service. He might have gone to it, and fallen to pieces. Or else he might not have gone and then felt guilty, or been upset that she'd attended without him. He knew Zenia was dead though, he'd seen it in the paper: a small oblong, hidden in the middle. *Canadian Killed in Terrorist Blast.* When they'd been young, *blast* had been a name for a party. He hadn't said anything to Tony, but she'd found that page with the piece cut out of it. They had a tacit agreement never to mention Zenia.

Tony presents the eggs in two ceramic eggcups shaped like chickens that she picked up in France a few years ago. The French liked to make dishes in the shapes of the things that were going to be served in them; when it came to eating they rarely beat about the bush. Their menus read like a vegetarian's nightmare—hearts of these, brains of that. Tony appreciates this directness. She has a French fish platter too, in the shape of a fish.

Shopping in general is not her thing, but she has a weakness for souvenirs. She bought these eggcups near the site of the battlefield where General Marius of Rome wiped out a hundred thousand Teutones—or two hundred thousand, depending on who was doing the chronicling—a century before the birth of Christ. By dangling a small advance contingent of his forces in front of the enemy like bait, he'd decoyed them to his chosen slaughtering-ground. After the battle, three hundred thousand Teutones were sold into slavery, and ninety thousand others may or may not have been thrown into a pit on Mont Sainte Victoire at the urging of a possibly Syrian prophetess, whose name may or may not have been Martha. She was said to have worn purple robes.

This clothing detail has been passed down through the centuries with firm authority, despite the vagueness of other parts of the story. The battle itself, however, definitely took place. Tony has inspected the terrain: a flat plain, hemmed in on three sides by mountains. A bad place to fight if you were on the defensive. Pourrières is the name of the nearby town; it's still called that, after the smell of the rotting corpses.

Tony does not mention (and has never mentioned) this eggcup connection to West. He would be dismayed, not so much by the rotting Teutones as by her. She once remarked to him that she could understand those kings of old who used to have their enemies' skulls made into wine cups. This was a mistake: West likes to think of her as kind and beneficent. And forgiving, of course.

Tony has made coffee, grinding the beans herself; she serves it with cream, in defiance of cholesterol. Sooner or later, as their arteries fill with sludge, they will have to give up cream, but not just yet. West sits eating his egg; he's absorbed in it, like a happy child. The bright primary colours—the red cups, the yellow tablecloth, the orange plates—give the kitchen a playground air. His grey hair seems a fluke, some unaccountable transformation that's been worked upon him overnight. When she first knew him he was blond.

"Good egg," he says. Small things like good eggs delight him, small things like bad eggs depress him. He's easy to please, but difficult to protect.

West, Tony repeats to herself. She says his name from time to time, silently, like a charm. He didn't use to be West. Once—thirty? thirty-two years ago?—he was Stewart, until he told her how much he hated being called *Stew*; so she reversed him, and he's been West ever since. She cheated a little, though: strictly speaking, he should have been *Wets*. But that's what happens when you love someone, thinks Tony. You cheat a little.

"What's on your agenda for today?" says West.

"Want some more toast?" says Tony. He nods and she gets up to tend the toaster, pausing to kiss the top of his head, inhaling his familiar scent of scalp and shampoo. His hair up there is thinning: soon he'll have a tonsure, like a monk's. For the moment she's taller than he is: it isn't often she gets such a bird's-eye view.

There's no need for West to be told who she's having lunch with. He doesn't like Roz and Charis. They make him nervous. He feels—rightly—that they know too much about him.

"Nothing very exciting," she says.

4

After breakfast West goes up to his third-floor study to work, and Tony changes out of her dressing gown, into jeans and a cotton pullover, and marks more papers. From upstairs she can hear a rhythmical thumping, punctuated by what sounds like a mixed chorus of mating hyenas, cows being hit with sledgehammers, and tropical birds in pain.

West is a musicologist. Some of what he does is traditional—influences, variants, derivations—but he's also involved in one of those cross-disciplinary projects that have become so popular lately. He's mixed up with a bunch of neurophysiologists from the medical school; together they're studying the effects of music on the human brain—different kinds of music, and different kinds of noises, because some of the things West comes up with can hardly be thought of as music. They want to know which part of the brain is listening, and especially which half of it. They think this information may be useful to stroke victims, and to people who have lost parts of their brains in car accidents. They wire people's brains up, play the music—or noises—and watch the results on a coloured computer screen.

West is very excited about all of this. He says it's

become clear to him that the brain itself is a musical instrument, that you can actually compose music on it, on someone else's brain; or you could, if you had free rein. Tony finds this idea distressing—what if the scientists want to play something that the person with the brain doesn't want to hear? West says it's only theoretical.

But he has a strong urge to wire up Tony, because of her left-handedness. Handedness is one of the things they study. They want to attach electrodes to Tony's head and then have her play the piano, because the piano is two-handed and the hands both work at the same time, but on different notations. Tony has avoided this so far by saying she's forgotten how to play, which is mostly true; but also she doesn't want West peering in at anything that might be going on in her brain.

She finishes the set of papers and goes back to the bedroom to change for lunch. She looks into her closet: there isn't a lot of choice, and no matter what she wears, Roz will narrow her eyes at it and suggest they go shopping. Roz thinks Tony goes in for too much floral-wallpaper print, although Tony has carefully explained that it's camouflage. Anyway, the black leather suit Roz once tried to convince her was her real self just made her look like an avant-garde Italian umbrella stand.

She finally settles on a forest green rayon outfit with small white polka dots that she bought in the children's section at Eaton's. She buys quite a few of her clothes there. Why not? They fit, and there's less tax; and, as Roz is never tired of remarking, Tony is a miser, especially when it comes to clothes. She would much rather save the money and spend it on airplane tickets for visits to the sites of battles.

On these pilgrimages she collects relics: a flower from each site. Or a weed rather, because what she picks are common things—daisies, clovers, poppies. Sentimentalities of this kind seem reserved, in her, for people she does not know. She presses the flowers between the pages of the Bibles left by proselytizing sects in the dresser drawers of the cheap hotels and *pensions* where she stays. If there's no Bible she flattens them under ashtrays. There are always ashtrays.

Then, when she gets home, she tapes them into her scrapbooks, in alphabetical order: *Agincourt. Austerlitz. Bunker Hill. Carcassonne. Dunkirk.* She doesn't take sides: all battles are battles, all contain bravery, all involve death. She doesn't talk about this practice of hers to her colleagues, because none of them would understand why she does it. She isn't even sure herself. She isn't sure what she's really collecting, or in memory of what.

In the bathroom she adjusts her face. Powder on the nose, but no lipstick. Lipstick is alarming on her, extra, like those red plastic mouths children stick onto potatoes. Comb through the hair. She gets her hair cut in Chinatown because they don't charge the earth, and they know how to do straight black short hair with a few straggly bangs over the forehead, the same every time. A pixie cut, it used to be called. With her big glasses and her big eyes behind them and her too-skinny neck, the effect is street urchin crossed with newly hatched bird. She still has good skin, good enough; it offsets the grey strands. She looks like a very young old person, or a very old young person; but then, she's looked that way ever since she was two.

She bundles the term papers into her outsized canvas tote bag and runs up the stairs to wave goodbye to West. *Headwinds,* says the sign on his study door, and that's what his answering machine says too—*Third floor, Headwinds.* It's what he'd call his high-tech recording studio if he had one. West has his earphones on now, he's hooked up to his tape deck and his synthesizer, but he sees her and waves back. She leaves by the front door, locking it behind her. She's always careful about the door. She doesn't want any drug addicts getting in while she's away, and bothering West.

The wooden porch needs repairing; there's a rotting board. She'll have it fixed next spring, she promises herself; it will take at least that long to get such a thing organized. Someone has tucked a circular under her doormat: another tool sale. Tony wonders who buys all these tools—all these circular saws, cordless drills, rasps, and screwdrivers—and what they do with them really. Maybe tools are substitute weapons; maybe they're what men go in for when they aren't waging war. West is not the tool-using type, though: the only hammer in the house belongs to Tony, and for anything other than simple nail-pounding she looks in the Yellow Pages. Why risk your life?

There's another tool circular cluttering the tiny front lawn, which is weed-ridden and needs cutting. The lawn is a neighbourhood blot. Tony knows this, and is embarrassed by it from time to time, and vows to have the grass dug up and replaced with some colourful but hardy shrubs, or else gravel. She has never seen the point of lawns. Given the choice she'd prefer a moat, with a drawbridge, and crocodiles optional.

Charis keeps making vague mewing noises about re-doing Tony's front lawn for her, transforming it into a miracle of bloom, but Tony has fended her off. Charis would make a garden like Tony's study drapes, which she calls "nourishing"—rampant blossoms, twining vines, blatant seed pods—and it would be too much for Tony. She's seen what happened to the strip of ground beside Roz's back walk when Roz gave in to similar pleas. Because Charis has done it, Roz can't possibly have it re-done, so now there's a little plot of Roz's yard that will be forever Charis.

At the street corner Tony turns to look back at her house, as she often does, admiring it. Even after twenty years it still seems like a mirage that she should own such a house, or any house at all. The house is brick, late Victorian, tall and narrow, with green fish-scale shingles on its upper third. Her study window looks out from the fake tower on the left: the Victorians loved to think they were living in castles. It's a large house, larger than it looks from the street. A solid house, reassuring; a fort, a bastion, a keep. Inside it is West, creating aural mayhem, safe from harm. When she bought it, back when the neighbourhood was more run down and the prices were low, she didn't expect anyone would ever live in it except her.

She goes down the subway steps, drops her token into the turnstile, boards the train, and sits on the plastic seat, with her tote bag on her knees like a visiting nurse. The car isn't crowded, so there are no heads of tall people blocking her view and she can read the ads. *Hcnurc!* says a chocolate bar. *Pleh uoy nac?* pleads the Red Cross. *Elas! Elas!* If she were to say these words out loud people would think it was another language. It is another language, an archaic language, a language she knows well. She could speak it in her sleep, and sometimes does.

If the fundamentalists were to catch her at it, they'd accuse her of Satan worship. They play popular songs in reverse, claiming to find blasphemies hidden in them; they think you can invoke the Devil by hanging the cross upside down or by saying the Lord's Prayer backwards. All nonsense. Evil doesn't require such invocations, such childish and stagy rituals. Nothing so complicated.

Tony's other language isn't evil, however. It's dangerous only to her. It's her seam, it's where she's sewn together, it's where she could split apart. Nevertheless, she still indulges in it. A risky nostalgia. *Aiglatson*. (A Viking chieftain of the Dark Ages? An up-market laxative?)

She gets off at St. George and takes the Bedford Road exit, makes it past the handout men and the street flower-seller and the boy playing the flute on the corner, avoids getting run over while she crosses at the green light, and heads along past Varsity Stadium and then across the grassy circle of the main campus. Her office is down one of the dingy old side streets and around the corner, in a building called McClung Hall.

McClung Hall is a solemn block of red brick, darkened to purple-brown by weather and soot. She lived in it once, as a student, for six years straight, when it was still a women's residence. She was told it was named after somebody or other who'd helped get the vote for women, but she didn't much care about that. Nobody did, back then.

Tony's first memories of the place are of an ancient fire-trap, overheated but drafty, with creaking floors and a lot of worn-out but stolid wood in it: massive banisters, heavy window seats, thickly panelled doors. It smelled—it still smells—like a damp pantry suffering from dry rot, with sprouting potatoes forgotten in it. At the time it also had a lingering, queasy odour that filtered up from the dining room: lukewarm cabbage, leftover scrambled eggs, burnt grease. She used to duck the meals there and smuggle bread and apples up to her room.

The Comparative Religion people got hold of it in the seventies, but since then it's been turned into makeshift offices for the overflow from various worthy but impoverished departments—people who are thought to use mostly their minds rather than pieces of glossy equipment, and who don't contribute much to modern industry, and who are therefore considered to be naturally adapted to seediness. Philosophy has established a bridgehead on the ground floor, Modern History has claimed the second. Despite some half-hearted attempts at repainting (already in the past, already fading), McClung is still the same dour, circumspect building it always was, virtuous as cold oatmeal and keeping itself to itself.

Tony doesn't mind its shabbiness. Even as a student she liked it here—compared, that is, with where she could have been. A rented room, an anonymous studio apartment. Some of the other, more blasé students called it McFungus, a name that has been passed down over the years, but for Tony it was a haven, and she remains grateful.

Her own office is on the second floor, just a couple of doors down from her old room. Her old room itself has become the coffee room, a wilfully cheerless place with a chipped pressboard table, several mismatched straight chairs, and a yellowing Amnesty poster of a man tied up in barbed wire and stuck full of bent nails. There's a drip coffee machine that spits and dribbles, and a rack where they are all supposed to keep their environmentally friendly washable mugs, with their initials painted on them so they won't get one another's gum diseases. Tony has gone to some trouble with her own mug. She's used red nail polish, on black: it says *Gnissapsert On.* People occasionally use one another's mugs, by mistake or from laziness, but nobody uses hers.

She pauses at the coffee room, where two of her colleagues, both dressed in fleecy jogging suits, are having milk and cookies. Dr. Ackroyd, the eighteenth-century agriculture expert, and Dr. Rose Pimlott, the social historian and Canadianist, who by any other name would still be a pain in the butt. She wonders if Rose Pimlott and Bob Ackroyd are having a *thing,* as Roz would say. They've been putting their heads together quite frequently in recent weeks. But most likely it's just some palace plot. The whole department is like a Renaissance court: whisperings, gangings-up, petty treacheries, snits, and umbrage. Tony tries to stay out of it but succeeds only sometimes. She has no particular allies and is therefore suspected by all.

Especially by Rose. Tony continues to resent the fact that, two years ago, Rose accused one of Tony's graduate courses of being Eurocentric.

"Of course it's Eurocentric!" Tony said. "What do you expect in a course called Merovingian Siege Strategy?"

"I think," said Rose Pimlott, attempting to salvage her position, "that you might teach the course from the point of view of the victims. Instead of marginalizing them."

"Which victims?" said Tony. "They were all victims! They took turns! Actually, they took turns trying to avoid being the victims. That's the whole point about war!"

What Dr. Rose Pimlott knows about war you could stick in your ear. But her ignorance is willed: mainly she just wants war to get out of her way and stop being such a nuisance. "Why do you *like* it?" she said to Tony recently, wrinkling her nose as if talking about snot or farts: something minor and disgusting, and best concealed.

"Do you ask AIDS researchers why they like AIDS?" said Tony. "War is *there*. It's not going away soon. It's not that I like it. I want to see why so many other people like it. I want to see how it works." But Rose Pimlott would rather not look, she'd rather let others dig up the mass graves. She might break a nail.

Tony considers telling Rose that Laura Secord, whose portrait on the old chocolate boxes that bore her name had turned out, under X-ray, to be that of a man in a dress, really had been a man in a dress. No woman, she would tell Rose, could possibly have shown such aggressiveness, or—if you like—such courage. That would stick Rose on the horns of a dilemma! She'd have to maintain that women could be just as good at war as men were, and therefore just as bad, or else that they were all by nature lily-livered sissies. Tony is filled with curiosity to see which way Rose would jump. But there isn't time today.

She nods in at Rose and Bob, and they look at her askance, which is the peer-group look she's used to. Male historians think she's invading their territory, and should leave their spears, arrows, catapults, lances, swords, guns, planes, and bombs alone. They think she should be writing social history, such as who ate what when, or Life in the Feudal Family. Female historians, of whom there are not many, think the same thing but for different reasons. They think she ought to be studying birth; not death, and certainly not battle plans. Not routs and débâcles, not carnages, not slaughters. They think she's letting women down.

On the whole she fares better with the men, if they can work their way past the awkward preliminaries; if they can avoid calling her "little lady," or saying they weren't expecting her to be so feminine, by which they mean short. Though only the most doddering ones do that any more.

If she weren't so tiny, though, she'd never get away with it. If she were six feet tall and built like a blockhouse; if she had hips. Then she'd be threatening, then she'd be an Amazon. It's the incongruity that grants her permission. *A breath would blow you away,* they beam down at her silently. *You wish,* thinks Tony, smiling up. *Many have blown.*

She unlocks her office door, then locks it behind her to disguise the fact that she's in there. It's not her office hours but the students take advantage. They can smell her out, like sniffer dogs; they'll seize any opportunity to suck up to her or whine, or attempt to impress her, or foist upon her their versions of sulky defiance. *I'm just a human being,* Tony wants to say to them. But of course she isn't. She's a human being with power. There isn't much of it, but it's power all the same.

A month or so ago one of them—large, leather-jacketed, red-eyed, second-year undergraduate survey course—stuck a clasp knife into the middle of her desk.

"I need an A!" he shouted. Tony was both frightened

by him and angry. *Kill me and you won't even pass!* she wanted to shout back. But he might have been on something. Doped up or crazy, or both, or imitating those other berserk, professor-slaughtering students he'd seen on the news. Luckily it was only a knife.

"I appreciate your directness," she said to him. "Now, why don't you sit down, in that chair right over there, and we can discuss it?"

"Thank God for Psychiatric Services," she said to Roz on the phone, after he'd left. "But what gets into them?"

"Listen, sweetie," said Roz. "There's just one thing I want you to remember. You know those chemicals women have in them, when they've got PMS? Well, men have the very same chemicals in them *all the time.*"

Maybe it's true, thinks Tony. Otherwise, where would sergeants come from?

Tony's office is large, larger than it would be in a modern building, with the standard-issue scratched desk, the standard sawdusty bulletin board, the standard dust-laden venetian blinds. Generations of thumbtacks have woodwormed the pale green paint; leftover shards of cellophane tape glint here and there, like mica in a cave. Tony's second-best word processor is on the desk—it's so slow and outmoded she hardly cares if anyone steals it—and in her bookcase are a few dependable volumes, which she lends out to students sometimes: Creasy's *Fifteen Decisive Battles of the World,* a necessary chestnut; Liddell Hart; Churchill, of course; *The Fatal Decisions*; and, one of her own favourites, Keegan's *The Face of Battle.*

On one wall there's a bad reproduction of Benjamin

West's "The Death of Wolfe," a lugubrious picture in Tony's opinion, Wolfe white as a codfish belly, with his eyes rolled piously upwards and many necrophiliac voyeurs in fancy dress grouped around him. Tony keeps it in her office as a reminder, both to herself and to her students, of the vainglory and martyrologizing to which those in her profession are occasionally prone. Beside him is Napoleon, thoughtfully crossing the Alps.

On the opposite wall she's hung an amateurish pen-and-ink cartoon entitled "Wolfe Taking a Leak." The general is shown turned away from the viewer, with only his weak-chinned profile showing. He's wearing a peevish expression, and the balloon coming out of his mouth says, "Fuck These Buttons." This cartoon was drawn by one of her students, two years ago, and was presented to her by the whole class at the end of term. As a rule her students are mostly men: not a lot of women find themselves deeply attracted to such courses as Late Medieval Tactical Blunders or Military History as Artefact, which is what her graduate courses are entitled, this time around.

As she'd unwrapped the package, they'd all eyed her to see how she'd respond to the word *fuck*. Men of their age seem to think that women of her age have never heard such words before. She finds this touching. She has to make a conscious effort to stop herself from calling her students "my boys." If she doesn't watch it, she'll turn into a hearty, jocular den mother; or worse, a knowing, whimsical old biddy. She'll start winking, and pinching cheeks.

The cartoon itself is in honour of her lecture on the technology of fly-front fastenings, which—she's heard—has been dubbed "Tender Buttons," and which usually attracts an overflow crowd. *Writers on war*—she begins—

have tended to concentrate on the kings and the generals, on their decisions, on their strategy, and have overlooked more lowly, but equally important factors, which can, and have, put the actual soldiers—those on the sharp edge—at risk. Disease-carrying lice and fleas, for instance. Faulty boots. Mud. Germs. Undershirts. And fly-front fastenings. The drawstring, the overlap, the buttoned flap, the zipper, have all played their part in military history through the ages; not to mention the kilt, for which, from a certain point of view, there is much to be said. *Don't laugh,* she tells them. *Instead, picture yourself on the battlefield, with nature calling, as it frequently does in times of stress. Now picture yourselves trying to undo these buttons.*

She holds up a sketch of the buttons in question, a nineteenth-century set that would surely have required at least ten fingers and ten minutes each.

Now picture a sniper. Less funny?

An army marches on its stomach, but also on its fly-front fastenings. Not that the zipper—although improving the speed of opening—has been entirely blameless. *Why not? Use your heads—zippers get stuck. And they're noisy!* And men have developed the dangerous habit of striking matches on them. *In the dark! You might as well set a flare.*

Many have been the crimes committed—she continues—on helpless enlisted men by the designers of military clothing. How many British soldiers died needlessly because of the redness of their uniforms? And don't think that sort of thoughtlessness went out with the nineteenth century. Mussolini's criminal failure to provide shoes—shoes!—for his own troops was just one case in point. And, in Tony's opinion, whoever dreamed up those nylon pants for North Korea should have been court-martialled. You could hear the legs whisking together a mile away. And the sleeping bags—they rustled too, and you couldn't undo them easily from inside, and they froze shut! During night raids by the enemy, those men got butchered like kittens in a sack.

Murder by designer! She can get quite worked up about it.

All of which, in a more sedate and footnoted form, will be good for at least one chapter of her book-in-progress: *Deadly Vestments: A History of Inept Military Couture*.

Charis says it's bad for Tony to spend so much of her time on something as negative as war. She says it's carcinogenic.

Tony searches through her accordion file for the class list, locates it under B, for Bureaucracy, and enters the grade for each paper in the little square provided. When she's finished she drops the marked papers into the heavy manila envelope thumbtacked to the outside of her door, where the students can pick them up later today, as promised. Then she continues to the end of the hall, checks for mail in the squalid cubbyhole of a departmental office where there is sometimes a secretary, finds nothing but a renewal notice for *Jane's Defence Weekly* and her latest copy of *Big Guns,* and tucks both into her bag.

Next she makes a rest stop in the overheated women's washroom, which smells of liquid soap, chlorine, and partly digested onions. One of the three toilets is clogged, as is its long-standing habit, and the other two stalls lack toilet paper. There's some hidden in the non-functioning one, however, so Tony requisitions it. On the wall of the cubicle she prefers—the one next to the pebble-glass window—someone has scratched a new message, above *Herstory Not History* and *Hersterectomy Not Hysterectomy*: *FEMINIST DECONSTRUCTION SUCKS*. The sub-text of this, as Tony well knows, is that there's a move afoot to have McClung Hall declared a historic building and turned over to Women's Studies. *HISTORIC NOT HERSTORIC*, someone has added off to the side. Omens of a coming tussle Tony hopes to avoid.

She leaves a note on the secretary's desk: *The Toilet is Clogged. Thank you. Antonia Fremont*. She does not add, *Again*. There is no need to be unpleasant. Nothing will come of this note, but she has done her duty. Then she hurries out of the building and back to the subway, and heads south.

5

The lunch is at the Toxique, so Tony gets off at Osgoode and walks west along Queen Street, past Dragon Lady Comics, past the Queen Mother Café, past the BamBoo Club with its hot graphics. She could wait for a streetcar, but in streetcar crowds she tends to get squashed, and sometimes pinched. She's done enough shirt-button and belt-buckle surveys to last her for a while, so she chooses the more random hazards of the sidewalk. She's not very late, anyway; no later than Roz is, always.

She keeps to the outside of the sidewalk, away from the walls and the ragged figures who lean against them. Ostensibly they want small change, but Tony sees them in a more sinister light. They are spies, scouting the territory before a mass invasion; or else they are refugees, the walking wounded, in retreat before the coming onslaught. Either way she steers clear. Desperate people alarm her, she grew up with two of them. They'll hit out, they'll grab at anything.

This part of Queen has settled down a little. Several years ago it was wilder, more risky, but the rents have gone up and a lot of the second-hand bookstores and scruffier artists are gone. The mix is still fringe fashion, Eastern

European deli, wholesale office furniture, country-and-western beer drinkers' bars; but there are brightly lit doughnut shops now, trendy nightspots, clothes with meaningful labels.

The Recession however is deepening. There are more buildings for sale; there are more closed-out boutiques, and saleswomen lurk in the doorways of those still open, aiming defeated, pleading stares at the passers-by, their eyes filled with baffled rage. *Prices Slashed,* say the windows: that would have been unheard of at this time last year, two months before Christmas. The glistering dresses on the blank-faced or headless mannequins are no longer what they seemed, the incarnation of desire. Instead they look like party trash. Crumpled paper napkins, the rubble left by rowdy crowds or looting armies. Although nobody saw them or could say for certain who they were, the Goths and the Vandals have been through.

So thinks Tony, who could never have worn those dresses anyway. They are for women with long legs, long torsos, long graceful arms. "You're not short," Roz tells her. "You're *petite.* Listen, for a waist like that I'd kill."

"But I'm the same thickness all the way down," says Tony.

"So, what we need is a blender," says Roz. "We'll put in your waist and my thighs, and we'll split the difference. Fine by you?"

If they had been younger such conversations might have pointed to serious dissatisfactions with their own bodies, serious longings. By this time they're just repertoire. More or less.

● ● ●

There's Roz now, waving to her outside the Toxique. Tony comes up to her and Roz stoops, and Tony stretches up her face, and they kiss the air on both sides of each other's heads, as has lately become the fashion in Toronto, or in certain layers of it. Roz parodies the ritual by sucking in her cheeks so her mouth is a fish-mouth, and crossing her eyes. "Pretentious? *Moi?*" she says. Tony smiles, and they go in together.

The Toxique is one of their favourite places: not too expensive, and with a buzz; though it's a little arch, a little grubby. Plates arrive with strange textures sticking to their undersides, the waiters may have eye shadow or nose rings, the waitresses tend to wear fluorescent leg-warmers and leather mini-shorts. There's a long smoked-glass mirror along one side, salvaged from some wrecked hotel. Posters of out-of-date alternative-theatre events are glued to the walls, and people with pallid skin and chains hanging from their sombre, metal-studded clothing slouch through to the off-limits back rooms or confer together on the splintering stairs that lead down to the toilets. The Toxique specials are a chèvre-and-roasted-pepper sandwich, a Newfoundland cod-cake, and a sometimes mucilaginous giant salad with a lot of walnuts and shredded roots in it. There's baklava and tiramisù, and strong, addictive espresso.

They don't go there at night, of course, when the rock groups and the high decibels take over. But it's good for lunch. It cheers them up. It makes them feel younger, and more daring, than they are.

Charis is already there, sitting in the corner at a red formica table with gold sprinkles baked into it and aluminum legs and trim, which is either authentic fifties or else a reproduction. She's got them a bottle of white wine already, and a bottle of Evian water. She sees them and smiles, and airy kisses go round the table.

Today Charis is wearing a sagging mauve cotton jersey dress, with a fuzzy grey cardigan over top and an orange-and-aqua scarf with a design of meadow flowers draped around her neck. Her long straight hair is grey-blonde and parted in the middle; she has her reading glasses stuck up on top of her head. Her peach lipstick could be her real lips. She resembles a slightly faded advertisement for herbal shampoo—healthful, but verging on the antique. What Ophelia would have looked like if she'd lived, or the Virgin Mary when middle-aged—earnest and distracted, and with an inner light. It's the inner light that gets her in trouble.

Roz is packed into a suit that Tony recognizes from the window of one of the more expensive designer stores on Bloor. She shops munificently and with gusto, but often on the run. The jacket is electric blue, the skirt is tight. Her face is carefully air-brushed, and her hair has just been re-coloured. This time it's auburn. Her mouth is raspberry.

Her face doesn't go with the outfit. It isn't insouciant and lean, but plump, with cushiony pink milkmaid's cheeks and dimples when she smiles. Her eyes, intelligent, compassionate, and bleak, seem to belong to some other face, a thinner one; thinner, and more hardened.

Tony settles into her chair, parking her big tote bag under it where she can use it as a footstool. Short kings once had special foot cushions so their legs wouldn't dangle as they sat on their thrones. Tony sympathizes.

"So," says Roz after the preliminaries, "we're all in our places, with bright shiny faces. What's new? Tony, I saw the cutest outfit in Holt's, it would be so good for you. A mandarin collar—mandarin collars are back!—and brass buttons down the front." She lights her usual cigarette, and Charis gives her usual tiny cough. This part of the Toxique is not a smoke-free zone.

"I'd look like a bellhop," says Tony. "Anyway, it wouldn't fit."

"You ever consider spike heels?" says Roz. "You'd add four inches."

"Be serious," says Tony. "I want to be able to walk."

"You could get a leg implant," says Roz. "A leg *enhancement*. Well, why not? They're doing everything else."

"I think Tony's body is appropriate the way it is," says Charis.

"I'm not talking about her body, I'm talking about her wardrobe," says Roz.

"As usual," says Tony. They all laugh, a little boisterously. The wine bottle's now half empty. Tony's had only a few squirts of wine, mixed with Evian water. She's wary of alcohol in any form.

The three of them have lunch once a month. They've come to depend on it. They don't have much in common except the catastrophe that brought them together, if Zenia can be called a catastrophe; but over time they've developed a loyalty to one another, an *esprit de corps*. Tony has come to like these women; she's come to consider them close friends, or the next thing to it. They have gallantry, they have battle scars, they've been through fire;

and each of them knows things about the others, by now, that nobody else does.

So they've continued to meet regularly, like war widows or aging vets, or the wives of those missing in action. As with such groups, there are more people present around the table than can be accounted for.

They don't talk about Zenia, though. Not any more, not since they buried her. As Charis says, talking about her might hold her on this earth. As Tony says, she's bad for the digestion. And as Roz says, why give her the air time?

She's here at the table all the same, thinks Tony. She's here, we're holding her, we're giving her the air time. We can't let her go.

The waitress comes for their order. Today she's a dandelion-haired girl in leopard-pattern tights and calf-high lace-up silver boots. Charis has the Rabbit Delite—for rabbits, not of them—with grated carrots, cottage cheese, and cold lentil salad. Roz has the Thick-cut Gourmet Toasted Cheese Sandwich, on Herb and Caraway Seed Bread, with Polish Pickle; and Tony has the Middle East Special, with falafel and shashlik and couscous and hummus.

"Speaking of the Middle East," says Roz, "what's happening there? That thing with Iraq. Your specialty, I guess, Tony."

The two of them look at Tony. "Actually, it's not," says Tony. The whole point about being a historian, she's tried to tell them, is that you can successfully avoid the present, most of the time. Though of course she's been following the situation; she's been following it for years. Some interesting new technology will be tested, that much is certain.

"Don't be coy," says Roz.

"You mean, is there going to be a war?" says Tony. "The short answer is yes."

"That's terrible," says Charis, dismayed.

"Don't shoot the messenger," says Tony. "I'm not doing it, I'm just telling you."

"But how can you *know*?" says Roz. "Something could change."

"It's not like the stock market," says Tony. "It's already been decided. It was decided as soon as Saddam crossed that border. Like the Rubicon."

"The what?" says Charis.

"Never mind, sweetie, it's just something historical," says Roz. "So is this really bad, or what?"

"Not in the short run," says Tony. "In the long run— well, a lot of empires have folded because they overextended themselves. That could go for either side. But right now the States isn't thinking about that. They love the idea. They'll get a chance to try out their new toys, drum up some business. Don't think of it as a war, think of it as a market expansion."

Charis forks up the grated carrot; she has a shred of it on her upper lip, an endearing orange whisker. "Well, anyway, it won't be *us* doing it," she says.

"Yes it will," says Tony. "Our attendance will be required. If you take the king's shilling, you kiss the king's ass. We'll be there, us and our falling-apart, rusty old navy. Now *that's* a disgrace." Tony is in fact indignant about this: if you're going to make men fight, you ought to give them decent equipment.

"Maybe he'll back down," says Roz.

"Who?" says Tony. "Uncle Sam?"

"Uncle Saddam, pardon the pun," says Roz.

"He can't," says Tony. "He's gone too far. His own folks would murder him. Not that they haven't tried."

"This is depressing," says Charis.

"You bet," says Tony. "The lust for power will prevail. Thousands will die needlessly. Corpses will rot. Women and children will perish. Plagues will rage. Famine will sweep the land. Relief funds will be set up. Officials will siphon off the cash from them. It's not all bad, though— the suicide rate will fall. It always does during wars. And maybe women soldiers will get a crack at front-line combat, strike a blow for feminism. Though I doubt it. They'll probably just be doing bandages-as-usual. Let's order another bottle of Evian."

"Tony, you are *so* cold-blooded," says Roz. "Who's going to win?"

"The battle, or the war?" says Tony. "For the battle, it'll definitely be technology. Whoever's got air superiority. Now who could that be?"

"The Iraqis have some kind of a giant gun," says Roz. "I read something about it."

"Only part of one," says Tony, who knows quite a lot about this because it interests her. Her, and *Jane's Defence Weekly,* and persons unknown. "The Supergun. It would have been a technological breakthrough all right; done away with medium-range aircraft and expensive rockets, cut down on the cost. Guess what they called it? Project Babylon! But the guy who was making it got himself murdered. A mad weapons genius—Gerry Bull. Best ballistics man in the world—one of ours, by the way. He'd been warned, sort of. Stuff kept moving around inside his apartment when he wasn't there. More than a hint, I'd say. But he kept right on building the gun, until bang—five bullets in his head."

"That's awful," said Charis. "I hate that."

"Take your choice," says Tony. "Think how many people the Supergun would have killed."

"Well anyway, I hear they're dug in," says Roz. "I hear they have deep cement bunkers. Bomb-proof."

"Only for the generals," says Tony. "Wait and see."

"Tony, you're such a cynic," says Charis, with a pitying sigh. She keeps hoping for Tony's spiritual improvement, which would consist, no doubt, of a discovery of previous lives, a partial lobotomy, and an increased interest in gardening.

Tony looks at her, sitting in front of her pretty dessert, the Assorted Sorbets, a ball of pink, a ball of red, a ball of curranty purple, spoon at the ready like a kid at a birthday party. Such innocence pains Tony, two ways at once. She wants to console Charis; also to shake her. "What do you want me to say? That we should all try for a more positive attitude?"

"It might help," says Charis solemnly. "You never know. If everyone did it."

Sometimes Tony would like to take Charis by the lily-white hand and lead her to the piles of skulls, to the hidden pits filled with bodies, to the starved children with their stick arms and ballooning stomachs, to the churches locked up and then burned with their sizzling prisoners howling inside, to the crosses, row on row on row. Century after century, back and back, as far as you can go. *Now tell me,* she'd say to Charis. *What do you see?*

Flowers, Charis would say.

Zenia would not have said that.

●   ●   ●

Tony feels a chill. The door must have opened. She looks up, and into the mirror.

Zenia is standing here, behind her, in the smoke, in the glass, in this room. Not someone who looks like Zenia: Zenia herself.

It's not a hallucination. The leopard-skinned waitress has seen her too. She's nodding, she's going over, she's indicating a table at the back. Tony feels her heart clench, clench like a fist, and plummet.

"Tony, what's wrong?" says Roz. She clutches Charis's arm.

"Turn your head slowly," says Tony. "Don't scream."

"Oh shit," says Roz. "It's her."

"Who?" says Charis.

"Zenia," says Tony.

"Zenia's dead," says Charis.

"God," says Roz, "it really is. Charis, don't stare, she'll see you."

"And after putting us through that idiotic service," says Tony.

"Well, *she* wasn't at it," says Roz. "There was only that tin can, remember?"

"And that lawyer," says Tony. After the first shock, she finds she is not surprised.

"Yeah," says Roz. "Lawyer, my fanny."

"He looked like a lawyer," says Charis.

"He looked too much like a lawyer," says Roz. "Face it, we were had. It was one of her numbers."

They're whispering, like conspirators. Why? thinks Tony. We have nothing to hide. We should march up to her and demand—what? How she could have the brass-plated nerve to still be alive?

They ought to go on talking, pretending they don't see her. Instead they're gazing at the tabletop, where the remains of their Assorted Sorbets have melted in pink and raspberry smears, floating on the white plates like the evidence of a shark attack. They feel caught out, they feel trapped, they feel guilty. It should be Zenia who feels like that.

But Zenia strides past their table as if they aren't there, as if nobody is. Tony senses them all fading in the glare that spreads out from her. The perfume she's wearing is unrecognizable: something dense and murky, sullen and ominous. The smell of scorched earth. She goes to the back of the room and sits down, and lights a cigarette and stares above their heads, out the window.

"Tony, what's she doing?" Roz whispers. Tony is the only one with a clear view of Zenia.

"Smoking," says Tony. "Waiting for someone."

"But what's she doing *here*?" says Roz.

"Slumming," says Tony. "The same as us."

"I don't believe this," says Charis plaintively. "I liked this day until now."

"No, no," says Roz. "I mean this city. Shit, I mean this entire *country*. She's burnt all her bridges. What's left for her?"

"I don't want to talk about her," says Tony.

"I don't even want to *think* about her," says Charis. "I don't want her messing up my head."

But there is no hope of thinking about anything else.

Zenia is as beautiful as ever. She's wearing black, a tight outfit with a scoop neck that shows the tops of her breasts.

She looks, as always, like a photo, a high-fashion photo done with hot light so that all freckles and wrinkles are bleached out and only the basic features remain: in her case, the full red-purple mouth, disdainful and sad; the huge deep eyes, the finely arched eyebrows, the high cheekbones tinged with terracotta. And her hair, a dense cloud of it, blown around her head by the imperceptible wind that accompanies her everywhere, moulding her clothes against her body, fitfully moving the dark tendrils around her forehead, filling the air near her with the sound of rustling. In the midst of this unseen commotion she sits unmoving, as still as if she were carved. Waves of ill will flow out of her like cosmic radiation.

Or this is what Tony sees. It's an exaggeration, of course; it's overdone. But these are the emotions that Zenia mostly inspires: overdone emotions.

"Let's leave," says Charis.

"Don't let her frighten you," says Tony, as if to herself.

"It's not fear," says Charis. "She makes me sick. She makes me sick of myself."

Roz says, reflectively, "She does have that effect."

The two others gather their purses and begin the ritual of dividing up the bill. Tony is still looking at Zenia. It's true she's as beautiful as ever; but now Tony can detect a slight powdery dullness, like the bloom on a grape—a slight contracting of the pores, a shrinkage, as if some of the juice has been sucked out from under her skin. Tony finds this reassuring: Zenia is mortal after all, like the rest of them.

Zenia blows out smoke, lowers her gaze. She stares at Tony. She stares right through her. But she sees her all right. She sees all three of them. She knows how they feel. She's enjoying it.

Tony stops looking. Her heart inside her is cold and dense, packed together like a snowball. At the same time she's excited, tense, as if waiting for a short word, a command, clipped and deadly. *Forward! Charge! Fire!* Or something of the sort.

But also she's tired. Maybe she no longer has the energy for Zenia. She may not be up to her, this time. Not that she ever has been.

She focuses on the slick red tabletop, the black ashtray with its crumpled butts. The name of the restaurant is stamped on it in silver script: *Toxique.*

Euqixot. It looks Aztec.

What is she up to? thinks Tony. What does she want? What is she doing here, on this side of the mirror?

6

The three of them troop out the door, one by one. Beating a retreat. Tony resists the impulse to walk out backwards: the casualty rates go up when you turn tail.

It's not as if Zenia has a gun. Still, Tony can sense the contemptuous ultramarine gaze drilling through the back of her flimsy little dotted-rayon dress like a laser. *Pathetic,* Zenia must be thinking. She must be laughing; or smiling, with the corners of her lush mouth upcurled. The three of them aren't major enough for a laugh. *Shorn,* Tony murmurs, to herself. As in armour, as in dignity, as in hair.

Tony felt safe this morning, safe enough. But she doesn't feel safe now. Everything has been called into question. Even in the best of times the daily world is tenuous to her, a thin iridescent skin held in place by surface tension. She puts a lot of effort into keeping it together, her willed illusion of comfort and stability, the words flowing from left to right, the routines of love; but underneath is darkness. Menace, chaos, cities aflame, towers crashing down, the anarchy of deep water. She takes a breath to steady herself and feels the oxygen and car fumes rushing into her brain. Her legs are wavery, the façade of the street ripples, tremulous as a reflection on a pond, the weak sun-light blows away like smoke.

Nevertheless, when Roz offers to drive her home, or wherever she's going, Tony says she'll walk. She needs the interlude, she needs the space, she needs to ready herself for West.

This time the three of them don't kiss the air. Instead they hug. Charis is shivering, despite her attempt at seren-ity. Roz is flippant and dismissive, but she's holding back tears. She'll sit in her car and cry, blotting her eyes on her bright jacket sleeve, until she's ready to drive back to her penthouse office. Charis on the other hand will amble down to the Island ferry dock, peering into store windows and jay-walking. On the ferry she'll watch the gulls and visualize being one, and try to put Zenia out of her mind. Tony feels protective towards the two of them. What do they know about the hard dark choices? Neither one of them is going to be a whole lot of help in the coming struggle. But then, they have nothing to lose. Nothing, or nobody. Tony does.

She makes her way along Queen, then turns north on Spadina. She wills her feet to move, she wills the sun to shine. *He either fears his fate too much, Or his deserts are small, Who puts it not unto the touch, To win, or lose it all,* she repeats in her head. A bracing verse, a general favourite, a favourite of generals. What she needs is some perspective. Some *evitcepsrep*. A medicinal word.

Gradually her heart settles. It's soothing to be among strangers, who require from her no efforts, no explanations, no reassurances. She likes the mix on the street here, the mixed skins. Chinatown has taken over mostly, though there are still some Jewish delicatessens, and, further up and off to the side, the Portuguese and West Indian shops of the Kensington Market. Rome in the second century, Constantinople in the tenth, Vienna in the nineteenth. A crossroads. Those from other countries look as if they're trying hard to forget something, those from here as if they're trying hard to remember. Or maybe it's the other way around. In any case there's an inturned, preoccupied cast to the eyes, a sideways glancing. Music from elsewhere.

The sidewalk is crowded with lunchtime shoppers; they avoid bumping into one another without seeming to look, as if they're covered with cat whiskers. Tony weaves in and out, past the vegetable stores with their star fruit and lichees and long crinkly cabbages set out on stands at the front, the butchers with their glazed reddish ducks dangling in the windows, the linen shops with their cut-work tablecloths, their silk kimonos with good-luck dragons embroidered on the backs. Among Chinese people she feels the right height, although she is not unaware of how she might be viewed by some of them. A hairy white foreign devil; though she is not very hairy, as such things go, or very devilish either. Foreign, yes. Foreign here.

It's nearly time for her to get her hair cut, at Liliane's, two blocks up and around the corner. They make a fuss of her there: they admire, or pretend to admire, her small feet, her tiny mole-paw hands, her flat bum, her heart-shaped mouth, so out of date among the pouty bee-stung lips of the fashion magazines. They tell her she is almost Chinese.

Only almost, though. *Almost* is what she has always

felt; approximate. Zenia has never been *almost,* even at her most fraudulent. Her fakery was deeply assumed, and even her most superficial disguises were total.

Tony walks and walks, up Spadina, past the old Victory Burlesque—which victory, whose victory, she wonders— now stuck with posters advertising films in Chinese, past Grossman's Tavern and across College Street, where the Scott Mission offers Christian soup, to more and more people with less and less money. She can walk all the way home, she has no classes today. She needs to regroup her forces, she needs to ponder, she needs to plan her strategy. Though how much strategy can you plan with so little to go on? For instance, why has Zenia chosen to resurrect herself? Why did she go to the trouble of blowing herself up in the first place? For her own reasons, perhaps; nothing to do with the three of them. Or with the two of them, with her and West. Still, it's bad luck that Zenia spotted her in the Toxique.

Maybe Zenia has forgotten all about West by now. *He's small game,* pleads Tony silently. *A tiny fish. Why bother?* But Zenia likes hunting. She likes hunting anything. She relishes it.

Imagine your enemy, say the experts. *Put yourself in his place. Pretend you are him. Learn to predict him.* Unfortunately, Zenia is a bugger to predict. It's all in the old children's game—scissors, paper, stone. Scissors cut paper, but break on stone. The trick is to know what your opponent is concealing, what fist or nasty surprise or secret weapon he's hiding behind his back. Or hers.

•   •   •

The sun declines and Tony walks along her own quiet street, scuffing through the fallen leaves of the maple and chestnut trees, back to her own house. Her stronghold. In the waning light the house is no longer thick, solid, incontrovertible. Instead it looks provisional, as if it's about to be sold, or to set sail. It flickers a little, sways on its moorings. Before unlocking the door Tony runs her hand over the brickwork, reassuring herself that it exists.

West hears her come in, and calls down to her. Tony checks her face in the hall mirror, settling it into what she hopes is her normal expression.

"Listen to this," says West, when she's climbed the third-floor stairs.

Tony listens: it's another noise, much the same—as far as she can tell—as yesterday's. Courting male penguins bring rocks, held between their rubber-boot feet; West brings noises. "That's wonderful," she says. It's one of her more minor lies.

West smiles, which means he knows she can't hear what he hears but likes her for not saying so. She smiles back, scanning his face anxiously. She checks each wrinkle, each lift and inflection. All is as usual, from what she can tell.

Neither of them feels like cooking, so West goes around the corner for Japanese take-out—barbecued eel, yellowtail, and salmon sushi—and they eat it sitting on cushions, in front of the television set in West's third-floor study, with their shoes off, licking their fingers.

West has the TV in there so he can play videos on it in which sounds are rendered as colours and wavy lines, but they also use it for watching old movies and junky late-night crime series. West usually prefers the movies, but tonight it's Tony's turn to choose, and they settle on a rerun of a cop show, high on the offensive-and-tacky scale and punctuated with bursts of gratuitous violence.

Tony's students would smile if they caught her doing this; they're under the illusion that their elders and teachers can't possibly be as frivolous and lazy-minded as they are themselves. Tony watches as a woman brushes her freshly washed hair, and as another extols a new sanitary napkin, curved to catch the drips. She continues to watch as, for the hundredth, for the thousandth time, one man prepares to kill another.

Such men always have something appropriate to say before throwing the knife or breaking the neck or pulling the trigger. This may be just a screen phenomenon, a fantasy of scriptwriters; or maybe men really do say such things, under such circumstances. How would Tony know? Is there an urge to warn, to gloat, to intimidate the foe, to boost oneself into action? *Dieu et mon droit. Nemo me impune lacessit. Dulce et decorum est pro patria mori. Don't mess with me.* Challenges, battle cries, epitaphs. Bumper stickers.

This man says, "You're history."

Tony has compiled a mental list of these televised synonyms for death. *You're toast, you're fried, you're wasted, you're steak, you're dead meat.* It's odd how many of them have to do with food, as if being reduced to nutrients is the final indignity. But *you're history* has long been one of her favourites. It makes such an exact equation between the past—any of the past, all of the past—and a deserved and shoddy oblivion. *That's history,* the young announce, with self-righteous scorn. *This is now.*

There's a close-up of the bug-eyed fear on the face of the man who will soon be history if things go the way they're going, and then the scene shifts to a view of nasal passages, with smile-button medicated orange bubbles percolating through them.

"This is awful," says West. Tony doesn't know whether he means the cop show or the cross-sectioned nose. She mutes the sound, and takes up his large hand, holding two of his soy-sauced fingers. "West," she says. What is it she would like to convey? *You're so large?* No. *I don't own you?* No. *Please stay?*

Mutt and Jeff, he sometimes calls them. *Ttum and Ffej,* Tony replies. Cut that out, says West. When they go walking together, they always look as if one of them is on a leash; but which one? A bear and its handler? A poodle and its trainer?

"Want a beer?" says West.

"Apple juice," says Tony, "please," and West unfolds himself from his cushion and pads down the stairs in his sock feet.

Tony sits watching a new car scream around, silently, in the mountainous desert, overlooked by flat-topped buttes. Good ambush country. She has only one decision to make right now: whether or not to tell West. How could she put it? *Zenia lives.* And then what? What would West do? Run from the house, without his coat, without his shoes? It's possible. Tall people's heads are too far from the ground, their centre of gravity is too high. One shock and they topple. As Zenia said once, West is a pushover.

On a hunch, she gets up and tiptoes over to West's desk, where he keeps his phone. He has nothing so coherent as a phone pad, but on the back of a discarded sheet of musical notations she finds what she's afraid of. *Z. A. Hotel. Ext. 1409.*

The Z floats on the page as if scrawled on a wall, as if scratched on a window, as if carved in an arm. Z for Zorro, the masked avenger. Z for Zero Hour. Z for Zap.

It's as if Zenia has already been here, leaving a taunting signature; but the handwriting is West's. How sweet, she thinks; he just left it there for anyone to see, he doesn't even know enough to flush it down the toilet. What is not so sweet is that he hasn't told her. He is less transparent than she thought, less candid; more perfidious. The enemy is already within the walls.

The personal is not political, thinks Tony: the personal is military. War is what happens when language fails.

Zenia, she whispers, trying it out. *Zenia, you're history. You're dead meat.*

7

Charis

Charis gets up at dawn. She makes her bed neatly, because she respects this bed. After working her way through time from one bed to another— a mattress on the floor, or several mattresses on several floors, a second-hand box bed with screw-on tapered wooden legs that kept breaking, a spine-wrecking futon, a chemical-smelling foam pad—she has finally achieved a bed that pleases her: firm, but not too firm, with a wrought-iron bedstead painted white. She bought it cheap from Shanita, at work, who was getting rid of it in one of her periodic transformations. Anything from Shanita is good luck, and this bed is good luck too. It's clear, it's fresh, like a mint candy.

Charis has covered the bed with a beautiful print spread, dark pink leaves and vines and grapes, on white. A Victorian look. Too fussy, says her daughter Augusta, who has an eye for leather chairs as smooth as the backs of knees, for tubular-chrome-and-glass coffee tables, for nubbly-cotton designer sofas with pillows in greys and ivories and milky-tea browns: minimalist opulence like that in corporate lawyers' offices. Or so Charis imagines; she doesn't in fact know any corporate lawyers. Her daughter cuts pictures of these intimidating chairs and tables and sofas out of magazines and pastes them into her furniture scrapbook, and leaves the scrapbook lying around, open, as a reproach to Charis and her slovenly ways.

Her daughter is a hard girl. Hard to please, or hard for Charis to please. Maybe it's because she has no father. Or not *no father*: an invisible father, a father like a dotted outline, which has had to be coloured in for her by Charis, who didn't have all that much to go on herself, so it's no wonder his features have remained a little indistinct. Charis wonders whether it would have been better for her daughter to have a father. She wouldn't know, because she never had one herself. Maybe Augusta would go easier on Charis if she had two parents she could find inadequate, and not just one.

Maybe Charis deserves it. Maybe she was the matron of an orphanage in a previous life—a Victorian orphanage, with gruel for the orphans and a cosy fire and a warm four-poster bed with a down-filled quilt for the matron; which would account for her taste in bedspreads.

She remembers her own mother calling her *hard*, before she was Charis, when she was still Karen. *You're hard, you're hard,* she would cry, hitting Karen's legs with a shoe or a broom handle or whatever was around. But Karen wasn't hard, she was soft, too soft. A soft touch. Her hair was soft, her smile was soft, her voice was soft. She was so soft there was no resistance. Hard things sank into her, they went right through her; and if she made a real effort, out the other side. Then she didn't have to see them or hear them, or touch them even.

Maybe it looked like hardness. *You can't win this fight,* said her uncle, putting his meaty hand on her arm. He thought she was fighting. Maybe she was. Finally she changed into Charis, and vanished, and reappeared elsewhere, and she has been elsewhere ever since. After she became Charis she was harder, hard enough to get by, but she's continued to wear soft clothes: flowing Indian muslins, long gathered skirts, flowered shawls, scarves draped around her.

Whereas her own daughter has gone for polish. Lacquered nails, dark hair gelled into a gleaming helmet, though not a punk look: efficient. She's too young to be so shiny, she's only nineteen. She's like a butterfly hardened into an enamelled lapel pin while still half out of the chrysalis. How will she ever *unfold*? Her brittle suits, her tidy little soldiers' boots, her neat lists in crisp computer printout just break Charis's heart.

August, Charis named her, because that's when she was born. Warm breezes, baby powder, languorous heat, the smell of mown hay. Such a soft name. Too soft for her daughter, who has added an *a. Augusta,* she is now—a very different resonance. Marble statues, Roman noses, tight-lipped commanding mouths. Augusta is in first year in the business course at Western, on scholarship, luckily, because Charis could never have afforded to pay for it; her vagueness about money is another source of complaint, for Augusta.

But despite the lack of cash Augusta has always been well fed. Well fed, well nourished, and every time Augusta comes home for a visit Charis cooks her a nutritious meal, with leafy greens and balanced proteins. She gives Augusta small presents, sachets stuffed with rose petals, sunflower-seed cookies to take back to school with her. But they never seem to be the right things, they never seem to be enough.

Augusta tells Charis to straighten her shoulders or she'll be a bag lady in old age. She goes through Charis's cupboards and drawers and throws out the candle ends Charis has been saving to make into other candles, sometime when she gets around to it, and the partly used soaps she's been intending to cook into other soaps, and the twists of wool destined for Christmas tree decorations that got moths in them by mistake. She asks Charis when she last cleaned the toilet, and orders her to get rid of the clutter in the kitchen, by which she means the bunches of dried herbs grown so lovingly by Charis every summer, and dangling—somewhat dusty, but still usable—from the nails of different sizes that stud the top of the window frame, and the hanging wire basket for eggs and onions where Charis tosses her gloves and scarves, and the Oxfam oven mitts made by mountain peasant women, somewhere far away, in the shape of a red owl and a navy blue pussycat.

Augusta frowns at the owl and the pussycat. Her own kitchen will be white, she tells Charis, and very functional, with everything stored in drawers. She's already cut out a picture of it, from *Architectural Digest*.

Charis loves Augusta, but decides not to think about her right now. It's too early in the morning. Instead she will enjoy the sunrise, which is a more neutral way to begin the day.

She goes to the small bedroom window and flings aside the curtain, which is a piece of the same print that covers her bed. She hasn't got around to hemming it, but she will, later. Several of the thumbtacks holding its top end to the wall pop out and scatter on the floor. Now she will have to remember, and avoid stepping on them in her bare feet. She should get a curtain rod, or something, or two hooks with a piece of string: that wouldn't be very expensive. In any case the curtain has to be washed before Augusta comes home again. "Don't you ever *wash* this thing?" she said the last time she was here. "It looks like poor people's underpants." Augusta has a graphic way of putting things that makes Charis wince. It's too sharp, too bright, too jagged: shapes cut from tin.

Never mind. The view from her bedroom window is there to soothe her. Her house is the end one in the row, and then comes the grass and then the trees, maple and willow, and through a gap in the trees the harbour, with the sun just beginning to touch the water, from which, today, a vapoury mist is rising. So pink, so white, so softly blue, with a slice of moon and the gulls circling and dipping like flights of souls; and on the mist the city floats, tower and tower and tower and spire, the glass walls of different colours, black, silver, green, copper, catching the light and throwing it back, tenderly at this hour.

From here on the Island, the city is mysterious, like a mirage, like the cover on a book of science fiction. A paperback. It's like this at sunset too, when the sky turns burnt orange and then the crimson of inner space, and then indigo, and the lights in the many windows change the darkness to gauze; and then at night the neon shows up against the sky and it gives off a glow, like an amusement park or something safely on fire. The only time Charis doesn't care to look at the city is noon, in the full glare of the day. It's too clear-cut, too brash and assertive. It juts, it pushes. It's just girders then, and slabs of concrete.

Charis would rather look at the city than go there, even at dusk. Once she's in it she can no longer see it; or she sees it only in detail, and it becomes harsher, pock-marked, crisscrossed with grids, like a microscopic photo-graph of skin. She has to go into it every day, however; she has to work. She likes her job well enough as jobs go, but it's a job, and every job has shackles attached to it. Square brackets. So she tries to plan a small respite for each day, a small joy, something extra.

Today she's having lunch at the Toxique, with Roz and Tony. In a way they are inappropriate friends for her to have. It's odd to think that she's known them so long, ever since McClung Hall. Well, not known. She didn't truly know anybody back then, just their appearances. But Tony and Roz are friends now, that's beyond a doubt. They're part of her pattern, for this life.

She steps away from the window, and pauses to remove a thumbtack from her foot. It doesn't hurt as much as she would have expected. She flashes briefly on the image of a bed of nails, with herself lying on it. It would take some getting used to, but it would be good training.

She pulls off her white cotton nightgown, drinks the glass of water she leaves beside her bed every night to remind herself about drinking enough water, and does her yoga exercises in nothing but her underpants. Her leotard is in the wash, but who cares? Nobody can see her. There are some good things about living alone. The room is cool, but cool air tones up the skin. One nice thing about her job is that it doesn't start until ten, which gives her a long morning, time to grow slowly into her day.

She cheats a little on the exercises because she doesn't feel like lying down on the floor right now. Then she goes downstairs and has her shower. The bathroom is off the kitchen, because it was added on after the house was built. A lot of the Island houses are like that; at first they would have had outhouses, because they were just summer cottages then. Charis has painted her bathroom a cheerful shade of pink, but that's done nothing to improve the slanting floor. Possibly the bathroom is coming away from the rest of the house, which would account for the cracks, and the drafts in winter. She may have to get it propped up.

Charis washes herself with Body Shop shower gel, the Dewberry flavour: her arms, her neck, her legs with their nearly invisible scars. She likes to be clean. There's clean outside and there's clean inside, her grandmother used to say, and clean inside is better. But Charis is not altogether clean inside: shreds of Zenia cling to her still, like dirty spangled muslin. She sees the name *Zenia* in her head, glowing like a scratch, like lava, and draws a line through it with a thick black crayon. It's too early in the morning to think about Zenia.

She scrubs her hair in the shower, then gets out and towel-dries it and parts it in the middle. Augusta is pestering her to get it cut. Coloured also. Augusta doesn't want an old washed-out mother. *Washed-out* is her phrase. "I like myself the way I am," Charis tells her; but she wonders if that's altogether true. However, she refuses to dye her hair, because once you begin you have to keep on doing it, and that's just one more heavy chain. Look at Roz.

She does her breast self-examination in the bathroom mirror—she has to do it every day, or she'll forget and never do it—and doesn't find any lumps. Maybe she should start wearing a brassiere. Maybe she should always have worn one; then she wouldn't have become so floppy. Nobody tells you about aging, in advance. No, that's not right. People tell you but you don't hear them. "Mum's on another channel," August used to say to her friends, before she added the *a*.

Charis takes her quartz pendulum out of its blue Chinese silk drawstring bag—silk conserves the vibrations, says Shanita—and holds it over her head, watching it in the mirror. "Will this be a good day?" she asks it. Round and round means yes, back and forth means no. The pendulum hesitates, begins to swing: a sort of ellipse. It can't make up its mind. *Normal,* thinks Charis. Then it gives a sort of jump, and stops. Charis is puzzled: she's never seen it do that before. She decides to ask Shanita; Shanita will know. She tucks the pendulum back into its bag.

To get another angle, she takes down her grandmother's Bible, closes her eyes, and pokes at the pages with a pin. She hasn't done this for a while, but she hasn't lost the knack. Her hand is drawn down, and she opens her eyes and reads: *For now we see through a glass, darkly; but then face to face.* First Corinthians, and, as a daily forecast, not one whole lot of help.

•   •   •

For breakfast she has muesli, with yogurt mixed in and half an apple cut up in it. When Billy was here they used to have eggs, from the long-vanished hens, and bacon. Or Billy would have bacon. He liked it.

Charis quickly wipes from her mind—*Wipe it! Like a video!* says Shanita—the image of Billy, and of the things he liked. She considers bacon instead. She stopped eating bacon when she was seven, but other kinds of meat went later. *The Save Your Life Cookbook* advised her, back there, back then, to visualize what any given piece of fat would look like in her stomach. A pound of butter, a pound of lard, a strip of bacon, uncooked, white and limp and flat like a tapeworm. Charis is all too good at visualizing; she hasn't been able to stop with fat. Every time she puts something into her mouth she's likely to see it in living colour, as it makes its way down her esophagus into her stomach, where it churns unpleasantly and then inches through her digestive tract, which is the shape of a long snarled garden hose covered inside with little rubbery fingers, like foot massage sandals. Sooner or later it will come out the other end. This is what her concentration on healthy eating can lead to: she sees everything on her plate in the guise of a future turd.

Wipe the bacon, she tells herself sternly. It's sunny outside now, she should think about that. She sits at her kitchen table, a round oak one she's had ever since August was born, in her Japanese cotton kimono with the bamboo shoots on it, and eats her muesli, giving it the recommended number of chews and looking out the kitchen window. She used to be able to see the henhouse from here. Billy built that himself and she left it there as a sort of monument, even though there were no hens in it any more, until August changed into Augusta and made her take it down. The two of them did it with crowbars, and she cried afterwards, on her white bedspread with the vines. If only she knew where he'd gone. If only she knew where they'd taken him. He must have been taken somewhere, by force, by someone. He wouldn't have just gone away like that, without telling her, without writing. . . .

Pain hits her in the neck, right across the windpipe, before she can stop it. *Wipe the pain.* But sometimes she just can't. She bangs her forehead softly on the edge of the table.

"Sometimes I just can't," she says out loud.

All right then, says Shanita's voice. *Let it wash. Let it just wash over you. It's only a wave. It's like water. Think about what colour that wave is.*

"Red," says Charis out loud.

Well then, says Shanita, smiling. *That can be a pretty colour too, can't it? Just hold that. Just hold that colour.*

"Yes," says Charis meekly. "But it hurts."

Well of course it hurts! Who ever said it wouldn't hurt? If it hurts, that means you are still alive! Now—what colour is that hurt?

Charis breathes in, breathes out, and the colour fades. It works with headaches, too. She once tried to explain this to Roz, when Roz was in deep pain, a deeper and more recent pain than Charis's. Though maybe not deeper. "You can heal yourself," she told Roz, keeping her voice level and confident, like Shanita's. "You can control it."

"That is such *horse*shit," said Roz angrily. "It is

absolutely *no use* saying you should stop *loving* someone. It doesn't work like that!"

"Well, you should, if you know it's bad for you," said Charis.

"Bad for you has nothing to do with it," said Roz.

"I like hamburgers," said Charis, "but I don't eat them."

"Hamburgers are not an *emotion,*" said Roz.

"Yes they are," said Charis.

Charis gets up to put on the kettle. She'll make some Morning Miracle tea, a special blend from work. To light the gas stove she stands sideways, because at some times—and this is one of them—she doesn't like to turn her back to the kitchen door.

The kitchen door has a glass panel in it, at head height. A month ago, when she came home for the weekend, Augusta gave Charis a scare. Not in the morning, but at night, at dusk. It was drizzling, a fine Scotch mist; the city and part of the lake were blotted out, and there was no light from the hidden sunset. Charis wasn't expecting Augusta until later, or possibly not until the next day; she was expecting her to phone, from the mainland, though she didn't know just when. Augusta has become fairly off-hand about her comings and goings.

But suddenly there was a woman's face framed in the glass panel of the door. A white face, indistinct in the murkiness, in the cloudy air. Charis turned away from the stove and caught sight of it, and the back of her neck bristled.

It was only Augusta, but that's not what Charis thought. She thought it was Zenia. Zenia, with her dark hair sleeked down by the rain, wet and shivering, standing on the back step as she had done once before, long ago. Zenia, who had been dead for five years.

The worst thing, thinks Charis, was that she'd confused Zenia with her own daughter, who is nothing like Zenia at all. What a terrible thing for her to have done.

No. The worst thing was that she hadn't really been all that surprised.

8

Not surprised, because people don't die. Or so Charis believes. Tony asked her once what she meant by *die,* and Charis—who is made nervous by Tony's way of pinning her down, and frequently gets out of it by pretending she hasn't heard the question—had to admit that they did go through a process that everyone was in the habit of calling *death.* Certainly some fairly terminal things happened to the body, things that Charis would rather not dwell on because she hasn't decided whether it would be better to mingle with the earth, or—through cremation—with the air. Each of these possibilities is appealing as a sort of general idea, but when it comes right down to it, to particulars such as her own fingers, toes, and mouth, then less.

But death was just a stage, she tried to say. It was just a sort of state, a transition; it was—well, a learning experience.

She isn't very good at explaining things to Tony. She usually stutters to a halt, especially with Tony's huge and slightly chilly eyes fixed on her, magnified by those glasses, and with Tony's little pearly-toothed mouth slightly open. It's as if Tony is amazed by everything Charis says. But amazement is not—she suspects—what is really going on in that delicate head of Tony's. Though Tony never laughs at her, not up front.

"What do you learn?" said Tony.

"Well, you learn—how to be better, next time. You join the light," said Charis. Tony leaned forward, looking interested, so Charis fumbled on. "People have after-death experiences, and that's what they say, that's how we know. When they come back to life again."

"They come back to life?" said Tony, her eyes enormous.

"People pound their chests. And breathe into them, and warm them up, and, and, bring them back," said Charis.

"She means *near-death*," said Roz, who often tells Tony what Charis means. "You must have read those articles! It's a number lately. You're supposed to get a sort of *son et lumière*. Tunnels and fireworks and baroque music. My father had one, when he had the first heart attack. His old bank manager showed up, lit like a Christmas tree, and told my father he couldn't die yet because he had unfinished business."

"Ah," said Tony. "Unfinished business."

Charis wanted to say that this wasn't what she meant, she did mean *after* death. "Some people don't get as far as the light," she said. "They get lost. In the tunnel. Some of them don't even know they're dead." She did not go on to say that these sorts of people could be quite dangerous because they could get into your own body, more or less move into it, like squatters, and then it could be difficult to get them out again. She didn't go on to say this, because it would have been futile: Tony was a proof addict.

"Right," said Roz, who was made very uncomfortable by this sort of conversation. "I know people like that. My *own* bank manager, for instance. Or the government. Dead all right, but do they know it?" She laughed, and asked Charis what could be wrong with her delphiniums, because they were turning black. "It's a mildew," said Charis. That was how Roz handled the afterlife: perennial borders. It was the one subject about which Charis had a good deal more hard data than Tony did.

But when Zenia appeared at the back door, in the rain, this is what Charis thought. She thought, Zenia is lost. She can't find the light. Maybe she doesn't even know she's dead. What would be more natural than for her to show up at Charis's house, to ask for help? Help was what she had come for, at first.

Then of course it turned out that Zenia wasn't Zenia at all, but only Augusta, home for the weekend and slightly forlorn, because—Charis suspected—some other plan of hers had fallen through, something involving a man. There are men in Augusta's life, Charis divines this; though they are not produced, they are not presented to Charis. Most likely they are in the business course too, fledgling entrepreneurs who would take one look at Charis in her not yet fully organized house and run like crazy. Most likely Augusta heads them off. Maybe she tells them her mother is ill, or in Florida or something.

But Augusta is not completely lacquered yet; she does have moments of soft guilt. That time, she'd brought a loaf of bran bread with her as a peace offering, and some dried figs. Charis gave her an extra hug and made her some zucchini muffins, and a hot-water bottle for her bed, as she used to do when Augusta was little, because she was so thankful that Augusta was not Zenia after all.

Still, it's almost as if Zenia really has been here. As if she came and then went away without getting what she wanted. As if she'll be back.

When she materializes the next time, Charis will be expecting her. Zenia must have something she wants to say. Or no. Maybe it's Charis who has something to say; maybe this is what's holding Zenia to this earth. Because Zenia's around, she's around somewhere, Charis has known it ever since that funeral. She looked at the canister with Zenia's ashes in it, and she knew. The ashes might be in there, but ashes were not a person. Zenia was not in that canister, or with the light either. Zenia was loose, loose in the air but tethered to the world of appearances, and it's all the fault of Charis. It's Charis who needs her to be here, it's Charis who won't cut her free.

Zenia will appear, her white face looming in the glass oblong, and Charis will open the door. *Come in,* she will say, because the dead can't cross your threshold unless you invite them. *Come in,* she will say, risking her own body, because Zenia will be searching for a new flesh dress. *Come in,* she will say, for the third and crucial time, and Zenia will drift through the doorway, her eyes cavernous, her hair like cold smoke. She will stand in the kitchen and the light will darken, and Charis will be afraid.

But she won't back down, she won't back away this time. *What did they do with Billy?* she'll ask her. Zenia is the only one who knows.

●　　●　　●

Charis goes back upstairs and gets dressed for work, trying not to look over her shoulder. Sometimes she thinks
it's not such a great idea for her to live alone. The rest of
the time she likes it, though. She can do what she wants,
she can be who she is, and if she talks out loud to herself
there's nobody to stare. Nobody to complain about the
dustballs, except maybe Augusta, who gets out the broom
and sweeps them up.

She steps on another thumbtack and this one hurts
more, so she puts on her shoes. When she has all of her
clothes on she goes in search of her reading glasses,
because she'll need them at work, when she's making out
invoices, and to read the menu at the Toxique.

She looks forward to that lunch. She wills herself to
look forward to it, although there's something tugging at
her, some intuition . . . a sinking feeling. Not something
violent, like an explosion or a fire. Something else. She
often has these feelings, but since nothing ever comes of
half of them they aren't dependable. Shanita says it's
because she has a Solomon's Cross on her palm but it's
fuzzed over; too many wispy hairlines. "You are picking up
a lot of stations," is what Shanita says. "Cosmic static."

She finds the reading glasses under the tea cosy in the
kitchen; she doesn't remember putting them there.
Objects have a life of their own, and the ones in her house
move around at night. They've been doing it more, recently. It's the ozone layer, probably. Unknown energies are
getting through.

• • •

She has twenty minutes to walk to the ferry. That's ample. She goes out the back door as a matter of course; the front one is nailed shut, with plastic sheeting on the inside for insulation and an Indian hand-woven bedspread over top of it, in a paisley green-and-blue print. The insulation is for winter. In the summers she takes it down, except last summer she didn't get around to it. There's always a bunch of dead flies underneath the plastic, and she doesn't enjoy them a lot.

The air on the Island is so good. Compared, that is. At least there's usually a breeze. She pauses outside her back door, breathing in the comparatively good air, feeling its crispness fill her lungs. Her vegetable garden is still pushing up the Swiss chard, there are still carrots and green tomatoes; a rusty-orange chrysanthemum blooms in one corner. The soil is rich here; traces of henshit still linger, and she digs in compost from her compost heap every spring and fall. It's almost time to do it, now, before the first frost comes.

She loves her garden; she loves kneeling in the dirt, with both hands deep in the ground, rummaging among the roots with the earthworms slipping away from her groping fingers, enveloped in the smell of mudpies and slow ferment and thinking about nothing. Helping things grow. She never uses gardening gloves, much to Augusta's despair.

Shanita says her grandmother used to eat dirt, a handful or two every spring. She said it was good for you. (Although it's been impossible for Charis to figure out exactly which grandmother she means: Shanita seems to have more than two.) But eating dirt is the sort of thing that Charis's own grandmother might have done, because that grandmother, grubby and terrifying though she had been, was a woman who knew about such things. Charis hasn't got around to trying it herself yet, but she's working up to it.

At the front of her house there's more to be done. She pulled out the lawn last spring, and tried for a sort of English cottage effect, which she thought would go well with the house itself, with its white clapboard and slightly falling-apart look; but she planted too many species and didn't thin out, nor did she weed as much as she should have, and what resulted was a sort of scramble. Mostly the snapdragons won; they're still blooming, some of the tall spikes fallen over (she should have staked them), with leggy offshoots coming up from them. Next year she'll put the tall things in the back, and have fewer colours.

If there is a next year, that is. Next year she may not even have a house. The Island's war with the city is still going on. The city wants to tear down all these houses, level everything, turn it into a park. A lot of the houses here went that way, years ago, before people dug in their heels. Charis sees it as envy: if the city people can't live here themselves they don't want anyone else to be able to do it either. Well, it kept the property prices low. If not for that, where would Charis be?

And if no one lived on the Island, who would ever be able to look at the city from a distance, the way Charis does every morning at sunrise, and find it so beautiful? Without such a vision of itself, of its loveliness and best possibilities, the city would decay, would crack apart, would collapse into useless rubble. It's only sustained by belief; belief, and meditation, the meditation of people like her. Charis knows this for a certainty, but so far she has been unable to put it that way, exactly, in her frequent letters to the city councillors, only two of which she has actually got around to mailing. But just writing it down helps. It beams out the message, which gets into the city councillors' heads without their awareness. It's like radio waves.

When she reaches the dock the ferry is already boarding. People are going on, singly and in twos; there's something processional about their entrance, in the way they step from land to water. Right here was where she last saw Billy; and also Zenia, in the flesh. They were already aboard, and as Charis came heavily running, gasping, hands on her belly to hold it attached to her, it was dangerous for her to run like that, she could have fallen and lost the baby, the ferry men were hoisting up the gangway, the ferry was hooting and backing out, the deep water churning to a whirlpool. She couldn't have jumped.

Billy and Zenia were not touching. There were two strange men with them; or there were two strange men standing nearby. Men in overcoats. Billy saw her. He didn't wave. He turned away. Zenia didn't move. Her aura was deep red. Her hair blew out around her head. The sun was behind her, so she had no face. She was a dark sunflower. The sky was hugely blue. The two of them got smaller, going away.

Charis doesn't remember the sound that came out of

her. She doesn't want to. She tries to hold the image of the two of them receding, a moment of time stilled and devoid of content, like a postcard with nothing written on the back.

She walks to the main deck and settles herself for transition. In her cardigan pocket she has a crust of bread; she will feed it to the gulls, who are already circling, eyeing her, crying like hungry spirits.

Maybe you don't enter the light through a tunnel, she thinks. Maybe it's a boat, as the ancients said it was. You pay your fare, you cross, you drink of the River of Forgetfulness. Then you are reborn.

9

The place where Charis works is called Radiance. It sells crystals of all kinds, big and small, made into pendants and earrings or just raw, and seashells; and essential oils imported from Egypt and southern France, and incense from India, and organic body creams and bath gels from California and England, and sachets of bark and herbs and dried flowers, from France mainly, and Tarot cards in six different patterns, and Afghan and Thai jewellery, and tapes of New Age music with a lot of harp and flute sounds in them, and CDs of seashores, waterfalls, and loon calls, and books on Native Indian spirituality and Health Secrets of the Aztecs, and mother-of-pearl inlaid chopsticks and lacquered bowls from Japan, and tiny carvings of Chinese jade, and recycled handmade-paper greeting cards with arrangements of dried weeds stuck onto them, and packets of wild rice, and non-caffeine teas from eight different countries, and necklaces of cowries, dried plant seeds, polished stones, and carved wooden beads.

Charis remembers this place from the sixties. It was called The Blown Mind Shoppe then, and had hash pipes and psychedelic posters and roach clips and tie-dyed undershirts and dashikis. In the seventies it was called Okkult, and had books on demonology, as well as on women's ancient religions and Wicca and the lost kingdoms of Atlantis and Mu, and some unappealing bone artefacts, and smelly—and in Charis's opinion, fraudulent—bundles of ground-up animal parts. There was a stuffed alligator in its window then, and for a while it even sold fright wigs and horror makeup kits, with fake blood and glue-on scars. That was a low point for it, although popular with the punk set.

It changed again in the early eighties. That was when Shanita took over, when it was still Okkult. She quickly got rid of the stuffed alligator and the bones and the demonology books—why borrow trouble, she says, and she didn't want any run-ins with the animal-rights folks, or any Christian weirdos spray-painting the window. It was her idea to start up the crystals, and to change the name to Radiance.

It was the name that attracted Charis. First she was just a customer: she came in for the herbal teas. But then the sales position came open, and since she was tired of her job filing reports at the Ministry of Natural Resources—too impersonal, too much pressure, and besides she wasn't very good at it—she applied. Shanita hired her because she had the right look, or so Shanita told her.

"You won't bug the customers," said Shanita. "They don't like to be pushed. They like to just sort of float around in here, know what I mean?"

Charis did. She likes to float around in Radiance herself. She likes the way it smells, and she likes the things in it. Sometimes she does a trade, taking goods—at a discount price—instead of pay, much to Augusta's disgust.

More of that junk? she says. She does not see how many more Japanese lacquered bowls and tapes of loon calls Charis really needs. Charis says it isn't a matter of need, material need that is. It's a matter of spiritual need. Right now she has her eye on a truly lovely amethyst geode, from Nova Scotia. She will keep it in her bedroom, to ward off bad dreams.

She can picture Augusta's response to this geode. *Mom! What's this hunk of rock doing in your bed?* She can picture Tony's interested scepticism—*Does it really work?*—and Roz's maternal indulgence—*Honey, if it makes you happy I'm all for it!* This has been her problem all her life: picturing other people's responses. She's too good at it. She can picture the response of anyone—other people's reactions, their emotions, their criticisms, their demands—but somehow they don't reciprocate. Maybe they can't. Maybe they lack the gift, if it is one.

Charis walks away from the ferry dock, up to King and then Queen, sniffing the turgid city air, so different from the air on the Island. This air is full of chemicals, and also of breath, the breath of other people. There are too many people breathing in this city. There are too many people breathing on this planet; maybe it would be beneficial if a few million of them would make the transition. But this is an appallingly selfish thought, so Charis stops thinking it. Instead she thinks about sharing. Every single molecule that Charis is taking into her lungs has been sucked in and out of the lungs of countless thousands of other people, many times. Come to that, every single molecule in her body has once been part of someone else's body, of the bodies of many others, going back and back, and then past human beings, all the way to the dinosaurs, all the way to the first planktons. Not to mention vegetation. We are all a part of everybody else, she muses. We are all a part of everything.

That's a cosmic insight, if you can keep it at arm's length. But then Charis has an unpleasant idea. If everyone is part of everyone else, then she herself is a part of Zenia. Or the other way around. Zenia may be what she's breathing in. The part of Zenia that went up in smoke, that is. Not her astral body, which is still hovering near earth, and not the ashes either, which are safely in that canister under the mulberry tree.

Maybe that's what Zenia wants! Maybe she's bothered by her partial state, some of her energy in the canister and some wafting around. Maybe she wants to be let out. Maybe Charis should go to the cemetery some night, with a shovel and a can-opener, and dig her up and sprinkle her. Mingle her with the Universe. That would be a kindly thing to do.

She reaches Radiance at ten to ten, early for once, and lets herself in with her key, and puts on the mauve-and-aqua smock that Shanita designed for them so the customers will know they aren't customers themselves.

Shanita is already there. "Hi, Charis, how're you doing?" she calls out, from the stockroom at the back. It's Shanita who does all the ordering. She has a knack for it; she goes to crafts fairs and takes trips to little-known corners, and finds things, wonderful things that no other store in town has. She seems to know in advance what people will want.

Charis admires Shanita a lot. Shanita is smart and practical, as well as being psychic. Also she's strong, and also she's one of the most beautiful women Charis has ever seen. Though she isn't young—she must be well over forty. She refuses to tell her age—the one time Charis asked her, she only laughed, and said age was in the mind and in her mind she was two thousand—but she's getting a white streak in her hair. That's another thing Charis admires: Shanita doesn't dye.

The hair itself is black, neither curly nor frizzy but wavy, thick and shining and luscious, like pulled taffy or lava. Like hot black glass. Shanita coils it, and winds it here and there on her head: sometimes on top, sometimes on one side. Or else she lets it hang down her back in one thick curl. She has wide cheekbones, a trim high-bridged nose, full lips, and large darkly fringed eyes, which are a startling shade that shifts from brown to green, depending on what colour she's wearing. Her skin is smooth and unwrinkled, an indeterminate colour, neither black nor brown nor yellow. A deep beige; but beige is a bland word. Nor is it chestnut, nor burnt sienna, nor umber. It's some other word.

People coming into the store frequently ask Shanita where she's from. "Right here," she says, smiling her ultra-bright smile. "I was born right in this very city!" She's nice about it to their faces, but it's a question that bothers her a lot.

"I think they mean, where were your parents from," says Charis, because that's what Canadians usually mean when they ask that question.

"That's not what they mean," says Shanita. "What they mean is, when am I leaving."

Charis cannot see why anyone would want Shanita to leave, but when she says so, Shanita laughs. "You," she says, "have led one damn sheltered life." Then she tells Charis about the rudeness of white streetcar conductors towards her. "*Move to the back,* they tell me, like I was dirt!"

"Streetcar conductors are *all* rude! They say *Move to the back* to everybody, they're rude to *me!*" says Charis, intending to console Shanita—although she's being slightly dishonest, it's only some streetcar conductors, and she herself hardly ever takes the streetcar—and Shanita throws her a glance of contempt, for being unable to acknowledge the racism of almost everybody, almost everybody white, and then Charis feels bad. Sometimes she thinks of Shanita as a dauntless explorer, hacking her way through the jungle. The jungle consists of people like Charis.

So she stops herself from being too curious, from asking too much about Shanita, about her background, about where she's *from.* Shanita teases her, though; she throws out hints, changes her story. Sometimes she's part Chinese and part black, with a West Indian grandmother; she can do the accent, so maybe there's something to it. That might be the grandmother who used to eat dirt; but there are other grandmothers too, one from the States and one from Halifax, and one from Pakistan and one from New Mexico, and even one from Scotland. Maybe they are step-grandmothers, or maybe Shanita moved around a lot. Charis can't sort them out: Shanita has more grandmothers than anyone she knows. But sometimes she's part Ojibway, or else part Mayan, and one day she was even part

Tibetan. She can be whatever she feels like, because who can tell?

Whereas Charis is stuck with being white. A white rabbit. Being white is getting more and more exhausting. There are so many bad waves attached to it, left over from the past but spreading through the present, like the killing rays from atomic waste dumps. There's so much to expiate! It gives her anemia just to think about it. In her next life she's going to be a mixture, a blend, a vigorous hybrid, like Shanita. Then no one will have anything on her.

The store doesn't open till eleven, so Charis helps take stock. Shanita goes through the shelves, counting, and Charis writes down the numbers on a clipboard. It's a good thing she found her reading glasses.

"We'll have to bring down the prices," says Shanita, frowning. "Stuff is not moving. We'll have to do a sale."

"Before Christmas?" says Charis, astonished.

"It's the Recession," says Shanita, pursing her lips. "That's reality. This time of year, we usually have to re-order for Christmas, right? Now, just look at all this!"

Charis peers: the shelves are upsettingly full. "You know what's moving?" says Shanita. "This thing."

Charis is familiar with it, because she's sold a lot of them lately. It's a little pamphlet-like book, a cookbook, done on grey recycled paper with black-and-white line drawings, a do-it-yourself home publishing effort: *Pot Luck: Penny-Pinching Soups & Stews.* It doesn't appeal to her, personally. Penny-pinching as a concept she finds very blocking. There's something hard and grinding about it, and *pinching* is a hurtful word. True, she saves candle ends and pieces of wool, but that's because she wants to, she wants to create things with them, that's an act of love towards the earth.

"I need more stuff like this," says Shanita. "Fact is, I'm thinking of changing the store. Changing the name, the concept, everything."

Charis's heart sinks. "What would you change it to?" she asks.

"I was thinking, Scrimpers," says Shanita.

"Scrimpers?" says Charis.

"You know. Like the old five-and-dime, all cheap stuff," says Shanita. "Only more creative. It could work! A few years ago, you could trade on the impulse buy. Mad money, you know? Folks were flinging it around. But the only way you make it through a recession is by getting people to buy stuff about how not to buy stuff, if you know what I mean."

"But Radiance is so lovely!" cries Charis unhappily.

"I know," says Shanita. "It was a lot of fun while it lasted. But *lovely* is luxury goods. How many of these dinky toys you think people are going to buy, right now? Maybe some, but only if we keep the price down. In these times you cut your losses, you cut your overheads, you do what you have to. This is a lifeboat, you know? It's my lifeboat, it's my life. I have worked damn hard, I know which way the wind is blowing, and I do not intend to go down with the sinking ship."

She's defensive. She looks at Charis, her gaze level— her eyes are green today—and Charis realizes that she herself is an overhead. If things get much worse, Shanita will cut her, and run the store by herself, and Charis will be out of a job.

• • •

They finish taking stock and open the door for the day, and Shanita's mood changes. She's friendly now, almost solicitous; she makes them both some Morning Miracle, and they sit at the front counter drinking it. There is not exactly a stampede of customers, so Shanita passes the time by asking Charis all about Augusta.

To Charis's discomfort, Shanita approves of Augusta; she thinks Augusta is smart to be taking a business course. "A woman needs to be prepared to make her own way," she says. "Too many lazy men around." She even approves of the furniture scrapbook, which Charis herself finds so grasping, so materialistic. "That's a girl with a head on her shoulders," Shanita says, pouring them out more tea. "Wish I'd had one, at her age. Would've saved myself a lot of trouble." She has two daughters of her own, and two sons, grown up. She's a grandmother, even; but she doesn't talk much about that part of her life. By now she knows a great deal about Charis, whereas Charis knows almost nothing about her.

"My pendulum went funny this morning," says Charis, to get off the subject of Augusta.

"Funny?" says Shanita. The pendulums are sold in the store, five different models, and Shanita is an expert at interpreting their movements.

"It just stopped," says Charis. "Stock-still, right over my head."

"That's a strong message," says Shanita. "That's something real sudden, something you weren't looking for. Maybe it's some entity, trying to get a message through. Today is the cusp of Scorpio, right? It's like, the pendulum is pointing a finger and saying, watch out!"

Charis is apprehensive: could it be Augusta, an accident? That's the first thing she thinks of, so she asks.

"It's not what I get," says Shanita reassuringly, "but let's just see." She takes the Tarot she keeps under the counter, the Marseilles deck she favours, and Charis shuffles and cuts.

"The Tower," says Shanita. "Sudden, like I said. The Priestess. An opening, something hidden is revealed. The Knight of Swords—well, that could be interesting! The Knights all bring messages. Now, the Empress. A strong woman! Not you, though. Somebody else. But I wouldn't say this is Augusta, no. The Empress is not a young girl."

"Maybe it's you," Charis says, and Shanita laughs and says, "Strong! I am a broken reed!" She puts down another card. "Death," she says. "A change. Could be a renewal." She crosses that card again. "Oh. The Moon."

The Moon, with its baying dogs, its pool, its lurking scorpion. Just then the bell tinkles and a customer comes into the store; she asks Charis for two copies of *Pot Luck,* one for herself, one for a gift. Charis agrees with her that it's very useful and not too expensive, and that the hand-done illustrations are sweet, and tells her that yes, Shanita is truly stunning but she's not from any place except just plain old Toronto, and takes the money and wraps the books, her mind elsewhere.

The Moon, she thinks. Illusion.

10

At noon Charis takes off her flowered smock and says goodbye to Shanita—it's her half-day, Tuesday, so she won't be back after lunch—and heads out into the street, trying not to breathe too much. She has seen bicycle messengers wearing white paper nose masks, like nurses. It's a trend, she thinks; maybe they should order some for the store, only coloured and with some nice patterns printed on.

As soon as she walks into the Toxique her head starts to crackle. It's as if there's a thunderstorm around somewhere, or a loose connection. Ions are bombarding her, wavelets of menacing energy. She brushes her forehead, then shakes her fingers to get rid of them.

She cranes her neck, looking around for the source of the disturbance. Sometimes it's the people who come in to deal drugs on the stairs going down to the washrooms, but none of them seem to be around right now. The waitress comes up to her, and Charis asks for the corner near the mirror. Mirrors deflect.

The Toxique is Roz's latest discovery. Roz is always discovering things, especially restaurants. She likes eating in places where no one from her office would ever eat, she likes being surrounded by people wearing clothes she'd never wear herself. She likes to think she's mingling with real life, *real* meaning poorer than her. Or that's the impression Charis sometimes gets. She's tried telling Roz that all life is equally real, but Roz doesn't appear to understand what she means; though maybe Charis doesn't put it clearly enough.

She glances at the leopard-skin tights of the waitress, wrinkles her nose—these clothes are too tough for her— tells herself not to be judgmental, orders a bottle of Evian and some white wine, and settles down to wait. She opens the menu, squints at it, rummages in her bag for her reading glasses, can't find them—has she left them at the store?—and finally locates them on top of her head. She must have walked along the street like that. She puts them on her nose and scans the daily specials. At least they always have something vegetarian; though who knows where the vegetables come from? Probably off some irradiated chemical-saturated agro-business maxi-farm.

The truth is that she doesn't much like the Toxique. It's partly the name: she considers it damaging to the neurons to spend time around such a poisonous name. And the clothes on the waiters, the *servers,* remind her of some of the things they used to sell in Okkult. At any moment there could be rubber scars and fake blood. But she's willing to eat here once in a while for the sake of Roz.

As for Tony, who knows what she thinks of this place? Tony's hard for Charis to read; she always has been, ever since they first met, back in the McClung Hall days. But most likely Tony would have exactly the same attitude if it were the King Eddie, or else McDonald's: a kind of goggle-eyed, incredulous note-taking, like a Martian on a time-travel holiday. Collecting specimens. Freeze-drying them. Sticking everything into labelled boxes. Leaving no space, no space for the unsayable.

Not that she doesn't like Tony. No, wrong. There are quite a few times when she doesn't like Tony. Tony can use too many words, can grate on her, can rub her electrical field the wrong way. But she loves Tony all the same. Tony is so calm, so clear-headed, so grounded. If Charis ever hears any more voices telling her to slit her wrists, Tony is the one she'd call, to come over on the Island ferry and take charge of her, to defuse her, to tell her not to be an idiot. Tony would know what to do, step by step, one thing at a time, in order.

She wouldn't call Roz at first, because Roz would freak out, would cry and sympathize and agree with her about the unbearability of it all, and would be late for the ferry as well. But afterwards, after she felt safe again, she would go to Roz for the hug.

Roz and Tony come in together, and Charis waves at them, and there's the flurry there always is when Roz enters a restaurant, and the two of them sit down and Roz lights a cigarette, and they start talking at once. Charis tunes out because she isn't that interested in what they're saying, and just lets their presences wash over her. Their presences are more important to her anyway than what comes out of their mouths. Words are so often like window curtains, a decorative screen put up to keep the neighbours at a distance. But auras don't lie. Charis herself doesn't see auras as often as she used to. When she was little, when she was Karen, she saw them effortlessly; now it's only at moments of stress. But she can sense them, the way blind people can sense colour through the ends of their fingers.

What she senses about Tony today is coolness. A transparent coolness. Tony reminds her of a snowflake, so tiny and pale and fastidious, but cold; a mind like an ice cube, clear and square; or cut glass, hard and sharp. Or ice, because it can melt. In the school play, Tony would have been a snowflake: one of the smallest children, too little for a speaking part but taking it all in. Charis herself was usually cast as a tree or a shrub. She wasn't given anything that involved moving around because she would have bumped into things, or that's what the teachers said. They didn't realize that her clumsiness was not the ordinary kind, not poor coordination. It was just because she wasn't sure where the edges of her body ended and the rest of the world began.

What would Roz have been? Charis visualizes Roz's aura—so golden and many-coloured and spicy—and her air of command, but also that undercurrent of exile, and casts her in the role of one of the Three Kings, wearing brocade and jewels, carrying a splendid gift. But would Roz ever have been in such a play? Her early life is such a jumble, with all those nuns and rabbis in it. Maybe she wouldn't have been allowed.

Charis herself gave up Christianity a long time ago. For one thing, the Bible is full of meat: animals being sacrificed, lambs, bullocks, doves. Cain was right to offer up the vegetables, God was wrong to refuse them. And there's too much blood: people in the Bible are always having their blood spilled, blood on their hands, their blood licked up by dogs. There are too many slaughters, too much suffering, too many tears.

She used to think some of the Eastern religions would be more serene; she was a Buddhist for a while, before she discovered how many Hells they had. Most religions are so intent on punishment.

She realizes that she's halfway through her lunch without having noticed. She's having the grated carrot and cottage cheese salad, a wise choice; not that she can remember having ordered it, but sometimes it's useful to have an automatic pilot like that, to take care of the routines. For a moment she watches Roz eat a piece of French bread; she likes to watch Roz eat French bread, cracking it open, burying her nose in it—*This is so good, this is so good!*— before sinking her firm white teeth into it. It's like a small prayer, a miniature grace, what Roz does with bread.

"Tony," says Charis, "I could really make something good, with your back garden." Tony has a great space back there, but there's nothing in it except patchy lawn and some diseased trees. What Charis has in mind would be fixing up the trees, and making a sort of woodland, with jack-in-the-pulpits, violets, mayapples, Solomon's seal, things that grow in shade. Some ferns. Nothing that Tony would have to weed, she could never be depended on for that. It would be special! Perhaps a fountain? But Tony doesn't answer her, and after a moment Charis realizes it's because she hasn't spoken out loud. Sometimes it's hard for her to remember whether she's actually said a thing or not. Augusta has complained about this habit of hers, among others.

She tunes back in to the conversation: they're talking about some war. Charis wishes they wouldn't get going on war, but they often do these days. It seems to be in the air, after a long time of not being there much at all. Roz starts it; she asks Tony questions, because she likes to ask people questions about things they're supposed to know about.

One of their lunches a few months ago was all about genocide, and Roz wanted to talk about the Holocaust, and Tony launched into a detailed thing about genocides through the ages, Genghis Khan and then the Cathars in France, and then the Armenians being butchered by the Turks, and then the Irish and the Scots and what the English did to them, death after horrible death, until Charis thought she was going to throw up.

Tony can deal with all of that, she can handle it, maybe to her it's just words, but for Charis the words are pictures and then screams and moans, and then the smell of rotting meat, and of burning, of burning flesh, and then physical pain, and if you dwell on it you make it happen, and she can never explain this to Tony in a way that Tony will understand, and also she's afraid they'll decide she's being silly. Hysterical, a nitwit, a flake. She knows they both think that sometimes.

So she'd got up and gone down the dark splintery stairs to the washroom, where there was a Renoir poster on the wall, a rounded pink woman drying herself leisurely after the bath, with blue and mauve highlights on her body, and that was peaceful; but when she'd gone back upstairs Tony was still in Scotland, with the Highland women and children being hunted down in the hills and spitted like pigs and shot like deer.

"The Scots!" said Roz, who wanted to get back to the Holocaust. "They've done very well for themselves, look at all those bankers! Who cares about *them*?"

"I do," said Charis, surprising herself as much as she did the two of them. "I care." They looked at her in amazement, because they were used to her taking mental time off when they talked about war. They thought it didn't interest her.

"You do?" said Roz, her eyebrows up. "Why, Charis?"

"You should care about everybody," said Charis. "Or maybe it's because I'm part Scottish. Part Scottish, part English. All those people who used to kill one another so much." She leaves out the Mennonites because she doesn't want to upset Roz, although the Mennonites don't count as real Germans. Also they never kill people; they only get killed, instead.

"Sweetie, I'm sorry," said Roz, contrite. "Of course! I keep forgetting. Stupid *moi,* thinking of you as pure *crème de la WASP.*" She patted Charis's hand.

"Nobody's killed them recently, though," said Charis. "Not all at once. But I guess that's how we ended up here."

"Ended up *here*?" said Tony, looking around. Did Charis mean the Toxique, or what?

"Because of wars," said Charis, unhappily; it's an insight she doesn't like much, now that she's had it. "In this country. Wars of one sort or another. But that was then. We should try to live in the *now*—don't you think? Or at least, I try to."

Tony smiled at Charis with affection, or the closest she usually got to it. "She's absolutely right," she said to Roz, as if this were a noteworthy event.

●　●　●

Right about what though, Charis wonders. The wars, or the *now*? Tony's standard response to the *now* would be to tell Charis how many babies are being born per minute, in the *now* she's so fond of, and how all that excess birth will inevitably lead to more wars. Then she would add a footnote about the crazed behaviour of overcrowded rats. Charis is grateful she isn't doing that today.

But she has it at last, the thread: it's Saddam Hussein and the invasion of Kuwait, and what will happen next. "It's already been decided," says Tony, "like the Rubicon," and Charis says, "The what?"

"Never mind, sweetie, it's just something historical," says Roz, because she at least does understand that this is not Charis's favourite topic of conversation, she's giving her permission to drift off.

But then it comes to Charis what the Rubicon is. It's something to do with Julius Caesar, they took it in high school. He crossed the Alps with elephants; another of those men who got famous for killing people. If they stopped giving medals to such men, thinks Charis, if they stopped giving them parades and making statues out of them, then those men would stop doing it. Stop all the killing. They do it to get attention.

Maybe that's who Tony was, in a previous life: Julius Caesar. Maybe Julius Caesar has been sent back in the body of a woman, to punish him. A very short woman, so he can see what it's like, to be powerless. Maybe that is the way things work.

•   •   •

The door opens, and Zenia is standing there. Charis goes cold all over, then takes a breath. She's ready, she's been readying herself, though lunch at the Toxique is the last place she would have expected this, this manifestation, this return. *The Tower,* thinks Charis. *A sudden event. Something you weren't looking for.* No wonder the pendulum stopped dead, right over her head! But why did Zenia bother opening the door? She could have walked right through it.

Zenia is in black, which is no surprise, black was her colour. But the strange thing is that she's fatter. Death has filled her out, which is not the usual way. Spirits are supposed to be thinner, hungry-looking, parched, and Zenia appears to be quite well. Especially, her breasts are larger. The last time Charis saw her in the flesh, she was skinny as a rake, a shadow practically, her breasts almost flat, like circles of thick cardboard stuck against her chest, the nipples buttoning them on. Now she's what you would call voluptuous.

She's angry, though. A dark aura swirls out from around her, like the corona of the sun in eclipse, only negative; a corona of darkness rather than of light. It's a turbulent muddy green, shot through with lines of blood red and greyish black—the worst, the most destructive colours, a deadly aureole, a visible infection. Charis will have to call on all her own light, the white light she's been working so hard at, storing up, for years and years. She will have to do an instant meditation, and what a place for it! Zenia has chosen the ground well for this encounter: the Toxique, the chattering voices, the cigarette smoke and wine fumes, the thick breath-filled air of the city, all are working for Zenia. She stands in the doorway, scanning the room with a scornful rancorous glance, pulling off a glove, and Charis closes her own eyes and repeats to herself: *Think about the light*.

"Tony, what's wrong?" says Roz, and Charis opens her eyes again. The waitress is moving towards Zenia.

"Turn your head slowly," says Tony. "Don't scream." Charis watches with interest, to see if the waitress will walk right through Zenia; but she doesn't, she stops short. She must sense something. A coldness.

"Oh shit," says Roz. "It's her."

"Who?" says Charis, doubt beginning to form. Roz hardly ever says "Oh shit." It must be important.

"Zenia," says Tony. So they can see her too! Well, why not? They have enough to say to her, each one of them. It isn't only Charis.

"Zenia's dead," says Charis. I wonder what she's come back for, is what she thinks. *Who* she's come back for. Zenia's aura has faded now, or else Charis can no longer see it: Zenia appears to be solid, substantial, material, disconcertingly alive.

"He looked like a lawyer," says Charis. Zenia is coming towards her, and she concentrates all her forces for the moment of impact; but Zenia strides right past them in her richly textured dress, with her long legs, her startling new breasts, her glossy hair nebulous around her shoulders, her purple-red angry mouth, trailing musky perfume. She's refusing to notice Charis, refusing deliberately; she's passing a hand of darkness over her, usurping her, blotting her out.

Shaken and feeling sick, Charis closes her eyes,

struggling to regain her body. *My body, mine,* she repeats. *I am a good person. I exist.* In the moonlit night of her head she can see an image: a tall structure, a building, something toppling from it, falling through the air, turning over and over. Coming apart.

11

The three of them stand outside the Toxique, saying goodbye. Charis isn't entirely sure how she got out here. Her body has walked her out, all by itself, her body has taken care of it. She's shivering, despite the sun, she's cold, and she feels thinner—lighter and more porous. It's as though energy has been drained out of her, energy and substance, in order for Zenia to materialize. Zenia has made it back across, back across the river; she's here now, in a fresh body, and she's taken a chunk of Charis's own body and sucked it into herself.

That's wrong though. Zenia must be alive, because other people saw her. She sat down in a chair, she ordered a drink, she smoked a cigarette. But none of these are necessarily signs of life.

Roz gives her a squeeze and says, "Take care of yourself, sweetie, I'll call you, okay?" and goes off in the direction of her car. Tony has already smiled at her and is going, gone, off down the street, her short legs moving her steadily along, like a wind-up toy. For a moment Charis stands there in front of the Toxique, lost. She doesn't know what to do next. She could turn around and march back in there, march up to Zenia, stand planted; but the things she was going to say to Zenia have evaporated, have flown up out of her head. All that's left is a whirring sound.

She could go back to the store, back to Radiance, even though it's her half-day and Shanita isn't expecting her. She could tell Shanita what happened; Shanita is a teacher, maybe she can help. But possibly Shanita won't be too sympathetic. *A woman like that,* she'll say. *She's nothing. Why are you concerned about her? You are giving her the power, you know better than that! What colour is she? What colour is the pain? Wipe the tape!*

Shanita has never had a dose of Zenia. She won't realize, she can't understand, that Zenia can't be meditated out of existence. If she could be, Charis would have done it long ago.

She decides to go home. She'll fill up the bathtub and put some orange peel into it, some rose oil, a few cloves; she'll pin up her hair and get into the tub and let her arms float in the scented water. Steering herself towards this goal, she walks downhill, in the general direction of the lake and the ferry dock; but a block along she turns left and makes her way by a narrow alley to the next street, and then she turns left again, and now she's back on Queen.

Her body doesn't wish her to go home right now. Her body is urging her to have a cup of coffee; worse than that, a cup of espresso. This is so unusual—her body's promptings of this kind are normally for fruit juice or glasses of water—that she feels obliged to do what it wants.

There's a café, right across the street from the Toxique. It's called the Kafay Nwar, and has a hot-pink neon sign in forties writing in the window. Charis goes into it and sits at one of the small round chrome-edged tables by the window, and takes off her cardigan, and when the waiter comes, wearing a pleated dress shirt, a black bow tie, and jeans, she orders an Espresso Esperanto—all the things on the menu have complicated names, Cappuccino Cappriccio, Tarte aux Tarts, Our Malicious Mudcake— and watches the door of the Toxique. It's clear to her now that her body doesn't want an espresso primarily. Her body wants her to spy on Zenia.

To make herself less obvious as a watcher she takes her notebook out of her tote bag, a lovely notebook she traded some of her paytime for. It has a hand-bound cover of marbled paper with a burgundy suede spine, and the pages are a delicate lavender. The pen she bought to go with it is pearl grey, and filled with grey-green ink. She got the pen at Radiance too, and the ink. It makes her sad to think of Radiance vanishing. So many gifts.

The notebook is for her to write her thoughts in, but so far she hasn't written any. She hates to spoil the beauty of the blank pages, their potential; she doesn't want to use them up. But now she uncaps her pearl grey pen, and prints: *Zenia must go back*. She once took a course in italic handwriting, so the message looks elegant, almost like a rune. She does one letter at a time, looking up between the words, over the tops of her reading glasses, so nothing going on across the street will escape her.

At first more people go in than out, and after that more people go out than in. None of the people who go in is Billy, not that she is realistically expecting him, but you never know. None of the people who come out is Zenia.

Her coffee arrives and her body tells her to drop two lumps of sugar into it, and so she does, and then she drinks the coffee quickly and feels the hit of caffeine and sucrose rush to her head. She's focused now, she has X-ray vision, she knows what she has to do. Neither Tony nor Roz can help her, they don't need to help her with this, because their stories, the stories with Zenia in them, have endings. At least they know what happened. Charis doesn't, Charis has never known. It's as if her story, the story with Billy and Zenia in it, was going along a path, and suddenly there were no more footprints.

At last, when Charis is beginning to think that Zenia must have slipped out the back or else vaporized, the door opens and she comes out. Charis lowers her eyes slightly; she doesn't want to rest the full weight of her super-charged eyes on Zenia, she doesn't want to give herself away. But Zenia doesn't even glance in her direction. She's with someone Charis doesn't recognize. A young fair-haired man. Not Billy. He's too slightly built to be Billy.

Though if it were Billy, he would hardly be young any more. He might even be fat, or bald. But in her head he has stayed the same age as he was the last time she saw him. The same age, the same size, everything the same. Loss opens again beneath her feet, the pit, the familiar trapdoor. If she were alone, if she weren't here in the Kafay Nwar but home in her own kitchen, she would bang her forehead softly on the edge of the table. The pain is red and it hurts, and she can't just wipe it away.

Zenia isn't happy, Charis thinks. It's not an insight, it's more like a charm, an incantation. She can't possibly be happy. If she were allowed to be happy it would be completely unfair: there must be a balance in the Universe. But Zenia is smiling up at the man, whose face Charis can't quite see, and now she's taking his arm and they're walking along the street, and from this distance at least she looks happy enough.

Compassion for all living things, Charis reminds herself. Zenia is alive, so that means compassion for Zenia.

This is what it does mean, though Charis realizes, on taking stock, that at the moment she feels no compassion whatsoever for Zenia. On the contrary she has a clear picture of herself pushing Zenia off a cliff, or other high object.

Own the emotion, she tells herself, because although it's a thoroughly unworthy one it must be acknowledged fully before being discarded. She concentrates on the image, bringing it closer; she feels the wind against her face, senses the height, hears the release of her arm muscles inside her body, listens for the scream. But Zenia makes no sound. She merely falls, her hair streaming behind her like a dark comet.

Charis wraps this image up in tissue paper and with an effort expels it from her body. All I want to do is talk to her, she tells herself. That's all.

There's a confusion, a rustling of dry wings. Zenia has left the oblong of the Kafay Nwar window. Charis gathers up her notebook, her grey pen, her cardigan, her reading glasses, and her tote bag, and prepares to follow.

12

Roz

In her dream Roz is opening doors. Nothing in here, nothing in there, and she's in a hurry, the airport limousine is waiting and she has no clothes on, no clothes on her big slack raw embarrassing body. Finally she finds the right door. There are clothes behind it all right, long coats that look like men's overcoats, but the overhead light won't turn on and the first coat she pulls from the hanger is damp and covered with live snails.

The alarm goes off, none too soon. "Holy Moly, Mother of God," Roz mutters groggily. She hates clothing dreams. They're like shopping, except that she never does find anything she wants. But she'd rather dream about snail-covered coats than about Mitch.

Or about Zenia. Especially Zenia. Sometimes she has a dream about Zenia, Zenia taking shape in the corner of Roz's bedroom, reassembling herself from the fragments of her own body after the bomb explosion: a hand, a leg, an eye. She wonders whether Zenia was ever actually in this bedroom, when Roz wasn't. When Mitch was.

Her throat tastes of smoke. She flings out an arm, groping for the clock, and knocks her latest trashy thriller off the night-table. Sex killings, sex killings; this year it's all sex killings. Sometimes she longs to be back in the sedate English country houses of her youth, where the victim was always some venomous old miser who deserved it rather than an innocent plucked at random off the street. The misers were killed by poison or a single bullet hole, the corpses did not bleed. The detectives were genteel grey-haired ladies who knitted a lot, or very smart eccentrics with no bodily functions; they focused on tiny, harmless-looking clues: shirt buttons, candle ends, sprigs of parsley. What she truly enjoyed was the furniture: rooms and rooms of it, and so exotic! Things she didn't know existed. Tea trollies. Billiard rooms. Chandeliers. Chaises longues. She wanted to live in houses like that! But when she goes back to these books, they no longer interest her; not even the décor can hold her attention. Maybe I'm getting hooked on blood, she thinks. Blood and violence and rage, like everyone else.

She rolls her legs over the side of her enormous four-poster bed—a mistake, she practically breaks her neck every time she has to climb down from the darn thing—and stuffs her feet into her terry-cloth slippers. Her land-lady slippers, the twins call them, not realizing what disturbing echoes this word has for her. They've never seen a landlady in their lives. Or their life. It's still hard for her to tell whether they have a life of their own each, or just one between the two of them. But she feels compelled to wear attractive shoes all day, shoes that match her outfits, shoes with high heels, so she deserves to have something more comfortable on her poor pinched feet at home, no matter what the twins say.

All this white in the bedroom is a mistake too—the white curtains, the white rug, the white ruffles on the bed. She doesn't know what got into her. Trying for a girlish look, maybe; trying to go back in time, to create the perfect pre-teen bedroom she once longed for but never had. It was after Mitch had gone, vamoosed, skedaddled, checked out is more like it, he always did treat this place like a hotel, he treated *her* like a hotel, she needed to throw everything out that was there when he was; she needed to reassert herself. Though surely this isn't herself! The bed looks like a bassinet or a wedding cake, or worse, like those huge ruffly altars they build in Mexico, for the Day of the Dead. She never found out (that time she was there, with Mitch, on their honeymoon, when they were so happy) whether it was all of the dead who came back, or just the ones you invited.

She can think of a couple of them she'd rather do without. That's all she needs, gate-crashing dead people coming to dinner! And herself lying in the bed like a big piece of fruitcake. She'll re-do the whole room, add some pizazz, some texture. She's had enough of white.

She shuffles into the bathroom, drinks two glasses of water to replenish her cells, takes her vitamin pill, brushes her teeth, creams, wipes, vivifies and resurfaces her skin, and scowls at herself in the mirror. Her face is silting up, like a pond; layers are accumulating. Every once in a while, when she can afford the time, she spends a few days at a spa north of the city, drinking vegetable juice and having ultrasound treatments, in search of her original face, the one she knows is under there somewhere; she comes back feeling toned up and virtuous, and hungry. Also annoyed with herself. Surely she isn't still trying; surely she isn't still in the man-pleasing business. She's given that up. *I do it for me,* she tells Tony.

"Screw you, Mitch," she says to the mirror. If it weren't for him she could relax, she could be middle-aged. But if he were still around, she'd still be trying to please him. The key word is *trying.*

The hair has to go, though. It's too red this time. It's making her look raddled, a word she has always admired. *Raddled harridan,* she would read in those English detective stories, crouching on the steamer trunk that served as a window seat in her attic room, her feet tucked under her, with the room darkened for secrecy, as in air raids, angling the book so that the light from the streetlamp fell on the page, in the dusk, in that Huron Street boarding house with the chestnut tree outside. *Roz! You still up? You get into that bed, right now, no fooling! Sneaky brat!*

How could she hear Roz reading in the dark? Her mother the landlady, her mother the improbable martyr, standing at the foot of the attic stairs, yelling up in her hoarse washerwoman voice, and Roz mortified because the roomers might hear. Roz the toilet cleaner, Roz the down-market Cinderella, sullenly scrubbing. *You eat here,* said her mother, *so you help out.* That was before her father the hero turned rags into riches. *Raddled harridan,* Roz would mutter, with no sense that she might ever become one herself. It wasn't that easy, growing up with one hero and one martyr. It didn't leave much of a role for her.

That house is gone now. No, not gone: Chinese. They don't like trees, she hears. They think the branches hold bad spirits, the sorrowful things that have happened to everyone who's ever lived there before. Maybe there's something of Roz herself, Roz as she was then, caught in the branches of that chestnut tree, if it still exists. Caught there and fluttering.

She wonders how much trouble it would be to have her hair dyed grey, the colour it would be if she let it grow in. With grey hair she'd get more respect. She'd be firmer. Less of a softie. An iron lady! Fat chance.

Roz's latest bathrobe is hanging on the back of the bathroom door. Orange velour. Orange is the new colour this year; last year it was an acid yellow that she really couldn't wear, try as she might. It made her look like a lemon lollipop. But the orange brings out a glow under her skin, or so she thought when she bought the darn thing. She believes in the little inner voice, the one that says, *It's you! It's you! Grab it now, or it may be gone!* But the little inner voice is getting less and less trustworthy, and this time it must have been talking to someone else.

She puts on the bathrobe, over her hand-embroidered white-on-white batiste nightgown, bought to go with the bed, so who did she think was going to notice? She finds her purse, and transfers her half-empty pack of smokes to her pocket. *Not* before breakfast! Then she makes her way down the stairs, the back ones, the ones that used to be for maids, for toilet cleaners like her, clutching the banister so she won't trip. The stairs go straight into the kitchen, the sparkling austere all-white kitchen (time for a change!), where the twins sit on high stools at the tile-topped counter, wearing long T-shirts and striped tights and gym socks. These are the outfits they find it chic to sleep in, these days. It used to be such fun to dress them up, when they were little; such ruffles, tiny hats you could die for! Gone are the downy sleepers with plastic soles to their feet, gone too the expensive English cotton flannel nighties with rows of Mother Geese in bonnets and aprons printed on them. Gone are the books Roz used to read to the two of them when they wore those nighties, snuggling up to her, one under each arm—*Alice in Wonderland, Peter Pan, The Arabian Nights,* the reissues of lavish turn-of-the-century fairy tales with Arthur Rackham illustrations. Or not completely gone: stored in the cellar. Gone are the pink jogging suits, the raccoon bedroom slippers, the velvet party dresses, each frill and extravaganza. Now they won't let her buy them a thing. If she brings home even a black top, even a pair of underpants, they roll their eyes.

The two of them are drinking the yogurt-and-skim-milk-and-blueberry smoothies they've just made in the blender. She can see the melting package of frozen blueberries, and the puddle of blue milk lying like pale ink on the counter.

"So, you'll do me a favour, for once you'll put it in the dishwasher," she can't help saying to them.

They turn their identical eyes towards her, lambent eyes like those of forest cats, and smile their identical heartless heart-crushing smiles, showing their slightly feral faun's teeth, blue at the moment, and shaking their moussey, fluffed-out manes; and she catches her breath, as she does almost every time she sees them, because they are so huge and so gorgeous and she still can't quite understand how she managed to give birth to them. One such creature would have been unlikely enough, but two!

They laugh. "It's the Big Mom!" one of them shouts, the one on the right. "The Big Mommy! Let's give her a hug!"

They leap down from their stools and grab hold of her and squeeze. Her feet lift from the ground, and she rises perilously into the air.

"Put me down!" she shrieks. They know she doesn't like this, they know she's afraid they'll drop her. They'll drop her and she'll break. Sometimes they have no sense of that; they think she's unbreakable. Roz the Rock. Then they remember.

"Let's put her on a stool," they say. They carry her over and deposit her, and climb back onto their own stools, like circus animals who have done their trick.

"Mom, you look like a pumpkin in that," says one. It's Erin. Roz has always been able to tell them apart, or so she claims. Two guesses and she's right every time. Mitch used to have trouble. But then, he only ever saw them for about fifteen minutes a day.

"Pumpkin, that's me," says Roz, with heavy jocularity. "Fat, orange, big friendly grin, hollow in the centre and glows in the dark." She needs her coffee, right now! She pulls open the freezer door, sticks the frozen blueberry package back in there, finds the bag of magic beans, and fumbles around in one of the roll-out drawers for the electric grinder. Having everything stowed away in drawers wasn't such a hot idea, she can never find anything any more. Especially not the pot lids. *The uncluttered look,* said that fool of a designer. They always intimidate her.

"Aww," says the other one. Paula. Errie and Pollie, they call each other, or Er and La, or, when they're speaking collectively, Erla. It's creepy when they do that. *Erla's going out tonight.* That means both of them. "Aww. You rotten twin! You hurt the Mommy's feelings! You are just rotten, rotten to the core!" This last is an imitation of Roz imitating her own mother, who used to say that. Roz feels a sudden need for her, for her harsh, embattled, once-scorned, long-dead mother. She's tired of being a mother, she wants to be a child for a change. She missed out on that. It looks like way more fun.

The twins laugh delightedly. "Selfish rotten cesspool," one says to the other.

"Unshaved armpit!"

"Festering tampon!"

"Used panty liner!" They can go on this way for hours, thinking up worse and worse insults for each other, laughing so hard they roll on the floor and kick their feet in the air with delight at their own outrageous humour. What puzzles her is how so many of their insults can be so—well, so sexist. *Bitch* and *slut* are among their mildest; she wonders if they'd let boys call them that. When they think she's not listening, they can get much more obscene, or what she thinks of as obscene. *Cunt gum.* Such a thing could never even have been thought of, when she was growing up. And they're only fifteen!

But people carry their vocabularies with them through their lives, like turtle shells, thinks Roz. She has a sudden flash of the twins at eighty, their beautiful faces raddled, their by-then-withered legs still encased in coloured tights, gym socks on their bunioned feet, still saying *cunt gum.* She shudders.

Touch wood, she corrects herself. They should live so long.

The coffee grinder isn't there; not where she put it yesterday. "Darn it, kids," she says. "Did you move my grinder?" Maybe it was Maria. Yesterday was one of Maria's days to clean.

"Darn it!" says Paula. "Oh, my darned *grinder*. Oh gosh darn to heck!"

"Oh golly jeez, oh Holy Moly," says Erin. They think it's hilarious, the way Roz can't bring herself to really swear. But she can't. The words are in her head, all right, but they don't come out. *You want people to think you're trash?*

She must seem so archaic to them. So obsolete, so foreign. She spent the first half of her life feeling less and less like an immigrant, and now she's spending the second half feeling more and more like one. A refugee from the land of middle age, stranded in the country of the young.

"Where's your big brother?" she says. This sobers them up.

"Where he usually is at this time of day," says Erin with a hint of scorn. "Stoking up on his energy."

"Zizzing," says Paula, as if she wants them to get back to joking.

"Dreamland," says Erin pensively.

"Larryland," says Paula. "Greetings, Earthling, I come from a distant planet."

Roz wonders whether she should wake Larry up, decides not to. She feels safer about him when he's asleep. He is the firstborn, the firstborn son. Not a lucky thing to be. Fingered for sacrifice, he would have been, once. It's very bad news that he was named after Mitch. Laurence Charles Mitchell, such a weighty and pompous combination for such a vulnerable little boy. Even though he's twenty-two and has a moustache, she can't help thinking of him as that.

Roz finds the coffee grinder, in the pull-out drawer under the convection oven, among the roasting pans. She should speak to Maria. She grinds her beans, measures the coffee, turns on her cute Italian espresso maker. While waiting she peels herself an orange.

"I think he's got something going," says Erin. "Some romance or other."

Paula has made herself some false teeth out of Roz's orange peel. "*Pouf, qui sait, c'est con ça, je m'en fiche,*" she says, with elaborate shrugs, lisping and spitting. That's about all the two of them have picked up from French immersion: loose talk. Roz doesn't know most of the words and she's just as glad.

"I think I spoiled you," Roz says to them.

"Spoiled, *moi*?" says Erin.

"Erla's *not* spoiled," says Paula with fake pouty innocence, taking out the orange-peel teeth. "Is she, Erla?"

"Holy Moly, gee whizzikers, Mommy, no!" says Erin. The two of them peer out at her through the underbrush of their hair, their bright eyes assessing her. Their kibitzing, their mimicry, their vulgar idiocies, their laughter, all of it is a distraction they put on, for her benefit. They tease her, but not too much: they know she has a breaking point. They never mention Mitch, for instance. They carry on as if he's never existed. Do they miss him, did they love him, do they resent him, did they hate him? Roz doesn't know. They don't let her know. Somehow that's harder.

They are so wonderful! She gazes at them with ferocious love. *Zenia,* she thinks, *you bitch! Maybe you had everything else, but you never had such a blessing. You never had daughters.* She starts to cry, resting her head in her hands, her elbows on the cold white tiles of the kitchen counter, the tears rolling hopelessly down.

The twins come round her, smaller than they were, anxious, more timid, patting her, stroking her orange back. "It's okay, Mom, it's okay," they say.

"Look," she tells them, "I put my elbow in your darned blue milk!"

"Oh heck!" they say. "Oh double darn!" They smile at her with relief.

13

The twins place their tall smoothie glasses ostentatiously in the dishwasher, head for the back stairs, forget the blender, remember it and come back, put it in too, forget the puddle of blue milk. Roz wipes it up as they take the stairs, two at a time, and barge along the hall to their rooms to get ready for school. They're more subdued than usual, though; normally it's an elephant stampede. Upstairs, two stereos go on at once, two competing drumbeats.

A couple more years and they'll be away at university, in some other city. The house will be quiet. Roz doesn't want to think about it. Maybe she'll sell this barn. Get a Grade A condo, overlooking the lake. Flirt with the doorman.

She sits at the white counter, drinking her coffee at last, and eating her breakfast. Two rusks. Just an orange and two rusks, because she's on a diet. Sort of a diet. A mini-diet.

She used to do all kinds of diets. Grapefruit ones, bran added to everything, all-protein. She used to wax and wane like the moon, trying to shake the twenty pounds that came on when the twins were born. But she's not so drastic any more. She knows by now that weird diets are bad for you, the magazines have been full of it. The body is like a besieged fortress, they say; it stores up food supplies in its fat cells, it stockpiles in case of emergency, and if you diet then it thinks it's being starved to death and stores up even more, and you turn into a blimp. Still, a little deprivation here and there can't hurt. Eating a little less, that's not a real diet.

It's not as if she's fat, anyway. She's just solid. A good peasant body, from when the women had to pull the ploughs.

Though maybe she shouldn't skimp so much, especially at breakfast. Breakfast is the most important meal of the day, and at this age, what they say is that you trim the body at the expense of the face. It comes off the hips, but off the neck first. Then you get chicken neck. She has no intention of turning into one of those fiftyish size 6 bimbos with faces like piles of scrap metal and string, each bone and tendon showing. Though *bimbo* isn't the right word for a woman of that age. *Bimbag,* maybe. That's what Zenia would have been, if she'd lived. A bimbag.

Roz smiles, and puts two pieces of whole wheat bread into the toaster. She finds it helpful to call Zenia names; helpful and reassuring. So who can it hurt, now?

So who did it hurt, then? she asks herself bitterly. Certainly not Zenia, who never gave two hoots about what Roz thought of her. Or said about her, even to Mitch. There were some things she had the sense not to say, however. *Can't you see those tits aren't real? She had them done, I know for a fact; she used to be a 34A. You're in love with two sacks of silicone gel.* No, that wouldn't have gone over all that well with Mitch, not in his besotted phase. And after his besotted phase it was too late.

Those things don't burn when they cremate you

either; that's the rumour going around, about artificial boobs. They just melt. The rest of you turns to ashes, but your tits to marshmallow goo; they have to scrape them off the bottom of the furnace. Maybe that's why they didn't scatter the ashes at Zenia's memorial service. Maybe they couldn't. Maybe that's what was in that sealed tin can. Melted tits.

Roz butters her two pieces of toast and spreads honey on them, and eats them with slow relish, licking her fingers. If Zenia were alive there's no doubt that she'd be dieting; you don't get a waist like Zenia's without hard work. So by now she'd have chicken neck. Or else she'd be going for surgery, more of it. She'd get a nip here, a tuck there; a lid-lift, puffed-up lips. That isn't for Roz, she can't stand the thought of someone, some strange man, bending over her with a knife while she's lying in bed conked out cold. She's read too many thrillers for that, too many sex-murder thrillers. He could be a depraved nut in a stolen doctor suit. It happens. Or what if they make a mistake and you wake up covered in bandages and then spend six weeks looking like a road-kill raccoon, only to emerge as some bit player from a botched-up horror movie? No, she'd rather just age quietly. Like good red wine.

She makes herself another piece of toast, with strawberry-and-rhubarb jam this time. Why punish the flesh? Why stint the body? Why incur its resentments, its obscure revenges, its headaches and hunger pains and growls of protest? She eats the toast, jam dripping; then, after glancing behind to make sure nobody is watching her—though who would be?—she licks the plate. Now she feels better. It's time for her cigarette, her morning reward. Reward for what? Don't ask.

The twins cascade down the stairs, wearing, more or less, their school uniforms, those outfits Roz has never fully understood, the kilts and ties that are supposed to turn them into Scottish men. Leaving your shirt untucked until the dire last minute is the current thing, she gathers. They kiss her on the cheek, big sloppy exaggerated kisses, and gallop out the back door, and their two shining heads go past the kitchen window.

Possibly they are trampling on the flower border Charis insisted on planting there last year, a deed of love so Roz can't lay a finger on it, even though it resembles a moth-eaten patchwork quilt and her regular gardener, an elegant Japanese minimalist, considers it an affront to his professional standing. But maybe the twins will mash it beyond repair, cross your fingers. She looks at her watch: they're running late, but not very late. They take after her: she has always had a flexible sense of time.

Roz drains her coffee and butts out her cigarette, and goes up the stairs in her turn, and along the hall to have her shower. On the way she can't resist peeking into the twins' rooms, though she knows they're off limits. Erin's room looks like a clothing explosion, Paula has left her lights on again. They make such a fuss about the environment, they bawl her out because of her poisonous cleaning products, they make her buy recycled stationery, but still they can't seem to turn off their darn lights.

She flicks off the light switch, knowing she's given herself away (*Mom! Who's been in my room? I can go in your room, sweetie, I'm your mother! You don't respect my privacy, and Mom, don't be such a conehead, don't call me sweetie! I'm entitled! So who pays the light bills around here?* and so forth), and continues on down the hall.

Larry's room is at the very end, past her own room. Maybe she should wake him up. On the other hand, if he wanted her to he'd have left a note. Maybe, maybe not. Sometimes he expects her to read his mind. Well, why wouldn't he expect that? She used to be able to. Not any more. With the twins, she'd know if something was wrong, though she wouldn't necessarily know what. But not with Larry. Larry has become opaque to her. *How are things going?* she'll say, and he'll say *Fine,* and it could mean anything. She doesn't even know what *things* are, any more, those things that are supposed to be going so fine.

He was a dogged kid. Through all the uproar with Mitch, when the twins were acting out, snitching from the supermarket, skipping school, he plodded faithfully on. He tended Roz, in a dutiful sort of way. He took out the garbage, he washed the car, her car, on Saturdays, like a middle-aged man. *You don't need to do that,* she'd tell him. *Ever heard of car washes? I like to,* he said, *it relaxes me.*

He got his driver's licence, he got his high school diploma, he got his university degree. He got a worried little furrow between his eyes. He did what he thought was expected of him, and brought the official pieces of paper home to her like a cat bringing dead mice. Now it's as if he's given up because he doesn't know what else to bring; he's run out of ideas. He says he's deciding what to do next, but she sees no signs of any decision being made. He stays out at night and she doesn't know where he goes. If it was the twins she'd ask, and they'd say she should mind her own business. With him, she doesn't even ask. She's afraid to, because he might tell her. He's never been a very good liar. An earnest kid, maybe too earnest. There's a joylessness in him that bothers her. She's sorry he's given up that drum set he used to practise on, down in the cellar, although it drove her crazy at the time. At least then he had something to hit.

He sleeps in late. He doesn't ask her for money; he doesn't need to, because of what's been left him, what's his own. He could afford to leave home, get an apartment somewhere, but he's not making a move. He shows so little initiative; when she was his age she could hardly wait to shake the ancestral dust off her sandals. Not that she managed it all that well.

Maybe he's on dope, she thinks. She sees no signs of that either, but what does she know? When she was growing up, *dope* was some guy you thought was stupid. She did find a packet once, a little plastic envelope with what looked like baking powder in it, and she decided not to know what it was, because what could she do? You don't tell your twenty-two-year-old son that you just happened to be going through his pants pockets. Not any more.

He has an alarm clock. But on the other hand, he turns it off in his sleep, the way Mitch used to. Maybe she should just tiptoe in, take a quick look at the alarm clock, and see what time it's set for. Then she'll know whether or not he's turned it off, and her way will be clear.

She eases open his door. There's a trail of clothes leading from it to the bed, like a shed cocoon, just left there: hand-tooled cowboy boots, socks, fawn suede jacket, jeans, black T-shirt. Her hands itch, but it's no longer her job to pick up their floors, and she's told Maria not to do it either. *If it's in your laundry hamper it gets washed,* she's told all of them. *Otherwise not.*

The room is a boy's room, still. Not a man's. The bookshelves filled with school textbooks; two pictures of eighteenth-century sailing ships, chosen by Mitch; their first boat, the *Rosalind,* with the three of them on it, her and Mitch and Larry when he was six, before the twins were born; the hockey team trophy from Grade Eleven; a picture of a fish he drew when he was nine, and that Mitch liked especially. Or praised, at least. Larry got more of Mitch than the twins did, because he was the first maybe, and a boy, and because there was only one of him. But Mitch was never fully at ease with him, or with any of them. He always had one foot out the door. He had a father act: too bluff, too hearty, too conscious of the time. He made jokes that were way over Larry's head, and Larry would gaze at him with his puzzled, suspicious child's eyes, and see right through him. Kids do.

Still, it's been hard on Larry. There's something missing. Dejection enters Roz, a familiar sense of failure. The one she's failed most is Larry. If she'd only been—what?—prettier, smarter, sexier even, better somehow; or else worse, more calculating, more unscrupulous, a guerrilla fighter—Mitch might still be here. Roz wonders how long it will take her kids to forgive her, once they've figured out exactly how much they need to forgive her for.

Larry is asleep in his bed, his single bed, one arm thrown over his eyes. His hair is feathery on the pillow, hair lighter than the twins', straighter, more like Mitch's hair. He's growing it longer, with a thin rat-tail braid at the back. It looks like heck, in her opinion, but not a word has she said.

Roz stands stock-still, listening for his breathing.

She's always done that, ever since he was a baby: listened to see if he was still alive. He had weak lungs, as a child; he had asthma. With the twins she didn't listen because it didn't seem called for. They were so robust.

He draws in a breath, a long sigh, and her heart turns over. Her love for him is different in quality from her love for the twins. They're tough and wiry, they have resilience; it's not that they won't get any wounds, they have wounds already, but they can lick their wounds and then bounce back. Also they have each other. But Larry has an exiled look to him, the look of a lost traveller, as if he's stuck in some no man's land, between borders and without a passport. Trying to figure out the road signs. Wanting to do the right thing.

Under the young moustache his mouth is tidy, and also gentle. It's the mouth that worries her the most. It's the mouth of a man who can be wrecked by women; by a whole bunch of women in succession. Or else by one woman: if she was mean enough, it would only take one. One really slick mean-minded woman, and poor Larry will fall in love, he'll fall in love earnestly, he'll trot around after her with his tongue hanging out, like a sweet, loyal, house-trained puppy, he'll set his heart on her, and then one flick of her bony gold-encircled wrist and he'll just be a sucked-out shell.

Over my dead body, thinks Roz, but what can she do? Against this unknown future woman she will be helpless. She knows about mothers-in-law, she knows about women who think that their sons are perfect, that no woman, no other woman, will ever be good enough for them. She's seen it, she knows how destructive it can be, she's sworn never to get like that.

Already she's weathered several of his girlfriends—
the one in high school who had crimped bangs and tiny
crazed eyes like a pit bull, who claimed she played the gui-
tar, who left her push-up French bra in his room; the near-
sighted stockbroker's daughter from summer camp with
aggressively hairy legs and B.O. of the head, who'd been
on an art tour to Italy and thought that gave her the right
to patronize Roz's living-room furniture; the plump
smart-mouth one in university, with hair like a man's
toupee, dyed a lifeless artificial black, shaved at the sides,
who wore three earrings in each ear and leather mini-
skirts up to her armpits, who perched at the kitchen
counter and crossed her bulgy thighs and lit up a cigarette
without offering Roz one, and used Roz's coffee cup for an
ashtray, and asked Roz if she'd read *Thus Spake Zarathustra.*

That was the worst; that was the one she'd caught
looking through the Victorian rosewood silver caddy in the
dining room; probably wanted to hock some small item
and get the cleaning lady blamed, and stuff the proceeds
up her nose. That was the one who considered it tactful to
inform Roz that her mother had known Mitch, a few years
back, and acted surprised when Roz said she'd never heard
of her. (Untrue. She knew exactly who that woman was.
Twice divorced, a real estate agent, a man-collector, a slut.
But that was in Mitch's blow-and-throw female-Kleenex
period, and she'd only lasted a month.)

Larry was way over his depth with that creature. *Thus
Spake Zarathustra,* indeed! Pretentious little shit. Roz heard
her telling the twins (and they were only thirteen then) that
their brother had great buns. Her son! Great buns! The
tawdry bitch was just using him, but try telling him that.

Not that she sees much of the girlfriends. Larry keeps

them well tucked away. *Is she a nice girl?* she'll probe. *Bring her to dinner!* Fat chance. And red-hot tongs wouldn't get any information out of him. She can tell, though, when they're up to no good. She bumps into those girls on the street, hooked onto Larry with their tiny jaws and claws, and Larry introduces her, and she can tell by their shifty little mascara-encrusted eyes. Who knows what evil lurks in the hearts of women? A mother knows.

She's waited them all out, biting her tongue, praying it wasn't serious. Now, according to the twins, she's in for another one. Down on your knees, Roz, she tells herself. Atone for your sins. *Dear God, send me a nice understanding girl, not too rich, not too poor, not too pretty but not ugly either, not too bright, bright he won't need, a kind, warm, sensible, generous girl who'll appreciate his good points, who understands about his work, whatever the heck it turns out to be, who doesn't talk too much, and most of all, who loves kids. And please, God: make her have normal hair.*

Larry sighs and shifts in his bed, and Roz turns away. She's given up her plan of checking out his alarm clock. Let him sleep. Real life will be digging into him soon enough, with its shiny pointed grasping red nails.

Standing barefooted and pink and steaming and wrapped in a bath sheet, flamingo pink, best British, Roz goes through her room-length mirror-door closet. There's plenty to wear, but nothing she wants to. She settles on the suit she got in that Italian boutique on Bloor: she has a meeting, and then she's having lunch with Tony and Charis, at the Toxique, and this outfit's not too informal, but not too formal either. Also it's not built like a mummy case across the shoulders. Shoulder pads are going out, thank heaven, though Roz routinely snips hers off anyway, she has enough shoulders for two. The twins have been recycling some of her discarded pads: they've recently converted to fountain pens because plastic ballpoints are too wasteful, and according to them shoulder pads make great pen-wipers. It was only ever the tall and willowy who could handle the darn things anyway; and though Roz is tall, willowy she's not.

The shoulders are shrinking, but the bosoms are swelling. Not without help. Roz adds to her list of desir-ables: *Please, God, let her not have breast implants.* Zenia was ahead of her time.

14

Roz takes the Benz, because she knows she's going to have to park on Queen, at lunchtime, and the Rolls would attract too much attention. Who needs slashed tires?

Anyway she hardly ever drives the Rolls, it's like driving a boat. One of those ancient weighty in-boards, with the mahogany trim and the motor that whispered *Old money, old money.* Old money whispers, new money shouts: one of the lessons Roz thought she had to learn, once. *Keep your voice down, Roz,* went her inner censor. Low tones, low profile, beige clothing: anything to keep from being spotted, located among the pushing hordes of new money, narrow-eyed, nervous money, bad-taste money, chip-on-the-shoulder money. Anything to avoid incurring the amused, innocent, milky and maddening gaze of those who had never had to scrimp, to cut a few legal corners, to twist a few arms, to gouge a few eyes, to prove a thing. Most of the new-money women were desperate, all dressed up and nowhere safe to go and nervous as heck about it, and most of the men were pricks. Roz knows about desperation, and about pricks. She's a quick learner, she's a tough negotiator. One of the best.

Though by now she's been new money for so long she's practically old money. In this country it doesn't take long. By now she can wear orange, by now she can shriek. By now she can get away with such things; she can pawn them off as charming eccentricities, and anyone who doesn't like it can kiss her fanny.

She wouldn't have bought the Rolls herself, though. Too ostentatious, to her mind. It's left over from the days of Mitch; he was the one who talked her into it, she'd done it to please him, and it's one of the few things of his she can't bear to get rid of. He was so proud of it.

Mostly it sits in the garage, but she drove it to Zenia's memorial service, out of spite. *There,* she thought. *You got away with a lot, bitch, but you never nabbed this car.* Not that Zenia had been around to see, but there had been an undeniable pleasure all the same.

Charis disapproved of the Rolls; you could tell by the way she sat in it, hunched over and anxious. But Tony hardly noticed. *Is this your big car?* she'd said. Tony is so sweet about cars, she knows all about historical things and guns and such, but she can't tell one car from another. *Your big car, your other car,* those are her categories. It's like that awful joke about the Newfies counting fish: *one fish, two fish, another fish, another fish.* . . . Roz knows she shouldn't laugh at jokes like that, it's not fair, but she does anyway. Among friends. Does it hurt the Newfies, to lower Roz's blood pressure, to make her feel good on a bad day? Who knows? At least nobody has tried to genocide them. Yet. And they're supposed to have the best sex lives of anybody in Canada, which is a darn sight more than Roz has these days, worse luck.

•   •   •

She heads south through Rosedale, past the fake Gothic turrets, the fake Georgian fronts, the fake Dutch gables, all melded by now into their own curious authenticity: the authenticity of well-worn money. With a single glance at each, she estimates them: a million five, two million, three, prices have gone down but these babies are holding more or less firm, and good for them, something has to in all this shift and flux. What can you trust these days? (Not the stock market, that's for sure, and lucky she rearranged her portfolio just in time.) Much as she used to resent these prim, WASPy, self-assured houses, she's become fond of them over the years. Owning one helps. That, and the knowledge that a lot of the people who live in them are no better than they should be. No better than her.

She goes down Jarvis, once the street of the upper crust, then the red-light district, now not very convincingly renovated, cuts west on Wellesley, and ducks onto the university campus, where she tells the guard she's just picking someone up at the library. He waves her through—she's plausible, or rather her car is—and she goes around the circle and past McClung Hall, scene of boisterous memories. It's funny to think she lived in there once, when she was young and bright green, and bounding with canine enthusiasm. Big doggy paws on the furniture, big doggy tongue bestowing slurps of hope on any available face. *Like* me! *Like* me! Not any more. Times have changed.

She turns down to College, and makes a right on University. What a design fiasco! One clunky block of sterile brick and glass and then another one, no sidewalk interest, though they keep trying to tart the thing up with those constipated little flower beds. What would Roz do with it, if she had the contract? She doesn't know. Maybe grape arbours, or else round kiosks, like Paris; though whatever you did it would come out like something escaped from a theme park. But then everything does, nowadays. Even the real thing looks constructed. When Roz saw her first Alp, she thought, Bring out the chorus line in bodices and dirndls, and let's all yodel.

Maybe that's what people mean by a national identity. The hired help in outfits. The backdrops. The props.

Roz's head office is in a converted brewery, nineteenth-century. Red brick, with factory windows and a carving of a lion's head over the main entrance, for a touch of class. One of her father's cute ideas, to do it over; otherwise it would have been torn down. It was his first really big thing, his first indulgence; when he began playing with his money, finally, instead of just accumulating it.

She parks in the company lot, *Unauthorized Vehicles Will Be Towed,* in her own space marked *Ms. President* with its gold-lettered sign—if you've got it, flaunt it, although Roz constantly has to remind herself that she's not as all-fired important as she might be tempted to think. It's true she occasionally gets recognized in restaurants, especially after she's been in the annual *Toronto Life* list of Toronto's Fifty Most Influential. But if that kind of recognition is the measure of power, then Mickey Mouse is a million times more powerful than she is, and Mickey Mouse doesn't even exist.

She checks her front teeth for lipstick in the rear-view mirror—well, these things count—and walks briskly, she hopes it looks briskly, into the reception area. Time to change the wall art in here, she's tired of those stupid coloured squares, it looks like a tablecloth, though the thing cost a mint. A corporate tax write-off, fortunately. Canadian Art.

"Hi, Nicki," she says to the receptionist. It's important to remember their names. Roz has been known to print the names of new receptionists and secretaries on her wrist, in ballpoint ink, like a high school crib. If she were a man she could get away with a brief nod; but she's not a man, and she knows a whole lot better than to try acting like one.

Nicki blinks at her and continues talking on the phone, and doesn't smile, the stony-faced bimbette. Nicki won't last long.

It's complicated, being a woman boss. Women don't look at you and think *Boss*. They look at you and think *Woman*, as in *Just another one, like me, and where does she get off?* None of their sexy little tricks work on you, and none of yours work on them; big blue eyes are no advantage. If you forget their birthdays your name is mud, if you bawl them out they cry, they don't even do it in the washroom the way they would for a man but right out where you can see them, they hang their hard-luck stories on you and expect sympathy, and just try getting a cup of coffee out of them. *Lick your own stamps, lady.* They'll bring it all right, but it'll be cold and also they'll hate you forever. *Who was your servant last year?* she used to say to her own mother, once she was old enough to be defiant. Exactly.

Whereas the very same women would fetch and carry

for a man boss, no question. Buy the wife's birthday present, buy the mistress's birthday present, make the coffee, bring his slippers in her mouth, overtime no problem.

Is Roz being too negative? Could be. But she's had some bad experiences.

Maybe she handled it wrong. She was dumber then. Threw her weight around, acted normal. Had a few tantrums. *I didn't say tomorrow, I said now! Let's see a little professionalism around here!* By now she knows that if you're a woman and you hire women, you have to make them into girlfriends, into pals; you have to pretend you're all equal, which is hard when you're twice their age. Or else you have to baby them. You have to mother them, you have to take care of them. Roz has enough people in her life to mother already, and who is there to baby and mother and take care of her? Nobody; which is why she hired Boyce.

She takes the elevator up, and gets off on the top floor. "Hi, Suzy," she says to the receptionist there. "How's tricks?"

"Great, Ms. Andrews," says Suzy, giving a dutiful smile. She's been around longer than Nicki.

Boyce is in his office, which is right beside her own office and has a gold-lettered title: *Assistant to Ms. President.* Boyce is always in his office when she gets to work. "Hi, Boyce," she says to him.

"Good morning, Ms. Andrews," says Boyce gravely, rising from behind his desk. Boyce is studiously formal. Every one of his thin chestnut-coloured hairs is in order, his shirt collar is impeccable, his suit is a masterpiece of understatement.

"Let's run over it," says Roz, and Boyce nods.

"Coffee?" he says.

"Boyce, you're an angel," says Roz, and Boyce disappears and comes back with some, it's hot and fresh, he's just made it. Roz has remained standing so she can now experience the pleasure of having Boyce pull out her chair for her, which he proceeds to do. Roz sits down, as gracefully as she can manage, in this skirt—Boyce brings out the lady in her, such as it is—and Boyce says, as he never fails to do, "I must say, Ms. Andrews, you're looking very well this morning, and that's an attractive ensemble you're wearing."

"Boyce, I love your tie," Roz says, "it's new, isn't it?" and Boyce beams with pleasure. Or rather he glows quietly. Boyce rarely shows his teeth.

She adores Boyce! Boyce is delicious! She gets such a kick out of him, she could give him such a hug, although she would never dare to do a thing like that. She doesn't think Boyce would stand for it. Boyce is nothing if not reserved.

Boyce is also twenty-eight, a lawyer by training, smart as a whip, and gay. He dealt with the gayness right up front, at the job interview. "You might as well know immediately," he said to her, "it saves time-wasting speculation. I'm gay as a grig, but I won't embarrass you in public. My straight act is impeccable. A *grig,* in case you ever wondered, can mean either a short-legged hen or a young eel. I prefer the young eel version, myself."

"Thanks," said Roz, who found she had not known the least thing about grigs; she'd thought it must be some ethnic slur, like *wop.* She could see at once that Boyce was a person who would fill in the blanks for her without being asked. "Boyce, you're hired."

• • •

"Cream?" says Boyce now. He always inquires, because he deduces Roz's intermittent diets. He is so courteous!

"Please," says Roz, and Boyce pours some and then lights her cigarette for her. It's amazing, she thinks, what you have to do to get treated like a woman in this town. No, not like a woman. Like a lady. Like a lady president. Boyce has a sense of style, that's what it is, and also a sense of decorum. He respects hierarchies, he appreciates good china, he colours within the lines. He likes the fact that there's a ladder, with rungs on it, because he wants to go up it. And up is where he's going, if Roz has anything to say about it, because Boyce has real talent, and she's perfectly willing to help him. In return for his loyalty, needless to say.

As for what Boyce thinks of her, she has no idea. Though she does hope that, please God, he doesn't see her as his mother. Maybe he pictures her as a large, soft-bodied man, in drag. Maybe he hates women, maybe he wants to be one. Who cares, as long as he performs?

Roz cares, but she can't afford to.

Boyce closes the office door to show the rest of the world that Roz is occupied. He pours a coffee for himself, buzzes Suzy to ask her to stop all calls, and gives Roz the first thing she wants to see every morning, namely his rundown of how her remaining stocks are doing.

"What d'you think, Boyce?" says Roz.

"Half a league, half a league, half a league onward, all in the valley of Death rode the Fortune Five Hundred," says Boyce, who likes both reading and quoting. "Tennyson," he adds, for Roz's benefit.

"That one I got," says Roz. "So it's bad, eh?"

"Things fall apart, the centre cannot hold," says Boyce. "Yeats."

"Sell, or hang on?" says Roz.

"The way down is the way up. Eliot," says Boyce. "How long can you wait?"

"No problem," says Roz.

"I would," says Boyce.

What would Roz do without Boyce? He's becoming indispensable to her. Sometimes she thinks he's a surrogate son; on the other hand, he might be a surrogate daughter. On rare occasions she's even weaselled him into going shopping with her—he has such good taste in clothes—though she suspects him of maybe egging her on, just a little, for his own concealed and sardonic amusement. He was implicated, for instance, in the orange bathrobe.

"Ms. Andrews, it's time to let loose," was what he said. "*Carpe diem.*"

"Which means?" said Roz.

"Seize the day," said Boyce. "Gather ye rosebuds while ye may. Though myself, I'd rather be the gatheree."

This surprised Roz, because Boyce never gets that explicit inside the office walls. He must have, of course, another life—an evening life, about which she knows nothing. A private life, into which she is sweetly but firmly not invited.

"What're you doing tonight?" she was so unwise as to ask him once. (Hoping for what? That he would maybe go to a movie with her, or something. She gets lonely, why not admit it? She gets hugely, cavernously lonely, and then she eats. Eats and drinks and smokes, filling up her inner spaces. As best she can.)

"Some of us are going to see the Clichettes," said Boyce. "You know. They do lip-sync parodies of songs, they dress up like women."

"Boyce," said Roz, "they *are* women."

"Well, you know what I mean," said Boyce.

Who was *some of us*? A group of men, probably. Young men, young gay men. She worries about Boyce's health. More specifically, and let's be frank—could he maybe have AIDS? He's young enough to have missed it, to have found out about it in time. She didn't know how to ask, but as usual Boyce divined her need. When she'd commented, once too often, on the flu he'd had trouble shaking last spring, he'd said, "Don't fret so much, Ms. Andrews. Time will not wither me, nor Acquired Immune Deficiency Syndrome stale. This little piggy can take care of himself." Which is only part of an answer, but it's all the answer she's going to get.

After the stocks rundown, Roz and Boyce go over this month's batch of beautifully typed pleas, with embossed letterheads and signatures in real ink (Roz always tests them, by licking her finger; it's just as well to know who's cheating, and who on the other hand is truly pretentious). This one wants her to be an honorary patron, a title she hates, because how can you be a patron without being patronizing, and anyway it should be honorary *matron*, but that would be something else again. This other one wants to soak her a thousand bucks to attend some body-parts fundraising dance. Hearts, Lungs and Livers, Eyes, Ears, and Kidneys, all have their proponents; some, knowing how Torontonians will do anything to disguise themselves, are even going into costume balls. Roz is waiting for the Testicle Society, herself. The Ball Costume Ball. She used to love masquerade parties; maybe it would perk her up some to come as a scrotum. That, or the Ovarian Cysts; for that, she'd make the effort.

Roz has her own list. She still does Battered Women, she still does Rape Victims, she still does Homeless Moms. How much compassion is enough? She's never known, and you have to draw the line somewhere, but she still does Abandoned Grannies. She no longer attends the formal dinner-dances though. She can hardly go alone, and it's too depressing, rounding up some sort of a date. There would be takers, but what would they want in return? She recalls the dispiriting period after Mitch's departure, when she was suddenly fair game and all those husbands-on-the-make came out of the woodwork, one hand on her thigh, one eye on her bank balance. Quite a few drinks she shouldn't have drunk, quite a few entanglements that did her no good at all, and how to get them out of her bleached-bone-coloured bedroom in the morning without the kids seeing? Thanks a bunch, she thinks, but no thanks.

"B'nai Brith?" says Boyce. "The Marian Society?"

"Nothing religious, Boyce," says Roz. "You know the rule." God is complicated enough without being used as a fundraiser.

•   •   •

At eleven they take a meeting in the boardroom, with a new company, a little something Roz is thinking of investing in. Boyce puts on his businessman look, solemn and dull, conservative as heck, Roz could hug him to bits and she sure hopes his own mother appreciates him. She remembers her very first meeting like this: she'd grown up thinking business was something mysterious, something way beyond her, something her father did behind closed doors. Something only fathers did, that girls were forever too dull-witted to understand. But it was just a bunch of men sitting in a room, frowning and pondering and twiddling their gold-filled pens and trying to fake each other out. She'd sat there watching, trying to keep her mouth from falling open in astonishment. *Hey! Is this all there is? Holy Moly, I can do this!* And she can, she can do it better. Better than most. Most of the time.

Canadian businessmen are such wimps, by and large; they think if they keep their money under the pillow the nickels will breed with the dimes and give birth to quarters. All that chest-thumping they did over the free trade thing! *We have to be aggressive,* they said, and now they're whining and sucking their thumbs and asking for tax breaks. Or else moving their businesses south of the border. *Aggressively Canadian,* what a contradiction in terms, it is to laugh! Roz herself is a gambler. Not reckless gambling—informed gambling; but gambling nonetheless. Otherwise, where's the fun?

This group is from Lookmakers: cheap but high-quality cosmetics, and no bunny-torturing, it goes without saying. They started as a house-party outfit, like

Tupperware, and then expanded with a special line for actresses and models; but now they're growing like mad and they want a retail outlet, with franchises a possibility. Roz thinks there's something to it. She's done her home-work, or rather Boyce has, and in a recession—let's not mince words, depression—women buy more lipsticks. A little prezzie to yourself, a little reward, not that expensive and it cheers you up. Roz knows all about it. She may be rich but she can still think poor, it's an advantage. She likes the name, too, *Lookmakers*. It's bracing, it implies effort, a striding forth, a rolling up of the sleeves. A taking of risks.

Lookmakers is two men and two women, thirty-odd, obsequious to break your heart, with a lot of diagrams and photos and samples and graphs. The poor sweeties have worked their tiny behinds off for this meeting, so although Roz has already made up her mind she lets them do their pitch, while she sits back in her chair and makes memo notes in her head about a fresh product line. She's tired of just moving money around the map, she's ready for some-thing more hands-on again. This could be quite exciting! She'll get them to do some different names, move away from the languor, the toxicity and musky heaviness that was all the rage a few years ago. She has a flair.

"What do you think, Boyce?" she says, after the quar-tet have bowed and scraped their way out and Boyce has said they'd call them tomorrow. Never make the deal on the same day, is Roz's motto. Let them cool their jets, it gets the price down. "Should we have a flutter?"

"My eyes, my ancient, glittering eyes, are gay," says Boyce. "Yeats."

"So are mine," says Roz. "A controlling interest, as

usual?" Roz has burned her fingers a few times, she doesn't buy anything now that she can't control.

"I must say, Ms. Andrews," says Boyce, admiringly, "you have a gourmet's taste for the underbelly."

"Darn it, Boyce," says Roz, "don't make me sound so bloodthirsty. It's just good business."

Roz goes back to her office and flips through the pink slips of her phone messages, shuffling them like cards: these for Boyce to answer, these for Suzy, these for herself. She scribbles on them, instructions, comments. She feels good, revved up for innovation.

Now there's a pause; she just has time for a quick smoke. She sits down in her expensive leather-upholstered chair, behind her expensive desk, sleek, modern, hand-made, no longer satisfying. It's time for a change of desk; what she'd like is something antique, with all those cute little hidden drawers. From her desktop the twins, age nine, look out at her from their photo, in their pink birth-day-party dresses, mauling a long-gone cat. Then later, in their black semi-formals, at the annual Father-Daughter Dance put on by the school, an odd event considering the widespread shortage of fathers. Roz made Larry go, and coerced Boyce into being the second man. The twins said he was a cool dancer. Next to the four of them, silver-framed, is Larry all by himself, in his graduation gown, so serious. A worry.

Next to him is Mitch.

Guilt descends, billowing softly like a huge grey para-chute, riderless, the harness empty. Her gold wedding ring weighs heavy as lead on her hand. She should dump this picture of him, grinning at her so jauntily from the art nouveau brass frame, but with that uncertainty in the eyes. Always, but she didn't see it. *Not my fault,* she tells him. Zenia is still here, in this building, in this room; tiny fragments of her burnt and broken soul infest the old woodwork like termites, gnawing away from within. Roz should have the place fumigated. What are those people called? Exorcists. But she doesn't believe in them.

On impulse she rummages in her desk drawer, finds the poisonous file, and buzzes next door for Boyce. She's never told him anything about this, never discussed it, and he's only worked for her two years; maybe he doesn't know the story. Though everyone must know it, surely: this is gossip city.

"Boyce, your honest opinion. What do you think?"

What she hands him is an eight-by-ten colour glossy of Zenia, a studio portrait, the same one they'd used for *WiseWomanWorld* when Zenia was the editor, and also the one Roz herself passed to the private detective when she was going through that humiliating snoop act. A dark dress with texture, plushy, V-necked of course—if you've got it, flaunt it, even if it's styrofoam; the long white throat, the dark electrical hair, the left eyebrow quirked, the mulberry-coloured mouth curved up at the edges in that maddening, secretive smile.

My own monster, thinks Roz. I thought I could control her. Then she broke loose.

Boyce assumes, or pretends to assume, that Zenia is someone Roz is considering as a model for Lookmakers. He holds the photo between thumb and forefinger as if it has germs, purses his lips. "The chair she sat in, like a burnished throne, etcetera," he says. "The leather garter-belt brigade, I'd say. Whips and chains, and overdone; I mean, that hair looks like a wig. Definitely not the nineties, Ms. Andrews. *Vieux jeu,* and don't you think she's a little old for our target market?"

Roz could cry with relief. He's wrong, of course; whatever Zenia had, whatever her magic was, it transcended image-of-the-month. But she loves what he just said. "Boyce," she tells him, "you're a goldarn jewel."

Boyce smiles. "I try to be," he says.

15

Roz parks the Benz in an outdoor lot off Queen and hopes that nobody will flatten her tires, jimmy her trunk, or scratch her clean, recently polished dark blue paint while she's in having lunch. True, it's broad daylight, the car's in a supervised lot, and this isn't New York. But things are deteriorating, and even while she locks the door she's conscious of a dozen shadowy forms, out there on the sidewalk, huddled cloth-covered shapes, undernourished red eyes sizing her up, calculating whether she's good for a touch.

It's the Hearts, the Eyes, the Kidneys, and the Livers, but at a more basic level. She carries a clutch of pink two-dollar bills, ready in her pocket so she doesn't even have to slow down to open her purse. She will dole to left and to right as she runs the gauntlet from here to the Toxique. To give is a blessing, or so her father used to say. Does Roz agree? Do chickens have lips? To give is basically a drag these days, because it doesn't get you anything, it won't even buy you a scratch-free car, and for why? Because those you give to hate you. They hate you because they have to ask, and they hate you for being able to give. Or else they're professionals and they despise you for believing them, for feeling sorry for them, for being such a gullible dork. What happened to the Good Samaritan, afterwards? After he'd rescued the man fallen among thieves, lugged him off the roadside, carted him home, fed him some soup, and tucked him into the guest room overnight? The poor sappy Samaritan woke up in the morning to find the safe cracked and the dog strangled and the wife raped and the gold candlesticks missing, and a big pile of shit on the carpet, because it was just stick-on wounds and fake blood in the first place. A put-up job.

Roz has a quick flashback to Zenia, Zenia standing on their front steps, hers and Mitch's, after one of those dinner parties in the early eighties, the ones when Roz was still susceptible to Zenia's act, still promoting her, still inviting her. Zenia, in a tight red suit with jutting shoulders, a flared peplum at the back of the jacket skirting the curve of her neatly packed bum; Zenia in spike heels, hip cocked, one hand on it. She was only a little drunk; same with Roz. Zenia kissed Roz on the cheek because they were such friends, such pals and cohorts, and smiled mischievously at wretched Mitch, whose wretchedness Roz had stupidly failed to recognize. Then she turned to go down the steps, lifting her hand in a gesture oddly reminiscent of a newsreel general saluting the troops, and what was it she'd said? *Fuck the Third World! I'm tired of it!*

So much for the proprieties. So much for earnest old Roz and her poky, boring charities, her handouts to the Raped Moms and Battered Grannies, and, at that time, the whales and the famine victims and the village self-helpers, dowdy plump mommy Roz, shackled to her boring old conscience. It was a selfish, careless remark, a daring remark, a liberated remark—to hell with guilt! It was like speeding in a convertible, tailgating, weaving in and out without signalling, stereo on full blast and screw the neighbours, throwing your leftovers out the window, the ribbons, the wrapping paper, the half-eaten filo pastries and the champagne truffles, things you'd used up just by looking at them.

The worst of it was that Roz—although shocked, although gabbling, *Oh Zenia, you don't mean that!*—had felt an answering beat, in herself. A sort of echo, an urge to go that fast, be that loose, that greedy, herself, too. *Well, why not? You think they'd lift a finger, in the Third World, if it was you?* It was like that ad, for a car if she remembers rightly: *Make Dust Or Eat It.* Those were the choices on offer, then.

And Roz made dust, a lot of it, gold dust, and Zenia made a lot of dust too, though of a different kind. And now she is dust. And ashes, and so is Mitch. That's the taste Roz has now, in her mouth.

Roz teeters across the gravel, hits the sidewalk, and hurries towards the Toxique, as fast as her tight skirt will let her. There's a random flutter of hands held out, of thin murmuring voices, pale unhappy voices like those at the edge of sleep. She presses crumpled balls of money into the shaking fingers, the worn gloves, without looking, because if there's anything they resent it's your curiosity. So would she in their place. Ahead of her she spots Tony, coming along at her even-footed pony's trot. Roz waves an arm and yoo-hoos, and Tony stops and smiles, and Roz feels a warm rush of pleasure. Such a comfort!

And Charis is a comfort, too, sitting at the table already, flapping her hand in welcome. *Kiss kiss,* goes Roz, to either cheek, and plops herself into a chair, digging in her purse for her cigarettes. She intends to enjoy this lunch, because these two women are safe: of everyone she knows, her kids included, these two alone want nothing from her. She can slip her shoes off under the table, she can hold forth and laugh and say whatever she likes, because nothing's being decided, nothing's being demanded; and nothing's being withheld either, because the two of them know everything already. They know the worst. With them, and with them alone, she has no power.

Along comes the waitress—where do they get these clothes? Roz truly admires the nerve, and wishes she had some of it herself. Leopard-skin tights and silver boots! These are not outfits, these are costumes, but who are these people trying to be? Celebrants. But of what? What strange religion? Roz finds the Toxique denizens fascinating, but also a little scary. Every time she goes to the ladies' she's afraid of opening the wrong door down there, by mistake, and stumbling upon some kind of unholy rite. Orgies! Human sacrifices! No, that's going too far. But something she shouldn't know about, something that will get her in trouble. Some awful movie.

That's not the real reason she's drawn to the Toxique, however. The real reason is that, try as she may, she can't keep her hands off the laundry. She cruises her kids' rooms like a bottom-feeding fish, retrieving a dirty sock here, some underpants there, and she found a Toxique match folder in the pocket of Larry's crumpled shirt, and another one the next week. Is it so unnatural, to want to know where your son spends his time? At night, of course; he wouldn't be there at lunch. But she's compelled to keep an eye on the place, check in once in a while. It gives her more of a handle: at least he goes somewhere, he doesn't just vanish into thin air. But what does he do here, and who does he do it with?

Nothing and nobody, maybe. Maybe he just eats here, like her.

Speaking of which. She runs a finger down the menu—she's so hungry she could eat a horse, though she knows better than to use such an expression in front of Charis. What she settles on is the Thick-cut Gourmet Toasted Cheese Sandwich, on Herb and Caraway Seed Bread, with Polish Pickle. Solid peasant food, or an imitation of it. The Poles should have it so good, right now they're probably exporting all their pickles for hard currency. She gives her order to the tousle-haired waitress— could this be the attraction, for Larry? a serving wench?— and settles down to pick Tony's brain on the subject of the Middle East. Whenever something major happens there, the business world ripples.

Tony is so satisfying too, because however pessimistic Roz may be about current affairs, Tony is worse. She makes Roz feel like a naive young bubblebrain, such a refreshing change! Over the years they have deplored the U.S. presidency, shaken their heads while the Tories shredded the country, cast dire auguries from their analysis of Margaret Thatcher's hairdo, a militaristic sheet-iron coiffure if ever there was one, said Tony. When the Wall fell, Tony predicted waves of outgoing East Bloc immigrants, and rising resentment of them in the West, and Roz said, *Oh surely not,* because the thought of immigrants being resented bothers her a lot. *None is too many,* is what some Canadian government pooh-bah said about the Jews, during the war.

But things are getting more confusing: for instance,

how many immigrants can you fit in? How many of them can you handle, realistically, and who is *them,* and where do you draw the line? The mere fact that Roz is thinking this way shows the extent of the problem, because Roz knows very well what it's like to be *them.* By now, however, she is *us.* It makes a difference. She hates to be dog-in-the-manger, but she has to admit that Tony has been—however discouragingly—right on the money. Roz admires that. If only Tony would turn her predictive abilities to something more lucrative, like the stock market.

Tony's always so cool about everything, though. So matter-of-fact. *What did you expect?* she asks, with her round surprised eyes. Her surprise is for other people's hopefulness, their innocence, their mushy desire that everything will somehow turn out for the best.

Meanwhile, Charis, who doesn't believe in deaths, only in transitions, gets upset at the thought of all the riots and wars and famines Tony goes on about, because so many people will be killed. It isn't the deaths themselves, she tells them—it's the nature of the deaths. They aren't *good* deaths, they are violent and cruel, they are incomplete and damaged, and the evil effects will linger on like a sort of spiritual pollution for years and years. It's contaminating merely to think about this stuff, according to Charis.

"It's already been decided," says Tony. "It was decided as soon as Saddam crossed that border. Like the Rubicon."

The Rubicon, the Rubicon. Roz knows she's heard that word before. A river; somebody crossed it. Tony has a whole list of rivers that people crossed, with world-changing results, at some time or another. The Delaware, that was Washington. The Germanic tribes crossing the Rhine and overthrowing the Roman Empire. But the Rubicon? Well, how stupid of Roz! Julius Caesar, for a full ten points!

Then it comes to Roz in a flash of light—what a great lipstick name! A great series of names, names of rivers that have been crossed, crossed fatefully; a mix of the forbidden, and of courage, of daring, a dash of karma. *Rubicon,* a bright holly-berry. *Jordan,* a rich grape-tinged red. *Delaware,* a cerise with a hint of blue—though perhaps the word itself is too prissy. *Saint Lawrence*—a fire-and-ice hot pink—no, no, out of the question, saints won't do. *Ganges,* a blazing orange. *Zambezi,* a succulent maroon. *Volga,* that eerie purple that was the only shade of lipstick those poor deprived Russian women could lay their hands on, for decades—but Roz can see a future for it now, it will become avant-retro, a collector's item like the statues of Stalin.

Roz carries on with the conversation, but in her head she's furiously planning. She can see the shots of the models, how she wants them to look: seductive, naturally, but challenging too, a sort of meet-your-destiny stare. What was it Napoleon crossed? Only the Alps, no memorable rivers, worse luck. Maybe a few snippets from historical paintings in the background, someone waving a gusty, shredded flag, on a hill—it's always a hill, never for instance a swamp—with smoke and flames boiling around. Yes! It's right! This will go like hotcakes! And there's one final shade needed, to complete the palette: a sultry brown, with a smouldering, roiling undernote. What's the right river for that?

Styx. It couldn't be anything else.

• • •

It's at this moment that Roz catches the look on Tony's face. It isn't fear, exactly: it's an intentness, a focusing, a silent growl. If Tony had hackles they'd be raised, if she had fangs they'd be bared. This expression is so unlike the normal Tony that it scares Roz to bits.

"Tony, what's wrong?" she says.

"Turn your head slowly," says Tony. "Don't scream."

Oh shit. It's her. In the flesh.

Roz has no doubt, not a moment of it. If anyone can come back from the dead, if anyone would be determined to do it, it's Zenia. And she's back, all right. She's *back in town,* like the guy in the black hat in Western movies. The way she's striding through the room proclaims her sense of re-entry, of staking out the territory: a tiny contemptuous upcurved smirk, a conscious pelvic swagger, as if she's got two pearl-handled revolvers slung on her hips and is just waiting for an excuse to use them. Her perfume trails behind her like the smoke from an insolent cigar. While the three of them sit huddled at their table, cowards all, pretending not to notice and avoiding eye contact and acting like the Main Street folks who dive for cover behind the dry-goods counter, keeping out of the line of fire.

Roz reaches down for her purse, sneaking a peek at Zenia over her lowered shoulder, taking her measure, as Zenia undulates into a chair. Zenia is still magnificent. Though Roz knows how much of her is manufactured, it makes no difference. When you alter yourself, the alterations become the truth: who knows that better than Roz, whose hair tints vary monthly? Such things are not illusions, they are transformations. Zenia is no longer a small-titted person with two implants, she's a big-breasted knockout. The same goes for the nose job, and if Zenia's hair is turning grey it's invisible, she must have a top-notch colourist. You are what they see. Like a reno-vated building, Zenia is no longer the original, she's the end result.

Still, Roz can picture the stitch marks, the needle tracks, where the Frankenstein doctors have been at work. She knows the fault lines where Zenia might crack open. She would like to be able to say a magic word—*Shazam!*—that would cause time to run backwards, make the caps on Zenia's teeth pop off to reveal the dead stumps under-neath, melt her ceramic glaze, whiten her hair, shrivel her amino-acid-fed estrogen-replacement skin, pop her breasts open like grapes so that their silicone bulges would whiz across the room and splat against the wall.

What would Zenia be then? Human, like everyone else. It would do her good. Or rather it would do Roz good, because it would even the odds. As it is, Roz is going to war armed only with a basketful of nasty adjectives, a handful of ineffectual pebbles. What exactly can she do, to Zenia? Not a heck of a lot, because there can't be anything Zenia wants from her. Any more.

In the midst of her vengeful and fatalistic meditations, it occurs to her that Zenia may not just sit there and wait for Roz to attack. She may be here for a reason. She may be on the prowl. Hide the silver! What does she want, who is she out to get? At the thought that it might be her—though how, though why?—Roz shivers.

16

How did Roz get here, outside the Toxique? It must have been via her feet, but she can't recall gathering her purse, getting up, bravely, stupidly turning her back on Zenia, walking; she's been teleported, as in sci-fi movies of the fifties, reduced to a swirl of black-and-white zits, then reconstituted outside the door. She hugs Tony goodbye, and then Charis. She doesn't kiss their cheeks. Kisses are show-off, hugs are for real.

Tony is so little, Charis is so thin, both are shaken. She feels as if she's hugging the twins, one and then the other, on the morning of their first day at school. She wants to spread her hen wings over them, reassure them, tell them that everything will be all right, they just have to be courageous; but these are grown-ups she's dealing with, both of them smarter than she is in their different ways, and she knows they wouldn't believe a word of it.

She watches them walk away, Tony scuttling along her invisible trajectory, Charis ambling, a hesitant lope. Both smarter than she is, yes; Tony has a brilliant mind, within limits, and Charis has something else, harder to put your finger on but uncanny; sometimes she gives Roz the creeps because she knows things she has no way of knowing. But neither one of them has any street smarts. Roz keeps expecting them to wander out into the traffic and be squashed by trucks, or to be mugged, right before her very eyes. *Excuse me, ma'am, this is a mugging. Pardon? A what? What is a mugging? Can I help you with it?*

No street smarts at all, and Zenia is a street fighter. She kicks hard, she kicks low and dirty, and the only counterploy is to kick her first, with metal cleats on your boots. If there's going to be knife play, Roz will have to rely on herself alone. She doesn't need Tony's analysis of knives through the ages or Charis's desire not to discuss sharp items of cutlery because they are so negative. She just needs to know where the jugular is, so she can go for it.

The difficulty is that Zenia doesn't have a jugular. Or if she does Roz has never been able to figure out where it is, or how to get at it. Zenia of old had no discernible heart, and by now she may not even have blood. Pure latex flows in her veins. Or molten steel. Unless she's changed, and it hardly looks that way. In any case this is the second time round, and Roz is ready for it, and much less vulnerable, because this time there's no more Mitch.

All of this resolution and bravura is very well, but when Roz gets back to her car she finds a little message scratched in her paint, on the driver's door. *Rich Bitch*. A neatly lettered message, relatively polite—in the States it would have been *Cunt*—and ordinarily Roz would merely have calculated the cost of the repair and how much time it would take to get it done, and whether it's deductible. Also she would take out her annoyance by making a scene with the parking lot attendant. *Who did this? What do you mean, you don't know? What were you, asleep? Darn it, what the heck do they pay you for?*

But today she's not in the mood. She unlocks her car, checks the back seat to make sure nobody's in there—she hasn't read all those sex-killing thrillers for nothing—gets in, locks the door again, and has a small cry, in her usual position, with her forehead on the steering wheel and her new cotton hankie at the ready. (The twins have outlawed paper tissues. They're relentless, they don't give two hoots about Maria's extra ironing. Pretty soon Roz won't even be allowed toilet paper, they'll make her use old T-shirts. Or something.)

Her tears are not tears of mourning, nor of despair. They are tears of rage. Roz knows the flavour well. But at her age, rage for the sake of rage is becoming less and less worth it, because every time you grind your teeth a few of them could break off. So she blots her face, finishing with her sleeve because her hankie is soaked, re-does her lipstick (*Rubicon, here I come*), touches up her mascara, and guns her motor, gravel spewing from beneath her wheels. She half hopes she can graze a fender on the way out, pass along some anger—*Oops! So-o-o sorry!* It would be a substitute, the next best thing to strangling Zenia. But there's no car in a prime position, and the attendant's looking. Oh well, it's the thought that counts.

Roz goes up to her office—*Hi Nicki, Hi Suzy, How's it going Boyce, anything important, is there some more coffee, hold the calls, say I'm in a meeting*—and shuts the door. She sits in her leather chair and lights up, and ferrets in her in-basket for a chocolate, one of those round Viennese things with portraits of Mozart on them, Mozart Balls is what the kids call them, and chews and swallows, and drums her fingers on her unsatisfactory desk. Mitch is staring at her and it bothers her, so she gets up and turns the picture around, averting his gaze. *You aren't going to like this,* she tells him. He didn't the last time, either. Once he found out what she'd been doing.

She opens her file drawer and takes out the Z file, the same one with the glossy in it, and turns a few pages. There it all is, the skeleton of the skeleton in the closet: days, hours, places. It still hurts.

Why not use the same detective, less explaining to be done, and she was super good, Harriet, Harriet Thing, Hungarian but she WASPed her name—Harriet Bridges. Used to say she got to be a detective because if you were a Hungarian woman dealing with Hungarian men, you had to be one anyway. Roz finds the number, picks up the phone. She has to go through a gatekeeper to get through—Harriet must be doing better if she has a secretary, or probably it's one of those service-sharing offices—but she wheedles and pushes, and Harriet is finally not in a meeting any more, but there on the line.

"Hi, Harriet, this is Roz Andrews. Yeah, I know, it's been years. Listen, I want you to do something for me. Actually, the same thing you did before, sort of. The same woman. Well, I know she's dead. I mean, she *was* dead, but now she isn't. I saw her! In the Toxique. . . .

"I haven't the faintest. That's where you come in!

"If I were you I'd start with the hotels, but you can't count on her using her own name. Remember?

"I'll send over the photo by courier. Just find her.

Find out what she's up to. Who she's seeing. Phone me as soon as you know anything. Anything! What she has for breakfast. You know how nosy I am.

"Mark the bill Personal. Thanks. You're a doll. We'll do lunch!"

Roz hangs up. She ought to feel better but she doesn't, she's too keyed up. Now that she's set the thing in motion she can hardly wait for the results, because until she knows exactly where Zenia is, Zenia might be anywhere. She might be outside Roz's house right now, she might be climbing in through the window, gunny sack over her shoulder to carry away the loot. What loot? That's the question! Roz is almost ready to go out there and do the rounds herself, mooch from hotel to hotel with her precious glossy photo under her arm, lie, insinuate, bribe the desk clerks. She's impatient, she's irritable, she's avid, her skin is crawling with curiosity.

Maybe it's menopause, now wouldn't that be nice for a change? Maybe she'll get that surge of energy and *joie de vivre* they're always talking about. It's long overdue.

Or maybe this isn't raging hormones. Maybe it's sin. One of the Seven Deadlies, or rather two of them. The nuns were always keen on Lust, and Roz has thought recently that maybe Greed was the one with her own name on it. But here comes Anger, blindsiding her; and Envy, the worst, her old familiar, in the shape of Zenia herself, smiling and triumphant, an incandescent Venus, ascending not from a seashell but from a seething cauldron.

Let's face it, Roz, you're envious of Zenia. You always have been. Envious as Hell. Yes God, but so what? Judas Priest, what do I do about it? Down on your knees! Humiliate yourself! Mortify your soul! Scrub the toilet!

How long do I have to live before I'm rid of this junk, thinks Roz. The garage sale of the soul. She'll go home early, have a snack, pour herself a small drink, run a bath, put in some of the stuff Charis keeps deluging her with, from that hophead store where she works. Ground-up leaves, dried flowers, exotic roots, musty-hayfield aromas, snake oil, mole bones, age-old recipes brewed by certified crones. Not that Roz has a thing against crones, since at the rate she's going she'll soon be one herself.

It'll relax you, says Charis, though Roz, you have to help out! Don't fight it! Go with it. Lie back. Float. Picture yourself in a warm ocean.

But every time Roz tries this, there are sharks.

Black Enamel

17

All history is written backwards, writes Tony, writing backwards. We choose a significant event and examine its causes and its consequences, but who decides whether the event is significant? We do, and we are here; and it and its participants are there. They are long gone; at the same time, they are in our hands. Like Roman gladiators, they are under our thumbs. We make them fight their battles over again for our edification and pleasure, who fought them once for entirely other reasons.

Yet history is not a true palindrome, thinks Tony. We can't really run it backwards and end up at a clean start. Too many of the pieces have gone missing; also we know too much, we know the outcome. Historians are the quintessential voyeurs, noses pressed to Time's glass window. They can never actually be there on the battlefield, they can never join in those moments of supreme exaltation, or of supreme grief either. Their re-creations are at the best just patchy waxworks. Who'd choose to be God? To know the whole story, its violent clashes, its mêlées, its deadly conclusions, before it even begins? Too sad. And too demoralizing. For a soldier on the eve of battle, ignorance is the same as hope. Though neither one is bliss.

Tony sets down her pen. Such thoughts are as yet too nebulous to be formulated for the present purpose, which is a lecture she's promised to deliver to the Society of Military Historiographers two months from now. What she's leading up to is the defeat of Otto the Red at the hands of the Saracens on July 13, 982, and its inscription by later chroniclers as moral exemplum. It will be a good lecture, good enough—her lectures are always good enough—but as time goes on she has come to feel, at these events, more and more like a talking dog. Cute, no doubt; a clever trick; a *nice* dog; but nonetheless a dog. She used to think that her work was accepted or rejected on its own merits, but she's begun to suspect that the goodness of her lectures is somehow not the point. The point is her dress. She will be patted on the head, praised, fed a few élite dog biscuits, and dismissed, while the boys in the back room get down to the real issue, which is which one of them will be the next society president.

Such paranoia. Tony banishes it, and goes to get herself a drink of water.

She's in the cellar, in her dressing gown and raccoon slippers, in the middle of the night. She couldn't sleep, and she didn't want to disturb West by working in her office, which is down the hall from the bedroom. Her computer makes beeping sounds, and the light could wake him. When she eased herself down from the bed, when she tiptoed from the room, he was sleeping like an innocent, and also snoring like one, in a regular, gentle, maddening way.

Perfidious West. Indispensable West.

The real reason she came downstairs is that she

wanted to consult the phone book, the Yellow Pages, under Hotels, and she didn't want him to catch her doing it. She didn't want him to realize that she's been snooping on him, on him and Zenia, on his beside-the-phone scribblings. She didn't want to disappoint him, or, worse, alarm him. She's now looked up every hotel in the city beginning with A. She's made a list: the Alexandra, the Annex, the Arnold Garden, the Arrival, the Avenue Park. She could phone them all, ask for the room number, disguise her voice—or she wouldn't have to say a word, she could pose as a heavy-breathing phone pervert—and see if it's Zenia.

But there's a phone in the bedroom, right beside the bed. What's to stop West from hearing the tiny ping it makes when you hang up the other phones, and from listening in? She could use West's own phone, the Headwinds line; but it's just above the bedroom, and how to explain herself if surprised in the act? Better to wait. If Zenia is to be headed off—and Tony at the moment does not have the faintest idea how this is to be accomplished—West must be kept out of it as much as possible. He must be insulated. He's already been damaged enough. For kindly and susceptible souls like West's, the real world, especially the real world of women, is far too harsh a place.

The room Tony is writing in is the games room; or that's what she and West call it. It's the big part of the cellar, between the furnace room and the laundry room, and unlike these has indoor-outdoor carpet on the floor. West's game is a pool table, which takes up a relatively large amount of space and has a fold-up plywood pingpong overlay that can be added to it; which is what Tony is

writing on. Tony isn't much good at pool—she can understand the strategy, but she pokes too hard, she has no
finesse; however, she's a whiz at ping-pong. West is the
opposite—despite his amazing spider-monkey reach, he's
clumsy at high speeds. Sometimes, to give herself a hand-
icap, Tony will play a game with her right hand, not quite
as good as her left, though she can beat him that way also.
When Tony's been wiped out too often at pool, West will
suggest a game of ping-pong, though it's a foregone conclusion that he'll get creamed. He's always been very considerate, that way. It's a form of chivalry.

Which is a measure of how much, right now, Tony
stands to lose.

But ping-pong is a diversion. Tony's real game is off in a
corner, beside the tiny refrigerator they keep down there
for ice-water and West's beer. It's a large sand-table,
bought at a daycare-centre garage sale some years ago, but
it isn't full of sand. Instead it contains a three-dimensional
map of Europe and the Mediterranean, made of hardened
flour-and-salt paste, with the mountain ranges in relief and
the major bodies of water done in blue Plasticine. Tony has
been able to use this map over and over, adding and sub-
tracting canals, removing marshes, altering coastlines,
building and unbuilding roads and bridges and towns and
cities, diverting rivers, as occasion has demanded. Right
now it's set up for the tenth century: the day of Otto the
Red's fateful battle, to be exact.

For the armies and the populations, Tony doesn't use
pins or flags, not primarily. Instead she uses kitchen spices,
a different one for each tribe or ethnic grouping: cloves for

the Germanic tribes, red peppercorns for the Vikings, green peppercorns for the Saracens, white ones for the Slavs. The Celts are coriander seeds, the Anglo-Saxons are dill. Chocolate sprinkles, cardamom seeds, four kinds of lentils, and little silver balls indicate the Magyars, the Greeks, the North African kingdoms, and the Egyptians. For each major king, chief, emperor, or pope, there's a Monopoly man; areas in which each has sovereignty, actual or nominal, are marked by lengths of cut-up plastic swizzle stick, in matching colours, stuck into squares of gum eraser.

It's a complex system, but she prefers it to more schematic representations or to ones that show the armies and the strongholds only. With it she can depict interbreeding and hybridization, through conquest or through the slave trade, because populations are not in fact homogeneous blocks, but mixtures. There are white peppercorns in Constantinople and Rome, traded as slaves by the red peppercorns, who rule them; the green peppercorns trade from south to north, as well as from east to west and back again, using lentils. The Frankish rulers are really cloves, the green peppercorns have infiltrated the Celto-Ligurian corianders. There is a continuous ebb and flow, a blending, a shift of territories.

To keep the lighter spices from rolling around, she uses a touch of hairspray. Gently, though; otherwise they will be blown away. When she wants to change the year or the century, she scrapes off this or that population and sets up again. She uses tweezers; otherwise her fingers get covered with seeds. History isn't dry, it's sticky, it can get all over your hands.

• • •

Tony pulls a chair over to her sand-table and sits down to study it. On the west coast of Italy, near Sorrento, a group of cloves is pursuing a smaller group of fleeing green peppercorns: the Teutons are out to get the Saracens, or so they intend. The Monopoly man among the cloves is Otto the Red—impetuous, brilliant Otto, Otto the Second, the Germanic emperor of Rome. On and on ride Otto and the cloves, between the indifferent sea and the wrinkly dry mountains, sweating under the gruelling sun; they are buoyant with adrenalin, high on the prospect of bloodshed and loot, dizzy with imminent winning. Little do they know.

Tony knows more. Behind the folds of dry earth and stone, out of sight, a large force of Saracen peppercorns is lying in ambush. The band of fleeing green peppercorns running away up front are only decoys. It's the oldest trick in the book, and Otto has fallen for it. Soon his men will be attacked from three sides, and the fourth side is the sea. They will all be killed, or most of them will be; or they'll be pushed back into the sea, where they'll drown, or they'll crawl away wounded and die of thirst. Some of them will be captured and sold for slaves. Otto himself will escape with barely his life.

Go back, Otto, thinks Tony. She is fond of Otto, he's a favourite of hers; also she feels sorry for him because he had a fight with his wife that morning, before he left on this ill-starred expedition, which may account for his recklessness. Losing your temper is bad for war. *Otto, go back!* But Otto can't hear her, and he can't see the world from above, as she can. If only he'd sent out scouts, if only he'd waited! But waiting can also be fatal. So can going back. He who fights and runs away may live to fight another day, or else he may just get speared from behind.

Already Otto has come too far. Already the great tweezers in the sky descend, and the green peppercorns rise up from behind the hot rocks, ride out of hiding, and give chase along the arid shore. Tony feels awful about this, but what can she do? She's helpless. It's too late. It was too late a thousand years ago. All she can do is visit the beach. She has done that, she has seen the hot dry mountains, she has pressed a small spiky flower for her scrapbook. She has bought a souvenir: a pair of salad servers, carved from olive wood.

Absent-mindedly she picks up one of Otto's fallen cloves, dips it into her glass of water to get rid of any hairspray, and pops it into her mouth. It's a bad habit of hers, eating parts of the armies on her map; luckily there are always replacements in the bottles on the spice shelves upstairs. But the dead soldiers would have been eaten too, one way or another; or at least dismembered, their possessions dispersed. That's the thing about war: the polite formalities go by the wayside, and the proportion of funerals to actual deaths tends to be low. Already the Saracens are finishing off the wounded, a mercy under the (nurseless, waterless) circumstances, and stripping them of their armour and weapons. Already the scavenging peasants wait their turn. Already the vultures have gathered.

It's too late for Otto, but what about her? And if she had another chance, another turn, another beginning, with Zenia, would she have acted differently? She doesn't know, because she knows too much to know.

18

Tony was the first one of them to befriend Zenia; or rather, Tony was the first one to let her in, because people like Zenia can never step through your doorway, can never enter and entangle themselves in your life, unless you invite them. There has to be a recognition, an offer of hospitality, a word of greeting. Tony has come to realize this, although she didn't at the time. The question she asks about herself now is simply: why did she do it? What was there about her, and also about Zenia, that made such a thing not only possible but necessary?

Because she did issue an invitation, there's no doubt about it. She didn't know she was doing it, but ignorance in such matters is no defence. She opened the door wide, and in came Zenia, like a long-lost friend, like a sister, like a wind, and Tony welcomed her.

It was a long time ago, in the early sixties, when Tony was nineteen; not a period she remembers with much pleasure, before the advent of Zenia. In retrospect it seems to her empty, cindery, devoid of comforts; though while she was undergoing it she considered that she was doing all right.

She studied a lot, she ate and slept, she rinsed out her stockings in the McClung Hall second-floor washbasin and twisted them up in a towel and hung them neatly above the clanking radiator in her room, on a coat-hanger suspended from the curtain rod by a string. She had various little well-worn runways that got her through the weeks, like mice through a field; as long as she stayed on them she was safe. She was dogged, she plodded on, nose to the ground, wrapped in a protective numbness.

As she recalls, it was November. (She had a wall calendar on which she crossed off the days, though there was no special date she was heading towards or anticipating; but it gave her the feeling of moving forward.) She'd been living in McClung Hall for the past three years, ever since the death of her father. Her mother had died earlier and was presently in a metal canister the shape of a miniature depth charge, which she kept on a closet shelf, tucked in behind her folded sweaters. Her father was in the Necropolis, although his 1940s German pistol was in a box of old Christmas tree decorations, about all she'd kept from the family house. She'd been intending to reunite her parents—take a trowel to the Necropolis one day, plant her mother beside her father like an aluminum-alloy tulip bulb—but she was held back by the suspicion that her mother, at least, would have gone a long way to avoid such a thing. Anyway, she didn't at all mind having her mother in her room, on her shelf, where she could keep an eye on her. (Assign her a location. Tether her down. Make her stay put.)

Tony had a room to herself because the girl who was supposed to be sharing with her had taken an overdose of sleeping pills and had had her stomach pumped, and had then disappeared. People tended to, in Tony's experience.

For weeks before she left, the roommate had stayed in bed all day with her clothes on, reading paperback novels and weeping softly. Tony hated that. It bothered her more than the sleeping pills.

Tony had the sensation of living by herself, but of course she was surrounded by others; other girls, or were they women? McClung Hall was called a women's residence, but *girls* was what they said to one another. *Hey girls,* they would call, running up the stairs. *Guess what!*

Tony did not feel she had much in common with these other girls. Groups of them would spend the evenings—when they weren't out on dates—in the Common Room, sprawled on the dispirited orangy-brown chesterfield and the three overstuffed and leaking easy chairs, in their pyjamas and housecoats and big bristly hair rollers, playing bridge and smoking and drinking coffee, and dissecting their dates.

Tony herself did not go out on dates; she did not have anybody to go with. She did not mind this; in any case, she was happier in the company of people who had died a long time ago. That way there was no painful suspense, no disappointment. Nothing to lose.

Roz was one of the Common Room girls. She had a loud voice, and called Tony Toinette, or, worse, Tonikins; even then she'd wanted to dress Tony up, like a doll. Tony hadn't liked her, at that period. She'd considered her intrusive and crude and smothering.

The girls in general thought Tony was odd, but they weren't hostile towards her. Instead they made a pet of her. They liked to feed her bits of the contraband food they kept hidden in their rooms—chocolate bars, cookies, potato chips. (Food in the rooms was officially forbidden, because of the cockroaches and mice.) They liked to give her little rumplings of the hair, little squeezes. People find it hard to keep their hands off the small—so like kittens, so like babies. *Tiny Tony.*

They would call out to her as she scuttled past them on her way to her room: *Tony! Hey! Hey Tone! How's it goin'?* Frequently Tony resisted them, or avoided them altogether. But sometimes she would go into the Common Room and drink their sedimentary coffee and nibble their sandy cookies. Then they would get her to write their names for them, backwards and forwards at the same time, one name with each hand; they would crowd around, marvelling at what she herself felt to be self-evident, a minor and spurious magic.

Tony wasn't the only girl with a specialty. One of them could make a sound like a motorboat starting up, several—including Roz—were in the habit of drawing faces on their stomachs with eyebrow pencils and lipsticks and then performing a belly dance that made the painted mouths open and close grotesquely, and another did a trick involving a glass of water, an empty toilet-paper roll, a broomstick, an aluminum pie pan, and an egg. Tony found these accomplishments much more valid than her own. What she did required no skill, no practice; it was merely like being double-jointed, or being able to wiggle your ears.

Sometimes they would beg her to sing backwards for them, and if they pestered enough and if Tony was feeling strong, she would oblige. In her off-key, surprisingly raspy voice, the voice of a choir-child with a cold, she would sing:

Gnilrad ym ho,
Gnilrad ym ho,

> *Gnilrad ym ho,*
> *Enitn(e)melc,*
> *Reverof (e)nog dna tsol er(a) uoy,*
> *Yrros lufdaerd,*
> *Enitn(e)melc.*

In order to make it scan she would claim that three of the vowels were silent, and that *uo* was a diphthong. Why not? All languages had such tics, and this was her language; so its rules and its irregularities were at her mercy.

The other girls found this song hilarious, especially since Tony never cracked a smile, never twinkled, never twitched. She did it straight. The truth was that she didn't find it funny, this song about a woman who had drowned in a ludicrous fashion, who was not mourned, who was ultimately forgotten. She found it sad. *Lost and gone forever.* Why did they laugh?

When she wasn't with these girls she didn't think much about them—about their edgy jokes, their group smell of pyjamas and hair gel and damp flesh and talcum, their welcoming chirps and clucks, their indulgent smirks behind her back: *droll Tony.* Instead she thought about wars.

Wars, and also battles, which were not the same thing.

What she liked was to replay decisive battles, to see if they could conceivably have been won by the losing side. She studied the maps and the accounts, the disposition of troops, the technologies. A different choice of ground could have tipped the scales, or a different way of thinking, because thought could be a technology. A strong religious faith, because God too was a military weapon. Or a different weather, a different season. Rain was crucial; snow also. So was luck.

She had no biases, she was never for one side and against the other. The battles were problems that might have been solved in another way. Some had been unwinnable, no matter what; others not. She kept a battle notebook, with her alternative solutions and the scores. The scores were the men lost. "Lost," they were called, as if they had been forgetfully misplaced somewhere and would be found again later. Really it meant killed. Lost and gone forever. *Dreadful sorry,* the generals would say afterwards, if they themselves were still alive.

She was smart enough not to mention this interest of hers to the other girls. If known about, it would have pushed her over the edge: from strange but cute to truly pathological. She wanted to retain the option of cookies.

There were a few other girls in residence who were like Tony, who snuck past the housecoated bridge players and avoided communal meals. These girls didn't band together; they didn't even speak to one another, apart from nods and hellos. Tony suspected them of having secret preoccupations, secret and risible and unacceptable ambitions, like her own.

One of these isolates was Charis. Her name wasn't Charis then, but plain Karen. (It changed sometime in the sixties, when there were a lot of nomenclatural mutations.) Charis-Karen was a thin girl; *willowy* was one of the words that came to mind, like willows, with their swaying branches, their shivering fountains of blonde leaves. The other word was *amnesiac.*

Charis meandered: Tony saw her sometimes, on the way to and from classes, wandering slantways across the street, always—it seemed—in danger of being run over. She wore long dirndl skirts with wedges of slip showing beneath them; things fell out of her purses, or rather her bags, which were woven, ravelling, and embroidered. When she strayed into the Common Room it was always to ask if anyone had seen her other glove, her mauve scarf, her fountain pen. Usually no one had.

One evening when Tony was coming back from the library she saw Charis climbing down the McClung fire escape at the side of the building. She was wearing what looked like her nightgown; at any rate it was long and white and billowy. She reached the bottom platform, hung by her hands for a minute, then dropped the last few yards and began to walk towards Tony. Her feet were bare.

She was sleepwalking, Tony decided. She wondered what to do. She knew you weren't supposed to wake sleepwalkers, although she had forgotten why. Charis was none of her business, she'd never said more than two words to her, but she felt she ought to follow her to make sure no moving vehicles bumped into her. (If this had been happening now Tony would have included rape among the possibilities: a young woman in a nightgown, outside in the dark, in downtown Toronto, would be heavily at risk. Charis might have been at risk then too, but rape was not among Tony's daily-life categories at that time. Rape went with pillage, and was historical.)

Charis didn't go far. She walked through several piles of raked-up leaves, from the maples and chestnuts on the McClung lawn; then she turned around and walked back through them again, with Tony sneaking along behind her like a butterfly collector. After that she sat down under one of the trees.

Tony wondered how long she was going to stay there. It was getting cold, and she wanted to go inside; but she couldn't just leave Charis out on the lawn, sitting under a tree in her nightgown. So she sat down under the tree next to Charis's. The ground was not dry. Tony hoped nobody would see her out there, but luckily it was quite dark and she had on a grey coat. Unlike Charis, who glimmered faintly.

After a while a voice spoke to Tony out of the darkness. "I'm not asleep," it said. "But thank you anyway."

Tony was annoyed. She felt she had been led on. She didn't find this behaviour of Charis's—traipsing around in her bare feet and her nightgown—at all mysterious or intriguing. She found it theatrical and bizarre. Roz and the girls in the Common Room might be abrasive, but at least they were solid and uncomplicated, they were known quantities. Charis on the other hand was slippery and translucent and potentially clinging, like soap film or gelatin or the prehensile tentacles of sea anemones. If you touched her, some of her might come off on you. She was contagious, and better left alone.

19

None of the McClung Hall girls had anything to do with Zenia. And Zenia would have nothing to do with them. She wouldn't have lived in a women's residence if forced at gunpoint, as she said to Tony the first time she set foot in the place. *This dump,* she called it.

(Why had she come? To borrow something. What was it? Tony doesn't wish to remember, but remembers anyway: it was money. Zenia was always running short. Tony found it embarrassing to be asked, but she would have found it more embarrassing still to refuse. What she finds embarrassing now is that she so naively, so tamely, so obligingly forked over.)

"Residence is for small people," Zenia said, gazing contemptuously around her, at the institutional paintwork, the shoddy chairs in the Common Room, the comic strips cut out of the newspaper and Scotch-taped to the girls' doors.

"Right," said Tony, heavily.

Zenia looked down at Tony, smiling, correcting herself. "Imaginatively small. I don't mean *you.*"

Tony was relieved, because Zenia's contempt was a work of art. It was so nearly absolute; it was a great privilege to find yourself excluded from it. You felt reprieved, you felt vindicated, you felt grateful; or this is what Tony felt, pattering off to her room, locating her little chequebook, writing out her little cheque. Offering it up. Zenia took it carelessly, folded it twice, and stuck it into her sleeve. Both of them tried to act as if nothing had happened; as if nothing had changed hands, as if nothing at all was owed.

How she must have hated me for that, thinks Tony.

So Tony did not meet Zenia among the girls at McClung Hall. She met her instead through her friend West.

She was not sure, exactly, how West had become her friend. He had more or less materialized. He began by sitting beside her in class and borrowing her Modern History notes because he'd missed the lecture before that one, and then all of a sudden he was a part of her routine.

West was the only person she could talk to about her interest in war. She hadn't done it yet, but she was working up to it gradually. Such a thing might take years, and he'd only been her friend for a month. For the first two weeks of this period she'd called him Stewart, like his other, his male friends, who would slap him on the shoulder, give him small punches on the arm, and say, *Hey Stew, what's new?* But then he'd come across a few of the cryptic comments she'd written in the margins of her notes—*egabrag tahw, poop dlo gnirob*—and she'd had to explain them. He was impressed with her ability to write backwards—*That's something,* was what he said—and he'd wanted his own name reversed. He claimed to like his new name a lot better.

The girls in the residence began referring to West as Tony's boyfriend, although they knew he wasn't. They did it to tease. "How's your boyfriend?" Roz would yell, grinning at Tony from the saggy depths of the orange sofa, which sagged even more when it was Roz who was sitting on it. "Hey, Tonikins! How's your secret life? How's Mr. Beanpole? Poor me! The tall guys always go for shrimps!"

West was tall enough, but walking beside Tony made him look even taller. He lacked the solidity of the word *giant*; instead he was skinny, loosely strung. His legs and arms were only tentatively attached to the rest of him, and his hands and feet seemed larger than they were because his sleeves and pant legs were always an inch or two short. He was handsome in an angular, an attenuated way, like a medieval stone saint or an ordinarily handsome man who had been stretched like rubber.

He had shaggy blond hair then, and wore dark, tarnished clothing—a frayed turtleneck, sullied jeans. This was unusual for the time: most men at university still wore ties, or at least jackets. His clothes were a badge of the fringe, they gave him an outlaw's lustre. When Tony and West had coffee together after their Modern History lecture, in one of the student coffee shops they frequented, the girls would stare at West. Then their eyes would move downwards and they would spot Tony, in her kiddie pageboy, her horn-rimmed glasses and kilty skirt and penny loafers. Then they would be puzzled.

Drinking coffee was about all Tony did with West. As they drank the coffee, they talked; although neither of them was what you would call loquacious. Most of their talk was an easy silence. Sometimes they drank beer, in various dark beer parlours, or rather West did. Tony would sit on the edge of her chair, her toes barely touching the floor, and lick the froth off the top of her draft, her tongue exploring it thoughtfully, like a cat's. Then West would drink the rest of the beer and order two more. Four was his limit. To Tony's relief he never drank any more than that. It was surprising that the beer parlours let Tony in, because she looked so under-age. She *was* under-age. They must have thought she would never dare to set foot in such places unless she was in reality twenty-two. But she was disguised as herself, one of the most successful disguises. If she'd tried to look older it wouldn't have worked.

West said nobody took better history notes than Tony. That made her feel useful—even better, indispensable. Praised.

West was taking Modern History—which wasn't modern history at all, it was simply not Ancient History, which ended with the fall of Rome—because he was interested in folk songs and ballads, and in antique musical instruments. He played the lute, or so he said. Tony had never seen his lute. She'd never been to his room, if in fact he lived in a room. She didn't know where he lived, or what he did in the evenings. She told herself she wasn't interested: theirs was a friendship of the afternoons.

As time went on, however, she began thinking about the rest of his life. She found herself wondering what he ate for dinner, and even breakfast. She assumed he lived with other men, or boys, because he'd told her about a guy he knew who could set fire to his own farts. He didn't tell her this in a sniggering way, but regretfully somehow. "Imagine having that engraved on your tombstone," he said. Tony recognized the fart-lighting as a variant of the more sedate tricks that went on in McClung Hall with the eggs and lipstick faces, and postulated a men's residence. But she didn't ask.

When West appeared, he said *Hi*. When he disappeared, he said *See you*. Tony never knew when either of these things was going to happen.

In this fashion they reached November. Tony and West were sitting in a beer parlour called Montgomery's Inn, after one of the skirmishes of the 1837 Rebellion in Upper Canada, which, in Tony's opinion, should have gone the other way, but had been lost through stupidity and panic. Tony was licking the foam off the top of her draft beer as usual, when West said something surprising. He said he was having a party.

What he actually said was *we*. And he didn't say *party*, he said *bash*.

Bash was an odd word, coming from West. Tony did not think of West as a violent person, and *bash* was harsh, a body-blow term. He sounded as if he were quoting someone.

"A bash?" Tony said uncertainly. "I don't know." She had heard the girls in the residence talking about bashes. They took place at men's fraternities, and frequently ended with people being sick—men mostly, but sometimes girls too, either at the fraternity itself or later, in one of the McClung washrooms.

"I think you should come," said West, gazing at her benevolently with his blue eyes. "I think you're looking pale."

"This is the colour I am," said Tony defensively. She was taken aback by the sudden concern for her health on West's part. It seemed too polite; although, in contradiction to his offhand and sullen clothing, he always opened doors. She wasn't used to such concern from him, or from anyone else. She found it alarming, as if he had touched her.

"Well," said West, "I think you should get out more."

"Out?" said Tony. She was confused: what did he mean by *out*?

"You know," said West. "Meet people."

There was something almost sly about the way he said this, as if he were concealing a more devious purpose. It occurred to her that he might be trying to set her up with some man, out of misplaced solicitude, the way Roz might. *Toinette! There's someone I want you to meet!* Roz would say, and Tony would sidestep and evade.

Now she said, "But I wouldn't know anyone there."

"You'd know me," said West. "And you could meet the others."

Tony didn't say she did not want to meet any more people. It would have sounded too strange. Instead she let West write down the address for her, on a corner of paper torn from his *Rise of the Renaissance* textbook. He didn't say he would pick her up, so at least it wasn't a date. Tony couldn't have handled a date with anyone, much less West. She couldn't have handled the implications, or the hope. Hope of that kind might unbalance her. She didn't want to get involved, with anyone, underlined, full stop.

The bash is up two flights of stairs, in a narrow asphalt-shingled building far downtown that forms part of a row of cut-price and army surplus stores, and fronts on the railway tracks. The stairs are steep; Tony climbs them one step at a time, helping herself up by the banister. The door at the top is open; smoke and noise are billowing out through the doorway. Tony wonders whether to knock, decides against it on the grounds that no one would hear her, and goes in.

Right away she wishes she hadn't, because the room is thick with people, and they are the kind of people who, taken *en masse,* are most likely to frighten her, or at least make her very uneasy. Most of the women have straight hair, worn long in a ballerina ponytail or wound into austere buns. They have black stockings and black skirts and black tops, and no lipstick; their eyes are heavily outlined. Some of the men have beards. They wear the same kind of clothes that West does—work shirts, turtlenecks, jean jackets—but they lack his candour, his sweetness, his air of hairlessness. Instead they are compacted, matted, dense with supercharged matter. They hulk, they loom, they bristle with static energy.

The men are talking mostly to one another. The women aren't talking at all. They're leaning against the wall, or standing with their arms folded under their breasts, a cigarette carelessly in one hand, dropping ashes on the floor, looking as if they're bored and about to leave for some other, better party; or they're gazing expressionlessly at the men, or staring past their shoulders as if searching intently for someone else, some other man, a more important one.

A couple of the women glance over at Tony as she comes in, then shift their eyes quickly away. Tony is wearing the sort of clothes she usually wears, a dark green corduroy jumper with a white blouse under it, a green velvet hairband, and knee socks and brown loafers. She has kept a lot of her clothes from high school, because they still fit.

She knows at this moment that she will have to acquire other clothes. But she is not sure how.

She stands on tiptoe and peers through the intertwined hedge of arms and shoulders and heads, of black wool rib-knit breasts and denim chests and torsos. But West is nowhere in sight.

Maybe it's because the room is so dark; maybe that's why she can't see him. Then she realizes that the room is not only dark, it's black. The walls, the ceiling, even the floor are a glossy, hard enamel black. Even the windows have been painted over; even the light fixtures. Instead of electric lights there are candles, stuck in Chianti bottles. And all over the room there are big silvery juice tins, peeled of their labels and filled with bunches of white chrysanthemums that waver and shine in the light from the candles.

Tony wants to leave, but she wouldn't like to do that without seeing West. He might think she'd refused his invitation, had failed to come; he might think she was being snobby. Also she wants to be soothed and reassured: with him there she will not be so out of place. She goes in search of him, down a hallway that leads off to the left. This terminates in a bathroom. A door opens, there's a flushing sound, and a large, hair-covered man comes out. He gives Tony an unfocused look. "Shit, the Girl Guides," he says.

Tony feels about two inches tall. She flees into the bathroom, which will at least be a refuge. It too has been painted black, even the bathtub, even the sink, even the mirror. She locks the door and sits down on the black toilet, touching it first to make sure the paint is dry.

She's not sure she's in the right place. Perhaps West

doesn't live here at all. Perhaps she has the wrong address; perhaps this is some other bash. But she checked the scrap of paper before coming up the stairs. Perhaps, then, it's the time that's wrong—perhaps she's too early for West, or too late. There's no way of knowing, since his comings and goings have always been so unpredictable.

She could go out of the bathroom and ask someone— one of the enormous, furry men, one of the tall supercilious women—where he might be, but she dreads doing this. What if nobody knows who he is? It would be safer to stay in here, replaying the Battle of Culloden to herself, calculating the odds. She arranges the terrain—the hill that slopes downwards, the line of the stone wall with the tidy British soldiers and their tidy guns in a row behind it. The raggedy clans charging, plunging down the hill yelling, with nothing but their heavy outdated swords and their round bucklers. Falling in picturesque, noble heaps. An abattoir. Courage is of use only when technologies are evenly matched. Bonnie Prince Charlie was an idiot.

Unwinnable, she thinks, as a battle. The only hope would have been to avoid a battle altogether. To reject the terms of the argument, refuse the conventions. Strike at night, then melt away into the hills. Disguise yourself as a peasant. Not a fair fight, but then, what is a fair fight? Nothing she's learned about yet.

Someone's knocking at the door. Tony gets up, flushes the black toilet, rinses her hands at the black sink. There's no towel so she wipes her hands on her corduroy jumper. She unlocks the door: it's one of the ballerina women.

"Sorry," Tony says to her. The woman stares coldly.

Tony goes back into the main room, intending to

leave. Without West, there's no point. But there, in the centre of the room, is Zenia.

Tony doesn't know Zenia's name yet, but Zenia doesn't seem to need a name. She isn't wearing black like most of the others. Instead she's in white, a sort of shepherd's smock that comes down to mid-thigh on the long legs of her tight jeans. The smock isn't thin but it suggests lingerie, perhaps because the front buttons are open to a point level with her nipples. In the V of cloth, a small firm half-breast curves away to either side, like back-to-back parentheses.

All the others, in their black, sink into the black background of the walls. Zenia stands out: her face and hands and torso swim against the darkness, among the white chrysanthemums, as if disembodied and legless. She must have thought it all out beforehand, Tony realizes—how she would glow in the dark like an all-night gas station, or— to be honest—like the moon.

Tony feels herself being sucked back, pushed back into the black enamel of the wall. Very beautiful people have that effect, she thinks: they obliterate you. In the presence of Zenia she feels more than small and absurd: she feels non-existent.

She ducks into the kitchen. It's black too, even the stove, even the refrigerator. The paint glistens moistly in the candlelight.

West is leaning against the refrigerator. He is quite drunk. Tony can see it at once, she's had enough practice. Something turns over inside her, turns over and sinks.

"Hi, Tony," he says. "How's my little pal?"

West has never called Tony his little pal before. He's never called her *little*. It seems a violation.

"Actually I have to go," she says.

"'Night's young," he says. "Have a beer." He opens the black refrigerator, which is still white inside, and digs out two Molson's Ex. "Where'd I put the fucker?" he asks, patting parts of his body.

Tony doesn't know what he's talking about or what he's doing, or even who he is, exactly. Not who she thought he was, that's for sure. He doesn't usually swear. She starts backing away.

"It's in your pocket," says a voice behind her. Tony looks: it's the girl in the white smock. She smiles at West, points her index finger at him. "Hands up."

Grinning, West puts his hands in the air. The girl kneels and fumbles in his pockets, leaning her head against his thighs, and after a very long moment—during which Tony feels as if she's being forced to peep through a keyhole at a scene far too intimate to be borne—brings out a bottle-opener. She opens both beers with it, flipping the tops off expertly, hands one to Tony, tilts the other one back and drinks from it. Tony watches her throat undulate as she swallows. She has a long neck.

"What about me?" says West, and the girl hands him the bottle.

"So, how do you like our flowers?" she says to Tony. "We stole them from the Mount Hope Cemetery. Some big cheese croaked. They're sort of wilted, though: we had to wait until everyone had buggered off." Tony notes the words—*stole, croaked, buggered*—and feels timid and lacking in style.

"This is Zenia," says West. There's a proprietary

reverence in his voice, and a huskiness, that Tony doesn't like at all. *Mine,* is what he means. Handfuls of *mine*.

Tony can see now that she was wrong about *we*. *We* had nothing to do with male roommates. *We* meant Zenia. Zenia is now leaning back against West as if he's a lamppost. He has his arms around her waist, under her smock; his face is half hidden in her smoky hair.

"They're great," Tony says. She tries to sound enthusiastic. She takes an awkward swallow from the bottle Zenia has given her, and concentrates to avoid spluttering. Her eyes are stinging, her face reddening, her nose is full of prickles.

"And this is Tony," says West's voice. His mouth is behind Zenia's hair, so it looks like the hair talking. Tony thinks about running: out the kitchen door, between the denim-covered legs in the main room, down the stairs. A stampeding mouse.

"Oh, *this* is Tony," says Zenia. She sounds amused. "Hi there, Tony. Do you like our black walls? Please get your cold hands off my stomach," she adds, to West.

"Cold hands, warm heart," West mutters.

"Heart," says Zenia. "Who cares about your *heart*? It's not your most useful body part." She lifts up the bottom of her smock, finds his two big hands, extracts them, and holds them in hers, caressing them, all the time smiling at Tony. "It's revenge," she says. Her eyes aren't black, as Tony thought at first: they're navy blue. "This is a revenge party. The landlord's kicking us out, so we thought we'd give the old fucker something to remember us by. It'll take him more than two coats to cover *this* up. The lease said we had the right to paint, but it didn't say what colour. Did you see the toilet?"

"Yes," says Tony. "It's very slippery." She doesn't mean this to be funny, but Zenia laughs.

"You're right," she says to West. "Tony's a scream."

Tony hates being talked about in the third person. She's always hated it; her mother used to do the same thing. West has been discussing her with Zenia, the two of them, analyzing her behind her back, sticking adjectives onto her as if she's a child, as if she's anyone at all, as if she's a topic. It occurs to her also that the only reason West asked her to their party is that Zenia told him to. She sets the beer bottle down on the black stove, noticing that it's half empty. She must have drunk the other half. How did she do that? "I should be going," she says, with what she hopes is dignity.

Zenia doesn't seem to have heard her. Neither does West. He's peering out now from the burrow of Zenia's hair; she can see his eyes gleaming in the light from the candles.

Tony's arms and legs are coming detached from the rest of her, and sounds are slowing down. It's the beer, she doesn't usually drink it, she isn't used to it. Longing sweeps through her. She wishes she knew someone who would bury his face in her own hair like that. She wishes it could be West. But she doesn't have enough hair for that. He would just hit scalp.

She's lost something. She's lost West. *Tsol. Reverof.* It's a dumb thought: how can you lose somebody you never really had?

"So, Tony," says Zenia. She says *Tony* as if it's a foreign word, as if it's in quotes. "West tells me you're brilliant. What's your direction?"

Tony thinks that Zenia is asking her where she's going from here. She could pretend there's another party, a better one, to which Zenia herself has not been invited. But it's not likely she would be believed. "I guess I'll take the subway back," she says. "I have to work."

"She's always working," says West.

"No," says Zenia, with a hint of impatience. "I mean, what do you want to do with your life? What's your obsession?"

Obsession. Tony doesn't know anyone who talks like that. Only criminals and creepy people have obsessions, and if you have one yourself you aren't supposed to admit to it. *I don't have to answer,* she tells herself. She pictures the girls in the Common Room, and what they would think of obsessions; and what they would think of Zenia, come to that. They would think she was full of it, and also a slut, with her buttons undone like that. They would disapprove of her slutty hair. Usually Tony finds their judgments on other women catty and superficial, but right now she finds them comforting.

She should smile a bored, dismissive smile. She should say, "My what?" and laugh, and act puzzled, as if it's a stupid question. She knows how to do this, she has watched and listened.

But it isn't a stupid question, and she knows the answer. "Raw," she says.

"What?" says Zenia. She's concentrating on Tony now, as if she is finally interesting. Something worth figuring out. "Did you say *law*?"

Tony realizes she's made a mistake, a slip of the tongue. She's reversed the word. It must be the alcohol.

"I mean *war*," she says, pronouncing this time carefully.

"That's what I want to do with my life. I want to study war." She shouldn't have said it, she shouldn't have told that much about herself, she's put it wrong. She's been ridiculous.

Zenia laughs, but it isn't a mocking laugh. It's a laugh of delight. She touches Tony's arm, lightly, as in a game of tag played with cobwebs. "Let's have coffee," she says. And Tony smiles.

20

That was it, that was the decisive moment. Rubicon! The die was cast, but who would have known it at the time? Not Tony, although she does remember a sensation, the sensation of having lost her footing, of being swept out into a strong current. And what, exactly, had acted as the invitation proper? What had beckoned to Zenia, shown her an opening in Tony's beetle-like little armoured carapace? Which was the magic word, *raw* or *war*? Probably it was the two of them together; the doubleness. That would have had high appeal, for Zenia.

But this may be just overcomplication, intellectual web-spinning, to which Tony knows she is prone. Doubtless it was something much simpler, much more obvious: Tony's confusion, her lack of defences under the circumstances, the circumstances being West; West, and the fact that Tony loved him. Zenia must have sensed this before Tony did, and known that Tony was no threat, and known as well that Tony had some feathers worth plucking.

But what about Tony herself? What was Zenia offering her, or appearing to offer, as she stood there in the black kitchen, as she smiled with her fingers lightly on Tony's arm, shimmering in the candlelight like a mirage?

Nature abhors a vacuum, thinks Tony. How inconvenient. Otherwise, we vacuums might lead our lives in relative security.

Not that Tony is a vacuum now. No, not at all. Now she's replete, now she wallows in plenitude, now she's guarding a castle full of treasure, now she's involved. Now she must take hold.

Tony paces the basement floor, her pen and notebook neglected on the ping-pong table, thinking of West sleeping upstairs, with the air going deeply into and out of him; West, shifting and groaning, with forlorn sighs, sighs that sound like heartbreak. She listens to the screams of the dying, to the cheering of the Saracens on the barren coast, to the refrigerator humming nearby, to the clunk of the furnace as it turns itself off and on, and to Zenia's voice.

A drawling voice, with a slight hesitation in it, a slight foreign flavour, the hint of a lisp; low, succulent, but with a hard surface. A glazed chocolate, with a soft, buttery, deceptive centre. Sweet, and bad for you.

"What would cause you to kill yourself?" says Zenia.

"Kill myself?" says Tony wonderingly, as if she's never thought of such a thing. "I don't know. I don't think I would."

"What if you had cancer?" Zenia says. "What if you knew you were going to die slowly, in unbearable pain? What if you knew where the microfilm was, and the other side knew you knew, and they were going to torture you to get it out of you and then kill you anyway? What if you had a cyanide tooth? Would you use it?"

Zenia is fond of such interrogations. Usually they are based on fairly extreme scripts: what if you'd been on the *Titanic,* going down? Would you have elbowed and shoved, or stood back and drowned politely? What if you were starving, in an open boat, and one of the others died? Would you eat him? If so, would you push the others overboard so you could keep him all to yourself? She seems to have her own answers fairly firmly in place, though she does not always reveal them.

Despite the weightless corpses strewn about in her head, despite her graph-paper wars and the mass bloodshed she contemplates daily, Tony finds herself taken aback by such questions. They aren't abstract problems—they're too personal for that—and there are no correct solutions to them. But it would be a tactical error to let her dismay show. "Well, you'd never know, would you?" she says. "Unless it happened."

"Granted," Zenia says. "Well then, what would cause you to kill someone else?"

Tony and Zenia are having coffee, as they have done almost every third day now for the past month, ever since they met. Or not every third day, every third evening: right now it's eleven o'clock, Tony's usual bedtime, and here she is, still up. She isn't even sleepy.

They aren't in a tame campus coffee shop, either; they're in a real coffee shop, near Zenia's new place. Zenia's and West's. *A dive,* says Zenia. This coffee shop is called Christie's, and it stays open all night. At the moment there are three men in it, two of them in trench coats, one in a greasy tweed jacket, sobering up, says Zenia; and two women, sitting in a booth together, talking in low voices.

Zenia says these women are prostitutes; *prosties,* she calls them. She says she can always tell. They don't seem like very attractive sexual produce, to Tony: they aren't young, they're stuccoed with makeup, and they have forties hairdos, shoulder length, stiffened with spray and with a parting of white scalp at the side. One of them has taken off a sling-backed shoe, and dangles her nyloned foot out over the aisle. The whole place, with its dirty linoleum floor and its out-of-order jukebox and its thick, chipped cups, has a discarded quality to it, a raffish and tawdry carelessness, that repels Tony and also thrills her deeply.

She's been signing out at McClung Hall for later and later hours. She says she's helping to paint the sets for a play: *The Trojan Women.* Zenia read for Helen, but instead she's Andromache. "All that wailing," she says. "Female whining. I hate it really." She says she once wanted to be an actress, but not any more. "Fucking directors think they're God," she says. "You're just dog food, as far as they're concerned. And the way they drool and paw at you!" She's thinking of quitting.

Drooling and pawing is a new concept, for Tony. She has never been drooled on or pawed. She would like to ask how it is done, but refrains.

Sometimes the two of them really do paint sets. Not that Tony's any good at painting—she's never painted anything before in her life—but the others give her a brush and the paint and show her where, and she puts on the base colours. She gets paint on her face and in her hair, and on the man's shirt they've provided, which comes down to her knees. She feels baptized.

By the others—the thin scornful straight-maned women, the black-sweatered, ironic men—she is almost accepted, which is naturally Zenia's doing. For some reason that none of these people can figure out, Zenia and Tony are thick as thieves. Even the girls in the residence have noticed it. They no longer call Tony Tonikins, or offer her cookie shards, or beg her to sing "Darling Clementine" in reverse. They have backed off.

Tony can't tell if this is dislike or respect; or possibly it's fright, because Zenia, it seems, has a certain reputation among them. Although none of them know her personally, she is one of the visible people—visible to everyone else, but unseen by Tony before now because she wasn't looking. It's partly her appearance: Zenia is the incarnation of how plainer, more oblong women wish to look, and therefore to be: it's a belief of theirs that such things can be arranged from the outside in. She is thought also to be brilliant, and she gets top marks—though she doesn't exert herself, she hardly ever attends a lecture, so how does she do it? Brilliant, and also fearsome. Wolfish, feral, beyond the pale.

Tony hears some of this from Roz, who barges into her room one morning while Tony is studying, trying to catch up on the time she's missed the night before. Mothering Roz descends with squawks and a flutter of feathers, and attempts to enlighten small Tony, towards whom she feels protective. Tony listens in silence, her eyes hardening, her ears closing over. She will not hear a word against Zenia. *Jealous bitch,* she thinks. *Hctib suolaej.*

She has different clothes now, too, because Zenia has redesigned her. She has black corduroy jeans, and a pullover with a huge rolled collar in which her head sits like an egg in its nest, and a gigantic wraparound green scarf. It's not as though you can't afford it, says Zenia, propelling her through the stores. The pageboy with the velvet hairband is gone; instead, Tony's hair is cut short and tousled on top, with artful wisps coming out of it. Some days Tony thinks she looks a little like Audrey Hepburn; other days, like an electrocuted mop. Much more sophisticated, Zenia has pronounced. She has also made Tony exchange her normal-sized horn-rimmed glasses for bigger ones, enormous ones.

"But they're too exaggerated," said Tony. "Unbalanced."

"That's what beauty is," said Zenia. "Exaggerated. Unbalanced. Pay more attention and you'll see."

This is the theory behind the outsized sweaters too, the blanket-like scarves: Tony, swimming within them, is rendered even scrawnier. "I look like a stick," she says. "I look ten!"

"Slender," says Zenia. "Juvenile. Some men like that."

"Then they're warped," says Tony.

"Listen to me, Antonia," says Zenia seriously. "*All* men are warped. This is something you must never forget."

The waitress comes, dollops of fat under her chin, support hose on her legs and clumpy shoes on her feet, a grey bibbed bosom with a stain of ketchup on it bulging out in front. Indifferently she refills their cups. "She's one too," says Zenia, when her back is turned. "A prostie. In her spare time."

Tony scans the stolid rump, the bored slope of the shoulders, the straggling bun of dead-squirrel-coloured hair. "No!" she says. "Who would want to?"

"Bet you anything," says Zenia. "Go on!"

She means that Tony should continue with whatever story she's been telling, but Tony can scarcely remember where she was. This friendship with Zenia has been very sudden. She feels as if she's being dragged along on a rope, behind a speeding motorboat, with the waves sloshing over her and her ears full of applause; or as if she's racketing downhill on a bicycle, with no hands and no brakes either. She's out of control; at the same time, she's unusually alert, as if the small hairs on her arms and on the back of her neck are standing straight up. These are perilous waters. But why? They're only talking.

Though it's making Tony dizzy, all this reckless verbiage. She's never listened so much to one person; also, she herself has never said so much, so heedlessly. She has hardly gone in for self-revelation, in her previous life. Who was there to tell? She has no idea what might come reeling out, the next time she opens her mouth.

"Go on," says Zenia once more, leaning forward, across the speckled-brown table, the half-empty cups, the butts in the brown metal ashtray. And Tony does.

21

What Tony is telling about is her mother. This is the first time Tony has ever said very much to anyone about her mother, beyond the bare bones, that is. *Lost and gone,* says Tony, and *Dreadful sorry,* says everyone else. Why say more? Who would be interested?

Zenia is, as it turns out. She can see it's a painful subject for Tony, but this doesn't deter her; if anything it spurs her on. She pushes and prods and makes all the right noises, curious and amazed, horrified, indulgent, and relentless, and pulls Tony inside out like a sock.

It takes time, because Tony has no single clear image of her mother. The memory of her is composed of shiny fragments, like a vandalized mosaic, or like something brittle that's been dropped on the floor. Every once in a while Tony takes out the pieces and arranges and rearranges them, trying to make them fit. (Though she hasn't spent very long at this yet. The wreck is too immediate.)

So all Zenia can get out of her is a handful of shards. Why does she want such a thing? That's for Zenia to know and Tony to find out. But, in the entranced and voluble moment, it doesn't occur to Tony even to ask.

• • •

Tony was hardened off early. This is what she calls it by now, ruefully, in her cellar, at three a.m., with the shambles of Otto the Red's clove army strewn on the sand-table behind her and West sleeping the sleep of the unjust upstairs, and Zenia raging unchecked, somewhere out there in the city. "Hardened off" is a term she's lifted from Charis, who has explained that it's what you do to seedlings to toughen them up and make them frost-resistant and help them to transplant better. You don't water them very much, and you leave them outside in the cold. This is what happened to Tony. She was a premature baby, as her mother was fond of telling her, and was kept in a glass box. (Was there a note of regret in her mother's voice, as if it was a pity that she was eventually taken out?) So Tony spent her first days motherless. Nor—in the long run—did things improve.

For instance:

When Tony was five, her mother decided she would take her tobogganing. Tony knew what tobogganing was, although she had never done it. Her mother had only a vague idea, gleaned from Christmas cards. But it was one of her romantic English images of Canada.

Where did she get the toboggan? Probably she borrowed it from one of her bridge club friends. She zipped Tony into her snowsuit and got them to the tobogganing hill in a taxi. The toboggan was just a small one, so it fit into the back seat, on a slant, along with Tony. Her mother sat in the front. Tony's father had the car that day, as he did most days. This was just as well, as the streets were icy and Tony's mother was at best a spontaneous driver.

By the time they got to the tobogganing hill the sun was low and huge and dimly pink in the grey winter sky, and the shadows were bluish. The hill was very high. It was on the side of a ravine, and covered with close-packed, icy snow. Groups of screaming children and a few adults were careering down it on sleighs and toboggans and large pieces of cardboard. Some had overturned, and there were pile-ups. Those that reached the bottom disappeared behind a clump of dark fir trees.

Tony's mother stood at the top of the hill, staring down, holding the toboggan by its rope as if restraining it. "There," she said. "Isn't that nice?" She was pleating her lips, the way she did when she put on lipstick, and Tony could tell that the scene before her was not exactly what she'd had in mind. She was wearing her downtown coat and hat, and nylon stockings and little boots with high heels and fur tops. She didn't have slacks or a ski suit or a Hudson's Bay coat and earmuffs like the other adults there, and it occurred to Tony that her mother expected her to go down the hill on the toboggan all by herself.

Tony felt an urgent need to pee. She knew how difficult this would be, considering her clumsy two-piece snowsuit with the elastic braces over the shoulders, and what annoyance it would cause her mother—there was not a washroom in sight—so she said nothing about it. Instead she said, "I don't want to." She knew that if she ever went down that hill she would flip over, she would crash into something, she would be crushed. One small child was being led up the hill, howling, with blood running from its nose.

Tony's mother hated having her scenarios foiled. People should enjoy themselves when she wanted them to. "*Come* on," she said. "I'll give you a push. It'll be lovely!"

Tony sat down on the ground, which was her habitual means of protest. Crying did not work, not with her mother. It was likely to produce a slap, or at best a shake. She had never been much of a crier.

Her mother glanced down at her with disgust. "I'll show you how!" she said. Her eyes were sparkling, her teeth were set: it was the look she got when she was willing herself to be brave, when she was refusing to be defeated. Before Tony knew what was happening her mother had picked up the toboggan and run with it to the brink of the hill. There she threw it onto the snow and hurled herself on top of it, and went whizzing down, flat on her belly, with her beige legs in their nylons and her fur-topped boots sticking straight up behind her. Almost immediately her hat came off.

She went at an astonishing speed. As she diminished down the slope, into the dusk, Tony clambered to her feet. Her mother was going away from her, she was vanishing, and Tony would be left alone on the cold hill.

"No! No!" she screamed. (Unusual for her to have screamed: she must have been terrified.) But inside herself she could hear another voice, also hers, which was shouting, fearlessly and with ferocious delight:

On! On!

As a child, Tony kept a diary. Every January she would write her name in the front of it, in block letters:

TONY FREMONT

Then under it she would write her other name:

TNOMERF YNOT

This name had a Russian or Martian sound to it, which pleased her. It was the name of an alien, or a spy. Sometimes it was the name of a twin, an invisible twin; and when Tony grew up and learned more about left-handedness she was faced with the possibility that she might in fact have been a twin, the left-handed half of a divided egg, the other half of which had died. But when she was little her twin was merely an invention, the incarnation of her sense that part of her was missing. Although she was a twin, Tnomerf Ynot was a good deal taller than Tony herself. Taller, stronger, more daring.

Tony wrote her outer name with her right hand and her other name, her inner one, with her left; although, officially, she was forbidden to write with her left hand, or to do anything else of importance with it. Nobody had told her why. About the closest she'd come to an explanation was a speech of Anthea's—of her mother's—in which she'd said that the world was not constructed for the left-handed. She also said that Tony would understand better when she grew up, which was just another of Anthea's assurances that failed to come true.

When Tony was younger the teachers at school would slap her left hand or hit it with rulers, as if she'd been caught picking her nose with it. One teacher tied it to the side of her desk. The other children might have teased her about this, but they didn't. They couldn't see the logic of it, any more than she could.

That was a school Tony got yanked out of quickly. Usually it took Anthea eight months or more before she got fed up with a school. It was true that Tony couldn't spell very well, or not according to the teachers. They said she reversed letters. They said she had trouble with numbers. They would say this to Anthea, and Anthea would say that Tony was gifted, and then Tony would know it would soon be time for a change because very shortly now Anthea would lose her temper and start insulting the teachers. *Nincompoops* was one of the nicer names she called them. She wanted Tony changed, fixed, turned right side up, and she wanted it to happen overnight.

Tony could do things easily with her left hand, things her right hand would stumble over. In her right-handed life she was awkward, and her handwriting was lumpish and clumsy. But that made no difference: despite its good performance her left hand was scorned, but her right hand was bribed and encouraged. It wasn't fair, but Anthea said that life wasn't fair.

Secretly Tony continued to write left-handed; but she felt guilty about it. She knew there must be something shameful about her left hand or it would not have been humiliated like that. It was the hand she loved best, all the same.

It's November, and the afternoon is already darkening. Earlier there was a dusting of snow, but now it's drizzling. The drizzle runs down the living-room windows in icy, sinuous trickles; a few brown leaves are stuck to the outside of the glass like leather tongues.

Tony kneels on the chesterfield with her nose pressed against the window, making fog patches with her breath. When the patch is big enough she writes on it, squeakily, with her index finger. Then she rubs out the words. *Kcuf,* she writes. This is a word too bad even for her diary. *Tihs*. She writes these words with fear and awe, but also with a superstitious relish. They are Tnomerf Ynot words. They make her feel powerful, in charge of something.

She breathes and writes and rubs out, breathes and writes. The air is unfresh, filled with the dry, burnt smell of the chintz curtains. All the time she's writing, she's listening to the silence of the house behind her. She's used to silences: she can distinguish between full silences and empty ones, between those that come before and those that come after. Just because there's a silence it doesn't mean that nothing is going on.

Tony kneels at the window as long as she dares. At last she sees her mother walking quickly along the street from the corner, head down against the drizzle, her fur collar turned up, her face hidden by her maroon hat. She's carrying a wrapped package.

Probably it's a dress, because clothes are a solace for Anthea; when she's feeling "blue," as she calls it, she goes shopping. Tony has been dragged downtown on these expeditions many times, when Anthea couldn't figure out where else to stash her. She's waited outside change rooms, sweating in her winter coat, while Anthea has tried things on and then more things, and has come out in her stocking feet and done a pirouette in front of the full-length mirror, smoothing the cloth down over her hips. Anthea doesn't often buy clothes for Tony; she says she could dress Tony in a potato sack and Tony wouldn't notice. But Tony does notice, she notices a great deal. She just doesn't think it would make any difference whether she wore a potato sack or not. Any difference to Anthea, that is.

Tony gets up from the chesterfield and begins her piano practice. Playing the piano is supposed to strengthen her right hand, though everyone including Tony knows that Tony isn't musical and that these lessons will lead nowhere. How could they? Tony, with her little rodent paws, can't even span an octave.

Tony practises doggedly, trying to keep time to the ticking metronome, and squinting at the music because she's forgotten to turn on the piano lamp, and because, without realizing it, she's becoming near-sighted. The piece she's playing is called "Gavotte." *Ettovag.* It's a good word; she will think of a use for it, later. The piano reeks of lemon oil. Ethel, who comes in to clean, has been told not to polish the keys with it—she's only supposed to use a damp cloth—but she pays no attention, and Tony's fingers will smell of lemon oil for hours. It's a formal smell, an adult smell, ominous. It comes before parties.

She hears the front door open and close, and feels the cold draft from it on her legs. After a few minutes her mother walks into the living room. Tony can hear the high heels, tapping on the hardwood floor, then muffled by the carpet. She plays on, banging the keys down to show her mother how studious she is.

"That's enough for today, don't you think, Tony?" her mother says gaily. Tony is puzzled: usually Anthea wants her to practise as long as possible. She wants her safely occupied, somewhere out of the way.

Tony stops playing and turns to look at her. She's taken off her coat, but she still has her hat on, and, oddly, her matching maroon gloves. The hat has a spotted half-veil that comes down over her eyes and part of her nose. Below the veil is her mouth, slightly blurred around the edges, as if her lipstick has run because of the rain. She puts her hands up behind her head, to unpin her hat.

"I haven't done a half-hour yet," says Tony. She still believes that the dutiful completion of pre-set tasks will cause her to be loved, although in some dim corner of herself she knows this hasn't worked yet and most likely never will.

Anthea takes down her hands, leaving her hat in place. "Don't you think you deserve a little holiday today?" she says, smiling at Tony. Her teeth are very white in the dim room.

"Why?" says Tony. She can see nothing special about this day. It isn't her birthday.

Anthea sits down beside her on the piano bench and slides her left arm with its leather-gloved hand around Tony's shoulders. She gives a little squeeze. "You poor thing," she says. She puts the fingers of her other hand under Tony's chin and turns her face up. The leather hand is lifeless and cool, like the hand of a doll.

"I want you to know," she says, "that Mother truly, truly loves you."

Tony pulls back within herself. Anthea has said this before. When she says it her breath smells the way it does now, of smoke and of the empty glasses left on the kitchen counter in the mornings after parties, and on other mornings as well. Glasses with damp cigarette butts in them, and broken glasses, on the floor.

She never says "I truly, truly love you." It's always *Mother,* as if Mother is someone else.

Rehtom, thinks Tony. *Evol.* The metronome ticks on.

Anthea gazes down at her, holding onto her with her two gloved hands. In the semi-dark her eyes behind the spots of her veil are sooty black, bottomless; her mouth is tremulous. She bends over and presses her cheek to Tony's, and Tony feels the rasp of the veil and the damp, creamy skin under it, and smells her, a smell of violet perfume and underarms mixed with dress cloth, and a salty, eggy smell, like strange mayonnaise. She doesn't know why Anthea is acting like this, and she's embarrassed. All Anthea does normally is kiss her goodnight, a little peck; she's shaking all over, and for a moment Tony thinks—hopes—it's with laughter.

Then she lets go of Tony and gets up and moves to the window, and stands with her back turned, unpinning her hat really this time. She takes it off and throws it down on the sofa, and fluffs out her dark hair at the back. After a moment she kneels and looks out. "Who's been making all these smudges?" she says, in a higher, tighter voice. It's the voice she uses for mimicking happiness, when she's angry with Tony's father and wants to show him she doesn't care. She knows the smudges are Tony's. Ordinarily she'd be irritated, she'd make some remark about how much it costs to have Ethel clean the windows, but this time she laughs, breathlessly, as if she's been running.

"Nose marks, just like a dog. Guppy, you are such a funny child."

Guppy is a name from long ago. Anthea's story is that she called Tony that right after she was born, because of her time in the incubator. Anthea would come and look at Tony through the glass, and Tony's mouth would be opening and closing but there wouldn't be any sound. Or

Anthea said she couldn't hear any. She kept the name because later, when Tony was out of danger and she'd taken her home, Tony scarcely cried; she just opened and closed her mouth. Anthea tells this story as if it's funny.

This nickname—enclosed by quotation marks—is pencilled in below Tony's baby pictures, in Anthea's white leather *My Baby* photo album: "'Guppy,' 18 months"; "'Guppy' and Me"; "'Guppy' and her Dad." After a while Anthea must have stopped taking these pictures, or stopped sticking them in, because there are just blank pages.

Tony feels a rush of longing for whatever it was that existed once between herself and her mother, in the photo album; but she feels annoyance as well, because the name itself is a trick. She used to think a guppy was something warm and soft, like a puppy, and she was hurt and insulted when she discovered it was a fish.

So she doesn't answer her mother. She sits on the piano bench, waiting to see what Anthea will do next.

"Is he here?" she says. She must know the answer: Tony's father wouldn't have left Tony in the house alone.

"Yes," says Tony. Her father is in his study at the back of the house. He's been there all along. He must have heard the silence, when Tony wasn't playing. He doesn't care whether Tony practises the piano or not. The piano, he says, is her mother's bright idea.

22

Tony's mother cooks supper as usual. She doesn't take off her good bridge club dress, but puts her apron over it, her best apron, the white one with ruffles over the shoulders. She has re-done her lipstick: her mouth shines like a waxed apple. Tony sits on the kitchen stool, watching her, until Anthea tells her to stop goggling: if she wants to be useful she can set the table. Then she can go and dig up her father. Anthea often puts it this way: *dig up,* as if he's a potato. Sometimes she says *root out.*

Tony has no particular desire to be useful, but she's relieved that her mother is acting more normally. She deals out the plates and then the forks, knives, and spoons, a left right right, a left right right, and then she goes into her father's study, knocking first, and sits down cross-legged on the floor. She can always go in there as long as she keeps quiet.

Her father is working at his desk. He has his desk lamp on, with its green shade, so his face has a greenish tinge. He's a large man with small neat handwriting that looks as if it's been done by fastidious mice. Beside it, Tony's own writing is that of a three-fingered giant. His long arrow nose is pointing straight down at the papers he's working on; his yellowy-grey hair is combed back, and the nose and the hair together make him seem as if he's flying through a strong headwind, hurtling down towards the target of his paper. He's frowning, as if braced for the impact. Tony is dimly aware that he isn't happy; but happiness isn't something she expects, in men. He never complains about not having it; unlike her mother.

His yellow pencil twiddles. He has a jarful of these pencils on his desk, kept very sharp. Sometimes he asks Tony to sharpen them for him; she turns them one by one in the businesslike sharpener clamped to the windowsill, feeling that she's preparing his arrows. What he does with these pencils is beyond her, but she knows that it's something of the utmost importance. More important—for instance—than she is.

Her father's name is Griff, but she doesn't think of him as *Griff*, the way she thinks of her mother as *Anthea*. He's somewhat more like the other fathers, whereas Anthea isn't very much like the other mothers, although occasionally she tries to be. (Griff is not her Dad, though. Griff is not a *Dad*.)

Griff was in the war. Anthea says that although he may have been in it, he didn't go *through* it, the way she did. Her parents' house in London was destroyed by a bomb during the Blitz and her parents were both killed. She'd come home—where had she been? She has never said—to find nothing but a crater, one standing wall, and a pile of rubble; and her own mother's shoe, with a foot in it.

But Griff missed all that. He only got into it at D-Day. (*It* meaning the danger, the killing; not the training, the waiting, the fooling around.) He was there for the landing, the advance, the easy bit, says Anthea. The winning.

Tony likes to think of him like that—winning—like

someone winning a race. Victorious. He has not been noticeably victorious lately. But Anthea says *the easy bit* in front of people, in front of their friends when they come over for drinks and Tony watches from doorways. Anthea says *the easy bit,* looking straight at Griff with her chin up, and he turns red.

"I don't want to talk about it," he says.

"He never does," says Anthea with mock despair, lifting her shoulders. It's the same gesture she makes when Tony refuses to play the piano for the bridge club.

"At the end it was just children," says Griff. "Children, in men's uniforms. We were killing children."

"Lucky you," says Anthea lightly. "That must have made it smoother for you."

"It didn't," says Tony's father. They stare at each other as if no one else is in the room: tense and measuring.

"He liberated a gun," says Anthea. "Didn't you, darling? He's got it in his study. I wonder if the gun feels *liberated.*" She gives a dismissive laugh, and turns away. A silence eddies behind her.

That was how Anthea and Griff met—during the war, when he was in England. *Stationed* in England, Anthea would say; so Tony pictures the two of them in a train station, waiting to depart. It would have been a winter train station; they had on their overcoats and her mother was wearing a hat, and their breath was turning to white fog as it came out of their mouths. Were they kissing, as in pictures? It's not clear. Perhaps they were going on the train together, perhaps not. They had a lot of suitcases. There are always a lot of suitcases in the story of Tony's parents.

•   •   •

"I was a war bride," Anthea says; she gives a self-deprecating smile, and then a sigh. She says *war bride* as if she's making fun of it—minor-key, rueful fun. What does she mean to imply? That she has fallen prey to an old trick, an old confidence trick, and knows it now and deplores it? That Tony's father took advantage of her in some way? That it was the fault of the war?

The *raw. A raw bride,* thinks Tony. Uncooked. Or, more like it: *rubbed raw,* like her own wrists by the frozen cuffs of her snowsuit.

"I was a war husband," her father says; or used to say, back when he still made jokes. He also said that he'd picked Anthea up in a dance hall. Anthea didn't like that.

"Griff, don't be vulgar," she would say.

"Men were scarce," he would add, to the audience. (There was usually an audience for these exchanges. They rarely said such things when they were alone.) "She had to grab what she could get."

Then Anthea would laugh. "Decent men were scarce, and who grabbed who? And it wasn't a dance hall, it was a dance."

"Well, you can't expect us poor barbarians to know the difference."

What happened after that? After the dance. It's unclear. But for some reason, Anthea decided to marry Griff. That it was her decision is frequently underlined by Tony's father: *Well, nobody forced you.* Her mother was somehow forced, however. She was forced, she was coerced, she was carried off by that crude thieving lout, Tony's father, to this too-cramped, two-storey, fake Tudor, half-timbered, half-baked house, in this tedious neighbourhood, in this narrow-minded provincial city, in this too-large, too-small, too-cold, too-hot country that she hates with a strange, entrapped, and baffled fury. *Don't talk like that!* she hisses at Tony. She means the accent. Flat, she calls it. But how can Tony talk the same way her mother does? Like the radio, at noon. The kids at school would laugh.

So Tony is a foreigner, to her own mother; and to her father also, because, although she talks the same way he does, she is—and he has made this clear—not a boy. Like a foreigner, she listens carefully, interpreting. Like a foreigner she keeps an eye out for sudden hostile gestures. Like a foreigner she makes mistakes.

Tony sits on the floor, looking at her father and wondering about the war, which is such a mystery to her but which appears to have been decisive in her life. She would like to ask him about battles, and if she can look at the gun; but she knows already that he will evade these questions, as if there's a sore place on him that he must protect. A raw place. He will keep her from putting her hand on it.

Sometimes she wonders what he did before the war, but he won't talk about that either. He has told only one story. When he was small he lived on a farm, and his father took him out into the woods, in winter. His father intended to chop firewood, but the tree was frozen so hard that the axe bounced off it and cut into his leg. He threw down the axe and strode away, leaving Griff by himself in the woods. But he followed the footprints home through the snow: a red one, a white one, a red one.

If it hadn't been for the war, Griff wouldn't have an education. That's what he says. He would still be on the farm. And then, where would Tony be?

Her father keeps on doing whatever it is he does. He works for an insurance company. Life insurance.

"So, Tony," her father says without looking up. "What can I do for you?"

"Anthea says to tell you supper is almost ready," she says.

"Almost ready?" he says. "Or really ready?"

"I don't know," says Tony.

"Then you'd better go and see," says her father.

The supper is sausages, as it often is when Anthea has been out in the afternoon. Sausages and boiled potatoes, and green beans from a can. The sausages are a little burned, but Tony's father doesn't say anything about it. He doesn't say anything when the food is really good either. Anthea says Tony and her father are two of a kind. Two cold fish.

She brings the serving dishes in from the kitchen, and sits down in her own chair still wearing her apron. Usually she takes it off. "Well!" she says brightly. "And how are we all today?"

"Fine," says Tony's father.

"That's good," says her mother.

"You look all dolled up," says her father. "Special occasion?"

"Not likely, is it?" says her mother.

After that there's a silence, which fills with the sound

of chewing. Tony has spent a good deal of her life listening to her parents chew. The noises their mouths make, their teeth grinding together as they bite down, are disconcerting to her. It's like seeing someone taking their clothes off through a bathroom window when they don't know you're there. Her mother eats nervously, in small bites; her father eats ruminatingly. His eyes are fixed on Anthea as if on a distant point in space; hers are narrowed a little, as if aiming.

Nothing moves, although great force is being exerted. Nothing moves yet. Tony feels as if there's a thick elastic band stretching right through her own head, with one end of it attached to each of them: any tighter and it would snap.

"How was the bridge club?" says her father at last.

"Fine," says her mother.

"Did you win?"

"No. We came second."

"Who won, then?"

Her mother thinks for a moment. "Rhonda and Bev."

"Rhonda was there?" says her father.

"This is not the Spanish Inquisition," says her mother. "I just said she was."

"That's funny," says her father. "I bumped into her, downtown."

"Rhonda left early," says her mother. She sets her fork down carefully on her plate.

"That's not what she told me," says her father.

Her mother pushes back her chair and stands up. She crumples her paper napkin and throws it on top of the sausage ends on her plate. "I refuse to discuss this in front of Tony," she says.

"Discuss what?" says Tony's father. He keeps on chewing. "Tony, you are excused."

"Stay where you are," says Anthea. "That you called me a liar." Her voice is low and quivering, as if she's about to cry.

"Did I?" says Tony's father. He sounds bemused, and curious about the answer.

"Antonia," says her mother warningly, as if Tony has been about to do something wrong or dangerous. "Couldn't you have waited until after dessert? I try every day to get her to eat a decent meal."

"That's right, make this my fault," says Tony's father.

The dessert is rice pudding. It stays in the fridge, because Tony says she doesn't want any. She doesn't, she isn't hungry. She goes up to her bedroom and climbs into her flannelette-sheeted bed, and tries not to hear or imagine what they are saying to each other.

Bulc egdirb, she murmurs to herself in the darkness. The barbarians gallop across the plains. At their head rides Tnomerf Ynot, her long ragged hair flying in the wind, a sword in each of her hands. *Bulc egdirb!* she calls, urging them forward. It's a battle cry, and they are on the rampage. They are sweeping all before them, trampling down crops and burning villages. They loot and plunder and smash pianos, and kill children. At night they put up their tents and eat supper with their hands, whole cows roasted on bonfires. They wipe their greasy fingers on their leather clothes. They have no manners at all.

Tnomerf Ynot herself drinks from a skull, with silver handles attached where the ears used to be. She raises the skull high in a toast to victory, and to the war god of the barbarians: *Ettovag!* she yells, and the hordes answer, cheering: *Ettovag! Ettovag!*

In the morning there will be broken glass.

●　　●　　●

Tony wakes up suddenly in the middle of the night. She gets out of bed, gropes under her night-table until she finds her rabbit-shaped slippers, and tiptoes across the room to the door. It opens easily.

She creeps along the hallway to her parents' room, but their door is closed and she can't hear anything. Maybe they are in there, maybe not. Though most likely they are. When she was younger she used to worry—or was it a dream?—that she would come home from school and find only a hole in the ground, and their shoes with feet in them.

She continues to the stairs and goes down them, guiding herself with one hand on the banister. She often gets up like this in the middle of the night; she often makes the rounds, checking for damage.

She gropes her way through the blurry darkness of the hushed living room. Items gleam here and there in the dull glow from the streetlights outside: the mirror over the fireplace, the two china dogs on the mantelpiece. Her eyes feel huge, her slippered feet are soundless on the carpet.

She doesn't turn on a light until she gets to the kitchen. There's nothing on the counter or on the floor, nothing broken. She opens the refrigerator door: the rice pudding is in there but it's intact, so she can't eat any of it without detection. She makes herself a piece of bread and jam instead. Anthea says that Canadian bread is a disgrace, all air and sawdust, but it tastes fine to Tony. The bread is like many of Anthea's hatreds—Tony doesn't get the point. Why is the country too big, or too small? What would "just right" be? What's wrong with the way she talks, anyways? *Anyway.* She wipes the crumbs up carefully, and goes back to bed.

When she gets up the next morning she doesn't have a chance to make a pot of tea—her one possible atonement to Anthea for failing to be English—because Anthea is already in the kitchen, cooking breakfast. She has on her daily apron, blue-and-white checks; she's frying things at the stove. (This is a sporadic activity, for her. Tony often makes her own breakfast, and her own brown-bag school lunch as well.)

Tony slides herself across the padded seat of the breakfast nook. Her father is already in there, reading the paper. Tony pours herself some cold cereal and spoons it into her mouth, with her left hand because nobody's watching. With her right hand she holds the cereal box close to her eyes. *Sekalf narb. Ytiraluger,* Tony whispers to herself. They never come right out and say "constipation." *Noitapitsnoc:* a much more satisfactory word.

She has a collection of palindromes—*Live evil, Madam I'm Adam, Able was I ere I saw Elba*—but the phrases she prefers are different backwards: skewed, odd, melodious. They belong to another world, where Tony is at home because she can speak the language. *Reffo eerf! Evas! Faol tun egnaro!* Two barbarians stand on a narrow bridge, hurling insults, daring their enemies to cross. . . .

"Tony, put that down," says her father tonelessly. "You shouldn't read at the table." He says this every morning, once he's finished with the paper.

Anthea comes with two full plates, bacon and eggs and toast, setting them down formally as if it's a restaurant. Tony cuts her egg open and watches the yolk run like yellow glue into her toast. Then she watches her father's Adam's apple go up and down while he swallows his coffee. It's like something stuck in his throat. *Madam I'm Adam's apple.*

Anthea has a bright enamelled cheerfulness this morning that makes her seem covered with nail polish. She scrapes the cereal bowls into the garbage can, singing: "Pack up your troubles in your old kit bag, and smile, smile, smile. . . ."

"You should have been on stage," says Tony's father.

"Yes, I should have, shouldn't I?" says her mother. Her voice is airy and careless.

There's been nothing out of place, nothing obvious; nevertheless, when Tony comes home from school that afternoon, her mother isn't there. She isn't just out, she's gone. She's left a wrapped package for Tony, on her bed, and a note in an envelope. As soon as Tony sees the note and the package she turns cold all over. She's frightened, but somehow she is not surprised.

The note is in the brown ink Anthea favours, on her initialled cream-coloured notepaper. In her curling handwriting with its florid capital letters she has written:

Darling, you know I would like to take you with me but I can't right now. When you are older you will understand why. Be a good girl and do well in school. I will write you lots. Your Mother who loves you very much.

P.S. See you soon!

(Tony kept this note, and marvelled over it later, when she was grown up. As an explanation it was of course inadequate. Also, nothing in it was true. To begin with, Tony was not *darling*. The only people who were *darling*, for Anthea, were men, and sometimes women if she was annoyed with them. She didn't want to take Tony with her: if she'd wanted to she would have done it, because she mostly did what she wanted. She didn't write Tony lots, she didn't love her very much, and she didn't see her soon. And although Tony did get older, she did not understand why.)

At the moment of finding this note, however, Tony wants to believe every word of it, and by an effort of will she does. She even manages to believe more than is there. She believes her mother will send for her, or else come back. She isn't sure which.

She opens the package; it's the same package Anthea was carrying yesterday, in the drizzle, on her way back from the bridge club, which means that all of this was planned out in advance. It isn't like the times she rushed out of the house, slamming the door, or locked herself in the bathroom and turned on the taps so that the tub overflowed out into the hall and down the stairs and through the ceiling, and Griff had to call the Fire Department to break in. It isn't a tantrum, or a whim.

Inside the package is a box, and inside the box there's a dress. It's navy blue, with a sailor collar piped in white. Since there's nothing else she can think of to do, Tony tries it on. It's two sizes too big for her. It looks like a dressing gown.

Tony sits down on the floor and pulls up her knees, and pushes her nose into the skirt of the dress, inhaling its smell, a rough chemical smell of broadcloth and sizing. The smell of newness, the smell of futility, the smell of noiseless grief.

All of this is her own fault, somehow. She hasn't made enough cups of tea, she's misread the signals, she has let go of the string or the rope or the chain or whatever it is that's been attaching her mother to this house, holding her in place, and like an escaped sailboat or a balloon her mother has come loose. She's out in the blue, she's blowing away with the wind. She's lost.

23

This is the story Tony tells to Zenia, as they sit in Christie's Coffee Shop, their heads leaning together across the table, drinking harsh acidy coffee in the dead of night. It seems a bleak story, as she tells it—starker and more dire than when it was actually happening to her. Possibly because she believes it, by now. Back then it seemed temporary—her motherlessness. Now she knows it was permanent.

"So she buggered off, just like that! Where'd she go?" says Zenia, with interest.

Tony sighs. "She ran off with a man. A life insurance man, from my father's office. His name was Perry. He was married to someone called Rhonda, from my mother's bridge club. They went to California."

"Good choice," says Zenia, laughing. In Tony's opinion it was not a good choice. It was a lapse of taste, and of consistency as well: if Anthea had to go anywhere, why didn't she go to England, *home* as she always called it? Why go to California, where the bread is even airier, the accent even flatter, the grammar even more spurious, than it is here?

So Tony doesn't think it's all that funny, and Zenia catches this reservation and changes her face immediately. "Weren't you furious?"

"No," says Tony. "I don't think so." She searches through herself, patting surfaces, testing pockets. She doesn't discover any fury.

"I would have been," says Zenia. "I would have been enraged."

Tony isn't sure what it would be like, to be enraged. Possibly too dangerous. Or else a relief.

No rage at the time: only a cold panic, a desolation; and fear, because of what her father would do, or say: would she be blamed?

Tony's father wasn't yet back from work. There was nobody else in the house, nobody but Ethel, mopping the floor in the kitchen. Anthea asked her to stay late on the afternoons when she went out so someone would be there when Tony came home from school.

Ethel was a craggy big-boned woman with lines on her face like those on other people's hands, and dry, wig-like hair. She had six children. Only four of them were still alive—diphtheria had killed the others—but if you asked her how many children she had, she would say six. Anthea used to tell this as if it were a joke, as if Ethel couldn't count properly. Ethel had a habit of groaning as she worked, and talking to herself: words that sounded like "Oh no, oh no," and "Pisspisspiss." As a rule Tony kept out of her way.

Tony went into her parents' bedroom and opened her mother's closet door. Aroma wafted out: there were little satin bags of lavender tied with mauve ribbons on every hanger. Most of Anthea's suits and dresses were still in there, with the matching shoes in their shoe-trees ranged beneath them. They were like hostages, these clothes. Anthea would never just leave them behind, not forever. She would have to come back and retrieve them.

Ethel was coming up the stairs; Tony could hear her grunting and mumbling. Now she had reached the bedroom door, dragging the vacuum cleaner by its hose. She stood still and looked at Tony.

"Your mother's run away," she said. She talked in regular language when anyone else was there.

Tony could hear the scorn in Ethel's voice. Dogs ran away, cats, horses. Mothers did not.

Here Tony's memory divides, into what she wanted to happen and what actually did happen. What she wanted was for Ethel to take her in her knobbly arms, and stroke her hair and rock her, and tell her that everything would be all right. Ethel, who had bulgy blue veins on her legs, who smelled of sweat and Javex, whom she didn't even like! But who might have been capable of providing comfort, of a sort.

What actually did happen was nothing. Ethel turned back to the vacuuming, and Tony went into her own room and shut the door and took off the baggy sailor dress and folded it, and put it back into its box.

After a while Tony's father came home and spoke with Ethel in the front hall, and then Ethel went away and Tony and her father had supper. The supper was a tin of tomato soup; her father warmed it up in a saucepan, and Tony put some crackers and cheddar cheese on a plate. Both of them felt at a loss, as if there were gaps in this meal that could not be filled in because they could not be identified.

What had happened was so momentous, and so unheard of, that it could not yet be mentioned.

Tony's father ate in silence. The little slurping noises he made scratched against Tony's skin. He was looking at Tony slyly, in a speculative way; Tony had seen the same expression on door-to-door salesmen, and on street beggars, and on other children who were about to tell outrageous and transparent lies. The two of them were in a conspiracy now, his look implied: they were going to gang up, have secrets together. Secrets about Anthea, of course. Who else? Although Anthea was gone, she was still there, sitting at the table with them. She was there more than ever.

After a while Tony's father put down his spoon; it clanked against the plate.

"We'll make out fine," he said. "Won't we?"

Tony was not convinced of this, but she felt under pressure to reassure him. "Yes," she said.

Tomato, she whispered to herself. *Otamot.* One of the Great Lakes. A stone war hammer used by an ancient tribe. If you said a word backwards, the meaning emptied out and then the word was vacant. Ready for a new meaning to flow in. *Anthea. Aehtna.* Like *dead,* it was almost the same thing, backwards or forwards.

And then what, and then what? Zenia wants to know. But Tony is at a loss: how can she describe emptiness? Acres of vacancy, which Tony filled up with whatever she could, with knowledge, with dates and facts, more and more of them, pouring them into her head to silence the echoes. Because whatever had been lacking when Anthea was there, it was much worse now that she wasn't.

Anthea was her own absence. She hovered just out of reach, a tantalizing wraith, an *almost,* endowed with a sort of gauzy flesh by Tony's longing for her. If only she loved Tony more, she would be here. Or Tony would be elsewhere, with her, wherever she was.

Anthea wrote, of course. She sent a postcard with a picture of palm trees and surf, and said that she wished Tony was there. She sent packages for Tony with clothes in them that never fit: sun suits, shorts, hot-weather dresses, too big or sometimes—after a while—too small. She sent birthday cards, late. She sent snapshots taken always, it seemed, in full sunlight; snapshots of herself wearing white, in which she looked fatter than Tony remembered, her face tanned and shining as if oiled, with a little moustache of shadow cast by her nose. In some of these, runaway, culpable Perry stood beside her with his arm around her waist: a flabby man with wrinkled knees and bags under his eyes and a lopsided, rueful smile. Then after a while Perry was no longer in the pictures, and another man was; and after a while, yet another. The shoulders on Tony's mother's dresses shrank, the skirts grew longer and fuller, the necklines scooped themselves out; Spanish-dancer ruffles appeared on the sleeves. There was talk of Tony visiting, during Easter holidays, during summer holidays, but nothing ever came of it.

(As for Anthea's other clothes, the ones she'd left behind in her closet, Tony's father had Ethel pack them into boxes and give them away to the Salvation Army. He did not warn Tony in advance. She was in the habit of checking the closet every few days, when she came back from school, and one day it was empty. Tony said nothing about it, but she knew. Anthea would not be coming back.)

Meanwhile the years became other years. At school, Tony was diagnosed as near-sighted and was supplied with glasses, which she did not particularly mind. They were a sort of barrier, and also she could now see the blackboard. For dinner she ate casseroles prepared in advance by Ethel and left on the kitchen counter to be warmed up. She made her own school lunches as usual; also she made caramel puddings out of a package and cakes from cake mixes, to impress her father, though they failed to have this result.

Her father gave her twenty-dollar bills for Christmas and told her to buy her own presents. She made him cups of tea, which he did not drink, any more than her mother had. He was frequently not there. During one of these years there was a girlfriend, a secretary from his company, who wore jangly bracelets and smelled of violets and warm rubber, who gushed over Tony and said she was cute as a button, and wanted to take her shopping or else to movies. *Girl stuff,* she called it. *We won't take big old Griff! I want us to be chums.* Tony despised her.

After the girlfriend was finished with, Griff began drinking more than ever. He would come into Tony's room and sit there watching her while she did her homework, as if he wanted her to say something to him. But by this time she was older and more hardened, and she expected nothing much from him. She had ceased to consider him her responsibility; she found him simply an irritating interruption. He was much less interesting than the siege techniques of Julius Caesar, which she was studying in Latin. Her father's suffering wore her out: it was too flat, it was too wordless, it was too powerless, it was too much like her own.

Once or twice, when he was drunker than usual, he chased her through the house, stumbling and shouting, overturning furniture. At other times he would become affectionate: he wanted to tousle her hair, to hug her as if she were still a child, though he had never behaved like that when she really was one. She would crawl underneath the dining-room table to escape from him: she was a lot smaller than he was, but she was also a lot more agile. The worst thing about these episodes was that he seemed to remember nothing about them the next day.

Tony took to avoiding him when possible. During the course of the evening she would monitor his level of drunkenness—she could tell by the smell partly, of sugary varnish—and plan her exit routes: into the bathroom, out the kitchen door, into her bedroom. The main thing was not to be cornered. Her bedroom had a lock, but she would also push her bureau in front of the door, taking all the drawers out first and then putting them back when the bureau was in place; otherwise it would have been too heavy for her. Then she would sit with her back against the bureau and her book open on her knees, trying to block out the sound of the knob turning, and of the muffled, broken voice, snuffling at her door: *I just want to talk to you! That's all! I just want. . . .*

Once she tried an experiment: she poured out all the liquor from his bottles so there was none when he came home from work—he had changed jobs, he had changed jobs again—and he threw all the wineglasses, all the glasses of every kind, against the kitchen wall, and there was a lot of broken glass in the morning. Tony was interested to note that this evidence of chaos no longer frightened her. She used to think that Anthea was the glass-breaker of the family; maybe she had been, once. They had to drink their orange juice out of teacups for a week, until Ethel could buy new glassware.

When Tony got her first period, it was Ethel who dealt with it. It was Ethel who explained that bloodstains would come out easier if you soaked them first in cold water. She was an authority on stains of all kinds. "It's only the curse," she said, and Tony liked that. It was a curse, but it was *only* a curse. Pain and distress were of scant importance, really. They could be ignored.

Tony's mother died by drowning. She dove off a yacht, at night, somewhere off the coast of Baja California, and didn't come back up. She must have become confused underwater, and surfaced in the wrong place and hit her head on the bottom of the boat and knocked herself out. Or this was the story told by Roger, the man she was with at the time. Roger was very sorry about it, in the way you would be if you'd lost someone's car keys or broken their best china plate. He sounded as if he wanted to buy a replacement but wasn't sure how. He also sounded drunk.

Tony was the one who took the phone call, because neither her father nor Ethel was there. Roger didn't seem to know who she was.

"I'm the daughter," she said.

"Who?" said Roger. "She didn't have any daughter."

"What was she wearing?" said Tony.

"What?" said Roger.

"Was she wearing a bathing suit, or a dress?"

"What kind of a dumb question is that?" said Roger. He was shouting by then, long distance.

Tony couldn't see why he should be angry. She just wanted to reconstruct. Had Anthea dived off the boat in her bathing suit for a midnight swim, or had she jumped off, wearing a long, entangling skirt, in a fit of anger? The equivalent of a slammed door? The latter seemed more probable. Or perhaps Roger had pushed her. This too was not out of the question. Tony was not interested in revenge, or even in justice. Merely in accuracy.

Despite his rambling vagueness, it was Roger who arranged for the cremation and shipped back the ashes in a metal cylinder. Tony thought there should be a service of some kind; but then, who would have gone to it except her?

Shortly after its arrival the cylinder disappeared. She found it again several years later, after her father had died too and she and Ethel were cleaning out the house. It was in the cellar, stuck in among some old tennis racquets. This gave it the proper period flavour: many of her mother's snapshots had shown her in a tennis dress.

After her mother died Tony went to boarding school, by her own request. She'd wanted to get out of the house, which she did not think of as home, where her father lurked and drank and followed her around, clearing his throat as if he was about to start a conversation. She didn't want to hear what he had to say. She knew it would be some kind of excuse, a plea for understanding, something maudlin. Or else an accusation: if it weren't for Tony he never would have married her mother, and if it weren't for him, Tony never would have been born. Tony had been the catastrophe in his life. It was for Tony he had sacrificed—what, exactly? Even he didn't seem to know. But all the same, didn't she owe him something?

From piecing things together, from checking dates, from a few stray comments dropped earlier, Tony had come to suspect something of the sort: a pregnancy, a hasty wartime marriage. Her mother was a war bride, her father was a war husband, she herself was a war baby. She was an accident. So what? She didn't want to hear about it.

Whatever he wanted to say to her remained unsaid. It was Ethel who found him, lying on the floor of his still-neat study, with his sharpened pencils lined up on the desk. He said in the note that Tony's high school graduation was all he'd been waiting for. He'd even come to the ceremony, that afternoon, and had sat in the auditorium with the other parents, and had given Tony a gold wristwatch after-wards. He kissed her on the cheek. "You'll do all right," he told her. After that he went home and shot himself in the head with his liberated gun. A Luger pistol, as Tony knows now, since she inherited it. He put newspapers down first because of the rug.

Ethel said that was what he was like: considerate, a gentleman. She cried at the funeral, unlike Tony, and talked to herself during the prayers. Tony thought at first that she was saying *Pisspiss* but actually it was *Pleaseplease.* Maybe it always had been. Maybe she wasn't crying about Griff at all, but about her two dead children. Or life in general. Tony could consider all possibilities, she had an open mind.

Griff's life insurance was no good, of course. It didn't cover suicide. But Tony had the money from the house, after the mortgage was paid off, and her mother's leftover money, which had been willed to her, and whatever else was in the bank. Maybe that's what her father meant when he said she would be all right.

So that's it, Tony tells Zenia. And it is, as far as she knows. She doesn't think about her parents very much. She doesn't have nightmares about her father appearing with half of his head blown off, still with something to tell; or of her mother, trailing wet skirts and salt water, her hair hanging over her face like seaweed. She thinks maybe she ought to have such nightmares, but she doesn't. The study of history has steeled her to violent death; she is well armoured.

"You've still got the ashes?" says Zenia. "Your mother's?"

"They're on my sweater shelf," says Tony.

"You are a gruesome little creature," says Zenia, laughing. Tony takes it as a compliment: it's the same thing Zenia said when Tony showed her the battle notebooks with the scores of the men lost. "What else have you got? The gun?" But then she turns serious. "You should get rid of those ashes right away! They're bad luck, they'll ill-wish you."

This is a new side to Zenia: she's superstitious. Tony would not have suspected it, and her high estimate of Zenia slips a notch. "They're just plain old ashes," she says.

"You know that's not true," says Zenia. "You *know* it isn't. Keep those, and she'll still have a hold on you."

So the next evening at twilight the two of them take the ferry across to the Island. It's December and there's a bitter wind, but no ice on the lake yet, so the ferry is still running. Halfway across Tony tosses the canister with her mother's ashes off the back of the ferry, into the dark choppy water. It's not something she'd have done on her own; it's just to please Zenia.

"Rest in peace," says Zenia. She doesn't sound altogether convinced. Worse, the metal cylinder isn't sinking. It's floating, bobbing along in the wake of the ferry. Tony realizes she should have opened it and dumped out the contents. If she had a rifle she could put a couple of holes through it. If she could shoot.

24

December darkens and dark-
ens, and the streets sprout forth their Christmas tinsel,
and the Salvation Army brass band sings hymns and jingles
its bells and stirs up its cauldron of money, and loneliness
blows in the snowflurries, and the other girls in McClung
Hall set off to join their families, in their homes, their
warm homey homes, and Tony stays behind. As she has
done before; but this time it's better, this time there's no
cold feeling in the pit of her stomach, because Zenia is
there with her heartening sneers. "Christmas is a bitch,"
says Zenia. "Screw Christmas, it is *so* bourgeois," and then
Tony feels all right again and tells Zenia about the controversy over Christ's birthdate, in the Dark Ages, and how
grown men were willing to kill one another over it, over
the exact timing of *Peace on earth, goodwill towards men,* and
Zenia laughs. "Your head is a card file," she says. "Let's
eat, I'll make us something." And Tony sits with content-
ment at Zenia's kitchen table, watching her measure and
blend and stir.

Where is West in all of this? Tony has relinquished
him, because how could she ever compete with Zenia?
And even if she could compete, she wouldn't think of it.

Such a thing would be dishonourable: Zenia is her friend. Her best friend. Her only friend, come to think of it. Tony has not been in the habit of having friends.

Or it may be otherwise; it may be that there's no room left for West, between the two of them. They're too close together.

So there's Zenia and Tony now, and Zenia and West; but no longer any West and Tony.

Sometimes there are the three of them together. Tony goes with Zenia and West to their place, the new one they moved into after painting their old one black. The new place isn't new, but dingy and cheap and falling apart, an over-the-store walk-up east on Queen. This apartment has a long living room with one window, its glass rattled by passing streetcars; a big raffish kitchen, with tattered orange wallpaper and a table, a wooden one with cracked blue paint, and four mismatched chairs; and a bedroom, where Zenia and West sleep together on a mattress on the floor.

Zenia makes them scrambled eggs, and strong, amazing coffee, and West plays his lute for them: he does have one, after all. He sits on a cushion on the floor, his long legs bent at the knees and sticking up like the back legs of a grasshopper, and fingers deftly, and sings old ballads.

> The water is wide, I cannot get over,
> And neither have I wings to fly,
> Build me a boat that can carry two,
> And both shall row, my love and I,

he sings. "There's an Irish version too," he adds, "with a boatman."

Really he is singing for Zenia, not for Tony at all. He is deeply in love with Zenia; Zenia has told Tony this, and indeed it's obvious. Zenia must feel the same way about West, because she praises him, she extols him, she strokes him with her eyes. He is such a gentle man, she's told Tony during their coffee talks; so thoughtful, unlike most men, who are slobbering brutes. He values her for the right reasons. He worships her! She is very fortunate to have found such a sweet man. Of course he's great in the sack as well.

The sack? thinks Tony. What is the sack? It takes her a minute. She has never been in the presence, before, of two people who are in love with each other. She feels like a stray child, ragged and cold, with her nose pressed to a lighted window. A toy-store window, a bakery window, with fancy cakes and decorated cookies. Poverty prevents her entrance. These things are for other people; nothing for her.

But Zenia seems to be aware of this, too—of Tony's singleness, her forlorn wistfulness—and smooths it over. She's very considerate. She distracts, she acts, she talks gaily of other things. Recipes, shortcuts, wrinkles, and twists: she hasn't lived from hand to mouth for nothing, she has a full supply of useful knacks. The secret of the scrambled eggs, for instance, is the fresh chervil and chives—she has several pots of herbs growing on the windowsill—and a little water added, and not too high a flame; the secret of the coffee is the coffee grinder, a wooden one with a handle and an enchanting pull-out drawer.

Zenia is full of secrets. She laughs, she throws her secrets casually this way and that, her teeth flashing white;

she pulls more secrets out of her sleeves and unfurls them from behind her back, she unrolls them like bolts of rare cloth, displaying them, whirling them like gypsy scarves, flourishing them like banners, heaping them one on top of another in a glittering, prodigal tangle. When she's in the room, who can look at anything else?

But Tony and West do look—just for a moment—when Zenia has her back turned. They look sadly at each other, a little shamefaced. *In thrall,* is what they are. They know they can no longer drink beer together calmly in the afternoons. It is Zenia, now, who borrows Tony's Modern History notes. West gets the benefit of them too, of course, but only second-hand.

Once Tony forgot to sign out of McClung Hall and then stayed at Zenia's too late. She ended up spending the night on Zenia's living-room floor, rolled in a blanket, on top of Zenia's coat and her own coat and West's. In the morning, very early, West went back with her to McClung Hall and gave her a boost onto the bottom platform of the fire escape, which was too high for her to reach otherwise.

It was a daring thing to do, staying out all night, but she doesn't want to do it again. For one thing it was too humiliating, coming back with West on the streetcar and then the subway, unable to think of what she should be saying to him, then being lifted up by him and deposited on the fire escape platform like a parcel. For another thing, sleeping outside the bedroom with both of them inside it made her too unhappy.

She didn't sleep, anyway. She couldn't, because of the sounds. Thick sounds, unknown sounds, deep sounds, hair-covered and snouted and root-like, muddy and hot and watery sounds from underneath the earth.

●　　●　　●

"I think your mother was a romantic," says Zenia, out of nowhere. She is mixing batter for the *langues de chat* she's making; Tony is sitting at the table copying out her own history notes for Zenia, who as usual is short of time. "I think she was in search of the perfect man."

"I don't think so," says Tony. She's a little taken aback: she thought the file on her mother was closed.

"She sounds fun-loving," says Zenia. "She sounds full of life."

Tony can't quite understand why Zenia wants to excuse her mother. She herself has not done so, she realizes now. "She liked parties," she says briefly.

"I bet she tried to have an abortion, and it didn't work out," says Zenia cheerfully. "Before she married your father. I bet she filled the bathtub up with boiling water and drank a lot of gin. That's what they used to do."

This is a darker view of her mother than Tony herself has ever taken. "Oh, no," she murmurs. "She wouldn't have done that!" Though it could be true. Maybe that's why Tony is so small. Neither of her parents was particularly diminutive. Maybe her growth got stunted by the gin. But then, wouldn't she be an idiot as well?

Zenia fills the shallow moulds and slides them into the oven. "The war was a strange time," she says. "Everybody screwed everybody, they just cut loose! The men thought they were going to die, and the women thought that too. People couldn't get used to being normal again, afterwards."

Wars are Tony's territory. She knows all this, she has read about it. Plagues have the same effect: a panic, a hothouse forcing, a sort of greedy hysteria. But it seems unfair that such conditions should have applied to her own parents. They should have been exempt. (Her father, the Christmas after her mother ran away, standing in the middle of the living room with an armful of glass ornaments, standing there in front of the naked Christmas tree as if paralyzed, not knowing what to do. Herself going for the stepladder, taking the ornaments gently from his hands. *Here. I can hang them on!* He would have thrown them, otherwise. Thrown them against the wall. Sometimes he would pause that way, in the middle of doing a simple thing, as if he'd gone blind or lost his memory. Or suddenly regained it. He was living in two times at once: hanging the Christmas tree ornaments, and blowing holes in enemy children. So no wonder, thinks Tony. Despite his increasingly drunken and fragmented and, yes, violent and frightening later years, she has more or less forgiven him. And if Anthea hadn't run away, would he have ended up on the floor, with his blood soaking into the morning paper? Not likely.)

"She abandoned me," says Tony.

"My own mother *sold* me," says Zenia, with a sigh.

"Sold you?" says Tony.

"Well, rented me out," says Zenia. "For money. We had to eat. We were refugees. She'd made it as far as Poland before the war but she'd seen what was coming; she got out somehow, bribery or something, forged passports, or else she went down for a bunch of train guards, who knows? Anyway, she made it as far as Paris; that's where I grew up. People were eating garbage then, they were eating cats! What could she do? She couldn't get a job, God knows she didn't have any skills! She had to have money somehow."

"Rented you to who?" says Tony.

"Men," says Zenia. "Oh, not out on the street! Not just anyone! Old generals and whatnot. She was a White Russian; I guess the family had money, once—back in Russia, I suppose. She claimed to be some sort of a countess, though God knows Russian countesses were a dime a dozen. There was a whole bunch of White Russians in Paris; they'd been there since the revolution. She liked to say she was used to good things, though I don't know when that would have been."

Tony hasn't known this—that Zenia's mother was Russian. She has only known Zenia's story of recent years: her foreground. Her life at the university, her life with West, and with the man before him and the one before that. Brutes, both of them, who wore leather jackets and drank, and hit her.

She examines the cast of Zenia's high cheekbones: Slavic, she supposes. Then there's her slight accent, her air of scornful superiority, her touch of superstition. The Russians go in for icons and so forth. It all makes sense.

"Rented?" she says. "But how old were you?"

"Who knows?" says Zenia. "It must've started when I was five, six, earlier maybe. Really I can't remember. I can't remember a time when I didn't have some man's hand in my pants."

Tony's mouth opens. "Five?" she says. She is horrified. At the same time she admires Zenia's candour. Zenia doesn't seem to get embarrassed by anything. Unlike Tony, she is not a prude.

Zenia laughs. "Oh, it wasn't obvious, at first," she says. "It was all very polite! They would come over and sit on the sofa—God, she was proud of that sofa, she kept a silk shawl draped over it, embroidered with roses—and she would tell me to sit beside the nice man, and after a while she'd just go out of the room. It wasn't real sex, at first. Just a lot of feeling up. Sticky fingers. She saved the big bang till I was what she called grown up. Eleven, twelve . . . I think she did fairly well on that one, though not many of those men were filthy rich. Penny-pinching shabby genteel, with a little put by, or some shady trade. They were all in the black market, they all had an angle, they lived in between the walls, you know? Like rats. She bought me a new dress for the occasion, on the black market too, I guess. I made my début on the sitting-room rug—she never let them use the bed. His name was Major Popov, if you can believe it, just like something out of Dostoevsky, with brown crusts up his nose from taking snuff. He didn't even take off his pants, he was in such a hurry. I stared at those embroidered roses on the fucking shawl the whole time. I offered up the pain to God. It isn't as though I was sinning for fun! I was very religious, at the time; Orthodox, of course. They still have the best churches, don't you think? I hope she got a hefty slice out of old Popov. Some men will give up a lot of lunches, for a virgin."

Zenia tells this story as if it's a piece of casual gossip, and Tony listens, electrified. She has never heard of such a thing. Correction: she has heard of such things, more or less, but she has heard of them only in books. Such baroque, such complicated European things don't happen to real people, or to people she might meet. But how would she know? These activities might be going on all around her, but she doesn't see them because she wouldn't know where to look. Zenia would know. Zenia is older than Tony, in years not so much, but in other ways a lot. Beside Zenia, Tony is a child, ignorant as an egg.

"You must have hated her," says Tony.

"Oh, no," says Zenia seriously. "That wasn't until later. She was very nice to me! When I was little she made me special meals. She never raised her voice. She was beautiful to look at, she had long dark hair braided and wound around her head like a saint, and big sorrowful eyes. I used to sleep with her in her big white feather bed. I loved her, I adored her, I would have done anything for her! I didn't want her to be so sad. That's how she was able to get away with it."

"How terrible," says Tony.

"Oh well," says Zenia, "who gives a shit? Anyway it wasn't only me—she rented herself out, too. She was a sort of bargain-basement mistress, I suppose. For gentlemen down on their luck. Only Russians though, and nobody below the rank of major. She had her standards. She helped them with their pretensions, they helped her with hers. But she wasn't very successful at the sex part, maybe because she didn't really like it. She preferred suffering. There was quite a turnover of men. Also she was sick a lot of the time. Coughing, just like an opera! Blood in the hankie. Her breath smelled worse and worse, she used to wear a lot of perfume, when she could get it. I suppose it was TB, and that's what killed her. What a corny death!"

"You were very lucky not to get it yourself," says Tony. All of this seems so archaic. Surely nobody gets TB any more. It's a vanished illness, like smallpox.

"Yes, wasn't I?" says Zenia. "But I was long gone by the time she finally croaked. As I got older I didn't love her any more. I did most of the work, she kept most of the money, and that was hardly fair! And I couldn't stand listening to her coughing, and crying to herself at night. She was so hopeless; I think she was stupid, as well. So I ran away. It was a mean thing to do, I suppose; she didn't have anybody by that time, any man; only me. But it was her or me. I had to choose."

"What about your father?" says Tony.

Zenia laughs. "What father?"

"Well, you must have had one," says Tony.

"I did better," says Zenia. "I had three! My mother had several versions—minor Greek royalty, a general in the Polish cavalry, an Englishman of good family. She had a photograph of him, just the one man—but three stories. The story about him changed, depending on how she felt; though in all three of the stories he died in the war. She used to show me where, on the map: a different place, a different death for each. Charging the German tanks on horseback, behind the French lines in a parachute, machine-gunned in a palace. When she could afford it she would put a single rose in front of the picture; sometimes she would light a candle. God knows whose photo it was really! A young man in a jacket, with a knapsack, sort of blurry, looking over his shoulder; not even in uniform. Pre-war. Maybe she bought it. Myself, I think she got raped, by a bunch of soldiers or something, but she didn't want to tell me. It would've been too much—for me to discover that my father was someone like that. But it would figure, wouldn't it? A woman with no money, on the run from one place to another, by herself—no protection. Women like that were fair game! Or else she had a Nazi lover, some German thug. Who can tell? She was quite a liar, so I'll never know. Anyway, she's dead now."

Tony's own little history has dwindled considerably. Beside Zenia's, it seems no more than an incident, minor, grey, suburban; a sedate parochial anecdote; a footnote. Whereas Zenia's life sparkles—no, it glares, in the lurid although uncertain light cast by large and portentous world events. (White Russians!)

So far Tony has seen Zenia as very different from herself, but now she sees her as similar too, for aren't they both orphans? Both motherless, both war babies, making their way in the world by themselves, trudging onwards with their baskets over their arms, baskets containing their scant, their only worldly possessions—one brain apiece, for what else do they have to rely on? She admires Zenia tremendously, not least for keeping her cool. Right now, for instance, when other women might be crying, Zenia is actually smiling—smiling at Tony, with perhaps a hint of mockery, which Tony chooses to interpret as a touching gallantry, a steely courage in the face of adverse destiny. Zenia has been through horrors, and has emerged victorious. Tony pictures her on a horse, cloak flying, sword-arm raised; or as a bird, a silver and miraculous bird, rising triumphant and unscathed from the cinders of burning and plundered Europe.

"There's one thing about being an orphan, though," says Zenia thoughtfully. Two jets of smoke come out of her perfect nostrils. "You don't have to live up to anyone else's good opinion of you." She drinks the dregs of her coffee, butts out her cigarette. "You can be whoever you like."

Tony looks at her, looks into her blue-black eyes, and sees her own reflection: herself, as she would like to be. *Tnomerf Ynot.* Herself turned inside out.

25

Under the circumstances, what can Tony withhold? Not very much.

Certainly not money. Zenia has to eat—Zenia, and West too, of course—and how are they to do that unless Tony, replete with the wealth of the dead, will lend Zenia the odd twenty, the odd fifty, the odd hundred, from time to time? And then how is Zenia to pay it back, things being what they are? She has a scholarship of some kind, or so she has implied, but it doesn't cover the whole shot. In the distant past she panhandled and to a certain extent hooked her way through Europe and across the ocean; although— she tells Tony, as Tony's eyes widen and blink—she'd much rather roll a nice middle-class drunk any time, it's quicker and a good deal cleaner. In the more recent past she's made extra cash by waiting on tables and by cleaning washrooms in second-rate hotels—drudgery is the price of virtue—but when she does that she's too tired to study.

She's too tired anyway. Love takes it out of you, and love-nests require feathering, and who does the cooking and laundry and cleaning up around Zenia's place? Not West, poor angel; man-like, he has trouble cooking an egg or making himself a cup of tea. (Ah, thinks Tony, I could make his tea! She longs for such simple domestic chores, to offer up to West. But she censors this almost immediately. Even the boiling of West's tea-water would feel like a betrayal of Zenia.)

Also, Zenia indicates, it costs to defy the social order: freedom is not free, it comes with a price. The front lines of liberation get the first bullets. Already Zenia and West are paying more than they should for that rat-bag of an apartment because the dirty-minded hypocrite of a landlord has come to suspect they aren't married. Toronto is so puritanical!

Then how can Tony refuse when Zenia comes to her room one evening, in tears and minus a term paper for Modern History, with barely a moment to spare? "If I flunk this course it's game over," she says. "I'll have to leave university, it's back on the streets for me. Shit, you don't know, Tony—you just don't *know*! It's such hell, it's so degrading, I can't go back to that!"

Tony is bewildered by her tears; she has thought of Zenia as tearless, more tearless even than herself. And now there are not only tears but many tears, rolling fluently down Zenia's strangely immobile face, which always looks made-up even when it isn't. On some other woman the mascara would run; but that isn't mascara, it's Zenia's real eyelashes.

It ends with Tony writing two term papers, one for herself and one for Zenia. She does this nervously: she knows it's highly risky. She's stepping over a line, a line she respects. But Zenia is doing Tony's rebelliousness for her so it's only fair that Tony should write Zenia's term paper. Or that is the equation Tony makes, at some level below words. Tony will be Zenia's right hand, because Zenia is certainly Tony's left one.

Neither of the term papers is about battles. The Modern History professor, bald-headed, squinty-eyed, leather-elbow-patched Dr. Welch, is more interested in economics than he is in bloodshed, and he has made it clear to Tony—who suggested the out-of-control sack of Constantinople by the Crusaders—that he does not consider war an appropriate subject for girls. So both of the papers are about money. Zenia's is on the Slavic slave trade with the Byzantine Empire—Tony picked this because of Zenia's Russian ancestors—and Tony's is about the tenth-century Byzantine silk monopoly.

Byzantium interests Tony. A lot of people died unpleasantly there, most of them for trivial reasons; you could be torn in pieces for dressing wrong, you could be disembowelled for smirking. Twenty-nine Byzantine emperors were assassinated by their rivals. Blinding was a favourite method; that, and joint-by-joint dismemberment, and slow starvation.

If the professor hadn't been so squeamish Tony would have chosen to write about the assassination of the Byzantine emperor Nicephorus Phocas by his beautiful wife, the empress Theophano. Theophano started life as a concubine and worked her way to the top. When her autocratic husband became too old and ugly for her she had him killed. Not only that, she helped to do it. On December 1, 969, she persuaded him to leave his bedroom door unlocked, promising sexual favours, no doubt, and in the middle of the night she entered his room with her younger, better-looking lover, John Tsimisces—who would later have her imprisoned in a convent—and a band of mercenaries. They woke Nicephorus up—he was sleeping on a panther skin, a nice touch—and then John Tsimisces split his head open with a sword. John was laughing.

How do we know that? thinks Tony. Who was there to record it? Was Theophano laughing, as well? She speculates about why they woke him up. It was a sadistic touch; or perhaps it was revenge. By all accounts Nicephorus was a tyrant: proud, capricious, cruel. She pictures Theophano on her way to the assassination, with a purple silk mantle thrown over her shoulders and gold sandals. Her dark hair swirls around her head; her pale face shines in the torchlight. She walks first, and quickly, because the most important element in any act of treachery is surprise. Behind her come the men with swords.

Theophano is smiling, but Tony doesn't see it as a sinister smile. Instead it's gleeful: the smile of a child about to put its hands over someone's eyes from behind. *Guess who?*

There's an element of sheer mischief in history, thinks Tony. Perverse joy. Outrageousness for its own sake. What is an ambush, really, but a kind of military practical joke? Hiding yourself, then jumping out and yelling *Surprise!* But none of the historians ever mentions it, this quality of giddy hide-and-seek. They want the past to be serious. Dead serious. She muses over the phrase: if *dead* is serious, is *alive* then frivolous? So the phrasemakers would have it.

Maybe Theophano woke up Nicephorus because she wanted him to appreciate her cleverness before he died. She wanted him to see how duplicitous she was, and how mistaken he had been about her. She wanted him to get the joke.

• • •

Both of the papers are up to Tony's usual standard; if any-thing, the silk monopoly one is better. But Zenia's gets an A and Tony's a mere A minus. Zenia's reputation for brilliance has affected even Professor Welch, it seems. Or perhaps it's the way she looks. Does Tony mind? Not particularly. But she notices.

She also feels remorseful. Up until now she has always paid the strictest attention to academic decorum. She never borrows other people's notes, although she lends them; her footnotes are impeccable; and she is well aware that writing a term paper for someone else is cheating. But it isn't as if there's any benefit to herself. Her motives are of the best: how could she turn away her friend? How could she condemn Zenia to a life of sexual bondage? It isn't in her. Nevertheless, her conscience troubles her; so maybe it's justice that she's received a mere A minus. If this is the only punishment in store for her she'll have got-ten off lightly.

Tony composed her two term papers in March, when the snow was melting and the sun was warming up, and the snowdrops were appearing through the mud and old newspapers and decaying leaves on front lawns, and peo-ple were becoming restive inside their winter coats. Zenia was becoming restive too. She and Tony no longer spent their evenings drinking coffee at Christie's Coffee Shop on Queen East; they no longer talked intensely, far into what Tony considered the night. Partly Tony didn't have the time, because the final exams were coming up and her own brilliance was something she had to work at. But also it was as if Zenia had learned all she needed to know about Tony.

The reverse was far from true: Tony was still curious, still fascinated, still avid for detail; but when Tony asked questions, Zenia's answers—although good-natured enough—were short, and her eyes wandered elsewhere. She had the same affable but absent-minded attitude towards West now, too. Although she still touched him whenever he came into the room, although she still doled out little flatteries, little praises, she wasn't concentrating on him. She was thinking about something else.

On a Friday in early April, Zenia climbs in through Tony's bedroom window in the middle of the night. Tony doesn't see her do it, because she's asleep; but suddenly her eyes open and she sits up straight in her bed, and there's a woman standing in the darkness of the room, her head outlined against the yellowy-grey oblong of the window. In the instant of waking Tony thinks it's her mother. Anthea could not be disposed of so easily, it appears: compressed into a cylinder, tossed into the lake, forgotten. She's come back to exact retribution, but for what? Or maybe she has returned, far too late, to collect Tony and take her away at last, to the bottom of the deep blue sea, where Tony has no desire to go, and what would she look like if Tony were to turn on the light? Herself, or a bloated watercolour?

Tony goes cold all over. *Where are my clothes?* Anthea is about to say, out of the middle of her faceless face. She means her body, the one that's been burned up, the one that's been drowned. What can Tony reply? *I'm sorry, I'm sorry.*

All this is wordless. What Tony experiences is a complex wave of recognition and dread, shock and the lack of it: the package that comes intact whenever unvoiced wishes come true. She is too paralyzed to scream. She gasps, and puts both hands over her mouth.

"Hi," says Zenia quietly. "It's me."

There's a pause while Tony recovers herself a little. "How did you get in?" she asks, when her heart is again inaudible.

"The window," says Zenia. "I climbed up the fire escape."

"But it's too high," says Tony. Zenia is tall, but not tall enough to reach the bottom platform. Is West down there, did he give her a boost? Tony moves to switch on her bedside light, then thinks better of it. She isn't supposed to have anyone in her room at this time of night, and dons and busybodies prowl the corridors, on the sniff for cigarette smoke and contraband sex.

"I went up that tree and swung over from the branch," says Zenia. "Any lunatic could do it. You should really get some sort of a lock on your window." She sits down, cross-legged, on the floor.

"What's the matter?" says Tony. There has to be something: even Zenia wouldn't just climb in through somebody's window in the middle of the night on a passing whim.

"I couldn't sleep," says Zenia. They are both almost whispering. "I needed to talk to you. I'm feeling so bad about poor Professor Welch."

"What?" says Tony. She doesn't understand.

"About how we cheated on him. I think we should confess. It was forgery, after all," says Zenia pensively. She's talking about the term paper, on which Tony spent so much time and generous care. There was nothing dishonest about the paper itself: just about the name on it, which was Zenia's.

Now Zenia wants to tell, and there goes Tony's life. Many large though shadowy possibilities loom ahead for Zenia—journalism, high finance, even politics have all been mentioned—but university professor has never been among them; whereas for Tony it's the only thing. It's her vocation; without it she'll be useless as an amputated hand. What else can she do? Where else can her pedlar's pack of knowledge, the doodads and odd fragments and frippery she accumulates like lint, be exchanged for an honest living? *Honest*: that's the key. Stripped of her intellectual honesty, her reputation, her integrity, she'll be exiled. And Zenia is in a position to strip her.

"But I did it to help you!" says Tony, aware even as she says it that her own motives will cut no ice with the authorities. (For a moment she thinks, I could simply deny I wrote the thing. But Zenia has the original, in Tony's back-slanted handwriting. Naturally she had to copy it out in her own.)

"I know," says Zenia. "But still. Well, maybe I'll think differently in the morning. I'm just depressed, I'm down on myself; sometimes I feel so shitty I just want to jump off a bridge, you know? I feel like such an impostor sometimes. I feel I don't belong here—that I'm just not good enough. Or for West, either. He's so squeaky clean. Sometimes I'm afraid I'll get him dirty, or break him, or something. You know the worst of it? Sometimes I *want* to. When I'm—you know. Under a lot of stress."

So it's not only Tony whose life is threatened, but West's too. From what she's seen of West and his unquestioning devotion, Tony is convinced that Zenia could indeed wreak havoc. One contemptuous flick of her hand could splatter him all over the sidewalk. How did Zenia get so much power without Tony noticing? Insofar as West is concerned, Tony did notice. But she trusted Zenia to use that power well. She trusted Zenia. Now both she and West are in danger, now she must save them both. "Stress?" she says faintly.

"Oh, the money thing. Tony, you wouldn't know, it's not something you've ever had to deal with. The fucking rent's a few months behind, and the fucking land-lord's threatening to have us evicted; he says he'll phone the university and make a stink. There's no point in even bothering West with any of it—he's such a baby, he just leaves all those practical things to me. If I told him how much we owe he'd go out and sell his lute, no question; I mean, what else does he have? He'd do anything for me, though it wouldn't even make a dint, poor lamb; but he's fond of those sacrificial gestures. I just don't know what to do. It's all such a *burden,* Tony. That's when I get so fucking depressed!"

Tony has given Zenia money for the rent, several times already. However, she knows what Zenia will say if she mentions this. *But Tony! We had to eat! You don't know what it's like, to be hungry. You just don't get it! You don't know what it's like to have no money at all!*

"How much?" she says in a cold, meticulous voice. It's a neat piece of blackmail. She's being bushwhacked.

"A thousand dollars would see us out of the woods," says Zenia smoothly. A thousand dollars is a great deal of money. It will make a definite hole in Tony's nest egg. Also it's much more than could possibly be needed for back rent. But Zenia doesn't beg, she doesn't plead. She knows that Tony's response is a foregone conclusion.

Tony gets out of bed in her polo pyjamas with blue mice in clown suits printed on them, sent to her from California by her mother, left over from when she was fourteen—her nocturnal wardrobe has not been upgraded, because who would ever see it, and one of the things she minds most about this evening in retrospect is that Zenia got a good look at her absurd pyjamas—and goes over to her desk and turns the desk lamp on, briefly, and writes the cheque. "Here," she says, thrusting it at Zenia.

"Tony, you're a brick," says Zenia. "I'll pay you back later!" Both of them know this isn't true.

Zenia exits via the window, and Tony goes back to bed. A brick: hard, foursquare, a potential murder weapon. You could bash in quite a few skulls, with a brick. No doubt Zenia will be back later for more money, and then more. Tony has gained nothing but time.

26

Two days later West comes to McClung Hall and seeks out Tony, and asks her if she's seen Zenia, because Zenia is gone. She's gone from the apartment, she's gone from the precincts of the university, she appears to be gone from the entire city, because nobody—not the bearded theatrical men, not the thin, ballet-faced, horse-maned women, and not the police, when West finally calls them—knows where she is. Nobody saw her go. She is simply not there any more.

Gone with her are the thousand dollars Tony gave her, plus the contents of her joint account with West—two hundred dollars, give or take. There would have been more, but Zenia took some out earlier on the pretext that their good friend Tony, who was not as rich as they'd all thought, had asked her for a temporary loan, being too shy to mention it to West. Gone also is West's lute, which is located several weeks later by Tony during a diligent and inspired search of second-hand stores, and is purchased by her on the spot. She carries it to the apartment herself and shoves it at West like a lollipop, hoping to soothe his unhappiness. But it makes scarcely any impact on him, where he sits by himself in the middle of the floor, on a large threadbare cushion, staring at the wall and drinking beer.

Zenia has left a letter for West. She did have that much consideration, or—Tony thinks, with her new insight into the twists of Zenia's soul—that much calculation. *My darling, I am not worthy of you. Some day you will forgive me. I will love you till I die. Your loving Zenia.* Tony, who has been the recipient of a similar letter, knows what these avowals are worth, which is nothing at all. She knows how such letters can be hung around your neck like lockets made of lead, heavy keepsakes that will drag you down for years. But she understands too West's need to rely on Zenia's assurances. He needs them like water, he needs them like air. He would rather believe that Zenia has renounced him out of misplaced nobility than that she's been taking him for a ride. Women can make fools of men, thinks freshly disabused Tony, even if they weren't fools to begin with.

West's desolation is palpable. It envelops him like a cloud of midges, it marks him like a slashed wrist, which he holds out to Tony (mutely, without moving) to be bandaged. Given the choice, she would not have elected the role of nurse and comforter, having been so bad at it with her father. But there isn't a lot else on offer, and so Tony makes cups of tea for West, and pries him off his cushion, and—not knowing what else to do—takes him out for walks, like a dog or invalid. Together they meander across parks, together they cross at the corners, holding hands like the babes in the wood. Together they silently lament.

West is in mourning, but Tony is in mourning too. They have both lost Zenia, although Tony has lost her more completely. West still believes in the Zenia he has lost: he thinks that if she would only come back and allow herself to be forgiven and cherished and cared for, all could go on as before. Tony knows better. She knows that the person she's lost has never really existed in the first place. She does not yet question Zenia's story, her history; indeed, she uses it to explain her: what can you expect of someone with such a mangled childhood? What she questions is Zenia's good will. Zenia was only using her, and she has let herself be used; she has been rummaged, she has been picked like a pocket. But she doesn't have much time to feel sorry for herself because she's too busy feeling sorry for West.

West's hand lies passively in Tony's. It's as if he's blind: he goes where Tony steers, sucked dry of any will of his own, careless of where he's headed. Precipice or safe haven, it's all the same to him. Once in a while he seems to wake; he peers around, disoriented. "How did we get here?" he says, and Tony's tenderized little heart is wrung.

What bothers her the most is West's drinking. It's still only beer, but there's a lot more of it going into him than there used to be. It's possible he's not ever completely sober. Zenia's absence is like a path, a path Tony recognizes because she's seen it before. It leads downwards and ends abruptly in a square of bloodstained newspaper, and West stumbles along it as if he's sleepwalking. She's powerless to stop him, or to wake him either. What sort of match is skinny, awkward, and bone-headed Tony, with her oversized spectacles and walks in the park and cups of tea, for the memory of shimmering Zenia that West carries next to his heart, or else instead of it?

Tony is worried sick about him. She loses sleep. Inky rings appear beneath her eyes, her skin turns to paper. She writes her final exams in a frantic trance rather than with her usual cool rationality, calling upon reserves of stashed-away knowledge she didn't even know she had.

West on the other hand doesn't even turn up, at least for the Modern History exam. The vortex is taking him down.

Roz passes Tony in the hallway of McClung and notes her dreadful appearance.

"Hey, Tone," she says. (She has reverted to this pet name since the defection of Zenia, which she knows about, of course. The grapevine here has many tendrils. Tony without Zenia is no longer viewed with trepidation, and can be treated as a diminutive again.) "Hey, Tone, how's it goin'? Holy cow, you look awful." She puts her big warm hand on Tony's pointy bird-shoulder. "It can't be that bad. What's the matter?"

Who else does Tony have to talk to? She can't talk to West about himself, and Zenia is absent. Once upon a time she would have talked to no one, but ever since Christie's Coffee Shop she has developed an appreciation for confidences. So they go to Roz's overstuffed room and sit on Roz's pillow-covered bed, and Tony disgorges.

She doesn't tell Roz about the forged term paper or the thousand dollars. In any case they are not the story. The story is about West. Zenia is gone, with West's soul stuffed into her over-the-shoulder bag, and without it West will die. He will kill himself, and then what will Tony do? How will she live with herself?

This isn't how she puts it though. She outlines the

bare facts, and facts they are. She isn't being melodramatic. Merely objective.

"Listen, sweetie," says Roz, when Tony stops talking. "I know you like him, I mean, he seems like a nice enough guy, but is he worth it?"

He is, says Tony. He is, he definitely is, but she is without hope. (He will dwindle and fade, as in ballads. He will pine and wane. Then he will blow off his head.)

"Sounds to me he's acting like a jerk! Zenia's a floozie, we all knew that. A couple of years ago she went through half the fraternities—more than half! You never heard that poem about her—'Trouble with your penia? Try Zenia!' He should wake up, eh?" says Roz, who has yet to encounter love, having yet to encounter Mitch. She has however just encountered sex and thinks it's the new wonder drug, and she's always had trouble keeping secrets. She lowers her voice. "You should take him to bed," she says, nodding her head sagely. She's enjoying the role of wise woman, counsellor to the afflicted. It helps not to be afflicted yourself.

"Me?" says Tony. The girls in McClung Hall, although they talk endlessly about their boyfriends, are never very specific about what they actually do with them. If they go to bed with them they don't mention it. Zenia is the only person Tony's ever known who has been at all open about sex, until right now.

"So who else?" says Roz. "You need to make him feel wanted. Give him an interest in life."

"Oh, I don't think I could do that," says Tony. The thought of going to bed with anyone at all is terrifying. What if they rolled over on her by mistake, and she got squashed? Also the thought of giving another person that much power over her makes her flinch. Let alone her reluctance to be pawed and drooled on. Zenia was frank about sex, but she didn't make it sound all that attractive.

Still, thinking about it, Tony has to admit that if there's one person she might be able to tolerate, it would be West. Already she holds his hand, on their walks; it's nice. But the concrete details defeat her. How would she lure West into such a place as bed, and which bed? Not her own narrow bed in McClung Hall—that's out of the question, too many eyes are on her, you can't even eat cookies in your room without everyone finding out—and surely not the same bed he's been sleeping in with Zenia. It wouldn't be right! Also, she doesn't know how such things are done. In theory, yes, she knows what goes where, but in practice? One of the hurdles is conversational: what would she say? And even if she could successfully manoeuvre West into the physical location, what would happen then? She is too small, and West is too big. She would be shredded.

She loves West, though. That much is very clear to her. And isn't it a matter of saving his life? It is. So heroism and self-sacrifice are called for.

Tony grits her teeth and sets out to seduce West. She is every bit as inept at it as she has feared she'll be. She tries bringing some candles over to West's apartment and cooking a candlelight dinner, but her activity in the kitchen seems only to depress West further, because Zenia was such a marvellous and inventive cook; in addition to which Tony burns the tuna casserole. She takes him to movies, leading him to cheap and silly horror films that give her a chance to clutch his hand in the dark when the vampires bare their fangs and the rubber head rolls down the staircase. But whatever she does West chooses to regard as simply the ministrations of friendship. Or so it appears to Tony. To her despair, but also—partly—to her relief, he views her as a loyal sidekick, and that is that.

It's June, it's warm, the university term is over but Tony has signed up for a summer course, as usual, so she won't have to move out of her room at McClung Hall. One afternoon she goes over to West's place to do his accumulated mildewed dishes and to take him out for his walk, and finds him asleep on his bed. His eyelids are curved and pure, like those on carved tombstone saints; one arm is thrown up over his head. Breath goes into him, breath goes out: she is so grateful that he is still, as yet, alive. His hair—uncut for weeks—is ragged on his head. He looks so sad lying there, so deserted, so lacking in threat, that she sits carefully down beside him, bends gingerly over, and gives him a kiss on the forehead.

West doesn't open his eyes, but his arms come around her. "You're so warm," he murmurs into her hair. "You're so kind to me."

Nobody has ever called Tony warm and kind before. No man has ever put his arms around her. While she is still getting used to it, West begins to kiss her. He gives her small kisses, all over her face. His eyes are still closed. "Don't go away," he whispers. "Don't move."

Tony can't move anyway, because she is paralyzed with apprehension. She is dismayed by her own lack of bravery, and also by the sheer magnitude of West's body, now that she's so close to it. She can actually see the stubs of whiskers coming out of his chin! Usually they're too high up for that. It's like seeing the ants on a falling boulder, just before it crushes you. She feels acutely menaced.

But West is very gradual. He slides off her glasses; then he undoes one button at a time, fumbling as if his fingers are asleep, and pulls his raspy blanket over her, and smooths her as if she's a velvet cushion, and although it does indeed hurt, as the books have said, it's less like being torn apart by wild beasts than she'd supposed, given all that growling that used to go on with Zenia, and more like falling into a river, because West is what other people call him, a long drink of water, and Tony is so thirsty, she's parched, she's been wandering in the desert all of these years, and now at last somebody truly needs her for something, and in the end she discovers what she's always wanted to know: she is bigger inside than out.

In this way Tony, proud of herself and filled with the joy of giving, drags West from the field of defeat and carts him off behind the lines, and tends his wounds, and mends him. He has been broken, but he knits together after a time. Though not perfectly. Tony is conscious of the scar, which takes the form of a low-level anxiety: West is convinced he's failed Zenia. He thinks she's been tossed out into the back alley of the world, to fend (badly) for herself, because he wasn't capable enough or smart enough or simply enough for her. He thinks she needs his protection, but Tony must keep her sneers about this to herself. There is no rival like an absent one. Zenia is not there to defend herself, and for this reason Tony can't attack her. Chivalry as well as wisdom ties her hands.

•   •   •

West goes back to university in the fall and makes up the courses he's missed. Tony is now in graduate school. They rent a small apartment together and share tidy breakfasts and sweet, kindly nights, and Tony is happier than she's ever been.

Time passes and they both get their first postgraduate degrees, and both of them acquire teaching assistantships. After a while they get married, at City Hall; the party afterwards is small and intellectual in tone, although Roz is there, married herself already. Her husband Mitch can't come, she explains; he's away on a business trip. She gives Tony an enveloping hug and a silver telephone cover, and after she leaves (early), Tony's historical and West's musical colleagues ask with ironic eyebrows who on earth that was. Her presence however has reassured Tony: although her own parents' marriage was a disaster, marriage itself must be possible and even normal if Roz is doing it.

West and Tony move into a larger apartment, and West buys a spinet, to go with his lute. He has a suit now, and several ties, and eyeglasses. Tony buys a coffee grinder and a roasting pan, and a copy of *The Joy of Cooking*, in which she looks up esoteric recipes. She makes a hazelnut torte, and buys a fondue dish with long forks, and some skewers for making shish kebab.

More time passes. Tony wonders about having babies, but doesn't bring up the subject because West has never mentioned it. There are peace marches in the streets now, and confused sit-ins at the university. West brings home some marijuana, and they smoke it together, and are frightened together by noises on the street outside, and don't do it again.

Their love is gentle and discreet. If it were a plant it would be a fern, light green and feathery and delicate; if a musical instrument, a flute. If a painting it would be a water lily by Monet, one of the more pastel renditions, with its liquid depths, its reflections, its different falls of light. "You're my best friend," West tells Tony, stroking her hair back from her forehead. "I owe you a lot." Tony is touched by his gratitude, and too young to be suspicious of it.

They never mention Zenia, Tony because she thinks it will upset West, West because he thinks it will upset Tony. Zenia does not go away, however. She hovers, growing fainter, true, but still there, like the blue haze of cigarette smoke in a room after the cigarette has been put out. Tony can smell her.

One evening Zenia appears at their door. She knocks like anybody else and Tony opens, thinking it is a Girl Guide selling cookies, or else the Jehovah's Witnesses. When she sees Zenia standing there she can't think of what to say. She's holding a skewer in her hand, with chunks of lamb and tomato and green pepper threaded onto it, and for an instant she has a vision of herself plunging the skewer into Zenia, into where her heart should be, but she doesn't do this. She just stands there with her mouth open, and Zenia smiles at her and says, "Tony darling, it was such work to track you down!" and laughs with her white teeth. She's thinner now, and even more sophisticated. She's wearing a black miniskirt, a black shawl with jet beading and long silken fringes, fishnet tights, and knee-high lace-up high-heeled boots.

"Come in," says Tony, motioning with her skewer. Lamb blood drips onto the floor.

"Who is it?" calls West from the living room, where he's playing Purcell on the spinet. He likes to play while Tony is making dinner: it's one of their little rituals.

Nobody, Tony wants to say. *They had the wrong address. They went away.* She wants to thrust her hands at Zenia, push her back, slam the door. But Zenia is already over the threshold.

"West! My God!" she says, striding into the living room, holding out her arms to him. "Long time no see!" West can't believe it. His eyes behind his rimless glasses are the shocked eyes of a burned baby, the amazed eyes of an interstellar traveller. He doesn't get up, he doesn't move. Zenia takes his upturned face in her two hands and kisses him twice, once on each cheek, and then a third time on the forehead. The fringes of her shawl caress him, his mouth is level with her chest. "It's so good to see old friends," says Zenia, breathing out.

Somehow or other she ends up staying for dinner, because who are Tony and West to hold grudges, and what is there to hold them about anyway? Wasn't it Zenia's defection that brought them together? And aren't they touchingly happy? Zenia tells them they are. They're just like a couple of kids, she says, kids on one long picnic, playing sand castles at the beach. So darling! She says she's delighted to see it. Then she sighs, implying that life has not treated her as well as it's been treating them. But then, she hasn't had their advantages. She's lived on the edges, out there where it's dark and sharp and there are scarcities. She's had to forage.

Where has she been? Well, Europe, she says, gesturing towards a higher, a deeper culture; and the States, where the big folks play; and the Middle East. (With a wave of her hand she invokes deserts, date palms, mystic knowledge, and better shish kebab than anything capable of being grilled in Tony's wee Canadian oven.) She avoids saying what she's been doing in these places. This and that, she says. She laughs, and says she has a short attention span.

About the money she made off with she tactfully says nothing, and Tony decides that it would be parochial of her to bring it up. Zenia does say, "Oh, there's your wonderful lute, I always loved it," as if she has no memory whatsoever of her own kidnapping of this instrument. West seems to have no memory of it either. At Zenia's request he plays a few of the old songs; though he doesn't do folksongs much any more, he says. By now he's into a cross-cultural study of polyphonal chants.

No memory, no memory. Does nobody but Tony have any memory at all? Apparently not; or rather West has no memory, and Zenia's is highly selective. She gives little nudges, little hints, and assumes a rueful expression: she has regrets, is what she implies, but she has sacrificed her own happiness for that of West. Hearth and home are what he needs, not a feckless, mossless rover like Zenia, and Tony is such a busy little housewife—isn't this cunning food! West is where he belongs: like a houseplant in the right window, just look how he's flourishing! "You two are so lucky," she whispers to Tony, a mournful catch in her voice. West overhears, as he is meant to.

"Where are you staying?" Tony asks politely, meaning, when are you leaving.

"Oh, you know," says Zenia with a shrug. "Here and

there. I live from hand to mouth—or from feast to famine. Just like the old days, remember, West? Remember our feasts?" She's eating a Viennese chocolate, from a box West brought home to surprise Tony. He often brings her little treats, little atonements for the part of himself he's unable to give her. Zenia licks the dark chocolate from her fingers, one by one, gazing at West from between her eyelashes. "Delicious," she says richly.

Tony can't believe that West doesn't see through all this, this blandishment and prestidigitation, but he doesn't. He has a blind spot: his blind spot is Zenia's unhappiness. Or else her body. Men, thinks Tony with new bitterness, can't seem to tell one from the other.

A few days after that, West comes home later than usual. "I took Zenia out for a beer," he tells Tony. He has the air of a man who is being scrupulously honest even though he's been tempted not to be. "She's having a rough time. She's a very vulnerable person. I'm quite worried about her."

Vulnerable? Where did West pick up that word? Tony thinks Zenia is about as vulnerable as a cement block, but she doesn't say so. Instead she says something almost as bad. "I suppose she wants some money."

West looks hurt. "Why don't you like her?" he asks. "You used to be such good friends. She's noticed, you know. She's upset about it."

"Because of what she did to *you*," says Tony indignantly. "That's why I don't like her!"

West is puzzled. "What did she do to me?" he asks. He really doesn't know.

• • • •

In no time at all—actually in about two weeks—Zenia has reclaimed West, in the same way she might reclaim any piece of property belonging to her, such as a suitcase left at a train station. She simply tucks West under her arm and walks off with him. It doesn't look like that to him, naturally; just to Tony. To West it looks as if he's on a rescue mission, and who is Tony to deny the attraction of that?

"I admire you a lot," he says to Tony. "You'll always be my best friend. But Zenia needs me."

"What does she need you for?" says Tony in a small clear voice.

"She's suicidal," says West. "You're the strong one, Tony. You've always been so strong."

"Zenia is as strong as an ox," says Tony.

"It's just an act," says West. "I always knew that about her. She's a deeply scarred person." *Deeply scarred,* thinks Tony. That can't be anyone's vocabulary but Zenia's. West has been hypnotized: it's Zenia talking, from the inside of his head. He goes on: "She's going to fall apart completely unless I do something."

Something means that West will move in with Zenia. This, according to West, will give Zenia back some of her lost confidence in herself. Tony wants to hoot with derisive laughter, but how can she? West is gazing at her earnestly, willing her to understand and to absolve him and to give him her blessing, just as if he were still in control of his own brain. But instead he's a zombie.

He's holding Tony's hands, at the kitchen table. She withdraws them and gets up and goes into her study, and shuts the door, and immerses herself in the Battle of Waterloo. After it was over the victorious soldiers celebrated, and drank all night, and roasted the flesh of the butchered cavalry horses on the metal breastplates of the dead, leaving the wounded to moan and scream in the background. Winning intoxicates you, and numbs you to the sufferings of others.

27

How well she did it, thinks Tony. How completely she took us in. In the war of the sexes, which is nothing like a real war but is instead a kind of confused scrimmage in which people change allegiances at a moment's notice, Zenia was a double agent. Or not even that, because Zenia wasn't working for one side or the other. She was on no side but her own. It's even possible that her antics—Tony is old enough, now, to think of them as *antics*—had no motive other than her own whim, her own Byzantine notions of pleasure. Maybe she lied and tortured just for the fun of it.

Though part of what Tony feels is admiration. Despite her disapproval, her dismay, all her past anguish, there's a part of her that has wanted to cheer Zenia on, even to encourage her. To make her into a saga. To participate in her daring, her contempt for almost everything, her rapacity and lawlessness. It's like the time her mother disappeared downhill on the toboggan. *No! No! On! On!*

But the recognition of that came later. At the time of West's defection she was devastated. (*Devastate,* verb, to lay waste, to render desolate; a familiar enough term in the literature of war, thinks Tony in the cellar, surveying her sand-table and the ruins of Otto's army, and eating another clove.) She refused to cry, she refused to howl. She listened to West's footsteps as he tiptoed around the apartment, as if in a hospital. When she heard the apartment door shut behind him she scuttled out and double-locked it, and put on the chain. Then she went into the bathroom and locked that door, too. She took off her wedding ring (simple, gold, no diamonds), intending to drop it down the toilet, but instead she placed it on a cabinet shelf, next to the disinfectant. Then she subsided onto the bathroom floor. American Standard, said the toilet. *Dradnats Nacirema*. A Bulgarian skin ointment.

After a while she came out of the bathroom because the phone was ringing. She stood there looking at it, it and its bridal silver telephone cover; it continued to ring. She lifted it, then dropped it down again. There was nobody she wanted to talk to. She wandered into the kitchen but there was nothing she wanted to eat.

Some hours later she found herself opening the box of old Christmas decorations where she also kept her father's German pistol, wrapped in red tissue paper. There were even some bullets for it, in a metal cough-drop tin. She'd never shot a gun in her life, but she knew the theory.

You need some sleep, she told herself. She could not stand the idea of sleeping in her desecrated bed, so she went to sleep finally in the living room, underneath the spinet. She had some thoughts of destroying it, with something—the meat cleaver?—but decided that could wait until morning.

When she woke up it was noon, and someone was pounding on the door. Probably it was West, come back because he'd forgotten something. (His underwear was gone from the drawer, his neatly arranged socks, washed by Tony and folded carefully in pairs. He'd taken a suitcase.)

Tony went to the door. "Go away," she said.

"Sweetie, it's me," said Roz on the other side. "Open the door, honey, I really need to go to the can, I'm about to flood this entire floor."

Tony didn't want to let Roz in because she didn't want to let anyone in, but she could not turn away a friend in urinary need. So she took off the chain and undid the locks and in waddled Roz, pregnant with her first baby. "This is just what I needed," she said ruefully, "a bigger body. Hey! I'm eating for five!" Tony didn't laugh. Roz looked at Tony's face, then put her fattening arms around Tony. "Oh honey," she said; then, with new-found knowledge, both personal and political, "Men are such pigs!"

Tony had a twinge of indignation. West was not a pig. He wasn't even shaped like one. An ostrich, perhaps. *It's not West's fault,* she wanted to say. *It's her. I loved him but he never really loved me. How could he? He was occupied territory, all along.* But she couldn't say anything about this, because she couldn't speak. Also she couldn't breathe. Or rather she could only breathe in. She breathed in and in and finally made a sound, a wail, a long wail that went on and on, like a distant siren. Then she burst into tears. *Burst,* like a paper bag full of water. She couldn't have burst like that if the tears hadn't been there all along, a huge unfelt pressure behind her eyes. The tears cascaded down her cheeks; she licked her lips, she tasted them. In the Middle Ages they thought that only those without souls could not cry. Therefore she had a soul. It was no comfort.

"He'll come back," said Roz. "I know he will. What does she need him for? She'll just take one bite out of him and throw him away." She rocked Tony back and forth, back and forth, the most mother that Tony had ever had.

Roz moved into Tony's apartment, just until Tony could function. She had a housekeeper, and her husband Mitch was away again, so she didn't need to be at her own house. She phoned the university and cancelled Tony's classes, saying that Tony had strep throat. She ordered in groceries, and fed Tony canned chicken noodle soup, caramel pudding, peanut butter and banana sandwiches, grape juice: baby food. She made her take a lot of baths and played soothing music to her, and told her jokes. She wanted to install Tony in her Rosedale mansion, but Tony didn't want to leave the apartment, even for a second. What if West should come back? She didn't know what would happen if he did, but she knew she needed to be there. She needed to have the choice of slamming the door in his face or falling into his arms. She didn't want to choose, though. She wanted to do both.

"He called you, didn't he?" said Tony after a few days of this, when she was feeling less gutted.

"Yeah," said Roz. "You know what he said? He said he was worried about you. That's kind of cute."

Tony didn't think it was cute. She thought it was Zenia, putting him up to it. Twisting the knife.

•　　•　　•

It was Roz who suggested Tony should give up the apartment and buy a house. "The prices are great right now! You've got the down payment—just cash in some of those bonds. Look—think of it as an investment. Anyway, you should move out of here. Who needs the bad memories, eh?" She got Tony a good real estate agent, drove around with her from house to house, clambered panting up and down the stairs, peering at furnaces and dry rot and wiring. "Now this—this is a deal," she whispered to Tony. "Ask low—see what they say! A few repairs and this could be gorgeous! Your study goes in the tower, just ditch the fake wood panelling, get rid of that linoleum—it's maple underneath, I looked. It's buried treasure, trust me! Once you're out of the old place, things will be tons better." She got a much bigger charge out of buying the house than Tony did. She found Tony a decent contractor, and dictated the paint colours. Even at the best of times Tony would have been incapable of making such arrangements herself.

After Tony moved in, things were indeed better. She liked the house, though not for any reasons that Roz would have approved. Roz wanted the house to be the centre of the new, outgoing life she envisaged for Tony, but for Tony it was more like a convent. A convent of one. She didn't belong in the land of the adults, the land of the giants. She shut herself up in her house like a nun, and went out only for supplies.

And for work, of course. Lots of work. She worked at school and also at home; she worked nights and weekends. She got pitying looks from her colleagues, because gossip travels through universities at the speed of influenza and they all knew about West, but she didn't care. She skipped regular meals and snacked on cheese food and crackers. She booked an answering service so she couldn't be disturbed while thinking. She did not answer the doorbell. It did not ring.

Tony in her turret room works late into the night. She wants to avoid bed, and sleep, and especially dreaming. She is having a dream, a recurring one; she has the feeling that this dream has been waiting for her a long time, waiting for her to enter it, re-enter it; or that it has been waiting to re-enter her.

This dream is underwater. In her waking life, she is no swimmer; she has never liked immersing herself, getting cold and wet. The most she'll trust herself to is a bathtub, and on the whole she prefers showers. But in the dream she swims effortlessly, in water as green as leaves, with sunlight filtering down through it, dappling the sand. No bubbles come out of her mouth; she is not conscious of breathing. Beneath her, coloured fish flit away, darting like birds.

Then she comes to an edge, a chasm. Like going down a hill she drops over it, slides diagonally through the increasing darkness. The sand falls away under her like snow. The fish here are larger and more dangerous, brighter—phosphorescent. They light up and dim, flash on and off like neon signs, their eyes and teeth glowing—a gas-flame blue, a sulphur yellow, a red the colour of embers. Suddenly she knows she isn't in the sea at all but miniaturized, inside her own brain. These are her neurons, the crackle of electricity touching them as she thinks about them. She looks at the incandescent fish with wonder: she is watching the electrochemical process of her own dreaming!

If so, then what is that, on the dim level white sand at the bottom? Not a ganglion. Someone walking away from her. She swims faster but it's no use, she's held in place, an aquarium goldfish bumping its nose against glass. *Reverof,* she hears. The backwards dream language. She opens her mouth to call, but there is no air to call with and water rushes in. She wakes up gasping and choking, her throat constricted, her face streaming with tears.

Now that she's started to cry it seems impossible to stop. In the daytime, in the lamplight, when she can work, she can keep this weeping locked away. But sleep is fatal. Fatal and unavoidable.

She takes off her glasses and rubs her eyes. From the street her room must look like a lighthouse, a beacon. Warm and cheerful and safe. But towers have other uses. She could empty boiling oil out the left-hand window, get a dead hit on anyone standing at the front door.

Such as West or Zenia, Zenia and West. She broods about them too much, them and their entangled bodies. Action would be better. She thinks about going over to their apartment (she knows where they're living, it wasn't hard to find out, West is listed in the university directory) and confronting Zenia. But what would she say? *Give him back?* Zenia would just laugh. "He's a free agent," she would say. "He's a grown-up, he can make his own choices." Or something like that. And if she were to turn up on Zenia's doorstep, to whine and beg and plead, wouldn't that be just what Zenia wanted?

She recalls a conversation she had with Zenia, early on, in the days when they were drinking coffee at Christie's and Zenia was such a friend.

"Which would you rather have?" said Zenia. "From other people. Love, respect, or fear?"

"Respect," said Tony. "No. Love."

"Not me," said Zenia. "I'd choose fear."

"Why?" said Tony.

"It works better," said Zenia. "It's the only thing that works."

Tony remembers having been impressed by this answer. But it wasn't fear through which Zenia had stolen West. Not a show of strength. On the contrary, it was a show of weakness. The ultimate weapon.

She could always take the gun.

For almost a year there was no word from West; no mention—for instance—of lawyers or divorce; not even any petitions about the spinet and the lute, which Tony was holding captive in her new living room. Tony knew why West was so wordless. It was because he felt too awful about what he'd done, or rather what had been done to him. He felt too ashamed.

After a while he began to leave timid messages with Tony's answering service, suggesting they get together for a beer. Tony did not reply, not because she was angry with him—she wouldn't have been angry with him if he'd been run over by a truck, and she viewed seduction by Zenia as analogous—but because she couldn't imagine what form any conversation between the two of them might take. *How are you* and *Fine* would about cover it. Thus when he finally turned up at her door, her new house door, the door of her nunnery, she simply stared at him.

"Let me in?" said West. Tony could tell at a glance that it was all finished between Zenia and West. She could tell from the colour of his skin, which was a light greenish grey, and from his sagging shoulders and dejected mouth. He'd been dismissed, sacked, ejected. He'd been kicked in the nuts.

He looked so pitiful, so pulled apart—as if he'd been on the rack, as if every one of his bones had been disconnected from every other bone, leaving only a kind of anatomical jelly—that of course she let him in. Into her home, into her kitchen, where she made him a hot drink, and ultimately into her bed, where he clutched her, shivering. It was not a sexual clutch, it was the clutch of a man drowning. But Tony was in no danger of being dragged down. She felt, if anything, strangely dry; strangely detached from him. He might be drowning, but this time she was standing on the beach. Worse: with binoculars.

She began again to cook small dinners, to boil breakfast eggs. She remembered how to care for him, how to pat him back into shape, and she did it again; but this time with fewer illusions. She still loved him, but she didn't believe he would ever love her in return, not to the same extent. How could he, after what he'd been through? Could a man with one leg tap-dance?

Nor could she trust him. He might crawl out of his depression, tell her how good she was, bring home treats for supper, go through the routines; but if Zenia were to return, from wherever she had gone—and even West didn't seem to know—then all of these fond habits would count for nothing. He was only on loan. Zenia was his addiction; one sip of her and he'd be gone. He'd be like a dog summoned by a supersonic whistle, inaudible to human ears. He would run off.

She never mentioned Zenia: to dwell on her might be to invoke her. But when Zenia died, when she was blown up and safely encapsulated and planted under a mulberry tree, Tony no longer needed to fear the doorbell. Zenia was no longer a menace, not in the flesh. She was a footnote. She was history.

Now Zenia is back, and hungry for blood. Not for West's blood: West is an instrument merely. The blood Zenia wants to drink is Tony's, because she hates Tony and always has. Tony could see that hatred in her eyes today, at the Toxique. There's no rational explanation for such hatred, but it doesn't surprise Tony. She seems to have been familiar with it for a long time. It's the rage of her unborn twin.

Or so thinks Tony, removing the vestiges of Otto the Red's fallen army with her tweezers, installing the Saracens in their freshly captured territory. The flag of Islam flies above the corpse-strewn Italian beaches, while Otto himself escapes by sea. His defeat will inspire the Slavic Wends to make another looting and pillaging foray into Germany; it will motivate uprisings, rebellions, a return to the old cannibal gods. Brutality, counter-brutality, chaos. Otto is losing his grip.

How could he have won this battle? Hard to say. By

avoiding recklessness? By drawing the enemy out first to estimate its strength? Strength and cunning are both essential, but each without the other is valueless.

Tony herself, lacking strength, will have to rely on cunning. In order to defeat Zenia she will have to become Zenia, at least enough to anticipate her next move. It would help if she knew what Zenia wanted.

Tony turns out the cellar lights and climbs the stairs to the kitchen, where she runs herself a glass of water out of the spring-water dispenser foisted on her by Charis. (As full of chemicals as anything else, she knows; but at least there's no chlorine. Eau de Swimming Pool, is what Roz calls the Toronto tap water.) Then she unlocks the back door and creeps out into the yard, into its flora of dry thistles and tree trunks and unpruned shrubs, its fauna of mice. Raccoons are regulars; squirrels make untidy nests in the branches. Once they had a skunk back here, hunting for grubs, rolling up what vestiges of turf remain; once a chipmunk, miraculous survivor of the neighbourhood gamut of cats.

It refreshes Tony to sneak around at night, from time to time. She enjoys being awake when others are asleep. She enjoys occupying dark space. Maybe she will see things other people can't see, witness nocturnal events, gain rare insights. She used to think that as a child, too—tiptoeing through the house, listening at doors. It didn't work then, either.

From this vantage point she has a novel view of her own house: the view of a lurking enemy commando. She thinks about how the house would look if she or anyone else were to blow it up. Study, bedroom, kitchen, and hall, suspended in fiery mid-air. Her house is no protection for her, really. Houses are too fragile.

The kitchen lights go on, the back door opens. It's West, a gangling silhouette, backlit, his face indistinct. "Tony?" he calls anxiously. "Are you out there?"

Tony savours his anxiety, just a little. True, she adores him, but there's no such thing as an unmixed motive. She waits for a moment, listening, in her moonlit weedy garden, blending—possibly—with the dappled silvery shadows cast by the trees. Is she invisible? The legs of West's pyjamas are too short, and so are the arms; they lend him an untended air, like that of a Frankenstein monster. Yet who could have tended him—over the years, and apart from finding some pyjamas that would fit—better than Tony? If she had done it unwillingly she might deserve to feel aggrieved. Is that how grievance works? *I've given you the best years of my life!* But for a gift you don't expect a return. And who would she have given them to otherwise, those years?

"I'm here," she says, and he comes outside and down the back porch steps. He has his slippers on, she's relieved to see, although not his dressing gown.

"You were gone," he says, stooping down towards her, peering. "I couldn't sleep."

"Neither could I," she says. "So I did some work, and then I came out for a breath of fresh air."

"I don't think you should wander around outside at night," he says. "It's not safe."

"This isn't wandering," she says, amused. "It's our backyard."

"Well, there might be muggers," he says.

She takes his arm. Under the thin cloth, under the flesh, within the arm itself, she can feel another arm forming: the arm of an old man. His eyes shine milky white in the moonlight. Blue eyes, she's read, are not the basic colour of human eyes; probably they grew from a mutation, and are therefore more prone to cataracts. She has a quick vision of West, ten years older and stone blind, herself leading him tenderly by the hand. Training the seeing-eye dog, arranging the library of books-on-tape, the collection of electronic noises. What would he do without her?

"Come inside," she says. "You'll catch cold."

"Is anything wrong?" he says.

"Not a thing," she lies pleasantly. "I'll make us some hot milk."

"Good," he says. "We can put some rum in it. Look at that moon! There's been men playing golf, up there."

He is so ordinary, so cherished, so familiar to her; like the smell of the skin on her own forearm, like the taste of her fingers. She would like to hang a sign on him, like the metal ones for liquor bottles or the plasticized ones at conventions: *Gnissapsert On*. She hugs him, standing on tiptoe, stretching her arms as far around him as they can go. They don't reach all the way.

How long can she protect him? How long before Zenia descends on them, with her bared incisors and outstretched talons and banshee hair, demanding what is rightfully hers?

Weasel Nights

28

Charis follows Zenia and the man who is not Billy along Queen Street, at a distance, dodging around her fellow pedestrians and occasionally bumping into them. She bumps into them because she feels that if she takes her eyes off Zenia, even for an instant, Zenia will vanish—not like a popped soap bubble, but like someone out of a TV kids' cartoon, turning into a bunch of dots and dashes and beaming herself off to some other locale. If you knew enough about matter you could walk through walls, and maybe Zenia does know enough; although any such knowledge must have been acquired by her in a sinister way. Something involving chicken blood, and the eating of still-alive animals. The collection of other people's toenails, pins driven in. Pain for someone.

Zenia must feel the stun-ray intensity of Charis's gaze burning into the small of her back, because at one point she turns around and looks, and Charis darts behind a lamppost, almost braining herself in the process. When she recovers from the bright red sensation in her head (*It's not a hurt, it's a colour*) and dares to peek, Zenia and the man have stopped and are talking.

Charis wends her way a little closer, leaving a trail of hostile glances and muttered comments on the sidewalk behind her and smiling weakly at those who, with frayed cuffs and hands held out and the swollen, sunken faces of those who eat too much refined sugar, ask her for the price of a meal. Charis doesn't have any small change, having left it as a tip at Kafay Nwar; she doesn't have very much money, period, although more than she thought she'd have after lunch, because it was Roz who figured out the bill and her accounting procedures always end up with Charis paying less, she suspects, than she ought to. Anyway, Charis doesn't believe in giving money to panhandlers, being of the opinion that money, like candy, is bad for people. But she would give them some of her home-grown carrots, if she could.

She makes her way to a good vantage point behind a hot dog vendor stand with a bright yellow umbrella, and lurks there, despite the offensive smell (pigs' innards!) and the sinful cans of pop (chemicals!) lined up beside the mustard and relish (pure salt!). The vendor asks her what she'd like today, but she hardly hears him; she's too engrossed in Zenia. Now the man with Zenia turns and his face is towards Charis, and with a jolt like putting her hand on a hotplate Charis recognizes him: he's Roz's son Larry.

It's always a jump in time for Charis to see Roz's children grown up, although of course they have grown up and she herself has watched them do it. But their aging is hard to believe. It's like the times Augusta is in the next room and Charis walks in, expecting to see her cross-legged on the floor playing house with her Barbie doll—Charis hadn't approved of that thing, but was too weak to forbid it—and instead finds her sitting in a chair in a wide-shouldered suit and sling-back high heels, painting her nails. *Oh August!* she wants to say. *Where did you get those weird dress-up clothes?* But those are her real clothes. It is a true head-bender to see your own daughter walking around in clothes that might have belonged to your mother.

There is Larry, then, in jeans and a fawn suede jacket, his taffy-haired head inclined towards Zenia, one of his hands on her arm. Little Larry! Serious little Larry, who would purse his mouth and frown at the very same time his twin sisters were laughing and pinching each other's arms and telling each other they had big snots coming out of their noses. Charis has never been altogether comfortable about Larry, or rather about his rigidity. She's always felt that a good massage therapist could do wonders. But Larry must have loosened up considerably if he's been having lunch at the Toxique.

But what is he doing with Zenia? What is he doing with Zenia right now? He's bending his face down, Zenia's own face is reaching up like a tentacle, they're kissing! Or so it appears.

"Listen lady, you want a hot dog or not?" says the vendor.

"What?" says Charis, startled.

"Crazy broad, shove off," says the vendor. "Get back in the bin. You're bothering the customers."

If Charis were Roz, she'd say, *What customers?* But if Charis were Roz she'd be in a state of deep shock. *Zenia and Larry! But she's twice his age!* thinks the vestige of Charis that remains from the time when age, in female-male relationships, was supposed to matter. The present Charis tells herself not to be judgmental. Why shouldn't women do what men have been doing for ages, namely robbing the cradle? Age is not the point. The point is not Zenia's age, but Zenia herself. Larry might as well be drinking liquid drain cleaner.

While Charis is having this uncharitable thought, Zenia steps sideways, off the curb, and disappears into a taxi. Larry gets in after her—so it was not a goodbye kiss—and the taxi is sucked out into the current of traffic. Charis dithers. What should she do now? Her urge is to phone Roz—*Roz! Roz! Help! Come quickly!*—but that would do no good, because she doesn't know where Zenia and Larry are going; and even if she did, so what? What would Roz do? Burst into their hotel room or whatever, and say *Let go of my son?* Larry is twenty-two, he is an adult. He can make his own decisions.

Charis sees another taxi and runs out into the street, flailing her arms. The taxi squeals to a stop in front of her and she hurries around, opens the door, and scrambles in. "Thank you," she gasps.

"You lucky you not dead," says the driver, who has an accent Charis can't identify. "So, what can I do for you?"

"Follow that taxi," says Charis.

"What taxi?" says the driver.

So that is that, and worse, Charis feels honour-bound to pay him three dollars, because she did after all get into his cab, but she only has a five-dollar bill and a ten, and he doesn't have change, and she doesn't want to ask the hot dog vendor, considering what he just called her, so it ends with him saying, "Time is money, lady, do me a favour, for-get it," and there are bad feelings all round.

Luckily they are digging up Queen Street, yet again, and Zenia's taxi is caught in the jam. After running down the street some more Charis manages to find another empty taxi, only two cars away from Zenia's, and she flings herself into it, and together the two taxis ooze slowly through the downtown core. Zenia and Larry get out at the Arnold Garden Hotel, and so does Charis. She watches the uniformed doorman nod to them, she watches Larry put his hand on Zenia's elbow, she watches them go through the brass-and-glass doors. She herself has never been through those doors. Anything with an awning intimidates her.

As she's trying to decide what to do next, a bicycle courier starts swearing at her for no reason at all. *Jesus lady, watch the fuck out!* It's an omen: she's done enough for today.

She walks down to the ferry dock, buffeted as if by wind. Being in the city is so abrasive; it's like dust blowing into your face, it's like dancing on sandpaper. Although she's not sure why, she minds being called *lady* even more than she minds being called *crazy broad*. Why is this word so offensive to her? (*Listen*, says Shanita's voice, with amused contempt. *If that's all you ever get called!*)

She's feeling baffled and inept, and slightly frightened. What is she supposed to do with what she knows? What is she supposed to do next? She listens, but her body tells her nothing, even though it was her body that got her into this, with its mischievous yen for caffeine, its adrenalin rushes, its megalomania. Some days—and this is becoming one of them—having a body is an inconvenience.

Although she treats her body with interest and consideration, paying attention to its whims, rubbing lotions and
oils into it, feeding it with selected nutrients, it doesn't
always repay her. Right now her back—for instance—
hurts, and there's a cold dark pool, an ominous pool, a
pool of browny-green septic acid, forming somewhere
below her navel. The body may be the home of the soul
and the pathway of the spirit, but it is also the perversity,
the stubborn resistance, the malign contagion of the material world. Having a body, being in the body, is like being
roped to a sick cat.

She stands on the ferry, leaning on the railing, facing
backwards, watching the wake rise and subside into the
notoriously poisonous lake, tracing and obliterating itself
in the same gesture. Light glitters on the water, no longer
white but yellowing; it's afternoon and there goes the sun,
there goes this day, down to where all the other days have
gone, each one carrying something away with it. She will
never get any of those days back, including the ones she
should have had but didn't, days with Billy in them. It was
Zenia who made off with those days. She took them away
from Charis, who now doesn't even have them to look
fondly back on. It's as if Zenia has crept into her house
when she wasn't there and torn the photos out of her
photo album, the photo album she doesn't possess except
inside her head. In one single snatch and grab, Zenia stole
both her future and her past. Couldn't she have left it a little longer? Just a month, just a week, just a little more?

In the spiritual world (which she has now entered,
because the ferry, with its soporific motor and gentle sway,
often has this effect on her), Charis's astral body falls to its

knees, raising imploring hands to the astral body of Zenia, which burns red, a red crown of flames like spiky leaves or old-fashioned pen nibs flaring around her head, with emptiness at the centre of each flame. *More time, more time,* Charis pleads. *Give back what you took!*

But Zenia turns away.

29

The history of Charis and Zenia began on a Wednesday in the first week of November in the first year of the seventies. *Seventy.* Charis finds both parts of this number significant, the seven and the zero as well. A zero always means the beginning of something and the end as well, because it is omega: a circular self-contained O, the entrance to a tunnel or the exit from one, an end that is also a beginning, because although that year saw the beginning of the end of Billy, it was also the year her daughter August began to begin. And seven is a prime number, composed of a four and a three—or two threes and a one, which Charis prefers because threes are graceful pyramids as well as Goddess numbers, and fours are merely box-like squares.

She knows it was a Wednesday, because Wednesdays were the days she went into town to earn some money by teaching two yoga classes. She did that on Fridays, too, except that on Fridays she also stayed late to put in her share of volunteer time at the Furrows Food Co-op. She knows it was November, because November is the eleventh month, the month of the dead, and also of regeneration. Sun sign Scorpio, governed by Mars, colour deep red. Sex, death, and war. Synchronicity.

• • •

The day begins as mist. Charis sees the mist as she gets out of bed, or rather off the bed, because the bed is a mattress on the floor. She goes to the window to look out. There's a miniature transparent rainbow stuck onto the glass, though Charis did not stick it there: it was left over from the previous tenants, a batch of burned-out hippies who also drew pictures in Magic Marker on the flowered, faded wallpaper—naked people copulating and cats with halos—and played the Doors and Janis Joplin at top volume in the middle of the night, and left mounds of human shit in the backyard. They were finally kicked out by the landlord with the help of the next-door neighbours after a screaming acid party, during which one of them set fire to a black plastic beanbag chair in the living room under the impression that it was a carnivorous puffball. The landlord—an old man who lives at the other end of the street—welcomed Charis and Billy, because there were only two of them and they did not have a big speaker system, and because Charis said she intended to plant a vegetable garden, which indicated some sort of decorous coupledom; and the neighbours were so grateful for the change that they didn't even make a fuss about the chickens, chickens that may or may not be illegal, but this is the Island and strict legality is not the norm here, witness the number of house additions that go up without a permit. Luckily they have a corner lot, so there are neighbours on only one side.

Charis painted over the naked people and cats and dug the human shit into her compost heap, telling herself that it was the right thing to do because the Chinese used it, in China, and everyone knew they were the world's best organic gardeners. Shit to food to shit, it was all part of the cycle.

They moved into this house in late spring, and from the very first Charis knew it was right. She loves the house and, even more, she loves the Island. It's infused with a vibrant, brooding, humid life; it makes her feel that everything—even the water, even the stones—is alive and aware, and her along with it. Some mornings she goes out before daybreak and just walks around, up and down the streets that are not real streets but more like paved bicycle paths, past the dilapidated or spruced-up former cottages with their woodpiles and hammocks and patchy gardens; or else she just lies on the grass, even when damp. Billy likes the Island too, or so he says, but not the same way she does.

The mist is rising from the ground and from the bushes, dripping from the old apple tree at the back of the yard. There are still a few brownish frostbitten apples, hanging from the twisted branches like burnt Christmas decorations. The fallen apples Charis was unable to use for jelly lie rotting and fermented at the base of the tree. Several of the chickens have been pecking at them; Charis can tell by the way those chickens stagger around, so drunk they have difficulty walking up the ramp into their chicken house. Billy thinks those drunken hens are cool.

The wide painted floorboards are cold under her bare feet; she hugs her goose-pimpled arms, shivering a little. She can't see the lake from here: the mist blots it out. She makes an effort to find the mist beautiful—everything made by nature should be beautiful—but succeeds only partly. The mist is beautiful, true, it's like solid light, but it's also ominous: when there's mist you can't see what's coming.

She leaves Billy sleeping on their mattress, under their opened-out sleeping bag, and puts on her embroidered Indian slippers, and pulls one of Billy's sweatshirts over her cotton nightgown. The nightgown is Victorian-style, second-hand; she bought it at a used-clothing place in Kensington Market. It would be cheaper to make such nightgowns, and she's bought a pattern and enough material for two, but there's something wrong with her sewing machine—a treadle model she traded some yoga lessons for—so she hasn't cut either of them out yet. The next thing she intends to trade for is a loom.

She tiptoes from the bedroom and along the narrow hallway, and down the stairs. When she moved in here with Billy, six months ago, there were several layers of worn linoleum covering the floorboards. Charis stripped off the linoleum and pulled out the nails that were holding it in place, and scraped away the black tarry goo that had oozed from it, and painted the hall floor blue. But she ran out of paint halfway down the stairs, and she hasn't got more paint yet, and the bottom stairs still have the outlines of the old linoleum stair treads. She doesn't mind them, the traces; they are like signals made by those who lived here long before. So she's left them alone. It's like leaving a wild patch in the garden. She knows she is sharing the space with other entities, even if they can't be seen or heard, and it's just as well to show them you're friendly. Or respectful. Respectful is what she means, because she does not intend to get too cosy with them. She wants them to respect her, as well.

She goes into the kitchen, which is freezing cold. There's a kind of furnace in the house, beside the water heater, in the dank, dirt-floored lean-to—the root cellar, Charis calls it, and she is indeed keeping some roots in it, some carrots and beets buried in a box of sand, the way her grandmother used to—but the furnace doesn't work very well. Mostly it blows lukewarm air through a series of grids in the floor, and makes dustballs; anyway, it seems like a waste of money and also like cheating to turn on the furnace before it's absolutely necessary. You should make use of what is naturally provided, if possible, so Charis has been scavenging dead wood from under the trees on the Island and using the ends of boards left over from building the henhouse, and breaking the odd dead branch off her apple tree.

She kneels before the cast-iron cookstove—it was one of the things that made her want this house, the wood stove—though it turned other people off, people who wanted electric stoves, so the rent was low. Figuring out how to work it was hard at first; it has its moods, and sometimes makes large clouds of smoke, or goes out completely even though it's packed with wood. You have to cajole it. She scrapes out yesterday's ashes, into a saucepan she keeps handy—she'll sprinkle some into the compost heap later, and sift the rest for a potter she knows, to make into glazes—and stuffs some crumpled newspaper and kindling and two thin logs into the firebox. When the fire has caught she crouches before the open stove door, warming her hands and appreciating the flames. The apple wood burns blue.

After a few minutes she gets up, feeling a stiffness in her knees, and goes over to the counter and plugs in the electric kettle. Although there's no electric stove the house has some basic wiring, a ceiling fixture in every room and a few wall sockets, though you can't plug in the kettle and anything else at the same time without blowing the fuses. She could wait for the iron kettle on the wood stove to boil, but that might take hours, and she needs her morning herbal tea right now. She remembers a time when she used to drink coffee, at university, a long time ago, in one of her other lives, when she lived in McClung Hall. She remembers the fuzzy feeling in her head, and the hankering for more. It was an addiction, she supposes. The body is so easily led astray. At least she never smoked.

Sitting at the kitchen table—not the round oak table she would like to have, but an interim table, an artificial table, an immoral table from the fifties, with chrome legs and black curlicues baked into its Formica top—Charis drinks her herbal tea and attempts to focus on the day ahead. The mist makes it more difficult: it's hard for her to tell the time, despite her wristwatch, when she can't see the sun.

The most immediate decision to make is: who will have breakfast first, herself or the chickens? If she does, the chickens will have to wait and then she will feel guilty. If the chickens do, she will be hungry for a while, but she will have her own breakfast to look forward to while she is feeding them. Also the chickens trust her. They are probably wondering where she is, right this minute. They are worrying. They are reproachful. How can she let them down?

Every morning she goes through this minor tug-of-war, in her head. Every morning the chickens win. She finishes her tea and fills a pail at the sink, then goes to the kitchen door where Billy's work overalls are hanging on a wall hook. She pulls them on, stuffing her nightgown down the legs—she could go upstairs and get dressed, but it might wake Billy, who needs his sleep because of the strain he's under—and kicks off her slippers and slides her bare feet into Billy's rubber boots. This is not the most attractive feeling: the rubber is chilly, and damp with old foot sweat. Sometimes there are wool work socks to put inside the boots, but these seem to have wandered off somewhere; and even with the socks these boots would be cold, and way too big for her. She might get some boots of her own, but this would violate the accepted version of reality, which is that Billy feeds the chickens. She picks up the water pail and waddles out into the yard.

The mist is less threatening when you're actually in it. It gives Charis the illusion of being able to walk through a solid barrier. Dripping grasses brush her legs; the air smells of leaf mould and damp wood, and of wet cabbages, from the half-dozen of them still in the garden. It's the autumnal smell of slow combustion. Charis breathes it in, breathing in also the ammonia and hot-feather scent of her chickens. Inside the henhouse they're making the sleepy crooning cooing sounds that show they are at ease, a sort of broody, meditative humming. Now they hear her, and change to excited cackles.

She unlatches the wire gate that leads to their enclosure. Charis's first idea had been to let the chickens range free, totally fenceless, but there turned out to be a cat and dog problem; and also the neighbours, although tolerant of the chickens in general, didn't much appreciate having stray ones in their own yards, scratching up their flower beds. The chickens don't like the fence and try to get out, so Charis always closes the gate behind her before opening the henhouse door.

Billy built the henhouse himself, working with his shirt off and the sun on his back, whacking the nails in. It was good for him, it gave him a sense of accomplishment. The house tilts a little but it does its job. It has one door for the hens, a small square one with a ramp going down, and another for the humans. Charis opens the chickens' door and they crowd and strut and cluck down their ramp, blinking in the light. Then she goes in by the human door, opens the metal garbage can where the chicken feed is kept, and scoops up a coffee tin of feed, which she takes outside and scatters on the ground. She prefers to feed the chickens outside. The book says you should let the straw litter and the chicken droppings build up on the henhouse floor because the heat of decomposition will keep the chickens warm in winter, but Charis does not think that food eaten under such circumstances can possibly be healthy. The cycle of nature is one thing, but you shouldn't confuse the different parts of it.

The chickens cluck hyperactively, mobbing her legs, making small fluttering hops, jostling and pecking one another, giving out yelps of anger. When they have settled down and are feeding she carries their water container outside too and tops it up from the pail.

Charis watches the chickens eat. They fill her with joy, a joy that has no rational source, because she knows—she has seen, also she remembers—how greedy chickens are, how selfish and unfeeling, how cruel they are to one another, how they gang up: at least two of them have naked scalps, from being picked on. Nor are they placid vegetarians: you can start a riot among them just by toss-ing them a few hot-dog ends or scraps of bacon. As for the rooster, with his eye of an insane prophet and his fanatic's air of outrage and his comb and wattles flaunted like gen-itals, he's an overbearing autocrat, and attacks her rubber boots when he thinks she's not looking.

Charis doesn't care; she excuses the chickens every-thing. She adores them! She has adored them ever since the moment they arrived, flowering out of the feed sacks in which they travelled, shaking their angels' feathers. She thinks they are miraculous. They are.

Inside the henhouse, she rummages through the straw in the boxes, hoping for eggs. In June the hens were bursting with eggs, laying two a day, huge milky ovals with double and triple yolks, but now, with the declining angle of the sun, they've fallen off badly. Their feathers and wat-tles are duller; several of them are moulting. She does manage to find one egg, an undersized one with a pebbly shell. She slips it into the breast pocket of her overalls; she will feed it to Billy for his breakfast.

Back in the kitchen she takes off her boots; she leaves the overalls on, because she's cold. She slides another stick of wood into the stove, warming her hands. Should she have her own breakfast first, or wait and have it while Billy has his? Should she wake him at all? Sometimes he's mad if she does, other times he's mad if she doesn't. But today is a city day for her, so if she wakes him up now she can get him fed before she catches the ferry. That way he won't spend the morning asleep, and blame her later.

• • •

She climbs the stairs and walks gently along the hall; when she gets to the doorway she stands for a moment, just looking. She likes looking at Billy in the same way that she likes looking at the hens. Billy too is beautiful; and just as the hens are the essence of hen-ness, Billy is the essence of Billy-ness. (Like the hens, too, he is a little frowsier now than when she first encountered him. This also may have something to do with the angle of the sun.)

He lies on their mattress, the sleeping bag pulled up to his neck. His left arm is flung across his eyes; the tan on it is fading, although it's still dark, this arm, and pelted with short golden hairs, like a honeybee covered with pollen. His short yellow beard shines in the white room, in the strange light from the mist outside—heraldic, the beard of a saint, or of a knight in an old picture. Or like something on a stamp. Charis loves to watch Billy at such moments, when he's quiet and still. It's easier to maintain her view of him that way than when he's talking and moving around.

Billy must sense her flashlight gaze on him. His arm moves away from his eyes, the eyes themselves open, such blue! Like forget-me-nots, like mountains in the distance, on postcards, like thick ice. He smiles at her, uncovering Viking teeth.

"What time is it?" he says.

"I don't know," says Charis.

"You've got a watch, don't you?" he says. *Don'tcha.* How can she explain about the mist? Also that she can't take the time to look at her watch, because she's looking at him? Looking is not a casual thing. It takes all her attention.

He gives a small sigh, of exasperation or desire, it's so hard to tell the difference. "Come here," he says.

It must be desire. Charis goes to the mattress, sits down beside Billy, smooths back the hair on his forehead, hair so yellow it looks painted. It's still amazing to her that the colour doesn't come off on her skin. Although her own hair is blonde as well, it's a different blonde, pale and bleached-out, moon to his sun. Billy's hair glows from within.

"I said *here*," says Billy. He pulls her down on top of him, zeroes in on her mouth, encircles her in his golden arms, squeezes her tight.

"The egg!" says Charis breathlessly, remembering it. The egg breaks.

30

That's what Billy was like, at the time. He was always after her then. In the mornings, in the afternoons, at night, it made no difference. Maybe it was just a sort of nervousness, or boredom, because he didn't have that much to fill up the time; or it might have been the tension of being there illegally. He would wait for her at the ferry dock and walk back to the house with her and grab her before she even had a chance to put the groceries down, pressing her back against the kitchen counter, his hands pulling up her long flimsy skirt. His urgency confused her. *God I love you, God I love you,* he would say at these times. Sometimes he did things that hurt—slapping her, pinching. Sometimes it hurt anyway, but since she didn't mention this, how was he supposed to know about it?

What had she felt, herself? It's hard to sort out. Maybe if there had been less, less plain old sex—if she had felt less like a trampoline with someone jumping up and down on it—she would have learned to enjoy it more, in time. If she could relax. As it was she merely detached herself, floated her spirit off to one side, filled herself with another essence—*apple, plum*—until he'd finished and it was safe to re-enter her body. She liked being held afterwards, she liked being stroked and kissed and told she was beautiful, a thing Billy sometimes did. Once in a while she cried, which Billy seemed to find normal. Her tears had nothing to do with Billy; he didn't make her sad, he made her happy! She told him that, and he was satisfied and didn't push her for answers. They talked about other things; they never talked about that.

But what was it supposed to be like? What would have been normal? She had no idea. Every so often they smoked dope—not a lot, because they couldn't afford much of it, and when they had some it usually came from one of Billy's friends—and at those times she got an inkling, an intimation, a small flutter. But it hardly count-ed, because her skin felt like rubber then anyway, like a rubber suit she had on with a grid of tiny electric wires running through it, and Billy's hands were like inflated comic-book gloves, and she would get involved with the convolutions of his ear or the whorl of golden hairs on his chest, and whatever her body was up to was no concern of hers. One of Billy's friends said that there was no sense in wasting good hash on Charis because she was stoned all the time anyway. Charis didn't think that was fair, although it was true that being stoned didn't make as much differ-ence for her as it seemed to make for other people.

Billy wasn't the first man she'd slept with, of course. She'd slept with several, because you were supposed to and she didn't want to be considered uptight, or selfish about her body, and she'd even lived with one man, although it hadn't lasted. He'd ended by calling her a frigid bitch, as if she was doing him some injury or other, which puzzled her. Hadn't she been affectionate enough, hadn't she nodded her head when he talked, hadn't she cooked the meals and laid herself down compliantly whenever he wanted her to, hadn't she washed the sheets afterwards, hadn't she tended him? She was not an ungiving person.

The good part about Billy was that this thing about her, this abnormality—she knew it must be one, because she'd listened to other women talking—didn't bother him. In fact he appeared to expect it. He thought women were like that: without urges, without needs. He didn't pester her about it, he didn't question her, he didn't try to fix her, as the other men had done—tinkering away at her as if she was a lawnmower. He loved her the way she was. Without anything being said, he simply assumed, as she did, that what she felt about it didn't matter. Both of them were agreed on that. They both wanted the same thing: for Billy to be happy.

Charis lies under the sleeping bag, propped on one elbow, touching lightly the face of Billy, who has his eyes closed and may be on his way back to sleep. Maybe one of these days she will have a baby, Billy's baby; it will look like him. She's thought about it before—how it would just happen, without any decision or plan, and how he would stay with her then, stay on and on, and they could keep living here, like this, forever. There's even a small room in the house where she could put the baby. At the moment it's full of stuff—some of it is Billy's, but most of it is Charis's, because despite her wish not to be pinned down by possessions she has a number of cardboard boxes full of them. But that could all be cleared out and she could put a little cradle in there, with rockers on it, or a rush laundry basket. Not a crib, though; nothing with bars.

She runs her fingers over Billy's forehead, his nose,

his gently smiling mouth; he doesn't know it, but this touching she does is not only tender, not only compassionate, but possessive. Although he is not a prisoner, he is in a way a prisoner of war. It's war that has brought him here, war that keeps him in hiding, war that makes him stay put. She can't help thinking of him as a captive; her captive, because his very existence here depends on her. He is hers, to do with as she will, as much hers as if he were a traveller from another planet, trapped on Earth in this dome of artificial interplanetary air that is her house. If she were to ask him to leave, what would happen to him? He'd be caught, deported, sent back, to where the air is heavier. He would implode.

He might as well be from another planet, because he's from the United States; not only that, but from some dim and esoteric part of it, as mysterious to Charis as the dark side of the moon. Kentucky? Maryland? Virginia? He's lived in all three places, but what do those words mean? Nothing to Charis, except that they verge on the South, a word also lacking in solid content. Charis has a few images connected with it—mansions, wisteria, and, once upon a time, segregation—she has seen movies, back in her other life, before she was Charis—but Billy does not seem to have lived in a mansion or to have segregated anybody. On the contrary, his father was almost run out of town (which town?) for being what Billy calls a "liberal," which is not at all the same thing as the solid, the orthodox, the bland-faced and interchangeable Liberals that appear on Toronto election posters with such stultifying monotony.

The United States is just across the lake, of course, and on clear days you can almost see it—a sort of line, a sort of haze. Charis has even been there, on a high-school day trip to Niagara Falls, but that part of it looked disappointingly similar; not like the part Billy comes from, which must be very strange. Strange, and more dangerous—that much is clear—and maybe because of that, superior. The things that happen there are said to matter in the world. Unlike the things that happen here.

So Charis runs her fingers over Billy, gloating a little, because here he is, in her bed, in her hands, her very own mythological creature, odd as unicorns, her very own captive draft dodger, part of a thousand headline stories, part of history, tucked away in secret in her house, the house for which she alone has had to sign the rental lease because nobody must know Billy's name or where he is. Some of the draft dodgers have visas, but others—such as Billy—don't, and once you're inside this country you can't get a visa, you'd have to go back across the border and apply from there, and then you'd be nabbed for sure.

Billy has explained all this; also that the Mounties are not really the Mounties of Charis's childhood, not the picturesque men on horseback, in red uniforms, upright and true, who always get their man. Instead they are devious and cunning and in cahoots with the U.S. government, and if they put their finger on Billy he's a dead duck, because—and she must never tell this to anyone, even his friends here don't know about it—dodging the draft wasn't the only thing he did. What else? He blew things up. A couple of people too, but they were an accident. That's why the Mounties are after him.

If he's lucky they'll go through the extradition process, and he might have a chance. If unlucky they'll just tip off the CIA and Billy will be kidnapped, some dark night, and whisked back across the border, maybe across the lake in a speedboat, the way the Canadians smuggled liquor during Prohibition, he's heard of guys they've done that to—he'll be spirited away and thrown into jail and that will be the end of him. Someone will cut his throat, in the shower, for being a draft dodger. That's what happens.

When he says things like this he holds onto Charis very tightly, and she puts her arms around him and says, "I won't let them," although she knows she has no power to prevent such a thing. But just saying this has a soothing effect, on both of them. She doesn't quite believe it anyway, this doom-laden scenario of Billy's. Things like that might happen in the United States—anything can happen there, where the riot police shoot people and the crime rate is so high—but not here. Not on the Island, where there are so many trees and people don't lock the door when they go out. Not in this country, familiar to her and drab, undramatic and flat. Not in her house, with the hens cooing peacefully in the yard. No harm can come to her, or to Billy either, with the hens watching over them, feathery guardian spirits. The hens are good luck.

So she says, "I'll keep you here with me," even though she knows that Billy is an unwilling voyager. She suspects something worse, as well: that she herself is just a sort of way station for him, a temporary convenience, like the native brides of soldiers who are posted abroad. Although he doesn't know it yet, she isn't his real life. But he is hers.

This is painful.

"Well," says Charis, sliding her mind quickly away, because pain is an illusion and should be circumvented, "how about some breakfast?"

"You're beautiful," says Billy. "Bacon, huh? We got any coffee?" Billy drinks real coffee, with caffeine in it. He makes fun of Charis's herbal teas and won't eat salad, not even the lettuce Charis grows herself. "Rabbit food," he calls it. "Fit for nothing but little bunnies, and women." *Li'l.*

"There would have been an egg," says Charis reproachfully, and Billy laughs. (The overalls with their breast pocket full of squished egg are of course no longer on Charis but on the floor. She will wash them, later. She will avoid hot water or the egg will scramble. She will have to turn the pocket inside out.)

"Can't make an omelette without breaking a few eggs," he says. *Cain't.* Charis turns the sound over, silently in her mouth, tasting it. Cherishing, storing away. She would like his name to be Billy Joe or Billy Bob, one of those double-barrelled Southern names, as in films. She hugs him.

"Billy, you are so . . ." she says. She wants to say *young,* because he is young, he's seven years younger than she is; but he doesn't like being reminded of it, he'd think she's pulling rank. Or she could say *innocent,* which he'd find even more of an insult: he'd think it was a comment on his sexual inexperience.

What she means is pristine. What she means is his unscratched surface. Despite the suffering he's gone through and is still going through, there's something shiny about him, shiny and new. Or else impermeable. She herself is so penetrable; sharp edges stick into her, she bruises easily, her inner skin is puffy and soft, like marshmallows. She's covered all over with tiny feelers like the feelers on ants: they wave, they test the air, they touch and recoil, they warn her. Billy has no such feelers. He doesn't need them. Whatever slams into him bounces right off— either he dismisses it, or instead of hurting him it makes him angry. It's a kind of hardness, which exists quite apart from any sadness or melancholy or even guilt that he may be experiencing at the time.

Maybe it's this: his own sadness and melancholy and guilt are his, and therefore important to him, but they're contained inside. Those of other people don't get in. Whereas Charis is a screen door, an open one at that, and everything blows right through.

"I'm so what?" says Billy, grinning. *Ah'm*. Charis smiles back at him.

"So . . . well, you know," she says.

Charis did not exactly meet Billy. Instead he was allotted to her, at the Furrows Food Co-op, where she knew a good many people although not well. It was a woman called Bernice who got her into it. Bernice was Peace Movement and in some church or other, and they were parcelling out the draft dodgers they had collected, sticking them here and there in people's houses, like the English children who were shipped across the ocean during the Second World War. Charis just happened to be at the co-op that day, and Bernice more or less raffled off the draft dodgers, and Billy was left over, him and another boy (Bernice called them "boys"), so Charis said she would put them up for a few nights, in her sublet Queen Street warehouse room, one on the broken-springed Goodwill sofa she had then and one on the floor, just until they could find some other place, if Bernice would supply the sleeping bags because Charis didn't have any extras.

Charis did not do this for political reasons: she didn't believe in politics, in getting involved in an activity that caused you to have such negative emotions. She didn't approve of wars, or of thinking about them. So she didn't understand the Vietnam War or want to understand it— although some of it had seeped into her head, despite her precautions, because it was in the air molecules—and above all she didn't watch it on TV. She didn't even have a TV, and she did not read newspapers because they were too upsetting and anyway there was nothing she could do about all that misery. So her reason for taking Billy in had nothing to do with any of that. Instead she did it out of a sense of hospitality. She felt an obligation to be kind to strangers, especially strangers who were down on their luck. Also it would have been too weird to have been the only person at the co-op who refused to take anyone in.

So that was how it started. After a few days the other boy moved out and Billy stayed; and then after a few more days she realized she was expected to go to bed with him. He didn't push it; in that early time he was diffident and shy, disoriented, uncertain of himself. He'd thought it was going to be more or less the same on this side of the border as on the other side, only safer, and when it turned out that it wasn't either one of those things he was confused and upset. He realized he'd done something monumental, something he couldn't reverse; that he'd landed himself in exile, perhaps forever. He'd made life hard for his family—they'd supported his decision about the draft but not about the other stuff, the explosives, and they were getting what he called "a lot of flak." Also he'd deserted his country, a notion that has a good deal more meaning for him than it does for Charis, because in Billy's schools they started the day with their hands over their hearts, saluting their flag, instead of praying to God as they did at Charis's schools. For Billy his country *was* a kind of God, an idea that Charis finds idolatrous and even barbaric. She finds the standard God with his white beard and anger and lamb sacrifices and death angels barbaric too, of course. She has gone beyond all that. Her God is oval.

Also Billy worried about his friends back there, back home, guys he'd gone to school with, who hadn't escaped with him and were probably, even now, on their way across the sea or being shot at in rice paddies or blown up by guerrillas as they walked along some hot mud road. He felt he'd betrayed them. He knew the war was wrong and that what he'd done was right, but he felt like a coward anyway. He was homesick. A lot of the time he wanted to go back.

This was how he talked to Charis, in fits and starts, in bits and pieces. He said he didn't expect her to understand, but she did understand some of it. She understood his emotions, which came at her in a deluge—watery, chaotic, a melancholy blue in colour, like a great wave of tears. He was so lost, so wounded, how could she refuse to offer him whatever comfort she had?

31

Things have changed since then. Since they moved to the Island, and into this house. Billy is still nervous, but less so. He seems more rooted. Also he has friends now, a whole network of exiles like himself. They even have meetings, on the mainland; Billy goes over there a couple of times a week. They help out the new arrivals, they pass them around and hide them out, and Charis has had to put up more than one of them, briefly, on the living-room sofa—a different sofa now, still second-hand but with better springs. Living with someone, Charis has discovered, leads to real furniture, although having real furniture was one of the things she renounced years ago.

Occasionally the exiles forgather at her house to drink beer and talk and smoke dope, though they take care to keep the parties quiet: the last thing they need is the police. They come across on the ferry and they bring their girlfriends, stringy-haired girls quite a lot younger than Charis, girls who take baths in Charis's bathroom because they live in places where they don't have bathrooms of their own, and they use up Charis's few towels and leave rings in Charis's old claw-footed bathtub. Dirt is an illusion, it's just one way of thinking about matter, and Charis knows she shouldn't be upset about it, but if she has to deal with an illusion of dirt she would rather it be her own dirt, not the dirt of these vacant-eyed girls. The men, or boys, refer to these girls as "my old lady," though they are the opposite of old, which makes Charis feel some better about the fact that Billy calls her by this name, as well.

Billy's group is always talking about plans. They think they should do something, take some action, but what kind? They've gone so far as to make up a list of names, the names of the others in the group, though they're first names only and false names at that. Charis—peeking at Billy's copy of the list, although she shouldn't have—was taken aback to discover that some of them were women's names: Edith, Ethel, Emma. During the parties, as she gets cold beer out of her tiny refrigerator, as she dumps chips and mixed nuts from the co-op into bowls, as she finds the shampoo for some girl who wants to wash her hair, as she sits on the floor beside Billy, breathing in second-hand pot smoke and smiling and gazing into space, she has listened in, she has overheard, and she knows that Billy is really Edith, or vice versa. He's named after Edith Cavell, some person in the past. There are telephone numbers, too; some of them are scrawled on the wall beside the phone, but Billy tells her it's safe because they're just the numbers of places where you can leave messages. They also have a plan to put out a newspaper, although there are several draft-dodger newspapers already. A lot of other guys got here before Billy and his new-found friends.

Charis isn't sure all these cloak-and-dagger props, the sneaking around and the codes and the pretend names, are really necessary. It's like kids playing. But the activity seems to give Billy more energy, and a purpose in life. He's venturing out more, he's less cooped up. On the days when Charis thinks the danger isn't real she rejoices in this, but on the days when she believes in it she worries. And every time Billy steps on board the ferry to go to the mainland, there's a corner of her that panics. Billy is like a tightrope walker, stepping carelessly blindfolded along a clothesline strung between two thirty-storey buildings, thinking he's only four feet above the ground. He believes that his actions, his words, his tiny little newspaper, can change things, can change things out there in the world.

Charis knows that there is no change possible in the world at large, no change for the better that is. Events are deceptive, they are part of a cycle; to get caught up in them is to be trapped in a whirlpool. But what does Billy know about the relentless malice of the physical universe? He is too young.

Charis feels that the only thing she herself can change is her own body, and through it her spirit. She wishes to free her spirit: this is what led her to yoga. She wants to rearrange her body, get rid of the heaviness hidden deep within it, that core of evil treasure she buried some time ago and has never dug up; she wants to make her body lighter and lighter, release it so that she's almost floating. She knows it's possible. She gives the yoga lessons because they pay for the rent and the phone and for the bulk food she gets cut-rate through her work at the co-op, but she gives them also because she wants to help other people.

Other women, really, because most of the people who take the classes are women. They too must have heavy metals hidden in them, they too must yearn for lightness. Although this class isn't about weight loss: she tells them that straight out, right at the beginning.

After she's dressed, after she's cooked Billy his bacon and toast and coffee, Charis packs her leotard and tights into her Peruvian carry-bag and runs around the house unearthing spare change for the trip from all the places where she's hidden it, for emergencies such as today, when she's run out of cash. The mist has evaporated now and the weak November sunlight is filtering through the grey overcast, so she can trust her watch again and she doesn't miss the ferry. She hardly ever misses it anyway unless it's a case of Billy, Billy and his spontaneous and overpowering urges. What can she tell him then? *I have to work or else we don't eat?* That doesn't go over too well: he thinks it's a criticism of him because he doesn't have a job, and then he sulks. He prefers to believe that she's like a lily of the field; that she neither toils nor spins; that bacon and coffee are simply produced by her, like leaves from a tree.

The yoga classes are held in the apartment above the co-op, or what used to be an apartment. Right now two of the rooms are offices, one for the co-op, one for a small poetry magazine called *Earth Germinations,* and the big front room is kept for meetings and for classes like the yoga ones. Charis will teach only ten people at a time: any more would overload her circuits, break her focus. They bring their own towels and mats, and usually they already have their leotards on under their clothes so they don't have to change. Charis gets there before the others, changes in the bathroom, and spreads out her mat, which she keeps in a cupboard in the co-op office. The old hardwood floor gives you splinters if you aren't careful.

Her first work is to abolish her surroundings. The faded wallpaper with the mauve trellis pattern on it must recede, the squares of darker wallpaper left by former pictures, the stale smell of used house and of the dank pee-stained carpet on the stairs coming up and of the lunch relics in the office wastebaskets, which nobody ever empties. The traffic noises from outside must go, the voices from the street and from downstairs—she erases them from her mind with a firm hand, as if they're on a blackboard. She lies down on her back, knees bent, arms loose overhead, and concentrates on her breathing, preparing, centring herself. The breath must go in and down, fully in and down to the solar plexus. The furtive scurrying trivial mind must be shut off. The *I* must be transcended. The self must be cut loose. It must drift.

The first class goes as usual. Charis knows she has a good voice for this, low and reassuring, and a good pace. "Honour the spine," she murmurs. "Salute the sun." The sun she means is inside the body. She uses her voice and also her hands, a touch here, a touch there, nudging the bodies into the right poses. To each individual woman she speaks in a whisper, so as not to call attention or embarrass her or interrupt the concentration of the others. The room fills with the sound of breathing, like wavelets on a shore, and with the scent of tensed muscles. Charis feels energy flowing out of her, through her fingers, into the other bodies. She doesn't move much—this is not what anyone else would call exertion—but at the end of the hour and a half she's exhausted.

She has an hour's break, to replenish herself. She drinks an orange-and-carrot juice from the juice bar downstairs to get some living enzymes into her system, and helps the others sort out the dried-bean pricing, and then it's time for her second class. Charis never much notices who is in which class; she counts to ten and registers the colours of the leotards, and once she's into the class she notes the particularities of the bodies and especially the spines and their wrong positioning, but the faces are not important to her, because the face is the individualism, the very thing Charis wants to help these women transcend. Also, the first exercises are done on the floor, with the eyes closed. So she's a quarter of the way through before she realizes that there's a new person, someone she's never seen before: a dark-haired woman in an indigo leotard and plum-coloured tights, who—strange for such a dimly lighted day—is wearing sunglasses.

This woman is tall, and thin as a razor, so thin Charis can see her ribcage right through the leotard, each rib in high relief as if carved, with a line of darkness beneath it. Her knees and elbows stick out like knots in rope, and the poses, as she performs them, are not fluid but practically geometrical, cages made of coat-hangers. Her skin is white as mushrooms, and a dark-light phosphorescence glimmers around her like the sheen on bad meat. Charis knows unhealth when she sees it: this woman needs a lot more than just one yoga class. A big hit of vitamin C and a dollop of sunlight would be a start, but they wouldn't even begin to touch what's wrong with her.

What's wrong with her is partly an attitude of the soul: the sunglasses are its manifestation, they symbolize a barrier to inner vision. So just before the lotus meditation Charis goes over and whispers to her, "Wouldn't you like to take your sunglasses off? They must be a distraction."

For answer the woman slips the glasses down, and Charis gets a shock. The woman's left eye is blackened. Black and blue, and half shut. The other eye regards her, hurt, wet, appealing.

"Oh," Charis breathes. "Sorry." She winces: she can feel the blow on her own flesh, her own eye.

The woman smiles, a harrowing smile in that emaciated and damaged face. "Aren't you Karen?" she whispers.

Charis doesn't know how to explain that she is but she isn't. She is once-Karen. So she says, "Yes," and looks more closely, because how would this woman recognize her?

"I'm Zenia," the woman says. And she is.

Charis and Zenia sit at one of the little tables beside the juice bar at the far end of the co-op. "What would you recommend?" says Zenia. "This is all new to me," and Charis, flattered by this call upon her expertise, orders her up a papaya-and-orange, with a dash of lemon in it and some brewer's yeast. Zenia keeps her glasses on and Charis doesn't blame her. Still, it's hard to talk with someone whose eyes she can't see.

She does remember Zenia, of course. Everyone in McClung Hall knew who Zenia was; even Charis, who drifted through her university years as if through an airport. Educationally she was a transient, and she left after three years without completing her degree: whatever it was that she needed to be taught, it wasn't on the curriculum there. Or maybe she wasn't ready for it. Charis believes that when you are ready to learn a thing the right teacher will appear, or rather will be sent to you. This has worked out for her so far, more or less, and the only reason she isn't learning anything at the moment is that she's so fully occupied with Billy.

Though maybe Billy is a teacher, in a way. She just hasn't figured out exactly what she's supposed to be learning from him. How to love, perhaps? How to love a man. Though she already does love him, so what next?

Zenia sips her juice, with the two ovals of her dark glasses turned towards Charis. Charis isn't sure what she can say to her. She didn't really know Zenia at university, she never spoke to her—Zenia was older, she was ahead of Charis, and she was in with all those artistic, intellectual people—but Charis remembers her, so beautiful and confident, striding around campus with her boyfriend Stew, and then later with short little Tony as well. What Charis remembers about Tony is that Tony followed her one night when Charis went outside to sit under a tree on the McClung lawn. Probably Tony thought Charis was sleepwalking; which showed some insight, because Charis had certainly done some sleepwalking in the past, though she wasn't doing it then.

This action of Tony's revealed a good heart; a quality much more important to Charis than Tony's academic brilliance, which was what she was known for. Zenia was known for other things as well—most notoriously for living with Stew, right out in the open, at a time when such things were not done. So much has changed. It's the married people, now, who are considered immoral. *The nukes,* they are called, for nuclear family. Radioactive, potentially lethal; a big leap from Home Sweet Home, but in Charis's opinion more appropriate.

Zenia too has changed. In addition to being thin she's ill, and in addition to being ill she is cowed somehow, beaten, defeated. Her shoulders hunch inwards protectively, her fingers are awkward claws, the corners of her mouth droop downwards. Charis wouldn't have known her. It's as if the former Zenia, the lovely Zenia, the Zenia of obvious flesh, has been burned away, leaving this bone core.

Charis doesn't like to question—she doesn't like to intrude on the selfhood of others—but Zenia is so drained of energy it's unlikely she will say anything at all, otherwise. So Charis chooses something non-invasive. "What brought you to my class?" she asks.

"I heard about it from a friend," says Zenia. Every word seems an effort. "I thought it might help."

"Help?" says Charis.

"With the cancer," says Zenia.

"Cancer," says Charis. It isn't even a question, because didn't she know it? There's no mistaking that whiteness, that sickly flicker. An imbalance of the soul.

Zenia smiles crookedly. "I beat it once before," she says, "but it's come back."

Now Charis remembers something: didn't Zenia disappear suddenly at the end of the year? The second year Charis lived in McClung Hall, that's when it was: Zenia vanished without an explanation, into thin air. The girls used to talk about it over breakfast and Charis would listen in, on the rare occasions when she bothered with listening, or with breakfast. They didn't have much there that she could eat: bran flakes was about it. The gossip was that Zenia had run away with another man, dumping Stew flat and taking some of his money as well, but now Charis divines the real truth: it was the cancer. Zenia went away without telling anyone about it because she didn't want a lot of fuss. She went away to cure herself, and to do that you need to be alone, to be free of interruption. Charis can understand that.

"How did you do it, the first time?" says Charis.

"Do what?" says Zenia, a little sharply.

"Beat it," says Charis. "The cancer."

"They did an operation," says Zenia. "They took out—they did a hysterectomy, I can never have babies. But it didn't work. So then I went to the mountains, by myself. I stopped eating meat, I cut out alcohol. I just had to concentrate. On getting well."

This sounds exactly right to Charis. Mountains, no meat. "And now?" she says.

"I thought I was better," says Zenia. Her voice has sunk to a hoarse whisper. "I thought I was strong enough. So I came back. I've been living with Stew—with West. I guess I let him take me back into our old way of living, you know, he drinks a lot—and the cancer came back. He can't take it—he really can't! A lot of people can't stand to be around sickness, they're afraid of it." Charis nods: she knows this, she knows this deeply, at the level of her cells. "He just denies that there's anything wrong with me," Zenia continues. "He tries to get me to eat . . . mounds of food, steak and butter, all those animal fats. They make me nauseated, I can't, I just can't!"

"Oh," says Charis. This is a horrible story, and one that has the ring of truth. So few people understand about animal fats. No, more: so few people understand about anything. "How awful," she says, which is only a pallid reflection of what she feels. She is troubled, she is on the verge of tears; above all she is helpless.

"Then he gets angry," Zenia goes on. "He gets furious with me, and I feel so weak . . . he hates me to cry, it just gets him angrier. He was the one who did this." She gestures towards her eye. "It makes me so ashamed, I feel like I'm the one responsible. . . ."

Charis tries to remember Stew, or West, whose name once changed so abruptly, just like her own. What she sees is a tall man, a somewhat inturned and unconnected man, gentle as a giraffe. She can't picture him hitting anyone, much less Zenia; but people can have deceptive exteriors. Men especially. They can put on a good act, they can make you believe they are model citizens and that they are right and you are wrong. They can fool everyone and make you seem like a liar. West, no doubt, is one of these. Indignation rises in her, the beginning of anger. But anger is unhealthy for her so she pushes it away.

"He says if I really have cancer I should have another operation, or else chemotherapy," says Zenia. "But I know I could heal myself again, if only . . ." she trails off. "I don't think I can drink any more of this right now," she says. She nudges the juice glass away. "Thank you . . . you've been really nice." She reaches across the table and touches Charis's hand. Her thin white fingers look cold but they are hot, hot as coals. Then she pushes back her chair, takes up her coat and purse, and hurries away, almost staggering.

Her head is bent, the hair is falling over her face like a veil, and Charis is sure she's crying.

Charis wants to jump up and run after her and bring her back. This desire is so strong in her it's like a fist on her neck. She wants to sit Zenia down again in her chair and put both hands on her, and summon up all her energy, the energy of the light, and heal her, right on the spot. But she knows she can't do that, so she doesn't move.

On Friday Zenia isn't in the yoga class, and Charis is anxious about her. Maybe she's collapsed, or maybe West has hit her again, this time more than once. Maybe she's in the hospital with multiple fractures. Charis takes the ferry boat to the Island, fretting all the way. Now she's feeling inadequate: there must have been something she could have said or done, something better than what she did do. A glass of juice was not enough.

That evening the fog returns, and with it a chilly drizzle, and Charis makes a good fire in the stove and turns on the furnace as well, and Billy wants her to come to bed early. She's brushing her teeth in the drafty bathroom downstairs when she hears a knock at the kitchen door. What she thinks is that it's one of Billy's group, with yet another draft dodger to be parked overnight on her living-room sofa. She has to admit she's getting a bit tired of them. For one thing, they never help with the dishes.

But it's not a draft dodger. It's Zenia, her head framed in the wet glass square of the door like a photo under water. Her hair is soaked and streaking down her face, her teeth are chattering, her sunglasses are gone, and her eye, purple now, is piteous. There's a fresh cut on her lip.

The door opens as if by itself, and she stands in the doorway, swaying slightly. "He threw me out," she whispers. "I don't want to disturb you . . . I just didn't know where else to go."

Mutely Charis holds out her arms, and Zenia stumbles over the threshold and collapses into them.

32

It's a sunless noon. Charis is in her garden, watched by the hens, who peer greedily through the hexagons of their wire fence, and by the remaining cabbages, goggling at her like three dull green goblin-heads emerging from the ground. The garden in November has a mangy, thumbed appearance: wilted marigolds, nasturtium leaves faded a pale yellow, the stumps of broccoli, the unripe tomatoes frost-killed and mushy, with silvery slug tracks wandering here and there.

Charis doesn't mind this vegetable disarray. It's all ferment, all fertilizer. She lifts her spade, shoves it into the earth, and steps on the top edge of its blade with her right foot in Billy's rubber boot, digging in. Then she heaves, grunting. Then she turns over the shovelful of soil. Worms suck themselves back into their tunnels, a white grub curls. Charis picks it up and tosses it relentlessly over the fence, in for the gabbling hens. All life is sacred but hens are more sacred than grubs.

The hens fluster and racket and abuse one another, and chase the one with the grub. Charis once thought it might be a good spiritual discipline to refuse to feed her hens anything she wouldn't eat herself, but she has since decided that this would be pointless. The ground-up shells, for instance, the crushed bones—hens need them to make eggs, but Charis doesn't.

It's the wrong season of the year to be turning the garden. She should wait till spring, when the new weeds poke through; she'll have to do it all over again at that time. But this is the only way she can be out of the house without either Zenia or Billy wanting to come with her. Each is eager to be with her alone, away from the other one. If she tries to go for a walk, just to be by herself for a short time, just to unwind, there's a rush for the door: a subdued, oblique rush (Zenia) or a gangling, obvious one (Billy). Then there's a psychic collision, and Charis is forced to choose. It's bothering her a lot. But luckily, neither one of them has any great desire to help her dig up the garden. Billy doesn't like mucking in the dirt—he says why do so much work, because all that comes up is vegetables—and Zenia of course is in no shape. She is managing to take feeble, occasional walks, down to the lakeshore and back, but even those exhaust her.

Zenia has been here for a week now, sleeping on the sofa by night, resting on it by day. The evening of her arrival was almost festive—Charis ran a hot bath for her and gave her one of her own white cotton nightgowns to put on, and hung her wet clothes up on the hooks behind the stove to dry, and after Zenia was finished with the bath and had put on the nightgown Charis wrapped her in a blanket and sat her in a chair beside the stove, and combed her wet hair, and made her a hot milk with honey. It pleased Charis to do these things; she experienced herself as competent and virtuous, overflowing with good will and good energy. It pleased her to give this energy to someone so obviously in need of it as Zenia. But by the time she'd settled Zenia on the sofa and had gone upstairs to bed, Billy was angry with her, and he's been angry ever since. He's made it clear that he doesn't want Zenia in the house at all.

"What's she doing here?" he whispered that first night.

"It's just for a bit," said Charis, whispering too because she didn't want Zenia to hear them and feel unwanted. "We've had lots of others. On the same sofa! It's no different."

"It's way different," said Billy. "They don't have any place else to go."

"Neither does she," said Charis. The different thing, she was thinking, was that the others were Billy's friends and Zenia was hers. Well, not friend exactly. Responsibility.

That was before Billy had even laid eyes on Zenia, or spoken a single word to her. The next day he'd grunted a surly "Morning" over the scrambled eggs—not home-grown, unfortunately, the hens had dried up—and the toast with apple jelly that Charis was serving to both of them. He'd hardly looked at Zenia where she sat hunched over, still in Charis's nightgown, with a blanket wrapped around her, sipping her weak tea. If he had looked, thought Charis, he would have relented, because Zenia was so pitiable. Her eye was still discoloured and swollen, and you could practically count the blue veins on the backs of her hands.

"Get her out of here," said Billy when Zenia had gone to the bathroom. "Just out."

"Shh," said Charis. "She'll hear you!"

"What do we know about her, anyway?" said Billy.

"She has cancer," said Charis, as if this was all anyone needed to know.

"Then she should be in a hospital," said Billy.

"She doesn't believe in them," said Charis, who didn't either.

"Bullshit," said Billy.

This remark struck Charis as not only ungenerous and crude, but faintly sacrilegious as well. "She has that black eye," she murmured. The eye was living proof of something or other. Of Zenia's neediness, or else her goodness. Of her status.

"I didn't give it to her," said Billy. "Let her go eat someone else's food." Charis was incapable of mentioning that if anyone ought to decide who ate what around this place it should be her, since she was the one who either grew it or paid for it herself.

"He doesn't like me, does he?" said Zenia, when Billy in his turn was out of hearing. Her voice quivered, her eyes were filling. "I'd better go. . . ."

"Of course he does! It's just his way," said Charis warmly. "Now you stay right where you are!"

It took Charis a while to figure out why Billy was so hostile to Zenia. At first she thought it was because he was afraid of her—afraid she would tell on him, tip off the wrong people, turn him in; or that she would just say something to someone by accident, something indiscreet. *Loose lips sink ships* used to be a slogan, during the war, the old war; it was on posters, and Charis's Aunt Viola used to quote it as a sort of joke, to her friends, in the late forties. So Charis explained all that to Zenia, how precarious Billy felt and how difficult things were for him. She even told Zenia about the bombs, about blowing things up, and about how

Billy might get kidnapped by the Mounties. Zenia promised not to tell. She said she understood perfectly.

"I'll be careful, cross my heart," she said. "But Karen—sorry, Charis—how did you get mixed up with them?"

"Mixed up?" said Charis.

"With the draft dodgers," said Zenia. "The revolutionaries. You never struck me as a very political person. At university, I mean. Not that there were a whole bunch of revolutionaries, around that dump."

It hadn't occurred to Charis that Zenia would have taken any notice of her at all, back then, back in her vague, semi-forgotten university days, when she was still Karen, outwardly at least. She hadn't participated in anything, she hadn't stood out. She had stayed in the shadows, but it turned out that Zenia at least had spotted her there and had considered her worthy of notice, and she was touched. Zenia must have been a sensitive person; more sensitive than people gave her credit for.

"I'm not," said Charis. "I wasn't political at all."

"I was," said Zenia. "I was totally anti-bourgeois, back then! A real bohemian fellow-traveller." She frowned a little, then laughed. "Why not, they had the best parties!"

"Well," said Charis, "I'm not *mixed up.* I don't understand any of those things. I just live with Billy, that's all."

"Sort of like a gun moll," said Zenia, who was feeling a little better. It was a warmish day, for November, so Charis had decided it was safe for Zenia to go out. They were down by the lake, watching the gulls; Zenia had walked the whole way without once holding onto Charis's arm. Charis had offered to get her some new sunglasses— Zenia had left the old ones behind, the night she ran away—but she hardly needed them any

faded to a yellowy-blue, like a washed-

"A what?" said Charis.

"Shit," said Zenia, smiling, "if t

isn't *mixed up*, I don't know what is.

care what people called things. Anyw

ing to Zenia, she was watching her smile.

Zenia is smiling more, now. Charis feels as if that smile has been accomplished single-handedly by her, Charis, and by all the work she's been putting in: the fruit drinks, the cabbage juice made from her own cabbages, ground up fine and strained through a sieve, the special baths she prepares, the gentle yoga stretches, the carefully spaced walks in the fresh air. All those positive energies are ranging themselves against the cancer cells, good soldiers against bad, light against darkness; Charis herself is taking meditation time every day, on Zenia's behalf, to visualize that exact same result. And it's working, it is! Zenia has more colour now, more energy. Although still very thin and weak, she is visibly improving.

She knows it and she's grateful. "You're doing so much for me," she says to Charis, almost every day. "I don't deserve it; I mean, I'm a total stranger, you hardly know me."

"That's all right," says Charis awkwardly. She blushes a little when Zenia says these things. She isn't used to people thanking her for what she does, and she has a belief that it isn't necessary. At the same time, the sensation is very agreeable; also at the same time, it strikes her that Billy could be showing a bit more gratitude himself, for thing she's done for him. Instead of which he scowls her and doesn't eat his bacon. He wants her to make two breakfasts—one for Zenia and a separate one for him—so he doesn't have to sit at the same table with Zenia in the mornings.

"The way she sucks up to you makes me puke," he said yesterday. Charis knows now why he says such things. He's jealous. He's afraid Zenia will come between them, that she'll somehow take Charis's full attention away from him. It's childish of him to feel like that. After all, he doesn't have a life-threatening illness, and he ought to know by now that Charis loves him. So Charis touches his arm.

"She won't be here forever," she says. "Just till she's a little better. Just till she can find a place of her own."

"I'll help her look," says Billy. Charis has told him about West punching Zenia in the eye, and his response was not charitable. "I'll do the other one for her," is what he said. "Wham, bam, thank you ma'am, a real pleasure."

"That's not very pacifist of you," said Charis reproachfully.

"I never said I was a goddamn pacifist," said Billy, insulted. "Just because one war's wrong doesn't mean they all are!"

"Charis," Zenia called fretfully, from the front room. "Is the radio on? I heard voices. I was just having a nap."

"I can't say spit in my own goddamn house," hisses Billy.

It's at moments like these that Charis goes out to dig in the garden.

•   •   •

She pushes her shovel down, lifts, turns the soil over, pauses to look for grubs. Then she hears Zenia's voice behind her.

"You're so strong," Zenia says wistfully. "I was that strong, once. I could carry three suitcases."

"You will be again," says Charis, as heartily as she can. "I just know it!"

"Maybe," says Zenia, in a small, sad voice. "It's the little everyday things you miss so much. You know?"

Charis feels suddenly guilty for digging in her own garden; or as if she ought to feel guilty. It's the same way with a lot of the other things she does: scrubbing the floor, making the bread. Zenia admires her while she does these things, but it's a melancholy admiration. Sometimes Charis senses that her own healthy, toned-up body is a reproach to Zenia's enfeebled one; that Zenia holds it against her.

"Let's feed the hens," she says. Feeding the hens is something Zenia can do. Charis brings out the hen feed in its coffee can, and Zenia scatters it, handful by handful. She loves the hens, she says. They are so vital! They are— well, the embodiment of the Life Force. Aren't they?

Charis is made nervous by this kind of talk. It's too abstract, it's too much like university. The hens are not an embodiment of anything but hen-ness. The concrete *is* the abstract. But how could she explain this to Zenia?

"I'm going to make a salad," she says instead.

"A Life Force salad," says Zenia, and laughs. For the first time Charis is not delighted to hear this laughter, welcome as it ought to be. There's something about it she doesn't understand. It's like a joke she's not getting.

•   •   •

The salad is raisins and grated carrots, with a lemon juice and honey dressing. The carrots themselves are Charis's own, from the box of damp sand in the root cellar lean-to; already they're beginning to grow small white whiskers, which shows they're still alive. Charis and Zenia eat the salad, and the lima beans and boiled potatoes, by themselves, because Billy says he has to go out that night. He has a meeting.

"He goes to a lot of meetings," murmurs Zenia, as Billy is putting on his jacket. She has given up trying to be nice to Billy, since she wasn't getting any results; now she's taken to speaking of him in the third person even when he's standing right there. It creates a circle, a circle of language, with Zenia and Charis on the inside of it and Billy on the outside. Charis wishes she wouldn't do it; on the other hand, in a way Billy has only himself to blame.

Billy gives Zenia a dirty look. "At least I don't just sit around on my butt, like some," he says angrily. He too speaks only to Charis.

"Be careful," Charis says. She means about going into the city, but Billy takes it as a reproof.

"Have a real good time with your sick friend," he says nastily. Zenia smiles to herself, a tiny bitter smile. The door slams behind him, rattling the glass in the windows.

"I think I should leave," says Zenia, when they are eating some of the applesauce Charis bottled earlier in the fall.

"But where would you live?" says Charis, dismayed.

"Oh, I could find a place," says Zenia.

"But you don't have any money!" says Charis.

"I could get a job of some sort," says Zenia. "I'm good at that. I can always lick ass somewhere, I know how to get jobs." She coughs, muffling her face in her spindly-fingered hands. "Sorry," she says. She takes a bird-sip of water.

"Oh, no," says Charis. "You can't do that! You're not well enough yet! You will be soon," she adds, because she doesn't want to sound negative. It's health and not sickness that must be reinforced.

Zenia smiles thinly. "Maybe," she says. "But Karen, really—don't worry about me. It's not your problem."

"Charis," says Charis. Zenia has trouble remembering her real name.

And yes, it is her problem, because she has taken it upon herself.

Then Zenia says something worse. "It's not just that he hates me," she says. Her tongue comes out, licking the applesauce off the tip of her spoon. "The fact is, he can hardly keep his hands off me."

"West?" says Charis. A cold finger runs down her back.

Zenia smiles. "No," she says. "I mean Billy. Surely you've noticed it."

Charis can feel the skin of her entire face sliding down in dismay. She has noticed nothing. But why hasn't she? It's obvious to her, now that Zenia's said it—the energy that leaps out of Billy's finger-ends and hair whenever Zenia is near. A sexual bristling, like tomcats. "What do you mean?" she says.

"He wants to haul me into bed," says Zenia. Her voice is lightly regretful. "He wants to jump me."

"He loves you?" says Charis. Her entire body has gone slack, as if her bones have melted. Dread is what she feels. *Billy loves me,* she protests silently. "Billy loves *me,*" she says, in a choked voice. "He says so." She sounds to herself like a whiny child. And when was the last time he said that?

"Oh, it's not love," says Zenia gently. "Not what he feels for me, I mean. It's hate. Sometimes it's so hard for men to tell the difference. But you knew that already, didn't you?"

"What are you talking about?" Charis whispers.

Zenia laughs. "Come on, you're not a baby. He loves your ass. Or some other body part, how would I know? Anyway, for sure it's not your soul, it's not *you*. If you didn't put out he'd just take anyway. I've watched him, he's a greedy shit, they're all just rapists at heart. You're an innocent, Karen. Believe me, there's only one thing any man ever wants from a woman, and that's sex. How much you can get them to pay for it is the important thing."

"Don't say that," says Charis. "Don't say it!" She can feel something breaking in her, collapsing, a huge iridescent balloon ripped and greying like a punctured lung. What's left, if you take away love? Just brutality. Just shame. Just ferocity. Just pain. What becomes of her gifts then, her garden, her chickens, her eggs? All her acts of careful tending. She's shaking now, she feels sick to her stomach.

"I'm just a realist, that's all," says Zenia. "The one reason he wants to stick his dick into me is that he can't. Don't worry, he'll forget all about it after I've left. They have short memories. That's why I want to go, Karen—it's for you." She's still smiling. She looks at Charis, and her face against the weak light of the ceiling bulb is in darkness, with only her eyes gleaming, red as in car headlights, and the look goes into Charis, down and down. It's a resigned look. Zenia is accepting her own death.

"But you'll die," says Charis. She can't let that happen. "Don't give up!" She starts to cry. She clutches Zenia's hand, or Zenia clutches hers, and the two of them hang onto each other's hands across the tableful of dirty dishes.

Charis lies awake in the night. Billy has come back, long after she went to bed, but he hasn't reached for her. Instead he turned away in bed and closed himself off and went to sleep. It's like that a lot, these days. It's as if they've had a fight. But now she knows there's another reason too: she is not wanted. It's Zenia who is the wanted one.

But Billy wants Zenia with his body only. That's why he's so rude to her—his body is divided from his spirit. That's why he's being so cold to Charis, as well: his body wants Charis out of the way, so he can grab Zenia, shove her up against the kitchen counter, take hold of her against her will, even though she's so ill. Maybe he doesn't know that's what he wants. But it is.

A wind has come up. Charis listens to it scraping through the bare trees, and to the cold waves slapping against the shore. Someone is coming towards her across the lake, her bare feet touching the tops of the waves, her nightgown tattered by the years of weathering, her colourless hair floating. Charis closes her eyes, focusing on the inner picture, trying to see who it is. Inside her head there's moonlight, obscured by scudding clouds; but now the sky lightens and she can see the face.

It's Karen, it's banished Karen. She has travelled a long distance. Now she's coming nearer, with that cowed, powerless face Charis used to see in the mirror looming up to her own face, blown towards her through the darkness like an ousted ghost, towards this house where she has been islanded, thinking herself safe; demanding to enter her, to rejoin her, to share in her body once again.

Charis is not Karen. She has not been Karen for a long time, and she never wants to be Karen again. She pushes away with all her strength, pushes down towards the water, but this time Karen will not go under. She drifts closer and closer, and her mouth opens. She wants to speak.

33

Karen was born to the wrong parents. That's what Charis's grandmother said could happen, and it is what Charis believes as well. Such people have to look for a long time, they have to search out and identify their right parents. Or else they have to go through life without.

Karen was seven when she met her grandmother for the first time. On that day she wore a cotton dress with smocking across the front and a sash, and matching hairbows on the ends of her pale blonde pigtails, which were braided so tight her eyes felt slanted. Her mother had starched the dress, and it was stiff and also a little sticky because of the damp late-June heat. They took the train, and when Karen got up off the hot plush seat she had to peel the skirt of the dress off the backs of her legs. That hurt, but she knew better than to say so.

Her mother wore an ivory-coloured linen outfit with a sleeveless dress and a short-sleeved jacket over it. She had a white straw hat and a white bag and shoes to match, and a pair of white cotton gloves, which she carried. "I think you'll enjoy this," she kept telling Karen anxiously. "You're a lot like your grandmother in some ways." This was news to Karen, because for a long time her mother and her grandmother had hardly been on speaking terms. She knew from listening in that her mother had run away from the farm when she was only sixteen. She'd worked at grinding hard jobs and saved up her money so she could go to school and become a teacher. She'd done this so she could be out from under the thumb of her own mother, the crazy old bat. Wild horses would not drag her back to that rubbish heap, or this was what she said.

Yet here they were, heading straight to the farm that Karen's mother hated so much, with Karen's summer clothes packed neatly into a suitcase and her mother's overnight bag beside it on the rack above their heads. They passed dirt fields, isolated houses, grey sagging barns, herds of cows. Karen's mother hated cows. One of her stories was about having to get up in the winter, in blizzards, before sunrise even, and go out shivering through the whirling snow to feed the cows. But, "You'll like the cows," she said now, in the too-sweet voice she used on the Grade Twos at school. She checked her lipstick in the mirror of her compact, then smiled at Karen to see how she was taking it. Karen smiled back uncertainly. She was used to smiling even when she didn't feel like it. She would be in Grade Two in September; she was hoping she wouldn't be put in her mother's class.

This wasn't her first time staying away from home. Other times she'd been sent to her aunt, her mother's older sister Viola. Sometimes it was just overnight, because her mother was going out; sometimes it was for weeks, especially in the summers. Her mother needed a long rest in the summers because of her nerves. *Well, who wouldn't have nerves, considering?* said Aunt Vi with disapproval, as if what could Karen's mother expect? She was speaking to Uncle Vern but looking sideways at Karen as if the nerves were Karen's doing. But surely not all of them were, because Karen tried to do what she was told, although sometimes she made mistakes; and there were other things, like the sleepwalking, that she couldn't help.

The nerves were the fault of the war. Karen's father was killed in the war when Karen wasn't even born yet, leaving Karen's mother to bring up Karen all by herself— a thing that was understood to be very hard, practically impossible. There was something else too, which had to do with Karen's mother's wedding, or else the absence of it. Whether her father and her mother were actually married was one of the many things Karen wasn't sure about, although her mother called herself Mrs. and wore a ring. There were no wedding photos, but things had been done differently during the war; everyone said so. There was something in Aunt Vi's tone of voice that alerted Karen: she was an embarrassment, someone who could only be spoken of obliquely. She wasn't quite an orphan but she had the taint of one.

Karen didn't miss her dead father, because how could you miss someone you never even knew? But she was told by her mother that she ought to miss him. There was a framed snapshot of him—not with her mother, but alone, in his uniform, his long bony face looking solemn and somehow already dead—which appeared and disappeared from the mantelpiece, depending on the state of Karen's mother's health. When she was up to looking at it, the picture was there; otherwise not. Karen used the picture of her father as a sort of weather report. When it vanished she knew there was going to be trouble, and she tried to keep out of the road, out from underfoot, out of her mother's hair (road, feet, hair, how could she be on or under or in all of them at the same time?). But she didn't always succeed, or else she succeeded too well and her mother would accuse her of daydreaming, of not helping, of not caring, of not giving a sweet Jesus about anyone but herself, and her voice would go up high, up higher, up dangerously high, like a thermometer, into the red part.

Karen tried to help, she tried to care. She would have cared except she didn't know what she was supposed to care about, and also there were so many things she needed to watch, because of the colours, and other things she needed to listen to. Hours before a storm, when the sky was still windless and blue, she would feel the whisper of the distant lightning running up her arms. She heard the phone before it rang, she heard pain gathering in her mother's hands, building up there like water behind a dam, getting ready to spill over, and she would stand terrified in the middle of the floor with her eyes elsewhere, looking—her mother said—like an idiot. *Stupid!* Maybe she was stupid, because sometimes she didn't understand what was being said to her. She wasn't hearing the words, she was hearing past the words; she heard the faces instead, and what was behind them. At night she would wake up, standing by the door, holding onto the door handle, and wonder how she got there.

Why do you do that? Why? said her mother, shaking her, and Karen couldn't answer. *My God, you're an idiot! Don't you know what could happen to you out there?* But Karen didn't know, and her mother would say, *I'll teach you! Little bitch!* Then she would hit the backs of Karen's legs with one of her shoes, or else the pancake flipper or the broom handle, whatever was nearby, and thick red light would pour out of her body and some of it would get on Karen, and Karen would squirm and scream. "If your Daddy was alive it'd be him doing this, and he'd do it a damn sight harder, believe you me!" Hitting Karen was the only function Karen's mother ever ascribed to her father, which made her secretly relieved that he wasn't there.

Ordinarily Karen's mother did not say *Jesus* and *God* and *bitch,* she didn't swear; only when she was heading into a patch of bad nerves. Karen cried a lot when her mother hit her, not just because it hurt but because she was supposed to show that she was sorry, although she was confused about why. Also, if she didn't cry her mother would keep right on hitting her until she did. *You hard girl!* But she had to stop at the right moment or her mother would hit her for crying. *Stop that noise! Stop right now!* Sometimes Karen couldn't stop and neither could her mother, and those were the worst times. Her mother couldn't help it. It was her nerves.

Then Karen's mother would fall on her knees and wrap her arms around Karen's body and squeeze her so she could scarcely breathe, and cry, and say, "I'm sorry, I love you, I don't know what got into me, I'm sorry!" Karen would try to stop crying then, she would try to smile, because her mother loved her. If someone loved you that made it all right. Karen's mother sprayed herself every day with Tabu perfume; she had a horror of smelling bad. So that was the smell in the room, during these beatings: warm Tabu.

● ● ●

Karen's Aunt Vi didn't like Karen very much, but at least she didn't touch her, and it wasn't bad at her place. Karen slept in the guest room, which had large disturbing roses on the curtains, orange and pink ones, like cauliflowers. She stayed out of the way as much as possible. She helped with the dishes without being asked, and kept her hand-kerchiefs folded in the top bureau drawer and her socks in pairs, and did not get dirty. "She's a nice enough little thing, but there's not that much to her," said Aunt Vi on the telephone. "Milk and water. Well, I keep her clean and fed, it's not that hard. Anyway it's only Christian charity, and it's not as if we have children of our own. I don't mind, really."

Uncle Vern went further than that. "Who's my girl?" he would exclaim. He wanted Karen to sit on his knee, he rubbed her head, he put his face down close to hers and grinned at her, and tickled her under the arms; Karen didn't like this but she laughed nervously anyway, because she could tell he wanted her to. "We have a good time, don't we?" he said boisterously; but he didn't believe it, it was only his idea of how he should behave towards her. "Don't pester her," said Aunt Vi coldly.

Uncle Vern's skin was white on top but red under-neath. He mowed the lawn in his shorts, on Sunday evenings when Aunt Vi was at church, and at those times he got even redder, though the light around his body was dim and a muddy green-brown. In the mornings, when she was still lying in bed, Karen could hear him grunting and groaning in the bathroom. She would put her pillow over her ears.

"She does sleepwalk, but not that much," said Aunt Vi

on the phone. "I just keep the doors locked, she can't get out. I don't know what Gloria makes such a fuss about. Of course her nerves are shot. Left with a—well, a child on her hands, like that—I feel I have to help out. But then, I'm her sister." She dropped her voice when saying this, as if it was a secret.

Her aunt and uncle did not live in an apartment, the way her mother did. They lived in a house, a new house in the suburbs, with carpets all over the floor. Uncle Vern was in the home furnishings business; there was a real demand for home furnishings because it was right after the war, so Uncle Vern was doing well, and right now Uncle Vern and Aunt Vi had gone on a vacation. They had gone to Hawaii. This was why Karen couldn't stay with them, but had to go to her grandmother's instead.

She had to go, because her mother needed a rest. She needed it badly; Karen knew how badly. When she peeled the starched skirt away from the backs of her legs, some of the skin came off too, because last night her mother had used the pancake flipper, not the flat way but sideways; she had used the cutting edge and there had been blood.

The grandmother met them at the train station in a battered blue pickup truck.

"How are you, Gloria," she said to Karen's mother, shaking hands with her as if they were strangers. Her hands were large and sunburned and so was her face; her head was topped with a straggly whitish grey nest, which Karen realized after a moment was her hair. She was wearing overalls, and not clean ones either. "So this is wee Karen." Her big, crinkly face swooped down, with a beak of a nose and two small bright blue eyes under wiry eyebrows, and her teeth appeared, large too and unnaturally even, and so white they were almost luminous. She was smiling. "I'm not going to eat you," she said to Karen. "Not today. You're too skinny, anyway—I'd have to fatten you up."

"Oh, Mother," said Karen's own mother reproachfully, in her sweet Grade Twos voice. "She won't know you're only joking!"

"Then she better find out fast," said the grandmother. "Part of it's true, anyway. She's too skinny. If I had a calf like that I'd say it was starving."

There was a black-and-white collie on the seat of the pickup truck, lying on a filthy plaid rug. "Into the back, Glennie," said the grandmother, and the dog pricked up its ears, wagged its tail, jumped down, and scrambled into the back of the truck via the back fender. "In you go," said the grandmother, picking Karen up as if she were a sack and hoisting her onto the seat. "Shove over for your mother." Karen slid along the seat; it hurt, because of her legs. Karen's mother looked at the dog hairs, hesitating.

"Get in, Gloria," said the grandmother drily. "It's just as dirty as it always was."

She drove the truck fast, whistling tunelessly, one elbow jauntily out the window. Both windows were open and the gravel dust billowed in, but even so the inside of the car stank of old dog. Karen's mother took off her white hat and stuck her head partway out the window. Karen, who was squashed in the middle and feeling a little sick, tried to imagine she was a dog herself, because if she was, then she would think the smell was nice.

"Home again, home again, jiggy jog jog," said the

grandmother jovially. She swung up a bumpy driveway, and Karen caught a glimpse of a huge skeleton, like a dinosaur skeleton, in the long weedy grass in front of the house. This thing was a rusty red, with sharp spines and many encrusted bones sticking out of it. She wanted to ask what it was but she was still too afraid of her grandmother, and anyway the truck was no longer moving and now there was a commotion, a barking and hissing and cackling outside, and a grunting, and her grandmother was yelling, "Be off, be off with you, shoo, shoo, boys and girls!"

Karen couldn't see out, so she looked at her mother. Her mother was sitting bolt upright, her hat on her knees, with her eyes tight shut, scrunching her white cotton gloves into a ball.

The grandmother's face appeared at the window. "Oh, for Christ's sake, Gloria," she said, jerking open the door. "It's only the geese."

"Those geese are killers," said Karen's mother, but she clambered down out of the truck. Karen thought that her mother shouldn't have worn her white shoes, because the yard in front of the house wasn't a lawn, it was an expanse of mud, some of it dry, some of it not, and some of it not mud at all but animal poo of various kinds. Karen was familiar only with the dog kind, because they had that in the city. There were now two dogs, the black-and-white collie and a larger, brown-and-white one, and at the moment they were herding a flock of geese back towards the barnyard, barking and waving their brushy tails. There were a lot of flies buzzing around.

"Yeah, they can give you a good peck," said Karen's grandmother. "You just have to stand up to them! Show some willpower!" She reached in for Karen, but Karen said, "I can get down by myself," and her grandmother said, "That's the ticket." Karen's mother had gone ahead, carrying her overnight case in one hand and waving her purse at the flies, picking her way across the yard through the clumps of poo in her high heels, and the grandmother took this opportunity to say, "Your mother's weak-minded. Hysterical. Always has been. I hope you're not."

"What's that thing?" said Karen, finding some courage because she saw that it was required of her.

"What thing?" said her grandmother. Leaning against her grandmother's legs was a medium-sized pig. It snuffled at Karen's socks with its alarming snout, wet and tender as an eyeball, drooly as a mouth. "This here's Pinky. She's a pig."

"No," said Karen. She could tell it was a pig, she'd seen pictures. "The big thing, at the front."

"Old cultivator," said her grandmother, leaving Karen to wonder what a cultivator was. "Come on!" She strode off towards the door with Karen's suitcase under one arm, and Karen trotted along behind. In the distance there was more barking and cackling. The pig followed as far as the house, and then, to Karen's surprise, came right in. It knew how to nose open the screen door.

They were in the kitchen, which was a lot less like a rubbish heap than Karen had thought it would be. There was an oval table covered with oilcloth—light green with a design of strawberries—with a huge teapot and some used plates on it. There were some chairs painted apple green, and a wood range and a saggy maroon velvet sofa piled with newspapers. On the floor there were more newspapers, with a ravelled afghan thrown on top of them.

Karen's mother was sitting in a rocking chair beside the window, looking exhausted. Her linen outfit was all creased. She had her shoes off and was fanning herself with her hat, but when the pig came into the room she gave a slight scream.

"It's okay, she's house-broken," said the grandmother.

"That is the limit," said Karen's mother, in a tight, furious voice.

"Cleaner than most people," said the grandmother. "Smarter, too. Anyways, this is my house. You can do what you like in yours. I didn't ask you to come here and I won't ask you to leave, but while you're here you can take things as you find them."

She scratched the pig behind the ears and gave it a slap on the rump, and it grunted gently and squinted up at her and then went over and flopped down sideways on the afghan. Karen's mother burst into tears and scrambled out of her chair, and headed out of the room in her stocking feet, with her white gloves crushed to her eyes. Karen's grandmother laughed. "It's okay, Gloria," she called. "Pinky can't climb stairs!"

"Why not?" said Karen. Her voice was almost a whisper. She'd never heard anyone talk to her mother like that.

"Legs're too short," said her grandmother. "Now, you can take off that dress, if you've got any other kind of clothes, and help me wash the potatoes." She sighed. "I should've had sons."

Karen opened her suitcase and found her long cotton pants, and changed into them in a room her grandmother called the back parlour. She didn't want to put on shorts because of the backs of her legs. They were a secret between her and her mother. She wasn't supposed to tell, about the broom handle or the pancake flipper, or there would be trouble, the way there was when her mother punched one of the Grade Two boys in the face and almost lost her job, and then what would they eat?

"I'll show you your own room later, when Gloria's over the sniffles," said her grandmother. Then Karen helped her grandmother wash the potatoes. They did this in a smaller kitchen off the main one where there was an electric stove, and a tin sink with a cold-water tap. Her grandmother called this room the pantry. The pig came in with them and grunted hopefully until it was sent away. "Not now, Pinky," said the grandmother. "Too many raw potatoes make her sick. She loves 'em, though. She'll take a drink too, and that's just as bad for her. Most animals like to go on a good drunk if they get the chance."

For dinner they had the potatoes, boiled, and chicken stew with biscuits. Karen wasn't all that hungry. She fed pieces of her dinner furtively to the pig and also to the two dogs, who were underneath the table. Her grandmother saw her doing it but didn't object, so she knew it was all right.

Her mother came down for dinner, still in the linen dress, with her face washed and a fresh mouth painted on and a grim set to her lips. Karen knew that expression: it meant her mother was going to see this through *or else*. Or else what? Or else things would not be so good, for Karen.

"Mother, are there any serviettes?" said Karen's mother. Her mouth jerked into a smile, as if there were strings pulling up the ends of it.

"Any what?" said the grandmother.

"Table napkins," said her mother.

"La-di-da, Gloria, use your sleeve," said the grandmother.

Karen's mother wrinkled her nose at Karen. "Do you see any sleeves?" she said. Her jacket was off, so her arms were bare. She was taking a new line: she'd decided that they would both find the grandmother comical.

The grandmother caught this look and frowned. "They're in the dresser drawer, same as always," she said. "I'm not a savage, but this is no dinner party neither. Those who wants can get them."

For dessert there was applesauce, and after that strong tea with milk in it. The grandmother passed a cup to Karen, and Karen's mother said, "Oh, Mother, she doesn't drink tea," and the grandmother said, "She does now." Karen thought there might be an argument, but her grandmother added, "If you're leaving her with me, you're leaving her with *me*. 'Course, you can always take her with you." Karen's mother clamped her mouth shut.

When Karen's grandmother had finished eating she scooped the chicken bones off the dinner plates, back into the stewpot, and set the plates down on the floor. The animals crowded around them, licking and slurping.

"Not from the dishes," said Karen's mother faintly.

"Less germs on their tongues than on a human's," said the grandmother.

"You're crazy, you know that?" said Karen's mother in a choking voice. "You should be locked up!" She jammed her hand over her mouth and ran out into the yard. The grandmother watched her go. Then she shrugged and went back to drinking her tea.

"There's clean inside and clean outside," she said. "Clean inside is better, but Gloria never could tell the difference."

Karen didn't know what to do. She thought about her stomach, with animal slobber and dog and pig germs in it; but strangely, she didn't feel sick.

When Karen went upstairs later, she heard her mother crying, a sound she had heard many times before. She went carefully into the bedroom where the sound was coming from. Her mother was sitting on the edge of the bed, looking more desolate than Karen had ever seen her. "She was never like a real mother," she sobbed. "She never was!"

She squeezed Karen tight and cried onto her hair, and Karen wondered what she meant.

Karen's mother left the next day, before breakfast. She said she had to get back to the city, she had a doctor's appointment. Karen's grandmother drove her to the station and Karen went too, to say goodbye. She wore her long pants, because of her legs, which were hurting again. Her mother kept one arm around her all the way to the station.

Before starting the truck the grandmother let the geese out of their pen. "They're watch-geese," she said. "Them and Cully'll take care of everything. Anyone tries to get in here, Cully'll knock them down and the geese'll poke out their eyes. Stay, Cully! Come, Glenn." She drove just as fast as before, almost in the centre of the road, but this time she didn't whistle.

When the time came to say goodbye at the station, Karen's mother kissed Karen on the cheek and squeezed her tight and said she loved her, and told her to be a good girl. She did not kiss the grandmother. She didn't even say goodbye to her. Karen watched the grandmother's face: it was shut tight like a box.

Karen wanted to wait until the train was actually moving, so they did. Her mother waved at her out of the train window, her white gloves fluttering like flags. That was the last she saw of her real mother, the one that could still smile and wave, although she didn't know it at the time.

Then Karen and her grandmother went back to the farmhouse and had their breakfast, which was oatmeal porridge with brown sugar and thick new cream on it. With Karen's mother gone, her grandmother was not so talkative.

Karen looked at her grandmother across the table. She looked thoroughly. The grandmother was older than Karen had thought the day before; her neck was bonier, her eyelids were more wrinkled. Around her head there was a faint pale blue light. Karen had already figured out that her teeth were false.

34

After breakfast Karen's grandmother says to her, "Are you sick?"

"No," says Karen. Her legs are still hurting but that isn't a sickness, it's nothing because her mother says it's nothing. She doesn't want to be put to bed, she wants to go outside. She wants to see the chickens.

Her grandmother looks at her sharply but only says, "Don't you want to put on your shorts? Today'll be a scorcher," but Karen says no again and they go to collect the eggs. The dogs and the pig aren't allowed to come with them, because the dogs would try to herd the hens, and the pig likes eggs. The three of them lie on the kitchen floor, the dogs' tails thumping slowly, the pig looking thoughtful. Karen's grandmother takes a six-quart basket with a dishtowel in it, to put the eggs in.

The sky is bright, bright blue like a fist pushed into an eye, that puddle of hot colour; the thin piercing voices of the cicadas go straight into Karen's head like wires. The edges of her grandmother's hair catch the sunlight and burn like fiery wool. They walk along the path, tall weeds beside them, thistles and Queen Anne's Lace, smelling deeper and greener than anything Karen has ever smelled before, mixing in with the sweet pungent barnyard smells so that she doesn't know whether it smells good or bad or just so powerful and rich it's like being smothered.

The henhouse is near the chicken-wire and rail fence that's around the garden; inside the fence are potato hills, and lettuce in a frilly row, and tripods of poles with climbing beans on them, their red flowers humming with bees. "Potatoes, lettuce, beans," Karen's grandmother says, to Karen, or possibly to herself. "Hens," she says, when they get as far as the henhouse.

The hens are two kinds: white with red wattles, and reddish brown. They scratch and cluck, and peer at Karen with their yellow lizards' eyes, one eye and then the other; sparkles of many-coloured light run off their feathers, like dew. Karen looks and looks at them, until her grandmother takes her arm. "No eggs out here," she says.

The henhouse is musty inside, and dim. Karen's grandmother gropes in the straw-filled boxes, and under the two hens still inside, and puts the eggs into her basket. She gives Karen one egg to carry, for herself. A tender glow comes from inside it. It is a little damp; there are bits of henshit and straw clinging to it. Also it's warm. Karen feels the backs of her legs throbbing and the heat running from the egg up into her head. The egg is soft in her hands, like a beating heart with a rubber shell around it. It's growing, swelling up, and as they walk back past the garden through the sun's glare and the vibration of the bees it gets so large and hot that Karen has to drop it.

After that she was in bed, lying on her stomach. Her grandmother was washing off her legs. "I wasn't the right mother for her," said the grandmother. "Nor she the right

daughter, for me. And now look. But it can't be helped."
She put her large nubbly hands on Karen's legs and at first
it hurt more, and then Karen got warmer and warmer, and
then cool, and after that she went to sleep.

When she woke up she was outside. It was quite dark
but there was a half moon; in the moonlight she could see
the trunks of trees, and the shadows the branches made. At
first she was afraid because she didn't know where she was
or how she'd got there. There was a deep sweet smell, a
glimmering of flowers, milkweeds as she learned later, and
a fluttering of many moths, the white flakes of their wings
kissing against her. Somewhere near was running water.

She heard breathing. Then she felt a wet nose pushed
into her hand, and something brushed against her. The
two dogs were with her, one on either side. Had they
barked when she came out of the house? She didn't know,
she hadn't heard them. But she didn't worry any more
because they would know the way back. She stood for a
long time, breathing in and breathing in, the scent of trees
and dogs and night flowers and water, because this was the
best thing, it was what she wanted, to be outside in the
night by herself. She wasn't sick any longer.

Finally the dogs nudged her gently, turning her
around, herding her back towards the dark bulk of the
house. No lights were on anywhere; she thought she might
go in and up the stairs and into her bed without her grandmother knowing. She didn't want to be shaken or told she
was hard, or hit with anything. But when she reached the
house her grandmother was standing beside it, in a long
pale nightgown with her hair feathery in the moonlight,
holding the door open, and she didn't say anything at all.
She simply nodded at Karen, and Karen went inside.

She felt welcomed, as if the house were a different house, at night; as if this was the first time she had entered it. She knew now that her grandmother walked in her sleep, too, and that her grandmother also could see in the dark.

In the morning Karen ran her hands over the backs of her legs. Nothing hurt. All she could feel, instead of the sticky welts that had been there before, were some tiny thin lines, like hairs; like the cracks in a mirror.

The room Karen slept in was the smallest bedroom upstairs. It used to be her mother's. The bed was narrow, with a scratched headboard of dark varnished wood. There was a white bedspread on it that looked like a lot of caterpillars sewn together, and a chest of drawers painted blue, with a straight-backed wooden chair to match. The drawers were lined with old newspapers; Karen put her folded clothes into them. The curtains were a faded forget-me-not print. In the mornings the sunlight came in through them, showing the dust on the surfaces, and on the rungs of the chair. There was a braided rug, shabby from use, and a dark wardrobe jammed into one corner.

Karen knew her mother hated this room; she hated the whole house. Karen didn't hate it, although there were some things about it she found strange. In the big front bedroom where her grandmother slept, there was a row of men's boots in the closet. There was no bathroom, only an outhouse, with a wooden box of lime and a little wooden paddle, to put the lime down the hole. There was a front parlour with dark curtains and a collection of Indian arrowheads picked up in the fields, and huge stacks of old newspapers all over the floor. On the wall was a framed photo of Karen's grandfather, from a long time ago, before he got crushed by a tractor. "He didn't grow up with tractors," said the grandmother. "Only horses. Damn thing rolled on him. Your mother saw it happen, she was only ten at the time. Maybe that's where she went off the rails. He said it was his own fault, for meddling with the Devil's inventions. He lived for a week, but there was nothing I could do. I can't do a thing about bones." She said these things more to herself than to Karen, as she said many things.

The tractor itself was still in the drive shed; her grandmother used to drive it before she got too old. Now the fields were worked by Ron Sloane from down the road, and he used his own tractor, his own baler, all his own stuff. The second week Karen was there one of the hens went broody and made a nest on the tractor seat instead of in her box. Karen found her, sitting on twenty-three eggs. "They'll do that," said the grandmother. "They know we take their eggs, so they sneak off by themselves. The other hens've been dropping their own eggs on her. Saving themselves the bother. Lazy sluts."

That hen had to be moved back into the henhouse though, because of the weasels. "They come at night," said Karen's grandmother. "They bite the chickens in the neck and suck out their blood." The weasels were so thin they could get through the smallest crack. Karen imagined them, long thin animals like snakes, cold and silent, slithering in through the walls, their mouths open, their sharp fangs ready, their eyes shining and vicious. Her grandmother sent her into the henhouse one night after dark, with the lantern, while she herself stayed outside, looking for cracks in the boards where the light shone through.

One weasel in a henhouse, she said, and that would be that. "They don't kill to eat," she said. "They kill for the pleasure of it."

Karen looked at the photo of her grandfather. She could never tell much from pictures; the bodies in them were just flat, made from black-and-white paper, and no light came out of them. The grandfather had a beard and heavy eyebrows and was wearing a black suit and a hat; he was not smiling. Karen's grandmother said he was a Mennonite, before he married her and broke with the rest of them. Karen was not able to make any sense of this at all, because she didn't know what a Mennonite was. Her grandmother said they were a religion. They wouldn't use anything newfangled, they kept themselves to themselves, they were good farmers. You could always tell a Mennonite farm because they farmed right to the edges of the fields. Also, they didn't hold with war. They wouldn't fight. "In wartime they aren't too popular," she said. "There's people on this line who still aren't speaking to me, because of him."

"I don't hold with war, either," said Karen solemnly. She had just decided that. It was the war that gave her mother so many nerves.

"Well, I know Jesus said turn the other cheek, but God said an eye for an eye," said her grandmother. "If people start killing your folks, you should fight back. That's my opinion."

"You could just go somewhere else," said Karen.

"That's what the Mennonites did," said her grandmother. "Trouble is, what happens when there's no place else to go? Answer that one, I say to him!" Her grandmother often spoke of the grandfather as if he were still alive—"He likes a good pot roast for dinner," or "He never cuts corners." Karen began to wonder whether he was indeed still alive, in some way. If anywhere, he would be in the front parlour.

Maybe that was why they never used the front parlour, only the back one. They would sit in it and Karen's grandmother would knit, one bright afghan square after another, and they would listen to the radio, the news and weather mostly. Karen's grandmother liked to know if it was going to rain, though she said she could tell better than the radio, she could feel rain in her bones. She fell asleep in there every afternoon, on the sofa, wrapped in one of the finished afghans, with her teeth in a glass of water and the pig and the two dogs guarding. In the mornings she was brisk and cheerful; she whistled, she talked to Karen and told her what to do, because there was a right and a wrong way to do everything. But in the afternoons, after lunch, she would droop and begin to yawn, and then she would say she was just going to sit down for a minute.

Karen didn't like being awake while her grandmother was asleep. This was the only part of the day she found frightening. The rest of the time she was busy, she could help. She pulled weeds out of the garden, she collected the eggs, at first with her grandmother and then by herself. She dried the dishes, she fed the dogs. But while her grandmother slept she didn't even go outside, because she didn't want to get too far away. She stayed in the kitchen. Sometimes she looked at the old newspapers. She would search for the weekend comic pages and study them: if you put your eye up close to the page, the faces dissolved into tiny coloured dots. Or she would sit at the kitchen table, drawing with the stub of a pencil on pieces of scrap paper. At first she tried to write letters to her mother. She knew how to print, she had learned at school. *Dear Mother, How are you, Love, Karen.* She would walk down to the mailbox beside the road and put the letter in, and lift the red metal flag. But no letters came in return.

So instead she would sit there drawing with the pencil stub; or else not drawing. Listening. Her grandmother snored, and mumbled in her sleep sometimes. There were flies buzzing, distant cows, chuckling of geese, a car going by, way down on the gravel road at the front of the property. Other sounds. The tap dripping into the sink, in the pantry. Footsteps in the front parlour, a creaking, what was it? The rocker in there, the hard sofa? She sat very still, chilled in the afternoon heat, with the small hairs on her arms lifting, waiting to see if the footsteps would come closer.

On Sundays her grandmother would put on a dress, but she didn't go to church—not like Aunt Vi, who went twice a day on Sundays. Instead she would take the huge family Bible out of the front parlour and stand it up on the kitchen table. She would close her eyes and poke between the pages with a pin, and then open to the page that the pin had chosen. "Now you," she would say to Karen, and Karen would take the pin and close her own eyes, and let her hand hover over the page until she felt it pulled down. Then her grandmother would read the part where the pin had stuck in.

"'If any man among you seemeth to be wise in this world, let him become a fool, that he may be wise,'" she read. "'For the wisdom of this world is foolishness with God.' Well now, I know who that must mean." And she would nod her head.

Sometimes though she would be puzzled. "'The dogs shall eat Jezebel by the wall of Jezreel,'" she read. "Now I don't know at all who that could be. Must be too far ahead." She only read one verse a Sunday. After that she would close up the Bible and put it back in the front parlour, and change into her overalls and go outside to do the chores.

Karen kneels in the garden. She's picking beans into a six-quart basket, yellow beans. She picks slowly, one bean at a time. Her grandmother can pick with both hands at once, not even looking, the same way she knits, but Karen has to look, to find the bean first and then pick it. The sun is white-hot; she's wearing her shorts and a sleeveless blouse, and the straw sunhat her grandmother makes her wear so she won't get sunstroke. Crouched down like that she's almost hidden, because the bean plants are so big. The sunflowers watch her with their huge brown eyes, their yellow petals like spikes of dry fire.

The air shimmers like cellophane, a clear sheet of it shaken over the flat fields; it crackles with grasshopper static. Good haying weather. From two fields over comes the drone of Ron Sloane's tractor, the clack and thump of the baler. Then it stops. Karen reaches the end of the bean row. She pulls a carrot up for herself, wipes off the dirt with her fingers, then rubs the carrot on her leg, then bites into it. She knows she's supposed to wash it first but she likes the earth taste.

There's a motor noise. A dark green pickup truck is coming up the drive. It comes fast, skewing from side to side on the gravel. Karen knows the truck: it's Ron Sloane's truck.

Why isn't he in the field, why is he coming here? Mostly nobody visits. Her grandmother has no opinion of the neighbours. She says they think stupid things and they gossip, and they stare at her when they pass her on the street, when she goes shopping in town. Karen has seen people doing that, all right.

The truck skids to a stop; there's a rush of geese, the dogs barking. The door of the truck opens and Ron Sloane falls out. Staggers out, holding his arm. The tanned skin of his face looks like a brown paper bag, all the pinky-red gone out of it. "Where is she?" he says to Karen. He smells of sweat and fear. His sleeve is torn, his arm is dripping blood. Pouring blood, she sees now. The hurt, the danger comes off the arm in shock waves of brilliant red. Karen wants to scream, but she can't, she can't move. She calls to her grandmother inside her head, and her grandmother comes around the corner of the house carrying a pail, and sees the blood too and drops the pail. "God Almighty," she says. "Ron."

Ron Sloane turns his face to her and it is a look of abject, helpless appeal. "Fuckin' baler," is what he says.

Karen's grandmother is hurrying towards him. "Boys and girls, boys and girls," she says to the dogs and geese. "Cully, out," and there is a barking, cackling retreat.

"It'll be fine," she says to Ron. She puts out her hand and touches him, touches his arm, and says something. What Karen sees is light, a blue glow coming out from her grandmother's hand, and then it's gone and the blood has stopped. "It's done," she says to Ron. "But you need to get to a hospital. All I can do is the blood. I'll drive you, you're not fit. That was a vein; it'll start again in half an hour. Get a wet cloth," she says to Karen. "A tea towel. Cold water."

Karen sits in the back of her grandmother's truck, with Glennie the dog. She always sits in the back now, if she can. The air whirls around her, her own hair ripples against her face, the trees blur by, it's like flying. They go to the hospital, twenty miles away, in the same town as the train station, and Ron gets out, and then he has to sit and put his head down, and then Karen's grandmother gets an arm around him and they hobble together into the hospital like people in a three-legged race. Karen and Glennie wait in the truck.

After a while her grandmother comes out. She says they're leaving Ron Sloane at the hospital to get sewed up, and he will be all right now. They drive back to tell Mrs. Sloane what's happened to Ron, so she won't worry. They sit at Mrs. Sloane's kitchen table and Karen's grandmother has tea and Karen has a glass of lemonade, and Mrs. Sloane cries and says thank you, and the grandmother doesn't say you're welcome. She only nods, a little stiffly, and says, "Don't thank me. It isn't me does it."

Mrs. Sloane has a fourteen-year-old daughter with pale hair, paler than Karen's, and pink eyes, and skin devoid of colour. She passes a plate of store cookies, and stares and stares at Karen's grandmother as if her pink eyes are about to fall out. Mrs. Sloane doesn't like Karen's grandmother, although she urges her to have more tea. Neither does the white-haired daughter. Instead they are afraid of her. Their fear is all around their bodies, little grey icy shivers, like wind blowing on a pond. They're afraid and Karen isn't; or not as much. She would like to touch blood too, she would like to be able to make it stop.

●   ◉   ●

In the evenings, when it's cooler, Karen and her grand-mother visit the cemetery. It's less than a mile away. At these times Karen's grandmother puts on her dress, but Karen doesn't have to.

They always walk, they never take the truck. They go along the gravel road beside the fences and the ditches and the dust-coated weeds, and Karen holds her grandmoth-er's hand. It's the only time she does. She holds it in a new way now, feeling its stringy veins and its knobs of bone and the loose skin on it not as *old* but as a colour. The colour of light blue. It's a hand with power.

The cemetery is small; the church beside it small too, and vacant. The people who used to be there have built a new church, a bigger one, out beside the main highway.

"That's where we put the women and children, when the Fenians came," says Karen's grandmother. "Inside that very church."

"What are Fenians?" says Karen. The word makes her think of a laxative, she's heard it on the radio. Feen-a-mints.

"Trash up from the States," says the grandmother. "Irish. They wanted war. Their eyes were bigger than their stomachs though." She talks about this event as though it just happened the other day, but really it was a long time ago. Over seventy years.

"We're not Irish," says Karen.

"Not by a long shot," says Karen's grandmother, "though your great-grandmother was." She herself is Scotch, partly, so Karen is part Scotch too. Part Scotch, part English, part Mennonite, and part of whatever her father was. According to her grandmother, Scotch is the best thing to be.

The cemetery is weedy, though people still come here: some of the graves are mowed. Grandmother knows where everyone's buried, and why: a car crash at a cross-roads, four dead, they'd been drinking; a man who blew himself in two with his own shotgun, everyone knew only they didn't want to say because then it would be suicide and that was a disgrace. A lady and her baby, the baby's grave smaller, like a tiny bedstead; another disgrace, because that baby had no real father. But "All fathers are real," says the grandmother, "though they're not all right." There are angel heads on the gravestones, urns with willow trees, stone lambs, stone flowers; real flowers too, wilting in jam jars. The grandmother's mother and father are in here, and her two brothers. She takes Karen to look at them; she doesn't say "their graves," she says "them." But mostly she wants to see Karen's grandfather. His name is carved on his stone, and his two numbers—when he was born, and when he died.

"Maybe I should've sent him back to the Mennonites," she says. "He might like to be with his own people. But most likely they wouldn't've took him. Anyways, he's best here with me."

Grandmother's own name is carved underneath his, but her right-hand date is a blank. "I had to get it fixed beforehand," she says to Karen. "Nobody around here to do it, after. That Gloria and that Vi would probably just dump me into the ditch, save the money. They're waiting for me to die so they can sell the farm. Or else they'd move me into that city, some hole in the ground. So I fooled them, I bought my own gravestone. I'm all set, come hell or high water."

"I don't want you to die," says Karen. She doesn't.

Her grandmother is a safe place for her, although hard. Or because hard. Not shifting, not watery. She doesn't change.

Her grandmother sticks out her chin. "I don't intend to die," she says. "Only the body dies." She glares at Karen; she looks almost ferocious. Her hair on top is like thistles, after they've gone to seed.

Did Karen love her grandmother? thinks Charis, halfway to the Island, sitting at the back of the ferry, remembering herself remembering. Sometimes yes, sometimes no. Love is too simple a word for such a mixture of harsh and soft colours, of pungent tastes and rasping edges. "There's more than one way to skin a cat," her grandmother would say, and Karen would flinch, because she could picture her grandmother actually skinning one. Her grandmother went out at dawn with her .22 rifle and shot woodchucks; also rabbits, which she made into stews. She killed the chickens when they were too old to lay or just when she wanted a chicken; she chopped their heads off with an axe, on the wooden chopping block, and they ran silently around the barnyard with their necks fountaining blood and the grey smoke of their life rising up from them and the rainbow of light around them fading and then going out. Then she plucked and gutted them and singed off their pinfeathers with a candle, and after they were cooked she saved their wishbones and dried them on the win-dowsill. She had five there already. Karen wanted them to break one, but her grandmother said, "Have you got a wish?" and Karen couldn't think of one. "You save these for when you need them," said her grandmother.

Karen asks more questions now; she does more

things. Her grandmother says she is toughening up. When she goes to the henhouse by herself to get the eggs, she swats at the hens if they hiss and try to peck her, and if the rooster jumps at her bare legs she kicks him; sometimes she carries a stick, to beat him off. "He's a mean old devil," her grandmother says. "Don't you take anything from him. Just give him a good whack. He'll respect you for it."

One morning they're eating bacon, and her grandmother says, "This here is Pinky."

"Pinky?" says Karen. Pinky the pig is lying on her afghan where she usually is during meals, blinking with her bristly-lashed eyes and hoping for scraps. "Pinky's right here!"

"This is last year's Pinky," says her grandmother. "There's a new one every year." She looks across the table at Karen. She has a sly expression; she's waiting to see how Karen will take it.

Karen doesn't know what to do. She could start to cry and jump up from the table and run out of the room, which is what her mother would do and is also what she herself feels like doing. Instead she sets her fork down and takes the rubbery chewed piece of bacon out of her mouth and places it gently on her plate, and that's the end of bacon for her, right then and there, forever.

"Well, for heaven's sake," says her grandmother, aggrieved but with some contempt. It's as if Karen has failed at something. "It's only pigs. They're cute when they're young, smart too, but if I let them stay alive they'd get too big. They're wild when they grow up, they're cunning, they'd eat you, yourself. They'd gobble you up as soon as look at you!"

Karen thinks about Pinky, running around the barn-yard with no head, the grey smoke of her life going up from her and her rainbow light shrinking to nothing. Whatever else, her grandmother is a killer. No wonder other people are afraid of her.

35

It was Labour Day. That was when Karen's mother was supposed to come on the train and take Karen back to the city. Karen had her suitcase all packed. She cried, in her narrow bed, under her chenille spread, under her pillow. She didn't want to leave her grandmother, but she wanted to see her mother, who—already—she couldn't remember clearly. All she could remember was her dresses, and the smell of Tabu, and one of her voices, her sweet voice, the too-sweet voice she used on the Grade Twos.

Her mother didn't come. Instead there was a phone call from Aunt Vi, and Karen's grandmother said there had been a hitch and Karen would be staying a little longer. "You can help me put up the tomatoes," she said. Karen picked tomatoes and washed them in the pantry, and her grandmother scalded them and peeled them and boiled them in jars.

Then it was time for school to begin, and still nothing happened. "There's no point starting you at that school," said Karen's grandmother. "You'd just be in and out." Karen didn't mind. She didn't much like school anyway, it was hard to pay attention to so many people in the same room at once. It was like the radio when there was a thunderstorm near: she could hardly hear a thing.

Her grandmother brought the Bible out of the front parlour and stood it on the kitchen table. "Let me see, said the blind man," she said. She closed her eyes and poked with a pin. "Psalm Eighty-eight. I've had that before. 'Lover and friend hast thou put far from me, and mine acquaintance into darkness.' Well, that's right enough; it means I should get ready to go, myself, pretty soon. Now you."

Karen took the pin and closed her eyes, and her hand followed the strong current that pulled it downwards. "Ah," said her grandmother, squinting. "Jezebel again. Revelations, Two, Twenty. 'Notwithstanding I have a few things against thee, because thou sufferest that woman Jezebel, which callest herself a prophetess, to teach and to seduce my servants to commit fornication, and to eat things sacrificed unto idols.' Now that's a strange thing, for a little girl." And she smiled at Karen, the smile of a withered apple. "You must be living ahead of yourself." Karen had no idea what she meant.

Finally it was Aunt Vi who arrived, not Karen's mother. She didn't even stay at the grandmother's house. She stayed at the one hotel in town, and the grandmother drove Karen in. Karen didn't sit in the back of the truck this time. She sat in the front seat with the dog hairs, wearing her dress, the same as the day she came, looking out the window and not saying a thing. Her grandmother whistled softly.

Aunt Vi wasn't all that pleased to see Karen but she pretended to be. She gave Karen a peck on the cheek. "Look how tall you've grown!" she said. It sounded like an accusation. "You've got her suitcase?" she said to the grandmother.

"Viola, I'm hardly senile yet," said the grandmother. "I'm not likely to forget her suitcase. Here you go," she said to Karen softly. "I put a wishbone in it." She crouched down and put her bony arms around Karen, and Karen could feel her square body, solid as a house, and then her grandmother wasn't there any longer.

Karen sat on the train beside Aunt Vi, who fussed and fussed. "We'll have to get you enrolled in school, right away," she said. "You've missed almost a month already! My goodness, you're brown as a berry!"

"Where's my mother?" said Karen. She couldn't think of any berries that were brown.

Aunt Vi frowned and looked away. "Your mother isn't well," she said.

When Karen got to Aunt Vi's house she went into her usual room with the orange-and-pink flowered curtains and opened up her suitcase right away. There was the hen wishbone, wrapped in a piece of wax paper, with a rubber band around it, from her grandmother's jar of saved-up rubber bands that was kept beside the sink. She took the wishbone out. It smelled sour, but rich and full, like a hand with dirt on it. She hid it in the hem of one of the curtains. She knew that if Aunt Vi found it she would throw it away.

Karen's mother is in a building, a new flat yellow building that looks like a school. Aunt Vi and Uncle Vern take

Karen to visit her. They sit in the waiting room, on hard chairs covered with a nubbly fabric, and Karen is frightened because Aunt Vi and Uncle Vern are so solemn; solemn, and at the same time avid. They are like the people who stop their cars and get out to see when there's been a car accident. Something is bad, something is wrong, but they want to participate in it, whatever it is. Karen would rather not, she would like to go back right now, back in time, back as far as the farm, but a door opens and her mother comes into the room. She walks slowly, putting a hand out to touch the furniture as if to guide herself. *Sleepwalking,* thinks Karen. Before, her mother's fingers were slim, the nails polished. She was proud of her hands. But now her hands are swollen and clumsy and there is no ring any more on her wedding finger. She's wearing a grey housecoat and slippers that Karen has never seen before, and also she has never before seen her mother's face.

Not this face. It's a flat face with a dull shine on it, like the dead fish in the white enamel trays at the fish store. A fading light, silvery, like scales. She turns this face towards Karen; it's expressionless as a plate. Eyes of china. Suddenly Karen is framed in those eyes, a small pale girl sitting on a nubbly chair, a girl her mother has never seen before. Karen brings her two hands up to her mouth and breathes in, a gasp, the reverse of a scream.

"Gloria. How're you feeling?" says Uncle Vern.

Karen's mother's head swings towards him, a ponderous head, heavy. The hair on it is pulled back, held with clips. Karen's mother used to do her hair up in pincurls, and when she combed it out it would be wavy. This hair is plain and straight, and filmed over, as if it's been kept in a cupboard. Karen thinks about her grandmother's root cellar, with its smell of indoor earth and its rows of preserve bottles, bright berries glassed over, powdered with dust.

"Fine," says Karen's mother, after a minute.

"I can't stand it," says Aunt Vi. She dabs at her eyes with a hankie. Then, in a firmer voice: "Karen, aren't you going to give your mother a kiss?"

Aunt Vi's questions are like orders. Karen slides off her chair and goes over to this woman. She doesn't put her arms around her, she doesn't touch her with her hands. She bends her body from the waist and places her lips against the woman's cheek. She hardly presses at all, but her mouth sinks in and down, on the cheek that is like cool rubber. She thinks of Pinky without a head, collapsing in the barnyard, becoming ham. Her mother has the texture of luncheon meat. She feels sick to her stomach.

Her mother receives the kiss passively. Karen steps back. There is no red light around her mother now. Only a faint mauve-brown shimmer.

In the car on the way home, Karen sits between Aunt Vi and Uncle Vern instead of in the back where she usually sits. Aunt Vi wipes at her eyes. Uncle Vern asks Karen if she wants an ice cream cone. She says no thank you, and he pats her knee.

"I felt so bad, my own little sister; but I had to do it," Aunt Vi says, on the phone. "It was the third time, and what could I do? I don't know where she got them! Lucky the empty bottle was right there beside her so at least we could tell the doctor what she took. It's just a wonder we were in time. Something in her voice, I guess; well, it's not like I hadn't heard it before! When we got there she was out cold. She had bruises on her mouth for weeks, they had to pry it open to get the hose down, and today it was like you wouldn't of known her. I don't know—shock treatments, I guess. If that doesn't work, they'll have to do an operation." She says *operation* in that solemn voice, the voice she uses for saying grace, as if it's a holy word. She wants it, this operation, Karen can tell. If her mother has an operation, some of that holiness will rub off on Aunt Vi.

Karen went to school, where she said little and did not make friends. She was not teased either, she was mostly ignored. She knew how to do that, make herself invisible. All she had to do was to suck in the light around her body; it was like sucking in her breath. When the teacher looked at her the look went right through, to whoever was sitting behind her. This way Karen hardly needed to be in the classroom at all. She let her hands do whatever was required: long rows of a's and b's, neat columns of numbers. She got gold stars for neatness. Her paper snowflake and her paper tulip were among the ten pinned up on the corkboard.

Every week, then every two weeks, then every three, she went with her aunt and uncle to visit her mother. Her mother was in a different hospital now. "Your mother is very ill," Aunt Vi told her, but Karen didn't need to be told. She could see the illness spreading on her mother's skin, like the hairs on arms, gone out of control; like filaments of lightning, only very small and slow. Like grey mould spreading through bread. When her mother was veined through and through like that, then she would die. Nobody could stop her, because that was what she wanted to do.

Karen thought about using her wishbone but she knew it wouldn't be any good. To make a wish work you had to really want it, and she didn't want this woman to stay alive. If she could have had her mother back the way she was before, during the good times, yes. But she knew this was impossible. There wasn't enough of that mother left. So she kept the wishbone in the hem of the curtain, checking once in a while to make sure it was still there.

Karen sat in her room. Sometimes she banged her head softly against the wall, so she wouldn't have to think. Or she looked out the window a lot. Or she looked out the window at school. What she looked at was the sky. She thought about the summer. Maybe next summer her aunt and uncle would go on a vacation and she could be back at her grandmother's farm, gathering the eggs, picking yellow beans in the sun.

On her eighth birthday Karen has a cake. Aunt Vi has baked it, and put sugar roses on it from the store, and eight candles. She asks Karen if she wants to have a little friend over, but Karen says no. So they eat the birthday dinner by themselves, the three of them, *Oh Lord, bless this food to our use, Amen,* and there are tuna and egg salad sandwiches, and peanut butter and jelly, and Aunt Vi says, "Isn't this nice," and then there is Neapolitan ice cream in three colours, white, pink, and brown. After that the cake. Aunt Vi lights the candles and tells Karen to blow them out and make a wish, but Karen just sits there, looking at the flames.

"I don't think she's ever had a cake before," Aunt Vi says to Uncle Vern, and Uncle Vern says, "Poor little tyke," and ruffles Karen's hair. He does this often these days and Karen doesn't like it. Uncle Vern's hands have a heavy luminescence around them, thick like jelly, sticky, brown-green. Sometimes Karen examines her blonde hair in the mirror to see if any of it has come off.

"Make a wish," says Uncle Vern heartily. "Wish for a bicycle!"

"You have to close your eyes," says Aunt Vi.

So to humour them Karen closes her eyes, and sees nothing but the sky, and opens her eyes again and obediently blows out the candles. Aunt Vi and Uncle Vern clap their hands, applauding, and Uncle Vern says, "Well, what do you know! Look what we have here!" and out of the kitchen he wheels a brand-new bicycle, bright red. It's decorated with pink ribbons and has a balloon tied to one handle. "What do you think of that?" says Uncle Vern eagerly.

It's dusk; the smell of mowed grass comes in through the open window, the June bugs batter themselves against the screen. Karen looks at the bicycle, at its glinting spokes and chains and its two black wheels, and knows that her mother is dead.

Her mother did not die for another three weeks, but it was the same thing, because sometimes (thinks Charis) there is a fold in time, like the way you fold the top bedsheet down to make a border, and if you stick a pin through at any spot, then the two pinholes are aligned, and that's the way it is when you foresee the future. There's nothing myste-rious about it, any more than there is with a backwash in a lake or with harmony in music, two melodies going on at the same time. Memory is the same overlap, the same kind of pleat, only backwards.

Or maybe the fold is not in time itself but in the mind of the person watching. In any case, Karen looks at the bicycle and sees her mother's death, and collapses onto the floor, crying, and Aunt Vi and Uncle Vern are baffled and then angry, and tell her she is a lucky girl, a lucky, ungrateful girl, and she can't explain.

There was a funeral but not very many people came. A few teachers from her mother's old school, some friends of Aunt Vi's. Her grandmother wasn't there, but Karen didn't find that strange—her grandmother in the city would have been out of place. There was another reason as well—*stroke,* said Aunt Vi, and *nursing home,* in the tone of voice that was supposed to enlist other people's sympathy for her—but these words meant nothing to Karen and she didn't want to hear them, so she put them out of her mind. She had on a navy blue dress, which was the closest Aunt Vi could get to black, at short notice, although—she said on the phone—she should've seen it coming. Karen wasn't allowed to visit her mother's body in the coffin because Aunt Vi said it was too shocking a thing for a young child, but she knew anyway what it would look like. The same as alive, only more so.

Uncle Vern and Aunt Vi have had part of their cellar re-done. They've had plasterboard put over the cement-block walls, linoleum with thick carpeting over it on the floor. They've made a rec room down there, *rec* not like *wreck* but like *recreation*. There's a bar with bar stools, and a set of Chinese chequers for Karen, and a television set. It's the second television set they've bought; the first one is kept in the living room. Karen likes to watch the set in the rec room, out of everyone's way. She doesn't actually have to pay attention to what's in front of her on the screen; she can be by herself, inside her head, and no one will ask what she's doing.

It's September, but outside, upstairs, it's still dry and hot. Karen sits on the carpet, in the rec room where it's cooler, in bare feet and shorts and a sleeveless top, watching *Kukla, Fran & Ollie* on TV. Kukla, Fran and Ollie are puppets, or two of them are. Overhead, Aunt Vi's shoes clack busily back and forth across the kitchen floor. Karen hugs her own knees, rocking gently. After a while she gets up and goes to the bar sink and runs herself a glass of water, and puts in an ice cube out of the little refrigerator, and sits back down on the rug.

Uncle Vern comes down the stairs. He's been mowing the lawn. He is a deeper red than usual, and the smell of sweat encircles him, like the water drops when a wet dog shakes itself. He goes to the bar and gets out a beer, takes the cap off the bottle and drinks down half, and wipes his wet face with the towel beside the sink. Then he sits down on the sofa. The sofa is a sofa-bed, in case they have visitors, because Karen has the room that used to be the guest room. That room is still called "the guest room," although Karen is living in it. They don't have visitors, though.

Karen gets up. She intends to go upstairs, because she knows what will happen next, but she isn't fast enough. "Come on," says Uncle Vern. He pats his huge, hairy knee, and Karen goes reluctantly towards him. He likes her to sit on his knee. He thinks it's fatherly. "You're our little girl now," he says fondly. But he isn't really fond of her, Karen knows that. She knows she is unsatisfactory to him, because she doesn't talk to him, she doesn't hug him, she doesn't smile enough. It's his smell she doesn't like. That, and his greeny-brown light.

She sits on Uncle Vern's knee and he pulls her higher up onto his lap and encircles her with one of his red arms. With the other hand he strokes her leg. He often does this, she's used to it; but this time he moves his hand up higher, between her legs. Kukla, Fran and Ollie continue to talk in their made-up voices; Kukla is some sort of a dragon. Karen squirms a little, trying to move herself away from the enormous fingers, which are inside her shorts now, but the arm tightens around her stomach and Uncle Vern says into her ear, "Hold still!" He does not sound hearty, wheedling, the way he usually does; he sounds angry. He has both hands on her now, he rubs her back and forth across himself as if she's a washcloth; his sticky breath is all over her ear. "You like your old Uncle Vern, don't you?" he says furiously.

"You two!" Aunt Vi calls gaily down the cellar stairs. "Suppertime! There's corn on the cob!"

"Be right there!" Uncle Vern yells hoarsely, as if the words have been expelled from him by a kick in the stomach. He shoves one finger right up inside Karen, and groans as if he's been stabbed. He holds Karen against himself for another minute: the energy is leaking out of him and he needs a bandage. Then he lets her go.

"Scamper upstairs," he tells her. He's trying for his fake voice, his uncle voice, but he hasn't got it back; his voice is desolate. "Tell your Auntie Vi I'll be up in a minute." Karen looks behind herself, to see if the back of her shorts is browny-green, but it isn't; only wet. Uncle Vern is wiping himself off with the bar towel.

Uncle Vern lurks, he lies in wait. Karen evades him, but she can't evade him all the time. The strange thing is that Uncle Vern never comes looking for her when Aunt Vi isn't in the house. Maybe he likes the danger; or maybe he knows that with Aunt Vi there, Karen won't dare to make a sound. It's unclear how he knows this, or why this is so, but it's true. Karen's fear of Aunt Vi's finding out is greater than her fear of Uncle Vern's sausage fingers.

Soon one finger isn't enough for him. He stands Karen in front of him, facing away so she can't see, a big knee holding her on either side, and puts his hands up under her pleated school skirts and slides her panties right down, shoving something hard in between her legs from behind. Or he uses two fingers, three. It hurts, but Karen knows that people who love you can do painful things to you, and she tries hard to believe that he does love her. He says he does. "Your old uncle loves you," he tells her, scraping his face against hers.

When they are having dinner afterwards he laughs more, he talks louder, he tells jokes, he kisses Aunt Vi on the cheek. He brings them both presents: boxes of chocolates for Aunt Vi, stuffed animals for Karen. "You're just like our daughter," he says. Aunt Vi smiles thinly. Nobody can say they aren't doing the right thing.

Karen loses her appetite: the effort of not thinking about Uncle Vern, both when he's there and when he isn't, is making her weak. She becomes thinner and paler, and

Aunt Vi discusses her on the phone—"It's the loss of her mother, she's the quiet type but you can tell she feels it. She just mopes around. I wasn't expecting it to go on this long. She's almost ten!" She takes Karen to the doctor to see if she has anemia, but she doesn't.

"Tell me what's wrong," says Aunt Vi. "It's better if you talk about it. You can tell me!" She has that solemn, avid look on her face, she's expecting to hear about Karen's mother. She urges and urges.

"I don't like Uncle Vern touching me," says Karen finally.

Aunt Vi's face goes slack, then hardens. "Touching you?" she says suspiciously. "What do you mean, *touching*?"

"Touching," says Karen miserably. "Down there." She points. She knows already she's done a wrong, an unforgivable thing. Up to now Aunt Vi has been willing to tolerate her, even to put on a show of liking her. Not any more.

Aunt Vi's lips are white, her eyes are sparkling dangerously. Karen looks down at the floor so as not to see. "You're exactly like your mother," says Aunt Vi. "A liar. I wouldn't be surprised if you went crazy, just like her. God knows it runs in the family! Don't you ever say such an evil thing about your uncle! He loves you like a daughter! Do you want to destroy him?" She starts to cry. "Pray to God to forgive you!" Then her face changes again. She wipes her eyes, she smiles. "We'll just forget you ever said that, dear," she says. "We'll both forget it. I know things have been hard on you. You never had a father."

After that, what can be done? Nothing at all. Uncle Vern knows Karen has told. He is nicer than ever to Aunt Vi. He is even nice to Karen, in front of people; but sadly, as if he's forgiving her. When Aunt Vi isn't looking he stares across the dinner table at Karen, his eyes in his face of uncooked beef shining with triumph. *You can't win this fight,* he's telling her. She can hear the words as clearly as if he's spoken them. For the time being he's avoiding her, he no longer tracks her through the house, but he's waiting. He's itching to get his hands on her, but not with any pleading whispers. Now he won't ask if she likes him, now he's more like her mother used to be, before she would start screaming and reach for the broom handle. That ominous lull, that softness.

Karen sleeps with her head under her pillow, because she doesn't want to hear or see; but she's sleepwalking again, more than ever. She wakes up in the living room, trying to get out through the French windows, or in the kitchen, shaking the back door handle. But Aunt Vi locks all the doors.

Karen is sitting straight up in her bed, holding her pillow against her chest. Her heart is beating with terror. There's a man standing in her dark bedroom; it's Uncle Vern, she can see his face in the light that comes through from the hall, just before he eases the door shut. His eyes are open, but he's sleepwalking; he has his striped pyjamas on, he has a glazed look. *Don't ever wake a person sleepwalking,* said her grandmother. *It breaks their journey.*

Uncle Vern sleepwalks quietly across the floor to Karen's bed. With him comes a smell of stale sweat and rancid meat. He kneels and the bed heaves like a boat, he pushes and Karen falls backwards. "You're a little bastard, that's what you are," he whispers softly. "A sly little bastard." He's talking in his sleep.

Then he falls on top of Karen and puts his slabby hand

over her mouth, and splits her in two. He splits her in two right up the middle and her skin comes open like the dry skin of a cocoon, and Charis flies out. Her new body is light as a feather, light as air. There's no pain in it at all. She flies over to the window and in behind the curtain, and stays there, looking out through the cloth, right through the pattern of pink and orange roses. What she sees is a small pale girl, her face contorted and streaming, nose and eyes wet as if she's drowning—gasping for air, going under again, gasping. On top of her is a dark mass, worrying at her, like an animal eating another animal. Her entire body—because Charis can see right through things, through the sheets, through the flesh to the bone—her body is made of something slippery and yellow, like the fat in a gutted hen. Charis watches in amazement as the man grunts, as the small child wriggles and flails as if hooked through the neck. Charis doesn't know she is Charis, of course. She has no name yet.

The man sits up, his hand over his heart, gasping for air now himself. "There," he says, as if he's completed something: a task. "Shut up now, I didn't hurt you. Shut up! You keep your dirty little mouth shut about this or I'll kill you!" Then he groans, the way he does in the bathroom in the mornings. "Oh God, I don't know what got into me!"

The small girl is rolling over onto her side. As Charis watches, she leans over and vomits onto the floor, onto the man's feet. Charis knows why. It's because that brown-green light is inside her body now, thick and sticky, like goose turds. It came out of Uncle Vern and went into Karen, and she has to get it out.

The door opens. Aunt Vi is standing there, in her nightgown. "What is it, what's going on?" she says.

"I heard her in here," says Uncle Vern. "She was calling—I think she's got the stomach flu."

"Well, for heaven's sake," says Aunt Vi. "You should've had sense enough to take her into the bathroom. I'll get the floor cloth. Karen, are you going to do that again?"

Karen has no speech, because Charis has taken all the words with her. Karen opens her mouth, and Charis is sucked back, it's as if she's being vacuumed into their shared throat. "Yes," she says.

After the third time Karen knows she is trapped. All she can do is split in two; all she can do is turn into Charis, and float out of her body and watch Karen, left behind with no words, flailing and sobbing. She will have to go on like this forever because Aunt Vi will never hear her, no matter what she says. She would like to take an axe and chop Uncle Vern's head off, and Aunt Vi's too, as if they were chickens; she would watch the grey smoke of their lives twist up out of them. But she knows she could never kill anything. She isn't hard enough.

She takes the wishbone out of the hem of her curtain and closes her eyes, and holds both stems of the wishbone, and pulls. What she wishes for is her grandmother. Her grandmother is far away now, almost like a story she was told once; she can hardly believe she once lived at such a place as the farm, or even that there is such a place. But she wishes anyway, and when she opens her eyes her grandmother is there, coming right into her room through the closed door, wearing her overalls and frowning a little, and smiling also. She walks towards Karen and Karen feels a cool wind against her skin, and the grandmother holds out both of her knobby old hands, and Karen puts out her own hands and touches her, and her hands feel as if sand is falling over them. There's a smell of milkweed flowers and garden soil. The grandmother keeps on walking; her eyes are light blue, and her cheek comes against Karen's, cool grains of dry rice. Then she's like the dots on the comic page, close up, and then she's only a swirl in the air, and then she's gone.

But some of her power stays there, in Karen's hands. Her healing power, her killing power. Not enough to get Karen out of the trap, but enough to keep her alive. She looks at her hands and sees a trace of blue.

What she has to do is wait. She must wait like a stone, until it's time. So this is what she does. As soon as Uncle Vern touches her she splits in two, and the rest of the time she waits.

Her grandmother is dead, or dead to this life, though Karen has seen her and she knows there isn't any death really. The Bible arrives in a large box, addressed to Karen, and Karen puts it in her suitcase under her bed, ready for when she can leave. Her grandmother has left her the farm, but because Karen's not old enough she can't have it or even go there, although she wants to. Uncle Vern and Aunt Vi are her guardians. They are in control.

When she grows breasts and hair under her arms and on her legs and between them, and has her first period, Uncle Vern leaves her alone. There is a space between them, but it isn't like an absence. It's a presence, transparent but thicker than air. Uncle Vern is afraid of her now, he's afraid of what she's going to do or say; he's afraid of what she remembers, he's afraid of being judged. Maybe it's because her eyes are no longer timid, no longer vacant or beseeching. Her eyes are stone. When she looks at him with her stone eyes it's as if she's reaching in through his ribs and squeezing his heart so it almost stops. He says he has a heart condition, he takes pills for it, but they both know it's a thing she's doing to him. Every time she looks at him she feels loathing, and a deep nausea. She's disgusted with him, but also with her body, because it still has his dirt inside it. She must think of ways to get clean inside.

When she feels those things she has to seal them off. She has to or else she will be destroyed. She splits herself in two and stays with the cooler part, the clearer part of herself. She has a name for this part now: she is Charis. She picked the hint for her new name out of the Bible, with a pin: "The greatest of these is Charity." Charity is better than Faith and Hope. She can use this new name only to herself, of course. Everyone else still calls her Karen.

Charis is more serene than Karen, because the bad things have stayed behind, with small Karen. She's polite to her aunt, but remote. One day, when she is over eighteen, she asks the two of them what they have done with her grandmother's money. Her uncle says he's invested it for her and she can have all of it when she's twenty-one, and meanwhile some of it can be used for her education. Aunt Vi acts as if this is an act of great generosity, as if the money belongs to them and they're giving it away. But nevertheless they're both relieved when she goes to university and moves into McClung Hall. Aunt Vi is nervous of her because of her stony eyes; as for Uncle Vern, he doesn't know what she remembers. He hopes she's forgotten it all, but he isn't sure.

She remembers everything, or rather Karen does; but Karen is in storage. Charis only remembers when she takes Karen out, from the suitcase under her bed where she has put her. She doesn't do this often. Karen is still little, but Charis is growing up.

Charis turned twenty-one, but nothing was said about her grandmother's money. She didn't care. She wouldn't take money from them anyway, because even though it was really her own money it had been in their hands, it was dirty. She wouldn't be able to get it anyway without a fight.

She didn't want to fight. Instead she wanted to go away somewhere else, and as soon as she felt ready she simply dropped out of sight. Out of their sight. It wasn't so hard when you knew no one would come looking for you. She left university before finishing—she was flunking her courses anyway, because they failed to hold her attention—and went travelling. She hitchhiked, she took buses. She worked as a waitress, she worked in an office. For a while she was in an ashram on the West Coast, for a while she stayed on a communal farm in Saskatchewan. She did various things.

Once she went back to the farm, her grandmother's farm; she wanted to see it. But it wasn't a farm any more, it was a subdivision. Charis tried not to mind, since nothing that was or had been would perish, and the farm was still inside her, it was still hers because places belonged to the people who loved them.

When she was twenty-six she dumped her old name. A lot of people were changing their names, then, because names were not just labels, they were also containers. *Karen* was a leather bag, a grey one. Charis collected everything she didn't want and shoved it into this name, this leather bag, and tied it shut. She threw away as many of the old wounds and poisons as she could. She kept only the things about herself that she liked or needed.

She did all of this inside her head, because the events there are just as real as the events anywhere else. Still inside her head, she walked to the shore of Lake Ontario and sank the leather bag into the water.

That was the end of Karen. Karen was gone. But the lake was inside Charis really, so that's where Karen was too. Down deep.

36

Until now, in her house on the Island, until this windy night with the scraping branches. Karen is coming back, Charis can't keep her away any more. She's torn away the rotting leather, she's come to the surface, she's walked through the bedroom wall, she's standing in the room right now. But she is no longer a nine-year-old girl. She has grown up, she has grown tall and thin and straggly, like a plant in a cellar, starved for light. And her hair isn't pale any more, but dark. The sockets of her eyes are dark too, dark bruises. She no longer looks like Karen. She looks like Zenia.

She walks towards Charis and bends, and blends into her, and now she's inside Charis's body. With her she brings the ancient shame, which feels warm.

Charis must have said something or made a sound, because Billy's awake now. He has turned over, he's pulling her to him, he's kissing her, burrowing into her with his old urgency. *It isn't me,* Charis wants to tell him, because she's no longer in charge of her own body. This other woman has taken over; but Charis doesn't float away, doesn't watch from behind the curtain. She's in the body too, she can feel everything. She can feel the body moving, responding;

she can feel the pleasure shoot through her like electricity, unfold in a hundred colours, like a peacock's tail on fire. She forgets about Karen, she forgets about herself. Everything in her has been fused together.

"Hey, that was different," Billy says. He's kissing her eyes, her mouth; she's lying in his arms, limp as a sick person; she can't move. *It wasn't me,* she thinks. But it was, partly. What she feels is difficult: guilt, relief. Anguish. Resentment, because Billy has the power to do that; resentment also, because she has lived for so many years without knowing about it.

Deep inside, far inside her body, something new is moving.

(That was the night her daughter was conceived. Charis is sure of it. She has always known who the father was, of course. There weren't any other choices. But the mother? Was it herself and Karen, sharing their body? Or was it Zenia, too?)

In the morning she feels more like herself, like Charis. She doesn't know where Karen has gone. Not back underneath the lake; it doesn't feel like that. Possibly Karen is hiding somewhere else inside their shared body; but when she closes her eyes and searches with the mind's eye, here and there within herself, she can't find her, although there is a dark patch, a shadow, something she can't see. When she makes love with Billy she doesn't think about being Karen, or Charis either. She thinks about being Zenia.

• • •

"Promise me she's leaving soon," says Billy. By now he's no longer angry. He's insistent, pleading, almost desperate.

"She's leaving soon," says Charis, as if reassuring a child. She loves Billy more now, in some ways; but in some ways less. Once greediness comes into a thing, the greediness of the body, it gets in the way of pure giving. She wants Billy's body now, for itself, not just as a manifestation of his essence. Instead of simply ministering to him, she wants something back. Maybe this is wrong; she doesn't know.

They're lying in bed, it's morning, she's stroking his face. "Soon, soon," she sings, crooning, to soothe him. She no longer thinks his body wants Zenia. How could he want Zenia, now that Charis wants him?

It's the middle of December. The frost is in the ground, the leaves are off the trees, the wind is gathering momentum. Tonight it's straight off the lake, hurling itself through the trees and bushes, tearing at the plastic sheeting that Charis has stapled over the windows to keep out the drafts. There are no storm windows for this house and the landlord has no intention of buying them any, because in his opinion all the houses on the Island will soon be bulldozed flat, so why spend the money? There's also no insulation.

Charis is beginning to see the drawbacks of living here. Already two of the houses on her street are empty, their windows boarded up. She wonders whether they will have enough wood to keep themselves warm when the real winter comes. There's a man at the co-op who might trade some yoga lessons for wood, but wood is heavy, so how will she get it to the Island?

They will all need winter clothing too. Billy is in the city tonight, at another one of those meetings. She pictures him at the ferry dock, waiting for the last boat back, shivering in his thin jacket. She should be knitting him something. She'll go to the Goodwill store, soon, and try for some second-hand coats.

One for Billy, one for herself, and one for Zenia as well, because Zenia has only the clothes on her back. She's afraid to go to West's place to get the rest of her clothes, or so she says. She's afraid West will kill her. He has an obsessive personality—gentle on the outside, but sometimes he goes berserk, and the thought of her dying drives him crazy. If he's going to lose her, if she's going to be dead, he wants to be in control of her death himself. A lot of men are like that, says Zenia, with a reminiscent stare into space, a tiny smile. Love drives them mad.

Once upon a time, Charis would never have understood a statement like that. Now she does.

Charis is certain she's pregnant. She's missed a period, but that isn't all: her body feels different, no longer taut and sinewy but sponge-like, fluid. Saturated. It has a different energy, a deep orangy-pink, like the inside of a hibiscus. She hasn't told Billy yet, because she isn't sure how he'll take it.

She hasn't told Zenia either. For one thing, she doesn't want to hurt her. Zenia can't have babies because of her hysterectomy for cancer, and Charis doesn't want to flaunt or boast. But also Zenia is now sleeping in the small room upstairs, the one that used to have all Charis's cardboard boxes in it. They moved her up there because Billy complained about never having any privacy in the living room. It's this little room that Charis wants to make over into a nursery for the baby, after Zenia is gone. So how can she tell Zenia she's pregnant without practically booting her out onto the street?

And she couldn't do that, not yet; although when Zenia mentions leaving, Charis no longer tells her not to even think about it. She is torn: she wants Zenia to go, but she doesn't want her to die. She would like to cure her and then never see her again. They don't have all that much in common, and now that she has part of Zenia inside herself, the only part that's necessary to her, she would rather not have the actual, fleshly Zenia around. Zenia takes up a lot of time. Also—though Charis hates to think this way— a certain amount of money. Charis doesn't really have enough money for the three of them.

Zenia is looking a lot better, but this can be deceptive. Sometimes she'll eat a good meal and then rush to the bathroom and throw up. And just yesterday, after they'd been discussing when Zenia might be ready to leave—after she'd been saying she was sure the tumours were shrinking, she was really getting on top of it—Charis walked into the bathroom and found the toilet bowl full of blood. If it were any other woman she'd have assumed that the woman was having her period and had forgotten to flush. But Zenia can't have periods. She has made that clear.

Charis was concerned, and asked about the blood; Zenia was offhand. It was just a hemorrhage, she said. More or less like a nosebleed. Minor. Charis admires her courage, but who is she trying to fool? Herself, maybe. She doesn't fool Charis. From time to time Charis wonders whether she should suggest a hospital. But she can't stand hospitals. Because her mother died in one she thinks of them as places where you go to die. She is already making plans to have the baby at home.

Charis and Zenia are sitting at the kitchen table. They're finishing supper: baked potatoes, mashed-up squash, a cabbage salad. This cabbage came from the market, because Charis's own cabbages have all been used up. They've been turned into juice and poured into Zenia, green transfusions.

"You're looking stronger today," says Charis hopefully.

"I'm strong as an ox," says Zenia. She puts her head down on the table for a moment, then raises it with an effort. "Really, I am."

"I'll make you a cup of ginseng," says Charis.

"Thanks," says Zenia. "So, where is he tonight?"

"Billy?" says Charis. "Some meeting, I guess."

"Don't you ever worry?" says Zenia.

"About what?" says Charis.

"That it's not just some meeting."

Charis laughs. She has more confidence lately. "You mean, some chick," she says. "No. Anyway, it wouldn't interfere." She believes that. Billy can do what he wants with other women, because it wouldn't count.

Billy has begun speaking to Zenia. He now says good morning to her, and when he comes into a room she's already in, he nods and grunts. What he calls his Southern manners are having a struggle with his aversion to Zenia, and the manners are winning. The other night he even offered her a puff on the joint he was smoking. But Zenia shook her head and Billy felt rebuffed, and that was that.

Charis would like to ask Zenia to take it easy on Billy, to meet him halfway, but after the way he's behaved she can hardly do that.

Behind Zenia's back, Billy is if anything even ruder than he was at first. "If she has cancer I'll eat my hat," he said two days ago.

"Billy!" said Charis, appalled. "She's had an operation! She has a big scar!"

"You seen it?" said Billy.

Charis hadn't. Why would she? Why would she ask to see a person's cancer scar? It wasn't something you could do.

"You want to place a little bet?" said Billy. "Five bucks there isn't one."

"No," said Charis. How could you prove such a thing? She had a short vision of Billy rushing into Zenia's room and tearing off her nightgown. That was not something she wanted.

"Penny for your thoughts," says Zenia.

"What?" says Charis. She is thinking about Zenia's scar.

"Billy's a big boy," says Zenia. "You shouldn't get too anxious about him. He can take care of himself."

"I was thinking about the winter," says Charis. "How we're going to get through it."

"Not how—if," says Zenia. "Oh, sorry, too morbid. One day at a time!"

Mostly Zenia goes to bed early because Charis tells her to, but sometimes she stays up. Charis makes a good fire in the wood stove and they sit at the kitchen table and talk. Sometimes they listen to music, sometimes they play solitaire.

"I can read the cards," Zenia says one evening. "Here, I'll read yours."

Charis isn't sure about this. She doesn't think it's such a good idea to know the future, because you can hardly ever change it, so why suffer twice? "Just for fun," says Zenia. She has Charis shuffle the deck three times and cut away from her so the bad luck won't come towards her, and then she lays the cards out in rows of three, for the past, the present, and the future. She studies the rows, then adds another set of cards, crossways.

"Someone new is coming into your life," she says. Oh, thinks Charis. That must be the baby. "And someone else is going out of it. There's water involved; a crossing of the water." Zenia herself, thinks Charis. She'll get better, she'll leave soon. And anyone who leaves here has to cross water.

"Anything about Billy?" she says.

"There's a jack," says Zenia. "Jack of Spades. That could be him. Crossed by the Queen of Diamonds."

"Is that money?" says Charis.

"Yes," says Zenia, "but it's a cross card. There's something off about the money. Maybe he'll take up dealing drugs or something."

"Not Billy," says Charis. "He's too smart." She doesn't really want to go on with this. "Where did you learn?" she asks.

"My mother was a Roumanian gypsy," says Zenia carelessly. "She said it ran in the family."

"It does," says Charis. This makes sense to her: she knows about gifts like that, there's her own grandmother.

Zenia's black hair and dark eyes, and also her fatalism—
they'd go with being a gypsy.

"She was stoned to death, during the war," says Zenia.

"That's terrible!" says Charis. No wonder Zenia has
cancer—it's the past lying inside her, an oppressive heavy-
metals past that she's never cleaned out of herself. "Was it
the Germans?" Being stoned to death seems worse to her
than being shot. Slower, more bruising, more painful; but
not very German. When she thinks of Germans she thinks
of scissors, of white enamel tables. When she thinks of
stoning, it's dust and flies and camels and palm trees. As in
the Old Testament.

"No, by a bunch of villagers," says Zenia. "In
Roumania. They thought she had the evil eye, they thought
she was hexing their cows. They didn't want to waste their
bullets so they used stones. Stones and clubs. Gypsies
weren't the most popular item, there. I guess they still
aren't. But she knew it was going to happen, she was a
clairvoyant. She handed me over to a friend she had, in
another village, the night before. That's what saved me."

"So you must speak some Roumanian," says Charis. If
she'd known all of this, she would have gone about curing
Zenia some other way. Not just with yoga and cabbages.
She would have tried more visualization, and not just
about the cancer: about the Roumanians. Perhaps the keys
to Zenia's illness are hidden in another language.

"I've repressed it," says Zenia. "You would too. I got
a look at my mother after they'd finished with her. They
left her there, lying in the snow. She was just a big lump of
rotting meat."

Charis flinches. This is a stomach-turning image. It
explains why Zenia throws up so much—if that's what's

inside her head. She needs to get such poisonous images out of her.

"Where was your father?" she says, to steer Zenia away from the dead mother.

"He was a Finn," says Zenia. "It's where I get my cheekbones."

Charis has only a vague notion of where Finland is. It has trees, and people with saunas and skin boots, and reindeer. "Oh," she says. "Why was he in Roumania?"

"He wasn't," says Zenia. "They were both Communists, before the war. They met at a youth congress in Leningrad. He was killed later, in Finland, fighting the Russians, in the Winter War. Ironic, isn't it? He thought he was on their side, but it was them who killed him."

"My father was killed in the war, too," says Charis. She's glad they have a bond in common.

"I guess a lot of people were," says Zenia dismissively. "But that's history." She has gathered up the cards and is laying out a new batch. "Ah," she says. "The Queen of Spades."

"Is that still my cards?" says Charis.

"No," says Zenia. "These are mine." She isn't looking at the cards now, she's looking at the ceiling, obliquely, out of her half-closed eyes. "The Queen of Spades is bad luck. Some say it's the death card." Her long black hair falls like a heavy veil around her head.

"Oh, no," says Charis, dismayed. "I don't think we should do this. This is too negative."

"Okay," says Zenia, as if she doesn't care what she does. "I think I'll go to bed."

Charis listens to her as she climbs up the stairs, dragging one foot after the other.

37

The winter wore on. It wore them down. Taking a bath was an arctic experience, feeding the chickens was a polar expedition: trudging through the snow, battling the fierce winds that swept in off the lake. The chickens themselves were cosy enough, inside the house that Billy built. The straw and droppings kept them warm, the way they were supposed to.

Charis wished there were a layer of straw under her own house. She tacked some old blankets over the walls, she stuffed some obvious cracks with wadded newspapers. Luckily they had enough wood: Charis had managed to acquire some, cheap, from a person who had given up and gone back to the mainland. It wasn't split, and Billy split most of it, working outside with the axe, on warmer days: he liked chopping. But the house was still cold, except when Charis built the fire up to danger level. At those times the air inside got muggy and smelled like heated mouse nest. There were real mice living under the floor, driven in by the cold; they came out at night to clean up crumbs and leave their droppings on the table. Zenia brushed the droppings off onto the floor, wrinkling her nose.

Nothing more was being said about her leaving. Every morning she gave Charis a bulletin on her health: better, worse. One day she felt up to a walk, the next day she told Charis that her hair was falling out. She no longer expressed any hope, she no longer seemed to be participating in her own body. She took the things Charis offered her—the carrot juice, the herb teas—passively and without much interest; she was humouring Charis, but she didn't really think they would do any good. She had periods of depression, when she would lie on the living-room couch, wrapped in a blanket, or slump at the table. "I'm a terrible person," she would tell Charis, her voice tremulous. "I'm not worth all this trouble."

"Oh, don't say that," Charis would say. "We all have those feelings. They're from the shadow side. Think of the best things about yourself." Zenia would reward her with a little wavering smile. "What if there isn't anything?" she would say weakly.

Zenia and Billy kept their distance from each other. Each still complained to Charis; they seemed to enjoy this, chewing each other over. Each liked the querulous taste of the other's name, the flavour of accusation, the bad taste. Charis would have liked to warn Billy not to be so harsh to Zenia: he could drive her to snitch on him, about the bombing. But Charis couldn't tell Billy this without admitting that she'd betrayed his confidence, that Zenia knew. Then he would be furious with her.

Charis didn't want fury. She wanted only happy emotions, because any other emotions would smudge her baby. She tried to spend time only with the things that gave her peace: the whiteness just after it snowed, before the soot of the city had a chance to fall; the gleam of icicles, the week they had the ice storm that took the telephone lines down. She walked around the Island by herself, being careful not to slip on the frozen paths. Her stomach was growing harder and rounder now, her breasts were swelling. She knew that most of her white-light energy was being directed into the baby now, not into Zenia or even Billy. The baby was responding, she could sense it; inside her it was listening, it was attentive, it was absorbing the light like a flower.

She hoped the other two didn't feel neglected, but there was nothing much she could do about it. She only had so much energy, and increasingly there was none to spare. She was becoming a more ruthless person, a harder one; she could feel her grandmother's ferociousness in her hands more strongly now. The baby inside her was Karen again, unborn, and with Charis watching over her she would have a better chance. She would be born to the right mother, this time.

In her head she spent time decorating the small room, the baby's room. She would paint it white, later, when she had the money, when Zenia was gone. In the summer, when it was hot, Billy could build a sauna in the backyard, beside the henhouse. Then next winter they could sit inside it and get heated through, and go outside and roll around in the snow. That would be a good way of using the snow; better than sitting inside and complaining about it, the way Zenia did. And Billy too.

In April, when the snow had melted and the shoots of Charis's three daffodil bulbs were poking up through the brown earth, and the chickens were outside again, scratching up the dirt, she told Billy and Zenia about the baby. She had to. Soon it would be obvious; also, soon there would have to be some changes. She wouldn't be able to carry on with the yoga classes, so the money would have to come from elsewhere. Billy would have to get a job of some sort. He didn't have the right papers but there were jobs to be had anyway, because some of his draft-dodging friends had them. Billy would have to get off his butt. Charis wouldn't have thought like this, before the baby, but now she did.

And Zenia would finally have to go. Charis had been a teacher to her, but if Zenia failed to take advantage of what Charis had given her, that was her own concern.

Enough is enough, said her grandmother's voice within her head. First things first. *Blood is thicker than water.*

She tells them one at a time, Zenia first. They're having dinner—baked beans from a can, frozen peas. Charis has not been so meticulous about organic lately; somehow she lacks the time. Billy's in the city, again.

"I'm going to have a baby," Charis blurts out over the canned peaches.

Zenia is not hurt, not the way Charis has feared she would be. Nor does she offer any wistful congratulations or woman-to-woman hugs or pats on the hand. Instead she's contemptuous. "Well," she says, "you've certainly screwed up!"

"What do you mean?" says Charis.

"What makes you think Billy wants a kid?" says Zenia.

This takes Charis's breath away. She recognizes that she's been going on a certain assumption: that everyone else will welcome this baby as much as she does. She also recognizes that she hasn't been taking Billy into account. She did make one attempt to imagine what it would be like to be a man, to be Billy, having a baby, but she just couldn't do it. After that she made no effort to divine his reaction.

"Well of course he does," she says, trying for conviction.

"You haven't told him yet, have you," says Zenia. It's not a question.

"How do you know?" says Charis. How *does* she know? Why are they fighting?

"Wait'll he finds out," says Zenia grimly. "This house is going to be one whole hell of a lot smaller with a screaming brat in it. You could've waited till I was dead."

Charis is amazed by her brutality and selfishness; amazed, and angry. But what comes out of her is close to appeasement. "There's nothing I can do about it now," she says.

"Sure there is," says Zenia, patronizingly. "You can get an abortion."

Charis stands up. "I don't want one," she says. She is close to tears, and when she goes upstairs—which she does right away, without for once doing the dishes—she does cry. She cries into their sleeping bag, wounded and confused. Something is going wrong and she isn't even sure what it is.

When Billy gets home she is still lying on the sleeping bag, with the light out and her clothes still on.

"Hey, what's the matter?" he says. "What's happening?" He kisses her face.

Charis heaves herself up, then throws her arms around him. "Haven't you noticed?" she says tearfully.

"Noticed what?" says Billy.

"I'm pregnant!" says Charis. "We're going to have a baby!" She's making it sound like a reproach; this isn't what she means. She wants him to celebrate with her.

"Oh shit," says Billy. He goes slack in her arms. "Oh Jesus Christ. When?"

"In August," says Charis, waiting for him to be glad. But he isn't glad. Instead he's treating this like a big catastrophe; like a death, not a birth. "Oh shit," he says again. "What're we gonna do?"

In the middle of the night Charis finds herself standing outside, in the garden. She's been sleepwalking. She's in her nightgown and her feet are bare; the mud and leaf mould crumble under her toes. She can smell a skunk, a distant one, like those run over on highways; but how could a skunk be here? This is the Island. But maybe they can swim.

Now she is fully awake. In her hand there's the imprint of another hand: it's her grandmother, trying to tell her something, trying to get through. A warning.

"What?" she says out loud. "What is it?"

She's aware that there's someone else in the garden, a dark shape leaning against the wall by the kitchen window. She sees a small glow. It wasn't a skunk she smelled, it was smoke.

"Zenia, is that you?" she says.

"I couldn't sleep," says Zenia. "So, how's Big Daddy taking it?"

"Zenia, you shouldn't be smoking," says Charis. She's forgotten she's angry with her. "It's so bad for your cells."

"Fuck my cells," says Zenia. "They're fucking me! I might as well enjoy myself while I've got the time." Her voice comes out of the darkness, lazy, sardonic. "And I have to tell you I'm sick to death of your do-gooder act. You'd be one hell of a lot happier if you'd mind your own business."

"I was trying to help you," Charis wails.

"Do me a favour," says Zenia. "Help someone else."

Charis can't understand it. Why was she brought out here to listen to this? She turns and goes inside, and gropes her way up the stairs. She doesn't turn on the light.

The next day Billy takes the early ferry into the city. Charis works feverishly in her garden, digging in the spring compost, trying to blank her mind. Zenia stays in bed.

When Billy comes back after dark, he is drunk. He's been drunk before but never this much. Charis is in the kitchen, doing the dishes, dishes left over from several days. She feels heavy, she feels clogged; there's something in her head that won't come clear. No matter how hard she looks, she can't see past the surfaces of things. She's being blocked, shut out; even the garden today wouldn't let her in. The earth has lost its shine and is just an expanse of dirt, the chickens are petulant and frowsy, like old feather dusters.

So when Billy comes in, she turns to look at him, but she doesn't say anything. Then she turns away from him, back to the dishes.

She hears him bump into the table; he knocks over a chair. Then his hands are on her shoulders. He turns her around. She hopes he's going to kiss her, tell her he's changed his mind, that everything is wonderful, but instead he begins to shake her. Back, forth, slowly. "You . . . are . . . just . . . so . . . goddamn . . . stupid," he says, in time to the shaking. "You are just so goddamn dumb!" His voice is almost fond.

"Billy, don't do that," she says.

"Why not?" he says. "Why the hell not? I can do what I like. You're too dumb to notice." He lets go of her shoulder with one hand and slaps her across the face. "Wake up!" He slaps her again, harder.

"Billy, stop that!" she says, trying to be firm and gentle, trying not to cry.

"Nobody . . . tells . . . me . . . what to do." He steps back from her, then brings his leg up, knee into her stomach. He's too drunk to aim well, but it hurts her.

"You'll kill it!" She's screaming now. "You'll kill our baby!"

Billy puts his head down on her shoulder and begins to cry, hoarse choking sobs that sound torn out of him. "I told you," he said. "I told you, but you wouldn't listen."

"Told me what?" she says, stroking his yellow hair.

"There's no scars," he says. "Nothing. There's no scars at all."

Charis doesn't put it together, what he's talking about. "Come on now," she says. "We're going up to bed." They do, and she rocks him in her arms. Then they are both asleep.

In the morning Charis gets up to feed the chickens, as she always does. Billy is awake: he stays warm underneath the sleeping bag, watching her dress. Before she goes downstairs she comes over to give him a kiss on the forehead. She wants him to say something, but he doesn't.

First she lights the stove, then she fills the pail at the sink. She can hear Billy moving around upstairs; also

Zenia, which is unusual. Maybe she's packing, maybe she'll leave. Charis certainly hopes so. Zenia can't stay here any more, she's causing too much disturbance in the air.

Charis goes outside and unlatches the gate to the chickens' compound. She can't hear them rustling around this morning, she can't hear their sleepy cooing. Sleepyheads! She opens the chickens' door, but none of them come out. Puzzled, she goes around to the door for humans and steps inside.

The chickens are all dead. Every single one of them, dead in their boxes, two of them on the floor. There is blood all over the place, on the straw, dripping down from the boxes. She picks up one of the dead hens from the floor: there's a slit in its throat.

She stands there, shocked and dismayed, trying to hold herself together. Her head is cloudy, red fragments are swirling behind her eyes. Her beautiful chickens! It must have been a weasel. What else? But wouldn't a weasel drink all the blood? Maybe it was a neighbour, not anyone right next to her but somebody else. Who hates them that much? The chickens; or her and Billy. She feels violated.

"Billy," she calls. But he can't hear her, he's inside. She walks unsteadily towards the house; she thinks she's going to faint. She reaches the kitchen, then calls again. He must have fallen asleep. Heavily she goes up the stairs.

Billy isn't there. He isn't anywhere in the room, and when she looks into Zenia's room he isn't there either. Why would she expect him to be?

Zenia is gone also. They are both gone. They aren't in the house.

Charis runs, she runs gasping, down towards the ferry dock. She knows now. It's finally happened: Billy has been kidnapped. When she reaches the dock the ferry is hooting, it's pulling away, and there is Billy standing on it, with two strange men close to him. Two men in overcoats, just the way they would look. Beside him is Zenia. She must have told, she must have turned him in.

Billy doesn't wave. He doesn't want the two men to know Charis has anything to do with him. He's trying to protect her.

She walks slowly back to the house, goes slowly into it. She searches it from top to bottom, looking for a note, but there is nothing. In the sink she finds the bread knife, with blood on the blade.

It was Zenia. Zenia murdered her chickens.

Maybe Billy wasn't kidnapped. Maybe he's run away. He's run away with Zenia. That's what he meant by no scars: there are no scars on Zenia. He knows because he's looked. He has looked at Zenia's body, all over it, with the light on. He knows everything there is to know about that body. He has been inside it.

Charis sits at the kitchen table, banging her head softly against it, trying to drive out thought. But she thinks anyway. If there are no scars there must be no cancer. Zenia doesn't have cancer, just as Billy said. But if that's true, what has Charis been doing for the past six months? Being a fool, that's what. Being stupid. Being so deeply stupid it's a wonder she has a brain at all.

Being betrayed. For how long, how many times? He tried to tell her. He tried to make Zenia go away, but then it was too late.

As for the dead chickens and the bread knife, it's a message. *Slit your wrists.* She hears a voice, a voice from a long time ago, more than one voice. *You are so stupid. You can't win this fight.* Not in this life. She's had almost enough of this life anyway; maybe it's time for the next one. Zenia has taken away the part of herself she needs in order to live. She is dumb, she is a failure, she is an idiot. The bad things that have happened to her are a punishment, they are to teach her a lesson. The lesson is that she might as well give up.

That is Karen speaking. Karen is back, Karen has control of their body. Karen is angry with her, Karen is desolate, Karen is sick with disgust, Karen wants them to die. She wants to kill their body. Already she has the bread knife in her hand, moving it towards their shared arm. But if she does that, their baby will die too, and Charis refuses to let that happen. She calls all of her strength, all of her inner healing light, her grandmother's fierce blue light, into her hands; she wrestles Karen silently for possession of the knife. When she gets it, she pushes Karen away from her as hard as she can, back down into the shadows. Then she throws the knife out the door.

She waits for Billy to come back. She knows he won't, but she waits anyway. She sits at the kitchen table, willing her body not to move, not moving. She waits all afternoon. Then she goes to bed.

By the next day she's no longer so spaced out. Instead she's frantic. The worst thing is not knowing. Maybe she's misjudged Billy, maybe he hasn't run away with Zenia. Maybe he's in prison, having his throat cut in the showers. Maybe he's dead.

She calls all the numbers scribbled on the wall beside their phone. She asks, she leaves messages. None of his friends has heard anything, or will admit to it. Who else could know where he is, where he might have gone? Him, or Zenia, or both of them together. Who else knows Zenia?

She can think of only one person: West. West was living with Zenia before she turned up on Charis's doorstep with a black eye. Charis views that black eye from a different angle, now. It could have had a valid reason for existing.

West teaches at the university, Zenia told her that. He teaches music or something. She wonders if he calls himself West, or Stewart. She will ask for both. It doesn't take her long to track down his home number.

She dials, and a woman answers. Charis explains that she's looking for Zenia.

"Looking for Zenia?" says the woman. "Now why in hell would anyone want to do that?"

"Who is this?" says Charis.

"Antonia Fremont," says Tony.

"Tony," says Charis. Someone she knows, more or less. She doesn't stop to wonder what Tony is doing answering West's phone. She takes a breath. "Remember when you tried to help me, on the front lawn of McClung Hall? And I didn't need it?"

"Yes," says Tony guardedly.

"Well, this time I do."

"Help with Zenia?" says Tony.

"Sort of," says Charis.

Tony says she'll come.

38

Tony takes the ferry to the Island. She sits at Charis's kitchen table and drinks a cup of mint tea and listens to the whole story, nodding from time to time, with her mouth slightly open. She asks a few questions, but she doubts nothing. When Charis tells her how stupid she has been, Tony says that Charis has not been particularly stupid; no more stupid than Tony was herself. "Zenia is very good at what she does," is how she puts it.

"But I was so sorry for her!" says Charis. Tears roll down her face; she can't seem to stop them. Tony hands her a crumpled Kleenex.

"So was I," she says. "She's an expert at that."

She explains that West couldn't have punched Zenia in the eye, not only because West would never punch anyone in the eye but because at that time West wasn't living with Zenia. He hadn't been living with Zenia for over a year and a half. He had been living with Tony.

"Though I suppose he might have done it just walking along the street," she says. "It would be a definite temptation. I don't know what I'd do if I ran into Zenia again. Soak her with gasoline maybe. Set fire to her."

As for Billy, Tony is of the opinion that Charis shouldn't

waste time looking for him; first, because she'll never find him; second, because what if she did? If he's been kidnapped by the Mounties she won't be able to rescue him, he's probably in some cement cubicle in Virginia by now, and if he wants to get in touch with her he will. They do allow letters. If he hasn't been kidnapped, but has been bagged by Zenia instead, he won't want to see Charis anyway. He'll be feeling too guilty.

Tony knows, Tony's been through it: it's as if Billy has been put under a spell. But Zenia won't be content with Billy for long. He's too small a catch, and—Charis will excuse Tony for saying so—he was too easy. Tony has thought a lot about Zenia and has decided that Zenia likes challenges. She likes breaking and entering, she likes taking things that aren't hers. Billy, like West, was just target practice. She probably has a row of men's dicks nailed to her wall, like stuffed animal heads.

"Leave him alone and he'll come home, wagging his tail behind him," says Tony. "If he still has a tail, after Zenia gets through with him."

Charis is astonished at the ease with which Tony expresses hostility. It can't be good for her. But it brings an undeniable comfort.

"What if he doesn't?" says Charis. "What if he doesn't come back?" She is still sniffling. Tony rummages under the sink and finds her a paper towel.

Tony shrugs. "Then he doesn't. There are other things to do."

"But why did she murder my chickens?" says Charis. No matter how she considers this, she just can't get her head around it. The chickens were lovely, they were innocent, they had nothing to do with stealing Billy.

"Because she's Zenia," says Tony. "Don't fret about motives. Attila the Hun didn't have motives. He just had appetites. She killed them. It speaks for itself."

"Maybe it was because her mother was stoned to death by Roumanians, for being a gypsy," says Charis.

"What?" says Tony. "No, she wasn't! She was a White Russian in exile! She died in Paris, of tuberculosis!"

Then Tony begins to laugh. She laughs and laughs.

"What?" says Charis, puzzled. "What is it?"

Tony makes Charis a cup of tea, and tells her to take a rest. She has to look after her health now, says Tony, because she is a mother. She wraps Charis up in a blanket and Charis lies on the living-room sofa. She feels drowsy and cared for, as if things are out of her hands.

Tony goes outside with some plastic garbage bags—Charis knows plastic is bad, but she's found no alternative—and collects up the dead chickens. She sweeps out the chicken house. She fills a pail of water and does the best she can with the blood.

"There's a hose," says Charis sleepily.

"I think I got most of it," says Tony. "What was this bread knife doing in the garden?"

Charis explains about trying to slit her wrists, and Tony doesn't scold her. She simply says that bread knives are not a viable solution, and washes it off and puts it back in the knife rack.

After Charis has had her rest, Tony sits her down at the table again. She has a sheet of paper and a ballpoint pen.

"Now, think of everything you need," she says. "Everything practical."

Charis thinks. She needs some white paint, for the nursery; she needs insulation for the house, because after the summer there will be a winter. She needs some loose dresses. But she can't afford any of these things. With Billy and Zenia eating up the groceries, she hasn't been able to save. Maybe she will have to go on welfare.

"Money," she says slowly. She hates to say it. She doesn't want Tony to think she's begging.

"Good. Now, let's think of all the ways you can get some."

With the help of her friend Roz, whom Charis remembers dimly from McClung Hall, Tony finds Charis a lawyer, and the lawyer goes after Uncle Vern. He's alive, though Aunt Viola is not. He's still living in the house with the wall-to-wall and the rec room. Charis doesn't have to go and see him—the lawyer does that for her, and reports to Tony. Charis doesn't have to tell the whole story about Uncle Vern because everything the lawyer needs is there in the wills, her mother's and her grandmother's. What has happened is perfectly clear: Uncle Vern has taken the money he got from selling the farm, Charis's money, and put it into his own business. He claims he tried to find Charis after her twenty-first birthday, but he couldn't. Maybe this is true.

Charis doesn't get as much money as she should have—she doesn't get interest, and Uncle Vern has spent some of the capital, but she gets more than she's ever had before. She also gets a creepy note from Uncle Vern, saying he'd love to see her again because she was always like a daughter to him. He must be going senile. She burns the note in the stove.

"I wonder if my life would've been better if I'd had a real father," she says to Tony.

"I had one," says Tony. "It was a mixed blessing."

Roz invests some of Charis's money for her. It won't bring in very much, but it will help. Charis spends part of what's left buying the house—the landlord wants it off his hands, he thinks the city will tear it down any day now, so he's happy to take a low price. After she's bought the house she fixes it up, not totally but enough.

Roz comes over to the Island, because she loves renovating houses, or so she says. She is even larger than Charis remembers her; her voice is louder, and she has a bright lemon-coloured aura that Charis can see without even looking hard.

"Oh, this is terrific," says Roz, "it's just like a doll's house! But sweetie—you need a different table!" The next day, a different table arrives. It's round and oak, just what Charis wants. Charis decides that—despite all appearances—Roz is a sensitive person.

Roz busies herself with the layette, because Tony doesn't like shopping and anyway wouldn't have a clue what to buy. Neither does Charis. But Roz has had a baby of her own, so she knows everything, even how many towels. She tells Charis how much it all costs so Charis can pay her back, and Charis is surprised at the lowness of the prices.

"Honey, I'm the original bargain hunter," says Roz. "Now, what you need is a Happy Apple. They're those plastic apples, they dingle in the bath—I swear by them!"

Charis, once so tall and thin, is now tall and bulgy. Tony spends the last two weeks of the pregnancy at Charis's house. She can afford to, she says, because it's the summer vacation. She helps Charis with her breathing exercises, timing Charis on her big-numbers wristwatch and squeezing Charis's hand in her own little hand, so strangely like a squirrel's paw. Charis can't quite believe she is actually having a baby; or she can't quite believe that the baby will soon be outside her. She knows it's in there, she talks to it constantly. Soon she will be able to hear its own voice, in return.

She promises it that she will never touch it in anger. She will never hit it, not even a casual slap. And she almost never does.

Charis goes to a hospital after all, because Tony and Roz decide it will be better: if there were complications Charis would have to be taken to the mainland in a police launch, which would not be appropriate. When August is born she has a golden halo, just like Jesus in the Christmas cards. No one else can see it, but Charis can. She holds August in her arms and vows to be the best person she can be, and praises her oval God.

Now that August is in the outside world Charis feels more anchored. Anchored, or tethered. She no longer blows around so much in the wind; all of her attention is on the *now*. She has been pushed back into her own milky flesh, into the heaviness of her breasts, into her own field of gravity. She lies under her apple tree on a blanket spread on the patchy grass, in the humid air, in the sunlight filtering through the leaves, and sings to August. Karen is far away, which is just as well: Karen would not be dependable around small children.

Tony and Roz are the godmothers. Not officially, of course, because there isn't a church in the world that would do things the way Charis wants. She performs the ceremony herself, with her grandmother's Bible and a very potent round stone she found on the beach, and a bayberry candle and some spring water from a bottle, and Tony and Roz promise to watch over August and to protect her spirit. Charis is glad she's able to give August two such hard-headed women as godmothers. They won't let her be a wimp, they'll teach her to stand up for herself—not a quality Charis is sure that she herself can provide.

There is a third godmother present, of course—a dark godmother, one who brings negative gifts. The shadow of Zenia falls over the cradle. Charis prays she will be able to cast enough light, from within herself, to wash it away.

August grows bigger, and Charis tends her and rejoices, because August is happy, happier than Charis ever was when she was Karen, and she feels the tears in her own life mending. Though not completely, never completely. At night she takes long baths, with lavender and rosewater in them, and she visualizes all of her negative emotions flowing out of her body into the bathwater, and when she pulls the plug they swirl down the drain. It's an operation she feels compelled to repeat frequently. She stays away from men, because men and sex are too difficult for her, they are too snarled up with rage and shame and hatred and loss, with the taste of vomit and the smell of rancid meat, and with the small golden hairs on Billy's vanished arms, and with hunger.

She is better just by herself, and with August. August's aura is daffodil yellow, strong and clear. Even by the age of five she has definite opinions. Charis is glad about that; she's glad August is not a Pisces, like her. August has few electric feelers, few hunches; she can't even tell when it's going to rain. Such things are gifts, true, but not without their drawbacks. Charis writes August's horoscope into one of her notebooks, a mauve one: sign, Leo; gem, the diamond; metal, gold; ruler, the Sun.

In all this time there is no word from Billy. Charis decides to tell August—when she is big enough—that her father died bravely fighting in the Vietnam War. It's the sort of thing she got told herself, and possibly just as accurate. She doesn't have a solemn picture of Billy in a uniform, though, for the simple reason that he didn't have such a thing. The only picture she has of him is a snapshot, taken by one of his buddies. In it he's holding a beer and wearing a T-shirt and shorts; it was when he was working on the henhouse. He looks hammered, and the top of his head is cut off. She doesn't consider it suitable for framing.

The ferry pulls into its dock and the gangway goes down, and Charis walks off, breathing in the clear Island air. Dry grass like reed pipes, loam like a cello. Here she is, back at her house, her fragile but steady house, her flimsy house that is still standing, her house with the lush flowers, her house with the cracked walls, her house with the cool white peaceful bed.

Her house, not theirs; not Billy's and Zenia's, even though this is where it all happened. Maybe it wasn't such a good idea to stay here. She has exorcised their fragments, she has burned sweetgrass, she has purified all the rooms, and the birth of August was an exorcism in itself. But she could never get rid of Billy, no matter what she tried, because his story was unfinished; and with Billy came Zenia. The two of them were glued together.

She needs to see Zenia because she needs to know the end. She needs to get rid of her, finally. She won't tell Tony or Roz about this need, because they would discourage her. Tony would say, keep out of the fire zone. Roz would say, why stick your head in a blender?

But Charis has to see Zenia, and very soon she will, now that she knows where Zenia is. She'll march right into the Arnold Garden Hotel and go up in the elevator and knock on the door. She's feeling almost strong enough. And August is grown up now. Whatever the truth turns out to be, about Billy, she's old enough not to be too hurt by it.

So Charis will confront Zenia and this time she won't be intimidated, she won't conciliate, she won't back down; she will stand her ground and fight back. Zenia, chicken murderer, drinker of innocent blood. Zenia, who sold Billy for thirty pieces of silver. Zenia, aphid of the soul.

From her bookshelf she takes down her grandmother's Bible and sets it on her oak table. She finds a pin, closes her eyes, waits for the pull downwards.

Kings Two, Nine, Thirty-five, she reads. *And they went to bury her, but they found no more of her than the skull, and the feet, and the palms of her hands.*

It's Jezebel thrown down from the tower, Jezebel eaten by dogs. *Again,* thinks Charis. Behind her eyes there is a dark shape falling.

The Robber Bride

39

Roz paces her office, to and
fro, back and forth, smoking and eating the package of
stale cheese straws she stashed in her desk last week and
then forgot about, and waiting. Smoking, eating, waiting,
the story of her life. Waiting for what? She can't expect
feedback this early. Harriet the Hungarian snoop is good,
but surely it will take her days to sniff out Zenia, because
Zenia won't have hidden herself in any obvious place, or
so you'd think. Though maybe she's not hiding. Maybe
she's out in plain sight. There's Roz, down on all fours
looking under the bed, at the fluff balls and the dried-out
bug carcasses that always seem to accumulate there despite
Roz's state-of-the-art vacuum cleaner, and all the time
Zenia is standing right there in the middle of the room.
What you see is what you get, she says to Roz. *Only you didn't
see it.* She likes to rub things in.

Over by the window Roz comes to a stop. Her office
is a corner office, naturally, and on the top floor. Toronto
company presidents are entitled to top-floor corner
offices, even small-potatoes presidents like Roz. It's a

status thing: in this city there's nothing higher on the totem pole than a room with a view, even if the view is mostly idle cranes and construction scaffolding and the freeway with its beetle-sized cars, and the spaghetti snarl of railroad tracks. But anyone who walks into Roz's office gets the message at once. *Let's have a little respect around here! Harrumph, harrumph!* Monarch of all she surveys.

Like shit. Nobody is monarch of anything any more. It's all out of control.

From here Roz can see the lake, and the future marina they're building out of termite-riddled landfill, and the Island, where Charis has her tiny falling-apart mouse nest of a house; and, from her other window, the CN Tower— tallest lightning rod in the world—with the SkyDome stadium beside it, nose and eye, carrot and onion, phallus and ovum, pick your own symbolism, and it's a good thing Roz didn't invest in that one, rumour has it the backers are losing a shirt or two. If she stands in the angle of the two windows and looks north, there's the university with its trees, golden at this time of year, and hidden behind it, Tony's red-brick Gothic folly. Perfect for Tony though, what with the turret. She can hole herself up in there and pretend she's invulnerable.

Roz wonders what the other two are doing right now. Are they pacing the floor like her, are they nervous? Seen from the air the three of them would form a triangle, with Roz as their apex. They could signal to each other with flashlights, like Nancy Drew the girl detective. Of course there's always the phone.

Roz reaches for it, dials, sets it down. What can they tell her? They don't know anything more about Zenia than she does. Less, most likely.

Roz's hands are damp, and her underarms. Her body smells like rusty nails. Is this a hot flash, or merely the old rage coming back? *She's just jealous,* people say, as if jealousy is something minor. But it's not, it's the worst, it's the worst feeling there is—incoherent and confused and shameful, and at the same time self-righteous and focused and hard as glass, like the view through a telescope. A feeling of total concentration, but total powerlessness. Which must be why it inspires so much murder: killing is the ultimate control.

Roz thinks of Zenia dead. Her actual body, dead. Dead and melting.

Not very satisfying, because if Zenia were dead she wouldn't know it. Better to think of her ugly. Roz takes Zenia's face, pulls down on it as if it's putty. Some nice jowls, a double chin, a permanent scowl. Blacken a few teeth, like children's drawings of witches. Better.

Mirror, mirror on the wall, who is the most beautiful of us all?

Depends, says the mirror. *Beauty is only skin deep.*

Right you are, says Roz, *I'll take some anyway. Now answer my question.*

I think you're a really terrific person, says the mirror. *You're warm and generous. You should have no difficulty at all finding some other man.*

I don't want some other man, says Roz, trying not to cry. *I want Mitch.*

Sorry, says the mirror. *Can't be done.*

It always ends like that.

Roz blows her nose and gathers up her jacket and purse, and locks her office door. Boyce is working late, bless his fussy little argyle socks: the light's on under his door. She wonders whether she should knock and invite him out for a drink, which he wouldn't find it politic to refuse, and take him to the King Eddie bar and bore the pants off him.

Better not. She'll go home and bore her kids, instead. She has a vision of herself, running down Bay Street in nothing but her orange bathrobe, tossing big handfuls of money out of a burlap bag. Divesting herself of her assets. Getting rid of all her filthy lucre. After that she could join a cult, or something. Be a monk. A monkess. A monkette. Live on dried beans. Embarrass everybody, even more than she does now. But would there be electric toothbrushes? To be holy, would you need to get plaque?

The twins are watching TV in the family room, which is decorated in Nouveau Pueblo—sand, sage, ochre, and with a genuine cactus looming by the window, wrinkling like a morel, dying from overwatering. Roz must speak to Maria about that. Whenever Maria sees a plant, she waters it. Or else she dusts it. Roz once caught Maria going over that cactus with the vacuum cleaner, which can't have done it any good.

"Hi Mom," says Erin.

"Hi Mom," says Paula. Neither of them looks at her; they're channel-changing, snatching the zapper back and forth. "Dumb!" cries Erin. "So-o-o stupid! Look at that geek."

"Brain snot!" says Paula. "*C'est con, ça!* Hey—my turn!"

"Hi kids," says Roz. She kicks off her tight shoes and flops down in a chair, a dull purple chair the colour of New

Mexican cliff rock just after sunset, or so said the decorator. Roz wouldn't know. She wishes Boyce were here; he'd mix her a drink. Not even mix: pour. A single malt, straight up, is what she'd like, but all of a sudden she's too tired to get it for herself. "What're you watching?" she says to her beautiful children.

"Mom, nobody *watches* TV any more," says Paula.

"We're looking for shampoo ads," says Erin. "We want to get rid of our flaky dandruff."

Paula pulls her hair over one eye, like a model. "Do you suffer from . . . flaky crotch dandruff?" she intones in a phoney advertising voice. They both seem to find this riotously funny. But at the same time they're scanning her, little fluttery sideways glances, checking for crisis.

"Where's your brother?" Roz says wearily.

"My turn," says Erin, grabbing the zapper.

"Out," says Paula. "I think."

"Planet X," says Erin.

"Dancing and romancing," they say together, and giggle.

If only they would settle down, rent a nice movie, something with duets in it, Roz could make popcorn, pour melted butter on it, sit with them in warm family companionship. As in days of yore. *Mary Poppins* was their favourite, once; back in their flannelette-nightie days. But now they've hit the music channel, and there's some man in a torn undershirt hopping up and down and wiggling his scrawny hips and sticking out his tongue in what he must assume is a sexual manner, although to Roz he just looks like a mouth-disease illustration, and Roz doesn't have the stamina for this, even without the sound, so she gets up and goes upstairs in her stocking feet and puts on her bathrobe and her trodden-down landlady slippers, then

ambles down to the kitchen, where she finds a half-eaten
Nanaimo bar in the refrigerator. She puts it on a plate—
she will not revert to savagery, she will use a fork—and
adds some individually wrapped Laughing Cow cheese tri-
angles she bought for the kids' lunches and a couple of
Tomek's Pickles, an Old Polish Recipe, drink the juice for
hangovers. No point in asking the kids to join her for dinner. They will say they've eaten, whether they have or not.
Thus provisioned, Roz wanders the house, from room to
room, munching pickles and revising the wall colours in
her head. Pioneer blue, she thinks. That's what I need.
Return to my roots. Her weedy and suspect roots, her
entangled roots. Inferior to Mitch's, like so many other
intangibles. Mitch had roots on his roots.

Some time later she finds herself holding an empty
plate and wondering why there is no longer anything on it.
She's standing in the cellar, the old part, the part she's
never had re-done. The storage part, with the poured
cement floor and the cobwebs. The remains of Mitch's
wine collection is over in one corner: not his best wines,
he took those with him when he flew the coop. Probably
he drank them with Zenia. Roz hasn't touched a single
bottle of what's left, she can't bear to. Nor can she bear to
throw it out.

Some of Mitch's books are down here, too; his old
law textbooks, his Joseph Conrads, his yacht manuals.
Poor baby, he loved his boats. He thought he was a sailor
at heart, though every time they went sailing something
conked out. Some motor part or piece of wood, search
Roz, she never got used to saying *prow* and *stern* instead of
front and *back*. She sees herself standing on one of those
boats, the *Rosalind* it must have been, the first one, named

after her, with her nose peeling from sunburn and her shoulders freckling and Mitch's cap tilted on her head, waving some wrench or other—*This one, honey?*—while they drifted towards a rocky shore—where? Lake Superior?—and Mitch bent over the motor, swearing under his breath. Was it fun? No. But she would rather be there than here.

She turns her back on Mitch's stuff so she won't have to look at it. It's too doleful. There are some of the twins' old things down here too, and some of Larry's: his baseball glove, his board games—Admirals, Strategy, Kamikaze—foisted on him by Tony because she thought those were the kind of games he should like. The children's books, fondly saved by Roz in the hope that someday she will have grandchildren and will read them these very same books. *Do you know, sweetie—this used to be your mommy's! When she was a little girl.* (Or *your daddy's.* But Roz, although she hopes, has trouble picturing Larry as a father.)

Larry used to sit gravely silent while she read to him. His favourites were about trains that talked and were a success, or good-for-you books about interspecies cooperation. *Mr. Bear helps Mr. Beaver build a dam.* Larry didn't comment much. But with the twins she could barely get a word in edgewise. They would fight her for control of the story—*Change the ending, Mom! Make them go back! I don't like this part!* They'd wanted *Peter Pan* to end before Wendy grew up, they'd wanted Matthew in *Anne of Green Gables* to live forever.

She remembers one phase, when they were, what? Four, five, six, seven? It went on for a while. They'd decided that all the characters in every story had to be female.

Winnie the Pooh was female, Piglet was female, Peter Rabbit was female. If Roz slipped up and said "he," they would correct her: *She! She!* they would insist. All of their stuffed animals were female, too. Roz still doesn't know why. When she asked them, the twins would give her looks of deep contempt. "Can't you *see*?" they would say.

She used to worry that this belief of theirs was some reaction to Mitch and his absences, some attempt to deny his existence. But maybe it was simply the lack of penises, on the stuffed animals. Maybe that was it. In any case, they grew out of it.

Roz sits down on the cellar floor, in her orange bathrobe, never mind the cement dust and silverfish and webs. She pulls books off the shelves at random. *To Paula and Erin, from Aunt Tony.* There on the cover is the dark forest, the dark wolfish forest, where lost children wander and foxes lurk, and anything can happen; there is the castle turret, poking through the knobbly trees. *The Three Little Pigs,* she reads. The first little pig built his house of straw. *Her* house, *her* house, shout the small voices in her head. The Big Bad Wolf fell down the chimney, right into the cauldron of boiling water, and got his fur all burned off. *Her* fur! It's odd what a difference it makes, changing the pronoun.

At one point the twins decided that the wolf should not be dropped into the cauldron of boiling water—it should be one of the little pigs, instead, because they had been the stupid ones. But when Roz suggested that maybe the pigs and the wolf could forget about the boiling water and make friends, the twins were scornful. Somebody had to be boiled.

It amazed Roz then, how bloodthirsty children could be. Not Larry; he didn't like the more violent stories, they gave him nightmares. He didn't take to the kinds of books Tony liked to contribute—those authentic fairy tales in the gnarly-tree editions, not a word changed, all the pecked-out eyes and cooked bodies and hanged corpses and red-hot nails intact. Tony said they were more true to life that way.

"*The Robber Bridegroom,*" reads Tony, long ago, a twin at each elbow. The beautiful maiden, the search for a husband, the arrival of the rich and handsome stranger who lures innocent girls to his stronghold in the woods and then chops them up and eats them. "One day a suitor appeared. He was . . ."

"She! She!" clamour the twins.

"All right, Tony, let's see you get out of this one," says Roz, standing in the doorway.

"We could change it to *The Robber Bride,*" says Tony. "Would that be adequate?"

The twins give it some thought, and say it will do. They are fond of bridal costumes, and dress their Barbie dolls up in them; then they hurl the brides over the stair railings or drown them in the bathtub.

"In that case," says Tony, "who do you want her to murder? Men victims, or women victims? Or maybe an assortment?"

The twins remain true to their principles, they do not flinch. They opt for women, in every single role.

Tony never talked down to the children. She didn't hug them or pinch their cheeks or tell them they were sweet. She spoke to them as if they were miniature adults.

In turn, the twins accepted her as one of themselves. They let her in on things, on their various plots and conspiracies, their bad ideas—stuff they would never have shared with Roz. They used to put Tony's shoes on and march around the house in them, one shoe for each twin, when they were six or seven. They were entranced by those shoes: grown-up shoes that fit them!

The Robber Bride, thinks Roz. Well, why not? Let the grooms take it in the neck for once. The Robber Bride, lurking in her mansion in the dark forest, preying upon the innocent, enticing youths to their doom in her evil cauldron. Like Zenia.

No. Too melodramatic for Zenia, who was, after all— who *is* surely nothing more than an up-market slut. The Rubber Broad is more like it—her and those pneumatic tits.

Roz is crying again. What she's mourning is her own good will. She tried so hard, she tried so hard to be kind and nurturing, to do the best thing. But Tony and the twins were right: no matter what you do, somebody always gets boiled.

40

The story of Roz and Zenia began on a lovely day in May, in 1983, when the sun was shining and the birds were singing and Roz was feeling terrific.

Well, not quite terrific. Baggy, to tell the truth: under the eyes, under the arms. But better than she'd felt when she'd turned forty. Forty had been truly depressing, she had despaired, she'd dyed her hair black, a tragic mistake. But she'd come to terms with herself since then, and her hair was back to auburn.

Also: the story of Roz and Zenia had actually begun some time before, inside Zenia's head, but Roz had no idea.

Not quite that, either. She had an idea, but it was the wrong idea. It was hardly even an idea, just a white idea balloon with no writing inside it. She had an idea that something was up. She thought she knew what, but she didn't know who. She told herself she didn't much care: she was past that. As long as it didn't disrupt, as long as it didn't interfere, as long as she could come out of it with not very many ribs broken. Some men needed their little escapades. It kept them toned up. As an addiction it was preferable to alcohol or golf, and Mitch's things—*things,* she called them, to distinguish them from people—never lasted long.

It was a lovely May day, though. That much was true.

Roz wakes up at first light. She often does this: wakes up, and sits up stealthily, and watches Mitch when he's still sleeping. It's one of the few chances she gets to look at him when he can't catch her doing it and interpose his opaque blue stare. He doesn't like being examined: it's too close to an evaluation, which is too close to a judgment. If there are judgments going around he wants to be making them himself.

He sleeps on his back, legs flung wide, arms spread out as if to possess as much of the space as possible. The Royal Posture, Roz saw it called once, in a magazine. One of those psycho-con articles that claim to tell all on the basis of how you tie your shoelaces. His Roman nose juts up, his slight double chin and the heaviness around his jaw disappear in this position. There are white lines around his eyes, wrinkles where he isn't tanned; some of the blunt hairs poking through his morning chin are grey.

Distinguished, thinks Roz. Distinguished as heck. Maybe she should've married someone ugly. Some ugly toad of a man who'd never be able to believe his good luck, who'd appreciate her sterling qualities of character, who'd worship her baby finger. Instead she had to go for distinguished. Mitch should have married a cold blonde with homicidal eyes and a double string of real pearls grafted onto her neck, and a built-in pocket behind the left breast, for the bankbook. Such a woman would've been up to him. She would not have taken the kind of crap Roz takes.

She goes back to sleep, dreams about her father standing on a black mountain, a mountain of coal or of something burnt, hears Mitch's alarm go off, hears it go off again, wakes finally. The space beside her is empty. She climbs out of bed, out of the king-sized bed with the brass bedstead in a curving art nouveau design and the raspberry-coloured sheets and duvet cover, onto the aubergine carpet, in the bedroom with its salmon walls and the priceless twenties dresser and mirror, *faux* Egyptian, and slips into her cream satin robe and pads barefoot into the bathroom. She loves this bathroom! It has everything: shower cubicle, Jacuzzi, bidet, a heated towel rack, His and Hers sinks so the hairs from Roz's head won't get mixed up with the stubble from Mitch's chin. She could live in this bathroom! So could several Southeast Asian families, come to that, she reflects morosely. Guilt sets in.

Mitch is already in here, taking a shower. His pink silhouette looms dimly through the steam and the pebble glass. Years ago—how many?—Roz would have scampered playfully into the shower, too; she would have soaped him all over, rubbed herself against his slippery body, pulled him down onto the tiled bathroom floor; back in the days when his skin fit him exactly, no sags, no bulges, and hers did too, and when he tasted like hazelnuts, a delicious roasted smell; but she doesn't do such things now, now that she has become more reluctant to be viewed by daylight.

Anyway, if what she suspects is true, this is the wrong time to be putting herself on display. In Mitch's cosmology

Roz's body represents possessions, solidity, the domestic virtues, hearth and home, long usage. Mother-of-his-children. The den. Whereas whatever other body may currently be occupying his field of vision will have other nouns attached to it: adventure, youth, freedom, the unknown, sex without strings. When the pendulum swings back—when that other body starts representing complications, decisions, demands, sulkiness, and weepy scenes—then it will be Roz's turn again. This has been the pattern.

Intuition is not one of Roz's strong suits, but she has intuitions about the onset of Mitch's attacks. She thinks of them as attacks, as in attacks of malaria; or else as attacks of a different nature, for isn't Mitch a predator, doesn't he take advantage of these poor women, who are surely becoming younger and younger as Mitch gets older and older, isn't it really more like a bear attack, a shark attack, aren't these women savaged by him? Judging from some of the tearful phone calls Roz has fielded, some of the shoulders she's patted in her hypocritical, maternal, there-there-ing way, they are.

It's amazing the way Mitch can just write these women off. Sink his teeth into them, spit them out, and Roz is expected to clean up the mess. Fire of his loins and then *wipe,* like a blackboard, and after that he can barely remember their names. Roz is the one who remembers. Their names, and everything else about them.

The beginnings of Mitch's flings are never obvious. He never says blatant things such as "I'm working late at the office"; when he says that, he really is working late at the office. Instead, his habits undergo a subtle change. The numbers of conferences he goes to, the numbers of showers he takes, the amount he whistles in them, the quantity and kind of aftershave he uses and the places where he splashes it—the groin is a sure giveaway—such things are minutely observed by Roz, looking pleasantly out of her indulgent eyes, bristling like a bottle-brush within. He stands up straighter, pulls in his stomach more; she catches him glaring at himself, at his profile, in hall mirrors, in store windows, his eyes narrowing as if for a leonine pounce.

He's more considerate of her, more attentive; he's alert to her, watching her to see if she's watching. He gives her little kisses on the back of her neck, on her fingertips—little homage kisses, little forgive-me kisses, but nothing that might be construed as foreplay, because in bed he becomes inert, he turns his back, he pleads minor illnesses, he takes up the jackknife position, oystering himself against her stroking fingers. His prick is a serial monogamist; a sure sign of a dyed-in-the-wool romantic, in Roz's books. No cynical polygamy for it! One more, it wants. Just one more woman, because a man's reach should exceed his grasp, and Mitch is afraid of dying, and if he were ever to pause, to see himself as a man married to Roz, married only to Roz, married to Roz forever, in that instant his hair would fall out, his face would wrinkle up like a thousand-year-old mummy's, his heart would stop. Or that is how Roz explains him, to herself.

She asks him if he's seeing someone.

He says no. He says he's just tired. He's under a lot of pressure, he says, a lot of stress, and to prove it he gets up in the middle of the night and goes into his study, where he shuts the door and works until dawn. Sometimes there is the murmur of his voice: dictating letters, or so he claims, offering unasked-for explanations at breakfast.

And thus it goes, until Mitch gets tired of whoever it is he really has been seeing. Then he becomes deliberately careless, then he starts to leave clues. The match folder from the restaurant where he and Roz have never been, the unknown-number long-distance phone-call entries on their home phone bill. Roz knows that at this point she is supposed to call him on it. She's supposed to confront him, to rave and scream, to cry and accuse and grovel, to ask him if he still loves her and whether the children mean anything to him at all. She's supposed to behave the way she did the first time (the second time, the fifth time), so he will be able to wriggle off the hook, so he can tell the other woman, the one with the haggard lines appearing around her eyes, the one with the pieces of love bitten out of her, that he will always adore her but he can't bear to leave the kids; and so he will be able to tell Roz—magnanimously, and with a heroic air of self-sacrifice—that she is the most important woman in his life, no matter how badly and foolishly he may behave from time to time, and he's given the other woman up for her, so how can she refuse to forgive him? The other women are just trivial adventures, he will imply: she's the one he comes home to. Then he will throw himself into her as into a warm bath, as into a deep feather bed, and exhaust himself, and sink again into connubial torpor. Until the next time.

Lately, however, Roz has been refusing her move. She's learned to keep her big fat mouth shut. She ignores the phone bills and the match covers, and after the midnight conversations she tells him sweetly that she hopes he's not overdoing it with too much work. During his conference absences she finds other things to do. She has meetings to go to, she has plays to attend, she has detective novels to read, tucked up in bed with her night cream; she has friends, she has her business to keep up; her time is fully occupied with items other than him. She adopts absent-mindedness: she forgets to send his shirts to the cleaners, and when he speaks to her she says, "What did you just say, sweetie?" She buys new dresses and new perfumes, and smiles at herself in mirrors when he can be supposed not to be looking, but is, and Mitch begins to sweat.

Roz knows why: his little piece of cotton candy is growing claws, she's saying she doesn't understand what's going on with him, she's whining, she's babbling about commitment and divorce, both of them things he is now supposed to be doing, after all he's promised. The net is closing around him and he's not being rescued. He's being thrown from the troika, thrown to the wolves, to the hordes of ravening bimbos snapping at his heels.

In desperation he resorts to more and more open ploys. He leaves private letters lying around—the women's letters to him, and, worse, his letters to the women—he actually makes copies!—and Roz reads them and fumes, and goes to the gym to work out, and eats chocolate mud cake afterwards, and puts the letters back where she found them and does not mention them at all. He announces a separate vacation—maybe he will take the boat on a short trip around Georgian Bay, by himself, he needs some time to unwind—and Roz pictures some loose-mouthed slut spread out on the deck of the *Rosalind II,* and mentally rips up the snapshot, and tells him she thinks that's a wonderful idea because each of them could use a little space.

God only knows how much she bites her tongue. She waits until the last minute, just before he really has to elope, or else get caught screwing his latest *thing* in Roz's raspberry-coloured bed in order to get Roz's attention. Only then will she reach out a helping hand, only then will she haul him back from the brink, only then will she throw the expected tantrum. The tears Mitch sheds then are not tears of repentance. They are tears of relief.

Does Roz secretly enjoy all this? She didn't at first. The very first time it happened she felt scooped out, disjointed, scorned and betrayed, crushed by bulldozers. She felt worthless, useless, sexless. She thought she would die. But she's developed a knack, and therefore a taste. It's the same as a business negotiation or a poker game. She's always been a whiz at poker. You have to know when to up the stakes, when to call a bluff, when to fold. So she does enjoy it, some. It's hard not to enjoy something you're good at.

But does her enjoyment make it all right? On the contrary. It's her enjoyment that makes it all wrong. Any old nun could tell you that, and many of them did tell Roz, once, in the earlier part of her life. If she could suffer through Mitch's attacks like a martyr, weeping and flagellating herself—if she could let them be imposed on her, without participating at all, without colluding, without lying and concealing and smiling and playing Mitch like an oversized carp, how right it would be. She'd be suffering for love, suffering passively, instead of fighting. Fighting for herself, for her idea of who she is. The right kind of love should be

selfless, for women at any rate, or so said the Sisters. The
Self should be scrubbed like a floor: on both knees, with a
harsh wire brush, until nothing is left of it at all.

Roz can't do that. She can't be selfless, she never
could. Anyway her way is better. It's harder on Mitch,
perhaps, but it's easier on her. She's had to give up some
love, of course; some of her once-boundless love for
Mitch. You can't keep a cool head when you're drowning
in love. You just thrash around a lot, and scream, and wear
yourself out.

The May sunlight comes in through the window, and
Mitch whistles "It Ain't Me, Babe," and Roz flosses her
teeth quickly so Mitch won't see her doing it when he gets
out of the shower. There is nothing so dampening to lust
as dental floss, in Roz's opinion: a wide-open mouth with
a piece of gooey string being manoeuvred around in it. She
has always had good teeth, they are one of her features.
Only recently has she begun to think they may not always
be where they are right now, namely inside her mouth.

Mitch steps out of the shower and comes up behind
her and encircles her with his arms, and presses her
against himself, and nuzzles her hair aside and kisses her
on the neck. If they hadn't made love last night she would
find this neck kiss conclusive: surely it is too courtly to be
innocent! But at this preliminary stage, you never know.

"Good shower, honey?" she says. Mitch makes the
noise he makes when he thinks Roz has asked a question
so meaningless it doesn't require an answer, not knowing
that what she said wasn't a question anyway but an

inverted wish: translation, *I hope you had a good shower, and here is your opening to complain about any little physical problems you may be having so I can offer sympathy.*

"I thought we could have lunch," says Mitch. Roz notes the formulation: not *Would you like to have lunch* or *I am inviting you to lunch.* No room here for a yes or no from her, no room for a rejection: Mitch is nothing if not directive. But at the same time her heart turns over, because she doesn't get invitations like this from him very often. She looks at his face in the mirror, and he smiles at her. She always finds his mirror reflection disconcerting. Lopsided, because she isn't used to seeing him that way around and he looks reversed. But nobody's symmetrical.

She suppresses the desire to say, *Judas Priest, how come I rate all of a sudden? Is hell freezing over, or what?* Instead she says, "Honey, that would be great! I'd love it!"

Roz sits on the bath stool, a converted Victorian commode, and watches Mitch while he shaves. She adores watching him shave! All that wild white foam, a sort of caveman beard, and the way he contorts his face to get at the hidden stubble. She has to admit he's not only distinguished, he's still what you'd call handsome, though his skin is getting redder and his blue eyes are paling. *Ruggedly handsome,* they might say in a men's clothing ad, though they'd be talking about the sheepskin coat. The sheepskin coat, the sheepskin gloves, the calfskin briefcase: that's Mitch's style. He has many items of good-taste expensive leather. He's not going bald yet, praise the Lord, not that Roz would mind but men seem to, and she hopes if he does start to shed that he won't get his armpit transplanted to the top of his head. Though he's showing some pepper and salt in the sideburns. Roz checks him over for rust spots, the way she would a car.

What she's really waiting for though is the aftershave. Which one will he pick, and where will he put it? Ah! Nothing too seductive, just some stuff he got in England, heather or something. The outdoor mode. And nothing below the neck. Roz sighs with relief.

She does love him. She loves him still. She can't afford to go overboard, is all.

But maybe, underneath, she loves him too much. Maybe it's her excessive love that pushes him away.

After Mitch is out of the bathroom Roz continues with her own preparations, the creams and lotions and perfumes that should never be seen by Mitch. They belong behind the scenes, as at theatres. Roz collects perfumes the way other people collect stamps, she's a sucker for anything new that comes out. She has three rows of them, three rows of cunning little bottles, sorted into categories that she thinks of as Flower Arranging, Executive Briskness, and Heavy Petting. Today, in honour of her lunch with Mitch, she chooses Shalimar, from the Heavy Petting section. But it's a bit too sultry for the middle of the day so she cuts it with something from Flower Arranging. Then, suited and made up but wearing her bedroom slippers and carrying her high heels, she descends to do her mother routine in the kitchen. Mitch, needless to say, is already out the door. He has a breakfast meeting.

"Hi, kids," says Roz. There they are, all three of them, bless their greedy overnourished hearts, gobbling down the Rice Krispies with brown sugar and bananas on top, supervised by Dolores, who is from the Philippines and is, Roz hopes, beginning to get over her culture shock. "Hi, Dolores."

Dolores fills Roz with anxiety and misgiving: should Dolores be here? Will Western culture corrupt her? Is Roz paying her enough? Does Dolores secretly hate them all? Is she happy, and, if not, is it Roz's fault? Roz has had spates of thinking they shouldn't have a live-in housekeeper. But when they don't, there's no one to do the kids' lunches and handle the illnesses and last-minute emergencies except Roz, and Roz becomes over-organized and can't pay enough attention to Mitch, and Mitch gets very short-tempered.

Roz makes the rounds of the kitchen table, bestowing smooches. Larry is fourteen going on fifteen and embarrassed by her, but he endures. The twins kiss her back, briefly, milkily. "Mom," says Erin, "you smell like room freshener."

How wonderful! How exact! Roz glances around the kitchen, done in warm wood panelling with chopping-block counters where the three school lunches sit in their matching lunch boxes, blue for Erin, green for Paula, black for Larry, and she lights up within, she glows! This is why she goes through it, this is what it's for! All the holy hell with Mitch has been worth it, for mornings like this, to be able to walk into the kitchen and say "Hi, kids," and have them continue scarfing down the breakfast food as if she's practically not there. She extends her invisible wings, her warm feathery angel's wings, her fluttery hen's wings, undervalued and necessary, she enfolds them. *Secure,* is what she wants them to feel; and they do feel secure, she's certain of it. They know this is a safe house, they know she's *there,* planted solidly, two feet on the ground, and Mitch is there too, more or less, in his own way. They know it's all right, so they can get on with whatever they're doing, they don't have to worry.

Maybe she's wrong about Mitch, this time. Maybe there's nothing going on. Maybe he's finally settled down.

41

The lunch is at a restaurant called Nereids. It's a small place, a done-over house on Queen East, with a large well-put-together stone man without any clothes on standing outside it. Roz has never been to it before, but Mitch has; she can tell by the way the hostess greets him, by the way he looks around with an amused, proprietorial eye. She can see too why he likes it: the whole place is decorated with paintings, paintings that twenty years ago could've got you arrested, because they are all of naked women. Naked women, and naked mermaids too, with enormous and statuesque breasts: not a droopy boob among them. Well, naked people, because the naked women do not lack for male company. Walking to their table Roz gets a cock right in the eye, and averts her gaze.

"What *is* this?" she whispers, alight with curiosity and appalled glee, and with the sheer pleasure of being taken out to lunch by Mitch. "Am I seeing what I think I'm seeing? I mean, is this a porn shop, or what?"

Mitch chuckles, because he likes to shock Roz a little, he likes to show that he's above her prejudices. (Not that she's a prude, but there's private and there's public, and this is public. Public privates!) He explains that this is a seafood restaurant, a Mediterranean seafood restaurant, one of the best in the city in his opinion, but that the owner is also a painter, and some of these paintings are by him and some are by his friends, who appear to share his interests. Venus is featured, because she was after all a goddess of the sea. The fish motif accounts too for the mermaids. Roz deduces that these are not just naked people, they are *mythological* naked people. She can deal with that, she took it at university. Proteus blowing his conch. Or getting it blown.

"Oh," says Roz in her mock-naive voice. "So this is capital-A Art! Does that make it legal?" and Mitch laughs again, uneasily, and suggests that maybe she should lower her voice because she wouldn't want to hurt people's feelings.

If anyone else told her to lower her voice, Roz would know what to do: scream louder. But Mitch has always been able to make her feel as if she were just off the boat, head wrapped in a shawl, wiping her nose on her sleeve, and lucky to have a sleeve at that. Which boat? There are many boats in her ancestral past, as far as she can tell. Everyone she's descended from got kicked out of somewhere else, for being too poor or too politically uncouth or for having the wrong profile or accent or hair colour.

The boat her father came over on was more or less recent, though far enough back to have arrived before the Canadian government walled out the Jews, in the thirties and during the war. Not that her father was even a whole Jew. *Why do you inherit Jewishness through the mother's side?* Tony once asked Roz. *Because so many Jewish women were raped by Cossacks and what-have-you that they could never be sure who the father was.* But her father was Jewish enough for Hitler, who hated mixtures more than anything.

The boat on her mother's side was much further back. Famine caused by landlessness caused by war drove them out, a hundred and fifty years ago, Irish and Scots both. One of those families set out with five children and arrived with none, and then the father died of cholera in Montreal and the mother remarried, as fast as she could— an Irishman whose wife had died, so he needed a new one. Men needed wives then, for such enterprises. Off they went into the semi-cleared bush, to be overtaxed and to have other children and to plant potatoes, and to chop down trees with implements they'd never used before, because how many trees were left in Ireland? A lot of legs got chopped into, by those people. Tony, who is more interested in these details than Roz is, once showed Roz an old picture—the men standing in metal washtubs, to protect their legs from their own axes. Low comedy for the English middle classes, back home, living off the avails. Stupid bogtrotters! The Irish were always good for a smirk or two, then.

All of them came steerage, of course. Whereas Mitch's ancestors, although not created by God from the sacred mud of Toronto—they had to have got here some-how—must have come cabin. Which means they threw up into a china basin instead of onto other people's feet, on the way across.

Big deal, but Roz is intimidated anyway. She opens the mermaid-festooned menu, and reads the items, and asks Mitch to advise her, as if she can't make up her own mind what to put into her mouth. *Roz,* she tells herself. *You are a suck.*

• • •

She remembers the time she first went out with Mitch. She was old, she was almost twenty-two, she was over the hill. A lot of girls she'd known in high school and then in university were already married, so why wasn't she? It was a question that looked out at her from her mother's increasingly baffled eyes.

Roz had already had a love affair, or rather a sex affair, and then another. She hadn't even felt too guilty about them. Although the nuns had ground it in about sex and what a sin it was, Roz was no longer a Catholic. She was once a Catholic, though, and once a Catholic, always a Catholic, according to her mother; so she'd had some qualms, after the first exhilarating sense of transgression had faded. Strangely enough, these qualms focused less on the sex itself than on the condoms—things you had to buy under the counter, not that she ever did, that was a man's job. Condoms seemed to her inherently wicked. But they were also inherently funny. They were like rubber gloves with only one finger, and every time she saw one she had to be severe with herself or she'd get the giggles, a terrifying thought because the man might think you were laughing at him, at his dick, at its size, and that would be fatal.

But the sex was great, it was something she was good at, though neither one of these men was her idea of bliss from the neck up. One had big sticking-out ears, the other one was two inches shorter than she was, and she didn't see going through life in flats. She wanted children, but not runty ones with jug ears.

So she hadn't taken either of them seriously. It helped that they hadn't taken her seriously either. Maybe it was the clown face she put on, fairly constantly by then. She needed it, that happy heedless party face, because there she was, on the shelf, still living at home, still working in her father's business. *You'll be my right-hand man,* he'd tell her. It was meant as a compliment, so she wouldn't feel bad about not being a son. But Roz didn't want to be a son. She didn't want to be a man at all, right-hand or otherwise. Such a strain, being one, from what she could see; such a pretence of dignity to maintain. She could never get away with her witless frivolity act if she were a man. But then, if she were one she might not need it.

Her job in the business was fairly basic; a moron could have done it. Essentially she was a glorified fetch-it. But her father believed that everyone, even the boss's daughter, should start at the bottom and progress up to the top. That way you got acquainted with the real workings of the business, layer by layer. If something was wrong with the secretaries, if something was wrong with Filing, there would be wrongness all the way through; and you had to know how to do those jobs yourself so you would know whether other people were doing them right or not. A lesson that has been useful to Roz, over the years.

She was learning a lot, though. She was watching her father's style. Outrageous but effective, soft but hard, uproarious but dead serious underneath. He waited for his moment, he waited like a cat on a lawn; then he pounced. He liked to drive bargains, he liked to cut deals. *Drive, cut,* these verbs had an appeal for him. He liked risk, he liked walking the edge. Blocks of property disappeared into his pocket, then came out magically transformed into office buildings. If he could renovate—if there was something worth saving—he did. Otherwise it was the wrecking ball, despite whatever clutch of woolly-headed protesters might be marching around outside with *Save Our Neighbourhood* signs, done in crayon and stapled onto rake handles.

Roz had some ideas of her own. She knew she could be good at this stuff if he'd give her the rope. But rope was not given by him, it was earned, so she was putting in her time.

Meanwhile, what about her love life? There was nobody. Nobody suitable. Nobody even close. Nobody who wasn't either a jerk-off or basically after her money, a factor she had to keep in mind. Her future money, because right then she was only on salary like everybody else, and a fairly measly salary at that. Her father believed you should know just how measly a measly salary was, so you could figure out what a pay-raise negotiation was all about. He thought you should know the price of potatoes. Roz didn't at the moment because she was still living at home, on account of her measly salary. She'd looked at studio apartments, one room with a mingy kitchenette tucked in the corner and a view into somebody else's bathroom, but too squalid! What price freedom? Higher than what she was making right then. She would rather stay where she was, in the former servants' flat over her parents' three-car garage, and spend her measly salary on new clothes and her own phone line.

She wanted to take a trip to Europe, by herself, but her father wouldn't let her. He said it was too dangerous. "What goes on over there, you don't need to know," he told her. He wanted to keep her walled up behind his money. He wanted to keep her safe.

●   ●   ●

Mitch was a neophyte lawyer then, working for the firm that papered her father's deals. The first time she saw him he was walking through the outer office where Roz sat grindstoning her nose. He was wearing a suit and carrying a briefcase, the end man in the almost-daily suit-and-briefcase parade that followed her father around like a tail. There was a pause at Roz's desk, handshakes all round: Roz's father always introduced everyone to everyone else. Mitch shook Roz's hand, and Roz's hand shook. She took one look at him and thought, There's ugly and there's gorgeous and there's in-between, but this is gorgeous. Then she'd thought: Dream on, babe. Slobber on your pillow. This is not for you.

But darned if he didn't phone her up! You didn't have to be Einstein to get the number, but it would've taken more than one step, because Roz had herself listed in the phone book as Rosie O'Grady, having tired of the hate calls that her father's last name sometimes attracted. The hoardings around the demolition sites didn't help, *Grunwald Developments* in foot-high print, she might as well go around with a red X painted on her forehead, *Spit here,* as list her right name in the phone book.

But all of a sudden there was Mitch on the phone, cool but persuasive, sounding as if he wanted to sell her some life insurance, reminding her of where she'd met him, as if she needed reminding, and he was so stiff at first that she'd wanted to yell at him, *Hey, I am not your granny! Slip that poker out of your bum!* Gorgeous or not, he sounded like a drag, a too-tight WASPy poop whose idea of a good time would be a hand of bridge with the crumbling in-laws or a walk in the cemetery on Sunday. It took him a lot longer to get to the point than it would've taken Roz, had she been leading, but he'd finally worked up to asking her out to dinner and then to a movie afterwards. Well, Hallelujah and Hail Mary, thought Roz. Wonders will never cease.

But while she was getting ready to go, her joy evaporated. She wanted to float, to fly, but she was beginning to feel heavier and heavier, sitting there at her dressing table dabbing Arpège onto her pulse points and trying to decide what earrings to wear. Something that would make her face look less round. True, she had dimples, but they were the kind of dimples you saw in knees. More like puckers. She was a big-boned girl, a raw-boned girl (her mother's words), a girl with backbone (her father's), and a full, mature figure (the dress shops'). Dainty she would never be. *Dear God, shrink my feet and I'll do anything for you. A size 6 would be nice, and while you're at it make me a blonde.*

The problem was that Mitch was simply too good-looking. The shoulders, the blue eyes, the bone structure—he looked like a movie mag starlet, male version, too good to be true. Roz was awed by this—nobody should be allowed out in public looking like that, it might cause car crashes—and by his aroma of decorum, and by his posture, bolt upright with squared corners, like a frozen fish fillet. She wouldn't be able to let herself go with him, crack jokes, fool around. She would worry about whether there were things caught in her teeth.

Plus, she would be so squirrelly with desire—out with it, *Lust,* capital L, the best of the Seven Deadlies—that she'd scarcely be able to sit still. She wasn't usually so out of control, but Mitch was off the top of the charts in the looks department. Heads would turn, people would stare, they'd wonder what such a dreamboat was doing with the runner-up in the Miss Polish Turnip Contest. All in all it was shaping up to be a purgatorial evening. *Get me through this, God, and I'll scrub a million toilets for you! Not that you'd be interested, because in Heaven, who shits?*

Things started out every bit as dreadful as Roz had expected. Mitch brought her flowers, not very many flowers but flowers, how old-fashioned could you get, and she didn't know what to do with the darn things, so she took them out to the kitchen—was she supposed to put them in a vase or what? Why hadn't he settled for chocolates?—and there was her mother brooding darkly over a cup of tea, in her dressing gown and metal curlers and hairnet, because she had to go out later to some banquet or other with Roz's father, some business thing, her mother hated that stuff, and she looked at Roz with the stricken gaze she'd been putting on ever since they got rich and moved into that barn of a house on Dunvegan, right near Upper Canada College, where male scions like Mitch were sent to be brainwashed and to have their spines fused so their pelvises would never move again, and she said to Roz, "Are you going out?" as in, "Are you dying?"

And Roz had left Mitch standing in the cavernous living room, in the centre of the half-acre of broadloom, surrounded by three truckloads of furniture in her mother's impeccable bad taste, it cost a mint but it looked straight out of a funeral parlour mail-order catalogue, in addition to which every single surface was covered with doilies, which didn't help, her mother had a doily fetish, she'd been deprived of them in youth, and what if Mitch were to follow Roz out to the kitchen and find Roz's mother sitting there and be given the once-over, the aim of which was to determine religious affiliation and financial prospects, in that order? So Roz dumped the flowers into the sink, she'd deal with them later, and kissed her mother on the firming cream, too little too late, and frogmarched Mitch out of the house before he could get waylaid by Roz's father, who would put him through the same third degree he put all of Roz's dates through if he could catch them—where were they going, what would they be doing, when would they be back, that was too late—and tell him cryptic ethnic parables illustrating Life. "Two cripples do not make one dancer," he would say to them, shooting out a meaningful look from underneath the bushy eyebrows, and what were the poor goofs supposed to think? "Papa, I wish you wouldn't say that," she'd tell him afterwards. That was another thing, she had to call him Papa, he wouldn't answer to Dad. "So?" he would say, grinning at her. "It's true, or not?"

Once they'd made it past the door it turned out that Mitch didn't have a car, and what was the etiquette? Was she supposed to offer hers, or what? She couldn't see the man of her dreams taking a bus; much less could she see herself taking one. What was the use of upward mobility if you had to take a bus anyway? There were limits! She was about to suggest a taxi when it occurred to her in a blinding flash that maybe Mitch didn't have the money for one.

In the end they took Roz's car, a little red Austin, a birthday present, Roz would've preferred a Jag but her father said that would have been spoiling her. Mitch didn't protest much when Roz gushingly urged the car keys on him so he could drive, because a man being driven by a woman might have felt diminished, she'd read the women's magazine articles about all the ways you could unwittingly diminish a man, it was terrible how easily they shrank, and though she usually liked to drive her own car herself she didn't want to scare Mitch off. This way too she could just sit back and admire his profile. He drove well—decisively, aggressively, but not without courtesy, and she liked that. She herself was a fast driver; a barger-in, a honker. But watching Mitch drive, she could see that there were smoother ways of getting where you wanted to go.

The dinner was at a small quasi-French restaurant, with a red plush décor like a turn-of-the-century whorehouse and not very good food. Roz had the onion soup, which was a mistake because of the filaments of stringy cheese that came looping down from each spoonful. She did what she could with it, but she felt she was not passing the gracefulness test. Mitch didn't seem to notice; he was talking to her about his law firm.

He doesn't like me, she thought, this is a fiasco, so she had another glass of white wine, and then she thought, What the hell, and told him a joke, the one about the girl who told another girl she'd got raped that summer, yes, and after that it was just rape rape rape, all summer long, and Mitch smiled at her slowly, and his eyes closed up a little like a cat when you stroke its ears, maybe despite the tin-soldier posture he had a hormone or two after all, maybe the WASPy façade was just that, a façade, and if it was she would be eternally grateful, and then she felt his hand on her knee, under the table, and that was the end of her self-control, she thought she was going to melt like a warm Popsicle, all over the red plush restaurant seat.

After dinner they did start out in the direction of the

movie, but somehow they ended up necking in Roz's car; and after that they were in Mitch's apartment, a three-bedroom he shared with two other law students who were conveniently out—*Did he plan this?* Roz thought fleetingly, because exactly who was seducing whom—and Roz was all set to wrestle with her panty girdle, having helped Mitch get the top half of her clothes off—no lady should ever be without a panty girdle, said her mother and the magazines both, control unsightly jiggle and you wouldn't want men to think you were a loose woman with a floppy bum, though the darn things were built like rat traps, pure cast-iron elastic, it was like trying to get out of a triple-wrapped rubber band—when Mitch took hold of her shoulders and gazed deeply into her eyes and told her he respected her too much. "I don't want to just make love with you," he said. "I want to marry you." Roz felt like protesting that these categories were not mutually exclusive, but that would have been immodest, in Mitch's eyes at least, and anyway she was too overcome with happiness, or was it fear, because was this a proposal?

"What?" she said.

He repeated the marrying part.

"But I hardly know you," Roz stammered.

"You'll get to know me better," said Mitch calmly. He was right about that.

And this is how things went on: mediocre dinners, heavy petting, delayed gratification. If Roz had been able to get it over with, get Mitch out of her system, maybe she wouldn't have married him. Wrong: she would have, because after that first evening she was in over her depth and no was not an option. But the fact that he reduced her to a knee-wobbling jelly every time they went out, then gripped her hands when she tried to unzip him, added a certain element of suspense. For *suspense* read *frustration*. Read also abject humiliation. She felt like a big loose floozie, she felt like a puppy being whacked with a newspaper for trying to climb up trouser legs.

When the time came—not in a church, not in a synagogue—considering the mixtures involved, in one of the banquet rooms of the Park Plaza Hotel—Roz didn't think she'd make it all the way down the aisle. She thought there might be an unseemly incident. But Mitch would never have forgiven her if she'd jumped him in public, or even given him a big smooch during the kiss-the-bride routine. He'd made it clear by then that there were jumpers and jumpees, kissers and kissees, and he was to be the former and she the latter.

Sex-role stereotyping, thinks Roz now, having learned a thing or two in the interim. The cunning bastard. He held out on me, he wore me down. He knew exactly what he was doing. Probably had a little side dish for himself tucked away in some typing pool so he wouldn't get gangrene of the male member. But he pulled it off, he married me. He got the brass ring. She knows by this time that her money has to have been a factor.

Her father was suspicious about that even at the time. "How much is he making?" he queried Roz.

"Papa, that is not the *point!*" cried Roz, in an excess of anti-materialism. Anyway, wasn't Mitch the golden boy? Guaranteed to do well? Wasn't he about to rise in his law firm like a soap bubble?

"All I'm asking is, do I need to support him?" said her father. To Mitch he said, "Two cripples do not make one dancer," glowering out from under his eyebrows.

"Pardon me, sir?" said Mitch, with urbanity, too much urbanity, urbanity that bordered on condescension and that meant he was willing to overlook Roz's parents, the immigrant taint of the one, the boiled-potato doily-ridden rooming-house aftertaste of the other. Roz was new money, Mitch was old money; or he would have been old money if he'd had any money. His own father was dead, somewhat too early and too vaguely for total comfort. How was Roz to know then that he'd blown the family fortune on a war widow he'd run away with and then jumped off a bridge? She was not a mind-reader, and Mitch didn't tell her, not for years, not for years and years. Neither did his prune of a mother, who was not dead yet but (thinks Roz, in the cellar) might as well have been. Roz has never forgiven her those delicate, cutting post-bridal hints about toning down her wardrobe and the proper way to set a dinner table.

"Papa, I am not a cripple!" Roz said to her father afterwards. "I mean, that is *so* insulting!"

"One cripple and one who is not a cripple don't make a dancer either," said her father.

What was he trying to tell me? thinks Roz, at this distance. What had he seen, what crack or fault line, what incipient limp?

But Roz wasn't listening then, she was holding her hands over her ears, she didn't want to hear. Her father gave her a long, sombre look. "You know what you're doing?"

•   •   •

Roz thought she did; or rather she didn't care whether she did or not, because this was it, this was *It,* and she was floating finally, she was up there on cloud nine, light as a feather despite her big raw bones. Her mother was on her side, because Roz was almost twenty-three now and any marriage was better than no marriage as far as she was concerned; though once she saw it was really going to happen, she became scornful of Mitch's good manners—*la-di-da and excuse me, and who does he think he is*—and made it known that she would have preferred a Catholic to an Anglican. But having married Roz's father, who was not exactly the Pope, she couldn't put up much of an argument.

Mitch didn't marry Roz just for her money. She's sure of that. She remembers their actual honeymoon, in Mexico, all those Day of the Dead sugar skulls in the market, the flowers, the colours, herself giddy with pleasure, her sense of novelty and release because look, she had done it, she wasn't a potential old maid any more but a bride, a married woman; and during the hot nights the window open to the sea, the curtains blowing, the wind moving over her skin like muslin, and the dark shape of Mitch above her, faceless and intense. It was different when you were in love, it was no longer a game; there was more at stake. She cried afterwards because she was so happy, and Mitch must have felt it too, because you can't fake that kind of passion completely. Can you?

So it wasn't only the money. But she could put it this way—he wouldn't have married her without it. Maybe that's what keeps him with her, what keeps him anchored. She hopes it's not the only thing.

Mitch raises his glass of white wine to her and says, "To us," and reaches across the table and takes her left hand, the one with the ring, a modest ring because that's what he could afford at the time and he'd refused to accept any contribution from her father for a bigger one, and smiles at her, and says, "It hasn't been so bad, has it? We're pretty good, together," and Roz knows he's consoling himself for hidden disappointments, for time that marches on, for all the worlds he will, now, never be able to conquer, for the fact that there are thousands of nubile young women in the world, millions of them, more every minute, and no matter what he does he will never be able to get into all of them, because art is long and life is brief and mortality looms.

And yes, they are pretty good together. Sometimes. Still. So she beams at him and returns the squeeze, and thinks they are as happy as can be. They are. They are as happy as they can be, given who they are. Though if they'd been different people they might have been happier.

A girl, a pretty girl, a pretty girl in a scoop-neck jersey, appears with a platter of dead fish, from which Mitch selects. He's having the Catch of the Day, Roz is having the pasta done in sepia, because she has never eaten such a thing before and it sounds so bizarre. Spaghetti in Ink. There's a salad first, during which Roz sees fit to ask, tentatively enough, whether there's a specific topic Mitch wants to discuss. At previous lunches there has been one, a business topic usually, a topic having to do with Mitch getting more power on the board of *Wise Woman World*, of which he is the chairman, oops, chairperson.

But Mitch says no, he was merely feeling that he hasn't been seeing enough of her lately, without the kids that is, and Roz, eager for scraps as always, laps it up. She will forgive, she will forget. Well anyway, forgive, because what you can or can't forget isn't under your control. Maybe Mitch has just been having a middle-aged crisis all these years; though twenty-eight was a little young to begin.

The salad arrives, on a large plate borne by yet another long-haired, scoop-necked lovely, and Roz wonders whether the waitresses are chosen to go with the paintings. With so many nipples around she has the sensation of being watched by a myriad alien eyes. Pink ones. She flashes briefly on some flat-chested woman bringing a discrimination case against this restaurant for refusing to hire her. Even better, a flat-chested man. She'd love to be a fly on the wall.

The waitress bends over, showing deep cleavage, and dishes out the salad, and stands there smiling while Roz takes a bite. "Terrific," says Roz, meaning the salad.

"Absolutely," says Mitch, smiling up at the waitress. Oh God, thinks Roz. He's starting to flirt with waitresses. What'll she think of him? Sleazy old fart? And how soon before he really is a sleazy old fart?

Mitch has always flirted with waitresses, in his restrained way. But that's like saying a ninety-year-old can-can dancer has always done the can-can. When do you know when to stop?

● ● ●

After the salad the main course arrives. It's a different girl this time. Well, a different woman; she's a little older, but with a ravishing cloud of dark hair and amazing great tits, and a tiny little waist Roz would kill for. Roz looks hard at her and knows she's seen her before. Much earlier, in another life. "Zenia!" she exclaims, before she can help it.

"Pardon me?" says the woman. Then she looks at Roz in turn, and smiles, and says, "Roz? Roz Grunwald? Is it you? You don't look like your pictures!"

Roz has an overwhelming urge to deny it. She shouldn't have spoken in the first place, she should have dropped her purse on the floor and dived after it, anything to stay out of Zenia's sightlines. Who needs the evil eye?

But the shock of seeing Zenia there, working as a waitress—a *server*—in Nereids, overrides all that, and "What the heck are you doing here?" Roz blurts out.

"Research," says Zenia. "I'm a journalist, I've been freelance for years, in England mostly. But I wanted to come back, just to see—to see what things were like, over here. So I got myself commissioned to do a piece on sexual harassment in the workplace."

Zenia must be different, thinks Roz, if she's writing about that stuff. She even looks different. She can't place it at first, and then she sees. It's the tits. And the nose too. The former have swelled, the latter has shrunk. Zenia's nose used to be more like Roz's. "Really?" says Roz, who has a professional interest. "Who for?"

"*Saturday Night,*" says Zenia. "It's mostly an interview format, but I thought it would be good to take a look at the locales." She smiles more at Roz than at Mitch. "I was in a factory last week, and the week before that I spent in a hospital. You wouldn't believe how many nurses get attacked by their patients! I don't mean just grabbing—they throw things, the bedpans and so forth, it's a real occupational hazard. They wouldn't let me do any actual nursing though; this is more hands-on."

Mitch is beginning to look peevish at being sidelined, so Roz introduces him to Zenia. She doesn't want to say "an old friend," so instead she says, "We were at the same school." Not that we were ever what you'd call best buddies, thinks Roz. She scarcely knew Zenia then, except as an object of gossip. Lurid, sensational gossip.

Mitch does nothing to help Roz out, in the conversation department. He simply mutters something and stares at his plate. He obviously feels he's been interrupted. "So, how're the occupational hazards in this place?" says Roz, covering for him. "Has anyone called you 'honeybun' and pinched your butt?"

Zenia laughs. "Same old Roz. She was always the life of the party," she says to Mitch.

While Roz is wondering what parties she ever attended at which Zenia was also present—none, as far as she can remember, but she used to drink more in those days, or more at once, and maybe she's forgotten—Zenia puts her hand on Roz's shoulder. Her voice changes, becomes lower, more solemn. "You know, Roz," she says, "I've always wanted to tell you this. But I never could before."

"What?" says Roz.

"Your father," says Zenia.

"Oh dear," says Roz, fearing some scam she's never found out about, some buried scandal. Maybe Zenia is her long-lost half-sister, perish the thought. Her father was a sly old fox. "What did he do?"

"He saved my life," says Zenia. "During the war."

"Saved your life?" says Roz. "During the war?" Wait a minute—was Zenia even born, during the war? Roz hesitates, unwilling to believe. But this is what she's longed for always—an eyewitness, someone involved but impartial, who could assure her that her father really was what he was rumoured to be: a hero. Or a semi-hero; at any rate, more than a shady trader. She's heard accounts from others, her uncles for instance, but the two of them were hardly reliable; so she's never been really sure, not really.

Now, finally, there's a messenger, bringing news from that distant country, the country of the past, the country of the war. But why does that messenger have to be Zenia? It grates on Roz that Zenia has this news and Roz does not. It's as if her father has left something in his will, some treasure, to a perfect stranger, some drifter he'd met in a bar, and nothing for his own daughter. Didn't he know how much she wanted to know?

Maybe there's nothing in it. On the other hand, what if there is? It's at least worth a listen. It's at least worth a flutter.

"It's a long story," says Zenia. "I'd love to tell you about it, when you've got the time. If you want to hear it, that is." She smiles, nods at Mitch, and walks away. She moves confidently, nonchalantly, as if she knows she's just made the one offer that Roz can't possibly refuse.

42

Roz's father, the Great Unknown. Great to others, unknown to her. Or let's just say—thinks Roz, in her orange bathrobe, in the cellar, finishing off the crumbs of the Nanaimo bar, hungrily licking the plate—that he had nine lives, and she herself was only aware of three or four of them. You never knew when someone from one of her father's previous lives might reappear.

Once upon a time Roz was not Roz. Instead she was Rosalind, and her middle name was Agnes, after Saint Agnes and also her mother, though she didn't tell the girls at school about that because she didn't want to be nick-named Aggie, the way her mother was, behind her back, by the roomers. No one would dare call her mother Aggie to her face. She was far too respectable for that. She was Mrs. Greenwood, to them.

So Roz was Rosalind Greenwood instead of Roz Grunwald, and she lived with her mother in her mother's rooming house on Huron Street. The house was tall and narrow and made of red brick, with a sagging porch on the front that Roz's father was going to fix, maybe, sometime.

Her father was away. He'd been away as long as Roz could remember. It was because of the war.

Roz could remember the war, although not very well. She remembered the air raid sirens, from before she went to school, because her mother had made her crawl underneath the bed and there was a spider. Her mother had saved up bacon fat and tin cans, though what the soldiers would do with those things Roz couldn't imagine, and later, at school everyone gave nickels to the Red Cross because of all the orphans. The orphans stood on piles of rubble, and had raggedy clothes and huge, unsmiling eyes, appealing eyes, accusing eyes, because their parents had been killed by bombs. Sister Mary Paul showed pictures of them, in Grade One, and Roz cried because she was so sorry for them and was told to control herself, and couldn't eat her lunch, and was told she had to finish it because of the orphans, and asked for a second helping because if finishing one lunch was going to help the orphans, then eating a second one would help them even more, although she wasn't sure how. Maybe God had ways of arranging such things. Maybe the solid, visible food Roz ate got turned into invisible spiritual food and flown through the air, straight into the orphans, sort of like Communion, where the Host looked like a round soda cracker but was really Jesus. In any case, Roz was more than willing to help out.

Somewhere over there, behind the piles of rubble, out of sight among the dark clumps of trees in the distance, was her father. She hoped some of the food she ate would bypass the orphans and get into him. That was how Roz thought when she was in Grade One.

But the war was over, so where was Roz's father now?

"On his way," said her mother. There was a third chair always placed ready at the kitchen table for him. Roz could hardly wait.

Because Roz's father was away Roz's mother had to run the rooming house all by herself. It was wearing her down, as she told Roz, almost every day. Roz could see it: her mother had a stringy look, as if the soft parts of her were being scraped away, as if her bones were getting closer and closer to the surface. She had a long face, grey-streaked brown hair pulled back and pinned, and an apron. She didn't talk much, and when she did talk it was in short, dense clusters of words. "Least said soonest mended," she would say. "A stitch in time saves nine. Scarce as hen's teeth. Blood is thicker than water. Handsome is as handsome does. Safe as houses. Money doesn't grow on trees. Little pitchers have big ears." She said Roz was a chatterbox and her tongue wagged at both ends.

She had hard hands with enlarged knuckles, red from washing. "Look at my hands," she would say, as if her hands proved something. Usually what they proved was that Roz had to help out more. "Your mother is a saint," said little Miss Hines, who lived on the third floor. But if Roz's mother was a saint, Roz did not especially want to be one.

When Roz's father came back he would help out. If Roz was good, he would come back sooner, because God would be pleased with her and would answer her prayers. But sometimes she couldn't always remember. When that happened, when she did a sin, she would get frightened; she would see her father in a boat, crossing the ocean, and a huge wave washing over him or a bolt of lightning striking him, which would be God's way of punishing her. Then she needed to pray extra hard, until Sunday when she could go to confession. She would pray on her knees, beside her bed, with the tears running down her face. If it was a bad sin she would also scrub the toilet, even if it had just been done. God liked well-scrubbed toilets.

Roz wondered what her father would be like. She had no real memory of him, and the photo her mother kept on her dark, polished, forbidden bureau was just of a man, a large man in a black coat whose face Roz could scarcely make out because it was in shadow. This photo revealed none of the magic Roz ascribed to her father. He was important, he was doing important, secret things that could not be spoken about. They were war things, even though the war was over.

"Risking his neck," said her mother.

"How?" said Roz.

"Eat up your supper," said her mother, "there are children starving in Europe."

What he was doing was so important that he didn't have much time to write letters, although letters did arrive at intervals, from faraway places: France, Spain, Switzerland, Argentina. Her mother read these letters to herself, turning an odd shade of mottled pink while she did it. Roz saved the stamps.

What Roz's mother did mostly was cleaning. "This is a clean, respectable house," she would say, when she was bawling out the roomers for something they'd done wrong, some mess they'd made in the hall or bathtub ring they'd failed to wipe off. She brushed the stair treads and vacuumed the second-floor hall runner, she scrubbed the linoleum in the front vestibule and waxed it and did the same with the kitchen floor. She cleaned the bathroom fixtures with Old Dutch cleanser and the toilets with Sani-Flush, and did the windows with Windex, and washed the lace curtains with Sunlight Soap, scrubbing them carefully by hand on a washboard, although she did the sheets and towels in the wringer-washer that was kept in the back shed adjoining the kitchen; there were a lot of sheets and towels, because of the roomers. She dusted twice a week and put drain cleaner down all the drains, because otherwise the roomers' hair would clog them up. This hair was an obsession of hers; she acted as if the roomers tore great handfuls of it out of their heads and stuffed it down the drains on purpose. Sometimes she stuck a crochet hook down the sink drain on the second floor and hauled up a wad of slimy, soap-covered, festering hair. "See?" she would say to Roz. "Riddled with germs."

She expected Roz to help her with all of this endless cleaning. "I work my fingers to the bone," she'd say. "For you. Look at my hands," and it was no good for Roz to say that she didn't really care whether the second-floor toilet was clean or not because she didn't use that one. Roz's mother wanted the house to be decent for her father when he came, and since they never knew when that might be, it had to be decent all the time.

There were three roomers. Roz's mother had the second-floor front room, and Roz had one of the two rooms on the third floor—the attic, her mother called it. Little Miss Hines lived in the other attic room, with her woolly slippers and her Viyella plaid bathrobe, which she wore to go down to take her bath because the bathroom on the third floor had only a sink and a toilet. Miss Hines was not young. She worked in a shoe store in the daytime, and played the radio softly in her room at night—dance music—and read a lot of paperback detective novels. "There's nothing like a good murder," she would tell Roz. She seemed to find these books comforting. She read them in bed, and also in the bathtub; Roz would find them, opened and face down on the floor, their pages slightly damp. She would carry them back upstairs for Miss Hines, looking at the covers: mansions with storm clouds and lightning, men with felt hats pulled down over their faces, dead people with knives sticking into them, young women with large breasts, in their nightgowns, done in strange colours, dark but lurid, with the blood shiny and thick as molasses in a puddle on the floor.

If Miss Hines wasn't in her room Roz would have a look inside her clothes closet, but Miss Hines didn't have very many clothes and the ones she did have were navy blue and brown and grey. Miss Hines was a Catholic, but she had only one holy picture: the Virgin Mary, with the Baby Jesus in her lap, and John the Baptist, wearing fur because he would later live in the desert. The Virgin Mary always looked sad in pictures, except when Jesus was a baby. Babies were the one thing that cheered her up. Jesus, like Roz, was an only child; a sister would have been nice for him. Roz intended to have both kinds when she grew up.

On the ground floor there was one bedroom that used to be the dining room. Mr. Carruthers lived in there. He was an old man with a pension; he'd been in the war, but it was a different one. He'd been wounded in the leg so he walked with a cane, and he still had some of the bullets inside him. "See this leg?" he'd say to Roz. "Full of shrapnel. When they run out of iron they can mine this leg." It was the one joke he ever made. He read the newspapers a lot. When he went out, he went to the Legion to visit with his pals. He sometimes came back three sheets to the wind, said Roz's mother. She couldn't stop that, but she could stop him from drinking in his room.

The roomers were not allowed to eat in their rooms or drink either, except water. They couldn't have hotplates because they might burn down the house. The other thing they couldn't do was smoke. Mr. Carruthers did, though. He opened the window and blew the smoke out of it, and then flushed the butts down the toilet. Roz knew this, but she didn't tell on him. She was a little afraid of him, of his bulgy face and grey bristling moustache and clumping shoes and beery breath, but also she didn't want to tell, because telling on people was ratting, and the girls who did it at school were despised.

Was Mr. Carruthers a Protestant or a Catholic? Roz didn't know. According to Roz's mother, religion didn't matter so much in a man. Unless he was a priest, of course. Then it mattered.

Miss Hines and Mr. Carruthers had been there as long as Roz could remember, but the third roomer, Mrs. Morley, was more recent. She lived in the other second-floor bedroom, down the hall from the one where Roz's mother slept. Mrs. Morley said she was thirty. She had low-slung breasts and a face tanned with pancake makeup, and black eyelashes and red hair. She worked in Eaton's cosmetics, selling Elizabeth Arden, and she wore nail polish, and was divorced. Divorce was a sin, according to the nuns.

Roz was fascinated by Mrs. Morley. She let herself be lured into Mrs. Morley's room, where Mrs. Morley gave her samples of cologne and Blue Grass hand lotion and showed her how to put her hair up in pincurls, and told her what a skunk Mr. Morley had been. "Honey, he cheated on me," she said, "like there was no tomorrow." She called Roz "honey" and "sweetie," which Roz's mother never did. "I wish I'd of had a little girl," she'd say, "just like you," and Roz would grin with pleasure.

Mrs. Morley had a silver hand mirror with roses on it and her initials engraved on the back: *G.M.* Her first name was Gladys. Mr. Morley had given her that mirror for their first anniversary. "Not that he meant a word of it," Mrs. Morley would say as she plucked out her eyebrows. She did this with tweezers, gripping each eyebrow stub and yanking hard. It made her sneeze. She plucked out almost all of them, leaving a thin line in the perfect curved shape of the new moon. It made her look surprised, or else incredulous. Roz would study her own eyebrows in the mirror. They were too dark and bushy, she decided, but she was too young yet to begin pulling them out.

Mrs. Morley still wore her wedding ring and her engagement ring as well, though occasionally she would take them off and put them into her jewel box. "I should just sell them," she would say, "but I don't know. Sometimes I still feel married to him, in spite of everything, you know what I mean? You want something to hang onto." On some weekends she went out on dates, with men who rang the front doorbell and were let inside, grudgingly, by Roz's mother, and who then had to stand in the vestibule and wait for Mrs. Morley because there was nowhere else for them to go.

Certainly Roz's mother would not ask them back to sit in the kitchen. She did not approve of them, or of Mrs. Morley in general; though she sometimes let Roz go to the movies with her. Mrs. Morley preferred films in which women renounced things for the sake of other people, or in which they were loved and then abandoned. She followed these plots with relish, eating popcorn and dabbing at her eyes. "I'm a sucker for a good weepie," she said to Roz. Roz didn't understand why the things in the movies happened the ways they did, and would have preferred to have seen *Robin Hood* or else Abbott and Costello, but her mother felt an adult should be present. Things could happen in the flickering, sweet-smelling dark of movie theatres; men could take advantage. This was one subject on which Mrs. Morley and Roz's mother were in agreement: the advantage men could take.

Roz went through Mrs. Morley's jewel box when she wasn't there, although she was careful not to move anything out of its place. It gave her a feeling of pleasure, not just because the things were pretty—they weren't real jewels, most of them, they were costume jewellery, rhinestones and glass—but because there was something exciting about doing this. Although the brooches and earrings were exactly the same when Mrs. Morley wasn't there as when she was, they seemed different in her absence—more alluring, secretive. Roz looked into the closet as well: Mrs. Morley had many brightly coloured dresses, and the high-heeled shoes that went with them. When she was feeling more than normally daring Roz would slip on the shoes and hobble around in front of the mirror on Mrs.

Morley's closet door. The pair she liked best had sparkling clips on the toes that looked as if they were made of diamonds. Roz thought they were the height of glamour.

Sometimes there would be a little pile of dirty underwear in the corner of the closet, just thrown in there, not even put into a laundry bag: brassieres, stockings, satin slips. These were the things Mrs. Morley washed out by hand in the bathroom sink and draped over the radiator in her room to dry. But she should have picked them up off the floor first, as Roz had to do. Of course Mrs. Morley was a Protestant, so what could you expect? Roz's mother would have liked to have had nobody in her rooming house except Catholics, nice clean well-behaved Catholic ladies like Miss Hines, but beggars couldn't be choosers and in such times you had to take what you could get.

Roz had a round face and dark straight hair and bangs, and she was big for her age. She went to Redemption and Holy Spirit, which used to be two schools but now just had two names, and the nuns in their black-and-white habits taught her to read and write and sing and pray, with white chalk on a black blackboard and a ruler across the knuckles if you got out of line.

Catholics were the best thing because you would go to Heaven when you died. Her mother was a Catholic too, but she didn't go to church. She would take Roz there and push her towards the door, but she wouldn't go in. From the set of her face Roz knew better than to ask why.

Some of the other kids on the street were Protestants, or else Jews; whatever you were, the others chased you on your way home from school, though sometimes the boys might play baseball together. Boys would chase you if you were a girl: the religion didn't matter then. There were a few Chinese kids as well, and there were also DPs.

The DP kids had the worst time of all. There was a DP girl at Roz's school: she could hardly speak English, and the other girls whispered about her where she could see them, and said mean things to her, and she would say "What?" Then they would laugh.

DPs meant Displaced Persons. They came from the east, across the ocean; what had displaced them was the war. Roz's mother said they should consider themselves lucky to be here. The grown-up DPs had odd clothes, dismal and shabby clothes, and strange accents, and a shuffling, defeated look to them. A confused look, as if they didn't know where they were or what was going on. The children would shout after them on the street: "DP! DP! Go back where you come from!" Some of the older boys would shout "Dog Poop!"

The DPs didn't understand, but they knew they were being shouted at. They would hurry faster, their heads hunched down into their coat collars; or they would turn around and glare. Roz would join the shouting packs, if she wasn't near her house. Her mother didn't like her running around on the street like a ragamuffin, screeching like a pack of hooligans. Afterwards, Roz was ashamed of herself for yelling at the DPs like that; but it was hard to resist when everyone else was doing it.

Sometimes Roz got called a DP herself, because of her dark skin. But it was just a bad name, like "moron," or—much worse—"bugger." It didn't mean you were one. If Roz could get those kids cornered, and if they weren't too much bigger than she was, she would give them a Chinese burn. That was two hands on the arm and then a twist, like wringing out the wash. It did burn, and it left a red mark. Or else she would kick them, or else she would yell back. She had a temper, said the nuns.

Still, even if Roz wasn't a DP, there was something. There was something about her that set her apart, an invisible barrier, faint and hardly there, like the surface of water, but strong nevertheless. Roz didn't know what it was but she could feel it. She wasn't like the others, she was among them but she wasn't part of them. So she would push and shove, trying to break her way in.

To school Roz wore a navy tunic and a white blouse, and on the front of the tunic there was a crest with a dove on it. The dove was the Holy Spirit. There was a picture of it in the chapel, coming down from Heaven with its wings outspread, on top of the Virgin Mary's head, while the Virgin Mary rolled her eyes upwards in a way that Roz's mother had told her never to do or they might get stuck that way; likewise crossing them. There was a second picture too, the Disciples and Apostles receiving the Holy Spirit at the Feast of Pentecost; this time the dove had red fire around it.

The dove made the Virgin Mary pregnant, but everyone knew that men couldn't have babies, so the Disciples and Apostles didn't get pregnant, they only talked in tongues and prophesied. Roz didn't know what talking in tongues meant, and neither did Sister Conception, because when Roz asked about it Sister Conception told her not to be impertinent.

The Pentecost picture was in the long main corridor

of the school, with its creaky wooden floors and smell of goodness, a smell composed of slippery floor wax and plaster dust and incense from the chapel that made a small cool pool of guilty fear collect in Roz's stomach every time she smelled it, because God could see everything you did and also thought and most of these things annoyed him. He seemed to be angry much of the time, like Sister Conception.

But God was also Jesus, who got nailed to the cross. Who nailed him? Roman soldiers, who wore armour. There they were, three of them, looking brutal and making jokes, while Mary in blue and Mary Magdalene in red wept in the background.

It wasn't really the Roman soldiers' fault because they were just doing their job. Really it was the fault of the Jews. One of the prayers in chapel was a prayer for the conversion of the Jews, which meant they would switch over to being Catholic and then get forgiven. In the meantime God was still mad at them and they would have to keep on being punished. That's what Sister Conception said.

Things were more complicated than that, thought Roz, because Jesus had arranged for himself to be crucified on purpose. It was a sacrifice, and a sacrifice was when you gave your life to save other people. Roz wasn't sure why getting yourself crucified was such a favour to everyone but apparently it was. So if Jesus did it on purpose, why was it the fault of the Jews? Weren't they helping him out? A question of Roz's that went unanswered by Sister Conception, though Sister Cecilia, who was prettier and on the whole nicer to Roz, took a crack at it: a bad deed remained bad, she said, even if the result was good. There were lots of bad deeds that turned out to have good results, because God was a mystery, which meant he switched things around, but humans weren't in control of that, they were only in control of their own hearts. It was what was in your heart that counted.

Roz knew what a heart looked like. She'd seen lots of pictures of hearts, mostly the heart of Jesus, inside his opened-up chest. They were nothing like Valentines; they were more like the cows' hearts in the butcher store, brownish red and clotted and rubbery-looking. The heart of Jesus glowed, because it was holy. Holy things glowed in general.

Every sin people did was like another nail pounded into the cross. That was what the nuns said, especially at Easter. Roz was less concerned about Jesus, because she knew it would come out all right for him, than she was about the two thieves. One of them believed right away that Jesus was God, so that one would sit on Jesus's right hand in Heaven. But what about the other one? Roz had a sneaking sympathy for the other thief. He must have been in just as much pain as Jesus and the first thief, but it wasn't a sacrifice because he didn't do it on purpose. It was worse to be crucified when you didn't want to be. And anyway, what had he stolen? Maybe something small. It never said.

Roz felt that he deserved a place in Heaven, too. She knew something about the seating plan: God in the middle, Jesus to the right of him, the good thief to the right of Jesus. The right hand was the *right* hand, and you always had to use it to make the sign of the cross, even if you were left-handed. But who sat on the left hand of God? There must have been someone, because God had a left hand as well as a right hand, and nothing about God could possibly be bad because God was perfect, and Roz couldn't see that side just being left empty. So the bad thief could sit there; he could feast along with the rest. (And where was the Virgin Mary in all of this? Was it a long dinner table, with maybe God at one end and the Virgin Mary at the other? Roz knew enough not to ask. She knew she would be called wicked and impious. But it was something she would have liked to know.)

Sometimes when Roz asked questions the nuns gave her funny looks. Or they gave each other funny looks, pursing their mouths, shaking their heads. Sister Conception said, "What can you expect?" Sister Cecilia took extra time to pray with Roz, when Roz had been bad and needed to do penance after school. "There is more joy in Heaven over the one lost lamb," she said to Sister Conception.

Roz added sheep to Heaven. They would be outside the window, naturally. But she was glad to know about them. That meant dogs and cats stood a chance, too. Not that she was allowed to have either; they would have made too much trouble for her mother, who had enough things to do as it was.

43

Roz is late coming home from school. She walks by herself, through the failing light, in the snow that is falling, not very much of it, down through the air like tiny white flakes of soap. She hopes the snow will stay around until Christmas.

She's late because she's been rehearsing for the Nativity play, in which she is the chief angel. She wanted to be the Virgin Mary, but she's the chief angel instead because she's so tall, and besides that she can remember all the lines. She has a white costume with a sparkly gold halo made out of a coat-hanger, and wings of stiff white cardboard with painted gold feather-tips, held on by straps.

Today was the first day they tried it with the costumes. Roz has to be careful walking or the wings will slip down, and she has to keep her head up and facing straight ahead because of the halo. She has to go up to the shepherds as they keep watch over their flocks by night, with a big tinsel Star of Bethlehem dangling from a string over their heads, and hold her right hand up while they are looking afraid, and say, *Fear not; for behold, I bring you good tidings of great joy, which shall be to all people.* Then she has to tell them about going to see the babe in swaddling clothes, lying in the manger, and then she has to say, *Glory to God in the highest, and on earth peace, good will towards men,* and then she has to point, with her whole arm held out, and guide the shepherds across the stage to where the manger is, while the school choir sings.

Roz is sorry for the girls who play the shepherds, because they have to wear grubby clothes and beards that hook over their ears with wires, like eyeglasses. These are the same beards that get used every year, and they're dirty. She feels even sorrier for the little kids who play the sheep. Their sheep costumes must have been white, once, but now they are grey, and they must be very hot.

The manger has blue curtains across the front. The shepherds have to stand in front of it until the choir is finished; meanwhile, Roz has gone around behind it and has climbed up on a stepstool, and is standing with both arms spread out. On her right side is Anne-Marie Roy, on her left is Eileen Shea; both of them are blowing trumpets, although they aren't really blowing them, of course. They have to stand that way the whole time, while two little kids with cherubs' wings open the curtains, showing stupid Julia Warden with her blonde hair and rosebud mouth and dumb simpering smile dressed up like the Virgin Mary, with a bigger halo than Roz's and a china-doll Jesus, and Saint Joseph standing behind her leaning on his staff, and a bunch of hay bales. The shepherds kneel on one side, and then along come the Wise Men in glittering robes and turbans, one of them with her face blackened because one of the Wise Men was black, and they kneel on the other side, and the choir sings "Angels We Have Heard on High," and then the main curtains close and Roz can put her arms down, which is a relief because it really hurts to keep them up in the air like that for so long.

After the rehearsal today Sister Cecilia told Roz she'd done very well. Roz had the only speaking lines in the whole play and it was important to say them clearly, in a nice loud voice. She was doing excellently and would be a credit to the school. Roz was pleased, because for once her loud voice wasn't getting her in trouble—mostly when the nuns speak to her in public it's about her rowdy behaviour. But while they were all taking their costumes off, Julia Warden said, "I think it's dumb to have an angel with black hair."

Roz said, "It's not black, it's brown," and Julia Warden said, "It's black. Anyways, you're not a real Catholic, my Mum says," and Roz told her to shut up or she'd make her, and Julia Warden said, "Where's your father anyways? My Mum says he's a DP," and Roz grabbed Julia Warden's arm and did the Chinese burn on her, and Julia Warden screamed. Sister Cecilia came rustling up and said what was all the commotion, and Julia Warden ratted, and Sister Cecilia told Roz that this was not the Christmas spirit and she shouldn't pick on girls smaller than her, and she was lucky Sister Conception wasn't there because if she was, Roz would get the strap. "Rosalind Greenwood, you just never learn," she said sadly.

Walking home from school, Roz spends her time thinking about what she will do to Julia Warden tomorrow, to get even; until the last block, when the two Protestant boys who live on the corner see her and chase her along the sidewalk, yelling "The Pope stinks!" Almost to her house they catch her and rub snow in her face, and Roz kicks their legs. They let her go, laughing and yelling with mock pain, or real pain—"Ouch, ouch, she kicked me"—and then she picks up her snowy books and runs the rest of the way, not crying yet, and scrambles up her front steps onto her porch. "You're not allowed on my *prop*erty!" she yells. A snowball whizzes past her. If Roz's mother were there, she would chase these boys off. "Ragamuffins!" she would say, and they would scatter. She sometimes takes the flat of her hand to Roz, but she won't let anyone else lay a finger on her. Except the nuns, of course.

Roz brushes off the snow—she's not supposed to track snow into the house—and goes inside, and down the hall to the kitchen. Two men are sitting at the kitchen table. They're wearing DP clothes, not shabby ones, not worn out, but DP clothes all the same, Roz can tell because of the shape. On the table is a bottle that Roz knows straight away has liquor in it—she's seen bottles like that on the sidewalk—and in front of each of the men there's a glass. Roz's mother is not in the room.

"Where's my mother?" she says.

"She went to get food," says one of the men. "She didn't have nothing to eat."

The other one says, "We're your new uncles. Uncle George, Uncle Joe."

Roz says, "I don't have any uncles," and Uncle George says, "Now, you do." Then both of them laugh. They have loud laughs, and strange voices. DP voices, but with something else, some other accent. Something that's like the movies.

"Sit," says Uncle George hospitably, as if it's his house, as if Roz is a dog. Roz is unsure of the situation—there have never been two men in the kitchen before—but she sits anyway.

Uncle George is the bigger one; he has a high forehead and light wavy hair slicked straight back. Roz can smell his hair goo, sweet, like theatres. He's smoking a brown cigarette in a black holder. "Ebony," he says to Roz. "You know what ebony is? It's a tree."

"She knows," says Uncle Joe. "She's a smart girl." Uncle Joe is smaller, with hunched-up shoulders and spindly hands, and dark hair, almost black, and huge dark eyes. He has a tooth missing, off to one side. He sees Roz staring, and says, "Once, I had a gold tooth in this place. I keep it in my pocket." And he does. He takes out a small wooden box, painted red with a design of tiny green flowers, and opens it, and there inside is a gold tooth.

"Why?" says Roz.

"You don't want to leave a gold tooth lying around in your mouth, people get ideas," says Uncle Joe.

Roz's mother comes in, carrying two brown paper grocery bags, which she sets down on the counter. She is flushed, and pleased-looking. She says nothing at all about the drinking, nothing about the smoke. "These are friends of your father's," she says. "They were all in the war together. He's coming, he'll be here soon." Then she bustles out again; she needs to go to the butcher's, she says, because this is an occasion. Occasions call for meat.

"What did you do in the war?" says Roz, eager to find out more about her father.

The two uncles laugh, and look at each other. "We was horse thieves," says Uncle George.

"The best horse thieves," says Uncle Joe. "No. Your father, he was the best. He could steal a horse—"

"He could steal a horse from right between your legs, you wouldn't notice," says Uncle George. "He could lie—"

"He could lie like God himself."

"Bite your tongue! God don't lie."

"You're right, God says nothing. But your father, he never blinked. He could walk through a border like it wasn't there," says Uncle Joe.

"What's a border?" asks Roz.

"A border is a line on a map," says Uncle Joe.

"A border is where it gets dangerous," says Uncle George. "It's where you need a passport."

"Passport. See?" says Uncle Joe. He shows Roz his passport, with his picture in it. Then he shows her another, with the same picture but a different name. He has three of them. He fans them out like a deck of cards. Uncle George has four.

"A man with only one passport is like a man with only one hand," he says solemnly.

"Your father, he has more passports than anyone. The best, like I said." They raise their glasses, and drink to Roz's father.

Roz's mother makes chicken, with mashed potatoes and gravy, and boiled carrots; she is cheerful, more cheerful than Roz has ever seen her, and urges the uncles to have more. Or maybe she's not cheerful, maybe she's nervous. She keeps looking at her watch. Roz is nervous, too: when will her father arrive?

"He'll be here when he's here," say the uncles.

● ● ●

Roz's father comes back in the middle of the night. Her mother wakes her up, and whispers, "Your father's back," almost as if she's apologizing for something, and takes Roz downstairs in her nightgown, and there he is, sitting at the table, in the third chair that was kept for him. He sits easily, filling the space, as if he's always been there. He's large and barrel-shaped, bearded, bear-headed. He smiles and holds out his arms. "Come, give Papa a kiss!"

Roz looks around: who is this *Papa*? Then she understands that he means himself. It's true, what Julia Warden said: her father is a DP. She can tell by the way he talks.

Now Roz's life has been cut in two. On one side is Roz, and her mother, and the rooming house, and the nuns and the other girls at school. This part seems already in the past, although it's still going on. That's the side where there are mostly women, women who have power, which means they have power over Roz, because even though God and Jesus are men it's her mother and the nuns who have the last word, except for the priests of course, but that's just on Sundays. On the other side is her father, filling the kitchen with his bulk, his loud voice, his multilayered smell; filling the house with it, filling up all the space in her mother's gaze so that Roz is pushed off to the edge, because her mother, who is so unbending, bends. She abdicates. She says, "Ask your father." She looks at Roz's father mutely, the same kind of mushy cow-eyed look the Virgin Mary gives the Baby Jesus or the Holy Spirit in the pictures; she dishes up his food and sets the plate before him as if it's some kind of offering.

And there isn't less work for her now, there's more, because there are three plates instead of two, there's three of everything, and Roz's father never has to clean up. "Help your mother," he tells Roz, "in this family we help each other"; but Roz doesn't see him helping. Roz catches them hugging and kissing in the kitchen, two days after he's arrived, her father's big bear arms around her thin angular mother, and is full of disgust at her mother for being so soft, and with sorrow and jealousy and the rage of banishment.

To punish her mother for such betrayals Roz turns away from her. She turns to the uncles, when they are there, and also, and especially, to her father. "Come sit on Papa's knee," he says. And she does, and from that safe place she regards her mother, working as hard as ever, hunched over the kitchen sink or kneeling in front of the oven, or scraping the bones off their plates into the pot of soup stock, or wiping the floor. "Make yourself useful," her mother snaps, and once Roz would have obeyed. But now her father's arms hold her tight. "I didn't see her for so long," he says. And her mother clenches her lips and says nothing, and Roz watches her with gloating triumph and thinks it serves her right.

But when her father isn't there she has to work, the same as usual. She has to scrub and polish. If she doesn't, her mother calls her a spoiled brat. "Who was your servant last year?" she jeers. "Look at my hands!"

The uncles move in. They've been having dinner every night, but now they move right into the house. They're living in the cellar. They have two beds down there, two army surplus cots, and two army sleeping bags as well.

"Just till they get on their feet," says Roz's father. "Till the ship comes in."

"What ship?" says Roz's mother. "It'll be a frosty Friday when any ship of theirs makes it to land." But she says this indulgently, and she cooks for them and asks them to have some more, and washes their sheets, and says not a word about the smoking, and the drinking too, which goes on down in the cellar with roars of laughter coming up the stairs. The uncles don't have to help clean up, either. When Roz asks why, all her mother will say is that they saved her father's life, during the war.

"We saved each other's life," says Uncle George. "I saved Joe's, Joe saved your father's, your father saved mine."

"They never caught us," says Uncle Joe. "Not once."

"*Dummkopf*, if they did we wouldn't be here," says Uncle George.

Aggie's grip on the roomers is slipping, because it's no longer the same rules for everyone. It doesn't help that the uncles don't pay rent, or that they slam the front door, hurrying in and out. They have places to go, they have things to do. Unnamed places, unspecified things. They have friends to meet, a friend from New York, a friend from Switzerland, a friend from Germany. They have lived in New York, and in London, and in Paris too. Other places. They refer with nostalgia to bars and hotels and racetracks in a dozen cities.

Miss Hines complains about the noise: do they have

to shout at each other, and in foreign languages too? But Mrs. Morley jokes around with them, and sometimes joins them for a drink, when Roz's father is home and they're all in the kitchen. She comes mincing down the stairs in her high heels, jingling her bracelets, and says she doesn't mind a drop, now and then.

"She can sure hold her liquor," says Uncle Joe.

"She's a babe," says Uncle George.

"What's a babe?" says Roz.

"There's ladies, there's women, and there's babes," says Uncle George. "Your mother is a lady. That one, she's a babe."

Mr. Carruthers knows about the drinking that's going on in the cellar, and in the kitchen too. He can smell the smoke. He's still not supposed to drink or smoke in his own room but he starts doing it, more than he did before. One afternoon he opens his door and corners Roz in the front hall.

"Those men are Jews," he whispers. Beer fumes fill the air. "We sacrificed our life for this country and they're handing it over to the Jews!"

Roz is galvanized. She runs to find the uncles, and asks them right away. If they really are Jews she might take a crack at converting them, and astonish Sister Conception.

"Me, I'm a U.S. citizen," says Uncle George, laughing a little. "I got the passport to prove it. Joe, he's a Jew."

"I'm a Hungarian, he's a Pole," says Uncle Joe. "I'm a Yugoslav, he's a Dutchman. This other passport says I'm

Spanish. Your father now, he's half a German. The other half, that's the Jew."

This is a shock to Roz. She feels disappointment—no spiritual triumphs for her, because she could never hope to change her father in any way, she can see that—and then guilt: what if the Sisters find out? Worse, what if they've known all along and haven't told her? She pictures the malicious glee on Julia Warden's face, the whisperings that will go on behind her back.

She must look dismayed, because Uncle George says, "Better to be a Jew than a murderer. They murdered six million, over there."

"Five," says Uncle Joe. "The rest was other things. Gypsies and homos."

"Five, six, who's counting?"

"Six what?" says Roz.

"Jews," says Uncle George. "They burnt them in ovens, they piled them up in heaps. Little Rozzie-lind, you wouldn't want to know. If they got their hands on you, back over there, they'd make you into a lampshade."

He doesn't explain to Roz that it would just be the skin. She has a picture of her entire body turned into a lampshade, with a lightbulb inside it and the light beaming out from her eyes and nostrils and ears and mouth. She must look terrified, because Uncle Joe says, "Don't scare the kid. All of that, it's over."

"Why?" says Roz. "Why would they?" But neither of them answers.

"It's not over till it's over," says Uncle George gloomily.

• • •

Roz has the feeling that someone has been lying to her. Not just about her father: about the war too, and about God. The starving orphans were bad enough but they weren't the whole story. What else has been going on, with the ovens and the heaps and the lampshades, and why has God allowed it?

She doesn't want to think about any of it any more because it's too sad and confusing. Instead she takes to reading murder mysteries. She borrows them from Miss Hines and reads them at night, beside the streetlight coming through her attic window. She likes the furniture, and the outfits of the people in them, and the butlers and the maids. But mostly she likes the fact that there's a reason for every death, and only one murderer at a time, and things get figured out at the end, and the murderer always gets caught.

44

Roz walks home from school in an expectant mood. There's something going on; she isn't sure what, but she knows there's something. Something is about to happen.

Last week, her mother said at breakfast: *Mrs. Morley has been fired.* What did that mean? Lost her job, but Roz had a brief vision of Mrs. Morley in flames, like an early martyr. Not that she wanted Mrs. Morley to burn up. She liked her, and also her accoutrements—her face cream samples, her costume jewellery, and especially her shoes.

Ever since then Mrs. Morley has been dragging around the house in her quilted pink satin dressing gown. Her eyelids are puffy, her face bare of makeup; the jingling from her usual festoons of necklaces and bangles has fallen silent. She isn't supposed to eat in her room but she's doing it anyway, out of paper bags brought to her by Mr. Carruthers; there are sandwich crusts and apple cores in her wastepaper basket, but although Roz's mother must be aware of this, she isn't knocking on Mrs. Morley's door to issue the commands she's normally so fond of giving. Sometimes these paper bags contain small flat bottles that don't turn up in the wastepaper basket. In the late afternoons, still in her dressing gown, she goes down to the kitchen for short, fraught talks with Roz's mother. What is she going to do? she asks. Roz's mother purses her lips, and says she doesn't know.

These talks are about money: without her job, Mrs. Morley won't be able to pay the rent. Roz feels sorry for her, but at the same time less friendly, because Mrs. Morley is whining and it makes Roz disdainful. If girls whine at school they get poked or slapped by the other children, or stood in a corner by the nuns.

"She should pull herself together," Roz's mother says to Roz's father at the dinner table. Once Roz would have been the audience for such comments, but now she is just a little pitcher with big ears.

"Have a heart, Aggie," says Roz's father. No one else ever calls Roz's mother Aggie to her face.

"Having a heart is all very well," says Roz's mother, "but it won't put food on the table."

But there is food on the table. Beef stew, mashed potatoes and gravy, and cooked cabbage. Roz is eating it.

On top of Mrs. Morley being fired, Miss Hines is down with a cold. "Just pray to God she doesn't catch pneumonia," says Roz's mother. "Then we'll have two useless women on our hands."

Roz goes into Mrs. Morley's room. Mrs. Morley is in bed, eating a sandwich; she shoves it under the covers, but smiles when she sees it's only Roz. "Honey, you should always knock before entering a lady's chamber," she says.

"I have an idea," says Roz. "You could sell your shoes." The ones Roz means are the red satin ones with the sparkly clips. They must be very expensive.

Mrs. Morley's smile wavers and falls. "Oh, honey," she says. "If only I could."

•   •   •

As she rounds the corner to her house Roz sees a strange sight. The front lawn is covered with snow like all the other lawns, but scattered over it there are a number of coloured objects. As she gets closer she sees what they are: Mrs. Morley's dresses, Mrs. Morley's stockings, Mrs. Morley's handbags, Mrs. Morley's brassieres and under-pants. Mrs. Morley's shoes. A lurid light plays round them.

Roz goes inside, into the kitchen. Her mother is sitting white-faced and bolt upright at the kitchen table; her eyes are still as stone. In front of her is an untouched cup of tea. Miss Hines is sitting in Roz's chair, patting her mother's hand with small fluttery pats. She has a spot in pink in either cheek. She looks nervous, but also elated.

"Your mother's had a shock," she says to Roz. "Would you like a glass of milk, dear?"

"What are Mrs. Morley's things doing on the lawn?" says Roz.

"What could I do?" says Miss Hines, to nobody in particular. "I couldn't help seeing them. They didn't even shut the door all the way."

"Where is she?" asks Roz. "Where's Mrs. Morley?" Mrs. Morley must have gone away without paying the rent. "Flown the coop," is how her mother would put it. Roomers have flown the coop in that way before, leaving possessions behind them, though never out on the lawn.

"She won't be showing her face in this house again," says her mother.

"Can I have her shoes?" says Roz. She's sorry she won't be seeing Mrs. Morley again, but there is no need for the shoes to go to waste.

"Don't touch her filthy things," says her mother.

"Don't lay a finger on them! They belong in the garbage, like her. That whore! If all that junk's not gone by tomorrow I'll burn it in the incinerator!"

Miss Hines looks shocked by such strong language. "I will pray for her," she says.

"I won't," says Roz's mother.

Roz connects none of this with her father until he appears, later, in time for dinner. The fact that he's on time is remarkable: he isn't usually. He is subdued, and respectful towards Roz's mother, but he doesn't hug her or give her a kiss. For the first time since his return he seems almost afraid of her.

"Here's the rent," he says. He dumps a little heap of money on the table.

"Don't think you can buy me off," says Roz's mother. "You and that slut! It's hush money. I'm not touching one dirty cent."

"It's not hers," says Roz's father. "I won it at poker."

"How could you?" says Roz's mother. "After all I gave up for you! Look at my hands!"

"She was crying," says Roz's father, as if this explains everything.

"Crying!" says Roz's mother with scorn, as if she herself would never do such a degrading thing. "Crocodile tears! She's a man-eater."

"I felt sorry for her," says Roz's father. "She threw herself at me. What could I do?"

Roz's mother turns her back on him. She hunches over the stove and dishes out the stew, hitting the spoon loudly on the side of the pot, and goes through the entire dinner without speaking. At first Roz's father hardly touches his dinner—Roz knows the feeling, it's anxiety

and guilt—but Roz's mother shoots him a look of concentrated disgust and points at his plate, meaning that if he
doesn't eat what she's spent her whole life cooking for him
he'll be in even worse trouble than he is. When her back
is turned Roz's father smiles a little smile at Roz, and
winks at her. Then she knows that all of this—his misery,
his hangdog air—is an act, or partly an act, and that he's
all right really.

The money stays on the table. Roz eyes it: she has
never seen so much money in a pile before. She would like
to ask if she could have it, since neither of them seems to
want it, but while she's clearing off the plates—"Help your
mother," says her father—it disappears. It's in one of their
pockets, she knows, but which one? Her mother's, she suspects—her apron pocket, because in the following days she
softens, and talks more, and life returns to normal.

Mrs. Morley however is never seen again. Neither are
her clothes and shoes. Roz misses her; she misses the pet
names and hand lotion; but she knows enough not to say so.

"A babe, like I said," says Uncle George. "Your father
has a strong weakness."

"Better he should close the door," says Uncle Joe.

A few years later, when she was a teenager and had the benefit of girlfriends, Roz put it together: Mrs. Morley was her
father's mistress. She'd read about mistresses in the murder
mysteries. *Mistress* was the word she preferred, because it
was more elevated than the other words available: "floozie,"
"whore," "easy lay." Those other words implied nothing but
legs apart, loose flabby legs at that—weak legs, legs that did
nothing but lie there, legs for sale—and smells, and random

coupling, and sexual goo. Whereas *mistress* hinted at a certain refinement, an expensive wardrobe, a well-furnished establishment, and also at the power and cunning and beauty it took to get such things.

Mrs. Morley hadn't had the establishment or the refinement and her beauty had been a matter of opinion, but at least she'd had the clothes, and Roz wanted to give her father some credit: he wouldn't have gone for just any old easy lay. She wanted to be proud of him. She knew her mother was in the right and her father was in the wrong; she knew her mother had been virtuous and had worked her fingers to the bone and had ruined her hands, and had been treated with ingratitude. But it was an ingratitude Roz shared. Maybe her father was a scoundrel, but he was the one she adored.

Mrs. Morley was not the only mistress. There were others, over the years: kindly, sentimental, soft-bodied women, lazy and fond of a drink or two and of tearful movies. In later life Roz deduced their presence, by her father's intermittent jauntiness and by his absences; she even bumped into them sometimes on downtown streets, on the arm of her aging but still outrageous father. But such women came and went, whereas her mother was a constant.

What was their arrangement, her mother and her father? Did they love each other? They had a history, of course: they had a story. They met just as the war began. Did he sweep her off her feet? Not exactly. She had the rooming house even then, she'd inherited it from her own mother, who had run it since the father died, at the age of twenty-five, of polio, when Roz's mother was only two.

Roz's mother was older than her father. She must have been already an old maid at the time she met him; already taciturn, already acid, already prim.

She had been walking home, carrying a bag of groceries; she had to pass a tavern. It was late afternoon, closing time, when the drinkers were expelled onto the streets so they would be sure to eat their dinners, or so the theory went. Ordinarily Roz's mother would have crossed over to avoid this tavern, but she saw a fight in progress. Four against one: *thugs,* was what she called them. The one was Roz's father. He was roaring like a bear, but one of the thugs came up behind him and hit him over the head with a bottle, and when he fell down they all started kicking him.

There were people on the street, but they just stood there watching. Roz's mother thought the man on the ground would be killed. She was by habit a silent woman, but she was not particularly timid, not in those days; she was used to telling men what for, because she had honed herself on the roomers, some of whom had tried to take advantage. Usually though she minded her own business and let other people mind theirs; usually she skirted bar fights and looked the other way. But that day was different. She could not just stand there and watch a man be killed. She screamed (for Roz, this was the best part—her laconic mother, screaming her head off, and in public too), and finally she waded in and swung her grocery bag, scattering apples and carrots, until a policeman came in sight and the thugs ran off.

Roz's mother picked up her fruits and vegetables. She was quite shaken, but she didn't want to waste her purchases. Then she helped Roz's father up off the sidewalk. "There was blood running all over him," she said. "He looked like something the cat dragged in." Her house was nearby, and being a devout Christian and familiar with the story of the Good Samaritan, she felt she had to take him to it and clean him off, at least.

Roz could see how it must have been. Who can withstand gratitude? (Although gratitude is a complicated emotion, as she has had reason to learn.) Still, what woman can resist a man she's rescued? There's something erotic about bandages, and of course clothing would have had to have been removed: jacket, shirt, undershirt. Then what? Her mother would have swung into her washing mode. And where was this poor man going to spend the night? He was on his way to join the army, he said (although he did not in fact join it, not officially); he was far from home—where was home? Winnipeg—and his money was gone. The thugs had taken it.

For her mother, who'd spent her twenties taking care of her own ailing mother, who'd never seen a man without his shirt on, this must have been the most romantic thing that had ever happened to her. The only romantic thing. Whereas for her father it was just an episode. Or was it? Maybe he fell in love with her, this screaming, silent woman who had come to his aid. Maybe he fell in love with her house, a little. Maybe she meant shelter. In her father's rendition, it was the screaming he always mentioned, with considerable admiration. Whereas her mother mentioned the blood.

Whatever it was, they did end up married, though it was not a Catholic wedding; which meant that in the eyes of the Church they were not married at all. For her father's sake, her mother had placed herself in an unremitting state of sin. No wonder she felt he owed her something.

●   ●   ●

Ah, thinks Roz, sitting in the cellar in her orange bathrobe. *God, you foxy old joker, you certainly do fool around. Changing the rules. Giving out contradictory instructions—save people, help people, love people; but don't touch.* God is a good listener. He doesn't interrupt. Maybe this is why Roz likes talking to him.

Soon after the ejection of Mrs. Morley, Mr. Carruthers vanishes too, leaving his room in a mess, taking only a suitcase, owing a month's rent. Uncle George moves into his room, and Uncle Joe into Mrs. Morley's old room, and then Miss Hines gives notice because the house is no longer respectable. "Where is the money going to come from?" asks Roz's mother.

"Don't worry, Aggie," says her father. And somehow money does appear, not very much money but enough, and out of nowhere, it seems, because her father doesn't have a job and neither do Uncle George and Uncle Joe. Instead they go to the racetrack. Occasionally they take Roz with them, on Saturdays when she's not at school, and put a dollar on a horse for her. Roz's mother never goes, and neither—Roz concludes, looking around at the outfits—do any other mothers. The women there are babes.

In the evenings the uncles sit at the card table in Uncle George's new room, and drink and smoke and play poker. If Roz's mother isn't home her father sometimes joins them. Roz hangs around, looking over their shoulders, and eventually they teach her how to play. "Don't show what you're thinking," they tell her. "Play close to your chest. Know when to fold."

After she's learned the game they show her how to gamble. At first it's just with poker chips; but one day Uncle George gives her five dollars. "That's your stake," he tells her. "Never bet more than your stake." It's not advice he follows, himself.

Roz gets good. She learns to wait: she counts the drinks they have, she watches the level in the bottle go down. Then she moves in.

"This little lady's a killer," says Uncle George admiringly. Roz beams.

It helps that she's playing seriously, whereas the uncles and her father aren't, not really. They play as if they're expecting a phone call. They play as if they're filling in the time.

All of a sudden there was a lot of money. "I won it at the track," said Roz's father, but Roz knew this couldn't be true because there was too much of it for that. There was enough for dinner at a restaurant, for all of them, her mother too, with ice cream afterwards. Her mother wore her best dress, which was a new best dress, pale green with a white daisy collar, because there was enough money for that as well. There was enough for a car; it was a blue Dodge, and the boys from down the street stood outside Roz's house for half an hour, gazing at it, while Roz watched them silently from her porch. Her triumph was so complete she didn't even have to jeer.

Where had the money come from? Out of thin air. It was like magic; her father waved his hand and presto, there it was. "The ship came in," said Roz's father. The uncles got some too. It was for all three of them, said her father. Equal shares, because the ship belonged to all.

Roz knew it wasn't a real ship. Still, she could picture it, an old-fashioned ship like a galleon, a treasure ship, its sails golden in the sunlight, pennants flying from its masts. Or something like that. Something noble.

Her parents sold the rooming house and moved north, away from the streets of narrow cheek-by-jowl old houses and tiny lawns, into an enormous house with a semi-circular driveway in front and a three-car garage. Roz decided that they had become rich, but her mother told her not to use that word. "We're comfortable," was what she said.

But she didn't seem comfortable at all. Instead she seemed afraid. She was afraid of the house, she was afraid of the cleaning lady Roz's father insisted on, she was afraid of the new furniture that she herself had bought—"Get the best," said Roz's father—she was afraid of her new clothes. She wandered around in her housecoat and slippers, from room to room, as if she was looking for something; as if she was lost. She had been much more comfortable back in the old neighbourhood, where things were the right size and she knew her way around.

She said she had nobody to talk to. But when had she ever talked that much, before? And who had she ever talked to? Roz, Roz's father, the uncles. Now the uncles had places of their own. The roomers? There were no roomers any more, for her to complain about and boss around. When men came to the door delivering things they took one look at her and asked to speak to the lady of the house. But she had to pretend to be happy, because of Roz's father. "This is what we waited for," he said.

Roz has new clothes too, and a new name. She's no longer Rosalind Greenwood, she's Roz Grunwald. This, her parents explain, has been her real name all along. "Why wasn't I called that before, then?" she asks.

"It was the war," they say. "That name was too Jewish. It wasn't safe."

"Is it safe now?" she asks.

Not entirely. Different things are safe, where they are living now. By the same token, different things are dangerous.

Roz goes to a new school. She's in high school now so she goes to Forest Hill Collegiate Institute. She's no longer a Catholic: she's renounced all of that—not without qualms, not without residue—in favour of being a Jew. Since there are so clearly sides, she would rather be on that one. She reads up on it because she wants to do it right; then she asks her father to buy two sets of dishes, and refuses to eat bacon. Her father buys the dishes to humour her, but her mother won't separate the meat dishes from the milk ones, and gives her a wounded look if she brings it up. Nor will her father join a temple. "I was never religious," he says. "Like I always said—who owns God? If there was no religions there won't be all this trouble."

There are a lot of Jewish kids at Roz's new school; in fact at this school Jewish is the thing to be. But whereas once Roz was not Catholic enough, now she isn't Jewish enough.

She's an oddity, a hybrid, a strange half-person. Her clothes, although expensive, are subtly not right. Her accent is not right either. Her enthusiasms are not right, nor her skills: Chinese burns and kicking people in the shins and playing a nifty hand of poker cut no ice here. Added to that, she's too big; also too loud, too clumsy, too eager to please. She has no smoothness, no boredom, no class.

She finds herself in a foreign country. She's an immigrant, a displaced person. Her father's ship has come in, but she's just off the boat. Or maybe it's something else: maybe it's the money. Roz's money is plentiful, but it needs to be aged, like good wine or cheese. It's too brash, too shiny, too exclamatory. It's too brazen.

She is sent off to Jewish summer camp by her father because he's found out that it's the right thing to do with your children, here, in this country, in this city, in this neighbourhood, in the summer. He wants Roz to be happy, he wants her to fit in. He equates these things. But at camp she's even more of an interloper, an obvious intruder: she has never played tennis, she's never ridden a horse, she doesn't know any of the cute folk dances from Israel or any of the mournful minor-key Yiddish songs. She falls off sailboats, into the freezing blue northern water of Georgian Bay, because she's never been on a boat before; when she tries to water-ski she chickens out at the last minute, just before they gun the motor, and sinks like a stone. The first time she appears in a bathing suit, not that she really knows how to swim, a graceless flail is her basic style, she realizes you're supposed to shave your armpits. Who could have been expected to tell her? Not her mother, who does not discuss the body. She has never been outside the city in her life. The other kids act as if they were born paddling a canoe and sleeping in smelly tents, but Roz can't get used to the bugs.

She sits at the breakfast table in the log-cabin dining room, listening in silence while the other girls complain languidly about their mothers. Roz wants to complain about her mother too, but she's found that her complaints don't count because her mother isn't Jewish. When she begins, with her rooming house stories, her stories of toilets and scrubbing, they roll their eyes and yawn delicately, like kittens, and change the subject back to their own mothers. Roz can't possibly know, they imply. She can't understand.

In the afternoons they do their hair up in rollers and lacquer their nails, and after the folk dances and singsongs and marshmallow roasts and Beatnik dress-up parties they are walked slowly back to their sleeping cabin by various boys, through the aromatic, painful dark, with its owl sounds and mosquitoes and its smell of pine needles, its flashlights blinking like fireflies, its languorous murmurs. None of these boys saunters over to joke with Roz, none stands with his arm propped on a tree, over her head. Well, not many of them are tall enough to do that, and anyway who wants to be seen with a part-*shiksa* hippo-hips fool? So Roz stays behind, to help clean up. God knows she's an expert at that.

During arts and crafts, which Roz is no good at—her clay ashtrays look like cow patties, her belt woven on a primitive Inca-type hand loom like the cat got into it—she says she has to go to the bathroom, and wanders off to the kitchen to wheedle a pre-dinner snack. She has befriended the pastry cook, an old man who can make a row of ducks across a cake with butter icing in one burst of calligraphy, without lifting the decorator once. He shows Roz how, and how to make an icing rose too, and a stem with a leaf. "A rose without a leaf is like a woman without honour," he says, bowing to her in a courtly, old-fashioned, European way, handing her the cake decorator to let her try. He lets her lick out the bowl, and tells her she is the right shape for a woman, not all bones like some here, he can tell she appreciates good food. He has an accent, like her uncles, and a faint blue number on his arm. It's left over from the war, but Rose doesn't ask about that, because nobody talks about the war here, not yet. The war is unmentionable.

Roz can see that she will never be prettier, daintier, thinner, sexier, or harder to impress than these girls are. She decides instead to be smarter, funnier, and richer, and once she has managed that they can all kiss her fanny. She takes to making faces; she resorts to the old rudeness of Huron Street, to get attention. Soon she has bulldozed a place for herself in the group: she is the joker. At the same time, she imitates. She picks up their accents, their intonations, their vocabulary; she adds layers of language to herself, sticking them on like posters on a fence, one glued over the top of the next, covering up the bare boards. As for the clothes, as for the accessories, those can be studied.

Roz made it through high school, which was not exactly an abode of bliss, understatement of the year. Much later she'd discovered—at a class reunion she couldn't resist, because she had a great outfit for it and wanted to show off—that most of the other girls there had been as miserable as she was. Nor could they credit her own distress. "You were always so cheerful," they said.

After high school Roz went to university. She took Art and Archaeology, which her father didn't consider practical but which came in handy later in the renovation business; you never knew which little doodads from the past could be recycled. She arranged to live in residence, even though, as her mother pointed out, she had a perfectly good home to live in. But she wanted out, she wanted out from under, and she got her father to spring for it by threatening to run away to Europe or to some other university a million miles away unless he did. She picked McClung Hall because it was non-denominational. By that time she had dumped her excess Jewishness overboard, along with her excess Catholicism. Or so she thought. She wanted to travel light, and was happiest in a mixed bag.

The day Roz got her degree her father took her out for a treat, along with her mother and her increasingly seedy uncles. They went to a fancy restaurant where the menu was in French, with the English in small print underneath. For dessert there was ice cream, in various French flavours: *cassis, fraise, citron, pistache.*

"French was not one of my passports," said Uncle Joe. "I'll have the pastiche."

That was me, thinks Roz. I was the pastiche.

45

A long time later, after Roz was a married woman, after her mother had died—slowly and disapprovingly, since death was immodest, male doctors prying into your body being next door to sin—and after her father had followed, in jerky, painful stages, like a train shunting—after all this had happened and Roz was an orphan, she found out about the money. Not the later money, she knew about that; the first money. The root, the seedling, the stash.

She'd gone to visit Uncle George in the hospital, because he too was dying. He didn't have a room of his own, or even a semi-private; he was in a ward. Neither of the uncles had done well at all. Both had ended up in rooming houses. After blowing their own money, they'd blown some of Roz's father's as well. They'd gambled, they'd borrowed; or they'd called it borrowing, though everyone must have known they would never pay it back. But her father never said no, to any request of theirs.

"It's the prostrate," Uncle Joe told her, over the phone. "Better you shouldn't mention it." So Roz didn't, because the uncles too had their areas of modesty. She took flowers, and a vase to put them in because hospitals never had vases; she put on a bright smile and a bustling, efficient manner, but she dropped both immediately when she saw how terrible Uncle George looked. He was shrivelled away, he was wasted. Already his head was a skull. Roz sat beside him, inwardly mourning. The man in the bed next to him was asleep and snoring.

"That one, he's not going anyplace," said Uncle George, as if he himself had plans.

"You want a private room?" said Roz. She could arrange it for him, easy.

"Nah," said Uncle George. "I like the company. I like to have people. You know? Anyway, it costs a bundle. I never had the talent."

"The talent for what?" said Roz.

"Not like your father," said Uncle George. "He could start in the morning with a dollar, end of the day he'd have five. Me, I'd always just take that dollar and put it on a horse. I was more for the good times."

"Where did he get it?" said Roz.

Uncle George looked at her out of his wizened yellow eyes. "Get what?" he said innocently, craftily.

"The first dollar," said Roz. "What did the three of you really do, in the war?"

"You don't need to know that," said Uncle George.

"I do," said Roz. "It's okay, he's dead now. You can tell me, you're not going to hurt my feelings."

Uncle George sighed. "Yeah, well," he said. "It's a long time ago."

"It's me who's asking," said Roz, having heard the uncles use this expression on each other, always with effect.

"Your father was a fixer," said Uncle George. "He fixed things. He was a fixer before the war, he was a fixer in the war, and after the war he was also a fixer."

"What did he fix?" said Roz. She took it he didn't mean broken refrigerators.

"To tell you the truth," says Uncle George slowly, "your father was a crook. Don't get me wrong, he was a hero, too. But if he hadn't of been a crook, he couldn't of been a hero. That's how it was."

"A crook?" said Roz.

"We was all crooks," said Uncle George patiently. "Everybody was a crook. They was stealing, all kinds of things, you wouldn't believe—paintings, gold, stuff you could hide and sell later. They could see how it was going, at the end they was grabbing anything. Every time there's a war, people steal. They steal whatever they can. That's what a war is—a war is stealing. Why should we be any different? Joe was the inside man, I was the driver, your father, he did the planning. When we would move, who to trust. Without him, nothing.

"So, we'd get it out for them—not legal, with laws like they had I don't need to tell you—but we'd bribe the guards, everyone was on the take. Hide it somewhere safe, till after the war. But how did they know what was what, how did they know where we were putting it? So we kept some things back, for ourselves. Took it to different places. Picked it up afterwards. Some of them was dead, too, so we got theirs."

"That's what he did?" said Roz. "He helped the Nazis?"

"It was dangerous," said Uncle George reproachfully, as if danger was the main justification. "Sometimes we took out stuff we weren't supposed to take. We took out Jews. We had to be careful, go through our regulars. They let us do it because if we was caught, it was their neck too.

Your father never pushed it too hard though. He knew when it was too dangerous. He knew when to stop."

"Thank you for telling me," Roz said.

"Don't thank me," Uncle George said. "Like I told you, he was a hero. Only, some wouldn't understand." He was tired; he closed his eyes. His eyelids were delicate and crinkled, like wet crêpe paper. He raised two thin desiccated fingers, dismissing her.

Roz made her way out through the white tiled maze of the hospital, heading for home and a stiff drink. What was she to conclude from all this, her new, dubious knowledge? That her money is dirty money, or that all money is? It's not her fault, she didn't do it, she was just a child. She didn't make the world. But she still has a sense of hands, bony hands, reaching up from under the earth, tugging at her ankles, wanting back what's theirs. And how old are those hands? Twenty, thirty years, or a thousand, two thousand? *Who knows where money has been? Wash your hands when you touch it,* her mother used to say. *It's riddled with germs.*

She didn't tell Mitch, though. She never told Mitch. It would've been one up for him, and he was one up already, him and his old-money fastidiousness, his pretence of legal scruples. Clipping coupons yes, smuggling Jews no. Or that's what Roz would be willing to bet. He sneered discreetly at her money as it was, though she'd noticed he didn't mind spending it. But old money made a profit from human desperation too, as long as the desperation and the flesh and the blood were at several removes. Where the heck did people like Mitch think those dividends really came from? And how about the South African gold stocks he'd advised her to buy? In every conversation between the two of them there was a third party present: her money, sitting between them on the sofa like some troll or heavy barely sentient vegetable.

At times it felt like part of her, part of her body, like a hump on her back. She was torn between the urge to cut it off from herself, to give it away, and the urge to make more of it, because wasn't it her protection? Maybe they were the same urge. As her father said, you couldn't give without getting first.

Roz got with the left hand and gave away with the right, or was it the other way around? At first she gave to the body items, the hearts because of her father, the cancer because of her mother. She gave to World Hunger, she gave to the United Way, she gave to the Red Cross. That was in the sixties. But when the women's movement hit town in the early seventies, Roz was sucked into it like a dust bunny into a vacuum cleaner. She was visible, that was why. She was high-profile, and there weren't many women then who were, except for movie stars and the Queen of England. But also she was ready for the message, having been sandbagged twice already by Mitch and his *things*. The first time—the first time she found out, anyway—was when she was pregnant with Larry, and lower he couldn't go.

Roz loved the consciousness-raising groups, she loved the free-ranging talk. It was like catching up on all the sisters she'd never had, it was like having a great big family in which the members, for once, had something in common; it was like being allowed, finally, into all the groups and cliques she'd never quite been able to crash before. No more mealy-mouth, no more my-hubby-is-better-than-your-hubby, no more beating about the bush! You could say anything!

She loved sitting in a circle, though after a while she noticed that the circle was not quite circular. One woman would tell her problem and admit her pain, and then another one would do it, and then Roz would take her turn, and a sort of disbelieving glaze would come down over their eyes and someone would change the subject.

What was it? Why was Roz's pain second-rate? It took her a while to figure it out: it was her money. Surely, they thought, anyone with as much money as Roz couldn't possibly be suffering. She remembered an old expression from her uncles: *My heart bleeds for him.* This was always said with extreme sarcasm, about someone who'd got lucky, which meant rich. Roz was expected to do the bleeding for, but she could not expect to be bled over in return.

Still, there was one area in which Roz was in demand. In a movement so perennially cash-starved you could almost say she was indispensable. So it was natural that she was the one they had come to when *WiseWomanWorld* was about to go under because it couldn't attract big glossy lipstick-and-booze advertising. It was more than a magazine then, it was a friend; a friend that combined high ideals and hope with the sharing of down-and-dirty secrets. The truth about masturbation! The truth about wanting, sometimes, to shove your kids' heads into the wall! What to do when men rubbed themselves against you from behind, in the subway, and when your boss chased you around the desk, and when you had those urges to take all the pills in the medicine cabinet, the day before your period! *WiseWomanWorld* was all the sleepover parties

Roz had once felt were going on behind her back, and of course she had to save it.

The others wanted the magazine to be a cooperative, the way it already was. They wanted Roz to just give them the money, period, and no tax write-off either because it was too political. It wasn't peanuts either, what it would take. There was no point in a small cash injection. Not enough would be the same as nothing, she might as well flush it down the toilet.

"I never invest in anything I can't control," she told them. "You have to issue shares. Then I'll buy a majority holding." They got angry at her for that, but Roz said, "Your leg's broken, you go to a doctor. You have money troubles, you come to me. You tried it your way and it didn't work, and frankly your books are a mess. This is something I know. You want me to fix it, or not?" She knew it would still lose money, but that being the case she at least wanted to take the business loss.

They didn't like it either when Roz put Mitch on the board of directors and stuck on a couple of his legal buddies to keep him company, but it was the only way. If they wanted her help they had to realize what her life conditions were, and if Mitch couldn't participate, he would sabotage. Her home life would be turned into a maze of snares and booby traps, more than it already was. "It's just three meetings a year," she told them. "It's the price you pay." As prices went—as prices had gone, here and there in world history—it wasn't all that high.

"I'm having Zenia over for a drink," Roz tells Mitch. If she doesn't tell him, he's sure to walk in on the two of them and then sulk because he's been left out of the picture. Being a woman with power doesn't mean Roz has to tread less softly around Mitch. She has to tread more softly, she has to diminish herself, pretend she's smaller than she is, apologize for her success, because everything she does is magnified.

"Zenia who?" says Mitch.

"You know, we ran into her in that restaurant," says Roz. She's pleased Mitch doesn't remember.

"Oh yes," says Mitch. "She's not like most of your friends."

Mitch isn't that keen on Roz's friends. He thinks they're a bunch of man-hating hairy-legged whip-toting feminists, because at one point, in his early days on the board of *WiseWomanWorld,* they were. In vain does Roz tell him that everyone was then, it was a trend, and the overalls were just a fashion statement—not that Roz ever wore them herself, she would've looked like a truck driver. He knows better, he knows it wasn't just overalls. The women at *WiseWoman* had put up with him because of Roz, but they hadn't suffered him gladly. They wouldn't let him tell them how to be good feminists, much as he tried. Maybe it was because he said they should use humour and charm because otherwise men would be frightened of them, and they weren't in the mood to be charming, not to him, not just then. He must have been badly traumatized by that whole phase; though he wasn't above trying a few twists and ploys of his own.

Roz remembers the dinner party she threw to celebrate the restructuring of *WiseWomanWorld,* when Mitch was sitting beside Alma the managing editor, and made the mistake of trying to run his hand up and down her leg under the table while carrying on a too-animated theoretical discussion with Edith the designer. Poor lamb, he thought Roz couldn't guess. But one look at Mitch's arm position—and his dampening, reddening, braised-looking face, and Alma's stern frown and the squint lines around her mouth—told all. Roz watched with furious interest as Alma struggled with her dilemma: whether to put up with it because Mitch was Roz's husband and she didn't want to jeopardize her job—a thing Mitch had counted on with others, in the past—or whether to call him on it. Principle won, and also outrage, and Alma said to him sharply, though in an undertone, "I am not a piccolo."

"Pardon?" said Mitch, distantly, politely, bluffing it out, keeping his hand under the table. The poor baby hadn't realized yet that women had really changed. In days of yore, Alma would have felt guilty for attracting this kind of attention, but not any longer.

"Get your goddamn hand off my fucking leg or I'll stab you with my fork," hissed Alma.

Roz went into coughing mode to cover up that she'd heard, and Mitch's hand shot up above ground as if he'd been scalded, and after that night he started referring to Alma with pity and concern, as if she were a lost soul. A drug addict or something. "Too bad about that girl," he would say sadly. "She has such potential, but she has an attitude problem. She'd be quite good-looking if it weren't for the scowl." He hinted that she might be a lesbian; he hadn't figured out that this was no longer an insult. Roz waited a decent interval and then pulled strings to get Alma a raise.

But that's how Mitch tends to see Roz's friends: scowly. And more lately, frumpy. He can't resist commenting on how their faces are sliding down, as if his isn't, though it's true men can get away with looking older. Probably it's revenge: he suspects Roz and her friends of talking him over behind his back, of analyzing him and providing remedies for him, as if he's a stomach ailment. This was true once, granted, when Roz still thought she could change him, or when her friends thought she could change herself. When he was a project. *Leave him,* they'd say. *Turf the bugger out! You can afford it! Why do you stay with him?*

But Roz had her reasons, among them the children. Also she was still enough of a once-Catholic to be nervous about divorce. Also she didn't want to admit to herself that she'd made a mistake. Also she was still in love with Mitch. So after a while she stopped discussing him with her friends, because what was left to say? It was an impasse, and chewing over solutions that she knew she would never implement made her feel guilty.

And then her friends gave up wearing overalls, and left the magazine, and went into dress-for-success tailored suits, and lost interest in Mitch, and discussed burnout instead, and Roz could permit herself to feel guilty about other things, such as being more energetic than they were. But Mitch keeps on saying, "Are you having lunch with that frumpy old man-hater?" whenever one of the friends from that era turns up again. He knows it gets to her.

He has a little more tolerance for Charis and Tony, maybe because Roz has known them so long and because they're the twins' godmothers. But he thinks Tony is a weirdo and Charis is a nut. That's how he neutralizes them. As far as Roz knows he has never made a pass at either of them. Possibly he doesn't place them in the category of *woman* but in some other category, not clearly defined. A sort of sexless gnome.

Roz calls up Tony at her History Department office. "You won't believe this," she says.

There is a pause while Tony tries to guess what it is she's being called upon not to believe. "Probably not," she says.

"Zenia's back in town," says Roz.

There's another pause. "You were talking to her?" says Tony.

"I ran into her in a restaurant," says Roz.

"You never just run into Zenia," says Tony. "Look out, is my advice. What's she up to? There must be something."

"I think she's changed," says Roz. "She's different from the way she used to be."

"A leopard cannot change its spots," says Tony. "Different how?"

"Oh, Tony, you're so pessimistic!" says Roz. "She seemed—well, nicer. More human. She's a freelance journalist now, she's writing on women's issues. Also"—Roz drops her voice—"her tits are bigger."

"I don't think tits can grow," says Tony dubiously, having once looked into it.

"Most likely they didn't," says Roz. "They're doing a lot of artificial ones now. I bet she got them implanted."

"That wouldn't surprise me," says Tony. "She's upping her strike capability. But tits or no tits, watch your back."

"I'm just having her over for a drink," says Roz. "I have to, really. She knew my father, during the war." The full implications of which Tony could hardly be expected to understand.

So nobody could say, later, that Roz wasn't warned. And nobody did say it, and nobody said, either, that Roz *was* warned, because Tony wasn't one of those intolerable serves-you-right friends and she never reminded Roz of the precautions she had urged. But once the chips were down, Roz reminded herself. You walked into it with your eyes open, she would berate herself. Dimwit! What led you on?

She knows now what it was. It was. Pride, deadliest of the Seven Deadlies; the sin of Lucifer, the wellspring of all the others. Vainglory, false courage, bravado. She must have thought she was some kind of a lion-tamer, some kind of a bullfighter; that she could succeed where her two friends had failed. Why not? She knew more than they'd known, because she knew their stories. Forewarned was fore-armed. Also she was overconfident. She must have thought she would be guarded and adroit. She must have thought she could handle Zenia. She'd once had pretty much the same attitude towards Mitch, come to think of it.

Not that she'd felt the pride working in her at the time. Not at all. That was the thing about sins—they could dress up, they could disguise themselves so you hardly knew them. She hadn't thought she was being proud, merely hospitable. Zenia wanted to say thank you, because of Roz's father, and it would have been very wrong of Roz to deny her the opportunity.

There had been another kind of pride, too. She'd wanted to be proud of her father. Her flawed father, her cunning father, her father the fixer, her father the crook. She'd told little bits of his war story when people were interviewing her for magazine profiles, Roz the Business Whiz, *how did you get your start, how do you juggle all your different lives, what do you do about daycare, how does your husband cope, what do you do about the housework,* but even while she was telling about him, her father the hero, her father the rescuer, she knew she was sprucing him up, shining a good light on him, pinning posthumous medals onto his chest. He himself had refused to discuss it, this shadowy part of his life. *What do you need to know for?* he'd say. *That time is over. People could get hurt.* Waiting for Zenia, she'd been more than a little nervous about what she might find out.

46

When Zenia does come for a drink, finally—she hasn't rushed it—it's a Friday and Roz is wiped because it's been a vile week at the office, input overload times ten, and the twins have chosen this day to give each other haircuts because they want to be punk rockers, even though they're only seven, and Roz has been intending to parade them for Zenia but now they look as if they have a bad case of mange, and they show no signs of repentance at all, and anyway Roz doesn't feel she should display anger because girls should not be given the idea that being pretty is the only thing that counts and that other people's opinions of how they ought to arrange their bodies are more important than their own.

So after her first yelp of surprise and dismay she has tried to act as if everything is normal, which in a way it is, although her tongue is just a stub because she's bitten it so hard, and she has dutifully repressed her strong desire to send them upstairs to take baths or play in their play-room, and when Zenia arrives at the front door, wearing amazing lizard-skin shoes, three hundred bucks at least and with heels so high her legs are a mile long, and a cunning fuchsia-and-black raw silk suit with a little nipped-in waist and a tight skirt well above the knees—Roz is so disgusted that mini-skirts have come back, what are you supposed to do if you have serious thighs, and she remembers those skirts from the last time around, in the sixties, you had to sit down with your legs glued together or all would be on view, the once-unmentionable, the central item, the foul and disgraceful blot, the priceless treasure, an invitation to male peering, to lustful pinching and leering, to foaming at the mouth, to rape and pillage, just as the nuns always warned—there are the twins, wearing Roz's cast-off slips from their dress-up box and running down the hall with Mitch's electric shaver, chasing the cat, because they want it to be a punk rock mascot, although Roz has told them before that the shaver is strictly out of bounds and they will be in deep trouble if Mitch discovers cat fur caught in it, it's bad enough when Roz can't find her own shaver and uses Mitch's on her legs and pits and isn't careful enough washing the stubble out of it. The twins pay no attention to her because they assume she'll cover for them, lie herself blue, hurl her body in front of the bullets, and they're right, she will.

Zenia sees them, and says, "Are those yours? Did they fall in the food processor?" and it's just like something Roz might have said herself, or thought at least, and Roz doesn't know whether to laugh or cry.

She laughs, and they have the drink in the sun room, which Roz refuses to call the conservatory even though she's always hankered after a conservatory, a conservatory with miniature orange trees in it, or orchids, like the ones in twenties murder mysteries, the kind with the map of the English mansion and an X where the body gets found, in the conservatory quite frequently. But although the sun room is glass and has a Victorian cupola thing on top it's too small to be a real conservatory, and the word itself is too highfalutin for the voice of Roz's mother, which lives on intermittently inside Roz's head and would sneer, although it's full of plants, plants with limited lifespans, because whose responsibility are they exactly? Mitch says he doesn't have the time, although he was the one who ordered all this vegetation; but Roz's thumb is not green, it's brown, the brown of withered sedges. It's not that she doesn't want the plants to live. She even likes them, though she can't tell the difference between a begonia and a rhododendron. But these things should be done by professionals: a plant service. They come, they see, they water, they cart away the dying, they bring fresh troops.

She has a service like that for the office, so why not here? Mitch says he doesn't want yet more strangers tramping through the house—he's suffering from decorator burnout—but it's possible that he likes the image of Roz with an apron and a watering can, just as he likes the image of Roz with an apron and a frying pan, and an apron and a feather duster, even though Roz can't cook her way out of a paper bag, why did God make restaurants if he intended her to cook, and she has a phobia about feather dusters, having been force-fed on them in childhood. The constant is the apron, the Good Housekeeping guarantee that Roz will always be home whenever Mitch chooses to get back there.

Or there may be another agenda, another nuance to the guilt Roz is supposed to feel, and does feel, over the *kaput* plants, because Mitch wanted a swimming pool instead of a sun room, so he could dive into a chlorine purification bath and sterilize his chest hair and kill whatever athlete's foot and crotch fungus and tongue rot he may have picked up from plucking the ripening floozies; but Roz said an outdoor swimming pool was ridiculous in Canada, two months of swelter and ten of freeze-your-buns-off, and she refused to have an indoor one because she knew people who did and their houses smelled like gas refineries on a hot day because of all the chemicals, and there would be complicated machinery that would break down and that Roz would somehow be responsible for getting fixed. The worst thing about swimming pools as far as Roz is concerned is that they are one step too close to the great outdoors. Wildlife falls into them. Ants, moths, and such. Like the lake at summer camp, she'd be flailing along and suddenly there would be a bug, right at nose level. Swimming, in Roz's opinion, is a major health hazard.

Zenia laughs and says she couldn't agree more, and Roz talks on, because she's nervous at seeing Zenia again after all these years, she remembers the reputation, the aura of green poison that encircled Zenia, the invisible incandescence, touch her and you'd get burned; and she remembers history, the stories of Tony and Charis. So she has to step carefully here, it's no wonder she's nervous, and when she's nervous she talks. Talks, and also eats, and also drinks. Zenia takes one olive and chews it daintily, Roz gobbles the lot, and touches up Zenia's martini, and pours herself another, and offers a cigarette, words pouring out of her like ink from a squid. Camouflage. She's relieved to note that Zenia smokes. It would be intolerable if she were thin and well-dressed and unwrinkled and a knockout, and a non-smoker as well.

• • •

"So," says Roz, when she's made a sufficient fool of herself to consider the ice broken. "My father." Because this is what she wants, this is the point of the visit. Isn't it?

"Yes," says Zenia. She leans forward and sets down her glass, and rests her chin thoughtfully on one hand and frowns slightly. "I was only a baby, of course. So I have no real memories of that time. But my aunt always talked about your father, before she died. About how he got us out. I guess if it weren't for him I'd just be ashes now.

"It was in Berlin. That's where my parents lived, in a good neighbourhood, in a respectable apartment—it was one of those old Berlin buildings with the mosaic tiles in the front hall and the oblong staircase with the wooden banister, and the maid's room and the back balcony overlooking a courtyard, for hanging out the wash. I know, because I saw it—I went back. I was there in the late seventies, I had an assignment in Berlin—the Berlin nightlife, for some travel magazine, you know the sort of thing, sexy cabaret, kinky strip clubs, telephones on the tables. So I took the afternoon off and I found it. I had the address, from some old papers of my aunt's. The buildings all around were newer, they'd been rebuilt after the bombing, the whole place was practically levelled; it was amazing, but that one old building was still there.

"I rang all the buzzers and someone opened the door, and I went in and up the stairs, just as my parents must have done hundreds of times. I touched the same banister, I turned the same corners. I knocked at the door, and when it opened I said some relatives of mine had once lived there and could I look around—I speak a little German, because of my aunt, though my accent's old-fashioned—and the people let me in. They were a young couple with a baby, they were very nice, but I couldn't stay long. I really couldn't stand it, the rooms, the light coming through the windows . . . they were the same rooms, it was the same light. I think my parents became real to me for the first time. Everything, all of it became real. Before that, it was just a bad story."

Zenia stops talking. This is what people often do when they come to the hard part, Roz has discovered. "A bad story," she prompts.

"Yes," says Zenia. "It was already the war. Things were in short supply. My aunt had never married, there was such a shortage of men after the first war a lot of women couldn't, so she thought of our family as her family too, and she used to do things for us. Mother us—that's how she put it. So on this one day, my aunt was going to my parents' apartment; she was taking them some bread she'd baked. She went up the stairs as usual—there was a lift, one of those lifts like an iron cage, I saw it—but it was out of order. As she was about to knock, the door on the other side of the landing opened and the woman who lived there—my aunt knew her only by sight—this woman came out and grabbed her by the arm, and pulled her inside. 'Don't go in, don't try to go in there,' she said. 'They've been taken away.'

"'Taken, where?' said my aunt. She didn't ask who by, she didn't need to ask that.

"'Don't try to find out,' said the woman. 'Better not.' She had me in there with her because my mother had seen them coming, she'd looked out the window and she'd seen them coming along the street, and then when they'd turned in at the doorway and started up the stairs she'd guessed where they were headed and she'd run out the back door, the maid's door, and along the back balcony, with me wrapped up in a shawl——the balconies at the back adjoined one another——and she'd pounded at this woman's kitchen door, and the woman had taken me in. It happened so fast she hardly knew what she was doing, and most likely if she'd had time to think she never would have done anything so dangerous. She was just an ordinary woman, obedient and so on, but I suppose if someone shoves a baby at you, you can't just step back and let it fall to the ground.

"I was the only one saved, the others were all taken. I had an older brother, and an older sister too. I was much younger, I was a late baby. I have their picture; it's something my aunt brought with her. See——" Zenia opens her purse, then her wallet, and slides out a snapshot. It's a square picture with a wide white border, the figures tiny and fading: a family group, father, mother, two young children, and another older woman, off to one side. The aunt, Roz assumes. Both of the children are blond.

What amazes Roz is how contemporary they look: the knee-high skirts on the women, from the late twenties? the early thirties?——the smart hats, the makeup, it could be the retro look, in some fashion magazine, right now. Only the clothes of the children are archaic; that, and their haircuts. A suit and tie and short back and sides for the boy, and a fussy dress and ringlets for the girl. The smiles are a little tight, but smiles were, in those days. They are dress-up smiles. It must have been a special occasion: a vacation, a religious holiday, somebody's birthday.

"That was before the war," says Zenia. "It was before things got really bad. I was never part of that world. I was born right after the war started; I was a war baby. Anyway, that's all I have, this picture. It's all that's left of them. My aunt searched, after the war. There was nothing left." She slides the photo carefully back into her wallet.

"What about the aunt?" says Roz. "Why didn't they take her, too?"

"She wasn't Jewish," says Zenia. "She was my father's sister. My father wasn't Jewish either, but after the Nuremberg laws were passed he was treated as one, because he was married to one. Hell, even my mother wasn't Jewish! Not by religion. She was Catholic, as a matter of fact. But two of her four grandparents were Jewish, so she was classified as a *mischling*, first degree. A mixture. Did you know they had degrees?"

"Yes," says Roz. So Zenia is a mixture, like herself!

"Some of those *mischlings* survived longer than the real Jews," says Zenia. "My parents, for instance. I guess they thought it wouldn't happen to them. They thought of themselves as good Germans. They weren't in touch with the Jewish community, so they didn't even hear the rumours; or if they did, they didn't believe them. It's astonishing what people will refuse to believe."

"How about your aunt?" says Roz. "Why did she get out? If she wasn't Jewish at all, wasn't she safe?" Though come to think of it, *safe* is a silly word to use in such a context.

"Because of me," says Zenia. "They would have figured out sooner or later that my parents had three children, not two. Or some neighbour of my aunt's would have seen or heard me, and turned us in. A baby, in the home of an unmarried woman who just a little while before had no baby at all. People get a huge bang out of denunciation, you know. It makes them feel morally superior. God, how I hate that smug self-righteousness! People patting themselves on the back for murder.

"So my aunt started looking for a way to get me out, and then she found herself in a whole other world—the underground world, the black market world. She'd always lived above ground, but she had to go into that other world in order to protect me. There isn't a place on earth where that world doesn't exist; all you have to do is take a few steps off to the side, a few steps down, and there it is, side by side with the world people like to think of as normal. Remember the fifties, remember trying to get an abortion? It only took three phone calls. Provided you could pay, of course. You'd get handed along the line, to somebody who knew someone. It was the same in Germany at that time, for things like passports, only you had to be careful who you asked.

"What my aunt needed was some fake papers saying I was her daughter, by a husband killed in France, and she got some; but they wouldn't have stood up to much scrutiny. I mean, look at me! I'm hardly Aryan. My brother and my sister were both blond, and my father had light hair; my mother too. I must be some kind of throwback. So she knew she had to get me away, she had to get me right out. If they caught her she'd be up for treachery, because she was helping me. Some treachery! Christ, I was only six months old!"

Roz doesn't know what to say. "Poor you," which is what she murmurs to the stories of workplace crises or personal mishap or romantic catastrophe, as told to her by her friends, hardly seems to cover it. "How awful," she says.

"Don't feel sorry for me," says Zenia. "I was hardly

conscious. I didn't know what was going on, so it was no strain on me; though I must have registered that things had changed and my mother wasn't there any more. Anyway my aunt got in touch with your father, or I should say your father's friends. It was through the man who arranged the papers for her—that man knew someone who knew someone else, and after they'd checked her out and skimmed some money off her they passed her on. All black markets work that way. Try buying drugs, it's the same thing: they check you out, they pass you on. Luckily my aunt had some money, and her desperation must have been convincing. As I said, she'd never married, so I became her cause; she risked her life for me. It was for her brother, too. She didn't know then he'd been killed, she thought he might come back. Then, if he did and if she'd failed, what could she say?

"So your father and his friends got her out, through Denmark and then through Sweden. They told her it was relatively easy. She didn't have an accent or anything, and she looked as German as they come.

"My aunt was a kind of mother to me. She brought me up, she did her best, but she wasn't a happy woman. She'd been ruined, destroyed really, by the war. The loss of her brother and his family, and then the guilt also—that she hadn't been able to stop any of it, that she had some-how participated. She talked about your father a lot— what a hero he was. It gave her back a little bit of faith. So I used to pretend that your father was my father, and that some day he would come to get me, and I'd move into his house. I wasn't even sure where he lived."

• • •

Roz is practically in tears. She remembers her father, the old rascal; she's glad to know that his dubious talents were of service, because he's still her favourite parent and she welcomes the chance to think well of him. The two martinis aren't helping, in the get-a-grip department. How lucky she herself has been, with her three children and her husband, her money, her work, her house. How unfair life is! Where was God when all of this was happening, in sordid Europe—the injustice, the merciless brutality, the suffering? In a meeting, is where. Not answering the phone. Guilt wells up out of her eyes. She would like to give Zenia something, just a little something, to make up to her for God's neglect, but what could possibly be adequate?

Then she hears a small voice, a small voice clear as ice-water, right at the back of her head. It's the voice of experience. It's the voice of Tony. *Zenia lies,* it says.

"Do you remember Tony?" Roz blurts out, before she can stop herself. "Tony Fremont from McClung Hall?" How can she be such a jerk, such a *shit,* as to question Zenia's story, even in her head? No one would lie about such a thing. It would be too mean, it would be too cynical, it would be virtually sacrilegious!

"Oh yes," Zenia laughs. "That was a million years ago! Tony and her funny war collection! I see she's written a couple of books. She was always a bright little thing."

Bright little thing causes Roz to feel, by comparison, large and dim. But she trudges forward. "Tony told me you were a White Russian," she says. "A child prostitute, in Paris. And Charis says your mother was a gypsy, and was stoned to death by Roumanian peasants."

"Charis?" says Zenia.

"She used to be Karen," says Roz. "You lived with her on the Island. You told her you had cancer," she adds, pressing relentlessly on.

Zenia looks out the window of the sun room, and sips at the edge of her martini. "Oh yes, Charis," she says. "I'm afraid I told some awful—I didn't always tell the truth, when I was younger. I think I was emotionally disturbed. After my aunt died I had some hard times. She had nothing, no money; we lived over storefronts. And when she was gone, nobody would help me. This was in Waterloo, in the fifties. It wasn't a good time or place for orphans who didn't fit in.

"So part of what I told Tony was true, I did work as a hooker. And I didn't want to be Jewish, I didn't want to be connected with all of that in any way. I guess I was running away from the past. That was then, this is now, right? I even got my nose done, after I'd gone to England and landed a magazine job and could afford it. I suppose I was ashamed. When those things get done to you, you feel more ashamed than if you'd done them yourself to other people. You think maybe you deserved it; or else that you should have been stronger—able to defend yourself, or something. You feel—well, beaten up.

"So I made up a different past for myself—it was better to be a White Russian. Denial, I guess you could call it. I lived with a White Russian, once, when I was sixteen, so I knew something about them.

"With Karen—with Charis—I must have been having some kind of a nervous breakdown. I needed to be mothered; my shrink says it was because my own mother was taken away. I shouldn't have said I had cancer, because I didn't. But I *was* sick, in another kind of way. Karen did wonders for me.

"It wasn't a good thing—it was terrible, I suppose, to tell those stories. I owe both of them an apology. But I didn't think I could've told them the real story, what really happened to me. They wouldn't have understood it."

She gives Roz a long look, straight out of her deep indigo eyes, and Roz is touched. She, Roz—she alone—has been chosen, to understand. And she does, she does.

"After I left Canada," Zenia says, "things got worse. I had big ideas, but nobody seemed to share them. Looking the way I do doesn't help, you know. Men don't see you as a person, they just see the body, and so that's all you see yourself. You think of your body as a tool, something to use. God, I'm tired of men! They're so easy to amuse. All you have to do to get their attention is take off your clothes. After a while you want a bit more of a challenge, you know?

"I worked as a stripper for a year or so—that's when I had my breasts done, this man I was living with paid for it—and I got into some bad habits. Coke first, and then heroin. It's a wonder I'm not dead. Maybe I was trying to be, because of my family. You'd think that because I didn't really know them it wouldn't hurt. But it's like being born minus a leg. There's this terrible *absence*.

"It took me a long time, but I've finally come to terms with myself. I've worked it through. I was in therapy for years. It was hard, but now I know who I am."

Roz is impressed. Zenia has not evaded, she hasn't wriggled or squirmed. She has owned up, she has admitted, she's confessed. That shows—what? Honesty? Good will? Maturity? Some admirable quality. The nuns used to put a high value on confessing, so much so that Roz once confessed to placing a dog turd in the cloakroom, something she had not actually done. They didn't let you off punishment for confessing, though—she got the strap, all the same, and when you confessed to the priest you had to do penance—but they thought more highly of you, or so they said.

Also Zenia has been out in the world. The wide world, wider than Toronto; the deep world, deeper than the small pond where Roz is such a large and sheltered frog. Zenia makes Roz feel not only protected, but lax. Her own battles have been so minor.

"You've done really well," Roz says. "I mean—what a story! It's great material!" She's thinking of the magazine, because this is the kind of story they like to run: inspirational, a success story. A story about overcoming fears and obstacles, about facing up to yourself and becoming a whole person. It's like the story they did two months ago, about the woman who fought bulimia to a standstill. Roz finds stories about the one lost sheep who caused more joy in Heaven hard to resist. There's a story in the aunt, as well: WiseWomanWorld appreciates real-life heroines, ordinary women who have been more than ordinarily courageous.

To her amazement, and also to her horror, Zenia begins to cry. Big tears roll from her eyes, which remain open and fixed on Roz. "Yeah," she says. "I guess that's all it amounts to. It's just a story. It's just material. Something to use."

Roz, for gosh sake, get your big fat foot out of your mouth, thinks Roz. Miss Tact of 1983. "Oh honey, I didn't mean it that way," she says.

"No," says Zenia. "I know. Nobody does. It's just, I'm so strung out. I've been on the edge, I've been out there so long; I've had to do it alone. I can't work it out with men, they all want the same thing from me, I just can't make those kinds of compromises any more. I mean, you've got all this, you've got a home, a husband, you've got your kids. You're a family, you've got solid ground under your feet. I've never had any of that, I've never fitted in. I've lived out of a suitcase, all my life; even now it's hand-to-mouth, that's what freelancing means, and I'm running out of energy, you know? There's just no base, there's no permanence!"

How badly Roz has misjudged Zenia! Now she sees her in a new light. It's a tempestuous light, a bleak light, a lonely, rainy light; in the midst of it Zenia struggles on, buffeted by men, blown by the winds of fate. She's not what she appears, a beautiful and successful career woman. She's a waif, a homeless wandering waif; she's faltering by the wayside, she's falling. Roz opens her heart, and spreads her wings, her cardboard angel's wings, her invisible dove's wings, her warm sheltering wings, and takes her in.

"Don't you worry," she says, in her most reassuring voice. "We'll work something out."

47

Mitch passes Zenia in the front hall as she is leaving and he is coming in. She gives him only the briefest and chilliest of nods.

"Your old friend is certainly hostile," he says to Roz.

"I don't think so," says Roz. "I think she's just tired."

She doesn't want to share Zenia's dismaying life story with him. It's a story told just to her, for her, for her ears alone, by one outsider to another. Only Roz can understand it. Not Mitch, because what would he know about being outside?

"Tired?" says Mitch. "She didn't look too tired."

"Tired of men coming on to her," says Roz.

"Don't believe it," says Mitch. "Anyway, I wasn't coming on to her. But I bet she'd like it if I did. She's an adventuress, she has the look."

"Poetess, songstress, adventuress," says Roz lightly. Mitch is such an authority, he can tell what a woman thinks by the shape of her bottom. "Why not just call her an adventurer?" Roz is teasing, she knows the feminist terminology stuff drives him nuts. But also she thinks of herself as an adventurer, at least in some areas of life. The financial ones. *Gentleman adventurer* was once a term.

"It's not the same," says Mitch. "Adventurers live by their wits."

"And adventuresses?" says Roz.

"By their tits," says Mitch.

"Point," says Roz, laughing. He set her up for it.

But he's wrong, thinks Roz, remembering. It was wits for Zenia also.

That was the beginning of the end of her marriage, although she didn't realize it at the time. Or maybe it was the end of the end. Who knows? The end must have been a long time coming. These things are not sudden.

Roz wouldn't have known it from Mitch, though. He made love to her that night with an urgency he hadn't shown for a long time. No voluptuous ease, no lordly walrus-like wallowing: it was snatch and grab. There was nothing he wanted her to give; instead he wanted to take. Roz finds herself being bitten, and is pleased rather than otherwise. She didn't know she was still that irresistible.

A week later she arranges an early dinner, at Scaramouche, for herself and Zenia and the current *WiseWomanWorld* editor, whose name is BethAnne, and they ingest radicchio salads and exotic parboiled vegetables and clever pastas, and go over Zenia's résumé and her file of magazine stories. First there are the ones written when she was on staff for a cutting-edge fashion magazine, in England. But she quit that job because she felt too tied down, and also she'd wanted to write about more political things. Libya, Mozambique, Beirut, the Palestinian camps; Berlin,

Northern Ireland, Colombia, Bangladesh, El Salvador—Zenia has been to most of the hot spots Roz can remember, and a few she can't. Zenia regales them with incidents, of stones and bullets that have whizzed past her head, of cameras that have been broken by policemen, of narrow escapes in Jeeps. She names hotels.

A lot of the stories are under other names, men's names, because, as Zenia says, the material in them is controversial, inflammatory even, and she didn't want to open the door in the middle of the night and find some enraged Arab or Irish hit man or Israeli or drug lord standing on the other side of it. "I wouldn't want this to get around," she says, "but that's the main reason I came back to Canada. It's kind of a safe haven for me—you know? Things were getting just a little too *interesting* for me, over there. Canada is such a—such a *gentle* place."

Roz and BethAnne exchange a look across the table. Both are deeply thrilled. A political reporter from the trouble zones of the world, right in their midst; and a female political reporter, at that! Of course they must shelter her. What are safe havens for? It doesn't escape Roz that the opposite of *interesting* is not *gentle*, but *boring*. However, *boring* has something to offer, these days. Maybe they should export a little *boring*. It's better than getting your head shot off.

"We'd love it if you'd do a story for us," says BethAnne.

"To tell you the truth," says Zenia, "I'm sort of emptied out for now, story-wise. But I have a better idea."

Her better idea is that she should help them out in the advertising department. "I've been through the magazine, and I've noticed you don't have many ads," she says. "You must be losing money, a lot of money."

"Absolutely," says Roz, who knows exactly how much because the money they're losing is hers.

"I think I could double your ads, in, say, two months," says Zenia. "I've had experience."

She makes good her word. Roz isn't sure quite how it happened, but Zenia is soon sitting in on editorial meetings, and when BethAnne leaves to have another baby, creating a power vacuum, Zenia is offered the job, because who else—be honest—is as qualified? It may even be that Roz set it up for her. Most likely; it was the kind of sucky shoot-yourself-in-the-foot thing she must have been doing around then. Part of her save-poor-Zenia project. She'd rather not remember the details.

Zenia has her photograph taken, a glamour shot in a V-necked outfit; it appears on the editorial page. Women figure out how old she is and wonder how she manages to stay looking so good. Circulation goes up.

Zenia goes to parties now, a lot of parties. Why not? She has *schlep,* she has clout, she has—the men on the board are fond of saying—balls. Sharp as a tack, smart as a whip, and a great figure too, they can never resist adding, causing Roz to go home and frown at her dimpling grapefruit-peel leg skin in the mirror, and then to reproach herself for making odious comparisons.

Some of the parties Zenia goes to are given by Roz. Roz supervises the passing of the filo-bundle and stuffed-mushroom nibbles, and greets her friends with hugs and airy kisses, and watches Zenia work the room. She works it seriously, thoroughly; she seems to know by instinct just how much time any one person is worth. She spends some of her precious moments on Roz, though. She gets her off to one side and murmurs to her, and Roz murmurs back. Anyone watching them would think they were conspirators.

"You're really good at this," Roz tells Zenia. "Me, I always end up stuck for hours with some hard-luck story, but you never get cornered."

Zenia smiles back at her. "All foxes dig back doors. I like to know where the exit sign is." And Roz remembers the story of Zenia's narrow escape from death, and feels sorry for her. Zenia always arrives alone. She leaves alone. It's sad.

Mitch works the room too. Surprisingly, he doesn't work the part of it with Zenia in it. Ordinarily he'd flirt with everyone; he'd flirt with a saluki if there was nothing else on offer. He likes to see his own charm reflected back at him from the eyes of every woman in the room; he goes from one to another as if they're bushes and he's a dog. But he stays away from Zenia, and, when she's watching, pays extra attention to Roz. He keeps a hand on her whenever possible. *Steadying himself,* Roz thinks later.

Roz grows increasingly uneasy. There's something not quite right about the turn things have taken, but what could it be? She set out to help Zenia, and it appears she has helped her, and Zenia is certainly grateful, and she's performing well; they have lunch once a week just to go over things, and so Zenia can ask Roz's advice, because Roz has been around the magazine so much longer than Zenia has. Roz dismisses her own reaction as simple envy.

Ordinarily if there was something bothering her, something she couldn't quite put her finger on, she'd discuss it
with Tony or Charis. But she can't do that, because she's
friends with Zenia now, and they might not understand
that part of it. They might not understand how Roz could
be friends with someone who is—face it—an enemy of
theirs. They might see it as betrayal.

"I've been giving it some thought," Zenia says at the next
board of directors meeting. "We're still losing money,
despite the new ads. We can't seem to hook the big
spenders—the perfume companies, the cosmetics, high
fashion. To be honest, I think we need to change the name.
The concept we're working with is too seventies. This is the
eighties—we're way beyond a lot of those old positions."

"Change the name?" asks Roz, with fond memories of
the early collective. What happened to those women?
Where did they go? Why has she lost touch with them?
Where did all these business suits come from?

"Yes," says Zenia. "I've had a small survey done. We'd
do better with *WomanWorld,* or, even better, just plain
Woman."

It's obvious to Roz what's being dropped. The wisdom part, for one thing. Also the world. But how can she
object to *Woman* without implying that there's something
wrong with being one?

So Zenia changes the name, and soon the magazine
changes too. It changes so much that Roz hardly recognizes it. Gone are the mature achievers, the stories about
struggling to overcome sexism and stacked odds. Gone too
are the heavy-hitting health care stories. Now there are

five-page spreads on spring fashions, and new diets and hair treatments and wrinkle creams, and quizzes about the man in your life and whether or not you're handling your relationships well. Are these things unimportant? Roz would be the last to say so, but surely there's something missing.

She no longer has lunch with Zenia once a week; Zenia is now too busy. She's a busy bee, she has a lot of iron maidens in the fire. So, at the next board meeting, Roz pushes her about the shift in content. "This wasn't the original idea," she says.

Zenia smiles gently at her. "Most women don't want to read about other women who achieve," she says. "It makes them feel unsuccessful."

Roz finds herself getting angry—surely this is a dig at her—but she controls herself. "What do they want to read about, then?"

"I'm not talking intellectuals," says Zenia. "I'm talking about the average woman. The average magazine-buying woman. According to our demographics, they want to read about how to look. Oh, and sex, of course. Sex with the right accessories."

"What are the right accessories?" asks Roz pleasantly. She thinks she'll choke.

"Men," says Zenia. The men on the board of directors laugh, Mitch included. So much for Roz. She has a flash of Zenia, wearing black fringed gloves with gauntlets, blowing the smoke off her six-shooter, sliding it back into her holster.

Roz is the majority shareholder. She could pull strings, she could stack the deck, she could force Zenia out. But she can't do that without looking like a vindictive shrew.

And let's face it, they're making money, finally, and money talks.

One day Mitch is gone. He is just gone, in a snap of the fingers, in a wink. No prelude, no hints, no letters left lying around, none of the usual. But looking back, Roz realizes he must have been gone for some time.

Where has he gone? He's gone to live with Zenia. A whole courtship, a whole romance, has taken place right under Roz's very nose and she hasn't noticed a thing. It must have been going on for months.

But no, that isn't it. Mitch tells her—he seems to want to tell her—that it was all very sudden. Unexpected to him. Zenia came to his office one evening, after work, to consult him about some financials, and then . . .

"I don't want to hear about it," says Roz, who is familiar with the pleasures of narration. She doesn't intend to give him the satisfaction.

"I just want you to understand," says Mitch.

"Why?" says Roz. "Why is that important? Who gives a shit whether I understand or not?"

"I do," says Mitch. "Because I still love you. I love both of you. This is really difficult for me."

"Get stuffed," says Roz.

Mitch came to the house when Roz wasn't there. He came furtively because he couldn't face her. He came and went, soft as a thief, and he removed things: his suits from the mirror-door bedroom closet, his boat clothes, his best bottles of wine, his pictures. Roz would come back after work to find these blanks, these piercing eloquent spaces, where something of Mitch's used to be. But he left some things behind: an overcoat, his anorak, some books, his old boots, boxes of this and that in the storage room down in the cellar. What was it supposed to mean? That he was of two minds? That he still had one foot in the door? Roz almost wished he would take everything away at once, make a clean sweep. On the other hand, where there were boots there was hope. But hope was the worst. As long as she had hope, how was she supposed to get on with her life? Which was what women in her situation were constantly urged to do.

Mitch didn't take anything that wasn't his. He didn't take anything Roz had bought for the house, bought for them to share. Roz was surprised to discover how little he had actually been involved in all that shopping, how few choices he'd helped her make; or, look at it another way, how little he'd contributed. Well, how could he have helped her? She'd always forestalled him; she'd seen a need or a desire and supplied it instantly, with a wave of her magic chequebook. Maybe it had grated on him after a while, her munificence, her largesse, her heaps of pearls, her outpourings. Ask and it shall be given. Heck, Mitch didn't even ask! All he had to do was lie on the lawn with his mouth open while Roz climbed the tree and shook down the golden apples.

Maybe that was Zenia's trick. Maybe she presented herself as vacancy, as starvation, as an empty beggar's bowl. Maybe the posture she'd assumed was on her knees, hands upstretched for alms. Maybe Mitch wanted the opportunity to do a little coin-scattering, an opportunity never provided by Roz. He was tired of being given to, of being forgiven, of being rescued; maybe he wanted to do a little giving and rescuing of his own. Even better than a beautiful woman on her knees would be a grateful beautiful woman on her knees. But hadn't Roz been grateful enough?

Apparently not.

Roz stoops low. She gives in to her gnawing hunger for dirt and hires a private detective, a woman named Harriet; Harriet the Hungarian, someone she learned about, way back, through Uncle Joe, who had some Hungarian connections. "I just want to know what they're up to," she tells Harriet.

"What sort of thing?" asks Harriet.

"Where they're living, what they do," says Roz. "Whether she's real."

"Real?" says Harriet.

"Where she came from," says Roz.

Harriet finds out sufficient. Sufficient to make Roz even more miserable than she is. Zenia and Mitch live in a penthouse apartment overlooking the harbour, near where Mitch moors his boat. That way they can go for quick little sails on it, Roz supposes, though she can't see Zenia putting up with too much of that. Getting wet, chipping her polish. Not as much as Roz put up with. What else do they do? They eat out, they eat in. Zenia goes shopping. What's to see?

The question of whether Zenia is real or not is more difficult to solve. She doesn't seem to have been born, at least not under that name; but how can anyone say, since so much of Berlin went up in smoke? Inquiries in

Waterloo produce nothing. She didn't go to school there, or not under her present name. Is she even Jewish? It's anybody's guess, says Harriet.

"But what about the picture?" says Roz. "Her family?"

"Oh, Roz," says Harriet. "Pictures are a dime a dozen. Whose word have you got for it that those people were her family?"

"She knew about my father," says Roz. She's reluctant to let go.

"So did I," said Harriet. "Come on, Roz, there are hints about all that in every magazine interview you've ever given. What did she tell you about him that any twelve-year-old with an active imagination wouldn't have been able to make up?"

"You're right," sighs Roz, "but there was so much detail."

"She's very good," Harriet agrees.

London proves more fruitful: Zenia did indeed work for a magazine there; she appears to have written some of the articles she's claimed as hers, though by no means all of them. The ones on clothing, yes; the ones on political hot spots, no. The ones with men's names actually seem to have been written by the men in question, although three out of the five are dead. She made a brief traverse through the gossip columns when her name was linked with that of a cabinet minister; the phrase "good friend" was used, and marriage was subsequently hinted at but did not take place. Then there was a scandal when it came to light that Zenia had been seeing a Soviet cultural attaché at the same time. "Seeing" was a euphemism. There was a lot of political name-calling, and the usual English tabloid fox-hunting and muckraking. After that incident Zenia had dropped out of sight.

"Did she really travel to all those countries?" says Roz.

"How much money do you want to spend?" asks Harriet.

Knowing about the flimsiness of Zenia's façade is no help to Roz at all. She's stalemated. If she tells Mitch about the lies it will just come across as jealousy.

It is jealousy. Roz is so jealous she can't think straight. Some nights she cries with rage, others with sorrow. She walks around in a red fog of anger, in a grey mist of self-pity, and she hates herself for both. She calls on her stubbornness, her will to fight, but who exactly is her enemy? She can't fight Mitch, because she wants him back. Maybe if she holds her fire long enough, this will all blow over. Mitch will fizzle out like a barbecue in the rain, he'll come back home as he has before, wanting her to disentangle him from Zenia, wanting to be saved. And Roz will do it, though this time it won't be so easy. He's violated something, some unwritten contract, some form of trust. He's never moved out before. The other women were a game to him but Zenia is serious business.

There's another way it could play: Zenia would divest herself of Mitch. She would throw him out the window, as he has thrown many. Mitch would get his comeuppance. Roz would get revenge.

In public Roz maintains her grin, her tooth-filled grin. The muscles of her jaws ache with it. She wishes to preserve her dignity, put up a bold front. But that's not so easy, with her chest ripped open like this and her heart exposed for all to surely see; her heart, which is on fire and dripping blood.

She can't expect much pity from her friends, the ones

who used to tell her to dump Mitch. She sees now what they'd meant: *Dump him before he dumps you!*

But she didn't listen. Instead she'd kept on playing the knife-thrower's assistant, in her sparkly costume, with her arms and legs splayed out, standing still and smiling while the knives thudded into the wall, tracing the outline of her body. *Flinch and you're dead.* It was inevitable that one day, by accident or on purpose, she'd get hit.

Tony phones her. So does Charis. She hears the concern in their voices: they know something, they've heard. But she puts them off, she holds them at arm's length. One touch of their compassion now would do her in.

Three months go by. Roz straightens her back and tightens her lips and clenches her jaws so hard she's sure her teeth are being ground to stumps, and tints her hair maroon, and buys a new outfit, an Italian leather suit in an opulent shade of vermilion. She has several unsatisfactory flings with men. She rolls about with them, fitfully, self-consciously, as if her bedroom's wired for sound: she knows she's acting. She hopes the news of her reckless unfaithfulness will get back to Mitch and make him writhe, but any writhing he does is in the privacy of his own home, if the viper's nest he's living in can be called that. Worst case: maybe he's not writhing. Maybe he's delighted at the possibility that some hapless fall guy might take her off his hands.

Harriet phones: she thinks Roz might like to know that Zenia is seeing another man, in the afternoons, while Mitch is out.

"What sort of other man?" says Roz. Adrenalin rushes through her brain.

"Let's just say he wears a black leather jacket and drives a Harley, and has two arrests but no convictions. Lack of witnesses willing to come forward."

"Arrests for what?" says Roz.

"Dealing coke," says Harriet.

Roz asks for a written report, and pops it into an envelope, and addresses it anonymously to Mitch, and waits for the other shoe to drop; and it does drop, because one Monday just before lunchtime Harriet calls her at the office.

"She's taken a plane," says Harriet. "Three big suitcases."

"Where to?" says Roz. Her whole body is tingling. "Was Mitch with her?"

"No," says Harriet. "To London."

"Maybe he'll join her there later," says Roz. Well, well, she thinks. Bye bye black sheep. Three bags full.

"I don't think so," says Harriet. "She didn't have that look."

"What look did she have?" says Roz.

"The dark glasses look," says Harriet. "The scarf-around-the-neck look. I'd lay money on a black eye, and two to one he tried to throttle her. Or somebody did. I'd say from all appearances she's on the run."

"He'll go after her," says Roz, who doesn't want to get her hopes up. "He's obsessed."

But that evening, when she walks into her house, into her living room with its deep pink-and-mauve carpets and its subtle off-green accents, neo-forties revival with post-mod undertones, there is Mitch, sitting in his favoured armchair as if he's never been away.

Sitting in his favoured armchair, at least. But as for *away*, yes, that's where he's been. Far away. Some cinder of a planet in a distant galaxy. He looks as if he's been drifting around in deep space, where it's cold and empty and there are things with tentacles, and has just barely made it back to Earth. A stunned look, a conked-on-the-head look. Mugged, pushed face first against a brick wall, crammed into a trunk, tossed half-naked onto the stony roadside, and he didn't even see who did it.

Glee leaps up in Roz, but she stifles it. "Mitch," she says, in her best hen voice. "Honey, what's wrong?"

"She's gone," says Mitch.

"Who is?" says Roz, because although she won't demand a pound of flesh, not at this juncture, she does want a little blood, just a drop or two, because she's thirsty.

"You know who," says Mitch in a choking voice. Is this sorrow or fury? Roz can't tell.

"I'll get you a drink," she says. She pours one for each of them, then sits down opposite Mitch in the matching armchair, their usual position for conversations like this. Have-it-out conversations. He will explain, she will be hurt; he will pretend to repent, she will pretend to believe him. They face each other, two card sharps, two poker players.

Roz opens. "Where did she go?" she says, although she knows the answer; but she wants to know if he knows. If he doesn't know it won't be her that tells him. He can hire his own detective.

"She took her clothes," says Mitch, in a sort of groan. He puts one hand to his head, as if he has a headache. So, he doesn't know.

What is Roz expected to do? Sympathize with her

husband because the woman he loves, loves instead of her, has flown the coop? Console him? Kiss him better? Yes, that's what, all right. She hovers on the edge of doing it— Mitch looks so battered—but she hangs back. Let him wait.

Mitch looks across at her. She bites her tongue. Finally he says, "There's something else."

Zenia, it appears, has forged some cheques, on the *Woman* operating account. She's made off with the entire allowable overdraft. How much? Fifty thousand dollars, give or take; but in cheques under a thousand dollars each. She cashed them through different banks. She knows the system.

Roz calculates: she can afford it, and the disappearance of Zenia is cheap at the price. "Whose name did she use?" she asks. She knows who the signing officers are. For small cheques like that, it's Zenia herself and any one of three board members.

"Mine," says Mitch.

What could be crystal clearer? Zenia is a cold and treacherous bitch. She never loved Mitch. All she wanted was the pleasure of winning, of taking him away from Roz. Also the money. This is obvious to Roz, but not, apparently, to Mitch. "She's in some kind of trouble," he says. "I ought to find her." He must be thinking about the coke dealer.

Roz loses it. "Oh, spare me," she says.

"I'm not asking *you* to do anything," Mitch says, as if Roz would be too mean-spirited to lend a helping hand. "I know where that envelope came from."

"You're not actually going after her," says Roz. "I mean, haven't you got the message? She's wiped her spikes on you. She's made a fool of you. She's lied and cheated and stolen, and she's written you off. Believe me, there's no place in her life for a used dupe."

Mitch shoots her a glance of intense dislike. This is far too much truth for him. He's not used to getting dumped, to being betrayed, because it's never happened to him before. Maybe, thinks Roz, I should give lessons.

"You don't understand," he says. But Roz does understand. What she understands is that no matter what went on before this, there was never anyone more important to Mitch than she was, and now there is.

Harriet calls: Mitch has taken the Wednesday-night plane to London.

Roz's heart hardens. It ceases to burn and drip. The rent in her chest closes over it. She can feel an invisible hand there, tight as a bandage, holding her body shut. That's it, she thinks. That finally tears it. She buys five murder novels and takes a week off, and goes to Florida, and lies in the sun crying.

48

Mitch comes back. He comes back from the hunt. He comes back in the middle of February, having phoned first; having booked himself a time slot, like any client or petitioner. He turns up on Roz's doorstep in his sheepskin coat, looking like an empty sack. In his hand he holds a plaintive bouquet of flowers.

For that, Roz would like to kick him—does he think she's such a cheap date?—but she's shocked by his appearance. He's rumpled like a park-bench drunk, his skin is grey from travel, dark hollows ring his eyes. He's lost weight, his flesh is loose, his face is starting to cave in, like some old guy without his false teeth, like the kids' Hallowe'en pumpkins a few days after the holiday is over and the candles inside have burned out. That softening, that subsiding inwards towards a damp central emptiness.

Roz feels she should stand in the doorway, a barrier between the cold outside air he brings with him and her own warm house, blocking him, keeping him out. The children need to be protected from this leftover, this sagging echo, this shadowy copy of their real father, with his sinkhole eyes and his smile like crumpled paper. But she owes him a hearing, at least. Wordlessly she takes the flowers—roses, red, a mockery, because she does not delude herself, passion is not what he feels. Not, at least, for her. She lets him in.

"I want to come back," he tells her, gazing around the high, wide living room, the spacious domain that Roz has made, that was once his to share. Not *Will you let me come back?* Not *I want you back.* Nothing to do with Roz, no mention of her at all. It's the room he's claiming, the territory. He is deeply mistaken. He thinks he has rights.

"You didn't find her, did you?" says Roz. She hands him the drink she's poured for him, as in days of yore: a single-malt scotch, no ice. That's what he used to like, long long ago; that's what she's been drinking these days, and more of it than she should. The gesture of handing the glass to him softens her, because it's their old habit. Nostalgia for him seizes her by the throat. She fights against choking. He has a new tie on, an unfamiliar one, with grisly pastel tulips. The fingerprints of Zenia are all over it, like unseen scorch marks.

"No," says Mitch. He won't look at her.

"And if you had," says Roz, hardening herself again, lighting her own cigarette—she won't ask him to do it, they are way beyond such whimsical courtship gestures, not that he's leaping forward with arm outstretched— "what would you have done? Beat the shit out of her, or sicced the lawyers onto her, or given her a big sloppy kiss?"

Mitch looks in her direction. He can't meet her eyes. It's as if she's semi-invisible, a kind of hovering blur. "I don't know," he says.

"Well, at least that's honest," says Roz. "I'm glad you aren't lying to me." She's trying to keep her voice soft, to avoid the bitter cutting edge. He isn't lying to her, he isn't doing anything to her. There is no *her*, as far as he's concerned; she might as well not be here. Whatever he's doing is to himself. She has never felt so non-existent in her life. "So, what do you want?" She may as well ask, she may as well find out what's being demanded of her.

But he shakes his head: he doesn't know that, either. He isn't even drinking from the glass she's poured. It's as if he can't take anything from her. Which means there's nothing she can give him. "Maybe when you figure it out," she says, "you could let me in on it."

Now he does finally look at her. God knows who he sees. Some avenging angel, some giantess with a bared arm and a sword—it can't be Roz, tender and feathery Roz, not the way he's staring at her. His eyes are frightening because they're frightened. He's scared shitless, of her or of someone or something, and she can't bear the sight. Whatever else has been going on, all those years he played In and Out the Bimbos and she raged at him and wept, she's always depended on him not to lose his nerve. But now there's a crack in him, like a crack in glass; a little heat and he'll shatter. But why should it be Roz's job to sweep up?

"Just let me stay here," he says. "Let me stay in the house. I could sleep downstairs, in the family room. I won't bother you."

He's begging, but Roz hears this only in retrospect. At the moment she finds the idea intolerable: Mitch on the floor, in a sleeping bag, like the twins' friends at group sleepovers, demoted to transience, demoted to adolescence. Locked out of her bedroom, or worse, not wishing to go into it. That's it—he's rejecting her, he's rejecting her big, eager, clumsy, ardent, and solid body; it's no longer good enough for him, not even as a feather bed, not even as a fallback. He must find her repellent.

But she does have some pride left, though God knows how she's managed to hang onto it, and if she's going to let him come back it has to be on full terms. "You can't treat me like a rest stop," she says. "Not any more."

Because that's exactly what he'd do, he'd move in, she'd dish out the nourishing lunches, feed him, build him up again, and he'd get his strength back and be off, off in his longboat, off in his galleon, scouring the seven seas for the Holy Grail, for Helen of Troy, for Zenia, peering through the spyglass, on the watch for her pirate flag. Roz can see it in his eyes, which are focused on the horizon, not on her. Even if he came back, into her bedroom, in between her raspberry-coloured sheets, into her body, it wouldn't be her underneath him, on top of him, around him, not ever again. Zenia has stolen something from him, the one thing he always kept safe before, from all women, even from Roz. Call it his soul. She slipped it out of his breast pocket when he wasn't looking, easy as rolling a drunk, and looked at it, and bit it to see if it was genuine, and sneered at it for being so small after all, and then tossed it away, because she's the kind of woman who wants what she doesn't have and gets what she wants and then despises what she gets.

What is her secret? How does she do it? Where does it come from, her undeniable power over men? How does she latch hold of them, break their stride, trip them up, and then so easily turn them inside out? It must be something very simple and obvious. She tells them they're unique, then reveals to them that they're not. She opens her cloak with the secret pockets and shows them how the magic trick is worked, and that it is after all nothing more than a trick. Only by that time they refuse to see; they think the Water of Youth is real, even though she empties the bottle and fills it again from the tap, right before their very eyes. They want to believe.

"It won't work," Roz tells Mitch. She isn't being vindictive. It's the simple truth.

He must know it, because he doesn't plead. He subsides into his crumpled clothing; his neck gets shorter, as though there's a steady but inexorable weight pushing slowly down on the top of his head. "I guess not," he says.

"Didn't you keep the apartment?" says Roz. "Isn't that where you're living?"

"I couldn't stay there," says Mitch. His voice is reproachful, as if it's crass of her, cruel of her even to suggest such a thing. Doesn't she realize how much it would hurt him to be in a place he once shared with the fled beloved, a place where he would be reminded of the dear departed at every turn, a place where he was so happy?

Roz knows. She herself lives in such a place. But he obviously hasn't thought of that. Those in pain have no time for the pain they cause.

Roz sees him out, into the front hall, into the overcoat, which almost does her in because it's her overcoat too, she helped him buy it, she shared the life he led in it, that good-taste leather, that sheepskin, one-time container of such a rascally wolf. No longer, no more; he's toothless now. *Poor lamb,* thinks Roz, and clenches her fists tight because she won't let herself be fooled like that again.

He takes himself off, off into the freezing February dusk, off into the unknown. Roz watches him walk towards his parked car, lurching a little although he didn't touch his drink. The sidewalks are icy. Or maybe he's on something, some kind of pill, a tranquillizer. Most likely he shouldn't be driving, though it's no longer any of her business to stop him. She tells herself it's not necessary to have qualms about him. He can stay at a hotel. It's not as if he doesn't have any money.

She leaves his red roses on the sideboard, still wrapped in their floral paper. Let them wilt. Dolores can find them tomorrow, and reproach Roz in her heart for carelessness, rich people don't know what things cost, and throw them out. She pours herself another scotch and lights another cigarette, then gets down her old photo albums, those pictures she took so endlessly at backyard birthday parties, at graduations, on vacations, winters in the snow, summers on the boat, to prove to herself they were all indeed a family, and sits in the kitchen going through them. Pictures of Mitch, in non-living colour: Mitch and Roz at their wedding, Mitch and Roz and Larry, Mitch and Roz and Larry and the twins. She searches his face for some clue, some foreshadowing of the catastrophe that has befallen them. She finds none.

Some women in her place take their nail scissors and snip out the heads of the men in question, leaving only their bodies. Some snip out the bodies too. But Roz will not do this, because of the children. She doesn't want them to come across a picture of their headless father, she doesn't want to alarm them, any more than she already has. And it wouldn't work anyway, because Mitch would still be there in the pictures, an outline, a blank shape, taking up the same amount of room, just as he does beside her in her bed. She never sleeps in the middle of that bed, she still sleeps off to one side. She can't bring herself to occupy the whole space.

On the refrigerator, attached to it by magnets in the

form of smiling pigs and cats, are the Valentines the twins made for her at school. The twins are clinging these days, they want her around. They don't like her going out at night. They didn't wait for Valentine's Day, they brought their Valentines home and gave them to her right away, as if there was some urgency. These are the only Valentines she will get. Probably they are the only ones she will get ever again. They should be enough for her. What does she want with glowing hearts, with incandescent lips and rapid breathing, at her age?

Snap out of it, Roz, she tells herself. You are not old. Your life is not over.

It only feels like that.

Mitch is in the city. He's around. He comes to see the children and Roz arranges to be out, her skin prickling the whole time with awareness of him. When she walks into the house after he's gone she can smell him—his aftershave, the English heather stuff, could it be he's sprinkled some of it around just to get to her? She glimpses him in restaurants, or at the yacht club. She stops going to those places. She picks up the phone and he's on the other line with one of the kids. The whole world is booby-trapped. She is the booby.

Their lawyers talk. A separation agreement is suggested, though Mitch stalls; he doesn't want Roz—or else he would be here, wouldn't he, on the doorstep again, wouldn't he at least be asking?—but he doesn't want to be separated from her either. Or maybe he's just bargaining, maybe he's just trying to get the price up. Roz grits her teeth and holds the line. This is going to cost her but it will be worth it to cut the string, the tie, the chain, whatever this heavy thing is that's holding her down. You need to know when to fold. At any rate she's functioning. More or less. Though she's done better.

She goes off to see a shrink, to see if she can improve herself, make herself over into a new woman, one who no longer gives a shit. She would like that. The shrink is a nice person; Roz likes her. Together the two of them labour over Roz's life as if it's a jigsaw puzzle, a mystery story with a solution at the end. They arrange and rearrange the pieces, trying to get them to come out better. They are hopeful: if Roz can figure out what story she's in, then they will be able to spot the erroneous turns she took, they can retrace her steps, they can change the ending. They work out a tentative plot. Maybe Roz married Mitch because, although she thought at the time that Mitch was very different from her father, she sensed he was the same underneath. He would cheat on her the way her father had cheated on her mother, and she would keep forgiving him and taking him back just the way her mother had. She would rescue him, over and over. She would play the saint and he the sinner.

Except that her parents ended up together and Roz and Mitch did not, so what went wrong? Zenia went wrong. Zenia switched the plot on Roz, from rescue to running away, and then when Mitch wanted to be rescued again Roz was no longer up to it. Whose fault was that? Who was to blame? Ah. Didn't Roz think that too much time was spent apportioning blame? Did she blame, perhaps, herself? In a word, yes. Maybe she still can't quite leave God out of it, and the notion that she's being punished.

Maybe it was nobody's fault, the shrink suggests. Maybe these things just happen, like plane crashes.

If Roz wants Mitch back that badly—and it appears that she does, now that she has a greater insight into the dynamics of their relationship—maybe she should ask him to come for counselling. Maybe she should forgive him, at least to that extent.

All this is very reasonable. Roz thinks of making the phone call. She is almost nerved up to it, she is almost there. Then, in drizzly March, Zenia dies. Is killed in Lebanon, blown up by a bomb; comes back in a tin can, and is buried. Roz does not cry. Instead she rejoices fiercely—if there was a bonfire she'd dance around it, shaking a tambourine if one was provided. But after that she's afraid, because Zenia is nothing if not vengeful. Being dead won't alter that. She'll think of something.

Mitch isn't at the funeral. Roz cranes her neck, scanning for him, but there's only a bunch of men she doesn't know. And Tony and Charis, of course.

She wonders whether Mitch has heard, and if he has, how he's taking it. She ought to feel that Zenia has been cleared out of the way, like a moth-eaten fur coat, a tree branch fallen across the path, but she doesn't. Zenia dead is more of a barrier than Zenia alive; though, as she tells the shrink, she can't explain why. Could it be remorse, because Zenia the hated rival is dead and Roz wanted her to be, and Roz is not? Possibly. *You aren't responsible for everything,* says the shrink.

Surely Mitch will now change, appear, react. Wake up, as if from hypnotism. But he doesn't phone. He makes no sign, and now it's April, the first week, the second week, the third. When Roz calls his lawyer, finally, to find out where he is, the lawyer can't say. Something was mentioned about a trip, he seems to recall. Where? The lawyer doesn't know.

Where Mitch is, is in Lake Ontario. He's been there a while. The police pick up his boat, the *Rosalind II,* drifting with sails furled, and eventually Mitch himself washes into shore off the Scarborough Bluffs. He has his lifejacket on, but at this time of year the hypothermia would have taken him very quickly. He must have slipped, they tell her. Slipped off and fallen in, and been unable to climb back on. There was a wind, the day he left harbour. An accident. If it had been suicide he wouldn't have been wearing his lifejacket. Would he?

He would, he would, thinks Roz. He did that part of it for the kids. He didn't want to leave a bad package for them. He did love them enough for that. But he knew all about the temperature of the water, he'd lectured her about it often enough. Your body heat dissipates, quick as a wink. You numb, and then you die. And so he did. That it was deliberate Roz has no doubt, but she doesn't say. *It was an accident,* she tells the children. Accidents happen.

●　　●　　●

She has to tidy up after him, of course. Pick up the odds and ends. Clean up the mess. She is, after all, still his wife.

The worst thing is the apartment, the apartment he shared with Zenia. He didn't go back to it after she left, after he chased off to Europe to find her. Some of his clothes are still in the closet—his impressive suits, his beautiful shirts, his ties. Roz folds and packs, as so often before. His shoes, emptier than empty. Wherever else he is, he isn't here.

Zenia is a stronger presence. Most of her things are gone, but a Chinese dressing gown, rose-coloured silk with dragons embroidered on it, is hanging over a chair in the bedroom. Opium, Roz thinks, smelling it. It's the smell that bothers Roz the most. The tumbled sheets are still on the unmade bed, there are dirty towels in the bathroom. The scene of the crime. She should never have come here, this is torture. She should have sent Dolores.

Roz gives up going to the shrink. It's the optimism that's getting to her, the belief that things can be fixed, which right now feels like just one more burden. All this and she's supposed to be hopeful, too? Thanks but no thanks. *So, God,* she says to herself. *That was some number. Fooled me! Proud of yourself? What else have you got up your sleeve? Maybe a nice war, some genocide—hey, a plague or two?* She knows she shouldn't talk this way, even to herself, it's tempting fate, but it gets her through the day.

Getting through the day is the main thing. She puts two pending real estate deals on hold; she's in no shape to make major decisions. The magazine can run itself until she can get around to selling it, which shouldn't be too hard, because ever since the changes Zenia brought in it's showing a profit. If she can't sell it she'll fold it up. She doesn't have the heart to go on with a publication that has made such extravagant claims, claims she has so calamitously failed to embody in herself. Superwoman she's not, and *failed* is the key word. She's been a success at many things, but not at the one thing. Not at standing by her man. Because if Mitch drowned himself—if there wasn't enough left for him to live for—whose fault was it? Zenia's, yes, but also her own. She should have remembered about his own father, who took the same dark road. She should have let him back in.

Getting through the day is one thing, getting through the night is another. She can't brush her teeth in her splendid double-sinked bathroom without sensing Mitch beside her, she can't take a shower without looking to see if his damp footprints are on the floor. She can't sleep in the middle of her raspberry-coloured bed, because, more than ever, more than when he was alive but elsewhere, he is almost there. But he's not there. He's missing. He's a missing person. He's gone off someplace where she can't get at him.

She can't sleep in her raspberry-coloured bed at all. She lies down, gets up, puts on her bathrobe, wanders downstairs to the kitchen where she burrows through the refrigerator; or she tiptoes along the upstairs hall, listening for the breathing of her children. She's anxious about them now, more than ever, and they are anxious about her. Despite her efforts to reassure them, to tell them that she is fine and everything will be all right, she frightens them. She can tell.

It must be the flatness of her voice, her face naked of makeup and disguise. She drags a blanket around the house with her in case sleep might choose to appear. Sometimes she falls asleep on the floor, in the family room, with the television on for company. Sometimes she drinks, hoping to relax herself, conk herself out. Sometimes it works.

Dolores quits. She says she's found another job, one with a pension plan, but Roz doesn't think it's that. It's the bad luck; Dolores is afraid of catching it. Roz will replace her, find someone else; but later, when she can think. After she's had some sleep.

She goes to the doctor, the GP, the same one she uses for the children's coughs, and asks for some sleeping pills. Just to get her through this period, she says. The doctor is understanding, the pills are granted. She's careful with them at first, but then they don't work so well and she takes more. One evening she takes a handful of them, and a triple scotch; not out of any desire to die, she doesn't want to do that, but out of simple irritation at being awake. She ends up on the kitchen floor.

It's Larry who finds her, coming back from a friend's. He phones the ambulance. He's old now, older than he should be. He's responsible.

Roz comes to, and finds herself being walked around between two large nurses. Where is she? In a hospital. How weak, how embarrassing, she didn't intend to end up in such a place. "I need to go home," she says. "I need to get some rest."

"She's coming out of it," says the one on the left.

"You'll be fine, dear," says the other.

Roz has not been *she* or *dear* for a long time. There's a flicker of humiliation. Then it subsides.

Roz floats up out of the fog. She can feel the bones of her skull, thin as a skin; inside them her brain is swollen and full of pulp. Her body is dark and vast as the sky, her nerves pinpricks of brightness: the stars, long strings of them, wavering like seaweed. She could drift, she could sink. Mitch would be there.

Then Charis is sitting beside her, beside her bed, holding her left hand. "Not yet," says Charis. "You need to come back, it's not your time. You still have things to do."

When she's herself, when she's normal, Roz finds Charis an endearing nincompoop—let's face it, a polymath she's not—and mostly dismisses her gauzy metaphysics. Now, though, Charis reaches down with her other hand and takes hold of Roz's foot, and Roz feels grief travelling through her like a wave, up through her body and along her arm and into her hand, and out into Charis's hand, and out. Then she feels a tug, a pull, as if Charis is a long way away, on the shore, and has hold of something—something like a rope—and is hauling Roz in, out of the water, the water of the lake, where she has almost drowned. That's life over there: a beach, the sun, some small figures. Her children, waving, shouting to her, though she can't hear them. She concentrates on breathing, on forcing the air down into her lungs. She's strong enough, she can make it.

"Yes," says Charis. "You will."

Tony has moved into Roz's house, to be with the children. After Roz is let out of the hospital Charis moves in as well, just for a time; just until Roz is back on her feet.

"You don't need to do this," Roz protests.

"Somebody does," says Tony briskly. "You have other suggestions?" She's already phoned Roz's office and told them that Roz has bronchitis; also laryngitis, so she can't speak on the phone. Flowers arrive, and Charis puts them in vases and then forgets to add water. She goes to the health food store and brings back various capsules and extractions, which she feeds to Roz or else rubs onto her, and some breakfast cereals made from unknown seeds that need to be boiled a lot. Roz longs for chocolate, and Tony smuggles some in for her. "That's a good sign," she tells Roz.

Charis has brought August with her, and the three girls play Barbie doll games together in the twins' play-room, violent games in which Barbie goes on the warpath and takes over the world and bosses everyone else around, and other games in which she comes to a nasty end. Or they dress up in Roz's old slips and sneak around the house, three princesses on an expedition. Roz rejoices to hear the loud voices again, the arguments; the twins have been far too quiet lately.

Tony makes cups of tea, and, for dinner, olden-days tuna casseroles with cheese and potato-chip toppings, Roz thought such things had vanished from the world, and

Charis massages Roz's feet with mint essence and rose oil. She tells Roz that she's an ancient soul, with connections to Peru. These things that have happened to her, which look like tragedy, are past lives working themselves out. Roz must learn from them, because that is why we return to earth: to learn. "You don't stop being who you are, in your next life," she says, "but you add things." Roz bites her tongue, because she's returning to herself again and she thinks this is diarrhea, but she would never dream of saying so because Charis means well, and Charis runs baths for her that have sticks of cinnamon and leaves floating in them, as if Roz is about to be turned into chicken stock.

"You're spoiling me," Roz tells them. Now that she's feeling better she's made uneasy by all the fussing. She is usually the one who does these things, the hen things, the taking care. She's not used to being on the receiving end.

"You've been on a hard journey," says Charis, in her gentle voice. "You used up a lot of your energy. Now you can let go."

"That's not so easy," says Roz.

"I know," says Charis. "But you've never liked easy things." By *never*, she means *not for the past four thousand years*. Which is about how old Roz feels.

49

Roz finds herself sitting on the cellar floor in the light from the one unshaded overhead bulb, an empty plate beside her, a children's storybook open on her knees. She's twisting and untwisting her wedding ring, the ring that once meant she was married, the ring that's weighing her down, turning it on her finger as if she's unscrewing it, or else expecting some genie or other to appear from nowhere and solve everything for her. Put the pieces back together, make everything right; slide Mitch alive back into her bed where she will find him when she goes upstairs—scrubbed and scented and brushed and cunning, filled to the brim with affectionate lies, lies she can see through, lies she can deal with, twenty years younger. Another chance. Now that she knows what to do she will do it better this time. *Tell me, God—why don't we get rehearsals?*

How long has she been down here, whimpering in bad light? She must go upstairs and deal with reality, whatever that may be. She must pull herself together.

She does this by patting the pockets of her bathrobe, where she always used to keep a tissue before the twins outlawed them. Not finding any, she blots her eyes on her orange sleeve, leaving a black smear of mascara, then wipes her nose on the other sleeve. Well, who's to see, except God? According to the nuns he had a preference for cotton hankies. *God,* she tells him, *if you hadn't wanted us to wipe our noses on our sleeves you wouldn't have given us sleeves.* Or noses. Or tears, as far as that goes. Or memory, or pain.

She slides the kids' books back onto the shelf. She should donate these books to some charity, or maybe lend them—let them loose in the world to warp some small child's mind, while she waits for her own grandchildren to appear. What grandchildren? *Dream on, Roz.* The twins are too young and will anyway probably grow up to be stock-car racers or women who go off to live among the gorillas, something fearless and non-progenitive; as for Larry, he's in absolutely no hurry, and if the *faux* women he's come up with so far are any sample of what the future holds in the daughter-in-law department, Roz would rather not hold her breath.

Life would be so much easier if there were still arranged marriages. She'd go out into the marriage market, cash in hand, bargain with a dependable marriage broker, secure a nice bride for Larry: bright but not bossy, sweet but not a pushover, and with a wide pelvic structure and a strong back. If her own marriage had been arranged, would things have turned out any worse than they did? Is it fair, to send inexperienced young girls out into the wild forest to fend for themselves? Girls with big bones and maybe not the smallest of feet. What would help would be a wise woman, some gnarly old crone who would step out from behind a tree, who would give advice, who would say *No, not this one,* who would say *Beauty is only skin deep,* in men as well as women, who would see down as far as the heart. Who knows what evil lurks in the hearts of men? An older woman knows. But how much older do you have to get before you acquire that kind of wisdom? Roz keeps expecting it to sprout in her, grow all over her, sort of like age spots; but it hasn't yet.

She hauls herself up off the floor and dusts her behind, a mistake because her hands are covered with book dirt, as she realizes too late when she looks at them, having encountered a squashed silverfish stuck to her velour-covered buttock, and Lord knows what's been crawling over her while she's been sitting here woolgathering. *Woolgathering,* her mother's word, a word so old, rooted so far back in time, that although everyone knows what it means nobody knows where it came from. Why was gathering wool supposed to be lazy? Reading and thinking were both woolgathering, to her mother. *Rosalind! Don't just sit there woolgathering! Sweep the front walk!*

Roz's legs have gone to sleep. Every step she takes sends pins and needles shooting into them. She limps towards the cellar steps, pausing to wince. When she gets up to the kitchen she will open the refrigerator, just to see if there's something in there she might like to eat. She hasn't had a proper dinner, she often doesn't. Nobody to cook for her, nobody to cook for, not that she ever cooked. Nobody to order in for. Food should be shared. Solitary eating can be like solitary drinking—a way of dulling the edge, of filling in the blanks. The blank; the empty man-shaped outline left by Mitch.

But there won't be anything in the fridge that she wants; or rather, a few things maybe, but she will not stoop so low, she will not eat spoonfuls from the jar of chocolate-rum ice cream sauce, as she has done before, or blitz the can of *pâté de foie gras* she's been saving up for God knows what mythical occasion, along with the bottle of champagne she keeps tucked away at the back. There's a bunch of raw vegetables in there, roughage she bought in a fit of nutritional virtue, but right now they don't appeal. She foresees their fate: they will turn slowly to green and orange goo in the crisper, and then she will buy more.

Maybe she could call up Charis or Tony, or both of them, invite them over; order up some red-hot chicken wings from the Indian tandoori take-out on Carlton, or some shrimp balls and garlic beans and fried won-ton from her favourite Szechuan place on Spadina, or both: have a sinful little multicultural feast. But Charis will already be back on the Island, and it's dark by now, and she doesn't like the thought of Charis out alone at night, there might be muggers, and Charis is such an obvious target, a long-haired middle-aged woman walking around covered with layers of printed textiles and bumping into things, she might as well have a sign pinned to her, *Snatch my purse,* and Roz can rarely persuade her to take taxis even if she offers to pay for them herself, because Charis goes on about the waste of gasoline. She will take a bus; or worse, she might decide to walk, through the wilds of Rosedale, past the rows of ersatz Georgian mansions, and get picked up by the police for vagrancy.

As for Tony, she'll be at home in her turreted fortress, cooking up West's dinner for him, some noodle casserole or other from *The Joy of Cooking,* the 1967 edition. It's odd how Tony's the only one of them who has actually ended up with a man. Roz can't quite figure it out: tiny Tony, with her baby-bird eyes and her acidulated little smile, and, you'd think, the sex appeal of a fire hydrant, with more or less the same proportions. But love comes in odd boxes, as

Roz has had occasion to learn. And maybe West was so badly frightened by Zenia in his youth that he's never dared look at any other woman since.

Roz thinks wistfully of the dinnertime tableau at Tony's house, then decides she is not exactly envious, because straw-bodied, strange-minded, lantern-jawed West isn't her own idea of what she'd like to have sitting across the table from her. Instead she's glad that Tony has a man, because Tony is her friend and you want your friends to be happy. According to the feminists, the ones in the overalls, in the early years, the only good man was a dead man, or better still none at all; yet Roz continues to wish her friends joy of them, these men who are supposed to be so bad for you. *I met someone,* a friend tells her, and Roz shrieks with genuine pleasure. Maybe that's because a good man is hard to find, so it's a real occasion when anyone actually finds one. But it's difficult, it's almost impossible, because nobody seems to know any more what "a good man" is. Not even men.

Or maybe it's because so many of the good men have been eaten, by man-eaters like Zenia. Most women disapprove of man-eaters; not so much because of the activity itself, or the promiscuity involved, but because of the greed. Women don't want all the men eaten up by man-eaters; they want a few left over so they can eat some themselves.

This is a cynical view, worthy of Tony but not of Roz. Roz must preserve some optimism, because she needs it; it's a psychic vitamin, it keeps her going. "The Other Woman will soon be with *us*," the feminists used to say. But how long will it take, thinks Roz, and why hasn't it happened yet?

Meanwhile the Zenias of this world are abroad in the land, plying their trade, cleaning out male pockets, catering to male fantasies. Male fantasies, male fantasies, is everything run by male fantasies? Up on a pedestal or down on your knees, it's all a male fantasy: that you're strong enough to take what they dish out, or else too weak to do anything about it. Even pretending you aren't catering to male fantasies is a male fantasy: pretending you're unseen, pretending you have a life of your own, that you can wash your feet and comb your hair unconscious of the ever-present watcher peering through the keyhole, peering through the keyhole in your own head, if nowhere else. You are a woman with a man inside watching a woman. You are your own voyeur. The Zenias of this world have studied this situation and turned it to their own advantage; they haven't let themselves be moulded into male fantasies, they've done it themselves. They've slipped sideways into dreams; the dreams of women too, because women are fantasies for other women, just as they are for men. But fantasies of a different kind.

Sometimes Roz gets herself down. It's her own worthiness that does it, the pressure on her to be nice, to be ethical, to behave well; it's the rays of good behaviour, of good nature, of cluck-clucking good-as-gold goody-goodness beaming out from around her head. It's her best intentions. If she is so goldarned worthy, why isn't she having more fun? Sometimes she would like to cast off her muffling Lady Bountiful cloak, stop tiptoeing through the scruples, cut loose, not in minor ways as she does now— a little swearing inside her head, some bad verbiage—but something really big. Some great whopping thoroughly despicable sin.

Random sex would have done the trick once, but plain garden-variety sex hardly counts any more, it's just a form of mood therapy or calisthenics, she'd have to go in for bloodthirsty kink. Or something else, something devious and archaic and complicated and mean. Seduction followed by slow poisoning. Treachery. Betrayal. Cheating and lies.

To do that she would need another body, it goes without saying, because the one she has is too clumsy, too lumberingly honest, and the sort of evil she has in mind would require grace. To be truly malevolent she would have to be thinner.

> *Mirror, mirror on the wall,*
> *Who is the evilest of us all?*
> *Take off a few pounds, cookie, and maybe I can*
> *do something for you.*

Or maybe she could go in for superhuman goodness, instead. Hair shirts, stigmata, succouring the poor, a kind of outsized Mother Teresa. Saint Roz, it sounds good, though Saint Rosalind would be classier. A few thorns, one or two body parts on a plate, to show how she'd been martyred: an eye, a hand, a tit, tits were favourites, the ancient Romans seemed to have a thing about cutting off women's breasts, sort of like plastic surgeons. She can see herself in a halo, with her hand languidly on her heart and a wimple, great for sagging chins, and her eyes rolled up in ecstasy. It's the extremes that attract her. Extreme good, extreme evil: the abilities required are similar.

Either way, she would like to be someone else. But not just anyone. Sometimes—for a day at least, or even for an hour, or if nothing else was available then five minutes would do—sometimes she would like to be Zenia.

She hobbles up the cellar stairs on prickling feet, one step at a time, holding onto the banister and wondering if this is what it will be like to be ninety, should she get that far. She makes it to the top finally, opens the door. Here is the white kitchen, just as she left it. She feels as if she's been away from it for a long time. Wandering lost in the dark wood with its twisted trees, enchanted.

The twins are sitting on high stools at the counter, wearing shorts with tights underneath, a fashionable hole in each knee, drinking strawberry smoothies out of tall glasses. Pink moustaches adorn their upper lips. The frozen yogurt container melts near the sink.

"Gollee, Mom, you look like a car accident!" says Paula. "What's that smeary stuff all over your face?"

"It's just my face," says Roz. "It's coming off."

Erin jumps down and runs over to her. "Sit down, sweetie," she says, in a parody of Roz herself in her mothering mode. "Do you have a temperature? Let us feel your forehead!"

The two of them propel her across the floor, up onto a stool. They wet the dishtowel and wipe her face—"Ooh, messy messy!" It's obvious to them she's been crying, but of course they don't mention it. Then they try to get her to drink one of their smoothies, laughing and giggling because it's funny to them, their mother as a big baby, themselves as mothers. Wait for it, Roz thinks. Wait till I lose my marbles and start to drool, and you find yourselves doing this for real. It won't be so funny then.

But what a burden it must be to them, her bereft condition. Why shouldn't they put on clown faces to cover up their distress? It's a trick they've learned from her. It's a trick that works.

The Toxique

50

Tony is playing the piano but no music comes out. Her feet don't reach the pedals, her hands don't span the keys, but she plays on because if she stops a terrible thing will happen. In the room is a dry burning smell, the smell of the flowers on the chintz curtains. They are large pink roses, they open and close their petals, which are now like flames; already they are spreading to the wallpaper. They aren't the flowers from her own curtains, they've come here from somewhere else, some place Tony can't remember.

Her mother walks into the darkening room, the heels of her shoes ticking on the floor, wearing her maroon hat with the spotted veil. She sits down on the piano bench beside Tony; her face glimmers, obscured, its features blurring. Her leather hand, cool as mist, brushes Tony's face, and Tony turns and holds onto her, holds on ferociously because she knows what happens next; but out of the front of her dress her mother takes an egg, an egg that smells like seaweed. If Tony can have this egg and keep it safe, the burning in the house will stop, the future can be avoided. But her mother lifts the egg up into the air, teasingly overhead, and Tony isn't tall enough to reach it. "Poor thing, poor thing," says her mother; or is it *poor twin*? Her voice is like a pigeon cooing, soothing and inexorable and infinitely mournful.

Somewhere out of sight the flowers have grown out of control and the house is on fire. Unless Tony can stop it, everything that once was will burn. The unseen flames make a fluttering sound, like ruffling feathers. A tall man is standing in the corner. It's West, but why is he wearing those clothes, why is his hair black, why does he have a hat? There's a suitcase beside him on the floor. He picks it up and opens it: it's full of sharpened pencils. *Reverof,* he says sadly; though what he means is *Farewell,* because Zenia is there at the door, wound in a silk shawl with a long fringe. In her neck there's a pinkish grey gash, as if her throat's been cut; but as Tony watches, it opens, then closes moistly, and she can see that Zenia has gills.

But West is going, he's putting his arm around Zenia, he's turning his back. Outside, the taxi is waiting to take them to the snowy hill.

Tony needs to stop them. She holds out her hand once more and her mother puts the egg into it, but the egg is too hot now because of the fire and Tony drops it. It rolls onto a newspaper and breaks open, and time runs out of it, wet and dark red. There are gunshots, coming from the back of the house, and marching boots, and shouting in a foreign language. Where is her father? Frantically she looks around for him but he is nowhere to be seen, and the soldiers are already here to take her mother away.

• • •

Charis is lying in her white vine-covered bed, arms at her sides, palms open, eyes closed. Behind her eyes she is fully aware. She feels her astral body rise out of her, rise straight up and hang suspended above her like a mask lifted from a face. It too is wearing a white cotton nightgown.

How tenuously we inhabit our bodies, she thinks. In her body of light—clear, like gelatin—she glides out through the window and across the harbour. Below her is the ferry; she swoops and follows in its wake. Around her she hears the rushing of wings. She looks, expecting sea-gulls, and is surprised to see a flock of chickens flying through the air.

She reaches the other shore and floats along over the city. Ahead of her is a large window, the window of a hotel. She fetches up against the glass and beats her arms for a moment, like a moth. Then the window melts like ice and she passes through.

Zenia is in here, sitting in a chair, wearing a white nightgown just like Charis's, brushing her cloudy hair in front of the mirror. The hair twists like flames, like the branches of dark cypresses licking heavenwards, it crackles with static electricity; blue sparks play from the tips. Zenia sees Charis and motions to her, and Charis goes close and then closer, and she sees the two of them side by side in the mirror. Then Zenia's edges dissolve like a watercolour in the rain and Charis merges into her. She slides her on like a glove, she slips into her like a flesh dress, she looks out through her eyes. What she sees is herself, herself in the mirror, herself with power. Her nightgown ripples in an invisible wind. Beneath her face are the bones, darker and darker through the glass, like an X-ray; now she can see into things, now she can change herself into energy and pass through solid objects. Possibly she's dead. It's hard to remember. Possibly this is rebirth. She spreads the fingers of her new hands, wondering what they will do.

She drifts to the window and looks out. Down below, among the fiery lights and many lives, there's a slow smouldering; the smell of it permeates the room. Everything burns eventually, even stone can burn. In the room behind her is the depth of outer space, where the atoms are blown like ashes, borne on the restless inter-stellar winds, the banished souls, atoning. . . .

There's a knock at the door. She goes to open, because it will be a maid with towels. But it isn't, it's Billy, in striped pyjamas, his body grown older, bloated, his face raw meat. If he touches her she will fall apart like a bun-dle of rotted leather. It's her new eyes doing this. She rubs and pulls at her face, trying to get out of these eyes, these dark eyes she no longer wants. But Zenia's eyes won't come off; they're stuck to her own eyes like the scales of a fish. Like smoked glass, they darken everything.

Roz is walking through the forest, through the shattered trunks and spiky undergrowth, wearing a sailor dress that is too big for her. She knows this dress isn't hers, she never had a dress like this. Her feet are bare, and cold too; pain shoots through them, because the ground is covered with snow. There's a track ahead of her: a red footprint, a white footprint, a red footprint. To the side there's a clump of trees. Many people have been that way; they've dropped the things they were carrying, a lamp, a book, a watch, a suitcase fallen open, a leg with a shoe, a shoe with a diamond buckle. Paper money blows here and there, like candy-bar wrappers tossed away. The footprints lead in among the trees but none come out. She knows not to follow them; there's something in there, something frightening she doesn't want to see.

She's safe though because here is her garden, the delphiniums drooping, black with mildew, forlorn in the snow. There are white chrysanthemums too but they aren't planted, they're in big cylindrical silver vases and she's never seen them before. Nevertheless this is her house. The back window is shattered, the door swings loose but she goes in anyway, she walks through the white kitchen where nothing moves, past the table with three chairs. Dust covers everything. She'll have to clean this up, because her mother is no longer here.

She climbs up the back stairs, her thawing feet tingling with pins and needles. The upstairs hallway is empty and silent; there is no music. Where are her children? They must be grown up, they must have gone away, they must be living elsewhere. But how can that be, how can she have grown-up children? She's too young for that, she's too small. There's something wrong with time.

Then she hears the sound of the shower. Mitch must be here, which fills her with joy because he has been away so long. She wants to run inside, to greet him. Through the open bedroom door steam billows.

But she can't go in, because a man in an overcoat is blocking her way. Orange light pours from his mouth and nostrils. He opens his coat and there is his sacred heart, orange too like a glowing jack-o'-lantern, flickering in the wind that has sprung up suddenly. He holds up his left hand to stop her. *Nun,* he says.

Despite appearances, despite everything, she knows this man is Zenia. From the ceiling it begins to rain.

51

It's after dark. There's a fine chilly drizzle, and the storefronts with their lit-up windows and the black streets with their red neon reflections have the slick, wet look that Tony associates with plastic raincoats and greased hair and freshly applied lipstick—a dubious, exciting look. Cars sizzle past, filled with strangers, going somewhere unknown. Tony walks.

The Toxique is different at night. The lights are dimmer, and squat candles in red glass holders flicker on the tables; the outfits of the waiters and waitresses are subtly more outrageous. There are a few men in suits, having dinner; businessmen, Tony guesses, though with their mistresses rather than their wives. She likes to think that such men might still have mistresses, though probably they don't call them that. Lovers. Main squeezes. Special friends. The Toxique is where you would take a special friend, but maybe not a wife. Though how would Tony know? It's not a world she moves in. There are more men in leather jackets than there are in the daytime. There's a subdued buzz.

She checks her big-numbers wristwatch: the rock band doesn't come on till eleven, and she hopes she'll be out of there by then. She's had enough noise at home; today she had to listen to a full thirty minutes of aural torture, put together by West and played to her at full volume, with considerable arm-waving and expressions of glee. "I think I've done it," was West's comment. What could she say? "That's good," was what she came out with. It's an all-occasion phrase, and appeared to suffice.

Tony is the first one here. She's never had dinner at the Toxique before, only lunch. This dinner is last-minute: Roz phoned in a state of breathlessness and said there was something she really needed to tell. At first she suggested that Tony and Charis should come over to her place, but Tony pointed out that such a thing was difficult without a car.

She's not that keen on going to Roz's anyway, though Roz's twins are—in theory—favourites of hers. She used to regret not having had children, though she wasn't sure she would have been all that good at it, considering Anthea. But being a godmother has suited her better than being a mother—for one thing it's more intermittent—and the twins have done her proud. They have a fine glittering edge to them, and so does her other goddaughter, Augusta. None of them is what you would call self-effacing—all three would be at home on horses, riding astride, hair flying, scouring the plains, giving no quarter. Tony isn't sure how they've come by their confidence, their straight-ahead level gazes, their humorous but remorseless mouths. They have none of the timidity that used to be so built in, for women. She hopes they will gallop through the world in style, more style than she herself has been able to scrape together. They have her blessing; but from a distance, because close up Augusta is faintly chilling—she's so intent on success—and the twins have become gigantic;

gigantic, and also careless. Tony is slightly afraid of them. They might step on her by mistake.

So it was Tony who suggested the Toxique, this time. Roz may have something to tell, but Tony has something to tell also and it's fitting that it should be told here. She has requested their usual table, the one in the corner by the smoked mirror. From the young woman, or possibly man, who appears beside her, dressed in a black cat-suit with a wide leather stud-covered belt and five silver earrings in each ear, she orders a bottle of white wine and a bottle of Evian.

Charis arrives at the same time as the bottles, looking strangely pale. Well, thinks Tony, she always looks strangely pale, but tonight she's even more so. "Something weird happened to me today," she tells Tony, shedding her damp woollen sweater-coat and her fuzzy knitted hat. But this is not an unusual thing for Charis to say, so Tony merely nods and pours her a glass of Evian. Sooner or later they will get the story of the dream about shiny people sitting in trees, or the odd coincidence involving street numbers or cats that look just like other cats that used to belong to someone Charis once knew and doesn't any more, but Tony would rather have it wait till Roz gets here. Roz is more tolerant of such intellectual wispiness, and better at changing the subject.

Roz comes in, waving and yoo-hooing and wearing a flame-red trench coat and matching sou'wester, and shaking herself. "Judas Priest!" she says, pulling off her purple gloves. "Wait till you hear! You won't *believe*!" Her tone is dismayed rather than jubilant.

"You saw Zenia today," says Charis.

Roz's mouth opens. "How did you know?" she says.

"Because, so did I," says Charis.

"And so did I," says Tony.

Roz sits heavily down, and stares at each one of them in turn. "All right," she says. "Tell."

Tony waits in the lobby of the Arnold Garden Hotel, which would not have been her own hotel of choice. It's a grace-less fifties construction, cement slabs on the outside and a lot of plate glass. From her vantage point she can see out through the double doors at the back, into a patio dotted with chunky planters and with a large circular fountain off in one corner, non-functional at this time of year and overlooked by tiers of balconies with orange-painted sheet-metal railings. The post-modern awning and brass at the front is just an add-on: the essence of the Arnold Garden is those balconies. Though efforts are being made: above Tony looms a prehensile arrangement of purplish dried flowers and wires and strange pods, daring the aes-thetically uninitiated to call it ugly.

The patio and the fountain must be the garden part of the Arnold Garden, Tony decides; but she wonders about the Arnold. Is it Arnold as in Matthew, he of the ignorant armies clashing by night? Or Arnold as in Benedict, trai-tor or hero depending on point of view? Or perhaps it's a first name, denoting some bygone city councillor, some worthy backroom fixer whose friends called him Arnie. The lobby, with its framed prints of rotund pink-coated fox-hunting Englishmen, gives no clue.

The chair Tony sits in is leathery and slippery and built for colossi. Her feet don't touch the ground even if she moves well forward, and if she slides herself all the way back, then her knees can't bend over the front edge and her legs stick out stiffly like the legs of a china doll. So she has adopted a compromise—a sort of hunched curvature—but she is far from comfortable.

Also, despite her demure navy blue coat and her sensible walking shoes and her wimpy Peter Pan collar, she feels conspicuous. Her bad intentions must be sticking out all over her. She has the sensation that she's growing hair, little prickles of it pushing out through the skin of her legs like the quills of a porcupine, hanks of it shoving through in tufts around her ears. It's Zenia doing this, the effort of tracking Zenia: it's fusing her neurons, rearranging the molecules in her brain. A hairy white devil is what she's becoming, a fanged monster. It's a necessary transformation perhaps, because fire must be fought with fire. But every weapon is two-edged, so there will be a price to pay: Tony won't get out of this unaltered.

In her outsized tote bag is her father's Luger, unearthed from the box of Christmas decorations where it's usually stored, and freshly oiled and loaded according to the instructions in the manual of forties weaponry she photocopied in the library. She took care to wear gloves while photocopying, so as not to leave fingerprints, just in case. In case they try to pin anything on her, afterwards. The gun itself is unregistered, she believes. It is after all a sort of souvenir.

Beside it is another implement. Tony has taken advantage of one of the many tool circulars littering her front lawn to purchase a cordless drill, with screwdriver attachment, at a third off. She has never used one of these before. Also, she's never used a gun before. But there's a first time for everything. Her initial idea was that she could use the drill to break into Zenia's room, if necessary. Unscrew the door hinges, or something. But it occurs to her, sitting here in the lobby, that the drill too is potentially lethal, and might be put to use. If she could murder Zenia with a cordless drill, what policeman would be smart enough to figure it out?

But the actual scenario is unclear in her mind. Maybe she should shoot Zenia first and then finish her off with the drill: the other way around would be cumbersome, as she would have to sneak up behind Zenia with the drill and then turn it on, and the whirring noise would be a give-away. She could always do an ambidextrous murder: gun in the left hand, cordless drill in the right, like the rapier-and-dagger arrangements of the late Renaissance. It's an appealing thought.

The catch is that Zenia is considerably taller than Tony, and Tony would of course be aiming for the head. Symmetrical retaliation: Zenia's pattern has been to attack her victims at the point of most vulnerability, and the most vulnerable point is the one most prized, and Tony's most vulnerable point is her brain. That's how she was trapped by Zenia in the first place: that was the temptation, the bait. Tony got suckered in through her own intellectual vanity. She thought she'd found a friend who was as smart as she was. *Smarter* was not a category.

Tony's love for West is her other most vulnerable point, so it stands to reason that it's through West that Zenia will attack her now. It's to protect West that she's doing this, really—he would not survive another slice cut out of his heart.

• • •

She hasn't shared her plans with Roz or Charis. Each of them is a decent person; neither would condone violence. Tony knows that she herself is not a decent person, she's known that ever since childhood. She does act like one, most of the time, because there's usually no reason not to, but she has another self, a more ruthless one, concealed inside her. She is not just Tony Fremont, she is also *Tnomerf Ynot,* queen of the barbarians, and, in theory, capable of much that Tony herself is not quite up to. *Bulc egdirb! Bulc egdirb! Take no prisoners,* because in order to protect the innocent, some must sacrifice their own innocence. This is one of the rules of war. Men have to do hard things, they have to do hard man-things. Hard-man things. They have to shed blood, so that others may live out their placid lives suckling their infants and rummaging in their gardens and creating unmusical music, free from guilt. Women are not usually called upon to commit such cold-blooded acts, but this does not mean they are incapable of them. Tony clenches her small teeth and invokes her left hand, and hopes that she will rise to the occasion.

In front of her face she holds the *Globe and Mail,* opened to the business section. She's not reading, however: she's watching the lobby for Zenia. Watching, and getting jittery, because it isn't every day she does something this risky. To cut the tension, to give herself some critical distance, she folds up the paper and takes her lecture notes out of her bag. It will focus her mind to review them, it will refresh her memory: she hasn't given this lecture since last year.

The lecture is a favourite among her students. It's the

one on the role of female camp-followers through the ages, before and after battles—their handiness as bodies-for-hire, rapees, and producers of cannon fodder, their tension-reducing, nursing, psychiatric, cooking and laundering and post-massacre looting and life-terminating skills—with a digression on venereal diseases. Rumour has it that the students' nickname for this lecture is "Mother Courage Meets Spotted Dick," or "Whores 'n' Sores"; it usually attracts a contingent of visiting engineers, who come for the visuals, because Tony has an impressive instructional film she always screens. It's the same one the army showed to its new recruits at the time of the Second World War to promote the use of condoms, and features many a rotted-off nose and green, leaking male organ. Tony is used to the nervous laughter. *Put yourself there,* she will tell them. *Pretend it's you. Now: less funny?*

At that time syphilis was considered to be a self-inflicted wound. Some guys used VD to get themselves invalided home. You could be court-martialled for having a dose, just as you could for shooting yourself in the foot. If the wound was the disease, then the weapon was the whore. Yet another weapon in the war of the sexes, the whore of the sexes, the raw of the sexes, the *raw sexes war.* A perfect palindrome.

Maybe that's what West found so irresistible about Zenia, Tony used to think: that she was raw, that she was raw sex, whereas Tony herself was only the cooked variety. Parboiled to get the dangerous wildness out, the strong fresh-blood flavours. Zenia was gin at midnight, Tony was eggs for breakfast, and in eggcups at that. It's not the category Tony would have preferred.

• • •

All these years Tony had refrained from asking West about Zenia. She hadn't wanted to upset him; also she was afraid of finding out any more about Zenia's powers of attraction, about their nature and their extent. But after the return of Zenia she couldn't help herself. On the edge of the crisis, she had to know.

"Remember Zenia?" she asked West at dinner, two nights ago. They were having fish, a *sole à la bonne femme* from Tony's *Basic French Cooking* book, bought to go with her battlefield-of-Pourrières fish platter.

West stopped chewing, just for a moment. "Of course," he said.

"What *was* it?" said Tony.

"What was what?" said West.

"Why you—you know. Why you went with her." Tony felt herself tensing up all over. *Instead of me,* she thought. *Why you abandoned me.*

West shrugged, then smiled. "I don't know," he said. "I can't remember. Anyway, that was a long time ago. She's dead now."

Tony knew that West knew that Zenia was far from dead. "True," she said. "Was it the sex?"

"The sex?" said West, as if she'd just mentioned some forgotten but unimportant shopping-list item. "No, I don't think so. Not exactly."

"What do you mean, not exactly?" said Tony, more sharply than she should have.

"Why are we talking about this?" said West. "It doesn't matter now."

"It matters to me," said Tony in a small voice.

West sighed. "Zenia was frigid," he said. "She couldn't help it. She was sexually abused in childhood, by a Greek Orthodox priest. I felt sorry for her."

Tony's mouth dropped open. "Greek Orthodox?"

"Well, she was part Greek," said West. "Greek immigrant. She couldn't tell anyone about the priest, because nobody would have believed her. It was a very religious community."

Tony could barely contain herself. She felt a raucous and unseemly merriment building up inside her. Frigid! So that's what Zenia had told poor West! It does not at all accord with certain confidences Zenia once saw fit to share with Tony on the subject of sex. Sex as a huge plum pudding, a confection of rich delights, whose pleasures she would enumerate while Tony listened, shut out, nose to the glass. Tony could just see white-knight West, dutifully huffing and puffing away, giving it his best shot, trying to save Zenia from the evil spell cast by the wicked, nonexistent Greek Orthodox priest, with Zenia having the time of her life. Probably she told him she was faking orgasm to please him. Double the guilt!

It would have been a challenge for him, of course. Warm up the Ice Maiden. The first man ever to successfully explore those polar climes. But of course there was no way he could win, because Zenia's games were always rigged.

"I never knew that," she said. She fixed West with her large wide-open eyes, trying to look sympathetic.

"Yeah, well," said West. "She found it really hard to talk about."

"Why did you break up with her?" said Tony. "The second time. Why did you move out?" Now that they'd crossed the border into the never-mentioned, now that West was talking, she might as well push her advantage.

West sighed. He looked at Tony with something close to shame. "To be honest," he said, and stopped.

"Yes?" said Tony.

"Well, to be honest, she kicked me out. She said she found me boring."

Tony appalled herself by nearly laughing out loud. Maybe Zenia was right: from a certain point of view, West *was* boring. But one woman's meat was another woman's boredom, and West was boring in the same way children were boring, and interesting in the same way, too, and that's what a woman like Zenia would never see. Anyway, what was true love if it couldn't put up with a little boredom?

"Are you all right?" West asked.

"Choked on a bone," said Tony.

West hung his head. "I guess I am boring," he said.

Tony felt contrite. She was cruel for finding this funny. It wasn't funny, because West had been deeply wounded. She got up from the table and put her arms around his neck from behind, and laid her cheek against the top of his sparsely covered head. "You aren't at all boring," she said. "You're the most interesting man I've ever known." This was correct, since West was in fact the only man Tony had ever known, in any way that counted.

West reached up and patted her hand. "I love you," he said. "I love you much more than I ever loved Zenia."

Which is all very well, thinks Tony, sitting in the lobby of the Arnold Garden Hotel, but if that's really true, why didn't he tell me that Zenia called? Maybe he's already seen her. Maybe she's already lured him into bed. Maybe her teeth are in his neck, right now; maybe she's sucking out his life's blood while Tony sits here in this perverse leather chair, not even knowing where to look, because Zenia could be anywhere, she could be doing anything, and so far Tony doesn't have a clue.

This is the third hotel she's tried out. She's spent two other mornings hanging around in the lobbies of the Arrival and the Avenue Park, with no results whatsoever. Her only lead is the extension number, the one scribbled by West and left beside his phone, but she's hesitated to call all the hotels and use it because she doesn't want to alert Zenia, she wants to take her by surprise. She doesn't want to ask for her at the desk either, because she knows in her bones that Zenia will be using a false name; and once Tony has asked, and has been told there's no guest of that name, it would look suspicious if she were to keep on sitting in the lobby. Also she doesn't want to be remembered by the staff, should Zenia be found later wallowing in a pool of blood. So she merely sits, trying to look like someone waiting for a business meeting.

Her theory is that Zenia—who is by habit a late riser—must at some point get out of bed, must take the elevator to the main floor, must walk through the lobby. Of course it's not beyond Zenia to stay in bed all day or sneak down the fire stairs, but Tony is betting on the law of averages. Sooner or later—supposing Tony is in the right hotel—Zenia will appear.

And then what? Then Tony will leap or slither out of her chair, will patter across the floor to Zenia, will chirp a greeting, will be ignored; will scuttle after Zenia as she sweeps out through the glass doors. Gasping for breath, her outmoded gun and silly cordless drill clanking together in her bag, she will catch up to Zenia as she strides along the sidewalk. "We need to talk," Tony will blurt.

"What about?" Zenia will say. At that point she will simply walk faster, and Tony will either have to trot ridiculously or give up.

This is the nightmare scenario. Just thinking about it makes Tony blush with the sense of her own future humiliation. There's another scenario, one in which Tony is persuasive and dexterous and Zenia is taken in, one that acts out some of Tony's more violent although hypothetical fantasies and includes a neat red hole placed competently in the exact centre of Zenia's forehead. But at the moment Tony doesn't have a lot of faith in it.

She isn't having much luck concentrating on her lecture notes, so she switches back to the *Globe* business section and forces herself to read. *Tsol Sboj Erom. Gnisolc Tnalp.* This has a satisfying Slavic ring to it. That, or Finnish, or some wild-haired tribe from Planet Pluto. As Tony is savouring it she feels a hand on her shoulder.

"Tony! There you are, finally!" Tony looks up, then stifles a small rodent-like shriek: Zenia is bending over her, smiling warmly. "Why didn't you call before? And why are you just sitting here in the lobby? I gave West the room number!"

"Well," says Tony. Her mind scrabbles, trying to fit all this together. "He jotted it down and then lost it. You know what he's like." Awkwardly she disentangles herself from the leather chair, which appears to have grown suction cups.

"I told him to *make* you call me *right away,*" says Zenia. "It was just after I saw you in the Toxique. I guess you didn't recognize me! But I called up and told him it was very important." She's no longer smiling: she's beginning to assume an expression Tony recalls well, something between a frown and a wince, urgent and at the same time beset. What it means is that Zenia wants something.

Tony is alert now, on her inner toes. Her darkest suspicions are being confirmed: this is obviously a fallback story, a story Zenia and West have concocted together just in case Tony should sniff the wind, or should run across Zenia in some unlikely place such as Tony's own bedroom. The story is that the message was for Tony, not for West. It's a cunning story, it has Zenia's paw-prints all over it, but West must be colluding. Things are worse than Tony thought. The rot has gone deeper.

"Come on," says Zenia. "We'll go up to my room; I'll order coffee." She takes Tony's arm. At the same time she glances around the lobby. It's a look of anxiety, of fear even, a look Tony is not intended to see. Or is she?

She cranes her neck, peering up at Zenia's still-amazing face. Mentally she adds something to it: a small red X, marking the spot.

Zenia's hotel room is unremarkable except for its largeness and its neatness. The neatness is unlike Zenia. There are no clothes in evidence, no suitcases strewn around, no cosmetic bags on the bathroom counter, as far as Tony can see in one sideways glance. It's as if no one is living here.

Zenia sheds her black leather coat and phones for coffee, and then sits down on the flowered pastel green sofa, crossing her endless black-stockinged legs, lighting a cigarette. The dress she wears is a clinging jersey wrap, the purple of stewed blueberries. Her dark eyes are enormous, and, Tony sees now, shadowed by fatigue, but her plum-coloured smile still quirks up ironically. She seems more at ease here than in the lobby. She raises an eyebrow at Tony. "Long time no see," she says.

Tony is at a loss. How should she play this? It would be a mistake to display her anger: that would tip Zenia off, put her on her guard. Tony shuffles her inner deck and discovers that in fact she's not angry, not at the moment. Instead she's intrigued, and curious. The historian in her is taking over. "Why did you pretend to die?" she says. "What was all that stuff, with the ashes and the fake lawyer?"

"The lawyer was real," says Zenia, blowing out smoke. "He believed it too. Lawyers are so gullible."

"And?" says Tony.

"And, I needed to disappear. Trust me, I had my reasons. It wasn't just the money! And I *had* disappeared, I'd set up about six dead ends for anyone trying to track me down. But that dolt Mitch was following me around, he just wouldn't stop. He was really messing up my life. He was so goddamn persistent! He had the money too, he hired people; not amateurs either. He would've found me, he was right on the verge.

"People knew that; the other people, the ones I didn't really want to see. I was a bad girl, I did a shell game involving some armaments that turned out not to be where I'd said they'd be. I don't recommend it—armaments types get sniffy, especially the Irish ones. They tend to be vengeful. They figured out that all they had to do was keep an eye on Mitch and sooner or later he'd dig me up. He was the one I needed to convince, so he'd quit. So he'd lay off."

"Why Beirut?" says Tony.

"If you were going to get yourself accidentally blown up back then, what better spot to pick?" says Zenia. "The place was festooned with body parts; there were hundreds they never identified."

"You know Mitch killed himself," says Tony. "Because of you."

Zenia sighs. "Tony, grow up," she says. "It wasn't *because* of me. I was just the excuse. You think he hadn't been waiting for one? All his life, I'd say."

"Well, Roz thinks it was because of you," says Tony lamely.

"Mitch told me that sleeping with Roz was like getting into bed with a cement mixer," says Zenia.

"That's cruel," says Tony.

"Just reporting," Zenia says coolly. "Mitch was a creep. Roz is better off without him."

This is a little too close to what Tony thinks herself. She finds herself smiling; smiling, and sliding back down, back in, into that state she remembers so well. Partnership. Pal-ship. The team.

"Why us, at your funeral?" says Tony.

"Window dressing," says Zenia. "There had to be somebody there from the personal side. You know, old friends. I figured you'd all enjoy it. And anything Roz knew, Mitch would know too. She'd make sure of that! He was the one I wanted. He ducked it though. Prostrate with grief, I guess."

"The place was crawling with men in overcoats," says Tony.

"One of them was mine," says Zenia. "Checking up for me, to see who was there. A couple of them were from the opposition. Did you cry?"

"I'm not a cryer," says Tony. "Charis sniffled a bit." She's ashamed, now, of what the three of them had said, and of how jubilant and also how mean-minded they had been.

Zenia laughs. "Charis always did have mush for brains," she says.

There's a knock at the door. "It's the coffee," says Zenia. "Would you mind going?"

It occurs to Tony that Zenia may have a few reasons for not wanting to open doors. A prickle of apprehension runs up her spine.

But it really is the coffee, delivered by a short brown-faced man. The man smiles and Tony takes the tray and scrawls a tip on the bill, and closes the door softly, and puts on the safety lock. Zenia must be protected from the forces that threaten her. Protected by Tony. Right now, in this room, with Zenia finally incarnate before her, Tony can hardly remember what she's been doing for the past week—the way she's been sneaking around in a state of cold fury with a gun in her purse, selfishly planning to bump off Zenia. Why would she want to do that? Why would anyone? Zenia sweeps through life like a prow, like a galleon. She's magnificent, she's unique. She's the sharp edge.

"You said you needed to talk to me," Tony says, creating an opening.

"Want some rum in your coffee? No?" says Zenia.

She unscrews a small bottle from the mini-bar, pours herself a dollop. Then she frowns a little and lowers her voice confidentially. "Yes. I wanted to ask a favour. You're the only one I could go to, really."

Tony waits. She's alarmed again. *Watch it,* she tells herself. She should get out of here, right now! But what harm can it do to listen? And she's avid to find out what Zenia wants. Money, probably. Tony can always say no.

"All I need is to stay somewhere," says Zenia. "Not here, here's no good. With you, I thought. Just for a couple of weeks."

"Why?" says Tony.

Zenia moves her hands impatiently, scattering cigarette ashes. "Because they're looking! Not the Irish, they're off my track. It's some other people. They're not here yet, not in this city. But they'll get around to it. They'll hire local professionals."

"Then why wouldn't they try my house?" says Tony. "Wouldn't that be the first place they'd look?"

Zenia laughs, the familiar laugh, warm and charming and reckless, and contemptuous of the idiocy of others. "The *last* place!" she says. "They've done their homework, they know you hate me! You're the wife, I'm the ex-girlfriend. They'd never believe you'd let me in!"

"Zenia," says Tony, "exactly who are these people and why are they after you?"

Zenia shrugs. "Standard," she says. "I know too much."

"Oh, come on," says Tony. "I'm not a baby. Too much about what? And don't say it would be healthier for me not to hear."

Zenia leans forward. She lowers her voice. "Does the name Project Babylon mean anything to you?" she says.

She must know it does, she knows what line of knowledge Tony is in. "The Supergun for Iraq," she adds.

"Gerry Bull," says Tony. "The ballistics genius. Of course. He got murdered."

"To put it mildly," says Zenia. "Well." She blows out smoke, looking at Tony in a way that is almost coy, a fan dancer's look.

"You didn't shoot him!" says Tony, aghast. "It wasn't you!" She can't believe Zenia has actually killed someone. No: she can't believe that a person sitting in front of her, in a real room, in the real world, has actually killed someone. Such things happen offstage, elsewhere; they are indigenous to the past. Here, in this California-coloured room with its mild furniture, its neutrality, they would be anachronisms.

"Not me," says Zenia. "But I know who did."

She's lighting another cigarette, she's practically chain-smoking. The air around her is grey, and Tony is slightly dizzy. "The Israelis," she says. "Because of Iraq."

"Not the Israelis," says Zenia quickly. "That's a red herring. I was there, I was part of the set-up. I was only what you might call the messenger; but you know what happens to messengers."

Tony does know. "Oh," she says. "Oh dear."

"My best chance," says Zenia eagerly, "is to tell everything to some newspaper. Absolutely everything! Then there won't be any point in killing me, right? Also I could make a buck, I won't say that wouldn't be welcome. But nobody's going to believe me without proof. Don't worry, I've got the proof; it's not in this city but it's on the way. So I figured I could just hole up with you and West until my proof comes through. I know how it's coming, I know when. I'd be really quiet, I wouldn't need more than a sleeping bag, I could stay upstairs, in West's study. . . ."

Tony snaps to attention. The word *West* cracks across her mind: that's the key, that's what Zenia really wants, and how does Zenia know that West has a study, and that it's on the third floor? She's never seen the inside of Tony's house. Or has she?

Tony stands up. Her legs are wobbling as if she's just been pulled back from a crumbling cliff-edge. How nearly she was taken in, again! The whole Gerry Bull story is nothing but a huge lie, a custom-designed whopper. Anyone could have cobbled such a thing together just by reading *Jane's Defence Weekly* and *The Washington Post,* and Zenia—knowing Tony's weaknesses, her taste for new twists in weapons technology—must have done just that.

There is no vendetta, there is no *them,* nobody's after Zenia but the bill collector. What she wants is to break into Tony's castle, her armoured house, her one safe place, and extract West from it as if he were a snail. She wants him fresh and wriggling, speared on the end of her fork.

"I don't think that will be possible," says Tony, trying to keep her voice even. "I think I should go now."

"You don't believe me, do you?" says Zenia. Her face has gone still. "Well, help yourself to some righteous indignation, you little snot. You always were the most awful two-faced hypocrite, Tony. A smug dog-in-the-manger prune-faced little shit with megalomaniac pretensions. You think you have some kind of an adventurous mind, but spare me! At heart you're a coward, you hole yourself up in that bourgeois playpen of yours with your warped little battle-scars collection, you sit on poor West as if he's your very own fresh-laid fucking egg! I bet he's bored out of his skull, with nobody but you to stick his boring dick into! Jesus, it must be like fucking a gerbil!"

Zenia's suave velvet cloak has dropped away; underneath is raw brutality. This is what a fist sounds like just as it smashes. Tony stands in the middle of the room, her mouth opening and closing. No sound comes out. The glass walls are closing in on her. Wildly she thinks about the gun in her purse, useless, useless: Zenia is right, she could never pull the trigger. All her wars are hypothetical. She's incapable of real action.

But Zenia's expression is changing now, from angry to cunning. "You know, I've still got that term paper, the one you forged. The Russian slave trade, wasn't it? Sounds like your brand of displaced sadism, all those paper dead bodies. You're an armchair necrophiliac, you know that? You should try a real dead body some time! Maybe I'll just pop that paper in the mail, send it to your precious History Department, stir up some shit for you, a tiny scandal! I'd like that! What price academic integrity?"

Tony feels the blunt objects whizzing past her head, the ground dissolving under her feet. The History Department would be pleased, it would be more than happy to discredit and disbar. She has colleagues but no allies. Ruin looms. Zenia is pure freewheeling malevolence; she wants wreckage, she wants scorched earth, she wants broken glass. Tony makes an effort to step back from the situation, to view it as if it's something that happened long ago; as if she and Zenia are merely two small figures on a crumbling tapestry. But maybe this is what history is, when it's really taking place: enraged people yelling at one another.

Forget the ceremony. Forget the dignity. Turn tail.

Tony walks unsteadily towards the door. "Goodbye,"

she says, as firmly as she can; but her voice, to her own ears, sounds like a squeak. She has a moment of panic with the lock. As she scuttles out she expects to hear a feral growling, the thud of a heavy body against the door. But there's nothing.

She goes down in the elevator with the odd sensation that she's going up, and meanders across the lobby as if drunk, bumping into the leather furniture. There's a bunch of men checking in at the front desk. Overcoats, briefcases, must be a convention. In front of her looms the dried flower arrangement. She reaches out, watching her left hand reaching, she breaks off a stem. Something dyed purple. She makes for the doors, but finds herself at the wrong set, the ones facing the patio and the fountain. This is not the way out. She's disoriented, turned around in space: the visual world looks jumbled. She likes to have things clearly sorted in her head, but they are far from sorted.

She stuffs her filched sprig into her tote bag and aims for the front door, and wavers through it, and is finally outside, breathing in the cold air. There was so much smoke up there. She shakes her head, trying to clear it. It's as if she's been asleep.

52

This is not how Tony tells it to Roz and Charis, exactly. She leaves out the part about the term paper, although she conscientiously includes all the other bad things Zenia said about her. She·includes the gun, which has a certain serious weight, but leaves out the cordless drill, which does not. She includes her own ignominious retreat. At the end of her account she produces the purple branch, as evidence.

"I must have been a little crazy," she says. "To think I could actually kill her."

"Not so crazy," says Roz. "To *want* to kill her, anyway. She does that to people. You were lucky to get out of there with both eyes, is what I think."

Yes, thinks Tony, checking herself over. No obvious parts missing.

"Is the gun still in your purse?" Charis asks anxiously. She wouldn't want such a dangerous object colliding with her aura.

"No," says Tony. "I went home after that, I put it back."

"Good plan," says Roz. "Now you go, Charis. I'll be last."

Charis hesitates. "I don't know whether I should tell all of it," she says.

"Why not?" says Roz. "Tony did. I'm going to. Come on, we have no secrets!"

"Well," says Charis, "there's something in it you won't like."

"Heck, I probably won't like *any* of it," says Roz jovially. Her voice is a little too loud. Charis is reminded of the earlier Roz, the one who used to draw lipstick faces on her stomach and do the bump-and-grind, in the Common Room at McClung Hall. Maybe Roz is getting overexcited.

"It's about Larry," says Charis unhappily.

Roz sobers up immediately. "It's okay, sweetie," she says. "I'm a big girl."

"Nobody is," says Charis. "Not really." She takes a deep breath.

After Zenia turned up at the Toxique that day, Charis spent about a week wondering what she should do. Or rather she knew what she should do, but she didn't know how to go about doing it. Also she needed to fortify herself spiritually, because an encounter with Zenia would be no casual thing.

What she foresaw was the two of them locked in a stand-off. Zenia would be shooting out blood-red sparks of energy; her black hair would be crackling like burning fat, her eyeballs would be cerise, lit up from within like a cat's in headlights. Charis on the other hand would be cool, upright, surrounded by a gentle glow. Around her would be drawn a circle of white chalk, to keep the evil vibrations at bay. She would raise her arms upwards, invoking the sky, and out of her would come a voice like tinkling bells: *What have you done with Billy?*

And Zenia, writhing and twisting and resisting, but mastered by the superiority of Charis's positive force-field, would be compelled to tell.

Charis was not yet strong enough for this trial of strength. All by herself she might never be. She would have to borrow some weapons from her friends. No, not weapons; merely armour, because she did not see herself attacking. She didn't want to hurt Zenia, did she? She just wanted Zenia to return stolen property: Charis's life, the part with Billy in it. She wanted what was rightfully hers. That was all.

She went through some of the cardboard boxes in the small room upstairs, once a storeroom, then Zenia's room, then August's nursery and playroom, now a spare room, for guests if any. It was still August's room really; that was where she stayed on weekend visits. In the boxes were a bunch of things Charis never used and had been meaning to recycle. She found a Christmas present from Roz—a horrifying pair of gloves, leather ones with real fur cuffs, dead animal skin, she could never wear those. From Tony she found a book, a book written by Tony herself: *Four Lost Causes.* It was all about war and killing, septic topics, and Charis has never been able to get into it.

She took the book and the gloves downstairs and put them on the small table under the main window in the living room—where the sunlight would shine in on them and dispel their shadow sides—and set her amethyst geode beside them, and surrounded them with dried marigold petals. To this arrangement she added, after some thought, her grandmother's Bible, always a potent object, and a lump of earth from her garden. She meditated on this collection for twenty minutes twice a day.

What she wanted was to absorb the positive aspects of her friends, the things that were missing in herself. From Tony she wanted her mental clarity, from Roz her high-decibel metabolism and her planning abilities. And her smart mouth, because then if Zenia started insulting Charis she would be able to think up something really neutralizing to say back. From the garden earth she wanted underground power. From the Bible, what? Her grandmother's presence alone would do; her hands, her blue healing light. The marigold petals and the amethyst geode were to contain these various energies, and to channel them. What she had in mind was something concentrated, like a laser beam.

At work, Shanita notices that Charis is more absent-minded than usual. "Something bothering you?" she says.

"Well, sort of," says Charis.

"You want to do the cards?"

They are busy designing the interior for the new store. Or rather Shanita is designing it, and Charis is admiring the results. In the window there will be a large banner made of brown paper with the store name done on it in crayon, "like kids' writing," says Shanita: *Scrimpers*. At either end of the banner will be an enormous bow, also of brown paper, with packing-twine streamers coming out of it. "The idea is, everything needs to look totally basic," says Shanita. "Sort of homemade. You know, affordable." She's going to sell the hand-rubbed maple display cabinets and have different ones made out of raw boards, with the nails showing. The orange-crate look, she calls it. "We can keep some of the rocks and herbal goop, but we'll put that stuff at the back, not in the window. Luxury is not our middle name." Shanita is busy ordering fresh stock items: little kits for making seedling-transplanting pots out of recycled newspaper, other kits for pasting together your own Christmas cards out of cut-up magazines, and yet other card kits involving pressed flowers and shrink wrap that you do with a hair dryer. Kitchen-waste composters with organic wooden lids are an item; also, needlepoint kits for cushion covers, with eighteenth-century flowers on them, a fortune if you buy them already made. Also coffee grinders that work by hand, beautiful wooden ones with a drawer for the ground coffee. Minor electrical kitchen items, says Shanita, are no longer the rage. Elbow grease is back.

"What we need is stuff that makes stuff you'd otherwise have to pay a lot more for," says Shanita. "Saving, is our theme. God, I know this junk backwards, been doing it all my life. Thing is, nobody ever told me what you can make out of a million rubber bands."

She's decided to change their outfits, too: instead of the flowered pastels they'll be wearing canvas carpenter's aprons, in beige, and square caps made of folded brown paper. A pencil stuck behind the ear will complete the look. "Like we mean business," says Shanita.

Despite the admiration she's giving out, because all creativity should be supported and this is certainly creative, Charis isn't sure she'll fit in. It will be a tight squeeze, but she'll have to give it a try, because what other jobs are out there, especially for her? She might not even be able to get a job filing; not that she wants one, she doesn't consider the alphabet to be an accurate way of classifying things. If she stays she'll have to be more forceful, though; she'll have to seize hold. Get a grip. Actively sell. Shanita says that service and competitive pricing are the watchwords of the future. That, and keeping down the overheads. At least they don't have debt. "Thank God I never borrowed a lot," she says. "Banks wouldn't lend it to me, is why."

"Why wouldn't they?" says Charis.

Shanita tosses her hair—worn hanging down today in a single long shining curl—and gives her a scornful glance. "Three guesses," she says.

They take a work break in the afternoon and Shanita makes them some Lemon Refresher from their stockroom and lays out the cards for Charis. "Big event, coming up soon," she says. "What I see is—your card is the Queen of Cups, right? It's the High Priestess crossing you. Does this mean a thing?"

"Yes," says Charis. "Will I win?"

"What is this *win*?" says Shanita, smiling at her. "That's the first time I ever heard that word from you! Maybe it's time you started saying it." She peers at the cards, lays down a few more. "Looks something like winning," she says. "Anyway, you don't lose. But! There's a death. Just no way around it."

"Not Augusta!" says Charis. She's trying to see for herself: the Tower, the Queen of Swords, the Magician, the Fool. But cards are a thing she's never been able to do.

"No, no, nowhere near her," says Shanita. "This is an older person. Older than her, I mean. Related to you somehow, though. You are not going to see this death happen, but you're going to be the one finding it out."

Charis is dismayed. Billy, it must be. She will go to see Zenia, and Zenia will tell her that Billy is dead. That's what she's always dreaded. But it will be better than not knowing. There's a good side to it, as well, because when it's her own turn to make the transition and she finds herself in the dark tunnel, in the cave, on the boat, and sees the light up ahead of her, it will be Billy's voice she will hear first. He will be the one helping her, on the other side. They will be together, and he wouldn't be able to meet her like that if he hadn't died first.

It helps her, to know about the High Priestess crossing her. Also it fits, because now, finally, she's come to the chosen day, the right day to confront Zenia. She realized it as soon as she got up, as soon as she stuck her daily pin into the Bible. It picked out Revelations Seventeen, the chapter about the Great Whore: *And the woman was arrayed in purple and scarlet colour, and decked with gold and precious stones and pearls, having a golden cup in her hand full of abominations and filthiness of her fornication: And upon her forehead was written, MYSTERY, BABYLON THE GREAT, THE MOTHER OF HAR-LOTS AND ABOMINATIONS OF THE EARTH.*

Behind Charis's closed eyelids the form took shape, the outline—crimson around the edges, with scintillations of diamond-hard light. She couldn't see the face; though who else could it be but Zenia?

• • •

"That's why I thought it was such a—well, so right," says Charis to Tony.

"That what was?" says Tony patiently.

"What you said. About Project Babylon. I mean, it couldn't just be a coincidence, could it?"

Tony opens her mouth to say that it could be, but shuts it again because Roz has given her a nudge under the table.

"Go on," says Roz.

Charis wades through the city, breathing airborne sludge. Past the BamBoo Club with its hot-coloured Caribbean graphics, past Zephyr with its shells and crystals, a place where she usually browses, but today she pushes past it with hardly a look, past the Dragon Lady comic book shop, hurrying because she has a deadline. It's her lunch break. She doesn't usually take much time for lunch because lunchtime is the busiest time, but they've closed the store for a few days while the new counters and the brown-paper bows are being put in place, so today she can make an exception. She's asked Shanita for an extra half-hour; she'll make it up by staying later, some day after they've reopened. That will give her time to get to the Arnold Garden Hotel, to see Zenia and ask what she needs to ask, to extract the answer. Supposing Zenia is at the hotel, of course. She could always be out.

When she was getting dressed this morning, washing herself in her drafty bathroom, it occurred to Charis that although she knew the name of the hotel she didn't know the room number. She could always go to the hotel and poke around, walk up and down the corridors feeling the doorknobs; perhaps she would be able to pick up the electrical currents by touching the metal, sense the presence of Zenia through her fingertips behind the right door. But the hotel would be full of people, and those other people would create static. She could so easily make a mistake.

Then it came to her during the ferry ride to the mainland that there was one person who would be sure to know what room Zenia was staying in. Roz's son Larry would know, because Charis had seen the two of them go into the hotel together.

"This is the part I didn't want to tell you," says Charis to Roz. "That day at the Toxique? I waited in the Kafay Nwar, across the street. I saw them come out. I followed them. Zenia and Larry."

"*You* followed them?" says Roz, as if somebody else has followed them too, and she knows who.

"I just wanted to ask her about Billy," says Charis.

Roz pats her hand. "Of course you did!" she says.

"I saw them kissing, on the street," says Charis, apologetically.

"It's okay, baby," says Roz. "Don't worry about me."

"Charis!" says Tony, with admiration. "You're a lot more cunning than I thought!" The idea of Charis tiptoeing around behind Zenia's back fills her with pleasure, because it's so unlikely. Whoever else Zenia might have suspected of shadowing her, it sure as hell wouldn't have been Charis.

●   ●   ●

When Charis arrived at the store that morning, and after Shanita had gone out to pick up some small change from the bank, she called Roz's house. If anyone answered at all it would be Larry, because by this time the twins would be at school and Roz would be at work. She was right, it was Larry.

"Hello, Larry, it's Aunt Charis," she said. She felt stupid calling herself Aunt Charis, but it was a custom Roz had begun when the kids were little and it had never been abandoned.

"Oh, hi, Aunt Charis," said Larry. He sounded half asleep. "Mom's at work."

"Well, but it was you I wanted to talk to," said Charis. "I'm looking for Zenia. You know, Zenia, maybe you remember her, from when you were little." (How little had Larry been? she wonders. Not that little. How much had Roz ever told him, about Zenia? She hopes not much.) "We were all at university together. I'm supposed to meet her at the Arnold Garden Hotel, but I've lost the room number." This was a big lie; she felt guilty about it, and at the same time resentful towards Zenia for putting her in such a position. That was the thing about Zenia: she dragged you down to her own level.

There was a long pause. "Why ask me?" Larry said finally, guardedly.

"Oh," said Charis, playing up her usual vagueness, "she knows what a bad memory I have! She knows I'm not the best organizer. She said if I lost it, to call you. She said you'd know. I'm sorry if I woke you up," she added.

"That was pretty dumb of her," said Larry. "I'm not her answering service. Why don't you just phone the hotel?" This was strangely rude, for Larry. As a rule he was more polite.

"I would have," said Charis, "but, you know, her last name isn't the same as it used to be and I'm afraid I've forgotten the new one." This is a guess—the new last name—but it's the right guess. Tony once said that Zenia probably had a different name every year. Roz said, No, every month, she probably subscribed to the Name-of-the-Month Club.

"She's in 1409," Larry said sulkily.

"Oh, just let me write that down," said Charis. "Fourteen-oh-nine?" She wanted to sound as dithery and forgetful as possible; as much like an aging feather-brained biddy, as least like a threat. She didn't want Larry phoning Zenia, and warning her.

The significance of the room number does not escape her. Hotels, she knows, never number the thirteenth floor, but it exists anyway. The fourteenth floor is really the thirteenth. Zenia is on the thirteenth floor. But the bad luck of that may be balanced by the good luck of nine, because nine is a Goddess number. But the bad luck will attach itself to Zenia and the good luck to Charis, because Charis is pure in heart—or she's trying to be—and Zenia is not. Calculating in her head and clothing herself with light, Charis reaches the Arnold Garden Hotel, and walks under the intimidating awning and in through the glittering brass-trimmed glass doors as if there is nothing to it.

She stands in the lobby for a moment, catching her breath, getting her bearings. It's not a bad lobby. Although there's a lot of murdered-animal furniture, she's pleased to see that there's a sort of vegetation altarpiece as well: dried flowers. And through the plate glass doors at the back there's a courtyard with a fountain, though the fountain isn't turned on. She likes to see urban space moving in a more natural direction.

· Then all of a sudden she has a discouraging thought. What if Zenia has no soul? There must be people like that around, because there are more humans alive on the earth right now than have ever lived, altogether, since humans began, and if souls are recycled then there must be some people alive today who didn't get one, sort of like musical chairs. Maybe Zenia is like that: soulless. Just a sort of shell. In this case, how will Charis be able to deal with her?

This idea is paralyzing. In its grip Charis stands stock-still in the middle of the lobby. But she can't turn back now. She closes her eyes and visualizes her altar, with the gloves and the earth and the Bible, calling upon its powers; then she opens them and waits for an omen. In one corner of the lobby there's a grandfather clock. It's almost noon. Charis watches until both hands of the clock are aligned, pointing straight up. Then she gets onto the elevator. With every floor she passes, her heart beats harder.

On the fourteenth floor, really the thirteenth, she stands outside 1409. A reddish grey light oozes out through the crack under the door, pushing her backwards with palpable force. She puts her palm against the wood of the door, which vibrates in silent menace. It's like a train going by at a distance, or a slow explosion far away. Zenia must be in there.

Charis knocks.

After a moment—during which she can feel Zenia's

eye on her, through the glass peephole—Zenia opens the door. She's wearing one of the hotel bathrobes, and has her hair wrapped in a towel. She must have been taking a shower. Even with the terry-cloth turban on her head she is shorter than Charis remembers. This is a relief.

"I was wondering when you'd get here," she says.

"You were?" says Charis. "How did you know?"

"Larry told me you were on your way," says Zenia. "Come in." Her voice is flat, her face is weary. Charis is surprised at how old she looks. Maybe it's because she isn't wearing any makeup. If Charis didn't know better by now than to leap to such conclusions, she would think Zenia is ill.

The room is a mess.

"Just a minute," says Tony. "Go over that part again. You were there at noon and the room was a mess?"

"She was always messy when she lived with me, that time, on the Island," says Charis. "She never helped with the dishes or anything."

"But when I was there earlier, everything was really neat," says Tony. "The bed was made. Everything."

"Well, it wasn't," says Charis. "There were pillows on the floor, the bed was a wreck. Dirty coffee cups, potato chips, clothes lying around. There was broken glass on the coffee table, the rug too. It was like there'd been a party all night."

"You sure it was the same room?" says Tony. "Maybe she lost her temper and smashed a few glasses."

"She must have gone back to bed," says Roz. "After you left."

They all consider that. Charis goes on:

•   •   •

The room is a mess. The flowered drapes are pulled half shut, as if they've been closed recently against the light. Zenia steps over the items strewn on the floor, sits down on the sofa, and picks up a cigarette from the dozen or so that are scattered around in the broken glass on the coffee table. "I know I shouldn't smoke," she murmurs, as if to herself, "but it hardly matters, now. Sit down, Charis. I'm glad you've come."

Charis sits down in the armchair. This is not the charged confrontation she's been imagining. Zenia isn't trying to evade her; if anything, she seems mildly pleased that Charis is here. Charis reminds herself that what she needs is to find out about Billy, where he is, whether he's alive or dead. But it's hard to concentrate on Billy; she can scarcely remember what Billy used to look like, whereas Zenia is sitting right here in the room. It's so strange to see her in the flesh, at last.

Now she's smiling wanly. "You were so good to me," she says. "I've always meant to apologize for going away like that, without saying goodbye. It was very thoughtless of me. But I was too dependent on you, I was letting you try to cure me instead of putting the energy into it myself. I just needed to get off somewhere, be alone so I could focus. It was—well, I got a sort of message, you know?"

Charis is amazed. Maybe she's been misjudging Zenia, all these years. Or maybe Zenia has changed. People can change, they can choose, they can transform themselves. It's a deep belief of hers. She isn't sure what to think.

"You didn't really have cancer," she says finally. She doesn't intend it as an accusation. Only she needs to be sure.

"No," says Zenia. "Not exactly. I *was* sick, though. It

was a spiritual illness. And I'm sick now." She pauses, but when Charis doesn't ask, she says, "That's why I'm back here—for the health care system. I couldn't afford treatment anywhere else. They've told me I'm dying. They've given me six months."

"Oh, that's too bad," says Charis. She's looking at Zenia's edges, to see what colour her light is, but she's not getting a reading. "Is it cancer?"

"I don't know if I should tell you," says Zenia

"It's okay," says Charis, because what if Zenia is telling the truth, this time? What if she really is dying? She does have a greyish tinge, around the eyes. The least Charis can do is listen.

"Well, actually, I've got AIDS," says Zenia and sighs. "It's really stupid. I had a bad habit, a few years back. I got it off a dirty needle."

Charis gasps. This is terrible! What about Larry, then? Will he get AIDS, too? *Roz! Roz! Come quickly!* But what could Roz do?

"I wouldn't mind spending a little time, somewhere peaceful," says Zenia. "Just to get my head in order, before, you know. Some place like the Island."

Charis feels the familiar tug, the old temptation. Maybe there's no hope for Zenia's body, but the body isn't the only factor. She could have Zenia over to stay with her, the way she did before. She could help her to move towards the transition, she could put light around her, they could meditate together. . . .

"Or maybe I'll just check myself out," says Zenia softly. "Pills or something. I'm doomed anyway. I mean, why wait around?"

In Charis's throat the familiar sentiments bubble up.

Oh no, you must try, you must try for the positive. . . . She opens her mouth to issue the invitation, *Yes, come,* but something stops her. It's the look Zenia is giving her: an intent look, head on one side. A bird eyeing a worm.

"Why did you pretend to me, about the cancer?" she says.

Zenia laughs. She sits up briskly. She must know that she's lost, she must know that Charis won't believe her, about having AIDS. "Okay," she says. "We might as well get this over. Let's just say I wanted you to let me into your house, and it seemed the quickest way."

"That was mean," says Charis. "I believed you! I was very concerned about you! I tried to save you!"

"Yes," says Zenia cheerfully. "But don't worry, I suffered too. If I'd had to drink one more glass of that foul cabbage juice it would've finished me off. You know what I did when I hit the mainland? First chance I got, I went out and had a big plate of fries and a nice raw juicy steak. I would've inhaled it, I was so starved for red meat!"

"But you really were sick, with something," Charis says hopefully. Auras don't lie, and Zenia's was diseased. Also, she doesn't want to think that every single one of those vegetables went to waste.

"There's a trick you ought to know about," says Zenia. "Just cut out all the vitamin C from your diet and you get the early symptoms of scurvy. Nobody's expecting scurvy, not in the twentieth century, so they don't spot it."

"But I fed you lots of vitamin C!" says Charis.

"Try sticking your finger down your throat," says Zenia. "Works wonders."

"But why?" says Charis helplessly. "Why did you?"

She feels so defrauded—defrauded of her own goodness, her own willingness to be of service. Such a fool.

"Because of Billy, naturally," Zenia says. "Nothing personal, you were merely the means. I wanted to get close to him."

"Because you were in love with him?" says Charis. At least that would be understandable, at least there would be something positive about it, because love is a positive force. She can understand being in love with Billy.

Zenia laughs. "You are such a dipstick romantic," she says. "By your age you ought to know better. No, I was not in *love* with Billy, though the sex was fun."

"Fun?" says Charis. In her experience, sex was never fun. It was either nothing, or it was painful; or it was overwhelming, it put you at risk; which is why she's avoided it all these years. But not *fun*.

"Yeah, it may come as a surprise," says Zenia, "that some people think it's fun. Not you, I realize that. From what Billy said, you wouldn't know fun if you fell over it. He was so hungry for a little good sex that he jumped me almost as soon as I walked into that pathetic shack of yours. What do you think we were doing when you were over on the mainland teaching that tedious yoga class? Or when you were downstairs cooking our breakfasts, or outside feeding those brain-damaged hens?"

Charis knows she must not cry. Zenia may have been *sex*, but Charis was *love*, for Billy. "Billy loved me," she says uncertainly.

Zenia smiles. Her energy level is up now, her body's humming like a broken toaster. "Billy didn't love you," she says. "Wake up! You were a free meal-ticket! He was eating off you even though he had money of his own; he was peddling hash, but I guess that one went right past you. He thought you were a cow, if you must know. He thought you were so stupid you'd give birth to an idiot. He thought you were a stunned cunt, to be exact."

"Billy would never say a thing like that," says Charis. She feels as if a net of hot sharp wires is being pulled tight around her, the hairline burns cutting into her skin.

"He thought having sex with you was like porking a turnip," Zenia goes on relentlessly. "Now listen to me, Charis. This is for your own good. I know you, and I can guess how you've been spending your time. Dressing up in hair shirts. Playing hermits. Mooning around after Billy. He's just an excuse for you; he lets you avoid your life. Give him up. Forget about him."

"I can't forget about him," says Charis in a tiny voice. How can she just sit here and let Zenia tear Billy to shreds? The memory of Billy. If that goes, what does she have left of all that time? Nothing. A void.

"Read my lips, he wasn't worth it," says Zenia. She sounds exasperated. "You know what I was really there for? To turn him around. And, believe me, he was easy to turn."

"Turn?" says Charis. She can hardly concentrate; she feels as if she's being slapped in the face, on one side of the face and then the other. *Turn the other cheek.* But how often?

"Turn, as in turncoat," says Zenia, explaining as if to a child. "Billy turned informer. He went back to the States and ratted on all his incendiary-minded little friends, the ones who were still there."

"I don't believe you," says Charis.

"I don't care whether you believe me or not," says

Zenia. "It's true, all the same. He traded his pals in to get himself off the hook and make a bit of cash. They paid him off with a new identity and a sordid little job as a third-rate spy. He wasn't very good at it, though. Last time I ran into him, in Baltimore or somewhere, he was pretty disillusioned. A broken-down acid-head and whining drunk, and bald as well."

"You did that to him," Charis whispers. "You ruined him." Golden Billy.

"Bullshit," says Zenia. "That's what *he* said, but I hardly twisted his arm! I just told him the choices. Billy's choice was either that, or something quite a lot worse. In the real world most people choose to save their own skins. It's something you can count on, nine times out of ten."

"You were with the Mounties," says Charis. This is the hardest thing to believe—it's so incongruous. Zenia on the side of law and order.

"Not quite," says Zenia. "I've always been a free agent. Billy was just a sort of opportunity I saw. Those sanctimonious liberal help-a-dodger groups were infiltrated up to their armpits, and I had connections, so I got a peek at the files. I remembered you from McClung Hall— they had a file on you, too, you know, though I told them why waste the paper, not to mention the taxpayers' hard-earned money, it was like having a file on a jar of jelly— and I was counting on it that you'd remember me. It wasn't hard to get myself a black eye and turn up in your yoga class. Hell, you did the rest! Now, if you don't mind, I have to get dressed, I've got things to do. Billy lives in Washington, by the way. If you want to stage a joyful reunion with him and his long-lost daughter, I'd be happy to give you his address."

"I don't think so," says Charis. Her legs are shaking; she's afraid, for a minute, to stand up. Billy lies shattered in her head. *Wipe the tape,* she tells herself, but the tape won't wipe. She realizes that she has no weapons, no weapons that will work against Zenia. All Charis has on her side is a wish to be good, and goodness is an absence, it's the absence of evil; whereas Zenia has the real story.

Zenia shrugs. "Up to you," she says. "If I were you, I'd scratch him right off my list."

"I don't think I can," says Charis.

"Suit yourself," says Zenia. She stands up and walks to the closet and starts checking through her dresses.

There is one more thing Charis wants to know, and she summons all of her strength to ask it. "Why did you kill my chickens?" she says. "They weren't hurting anyone."

"I did not kill your fucking chickens," says Zenia, turning around. She sounds amused. "Billy killed them. He enjoyed doing it, too. Tiptoed out before dawn when you were still in dreamland, and slit their throats with the bread knife. Said it was doing them a favour, the way you kept them in that filthy hen slum of yours. But the truth is, he hated them. Not only that, he had a good laugh, thinking about you going into the henhouse and finding them. Sort of like a practical joke. He got a kick out of that."

Inside Charis, something breaks. Rage takes her over. She wants to squeeze Zenia, squeeze her and squeeze her by the neck until Charis's life, her own life that she has imagined, all of the good things about her life that Zenia has drunk, come welling out like water from a sponge. The violence of her own reaction dismays her but she's lost control. She feels her body filled and surrounded with a white-hot light; wings of flame shoot out from her.

Then she is over behind the flowered drapes, near the door to the balcony, outside her own body, watching. The body stands there. Someone else is in charge of it now. It's Karen. Charis can see her, a dark core, a shadow, with long raggedy hair, grown big now, grown huge. She's been waiting all the time, all these years, for a moment like this, a moment when she could get back into Charis's body and use it to murder. She moves Charis's hands towards Zenia, her hands that flicker with a blue light; she is irresistibly strong, she rushes at Zenia like a silent wind, she pushes her backwards, right through the balcony door, and broken glass scatters like ice. Zenia is purple and red and flashing like jewels but she is no match for shadowy Karen. She lifts Zenia up—Zenia is light, she's hollow, she's riddled with disease and rotten, she's insubstantial as paper—and throws her over the balcony railing; she watches her flutter down, down from the tower, and hit the edge of the fountain, and burst like an old squash. Hidden behind the flowered drapes, Charis calls plaintively: *No! No!* Not bloodshed, not the dogs eating the pieces in the courtyard, she doesn't want that. Does she?

"Anyway, it's all ancient history," says Zenia conversationally. Charis is back in her own body, she's in control of it, she's moving it towards the door. Nothing has happened after all. Surely nothing has happened. She turns and looks at Zenia. Black lines are radiating out from her, like the filaments of a spider web. No. Black lines are converging on her, targeting her; soon she will be ensnarled. In the centre of them her soul flutters, a pale moth. She does have a soul after all.

Charis gathers up all her strength, all her inner light; she calls on it for what she has to do, because it will take a lot of effort. Whatever Zenia has done, however evil she has been, she needs help. She needs help from Charis, on the spiritual plane.

Charis's mouth opens. "I forgive you," is what she hears herself saying.

Zenia laughs angrily. "Who do you think you are?" she says. "Why should I give a flying fuck whether you forgive me or not? Stuff your forgiveness! Get a man! Get a life!"

Charis sees her life the way Zenia must see it: an empty cardboard box, overturned by the side of the road, with nobody in it. Nobody worth mentioning. This is somehow the most hurtful thing of all.

She invokes her amethyst geode, closes her eyes, sees crystal. "I have a life," she says. She straightens her shoulders and turns the doorknob, holding back tears.

Not until she is walking unsteadily across the lobby towards the front door does it cross Charis's mind that maybe Zenia was lying. Maybe she was lying about Billy, about the chickens, about everything. She has lied to Charis before, and just as convincingly. Why wouldn't she be doing it now?

53

Roz leans sideways and gives Charis a one-armed hug. "Of course she was lying," she says. "Billy wouldn't say such a thing." What does she know from Billy? Not a shred, she never met him, but she's willing to give him the benefit of the doubt, because what does it cost, and anyway she wants to lighten things up. "Zenia's just malicious. She says stuff like that just for the heck of it. She only wanted to bother you."

"But why?" says Charis, on the verge of tears. "Why would she, why did she say that? She was so negative. It really hurt. Now I don't know what to think."

"It's okay, babe," says Roz, giving Charis another squeeze. "The heck with her! We won't invite her to our birthday parties, will we?"

"For heaven's sake," says Tony, because Roz always goes too far and Tony is finding this scene much too infantile for her taste. "This is critical!"

"Yes," says Roz, getting a grip, "I know it is."

"I do have a life," says Charis, blinking wet eyes.

"You have a rich inner life," says Tony firmly. "More than most." She digs into her bag, finds a crumpled tissue, hands it to Charis. Charis blows her nose.

"Now, here's me," says Roz. "Ms. Mature Fuller Figure meets the Queen of the Night. On the enjoyment scale, it didn't get ten out of ten."

Roz is in her office, pacing, pacing. On her desk is a stack of files, project files and charitable-donation files both, the Livers, the Kidneys, the Lungs, and the Hearts all clamouring for attention, not to mention the Bag Ladies and the Battered Wives, but they will all have to wait, because in order to give you have to make, it doesn't grow on trees. She's supposed to be thinking about the Rubicon project, as presented by Lookmakers. *Lipsticks for the Nineties* is the concept they're proposing, which Boyce says translates as Oral Glues for Nonagenarians. But Roz can't get her teeth into it, she's too preoccupied. Preoccupied? Frenzied! Her body's a hormone-fuelled swelter, the inside of her head's like a car wash, all those brushes whirring around, suds flying, vision obscured. Zenia's on the prowl, and God knows where! She might be climbing up the side of this building even now, with suckers attached to the bottoms of her feet like a fly.

Roz has eaten all the Mozart Balls, she's smoked every single cigarette, and one of Boyce's drawbacks, his only one really, is that he doesn't smoke, so she can't bum a fag off him, oops, pardon the pun; his lungs at any rate are pure as the driven. Maybe the new downstairs receptionist—Mitzi, Bambi?—might have a pack tucked away; she could call down, but how demeaning, Ms. Boss clawing the walls for a cig.

She doesn't want to leave the building right now, because it's about time for Harriet the detective to call.

Roz has asked her to call every afternoon at three to fill her in on progress. "We're narrowing it down," was all Harriet said for the first few days. But yesterday she said, "There's two possibilities. One's at the King Eddie, the other one's at the Arnold Garden. The people we've been able to—the people who have kindly agreed to identify the photo—each one of them is sure it's got to be her."

"What makes you think you have to choose?" said Roz.

"Pardon?" said Harriet.

"Bet you anything she's got rooms at both of those hotels," said Roz. "It would be just like her! Two names, two rooms." *All foxes dig back doors.* "What're the room numbers?"

"Let us do a little more checking," said Harriet cautiously. "I'll let you know." She could evidently visualize an undesirable situation: Roz barging into some stranger's room, hurling furniture and accusations and breathing fire, and Harriet getting hit with a lawsuit for having given her the wrong room number.

So now Roz is on tenterhooks, whatever those are. Something her mother knew about, because it was her expression. She makes a mental note to ask Boyce about it, and shakes herself, and sits down at her desk, and opens up the Lipsticks for the Nineties file that Boyce has annotated for her. She likes the business plan, she likes the projections; but Boyce is right, the name itself is wrong, because they'll want to expand the line beyond lipsticks. An eye shadow that would also shrink puffy lids would be a breakthrough, she'd buy that, and if she would buy a thing it's a cinch that a lot of other women would, as well, if the price is right. For another thing, *the Nineties* has to go. The nineties have not been great news so far, even though there's only been a year of them, so why underline the fact that everyone's stuck in them?

No, Roz is agreed—reading Boyce's tidy notes in the margins of the proposal, he has real talent, that boy—that they should opt for time travel, some history, the big H, via the river names tie-in. Women always find it easier to visualize themselves as having a romantic fling of it in some other age, an age before flush toilets and Jacuzzis and electric coffee grinders, an age in which a bunch of tubercular, prematurely wrinkled servants would have had to wash the men's undershorts, if any, by hand, and empty the slop pots and heat up the water in big cauldrons, in filthy rat-infested kitchens, and trample the coffee beans underfoot like grapes. Give Roz appliances any day. Appliances with warranties, and dependable household help that comes in twice a week.

As for the ads, she wants a lot of lace in them. Lace, and a wind machine, to blow the hair around for that burning-of-Charleston dramatic-crisis look. It will help to shoot the models on an angle, with the camera slanted up. Statuesque, monumental, as long as you can't see up their nostrils, which is the problem Roz has always had with bronze heroes on horseback. She's thought of another river name too, another colour: *Athabasca*. A sort of bronzed pink. Frostbite crossed with exposure. How you get in the North without sunblock.

The phone rings and Roz practically falls on it. "Harriet," says Harriet. "It's the Arnold Garden for sure, Room

1409. I went there myself and pretended to be a chambermaid with towels. No doubt about it."

"Great," says Roz, and jots down the room number.

"There's one other thing you ought to know," says Harriet. "Before you rush in."

"What, where angels fear to tread?" says Roz impatiently. "What is it?"

"She appears to be having an affair, or something, with . . . well, with a much younger man. He's been with her in her room almost every day, according to our source."

Why is Harriet sounding so coy? thinks Roz. "That wouldn't surprise me," she says. "Zenia would rob anything, cradles included. As long as he's rich."

"He is," says Harriet. "So to speak. Or he will be." There's a hesitation.

"Why are you telling me this?" says Roz. "I don't care who she's screwing!"

"You asked me to find out everything," says Harriet reproachfully. "I don't know quite how to put it. The young man in question appears to be your son."

"What?" says Roz.

After hanging up, she grabs her purse and hits the elevator and then the sidewalk at a fast trot, the nearest she can get to a run, what with her wicked shoes. She makes it to the nearest Becker's and buys three packs of du Mauriers and tears one open with trembling fingers, and lights up so fast she practically sets fire to her hair. She'll kill Zenia, she'll kill her! The effrontery, the brass, the consummate *bad taste,* to go after small helpless Larry, Larry son of Mitch, after doing away with his father! Well, as good as doing away. *Pick on somebody your own size!* And Larry, a sitting duck, poor baby; so lonely, so scrambled. Probably he remembers Zenia from when he was fifteen; probably he had a jerk-off crush on her, back then. Probably he thinks she's glamorous, and warm and understanding. Zenia has a good line in the glamour and understanding department. Plus, she'll tell him a few hard-luck stories of her own and he'll think they're both orphans of the storm together. Roz can't stand it!

Smoke percolates through her, and after a while she feels a little calmer. She walks back to the office, her head sizzling slowly. What exactly, what the *fuck,* is she supposed to do now?

She knocks on Boyce's door. "Boyce? Mind if I pick your brain for a minute?" she says.

Boyce stands up courteously and offers her a chair. "Ask, and it shall be given you," he says. "God."

"Don't I know it," says Roz, "but I haven't been getting such great results from God lately, in the answer department." She sits down, crosses her legs, and takes the cup of coffee Boyce provides. The part in his hair is so straight it's almost painful, as if done with a knife. His tie has tiny ducks on it. "Let me put a theoretical case to you," she says.

"I'm all ears," says Boyce. "Is this about Oral Glues?"

"No," says Roz. "It's a story. Once upon a time there was a woman who was married to a guy who used to fool around."

"Anyone I know?" says Boyce. "The guy, I mean."

"With other women," says Roz firmly. "Well, this woman put up with it for the sake of the kids, and anyway these things never lasted long because the other women were just wind-up sex toys, or that's what the man kept saying. According to him our heroine was the real thing, the apple of his eyes, the fire in his fireplace, and so on. Then one day, along comes this bimbo—excuse me, this *person* about the same age as the woman in question, only, I have to admit it, quite a lot better-looking, though between you and me and the doorpost her tits were fake."

"She walks in beauty, like the blight," says Boyce with sympathy. "Byron."

"Exactly," says Roz. "She was smart, as well, but if she was a guy you'd have to call her a prick. I mean, there is no female name for it, because *bitch* doesn't even begin to cover it! She tells some story about being a half-Jewish war orphan rescued from the Nazis, and our heroine, who is all heart, falls for it and gets her a job; and Ms. Dirigible-chest pretends to be our pal's grateful buddy, and gives the husband the cold shoulder, implying by her body language that she finds him less attractive than a lawn dwarf, which turned out to be the ultimate truth, in the end.

"Meanwhile our two girl chums have a lot of cosy networking lunches together, discussing world affairs and the state of the business. Then the lady starts having it off with Mr. Susceptible, behind Ms. Numskull's back. For Ms. Lollapalooza it's just a *thing*—worse, a tactic—but for him it's the real item, the grand passion at last. I don't know how she did it, but she did. Considering it was him, and thousands before her had failed, she was nothing short of brilliant."

"Genius is an infinite capacity for causing pain," says Boyce sombrely.

"Right," says Roz. "So she cons everyone into putting

her in charge of the business in question, which is a medium-hefty enterprise, and before you know it she's moved in with Mr. Sticky Fingers, and they're living together in the Designer Love-nest of the Year, leaving the wee missus to gnaw her stricken little heart out, which she does. But passion wanes, on Vampira's part, not his, when he finds out she's been having nooners with some stud on a motorcycle and fusses up about it. So she forges a few cheques—using his signature, copied no doubt from countless drool-covered mash notes—and disappears with the cash. Does that cool his ardour? Do chickens have tits? He goes raving off after her as if his pants were plugged into the light socket."

"I know the plot," says Boyce. "Happens in all walks of life."

"Ms. Lightfingers disappears," says Roz, "but next thing you know, she turns up in a metal soup can. Seems she's met with a nasty accident, and now she's cat food. She gets planted in the cemetery, not that I—not that my friend shed any tears—and Mr. Sorrowful comes creeping back to wee wifey, who stands on her hind legs and refuses to take him in. Well, can you blame her? I mean, enough is enough. So, instead of getting his head shrunk, which was long overdue, or picking up some new little sex gadget, as he has done many times before, what does he do? He's dying of love, not for Mrs. Domestic but for Ms. Fiery Loins. So he goes out on his boat in a hurricane and gets himself drowned. Maybe he even jumped. Who knows?"

"A waste," says Boyce. "Bodies are so much nicer alive."

"There's more," says Roz. "It turns out this woman wasn't dead after all. She was just fooling. She turns up again, and this time she gets her hooks into the only son—the one and only well-beloved son—I mean, can you imagine? She must be fifty! She gets her hooks into the son of the woman she ripped off and the man she as good as killed!"

"This is turgid," Boyce murmurs.

"Listen, I didn't write the plot," says Roz. "I'm just telling you, and a literary criticism I don't need. What I want to know is—what would you do?"

"You're asking *me*?" Boyce says. "What would *I* do? First, I'd make sure she was really a woman. It could be a man in a dress."

"Boyce, this is serious," says Roz.

"I am serious," says Boyce. "But what you really mean is, what should *you* do. Right?"

"In a word," says Roz.

"Obsession is the better part of valour," says Boyce. "Shakespeare."

"Meaning?"

"You'll have to go and see her," Boyce sighs. "Have it out. Oh Roz, thou art sick. Have a scene. Shout and yell. Tell her what you think of her. Clear the air; believe me, it's necessary. Otherwise, the invisible worm that flies in the storm will find out thy bed of crimson joy, and its dark secret love will thy life destroy. Blake."

"I guess so," says Roz. "I just don't trust myself, is all. Boyce, what is a tenterhook?"

"A wooden frame covered with hooks, on which cloth was stretched for drying," says Boyce.

"Not a lot of help," says Roz.

"Though true," says Boyce.

● ● ●

Roz sets out for the Arnold Garden Hotel. She takes a taxi because she's too keyed up to drive. She doesn't even need to ask at the desk, which is clogged with what look to her like travelling salesmen; she just quick-steps through the deplorable lobby, with its tawdry retro leather sofas and *Canadian Woman* spray-paint-it-yourself tacky flower arrangement *circa* 1984, and the view of the tatty little patio and City Hall Modern cement fountain visible through the glass doors, this is to *garden* as prepackaged microwave meals are to *food,* and straight into the plastic-leather-padded elevator.

All the time she's rehearsing: *Wasn't one enough? You gonna kill my son, too? Get your claws off my child!* She feels like a tigress, defending her young. Or this is what tigresses are rumoured to do. *I'll huff and I'll puff,* she roars inwardly, *and I'll blow your house down!*

Except that Zenia was never much of a one for houses. Only for breaking into them.

At the back of her mind is another scenario: what happens when Larry finds out what she's done? He is, after all, twenty-two. That's well over the age of consent. If he wants to screw cheerleaders or St. Bernard dogs or aging vamps like Zenia, what business is it, really, of hers? She pictures his glance of patient, exasperated contempt, and flinches.

Knock, knock, knock, she goes on Zenia's door. Just making a noise recoups her strength. *Open up, you pig, you sow, and let me in!*

And clickety-clack, here comes somebody. The door opens a crack. It's on the chain. "Who is it?" says the smoky voice of Zenia.

"It's me," says Roz. "It's Roz. You might as well let me in, because if you don't I'm just going to stand here and scream."

Zenia opens the door. She's dressed to go out, in the same low-cut black dress that Roz remembers from the Toxique. Her face is made up, her hair is loose, waving and coiling and uncoiling itself in restless tendrils around her head. There's a suitcase open on the bed.

"A suitcase?" says Tony. "I didn't see any suitcases."

"Me neither," says Charis. "Was the room tidy?"

"Fairly tidy," says Roz. "But this was later in the afternoon. After you were there. Most likely the maid had come."

"What was in the suitcase?" says Tony. "Was she packing? Maybe she's planning to leave."

"It was empty," says Roz. "I looked."

"Roz!" says Zenia. "What a surprise! Come on in—you're looking terrific!"

Roz knows she is not looking terrific: anyway, *looking terrific* is what people say about women her age who are not actually dead. Zenia, on the other hand, really is looking terrific. Doesn't she ever age? thinks Roz bitterly. What kind of blood does she drink? *Just one wrinkle, just a little one, God; would it be so hard? Tell me again—why do the wicked prosper?*

Roz does not beat about the bush. "What do you think you're up to, having a thing with Larry?" she says. "Don't you have any, any *scruples* at all?"

Zenia looks at her. "A *thing*? What a delicious idea! Did he tell you that?"

"He's been seen, going into your hotel room. More than once," says Roz.

Zenia smiles gently. "Seen? Don't tell me you've got that Hungarian following me around again. Roz, why don't you sit down? Have a drink or something. I never had anything against you personally." She herself sits demurely down on the flowered sofa, as if there's nothing at all going on; as if they're two respectable matrons about to have afternoon tea. "Believe me, Roz. My feelings for Larry are only maternal."

"What do you mean, maternal?" says Roz. She feels stupid standing up, so she sits in the matching chair. Zenia is hunting for her cigarettes. She finds the pack, shakes it: empty. "Have one of mine," says Roz reluctantly.

"Thanks," says Zenia. "I ran into him by accident, in the Toxique. He remembered me—well, he would, he was—what? Fifteen? He wanted to talk to me about his father. So touching! You really haven't been very forthcoming on that subject with him, have you, Roz? A boy needs to know something about his father; something good. Don't you think?"

"So, what exactly have you been telling him?" says Roz suspiciously.

"Nothing but the best," says Zenia. She lowers her eyes modestly. "I think it's sometimes in everyone's best interests to bend the truth a little, don't you? It doesn't cost me anything, and poor Larry does seem to want a father he can look up to."

Roz can hardly believe what she's hearing. In fact she doesn't believe it. There must be more, and there is. "Of course, if this situation goes on much longer it might become more complicated," says Zenia. "I might forget, and tell a little too much of the truth. About what a twisted jerk poor Larry's father really was."

Roz sees red. She actually sees it, a red haze obscuring her eyes. It's one thing for her to criticize Mitch, but another thing for Zenia! "You used him," she says. "You cleaned him out, you sucked him dry, then you just threw him away! You're responsible for his death, you know. He killed himself because of you. I don't think you're in any position to stand in judgment."

"You want to know?" says Zenia. "You really want to know? After I told him it wasn't going to work out, because he was just too besotted—shit, I could hardly breathe, he was a control freak, I had no life of my own, he wanted to know what I had for breakfast, he wanted to come into the bathroom with me every time I needed to pee, I mean it!—he practically tried to kill me! I had the marks on my neck for weeks; good thing I wasn't too squeamish to kick him in the nuts, as hard as I could, to make him let go. Then he cried all over me; he wanted the two of us to make some stupid suicide pact, so we could be together in death! Oh, fun! Fuck that, I told him! So don't blame me. I wash my hands."

Roz can't stand hearing this, she can't stand it! Poor Mitch, reduced to that. An abject groveller. "You could have helped him," she said. "He needed help!" Roz could have helped him too, of course. She would have, if she'd known. Wouldn't she?

"Don't be a priss," says Zenia. "You should give me a medal for getting him off your back. Mitch was a sick lech. What he wanted out of me was sexual twist—he wanted to be tied up, he wanted me to dress up in leather underwear, and other stuff, stuff he would never ask you to do because he thought you were his angel wife. Men get like that after a certain age, but this was too much. I can't tell you the half of it, it was so ridiculous!"

"You led him on," says Roz, who wants by this time to run out of the room. It's too humiliating for Mitch. It shrinks him too much. It's too painful.

"Women like you make me sick," says Zenia angrily. "You've always owned things. But you didn't own him, you know. He wasn't your God-given *property*! You think you had rights in him? Nobody has any rights except what they can get!"

Roz takes a deep breath. Lose her temper and she loses the fight. "Maybe," she says. "But that doesn't alter the fact that you ate him for breakfast."

"The trouble with you, Roz," says Zenia, more gently, "is that you never gave the man any credit. You always saw him as a victim of women, just putty in their hands. You babied him. Did it ever occur to you that Mitch was responsible for his actions? He made his own decisions, and maybe those decisions didn't have much to do with me, or with you either. Mitch did what he wanted to do. He took his chances."

"You stacked the deck," says Roz.

"Oh please," says Zenia. "It takes two to tango. But why fight about Mitch? Mitch is dead. Let's get back to the main issue. I have a proposition for you: perhaps, for Larry's sake, I should leave town. Larry wouldn't be the only reason—I'll be frank with you, Roz, I need to leave town anyway. I'm in some danger here, so I'm asking you for old times' sake as well. But I can't afford it right now;

I won't hide from you that things are getting very tight. I'd go like a shot if I only had, say, a plane ticket and some pocket money."

"You're trying to blackmail me," says Roz.

"Let's not call names," says Zenia. "I'm sure you see the logic."

Roz hesitates. Should she buy it, should she buy Zenia off? And what if she doesn't? What exactly is the threat? Larry is no longer a child; there's a lot he must have guessed, about Mitch. "I don't think so," she says slowly. "I have a better proposition. How about you leave town anyway? I could still get you for embezzlement, you know. And there is this thing about cheque-forging."

Zenia frowns. "Money is too important to you, Roz," she says. "What I was really offering you was protection for yourself. Not for Larry. But you aren't worth protecting. Here's the real truth, then. Yes, I'm screwing Larry, but that's just a sideshow. Larry isn't primarily my lover, Larry is primarily my pusher. I'm surprised your inept private dick didn't figure that out, and I'm truly surprised you haven't figured it out yourself. You may not be pretty, but you used to be smart. Your mama's boy has been inflating his flat little ego by doing a brisk trade in coke, the recreational yuppie drug-of-choice. He's dealing, he's retailing to his well-heeled friends. He's been sampling the product pretty heavily too—you'll be lucky if he ends up with a nose. What do you think he does at the Toxique, night after night? The place is notorious! He's not doing it just for the money—he enjoys it! And you know what he enjoys most of all? Sneaking around behind your back! Pulling a fast one on Mom! Like father, like son. That boy has a problem, Roz, and his problem is you!"

Roz has gone limp. She doesn't want to believe any of
this, but parts of it ring true. She remembers the envelope
of white powder she found, she remembers Larry's secre-
cies, the blanks in his life that she can't fill in, and her fear
comes flooding back, with a big helping of guilt added in.
Has she been overprotective? Is Larry trying to escape
from her? Is she a devouring mother? Worse: is Larry a
hopeless addict?

"So I'd think twice, if I were you," says Zenia.
"Because if you won't pay for information, there are people who will. I think it would make a nice headline, don't
you? *Son of Prominent Citizen Jailed in Hotel Drug Bust.*
Nothing would be easier for me to arrange. Larry trusts
me. He thinks I need him. All I have to do is whistle and
your sonny-boy comes running with his pockets full. He's
really cute, you know. He's got cute buns. He'll be appreciated in the slammer. What do they give them now?
Ten years?"

Roz is stupefied; she can't take it all in. She gets up
out of her chair and walks to the window, to the French
doors leading onto the balcony. From here she can see a
new-moon sliver of the fountain, down below. It hasn't
been drained yet; brown dead leaves are floating in it.
Most likely the hotel has a staff shortage, because of the
Recession. "I need to talk to him," she says.

"I wouldn't do that if I were you," says Zenia. "He'll
panic, he'll do something rash. He's an amateur, he'll give
himself away. And right now he owes his suppliers quite a
lot of money. I know who they are and they aren't nice
people. They won't like it if he flushes the stuff down the
toilet. They won't get paid, and as a rule they react badly
to that. They don't like it either if people get caught and

then talk about them. They don't fool around. Your boy Larry could get his fingers burned. Actually, he could end up in a ditch somewhere, minus a few parts."

This can't be happening, thinks Roz. Sweet, serious Larry, in his boy's room with the school trophies and the pictures of boats? Zenia is a liar, she reminds herself. But she can't afford to dismiss her story, because what if—for once—it's true?

The thought of Larry dead is too much to bear. She would never survive it. This thought is lodged like a splinter of ice in her heart; at the same time she feels as if she's been teleported into some horrible daytime soap, with hidden iniquities and sinister intrigues and bad camera angles.

She could sneak up behind Zenia, bop her on the head with a lamp or something. Tie her up with pantyhose. Make it look like a sex killing. She's read enough trashy novels like that, and God knows it would be plausible, it's just the kind of sordid ending a woman like Zenia deserves. She populates the room with detectives, cigar-smoking detectives dusting the furniture for fingerprints, fingerprints she will have taken care to wipe away. . . .

"I don't have my chequebook with me," she says. "It'll have to be tomorrow."

"Make it cash," says Zenia. "Fifty thousand, and that's a bargain; if it wasn't a recession I'd ask double. Small old bills, please; you can send it by courier, before noon. Not here though, I'll call you in the morning and tell you where. Now, if you don't mind, I'm in a bit of a hurry."

Roz takes the elevator down. All of a sudden she has a crashing headache, and on top of that she feels ill. It's the fear and anger, churning around inside her like a salmonella dinner. *So, God, is this my fault or what? Is this the double-cross I have to bear? So you gave with one hand and now you're taking away with the other? Or maybe you think it's a joke!* It occurs to her, not for the first time, that if everything is part of the Divine Plan then God must have one heck of a warped sense of humour.

54

"What're you going to do?" says Tony.

"Pay up," says Roz. "What are my options? Anyway, it's only money."

"You could talk to Larry," says Tony. "After all, Zenia lies her head off. She could be making it all up."

"First I'll pay," says Roz. "Then Zenia will take a plane. Then I'll talk to Larry." It strikes her that Tony doesn't always get it, about kids. Even five per cent true would be too much; she can't take the risk.

"But what are we going to do about *her*?" says Charis.

"About Zenia?" says Roz. "After tomorrow she'll be somewhere else. Personally I would like her permanently removed, like a wart. But I don't see that happening." She's lighting another cigarette, from the candle in its red glass holder. Charis gives a timid cough and flaps a hand at the smoke.

"I don't see," says Tony slowly, "that there's anything we *can* do about her. We can't make her vanish. Even if she does go, she'll be back if she wants to come back. She's a given. She's just *there*, like the weather."

"Maybe we should give thanks," says Charis. "And ask for help."

Roz laughs. "Thanks for what? *Thank you, God, for creating Zenia? Only next time don't bother?*"

"No," says Charis. "Because she's going away, and we're still all right. Aren't we? None of us gave in." She's not sure exactly how to put it. What she means is, they were tempted, each one of them, but they didn't succumb. Succumbing would have been killing Zenia, either physically or spiritually. And killing Zenia would have meant turning into Zenia. Another way of succumbing would be believing her, letting her in the door, letting her take them in, letting her tear them apart. They did get torn apart some, but that was because they didn't do what Zenia wanted. "What I mean is. . . ."

"I think I know what you mean," says Tony.

"Right," says Roz. "So, let's give thanks. I'm always in favour of that. Who're we thanking and what do we do?"

"A libation," says Charis. "We've got everything here for it, even the candle." She lifts her wineglass, in which there's an inch of white wine left, and pours a thimbleful onto the pink remains of her Assorted Sorbets. Then she bows her head and closes her eyes briefly. "I asked for help," she says. "For all of us. Now you." She also asked for forgiveness, for all of them too. She feels this is right, but she can't say why, so she doesn't mention it.

"I'm not sure about this," says Roz. She can see the need for a celebration, touch wood it's not premature, but she'd like to know which God is being invoked here—or rather which version of God—so she can guard against lightning strikes by any of the others. But she pours. So does Tony, smiling a little tensely, her bite-your-tongue smile. If this were three hundred years ago, she thinks, we'd all be burned at the stake. Zenia first, though. Without a doubt, Zenia first.

"That's all?" she says.

"I like to sprinkle a little salt, into the candle flame," says Charis, sprinkling it.

"I just hope nobody's watching," says Roz. "I mean, how long before we are three genuine certified batty old crones?" She's feeling slightly light-headed; maybe it's the codeine pills she took for her headache.

"Don't look now," says Tony.

"Crones is not so bad," says Charis. "Age is just attitude." She's staring dreamily at the candle.

"Tell that to my gynecologist," says Roz. "You just want to be a crone so you can mix potions."

"She already mixes them," says Tony.

Suddenly Charis sits up straight in her chair. Her eyes widen. Her hand goes over her mouth.

"Charis?" says Roz. "What is it, sweetie?"

"Oh my God," says Charis.

"Is she choking?" says Tony. Possibly Charis is having a heart attack, or a fit of some kind. "Hit her on the back!"

"No, no," says Charis. "It's Zenia! She's dead!"

"What?" says Roz.

"How do you know?" says Tony.

"I saw it in the candle," says Charis. "I saw her falling. She was falling, into water. I saw it! She's dead." Charis begins to cry.

"Honey, are you sure that wasn't just wishful thinking?" says Roz gently. But Charis is too absorbed in her grief to hear.

"Come on," says Tony. "We'll go to the hotel. We'll

check. Otherwise," she says to Roz, over the top of Charis's head, which is bowed into her hands now and swaying back and forth, "none of us is going to get a decent night's sleep." This is true: Charis will worry about Zenia being dead, and Tony and Roz will worry about Charis. It's worth a short car ride to avoid that.

As they get their coats on, as Roz settles the bill, Charis continues to sob quietly. Partly it's the shock; the whole day has been a shock, and this an even bigger shock. But partly it's because she saw more than she's told. She didn't only see Zenia falling, a dark shape turning over and over, the hair spreading like feathers, the rainbow of her life twisting up out of her like grey gauze, Zenia shrinking to blackout. She also saw someone pushing her. Someone pushed Zenia, over the edge.

Although she couldn't see it clearly, she thinks she knows who that person was. It was Karen, who was left behind somehow; who stayed hidden in Zenia's room; who waited until Zenia had opened the door onto the balcony and then came up behind her and shoved her off. Karen has murdered Zenia, and it's Charis's fault for holding Karen away, separate from herself, for trying to keep her outside, for not taking her in, and Charis's tears are tears of guilt.

That is just one way of putting it, of course. What Charis means, she explains to herself, is that she wished Zenia dead. And now Zenia is dead. A spiritual act and a physical one are the same, from the moral point of view. Karen-Charis is a murderer. She has blood on her hands. She's unclean.

• • •

They go in Roz's car, the smaller one. There is some delay while Roz tries to find someone to park the car; as Roz complains to the man who is finally provided, the Arnold Garden is not exactly Johnny-on-the-spot when it comes to service. Then the three of them walk into the lobby. Charis has pulled herself together by now, and Tony has a steadying hand on her arm.

"She's in the fountain," Charis whispers.

"Shh," says Tony. "We'll see in a minute. Let Roz do the talking."

"I was here this afternoon, checking out your hotel as a convention possibility, and I think I left my gloves," says Roz. She's decided it would be a mistake to say they are looking for Zenia, on the outside chance that Charis may be right; not that Roz believes it for an instant, but still. Anyway, if they call the room and there's no answer, what would it prove? Nothing about death. Zenia could have checked out.

"Who were you talking to?" says the woman behind the counter.

"Oh, this was just preliminary," says Roz. "I think I left them out there in the courtyard. On the edge of the fountain."

"We keep that door locked at this time of year," says the woman.

"Well, it wasn't locked this afternoon," says Roz belligerently, "so I just had a look around. It's such a nice patio for cocktails, out by the fountain, is what I thought. That would be in June. Here's my card."

The card has an improving effect. "All right, Ms. Andrews, I'll have that unlocked for you right away," says the woman. "As a matter of fact we often use it for cocktails. We could do a buffet lunch out there for you, too; in the summer there's tables." She motions to the concierge.

"And could you have the outside lights turned on?" says Roz. "I might have dropped my gloves in the fountain. Or they could've blown in."

Roz's idea is to have the whole place lit up like a Christmas tree so Charis will be able to see as plain as day that Zenia is nowhere in view. The three of them go out through the glass patio door and stand together, waiting for illumination. "It's all right, honey, there's nothing," Roz whispers to Charis.

But when the lights go on, big floodlights from above and also from under the water, there is Zenia, floating face down among the dead leaves, her hair spread out like seaweed.

"My God," Tony whispers. Roz stifles a scream. Charis doesn't make a sound. Time has folded in upon itself, the prophecy has come true. But there are no dogs. Then it comes to her. *We are the dogs, licking her blood. In the courtyard, the Jezebel blood.* She thinks she is going to be sick.

"Don't touch her," says Tony, but Charis needs to. She reaches forward, reaches down and tugs, and Zenia revolves slowly, and looks straight at them with her white mermaid eyes.

55

She isn't really looking though, because she can't. Her eyes are rolled back into her head: that's why they're blank, like fish eyes. She's been dead for several hours, or at least that's what the police say when they arrive.

The hotel people are very worried. A dead woman in their fountain is not the kind of publicity they need, especially with business down the way it is. They seem to think it's all Roz's fault for suggesting that the lights be turned on, as if this is what caused Zenia to materialize in the fountain. But as Roz points out to the concierge, daylight would have been worse: hotel guests would be having breakfast in their rooms, going out on the balcony for a little fresh air and a cigarette, looking down, and you can imagine the uproar then.

Because they were the ones who found the body, Tony and Roz and Charis have to wait around. They have to answer questions. Roz grabs hold of the conversation and quickly sticks in her story about the gloves; it would not be at all wise to tell the police that they'd rushed over to the

Arnold Garden Hotel because Charis saw a vision while staring into a candle. Roz has read enough detective novels to know that such a story would immediately cast suspicion on Charis. Not only would the police think she's a nutbar—well, objectively speaking, Roz can see it—but they'd also think she's a nutbar capable of shoving Zenia off the balcony herself, and then having amnesia, followed by an attack of psychedelic vision-producing guilt.

At the back of Roz's mind there's a sliver of suspicion: maybe they'd be right. There was enough time for Charis to come back to the hotel before turning up at the Toxique for dinner. She could have done it. So could Tony, who has been frank about her murderous intentions. So could Roz herself, for that matter. No doubt the fingerprints of the three of them are all over the room.

Maybe it was someone they don't even know, some stranger, one of those pursuing gun-runners or whatever, in that yarn Zenia fobbed off on Tony. But Roz doesn't credit that. Instead, there's a worse possibility, much worse: it might have been Larry. If what Zenia said was true, he would have had a good motive. He was never a violent child, he would walk away from the other kids rather than argue; but Zenia could have threatened him in some way. She could have tried to blackmail him. He could have been on drugs. What does Roz really know about Larry, now that he's grown up? She needs to get home as soon as possible and find out what he's been up to.

Tony has dragged Charis off to one side to keep her out of harm's way. She just hopes Charis will shut up about her vision, which—Tony has to admit—was accurate enough, though somewhat after the fact. But what really happened? Tony counts the possibilities: Zenia fell, Zenia jumped, Zenia was pushed. Accident, suicide, murder. Tony inclines towards the third: Zenia was killed— surely—by person or persons unknown. Tony's glad she took her gun home, in case there are bullet holes, although she didn't see any. She doesn't think Charis could have done it, because Charis wouldn't hurt a fly—it being her belief that flies might be inhabited by someone related to you in a previous life—but she's not that sure about Roz. Roz has a temper, and can be impetuous.

"Did anyone know this woman?" says the policeman.

The three of them glance at one another. "Yes," says Tony.

"We all came to see her, earlier today," says Roz.

Charis starts to cry. "We were her best friends," she says.

Which, thinks Tony, is news to her. But it will have to do for now.

Roz drives Charis to the ferry terminal, and then she drives Tony home. Tony goes up the stairs to West's study, where he's plugged into two of his machines via the ear- phones. She turns off his switch.

"Did Zenia call here?" she says.

"What?" says West. "Tony, what is it?"

"This is important," says Tony. She knows she's sounding fierce but she can't help it. "Have you been talk- ing to Zenia? Has she been here?" She finds the idea of Zenia rolling around on the carpet with West among the synthesizers highly distasteful. No: unbearable.

Maybe, she thinks, West did it. Maybe he went over to Zenia's hotel room to beg and plead, hoping to run off with her again, and Zenia laughed at him, and West lost it and heaved her off the balcony. If that's what happened Tony wants to know. She wants to know so she can shield West, think up a watertight alibi for him, save him from himself.

"Oh, yeah," says West. "She did call, I don't know—a week ago. But I didn't talk to her, she just left a message on the machine."

"What did it say?" says Tony. "Why didn't you tell me? What did she want?"

"Maybe I should've mentioned it," says West. "But I didn't want you to get hurt. I mean, we both thought she was dead. I guess I would've liked her to stay that way."

"Really?" says Tony.

"She didn't want to talk to me," says West, as if he knows what Tony's been thinking. "She wanted you. If I'd had her on the phone in person I would've told her to forget it; I knew you wouldn't want to see her. I did jot it down—where she was staying—but after I thought things over, I threw it out. She's always been bad news."

Tony feels herself softening. "I saw her, though," she says. "I saw her this afternoon. She seemed to know that your study's on the third floor. How would she know that, if she's never been here?"

West smiles. "It's on my answering machine. "*Third floor, Headwinds.* Remember?"

By this time he's unwired and standing up. Tony goes over to him and he folds himself up like a bridge chair and wraps his knotted-rope arms around her, and kisses her on the forehead. "I like it that you're jealous," he says, "but you don't need to be. She's nothing, any more."

Little does he know, thinks Tony. Or else he does

know and he's pretending not to. Squashed up against his torso, she takes a sniff of him, to see if he's been drinking a lot. If he has, it will be a dead giveaway. But there's nothing besides the usual mild scent of beer.

"Zenia is dead," she tells West solemnly.

"Oh, Tony," says West. "Again? I'm really sorry." He rocks her to and fro as if she's the one who needs to be consoled, and not him at all.

When Charis gets back to her house, still shaky but under control, there's a light on in the kitchen. It's Augusta, taking a long weekend break, paying a visit. Charis is glad to see her, though she wishes she'd had time to tidy up first. She notes that Augusta has washed the dishes from the last couple of days and has done away with a couple of major spider webs, though she's known better than to disassemble Charis's meditational altar. She has noted it, however.

"Mom," she says, after Charis has greeted her and has put on the kettle for bedtime tea, "what's this chunk of stone and this pile of dirt and leaves doing on the living-room table?"

"It's a meditation," says Charis.

"Christ," Augusta mutters. "Can't you put it somewhere else?"

"August," says Charis, a little tersely, "it's my meditation, and it's my house."

"Don't snap at me!" says August. "And Mom, it's *Augusta.* That's my name now."

Charis knows this. She knows she should respect August's new name, because everyone has a right to rename herself according to her inner direction. But she chose August's original name with such love and care. She gave it to her, it was a gift. It's hard for her to let it go.

"I'll make you some muffins," she says, attempting to conciliate. "Tomorrow. The ones with the sunflower seeds. You always liked those."

"You don't have to keep giving me stuff, Mom," says Augusta, in an oddly grown-up voice. "I love you anyway."

Charis feels her eyes watering. Augusta hasn't said anything this affectionate for some time. And she does find it difficult to believe—that a person would love her even when she isn't trying. Trying to figure out what other people need, trying to be worthy. "It's just, I worry about you," she says. "About your health." This isn't really the part of Augusta that worries her, but it stands in for the other, more spiritual things. Though health is a spiritual thing too.

"No kidding," says Augusta. "Every time I come home you try to stuff me full of veggie burgers. I'm nineteen, Mom, I take care of myself, I eat balanced meals! Why can't we just have fun? Go for a walk or something."

It's unusual for Augusta to want to spend time with Charis. Maybe Augusta isn't totally hard, not lacquered and shiny all the way through. Maybe she has a soft spot. Maybe she is part Charis, after all.

"Did you mind a lot, not having a father?" Charis asks. "When you were little?" She's been on the verge of asking this for a long time, although she's feared the answer because surely it was her fault that Billy had left. If he'd run away it was her fault for not being appealing enough to keep him, if he'd been kidnapped it was her fault for not taking better care of him. Now, though, she has some other possible views of Billy. Whether Zenia was lying or not, maybe it's just as well Billy didn't stick around.

"I wish you'd stop feeling so guilty," says Augusta. "Maybe I minded when I was small, but look around you, Mom, this is the twentieth century! Fathers come and go—a lot of the kids on the Island didn't have them. I know some people with three or four fathers! I mean, it could have been worse, right?"

Charis looks at Augusta and sees the light around her. It's a light that's hard like a mineral and also soft, a glow like the luminosity of a pearl. Inside the layers of light, right at the centre of Augusta, there's a small wound. It belongs to Augusta, not to Charis; it's for Augusta to heal.

Charis feels absolved. She puts her hands on Augusta's shoulders, gently so Augusta will not feel seized, and kisses her on the forehead.

Before she goes to bed, Charis does a meditation on Zenia. She needs to do this, because although she has often thought about Zenia in relation to herself, or to Billy, or even to Tony and Roz, she has never truly considered what Zenia was in and by herself: the Zenia-ness of Zenia. She has no object, nothing belonging to Zenia, to focus on, so instead she turns off the lights in the living room and stares out the window, into the darkness, towards the lake. Zenia was sent into her life—was *chosen* by her—to teach her something. Charis doesn't know what it was yet, but in time she will uncover it.

She can see Zenia clearly, Zenia lying in the fountain, with her cloudy hair floating. As she watches, time reverses itself and life flows back into Zenia, and she lifts out of the water and flies backwards like a huge bird, up onto the orange balcony. But Charis can't hold her there, and she falls again; falls down, turning slowly, into her own future. Her future as a dead person, as a person not yet born.

Charis wonders whether Zenia will come back as a human being or as something else. Perhaps the soul breaks up as the body does, and only parts of it are reborn, a fragment here, a fragment there. Perhaps many people will soon be born with a fragment of Zenia in them. But Charis would rather think of her whole.

After a while she turns out the other downstairs lights and goes upstairs. Just before she climbs into her vine-covered bed, she gets out her notebook with the lavender paper and her pen with the green ink, and writes: *Zenia has returned to the Light.*

She hopes this is so. She hopes that Zenia is not still hovering around, alone and lost, somewhere out there in the night.

After Roz takes Tony home she goes home herself, as fast as she can because she's worried sick, what if there's cocaine stashed all over her house, tucked into the tea leaves or the cookie jar in little plastic bags, what if she finds the place full of sniffer dogs and men named Dwayne, who will address her as ma'am and say they are just doing their jobs? She even runs a red light, not a thing she normally does, although everyone else seems to these days. She shucks her coat in the hall, kicks off her shoes, and goes on the hunt for Larry.

The twins are in the family room, watching a rerun of *Star Trek.*

"Greetings, Earthmom," says Paula.

"Maybe she isn't Mom," says Erin. "Maybe she's a Replicant."

"Hi, kids," says Roz. "It's way past your bedtime! Where's Larry?"

"Erla's done our homework," says Erin. "This is our reward."

"Mom, what's wrong?" says Paula. "You look like shit."

"It's old age," says Roz. "Is he home?"

"He's in the kitchen," says Erin. "We think."

"Eating bread and honey," says Paula.

"That's the Queen, stupid," says Erin. They giggle.

Larry is sitting on one of the high stools, at the kitchen counter, wearing jeans and a black T-shirt and bare feet, and drinking a bottle of beer. Across from him on another high stool is Boyce, neat in his suit; he's got a beer, too. When Roz walks into the room they both look up. They both seem equally anxious.

"Hi, Boyce," says Roz. "What a surprise! Is something wrong at the office?"

"Good evening, Ms. Andrews," says Boyce. "Not at the office, no."

"I have something to discuss with Larry," says Roz. "If you don't mind, Boyce."

"I think Boyce should stay," says Larry. He looks dejected, as if he's failed an exam: there must be something to Zenia's story. But what's Boyce got to do with it?

"Larry, I'm concerned," says Roz. "What are you into with Zenia?"

"Who?" Larry says, too innocently.

"I need to know," says Roz.

"I dream of Zenia in her light brown lair," Boyce murmurs as if to himself.

"She told you?" says Larry.

"About the drugs?" says Roz. "Oh God, it's true! If you've got any drugs in this house, I want them out of here, right now! So you *were* having a thing with her!"

"Thing?" says Larry.

"Thing, fling, whatever," says Roz. "Holy Moly, don't you know how old she was? Don't you know how vicious she was? Don't you know what she did to your father?"

"Thing?" says Boyce. "I don't think so."

"What drugs?" says Larry.

"It was only a few times," says Boyce. "He was experimenting. My nose aches, and a drowsy numbness pains my sense. Keats. He's given it up, as of now—right, Larry?"

"Then you weren't her dealer?" says Roz.

"Mom, it was the other way around," says Larry.

"But Charis saw you kissing her, right out on the street!" says Roz. She feels very weird, talking this way to her own son. She feels like a snoopy old crock.

"Kissing?" says Larry. "I never kissed her. She was whispering in my ear. She was telling me that we were being followed around by this deranged older woman. Maybe it looked like kissing, to Aunt Charis, because that woman was definitely her."

"Not kissing, but hissing," says Boyce. "Like 'not waving but drowning.' Stevie Smith."

"Boyce, shut up for a minute," says Larry irritably. They seem to know each other quite a lot better than Roz has assumed. She's thought they'd just met the one time, at the Father-Daughter Dance, and then a few nods at the office, as Larry came and went. Apparently not.

"But you went to her hotel room a lot," says Roz. "I know it for a fact!"

"It's not what you think," says Larry.

"You realize she's dead?" Roz says, playing her ace. "I just came from there, they just fished her out of the fountain!"

"Dead?" says Boyce. "Of what? A self-inflicted snakebite?"

"Who knows?" says Roz. "Maybe somebody threw her off the balcony."

"Maybe she jumped," says Boyce. "When lovely woman stoops to folly, and finds too late that men betray, they jump off balconies."

"I just hope to God you had nothing to do with it," says Roz to Larry.

Boyce says quickly, "He couldn't have, he was nowhere near her tonight. He was with me."

"I was trying to talk her out of it," says Larry. "She wanted money. I didn't have enough, and I could hardly ask you for some."

"Talk her out of what? Money for what?" says Roz. She's almost yelling.

"For not telling you," says Larry miserably. "I thought I could keep it secret. I didn't want to make things any worse—I thought you'd been upset enough, because of Dad, and everything."

"Judas Priest, for not telling me *what*?" shouts Roz. "You'll be the death of me!" She sounds exactly like her own mother. All the same, so sweet, Larry trying to protect her. He doesn't want to come home and find her flopping around on the kitchen floor, the way he did before. "Boyce," she says, more gently, "have you got a cigarette?"

Boyce, ever prepared, hands her the package and flicks his lighter for her. "I think it's time," he says to Larry.

Larry gulps, stares at the floor, looks resigned. "Mom," he says, "I'm gay."

Roz feels her eyes bugging out like those of a strangled rabbit. Why didn't she see, why couldn't she tell, what's the matter with her anyway? Nicotine grabs at her lungs, she really must quit, and then she coughs, and smoke billows from her mouth, and maybe she's about to have a premature heart attack! That's what she'll do, fall to the floor in a heap and let everyone else deal with this, because it's way beyond her.

But she sees the distress in Larry's eyes, and the appeal. No, she can handle it, if she can bite her tongue hard enough. It's just that she wasn't prepared. What's the right thing to say? *I love you anyway? You're still my son? What about my grandchildren?*

"But all those bimbos you put me through!" is what she comes out with. She's got it now: he was trying to please her. Trying to bring home a woman, like some kind of dutiful exam certificate, to show Mom. To show he'd passed.

"A man can but do his best," says Boyce. "Walter Scott."

"What about the twins?" Roz whispers. They are at a formative stage; how will she tell them?

"Oh, the twins know," says Larry, relieved that he's got at least one corner covered. "They worked it out pretty fast. They say it's cool." That figures, thinks Roz: for them, the fences once so firmly in place around the gender corrals are just a bunch of rusty old wire.

"Think of it this way," says Boyce affectionately. "You're not losing a son, you're gaining a son."

"I've decided to go to law school," says Larry. Now that the worst is over and Roz hasn't croaked or burst, he looks relieved. "We want you to help us decorate our apartment."

"Sweetie," says Roz, taking a deep breath, "I'd be glad to." It's not that she's prejudiced, and her own marriage wasn't such a terrific argument for heterosexuality, and neither was Mitch, and she just wants Larry to be happy, and if this is how he plans to do it, fine, and maybe Boyce will be a good influence and make him pick his clothes up off the floor and keep him out of trouble; but it's been a long day. Tomorrow she'll be genuinely warm and accepting. For tonight, hypocrisy will have to do.

"Ms. Andrews, you're the glass of fashion and the mould of form," says Boyce.

Roz spreads her hands wide, raises her shoulders, pulls down the corners of her mouth. "Tell me," she says. "What are my options?"

Men in overcoats come to visit. They want to know a lot of things about Zenia. Which of her three passports is real, if any. Where she actually came from. What she was doing.

Tony is informative, Charis vague; Roz is careful, because she doesn't want Larry involved. But she needn't have worried, because none of these men seems to be the least interested in Larry. What they are interested in is Zenia's two packed suitcases, left neatly on the bed, one of them with eleven little plastic bags of white powder in them, or so they say. A twelfth bag was open, beside the phone. Not nose candy either: heroin, and ninety per cent pure. They look out from their immobile faces, their eyes like intelligent pebbles, watching for twinges, for hints of guilty knowledge.

They are also interested in the needle found on the balcony, they continue, and in the fact that Zenia died of an overdose before even hitting the water. Could she have been trying the stuff out, without knowing the unusual strength of what she was buying, or selling? There were track marks on her left arm, although they looked old. According to the overcoats, there have been more and more overdoses like that; someone is flooding the market with high-octane product, and even the experienced aren't prepared.

There were nobody's fingerprints on the needle, except Zenia's, they tell her. As for her swan dive into the fountain, she could have fallen. She was a tall woman, and the sheet-metal balcony railings were really too low for safety; standards should be improved. Such a thing is possible. If she'd been leaning over. On the other hand, the heroin could have been a plant. It might have been murder.

Or it might have been suicide, Tony tells them. She would like them to believe this. She tells them that Zenia may not have been a well person.

Of course, say the men in overcoats politely. We know about that. We found the prescriptions in her suitcase, we traced the doctor. Seems she had a fake health card as well as some fake passports, but the disease itself was real enough. Six months to live: ovarian cancer. But there was no suicide note.

Tony tells them there wouldn't have been: Zenia was not really the note-writing kind.

The men in overcoats look at her, their small eyes glinting with scepticism. They don't buy any of these theories, but they don't have another one, not one that holds water.

Tony sees how it will be: Zenia will prove too smart for the men in overcoats. She will outfox them, just as she's always outfoxed everyone else. She finds herself being pleased about this, elated even, as if her faith in Zenia—a faith she didn't realize she had—is being vindicated. Let them sweat! Why should everyone know everything? It's not as if there are no precedents: history teems with people who died in unclear ways.

Still, she feels honour-bound to report the conversation about Gerry Bull and Project Babylon, although it's not merely honour that impels her: she hopes very much that if Zenia was murdered it was by professionals, rather than by anyone she knows. The men tell her they are retracing Zenia's steps, as best they can, via her plane tickets; she has certainly been in some very odd places in the last little while. But there's nothing conclusive. They shake hands and depart, asking Tony to call them if she hears anything else. She says she will.

She's left facing the unlikely possibility that all three of Zenia's most recent stories—or parts of them, at least—may have been true. What if Zenia's cries for help really were cries for help, this time?

After the police are finished there is a cremation. Roz pays for it, because when she tracks down the lawyer, the one who arranged Zenia's funeral the first time around, he is quite annoyed. He takes it as a personal slight that Zenia has chosen to be alive all this time without consulting him about it. Her will was probated the first time around, not that there was anything to probate because she didn't leave an estate, only a small bequest to an orphanage near Waterloo that turned out not to exist any more, and on top of that he never got paid. So what do they expect from him?

"Nothing," says Roz. "It will all be taken care of."

"Well, what about it?" she says to Tony and Charis. "Looks like we got left holding the sack. She doesn't seem to have any relatives."

"Except us," says Charis.

Tony sees no point in contradicting her, because it is Charis's belief that everyone is related to everyone else through some kind of invisible root system. She says she will take charge of the ashes until the three of them can figure out something more suitable. She puts the canister with Zenia in it down in the cellar, in her box of Christmas tree decorations, wrapped up in red tissue paper, beside the gun. She doesn't tell West it is there, because this is a female matter.

Outcome

56

So now Zenia is History.

No: now Zenia is gone. She is lost and gone forever. She's a scattering of dust, blown on the wind like spores; she's an invisible cloud of viruses, a few molecules, dispersing. She will only be history if Tony chooses to shape her into history. At the moment she is formless, a broken mosaic; the fragments of her are in Tony's hands, because she is dead, and all of the dead are in the hands of the living.

But what is Tony to make of her? The story of Zenia is insubstantial, ownerless, a rumour only, drifting from mouth to mouth and changing as it goes. As with any magician, you saw what she wanted you to see; or else you saw what you yourself wanted to see. She did it with mirrors. The mirror was whoever was watching, but there was nothing behind the two-dimensional image but a thin layer of mercury.

Even the name Zenia may not exist, as Tony knows from looking. She's attempted to trace its meaning— *Xenia,* a Russian word for hospitable, a Greek one pertaining to the action of a foreign pollen upon a fruit; *Zenaida,* meaning daughter of Zeus, and the name of two early Christian martyrs; *Zillah,* Hebrew, a shadow; *Zenobia,* the third-century warrior queen of Palmyra in Syria, defeated by the Emperor Aurelian; *Xeno,* Greek, a stranger, as in *xenophobic; Zenana,* Hindu, the women's quarters or harem; *Zen,* a Japanese meditational religion; *Zendic,* an Eastern practitioner of heretical magic—these are the closest she has come.

Out of such hints and portents, Zenia devised herself. As for the truth about her, it lies out of reach, because—according to the records, at any rate—she was never even born.

But why bother, in this day and age—Zenia herself would say—with such a quixotic notion as the truth? Every sober-sided history is at least half sleight-of-hand: the right hand waving its poor snippets of fact, out in the open for all to verify, while the left hand busies itself with its own devious agendas, deep in its hidden pockets. Tony is daunted by the impossibility of accurate reconstruction.

Also by its futility. Why does she do what she does? History was once a substantial edifice, with pillars of wisdom and an altar to the goddess Memory, the mother of all nine muses. Now the acid rain and the terrorist bombs and the termites have been at it, and it's looking less and less like a temple and more and more like a pile of rubble, but it once had a meaningful structure. It was supposed to have something to teach people, something beneficial; some health-giving vitamin or fortune-cookie motto concealed within its heaped-up accounts, most of them tales of greed, violence, viciousness, and lust for power, because history doesn't concern itself much with those who try to be good. Goodness in any case is problematic, since an action can be good in intent but evil in result, witness missionaries. This is why Tony prefers battles: in a battle there are right actions and wrong actions, and you can tell them apart by who wins.

Still, there was once supposed to be a message. *Let that be a lesson to you,* adults used to say to children, and historians to their readers. But do the stories of history really teach anything at all? In a general sense, thinks Tony, possibly not.

Despite this she still plods on, still weaves together her informed guesses and plausible assumptions, still ponders over her scraps of fact, her potsherds and broken arrowheads and tarnished necklace beads, arranging them in the patterns she thinks they must once have made. Who cares? Almost nobody. Maybe it's just a hobby, something to do on a dull day. Or else it's an act of defiance: these histories may be ragged and threadbare, patched together from worthless leftovers, but to her they are also flags, hoisted with a certain jaunty insolence, waving bravely though inconsequently, glimpsed here and there through the trees, on the mountain roads, among the ruins, on the long march into chaos.

Tony is down in the cellar, in the middle of the night, because she doesn't feel like sleeping. She's wearing her dressing gown and her wool work socks and her raccoon slippers, which are finally on their last legs, although they don't have any legs and the legs they are on are hers. One of them has lost a tail, and they now have only one eye between them. Tony has become used to having eyes on her feet, like the eyes the ancient Egyptians painted on the prows of their boats. They provide extra guidance—extra spirit guidance, you might say—a thing Tony is coming to believe she needs. Maybe when these slippers kick the bucket she will buy some other ones, other ones with eyes. There's a choice of animal: pigs, bears, rabbits, wolves. She thinks she will get the wolves.

Her sand-table map of Europe has been rearranged. Now it's the second decade of the thirteenth century, and what will later be France is being torn apart by religious wars. By this time it's no longer the Christians versus the Muslims: instead it's the Catholics versus the Cathars. The dualist Cathars held that the world was divided between the forces of good and the forces of evil, the spiritual and the material, God and the Devil; they believed in reincarnation, and had female religious instructors. Whereas the Catholics ruled out rebirth, thought women unclean, and held by force of logic that since God was by definition all-powerful, evil was ultimately an illusion. A difference of opinion that cost many lives, though there was more at stake than theology, such as who was to control the trade routes and the olive crops, and the women, who were getting out of hand.

Carcassonne, stronghold of Languedoc and the Cathars, has just fallen to the bloodthirsty Simon de Montfort and his brutal army of crusading Catholics, after a siege of fifteen days and a failure of the water supply. Full-spectrum killing ensued. Tony's main focus of interest is not Carcassonne, however, but Lavaur, which was attacked next. It resisted for sixty days under the leadership of the castle's chatelaine, Dame Giraude. After the town finally succumbed, eighty knights were butchered like pigs and four hundred Cathar defenders were burned alive, and Dame Giraude herself was thrown down a well by de Montfort's soldiers, with a lot of stones piled on top of her to keep her down. Nobility in war gets a name for itself, thinks Tony, because there is so little of it.

Tony has chosen May 2, 1211, the day before the massacre. The besieging Catholics are represented by kidney beans, the defending Cathars by grains of white rice. Simon de Montfort is a red Monopoly man, Dame Giraude a blue one. Red for the cross, blue for the Cathars: it was their colour. Tony has already eaten several of the kidney beans, which strictly speaking she should not have done until after the battle. But nibbling helps her to concentrate.

What was Dame Giraude thinking as she looked out over the battlements, assessing the enemy? She must have known that this battle was unwinnable, that her town and all the people in it were doomed. Did she despair, was she praying for a miracle, was she proud of herself for having fought for what she believed in? Watching her co-religionists fry the next day, she must have felt that there was more evidence in support of her own theories of evil than of de Montfort's.

Tony has been there, she has seen the terrain. She has picked a flower, some sort of tough-stemmed vetch; she has pressed it in the Bible, she has stuck it into her scrapbook, under L for Lavaur. She has bought a souvenir, a small satin pillow stuffed with lavender. According to the local residents, Dame Giraude is still there, still down in the well. That was all they could think of to do, in those days, with women like her: throw them into wells, or off steep cliffs or parapets—some unrelenting vertical—and watch them splatter.

Maybe Tony will write something about Dame Giraude, sometime. A study of female military commanders. *Iron Hands, Velvet Gloves,* she could call it. But there isn't much material.

She doesn't want to go on with this battle right now; she's not in the mood for slaughter. She gets up from her chair and pours herself a glass of water; then, on top of Europe in the thirteenth century, she spreads out a street map, a map of downtown Toronto. Here is the Toxique, here is Queen Street, here is Roz's renovated office building; here are the ferry docks, and the flat Island where Charis's house still stands. Over here is the Arnold Garden Hotel, which is now a big clay-sided hole in the ground, a site of future development, because failing hotels go cheap and someone cut a good deal. Here is McClung Hall, and, to the north, Tony's own house, with West in it, upstairs in bed, groaning gently in his sleep; with the cellar in it, with the sand-table in it, with the map on it, with the city in it, with the house in it, with the cellar in it, with the map in it. Maps, thinks Tony, contain the ground that contains them. Somewhere in this infinitely receding headspace, Zenia continues to exist.

Tony needs the map for the same reason she always uses maps: they help her to see, to visualize the topology, to remember. What she is remembering is Zenia. She owes her this remembrance. She owes her an end.

57

Every ending is arbitrary, because the end is where you write *The end*. A period, a dot of punctuation, a point of stasis. A pinprick in the paper: you could put your eye to it and see through, to the other side, to the beginning of something else. Or, as Tony says to her students, *Time is not a solid, like wood, but a fluid, like water or the wind. It doesn't come neatly cut into even-sized lengths, into decades and centuries. Nevertheless, for our purposes we have to pretend it does. The end of any history is a lie in which we all agree to conspire.*

An ending, then. November 11, 1991, at eleven o'clock in the morning, the eleventh hour of the eleventh day of the eleventh month. It's a Monday. The Recession is thickening, there are rumours of big-company bankruptcies, famine is rolling over Africa; in what was once Yugoslavia there is ethnic feuding. Atrocities multiply, leaderships teeter, car factories grind to a halt. The war in the Gulf is over and the desert sands are spackled with bombs; the oil fields still burn, clouds of black smoke roiling out over the greasy sea. Both sides claim to have won, both sides have lost. It's a dim day, wreathed in mist.

• • •

The three of them stand at the back of the ferry as it churns its way through the harbour, outbound towards the Island, trailing the momentary darkness of its wake. From the mainland they can hear, faintly, the sound of bugles, and of muffled shots. A salute. The water is quicksilver in the pearl-coloured light, the wind is slight, cool, but mild for the time of year, the month. The pause month, the month of empty branches and held breath, the fog month, the greyish hush before winter.

Month of the dead, month of returning, thinks Charis. She thinks of the grey weeds waving, under the poisonous, guileless water, at the bottom of the lake; of the grey fish with lumpy chemical growths on them, wafting like shadows; of the lamprey eels with their tiny rasping teeth and sucking mouths, undulating among the husks of wrecked cars, the empty bottles. She thinks of everything that has fallen in, or else been thrown. Treasures and bones. At the beginning of November the French decorate their family graves with chrysanthemums, the Mexicans with marigolds, making a golden path so the spirits can find their way. Whereas we go in for poppies. The flower of sleep and forgetting. Petals of spilled blood.

Each one of them has a poppy stuck into the front of her coat. Flimsy plastic but who can resist, thinks Roz, though she liked the cloth ones better. It's like those awful daffodils for cancer, pretty soon every single flower will be hooked up with some body part or disease. Plastic lupins for lupus, plastic columbines for colostomies, plastic aspidistras for AIDS, you have to buy the darn things though, it protects you from getting hit up every time you walk out the door. *I have one already. See?*

It was Tony who insisted on this particular day. Remembrance Day. Bloody Poppy Day. Tony is getting more bizarre by the minute, in Roz's opinion; but then, so are they all.

Remembrance Day is only fitting, thinks Tony. She wants to do Zenia justice; but she's remembering more than Zenia. She's remembering the war, and those killed by it, at the time or later; sometimes wars take a long time to kill people. She's remembering all the wars. She craves some idea of ceremony, of decorum; not that she's getting one whole hell of a lot of cooperation from the others. Roz did wear black, as requested, but she's tarted it up with a red-and-silver scarf. *Black brings out my eye bags,* she said. *I needed something else right next to my face. Goes with my lipstick—this is Rubicon, hot off the press. Like it? You don't mind, do you honey?*

And as for Charis . . . Tony looks sideways at the receptacle Charis is holding: not the chintzy copper urn with the imitation Greek handles peddled by the crematorium, more like a stirrup cup really, but something even worse. It's a handmade ceramic flower vase, heavily artistic, in mottled shades of mauve and maroon, donated to Charis by Shanita, from the stockroom of Scrimpers, where it had been gathering dust for years. Charis insisted on something more meaningful than the tin can that Tony's been keeping in her cellar, so before they got their ferry tickets they transferred Zenia from canister to vase, in the Second Cup coffee shop. Roz poured; the ashes were stickier than Tony had expected. Charis couldn't bear to look, in case there were any teeth. But she's got her nerve back by now; she stands at the railing of the ferry, her pale hair spread out, looking like a ship's figurehead going backwards and cradling the lurid flower vase with Zenia's earthly remains inside it. If the dead come back for revenge, thinks Tony, the flower vase alone will be enough to do it.

"Would you say this is halfway?" asks Tony. She wants them to be over the deepest part.

"Looks right to me, sweetie," says Roz. She's impatient to get this over. When they reach the Island they are all going to Charis's house for tea, and, Roz trusts and hopes, some form of lunch: a piece of homemade bread, a whole wheat cookie, anything. Whatever it is will taste like straw—that brown-rice, dauntingly healthy, lipstickless taste that is the base note of everything Charis cooks—but it will be food. She has three Mozart Balls tucked into her purse as a sort of anti-vitamin supplement and starvation fallback. She intended to bring champagne but she forgot.

It will be a wake of sorts, the three of them gathered around Charis's round table, munching away at the baked goods, adding to the seven-grain crumbs on the floor, because death is a hunger, a vacancy, and you have to fill it up. Roz intends to talk: it will be her contribution. Tony has picked the day and Charis the container, so the vocals will be up to Roz.

The funny thing is, she actually feels sad. Now figure that out! Zenia was a tumour, but she was also a major part of Roz's life, and her life is past the midpoint. Not soon, but sooner than she wants, she'll begin to set like the sun, to dwindle. When Zenia goes into the lake Mitch will go too, finally; Roz will finally be a widow. No. She'll be something more, something beyond that. What? She will wait and see. But she'll take off her wedding ring, because Charis says it constrains the left hand and that's the hand Roz needs to draw on, now.

She feels something else she never thought she would feel, towards Zenia. Oddly enough, it's gratitude. What for? Who knows? But that's what she feels.

"Should I just pour it out or throw in the whole thing?" says Charis. She has a sneaking wish to keep the vase for herself: it has a strong energy.

"What would you do with it afterwards?" says Tony, looking at her sternly, and after a moment—in which she pictures the vase full of flowers, or standing empty on a shelf, giving off a baleful crimson light in both cases—Charis says, "You're right." It would be a mistake to keep the vase, it would be holding Zenia to the earth; she has already seen the results of that, she doesn't want a repeat. The mere absence of a body would not stop Zenia; she would just take somebody else's. The dead return in other forms, she thinks, because we will them to.

"Heave ho, then," says Roz, "last one in's a rotten stinker!" What on earth is she thinking of? Cold water! Summer camp! Talk about mood swings! Not to mention bad taste. How much more of her life is she going to spend showing off, playing for cheap laughs? How old do you have to get before wisdom descends like a plastic bag over your head and you learn to keep your big mouth shut? Maybe never. Maybe you get more frivolous with age. *Their eyes, their ancient glittering eyes, are gay.*

But this is death, and death is Death, capital D, never mind whose, so sober up, Roz. Anyway she is sober, it's only the way things come out of her. *Bite my tongue, God, I didn't mean it. It's just the way I am.*

Tony gives Roz an annoyed glance. What she herself would like is a little gunfire. A ritual cannon shot, the flag lowering to half-mast, a single bugle note quivering in the silvery air. Other dead fighters get that, so why not Zenia? She thinks of solemn moments, battlefield vignettes: the hero leaning on his sword or spear or musket, gazing down with noble and philosophical grief at his freshly killed opponent. Of equal rank, it goes without saying. *I am the enemy you killed, my friend.*

All very well, in art. In real battles, more likely a quick rifling of the watch pocket and the cutting off of ears as souvenirs. Old photographs of hunters with one foot on the bear carcass, clowning around with the sad sawed-off omnivorous ravenous head. Reduction of your sacred foe to a rug, with all the paintings and poems a kind of decorous curtain to disguise the gloating discourse going on behind.

"Okay," she says to Charis, and Charis thrusts both arms and both hands and the flower vase straight out from her body, over the railing, and there is a sharp crack, and the vase splits in two. Charis gives a little shriek and pulls her hands back as if they've been burned. She looks at them: there's a slight blue tinge, a flickering. The pieces of the vase splash into the water, and Zenia trails off in a long wavering drift, like smoke.

"Holy Moly!" says Roz. "What did that?"

"I think she hit it on the railing," says Tony.

"No," says Charis in a hushed voice. "It cracked by itself. It was her." Entities can cause things like that, they can affect physical objects; they do it to get your attention.

Nothing Roz or Tony is likely to say will change her mind, so they say nothing. Charis herself is oddly comforted. It pleases her that Zenia would attend her own scattering, make herself known. It's a token of her continuation. Zenia will now be free, to be reborn for another chance at life. Maybe she will be more fortunate next time. Charis tries to wish her well.

Nevertheless she's shaking. She takes the hands held out to her, one on either side, and grips them tightly, and in this way they glide in to the Island dock. Three dark-coated middle-aged women; women in mourning, thinks Tony. Those veils had a purpose—those outmoded veils, thick and black. Nobody could see what you were doing in there behind them. You could be laughing your head off. She isn't, though.

No flowers grow in the furrows of the lake, none in the fields of asphalt. Tony needs a flower, however. A common weed, because wherever else Zenia had been in her life, she had also been at war. An unofficial war, a guerrilla war, a war she may not have known she was waging, but a war nevertheless.

Who was the enemy? What past wrong was she seeking to avenge? Where was her battlefield? Not in any one place. It was in the air all around, it was in the texture of the world itself; or it was nowhere visible, it was in among the neurons, the tiny incandescent fires of the brain that flash up and burn out. An electric flower would be the right kind for Zenia, a bright, lethal flower like a short circuit, a thistle of molten steel going to seed in a burst of sparks.

The best Tony can do is a sprig of Queen Anne's lace from Charis's backyard, already dry and brittle. She picks it surreptitiously as the others go in the back door. She will take it home and press it as flat as possible, and tape it into her scrapbook. She'll place it at the very end, after Tallinn, after Valley Forge, after Ypres, because she is a sentimentalist about dead people and Zenia is dead, and although she was many other things, she was also courageous. What side she was on doesn't matter; not to Tony, not any more. There may not even have been a side. She may have been alone.

Tony stares up at Zenia, cornered on the balcony with her failing magic, balancing on the sharp edge, her bag of tricks finally empty. Zenia stares back down. She knows she has lost, but whatever her secrets are she's still not telling. She's like an ancient statuette dug up from a Minoan palace: there are the large breasts, the tiny waist, the dark eyes, the snaky hair. Tony picks her up and turns her over, probes and questions, but the woman with her glazed pottery face does nothing but smile.

From the kitchen she hears laughter, and the clatter of dishes. Charis is setting out the food, Roz is telling a story.

That's what they will do, increasingly in their lives: tell stories. Tonight their stories will be about Zenia.

Was she in any way like us? thinks Tony. Or, to put it the other way around: Are we in any way like her?

Then she opens the door, and goes in to join the others.

Notes for Further Thought

The Robber Bride
by Margaret Atwood

In *The Robber Bride* (1993), her eighth novel, Margaret Atwood uses her trademark virtuoso wit and trenchant gaze to tell the tale of three women, once classmates at the University of Toronto, and the influence wielded upon them by a fourth classmate—the seductive and destructive Zenia. According to Sandra Martin of *Quill and Quire,* "No fairy tale . . . has a villain more dastardly than Zenia," who "systematically befriends and betrays each of the women, metaphorically slaying one a decade, enabling Atwood to romp and rampage through the sexual and cultural history of the past thirty years."

Margaret Atwood's Presentation to the American Booksellers Association Convention

Miami, Florida

June 1, 1993

It's a great honour to be here this morning, and in such distinguished international company. I have always enjoyed talking with booksellers, though I usually do it in bookstores. I like to lurk around and pretend to be a customer, and ask searching questions, because who if not a bookseller lives where the rubber meets the road bookwise?

In fact, my first contact with the official world of books was not with publishers—it was with booksellers. This was in Canada, in the early sixties, which was when I began to write seriously—by which I mean that I myself took it seriously. Others, somehow, didn't. About the most positive comment I got was from a friend of my mother's who said, "That's nice, dear, because it's something you can do at home." She was right, too. My parents felt I should be a botanist. Not that they had anything against writing, but they didn't want me to starve to death.

I, on the contrary, was all in favour of starving to death, because wasn't that what artists did? Or they got TB, or consumption, or brain poisoning in Paris from drinking absinthe, or, at the very least, they suffered neglect in rat-infested garrets. These things were in the cards for me, so I was in a hurry. I might snuff it by the age of twenty-six, like John Keats, so I'd better get cracking.

At that time, the publishing world in Canada was a lot less pretentious than I was. It was small and cautious, and suspicious of wild-eyed twenty-one-year-olds, which I was—although I myself felt I was pushing late middle age, and couldn't understand why it was taking me so long to turn into Emily Brontë, or Herman Melville, or Samuel Beckett, or whoever I thought I would shortly become. Most young writers in that somewhat sparse publishing climate began self-publishing, me included. I had the use of a small flat-bed press, and with the help of a friend I painstakingly hand-set my first book—which was extremely short, luckily, because there was a shortage of As and we had to disassemble each poem before we could set up the next one. We ground out the enormous total of 250 books; and dressed in my long beatnik stockings and with my hair pinned back into an existentialist bun—it took about 200 hairpins and I looked like a porcupine, but nobody could say I wasn't earnest—I trotted around to all the bookstores I knew, and foisted my freshly minted books upon the bemused managers. They sold for fifty cents, retail.

Jump ten years to the early seventies. I wasn't dead yet; moreover, I didn't even have any romantic major diseases or life-threatening addictions. I'd tried the garrets, and opted for central heating. I wasn't Emily Brontë, but I did have a modest reputation as a distinguished woman of letters, and/or a rug-chewing radical maniac, depending on your point of view. By this time, I had published several volumes of poetry and a first novel—*The Edible Woman*—which some reviewers hailed as the cutting edge of feminism, and which others said showed an immaturity that I would doubtless grow out of later, once I had come to terms with the proper woman's role.

In 1972 I did a tour of four towns in the Canadian Near-North. "Near-North" means it isn't above the Arctic Circle but can still get fairly chilly. Some of these towns had never encountered a writer in the flesh, which meant

I had at least as much drawing power as that month's movie, which everyone had seen anyway. I read in high school gyms and Oddfellows Halls, and the question periods afterward were, to put it mildly, direct—or let us say that no one was too concerned about my water symbolism. My favourite author's question of all time—because it's so simple to answer—dates from one of those readings: "Is your hair really like that, or do you get it done?"

The other question I was asked a lot wasn't as easy to answer. It was: "Why do you write?" People were really puzzled, they really wanted to know—what would drive a person to it? I hadn't really thought about this before, so I didn't have much of an answer. I'm not sure I have one now, but here's a beginning of what I should have said in Arnprior, Ontario, in 1972.

I spent most of my early life in a forest. I don't mean a village in a forest, I mean a forest, pure and simple. My father was an entomologist; for three quarters of every year he did his insect research there. We lived in a cabin with a wood stove and several kerosene lanterns. There were bears and wolves and moose and loons. When my mother wanted fish for dinner she would just make a cast off the end of the dock.

This sounds like an idyllic childhood, and in a way it was. But in addition to no electricity and no running water, there were also no movies, no theatres, no art galleries, and no radios on which you could get much more than a crackling noise during thunderstorms. However, there were many books. Books were what you did when it was raining; they were the entertainment, they were the escape, they were the extended family, and I read them all, even when they weren't supposed to be for children. I was traumatized early in life by the death of that poor horse in Orwell's *Animal Farm,* which I thought was going to be about user-friendly bunnies, sort of like *Peter Rabbit,* and I became haunted by the accusing, voyeuristic eye-in-the-keyhole that used to be on the covers of the Dell murder mysteries. But whatever I was reading held my full bug-eyed attention.

So the short answer to "Why do you write?" is—I suppose I write for some of the same reasons I read: to live a double life; to go to places I haven't been; to examine life on earth; to come to know people in ways, and at depths, that are otherwise impossible; to be surprised. Whatever their other reasons, I think all writers write as part of this sort of continuum: to give back something of what they themselves have received.

One of my favourite books as a child was *Grimm's Fairy Tales,* the unexpurgated version—the one with the red-hot shoes. My parents sent away for it by mail order without knowing just how unexpurgated it was, and then worried that it would terrify my brother and myself. It didn't terrify us, but it did fascinate us; and it's from *Grimm's* that I've derived the title of my forthcoming novel, *The Robber Bride.*

In the original story, it's "The Robber Bride-groom"—a tale of a wicked maiden-devouring monster—so why did I change it? Well, I was sitting around one day thinking to myself, "Where have all the Lady Macbeths gone? Gone to Ophelias, every one, leaving the devilish tour-de-force parts to be played by bass-baritones." Or, to put it another way: If all women are well behaved by nature—or if we aren't allowed to say otherwise for fear of antifemaleism—then they are deprived of moral choice, and there isn't much left for them to do in books except run away a lot. Or, to put it another way: *Equality* means equally bad as well as equally good.

From what I've just said, you will realize that *The Robber Bride* is a book with a villainess in it. What kind of villainess? Well, to begin with, a villainess who knows how to make an entrance. On October 23—when, as you're aware, the sun passes from Libra into Scorpio—or, if you aren't aware, you'll find it out on page 4—three women friends are having lunch in a Toronto restaurant called The Toxique. A reader was once quoted as saying: "I like Atwood's books because I can depend on her characters to grow old along with me," and so it has come to be; thus all of these women are what the French refer to as "of a certain age." The first one is an ambidextrous military historian, whose specialty is siege techniques of the Middle Ages. The second one has psychic leanings, a complex past, and a good reason for never eating pigs. The third one is a business wheeler and dealer with gambling tendencies. When they have reached the dessert, which is assorted sorbets—I like to be specific about food—in comes a fourth woman, whose funeral service all three of the others attended five years before.

This returnee—who, due to the wonders of modern plastic surgery, is very well preserved—did awful things to the first woman in the sixties, awfuller things to the second one in the seventies, and the awfullest things to the third one in the eighties. In a novelistic structure based on nineteenth-century symphonies with leitmotifs, Russian dolls-within-dolls, "Goldilocks and the Three Bears," and boxed sets of gift soaps, we learn about the awful things. Then we return to the present to find out what happens next. Will the perambulating nemesis do more awful things to our three heroines? Or will they, for a change, do awful things to her? I don't mean to imply that there is no love, compassion, sex, plangent lyricism, deep insight, wit and humour, metaphysical speculation, and language wielded with the skill of a tightrope walker crossing Niagara Falls blindfold in this book; I certainly intended to put in some of those. But on top of that, there are awful things. Well, why not? Life contains awful things. By the time you've reached a certain age, you notice.

What do I hope the reader will get out of all this— and, indeed, out of any book she or he may read? Exactly what I myself like to receive—and frequently do receive— from the books of others. There's one word that sums it up. It's a quality without which all other qualities, in book or in life, ring hollow. It takes many forms of the mind, forms of the heart, forms of the soul. It includes both tragedy and comedy, and the play of language, and Memory, the mother of all nine Muses, and, above all, the experience of getting your socks knocked off. The desire for it explains—when we go back in our lives to look for causes—why we are all readers here, and why you do what you do, and why I do what I do, and why my vocation is also my obsession. It was a favourite word of the poet William Blake, and it's in the full sense of his use of it that I invoke it now. The word is Delight; and this is what I wish for you as my readers—Delight, in all of its bookly incarnations.

To Delight.

I thank you.

—Reprinted by permission of the author.

Selected Poem by Margaret Atwood

The Robber Bridegroom

He would like not to kill. He would like
what he images other men have,
instead of this red compulsion. Why do the women
fail him and die badly? He would like to kill them gently,
finger by finger, and with great tenderness, so that
at the end they would melt into him
with gratitude for his skill and the final pleasure
he still believes he could bring them
if only they could accept him,
but they scream too much and make him angry.
Then he goes for the soul, rummaging
in their flesh for it, despotic with self-pity,
hunting among the nerves and the shards
of their faces for the one thing
he needs to live, and lost
back there in the poplar and spruce forest
in the watery moonlight, where his young bride
pale but only a little frightened,
her hands glimmering with his own approaching
death, gropes her way towards him
along the obscure path, from white stone
to white stone, ignorant and singing,
dreaming of him as he is.

Questions for Contemplation or Discussion

1. In *The Robber Bride,* Tony says that people like Zenia don't get into your life unless you invite them in. What devices does Zenia use to first gain entry into the lives of Tony, Charis, and Roz? How does she alter her techniques to attract and control men?

2. On the surface, Tony, Charis, and Roz are not a bit alike yet similarities exist. For example, during childhood they each developed what could be called "dual" identities. How do the psychological devices developed as children help or hinder them?

3. While seeming all-powerful, the constantly changing Zenia lacks a centre of her own. Do women have to break rules and operate as outlaws to achieve the same level of power as men? Do women have a power that differs from male power?

4. Is there a difference between the lies Zenia tells and those told by the other characters in the novel? Are there "good" lies and "bad" lies? Do the hearers play a part in the construction of these lies?

5. Read the poem "The Robber Bridegroom," reversing the gender as you read. What does this poem tell us about the nature of evil?

6. The American writer Lewis Hyde has asked, "Why is the Trickster the Messenger of the Gods?" Is Zenia a trickster? Is she also a messenger of the gods, and how?

7. Think of female villains from literature and film. What do they seem to have in common? Is female villainy portrayed differently from that of men?

8. William Blake said of Milton's *Paradise Lost* that Milton often seemed to be of the devil's part without knowing it. Does Atwood have a sneaking sympathy for Zenia? Do you?

Biography

Margaret Atwood was born in 1939 in Ottawa and grew up in northern Ontario, Quebec, and Toronto. She received her undergraduate degree from Victoria College at the University of Toronto and her master's degree from Radcliffe College.

The daughter of a forest entomologist, Atwood spent a large part of her childhood in the Canadian wilderness. At sixteen she found that writing was "suddenly the only thing I wanted to do."

Throughout her career Margaret Atwood has received numerous awards and several honorary degrees, including the Governor General's Award, Le Chevalier dans l'Ordre des Arts et des Lettres in France, the National Arts Club Medal of Honor for Literature in the United States, and the Giller Prize. She is the author of more than thirty volumes of poetry, nonfiction, and fiction, including children's books and short stories. Her most recent works include the novels *Cat's Eye* (1989), *The Robber Bride* (1993), and *Alias Grace* (1996); the story collection *Good Bones* (1992); and a volume of poetry, *Morning in the Burned House* (1995).

Atwood's work has been published in more than twenty-five countries. She has travelled extensively and has lived in Boston, Vancouver, Montreal, London, Provence, Berlin, Edinburgh, and Ireland.

Margaret Atwood now lives in Toronto with novelist Graeme Gibson and their daughter.

Information

To discuss this novel online, visit our "Bold Type" Bulletin Board at http://www.boldtype.com.

The Margaret Atwood web site at http://www.web.net/owtoad has more detailed information about Margaret Atwood and her work.